The Roots of
Conservatism in Mexico

The Roots of
Conservatism in Mexico

Catholicism, Society, and
Politics in the Mixteca Baja, 1750–1962

BENJAMIN T. SMITH

University of New Mexico Press ❧ Albuquerque

17   16   15   14   13   12   1   2   3   4   5   6

LIBRARY OF CONGRESS CATALOGING-IN-PUBLICATION DATA

Smith, Benjamin T.
The roots of conservatism in Mexico : Catholicism, society, and politics in the
Mixteca Baja, 1750–1962 / Benjamin T. Smith.
p. cm.
Includes bibliographical references and index.
ISBN 978-0-8263-5172-2 (pbk. : alk. paper) — ISBN 978-0-8263-5173-9 (electronic)
1. Peasants—Political activity—Mexico—Oaxaca (State)—History. 2.
Peasants—Religious life—Mexico—Oaxaca (State)—History. 3. Conservatism—
Mexico—Oaxaca (State)—History. 4. Religion and politics—Mexico—Oaxaca
(State)—History. 5. Catholic Church—Mexico—Oaxaca (State)—History. 6. Oaxaca
(Mexico : State)—Politics and government. I. Title.
HD1531.M6S65 2012
972'.74—dc23
2012022350

BOOK DESIGN
Typeset by Lila Sanchez
Composed in 10.25/13.5 Minion Pro Regular
Display type is Minion Pro

To my daughter, Emilia

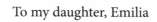

Contents

Acknowledgments
ix

INTRODUCTION
1

CHAPTER 1
The People of the Cross
The Mixteca Baja During the Colonial Period
19

CHAPTER 2
For "the peace and security of the pueblo"
The Roots of Provincial Conservatism, 1821–1867
75

CHAPTER 3
For a "government of Mexico, which protects
our religion, our persons, and our families"
The Counternarrative of Provincial Conservatism, 1821–1867
120

CHAPTER 4

"The spirit of God . . . in the hearts of everybody"

Liberalism Modified and Catholicism Resurgent, 1867–1910

159

CHAPTER 5

"No leaf of the tree moves without the will of God"

Regional Catholicism During the Revolution, 1910–1940

203

CHAPTER 6

"En el nombre de Dios, adelante"

From Resistance to Revolt, 1940–1962

246

CONCLUSION

294

Appendices

301

Notes

315

Bibliography

373

Index

419

Acknowledgments

—╀—

T HIS BOOK WOULD NOT HAVE BEEN POSSIBLE WITHOUT THE KIND help of many friends, relations, and acquaintances in Oaxaca and the Mixteca Baja. As befits a book at least in part about the church hierarchy, I shall start at the top. I would like to thank the bishop of the Diocese of Huajuapam de León, Teodoro Enrique Pino Miranda, who kindly allowed me to enter the diocesan archive and snoop around the region's rich parish documentation. I would also like to thank the many priests who let me into the church archives and helped me track down *libros de gobierno* and well-guarded *cofradía* records. A special mention must go to the priests of Tlacotepec Nieves, Miltepec, and Tequixtepec who were particularly generous with their time. Finally, I must thank the various communities and religious organizations that allowed me to view their histories. Special thanks must go to Manuel Barragán, head of the Museo Regional de Huajuapan, who first invited me to the Mixteca Baja and got me excited about the subject. Thanks also to the Catholic women's organizations of Miltepec and Tequixtepec, which gave me such interesting insights into contemporary church life.

Beyond priests and parishioners, I would also like to thank many of the professional archivists who helped me with their hard work, their patience, and their time. I would like to mention four in particular: Erika Ivette Gutiérrez Mosqueda at the Archivo General de la Nación, Claudia Ballesteros and María Isabel Grañen Porrúa at the Biblioteca Burgoa, and Elisa Garzón Balbuena at Apoyo al Desarrollo de Archivo y Bibliotecas de México. Without their work, this book would not have been possible. I would also like to thank the staff at the Archivo General del Poder Ejecutivo de Oaxaca, the Archivo del Registro Agrario Nacional in Oaxaca, and the Archivo Judicial de Oaxaca. Again, their help and kindness were invaluable. Special thanks must also go to the members of the municipal council of Tequixtepec, who allowed me to look through their archives, gave me the finest *barbacoa* I have ever tasted, and filled me with far too much mescal.

One of the principal joys of working in Oaxaca for a second time was that I was able to cement friendships with a wonderful group of local historians. Carlos Sánchez Silva, as always, was kind and helpful. Gregorio Eduardo

Rivera, a fine historian, and by all accounts a great priest, not only gave me some interesting inside information but also invited me to his *bodas de plata*. Michael Swanton at the Universidad Autónoma "Benito Juárez" de Oaxaca was always generous with his time, his advice, his friendship, and his encyclopedic knowledge of Oaxaca's indigenous groups. Jesús Edgar Mendoza García of the Centro de Investigaciones y Estudios Superiores en Antropología Social has not only produced two of the finest agrarian histories of the last decade, but was also kind enough to share with me his thoughts on events in his *patria chica* and the neighboring districts of the Mixteca Baja. Finally, my greatest thanks must go to Ricardo Ceballos Soto, teacher, historian, local archivist, and perhaps the most knowledgeable person I have ever met under thirty years old. His dissertation, which he finished at the Universidad Autónoma Nacional de México, was quite remarkable and his published book on the history of Chazumba fantastic. Over a couple of days Ricardo was kind enough to lend me copies of his private archive and help me gain entrance to the municipal archives of Chazumba and Tequixtepec. I hope that he chooses to pursue his career as a historian in the future.

Outside Oaxaca, the last six years in academia have allowed me the privilege of meeting many talented historians, and I cannot mention them all by name. Thank you to those who attended the conference "Authoritarianism and Resistance in Mexico" at Michigan State University and those who have offered me advice on papers and articles I have written in the past, especially Alan Knight and Tanalís Padilla. I would like to thank Antonio Escobar Ohmstede, Ben Fallaw, Brian Connaughton, Robert Curley, Adrian Bantjes, Roberto Blancarte, Wil Pansters, Paul Gillingham, and Matthew Butler, whose friendship and sage advice were invaluable. John Chance, Ben, Matthew, Wil, and Paul were particularly generous, lending me not only their time, but also their excellent manuscripts. Antonio and Brian, thanks so much for all the support, as well as the almost constant stream of thought-provoking books. Robert, thanks for the hospitality, the friendship, and the advice. We will all miss Adrian. The book itself benefitted immensely from the critiques of two UNM Press readers along with John Chance, Guy Thomson, Brian Connaughton, Edward Wright-Rios, Erika Pani, and William Taylor. Thank you so much for your time, your correspondence, and your advice. The book would have been far worse without them. I would like to thank Erika in particular for her invaluable insights on the messy reality of early nineteenth-century politics. I only hope I have done them justice.

I would like to thank the many friends in the United States and Oaxaca who have helped me over the last few years as I have struggled to get this book finished. Special thanks to John Wisti, Serafín Sánchez Hernández, Guillermo, and Miguel "el Diablo," who all accompanied me round the Mixteca Baja, walking the hills, eating the *tacos de barbacoa* and *pescado frito*, enjoying the music, and enduring the early morning chorus of a hundred angry fighting cocks. In the United States, I would like to give thanks to my colleagues at Michigan State University. Special thanks go to John, Abby, the two Peters, Erica, Liam, Monica, the two Davids, Sheila, Mark, Walter, Pero, Dylan, Estrella, Jerry, Charles, Ed, Cristina, Helen, Georgina, and Bob, who made the place such a pleasant place to live and work.

Finally, I would like to thank my ever-expanding family in the United Kingdom, the United States, and Mexico. Thanks to Ann, Claire, Patricia, Ernest, Nick, Sue, and Nigel Smith and Mary, Paul, Sue, Laura, Amy, and Alex. Agradesco mucho a mis suegros, Catalina Sánchez Ruiz y Eloy David Morales Jiménez; a mis cuñados, Efrain, Eloy, Avi, Edith, Elvia, y Michael; a mi concuños, Troy y Patricia; a mis sobrinos, Melissa y Ceilmor; y a todos mis primos, tíos, y tías. Sin ellos, no hubiera contraido matrimonio con mi esposa, y no hubiera estado tan contento en Oaxaca. Finally, I would like to thank my wife, Noemi, who was heavily pregnant when I started this book in 2007. Te agradesco tu apoyo, tu paciencia, y tu alegría. But most of all, thanks to Emilia for the enormous sense of joy you give me every day.

Introduction

✝

ON THE WALLS OF THE COMMUNITY MUSEUM OF TEQUIXTEPEC local artists have painted an account of the village's history from pre-Hispanic times to the present. Despite nearly a century of state attempts to institutionalize a distinct view of Mexico's past, culminating in that "indivisible combination of popular aspirations," the 1910 Mexican Revolution, Tequixtepec's painters have formulated a markedly different narrative of village history.[1] In the first of a series of vignettes, the mural shows the village's Mixtec Indians living hand to mouth from the fruits of the trees. In the second and third panels, the post-Conquest Mixtecs are shown clothed, surrounded by livestock, and worshipping a Christian saint. In the fourth panel, disaster strikes, as Zapatista soldiers are depicted burning the village to the ground. In the fifth and sixth sections, redemption arrives as a group of female villagers, clutching at crosses, worship the statue of Our Lord of Forgiveness and the priest hears the confession of a repentant community leader. This history, with its celebration of the "civilizing" aspects of Conquest, its condemnation of revolutionary violence, and its confirmation of the redemptive powers of Catholic ritual, stands in stark contrast to the state's unifying, emancipatory, secular narrative of revolutionary salvation.[2] Yet the mural is not simply a sharp visual rebuttal, it also reflects how the peasants of Tequixtepec and the rest of the Mixteca Baja have understood their relationship to their community and the broader Mexican nation for the past two hundred years. By recounting the history of the region's social, economic, and religious development, I explore this understanding and in so doing, suggest that certain regions under certain circumstances generated a political culture that I have termed "provincial conservatism."

1

Since Independence, the peasants of the Mixteca Baja have repeatedly sided with conservatives to defend the Catholic Church against state anticlericalism. After an initial burst of federalist fervor, Mixtec soldiers backed the centralist regime of the local caudillo, Antonio de León, until his death in the Mexican-American War. During the War of Reform, parishioners from the Mixteca Baja were one of the few groups in Oaxaca to support conservative rebels against the ruling liberal government. Although liberals negotiated a modus vivendi with the Mixtecs during the last days of the French Intervention, they never accepted the broad thrust of liberal policies and instead maintained cofradía lands and invested heavily in ecclesiastical infrastructure. During the Revolution, Mixtecs rejected Zapatista offers of land distribution and sought salvation in orthodox Catholic ritual. After the Revolution, priests and parishioners from the Mixteca Baja led a sustained campaign against state land reform and socialist education and continued to obey clerical commands and send their children to church establishments. During the 1940s and 1950s, Mixtec peasants militated on behalf of the Partido Acción Nacional (PAN), often winning municipal elections despite state repression. Finally, in 1962 Mixtecs led an armed religious uprising, the "last Cristiada," in a desperate bid to win local control and rid the region of impious "communist" governance.

This book recounts this long tradition of regional conservatism. As such, it follows another established convention, that of the Mexican regional history, reaching back to Luis González y González's *Pueblo en vilo*. The work examines the interplay of national political developments, regional socioeconomic structures, and local cultural practices over the *médian durée*.[3] As the introductory anecdote suggests, I emphasize the influence of religious belief, church ritual, and lay-clerical relations on both social relations and political affiliation. In doing so, I posit that the peasants of the Mixteca Baja embraced provincial conservatism, a regional variant of elite or metropolitan conservatism, which not only comprised ideas on property, hierarchy, and the state, but also acknowledged the overwhelming import of the church in maintaining this system. As a result, the book tries to offer a subtle counterpoint to Mexican history's dominant melody, with its crescendos of radical insurrection and its diminuendos of conservative rule. In doing so, I do not seek to validate either the church or conservatism or to compose a new national narrative. Rather, I hope to provide an explanation for why, since Independence, peasants throughout Mexico, like their peers in the Mixteca Baja, have taken up arms to cries of "¡Viva la religion!" "¡Viva Cristo Rey!"

or "¡En el nombre de Dios, adelante!" Although these groups were defeated and their histories often ignored, these stories help to clarify why the country's ruling coalitions, whether federalist, liberal, or revolutionary, have had to temper their most radical propositions in the face of popular opposition.

Until recently, historians dismissed these non-elite, prochurch conservatives as coerced and unwilling participants, irrational religious fanatics, or hoodwinked political illiterates. Gazing back over sixty years of civil strife, liberal historians of the late nineteenth century described their enemies—the centralists, conservatives, and imperialists—as "reactionaries" and "traitors" and their followers as "imbecilic," "primitive," "barbarians," and "bandits."[4] On the one hand, they blamed the propaganda power of the church. Thus Enrique Olavarria y Ferrari in the fourth volume of *México a través de los siglos* argued that the high clergy's alarmist claims, its "censures, excommunications, threats to take away the last rites, and other arms of the ecclesiastical arsenal," whipped up popular opposition to the 1834 anticlerical reforms.[5] On the other hand, liberal authors also condemned the innate credulity and "savagery" of their peasant adherents. Justo Sierra described conservative rebel leaders as reactionaries and bandits, their followers as "primitive hordes," and their clerical supporters as the "black beast of that great red devil."[6] Ciro B. Ceballos claimed that the *religioneros* of the 1870s were "cajoled, and excited by the stupid fanaticism of Mexican women."[7] José M. Vigil argued that the rebels of 1856 were simply a "considerable mass of individuals accustomed to the life of the guerilla."[8] Postrevolutionary historians, engaged in another bitter battle with prochurch groups, were equally condemnatory. Thus Alfonso Toro described popular conservatism as "a semi-savage movement," "undoubtedly" established "with the connivances of the clergy."[9] Similarly, these historians denounced members of contemporary conservative mobilizations, such as the First and Second Cristiadas, as "fanatical," "irrational," and incited to armed revolt by a cabal of reactionary white landowners and a greedy, immoral clergy.[10]

From the 1960s onward, a new generation of revisionists, heavily influenced by Marxist historiography, started to chip away at this skewed interpretation, questioning both liberal and revolutionary motivations. In an act of collective iconoclasm, they attempted to exorcise state-backed eidolons from the national pantheon, replacing them with the country's forgotten, plebian "heroés agachados"—caste war rebels like Jacinto Pat, land reformers like Emiliano Zapata, and martyred anarchists like Ricardo Flores Magón.[11] In doing so they shaped a powerful counternarrative of frustrated social change, culminating in the Partido Revolucionario Institucional's (PRI's) betrayal of the Revolution's distributive promises. But they also marginalized or misinterpreted popular prochurch groups. Few of these revisionist historians devoted their energies to analyzing conservative alliances, whether those of the mid-nineteenth or the early twentieth centuries. Those that did most often portrayed the clashes as interinstitutional struggles that pitched an aggressive secular state against a reactionary ecclesiastical hierarchy.[12] If they uncovered popular participation, they tended to view these exclamations of religious devotion and church support as convenient rhetorical devices, the political patina of what were essentially agrarian insurrections. Thus, Mario A. Aldana Rendon's work on Manuel Lozada aped Mariano Azuela's approach and distilled the rebellion and the subsequent decade of independent rule down to "the struggle for land": proto-Zapatismo, Nayarit style.[13] Similarly, scholars portrayed the Cristeros of the 1920s and 1930s as rural smallholders, motivated to revolt by the threat of state-backed agrarian capitalism.[14]

Still now, outside a handful of Catholic martyrologies, few contemporary historians examine popular conservative groups, except at times of extraordinary, and hence easily visible, tension. Furthermore, the church is usually relegated to a bit part, as the institutional bellwether of reactionary politics or the rhetorical carapace of antimodern revolt. Even the best contemporary historians, otherwise deeply concerned with the ramifications of peasant customs, have offered little insight.[15] For example, Peter Guardino in his work on post-Independence federalism sees centralist attempts to harness popular religious support as opportunist propaganda and concludes that "the church issue was considered relatively minor by many of the most important participants in politics." Moreover, despite devoting much of the work to laying out the relations between Mexico's "important" and "unimportant" political players, he leaves the question of whether "the church issue" was more significant for provincial peasants unanswered.[16] Similarly, although Florencia Mallon in her work on mid-nineteenth-century nationalism admits the possibility of "conservative populisms" and acknowledges the clergy's "clear conspiratorial role" in antiliberal insurgencies, religion remains superstructural flotsam, the surface detritus of "an entire articulation that connected political independence and participation to control of land, labor, and revenue." The ramifications of sustained histories of close lay-clerical partnerships or the growing distance between local priests and their parishioners are ignored. Instead, priests occasionally harness "community hegemony" through largesse or are beaten by angry liberal mobs as the local expression of the foreign, conservative alliance.[17] Finally, in recent works on socialist education, a government cultural program deliberately aimed at "exclud[ing] all religious doctrine" from school syllabi, the relationship between popular resistance and religion is viewed in a rather functionalist sense. Thus, although Mary K. Vaughan acknowledges that the peasants of Zacapoaxtla were "deeply religious" and that "religiosity, permeating a ceremonial social order, was lived culture," she concludes that city elites and caciques, not poor believers, "found in religion a means to put the brakes" on socialist education.[18]

Despite these broad historiographical trends, from the early 1970s onward some scholars began to bring religion back into political history, to piece together how religious cultures affected popular political affiliation. Starting with the extraordinary work of Jean Meyer, most have concentrated on the most visible outbreak of prochurch violence: the Cristiada. For Meyer, the peasants who formed the Cristero bands of the center-west were acting for explicitly religious motivations—to protect their orthodox expressions of religiosity, like Mass, Communion, and saints' celebrations, from secular state interference. The civil war itself was a clash of "two worlds": the traditional peasant world—that of the "pilgrims of Peter the Hermit"—and the modern revolutionary world—that of the "Jacobins of the Third Age."[19] Meyer's thesis, which he has extended and modified to cover the Cristero uprisings in Oaxaca, the Second Cristiada, Manuel Lozada's nineteenth-century rebellion, and the right-wing Sinarquismo movement, is still highly persuasive, a welcome counterpoint to secular understandings of peasant politics.[20] Meyer's assertion that "religion mattered," that peasant reactions to market forces and political interference depended on popular religious cultures, still provides the foundation for the scattered scholars of Mexico's prochurch groups.[21]

Yet Meyer's assertion is also problematic. First, by extricating the Cristeros from accusations of elite manipulation, from being what he terms "people of the church, political Catholics, the bishops' lay followers or instruments of the League," he downplays the influence of both local elites and the institutional church. For Meyer, peasant religion seems to exist in spite of rather than because of the ecclesiastical authorities. As a result, bishops and parish priests are conspicuous by their absence. Outside a "puñado" of co-conspirators, they offer lukewarm support at best; at worst they denigrate the uprising and eventually betray the rebellion.[22]

Second, by establishing this model of limited lay-clerical interaction, Meyer fails to explain the geographical reach of the rebellion. If peasants were merely protecting popular practices, why was the rebellion limited to the center-west? Or if rebels were guarding a particular type of orthodox religious observance, why were Cristeros so rare in clerical hubs like Querétaro, Puebla, or even the Mixteca Baja? Third, if the Cristeros were radical peasant defenders of age-old community customs, who were the country's anticlerical *agraristas*? Were they simply underchurched northerners and local opportunists?

Toward an Understanding of Provincial Conservatism

Building on Meyer's work, this book attempts to integrate the history of lay-clerical interaction into the region's socioeconomic and political developments and to discover why Mixtec peasants repeatedly supported conservatism, despite the attraction of other reformist or radical ideological currents. Uncovering such a telluric counternarrative over such a long period of time involves a certain methodological promiscuity, and this book includes the discussion of gender, ethnicity, and violence as well as the chronologically bound historiographies of relevant periods. Yet three distinct assumptions, drawn from agrarian and ethnohistory, religious history, and the "new political history," remain constant throughout the text and have regimented both the construction of the argument and the reading of the sources. First, I have adapted E. P. Thompson's and James Scott's ideas on the moral economy to describe the stable but changing economic, social, and cultural relations between the Mixteca Baja's elite and non-elite groups. Second, following the suggestions of contemporary historians of religion, I have attempted to establish a model of regional religious culture based on the dialectical relationship between local social relations and the institutional church. Third, using modern historical works on popular politics, I have started to disaggregate Mexico's tradition of political conservatism, to unearth its changing components and treat seriously its popular echo.

Traditionally, historians described relations between peasants and non-peasants in strictly materialist terms. Yet as E. P. Thompson argued, given that economic exploitation was a constant in most societies, this rationale failed to explain the cadence, intensity, and targeted nature of popular revolt. Instead, he claimed that relations between elites and non-elites were framed within what he termed "a moral economy"—a "view of social norms and obligations, [and] of the proper economic functions of several parties within the community."[23] Even when these mutual accords broke down, they still molded popular responses, channeling the poor not toward revolution but rather toward demands for the proper fulfillment of these perceived duties.[24] In his work, James Scott expanded this notion to explain peasant rebellions in Southeast Asia, arguing that the introduction of capitalist practices not only impoverished Burmese and Vietnamese peasants but, more importantly, broke down regional moral economies, severing paternalist links between elite and non-elite groups and undermining "common notions of what [was] just."[25] Over the past two decades Latin Americanists (particularly ethnohistorians) have embraced this idea, welding it to dependency theory economics to argue that foreign demand generated regional rhythms of agrarian capitalism, which in turn broke down the reciprocal ties between mercantile or landholding elites and peasants and provoked revolt.[26]

In importing Thompson's and Scott's original theses into a Latin American setting, scholars have offered some important revisions. On the one hand, they have broadened the concept of moral economy to encompass not only mutual agreements over the price of corn or bread, but also the broad array of cultural practices—what E. P. Thompson termed the "studied and elaborate hegemonic style"—that described and confirmed these accords.[27] Thus, Todd Diacon, in his work on Brazil's early twentieth-century Contestado rebellion, describes how the tradition of godparentage served to cement asymmetrical relations between landholders and their semi-independent peasant clients in southeastern Brazil. With the arrival of the railways and the increasing demand for commercial crops, these practices disintegrated as elites forsook their traditional duties in exchange for quick rewards. In response, the region's peasants rebelled, demanding not equality or autonomy but rather a "restoration of these unequal patron-client ties."[28] On the other hand, scholars have also started to insert religious expectations into these relationships. As Kevin Gosner points out, the legitimacy of Maya leaders depended not only on "how effectively they managed contact with colonial authorities" but also how "capably they fulfilled their ritual obligations and how convincingly they tapped into traditional ideas about the supernatural origins of secular power." In fact, the moral economy was so "embedded in beliefs about the supernatural" it might be better termed a spiritual economy.[29]

This idea of a broad, multivalent moral economy informs my description of connections between elites and non-elites in the Mixteca Baja. Chapter 1 delineates the economic, social, and cultural aspects of this intricate lattice of obligations and expectations that linked the region's colonial elites, indigenous nobles, and indigenous peasants. But I also go slightly further. Most historians have employed the notion of the moral economy to describe periods of crisis and upheaval, to outline the rationale, timing, and form of revolt. For Scott, the shift from a precapitalist to a capitalist agrarian economy was enacted through a "series of rude shocks" that, by demolishing regional moral economies, provoked a succession of profound dislocations and a frequent rhythm of peasant rebellions.[30] In many regions, from early nineteenth-century Yucatán through mid-nineteenth-century Vietnam to early twentieth-century Morelos, this model held true.[31] However, the idea can also be used to explain stability. Outside hubs of commercial agriculture, capitalism brought not shocks but rather "ambiguous shifts," the readjustment but not upending of these unequal interclass relations.[32] As Barrington Moore and E. P. Thompson suggest, in places elites could adjust their strategies to temper the sense of injustice that would otherwise generate revolt.[33] The Mixteca Baja, with its narrow, fertile valleys, sparse vegetation, and vast eroded mountainsides proved such a place. Here, geography provided little incentive for elites to tear up their contracts with the region's peasants. Instead, they adjusted "the balance of reciprocity" to maximize available profit, while at the same time minimizing the chances of revolt.[34] For example, from 1830 onward elites declined the opportunity to purchase indigenous nobles' lands. Instead, they encouraged Mixtec peasants to buy up the barren expanses as "agricultural societies," bartering away agrarian control in exchange for political allegiance and commercial wealth.

This cyclical reworking of the moral economy, repeated throughout the Mixteca Baja's history and reinforced through conscious pulpit promotion of stable interethnic relations, negated the attraction of radical revolt, buttressed cross-class cooperation, and became the foundation for the region's provincial conservatism. At the same time, the gradual and controlled percolation of capitalist relations also explains the flexible, hybrid nature of the region's agrarian base with its strange symbiosis of modern and traditional elements. For example, by encouraging peasant villages to become agricultural societies and buy up noble lands, elites inadvertently created closed-corporate communities of individualist ranchers. These were egalitarian, defensive, and broadly democratic, throwbacks in many ways to the traditional colonial *república*. Yet their members, as purchasers of the land, were also private property owners, paragons of the new liberal smallholder establishment. Unified yet undergirded by a common notion of private property, equitable yet in hock to the region's commercial elite, these agricultural societies were remarkably hardy institutions. Although they proved incomprehensible to the postrevolutionary state with its straightforward understanding of rural landholding, many survived until the 1960s.

As well as hijacking moral economy theory, this book also rests on new appreciations of Mexico's lay-clerical relations. Until very recently, most historians and anthropologists viewed the relationship between elite and popular (or official and folk) religion in oppositional terms. Catholicism's colonial stain confirmed this view. For many, the syncretism or blend of Spanish and indigenous traditions that constituted communities' religious rituals underscored the perpetual tension between ecclesiastical authorities and semipagan believers.[35] For Laura Lewis, late colonial religion comprised a culturally Spanish "sanctioned domain," expressed institutionally by the church and buttressed by the colonial legal system, and a culturally indigenous "unsanctioned domain," characterized by witchcraft and healing.[36] For Eric Van Young, the atavistic excesses of the Independence movement emerged from the "yawning cultural chasms" between Spanish and indigenous "views of the human and supernatural worlds" and the "deep-running incompatibility of popular and elite mentality and culture."[37] For Paul Vanderwood, writing about the Tomochic rebellion of the late nineteenth century, priests and parishioners "lived different realities," and "popular spirituality" operated "in a spirit of defiance towards authority."[38]

Although this static, Manichaean view of Catholicism works in certain regions, at certain times, and undoubtedly serves to explain the development of millenarian traditions, chiliastic uprisings, and clandestine pagan rituals, it fails to clarify why so many Mexicans not only continued to claim they were Catholic, but also fought for and died in defense of the Catholic Church. Instead, contemporary scholars of religion, following the work of European historians, have started to suggest that priests and parishioners were not involved in some sort of apocalyptic struggle, their relationship constantly on the point of anomie, rebellion, or collapse, but were rather engaged in perpetual, if occasionally fractious, dialogue.[39] William B. Taylor argues that although individual clergymen and communities continued to squabble over the tenor of religious ritual, late eighteenth-century Mexico was broadly Catholic, and the "magical invocations to natural forces, auguries, love potions, medicinal magic, and devotion to animal figures" that had petrified early missionaries were now judged "harmless superstitions." In fact, popular practices "existed with, more than against, the priest."[40] Matthew Butler in his work on the Cristada in Michoacán suggests adding nuance to the "basic elite-popular division by allowing for a measure of cross-class interaction."[41] Even Edward Wright-Rios in his study of apparition movements in early twentieth-century Oaxaca acknowledges that his evidence fails to "support the notion that popular religion in the archdiocese of Oaxaca exist[ed] in perpetual standoff with the institutional church." Instead, he suggests that these extempore Virgin cults and speaking Christs indicate "the ongoing processes of interaction and negotiation *within* the church."[42]

This vision of the clergy and the laity involved in constant dialogue over both religious meaning and practice offers some distinct advantages. First, it allows historians to study religion "in a creative encounter with other social activities."[43] Rather than viewing elite and popular religion as fixed poles, the former a convenient rhetorical tool for autocratic elites, the latter a symbolic refuge for suffering peasants, we are forced to ground our understanding of everyday religious practice in the shifting power relationships between these two groups. Such an approach dovetails easily with contemporary analyses of the dialectical relationship between structure and culture and ties in with the multivalent, shifting concept of the peasant moral economy outlined previously.[44] On the one hand it reaffirms our *Marxisant* impulse to contextualize religion within a region's distinct socioeconomic conditions, to draw out how tensions over land tenure, commercial supremacy, and social hierarchy, as interpreted by priests, landowners, and peasants, affected religious practices and meanings. How, for example, did the shift from noble landholding to agricultural societies and from a defined community hierarchy to a more equitable social system change lay-clerical relations, cofradía structures, and relationships to the local saint? On the other hand, such a dynamic conceptualization also demands that we ask how religious relationships influenced social, economic, and political expectations. How, for example, did the expansion of Marian cults and female lay organizations affect community politics?[45]

Second, such an approach permits historians to escape monolithic appreciations of the Catholic Church and focus our attention on power relationships within the institution.[46] As Talal Asad argues, ecclesiastical authorities managed the "authorizing discourses" that "defin[ed] and control[led]" religion. The church, in an effort to "subject all practice to a unified authority," could reject some practices and accept others, authenticate certain miracles and dismiss the rest, "regularize popular social movements into rule-following orders, or denounce them for heresy."[47] At the same time, individual priests could withdraw rites from, or spiritually banish noncompliant factions at their whim. However, parishioners were not entirely powerless. From the Reformation onward, bishops and priests throughout the Catholic world felt constantly threatened by non-Catholic groups. Enlightenment anticlericalism only heightened this fear. Despite ultramontane popish rhetoric, the local clergy, stripped of their tithes, their status, and their political roles, were increasingly willing to harness popular religious sentiment against these perceived threats.[48] To do so, they were often forced to, in the words of Timothy Tackett, "clericalize popular religion," to authorize more heterodox devotions, to allow for increased lay autonomy, and to hope that they could channel these enthusiasms in suitable directions.[49]

Such an approach highlights the importance of the omnipresent intermediary—the village priest. In Mexico clergymen were located at "the sensitive intersections between Indian subjects and higher authorities" and, as a result, at the heart of negotiations over acceptable religious practice.[50] As the buyers of saints, the innovators of lay organizations, and the blessers of caves, they, as much as their peasant charges, were the forgers of communities' religious identities. As Taylor points out, some were autocrats, some snobs, some down-on-their-luck chancers. Others were devoted, easygoing, accommodating, and even kind.[51] Yet distinct "clusterings of clerical attitudes" did emerge.[52] Some regions relied almost entirely on clerical outsiders, urban-born priests scarcely able to comprehend local religious rites and keen to leave their small parishes for the wealth and the status of the cities.[53] But other regions, including the Mixteca Baja, generated, taught, and then maintained their own priests.[54] Bilingual and often of indigenous descent, these local clergymen were more likely to engage with community beliefs and incorporate them into the rhythm of the Catholic calendar. Furthermore, prelates, like the first bishop of the Mixteca Baja, could institutionalize this practice, building seminaries, scouting the parishes for pious potential students, and encouraging flexibility in dealings with parishioners.

Third, by investigating the connections between religion and socioeconomic structure and taking seriously the role of the institutional church and the village clergy, we can start to construct appreciations of Mexico's regional religious cultures. Mapping out these cultures, with their roots in shifting socioeconomic relations, diocesan dictates, individual clerical prudence, and lay innovation, is extremely hard. Beyond some fairly basic data, the kind of cliometric indicators employed to build up clear pictures of religious practice in France or Spain are nearly non-existent.[55] At the same time, following Alan Knight's contention that there were as many local political cultures as there were municipalities, there were probably as many religious cultures as there were distinct parishes.[56] Looking back over the history of the Mixteca Baja, the oscillating popularity of certain shrines and pilgrimage routes can resemble the flickering of hundreds of tiny lights that shine brightly and then disappear from view. Yet local foci with their extralocal "fields of force" delineated broad trends, and by the end of the eighteenth century two overlapping archetypes of regional religiosity had emerged.[57] In some regions of rapid capitalist development and limited lay-clerical dialogue, priestly expectations and popular practices had diverged. Priests concentrated in local towns, fulfilling their duties to a thin tier of the commercial elite. In the villages clerical visits were few, the sacraments were rarely taken, church education was sparse, and agricultural prosperity was sustained through a mixture of unauthorized festivals and semipagan hilltop rituals. In other regions, like the Mixteca Baja, where cross-class relations remained intact, communities' religious rituals were far more dependent on the presence of the local clergy. Here, in these more clerical regions, priests supported local *cofradías*, shrines, and pilgrimage routes, the sacraments were fairly regularly taken, and church schools were widespread. Spanish, mixed-race, and indigenous groups shared religious spaces and religious beliefs and were often linked by regional cults.

These religious cultures were not set in stone. During the nineteenth and twentieth centuries, socioeconomic shifts, ecclesiastical strategies, and exterior threats promoted divergent dynamics of religious change. In regions of limited church influence, the growth of large landholdings and the loss of community lands strained class relations, often along ethnic lines, and pushed scattered priests out of the villages and into the nonindigenous commercial centers. In these same areas liberal or revolutionary anticlericalism often combined with popular anticlericalism to cleave lay-clerical relations. As a result, the church's power waned precipitously. Priests were scarce, church schools non-existent, and the power of pulpit preaching weak. Elite and popular religion split further as discussions over acceptable practice broke down. Here, two processes emerged. On the one hand, authorized "orthodox" rituals, including baptisms, church marriages, tithe payments, and the taking of sacraments, dwindled dramatically as natives "resist[ed] the imposition of clerical authority [and] the inculcation of approved Christian doctrine."[58] On the other hand, religious practice became increasingly "heterodox" as villagers usurped control over fiestas, village patrons, cofradías, and even aspects of the liturgy. These processes hardened existing tendencies, and as clerical expectations and lay practices diverged, peasants in these regions of "de-Christianization" became even more open to state anticlericalism.

In contrast, in regions of continuing church influence, like the Mixteca Baja, other social and political forces led to an alternate dynamic of "re-Christianization." In particular, violence or the threat of violence often brought clergy and laity together in an attempt to counter what they perceived as evidence of God's ire. Government attacks on the church also served to push the clergy and the laity into a closer alliance. In both of these situations, elites, local priests, and peasants sought the middle ground. As a result, popular and elite religions aligned. Again, two processes occurred. Peasants self-consciously adopted the sanctioned, orthodox expectations of the church, funneling money toward church construction, paying tithes, adopting (at least visibly) clerical ideals of morality, and taking the sacraments.[59] Concurrently, priests and elites also gave way, authorizing and channeling local cults, supporting cofradía autonomy, and celebrating popular pilgrimage routes. Again, these dynamics solidified existing dispositions, and as the clergy became increasingly subsumed into the general belief system, these regions in turn became even more resilient to anticlerical interference. Hierarchical yet flexible, orthodox yet regionally oriented, the disaggregated elements of this brand of re-Christianized regional religiosity often appeared paradoxical or even antithetical. Yet together they locked priests and parishioners into a tight lattice of mutual expectations around ritual practice.

These twin models of regional religious development are what social sociologists might term "border conditions," designed not to create another stable dichotomy nor offer static snapshots of religious cultures, but rather to order the spectrum of changing religious behavior under strain. As such, they serve to describe the religious expression of changing local identities.[60] At any one time, most regions contained elements of both dynamics. Within regions of de-Christianization, some peasants continued to resist an alliance with state anticlericals, to obey the priest, and to attend the sacraments regularly. Within regions of re-Christianization, some peasants employed government rhetoric and state force to undermine priestly power.

As Terry Rugeley states, "Some men [simply] hated priests."[61] Furthermore, they work best as interrelated models. Increasingly orthodox regions were generated as much by outside threats as by the inner mechanics of lay-clerical relations. Finally, both models are extremely dynamic and as a result often difficult to capture over the short term. The banishment of a single local priest or the adoption of some local ritual did not necessarily place a region in one or the other camp. Yet in describing Mexico's long history of political and religious conflicts, these opposing rhythms of lay-clerical interaction do help to define and explain regional allegiances. Whereas regions of de-Christianization embraced radical doctrines (whether federalist, liberal, or revolutionary) of social reform and anticlericalism, regions of re-Christianization resisted such changes and instead supported conservative groups.

Much of the book comprises a careful reconstruction of the Mixteca Baja's social relations and religious culture. Yet it is also concerned with the political interaction between local factions, opposition parties, and national governments. Here, recent work on popular politics proves extremely useful. Over the past two decades scholars have started to piece together the relationship between elite ideologies and popular political motivations, elaborating on the connections and tensions between the two. For example, countless historians have outlined how Mexico's peasants, artisans, and urban poor employed early nineteenth-century constitutionalist ideals to secure local rule.[62] Others have described how peasants used liberalism as a "menu à la carte," picking out principles, such as popular elections and the abolition of communal service, that suited local needs.[63] Most recently, scholars have delineated how the Cardenista ideology of radical *agrarismo* shaped approaches to socioeconomic and political shifts after 1940.[64] These same scholars have started to observe how these popular ideologies, transmitted through institutions, village traditions, and the teaching of parents and elders, could influence responses to political events over the long term. In doing so, they have often revealed the distance between elite and nonelite views. Thus, Emiliano Zapata invoked the popular liberalism of the 1857 Constitution to justify an assault on an avowedly liberal administration.[65] Rubén Jaramillo appealed to the promises of Cardenismo to attack the regime Cárdenas had helped create.[66]

Understandably, most scholars have concentrated on the local ramifications of broad national ideologies. Yet conservative political ideology also had its popular echo. This was often extremely difficult to ascertain.

Conservative writers, obsessed by order and stability, were keen to play down the taint of mass support. At the same time, if state policies were judged unobtrusive (such as during the Porfiriato in the Mixteca Baja or during the 1940s and 1950s in the Altos de Jalisco), conservatism as a generally reactive rather than a proactive political approach could remain under the radar. However, from the nineteenth century onward a popular ideology of conservatism, or what I term "provincial conservatism," also shaped regional political practices. Both elites and non-elites in the Mixteca Baja repeatedly supported national-level conservative leaders, from the centralists of the 1840s through the conservatives of the 1850s to the PAN of the 1950s. Throughout the period, two ideals linked these metropolitan and provincial groups. First, both rejected radical adjustments and instead embraced the need for gradual change. Whereas conservative elites employed the rhetoric of Edmund Burke, the neo-Thomists, or the Christian Democrats, provincial conservatives set about the pragmatic job of making subtle changes to the regional status quo.[67] Second, both groups conceived of the Catholic Church as the key moderator of this gradual change. For conservative elites, the church provided the nation with a unifying language, a common culture, and a well-known set of agreed-upon symbols. For provincial conservatives, religious rituals led by the clergy explained and ensured the rain, the harvest, and the smooth maintenance of regional socioeconomic relations. As a result, both groups shared a deep-seated clericalism and were willing to defend the church hierarchy from bishop down to parish priest.[68] Together, these ideals replicated what Georges Balandier has termed "the traditionalism of resistance," the introduction of slow structural and political change beneath the veneer of cultural, and predominantly religious, continuities.[69]

These twin constants of gradual change and church status not only provided the bond between metropolitan conservatives and their provincial counterparts but also molded all other aspects of the region's political ideology, including ideas about citizenship, political practice, and land tenure. Whereas early nineteenth-century Mixtecs supported a strong centralist state as the upholder of Catholic values and the bringer of stability and order, twenty years later they conceived of the liberal state, with its raft of anticlerical policies, as pernicious and invasive. These constants also shaped patterns of political behavior. When the state seemed to serve local interests, elites and non-elites towed the party line, couching their demands in the deferential language of compliant citizens.[70] In contrast, when the state threatened stable economic relations or church status, both groups vigorously opposed government policies, either through electoral contests (1930–1962) or armed revolt (1857–1867 and 1962). Finally, the drive to introduce change gradually, without conflict, and on terms on which both rich and poor could agree also regimented conceptions of land tenure. When radical rebels threatened reform, elites and non-elites defended the existing system through the discourse of reciprocal rights during the nineteenth century and through the rhetoric of private ownership during the twentieth. Yet as the shift suggests, neither group was averse to alteration. Between 1830 and 1890 indigenous nobles sold off the vast majority of their lands and created a new class of peasant smallholders.

At the same time, provincial conservatism, like its popular liberal or revolutionary equivalents, could also fall out of step with metropolitan ideals. On the one hand, provincial conservatism often melted away as soon as national or state governments pulled away from radical or anticlerical strategies. Catholics in the Mixteca Baja supported the Díaz regime until its final days, showing little enthusiasm for the church-backed Partido Católico Nacional. Twenty years later, the soft-pedaling of revolutionary anticlerical policy persuaded all but a few Mixtec Catholics to renounce support for the Cristero rebels. On the other hand, local habitus could also outstrip elite conservative pragmatism, often unsettling metropolitan leaders. Provincial conservatism was always selective. During the 1830s and 1840s, local centralists blended federalist respect for local rule with a centralist concern for priestly authority, church morality, and stability and order. Despite ecclesiastical dictates, peasants continued to struggle against state schooling beyond the official détente of 1940. A decade later PAN followers bucked official party policy and used violent means to resist PRI electoral impositions.

Together, the rejigging of moral economy theory, the interaction of elite and popular religion, and a political ideology of provincial conservatism serve to explain social relations, religious culture, and political allegiances in the Mixteca Baja in the two centuries since Independence. As readers will discover, the region was in many ways quite peculiar: dominated by a resilient indigenous noble class, cripplingly poor but covered in religious shrines, broadly indigenous yet comparatively literate, conservative but surrounded by radical liberals and revolutionaries. The longevity of the region's political culture and the continuity between events in the nineteenth and twentieth centuries certainly make the region stand out. Few areas have sustained such stable socioeconomic relations or church influence over the past two hundred years. However, as constant comparisons make clear, the situation in the Mixteca Baja was repeated elsewhere throughout Mexico's postcolonial period, in Nayarit under Manuel Lozada, in the Sierra Gorda under Tomás Mejía, and in the Bajío under the Sinarquistas.

Furthermore, although differing rhythms and forms of state anticlericalism make direct comparison less easy, the integration of socioeconomic, cultural, and political analyses outlined here can be employed to understand other prochurch peasantries throughout Europe and Latin America over the past two centuries. Despite protestations of Mexican exceptionalism, the country's Catholic rebels were not alone. Vendée peasants sided with local landholders to defend the church against French revolutionary reforms through armed rebellion and then prolonged passive resistance from the 1790s onward.[71] During the early nineteenth century Peruvian and Colombian indigenous groups and Guatemalan smallholders also allied with local priests to combat state radicalism.[72] In the "culture wars" of the second half of the nineteenth century, German, Polish, French, Spanish, and Mexican peasantries from Poznan in the east to Nayarit in the west did the same.[73] Finally, the early Cold War saw Catholics throughout the globe join together to oppose the communist threat. Although clear national differences emerged, comparison is nonetheless possible, especially because these popular reactions to state anticlericalism developed a disconcertingly familiar and repetitive pattern born of common ideological heritage, growing religious interaction, and a tradition of intellectual orthodoxy.[74]

Sources

Before launching the reader into the text, I should briefly describe my sources. Investigating conservatism over the past two hundred years in a dusty, mountainous, poorly studied, predominantly indigenous region, hours from the capital of one of Mexico's most liberal states, may appear quixotic. Yet there was a method to this madness. Unearthing the rhythm and focus of everyday religious life is notoriously difficult. As Butler points out, the usual source for such an understanding is the correspondence between diocesan authorities and parishioners. Yet these documents rarely mention the perfunctory ceremonies and regular festivities that make up the religious calendar and instead veer wildly in tone from overloaded condemnations of individual priests to bootlicking entreaties.[75] In this context, working in the Mixteca Baja has some distinct advantages. First, thanks to the work of Elisa Garzón Balbuena and the support of the Apoyo al Desarrollo de Archivos y Bibliotecas de México (ADABI), the region's parish records, not only of baptisms, marriages, and deaths but also of local cofradías and bishops' visits, are extremely well organized and accessible.[76] Second, from the 1890s onward, the future bishop of the Mixteca Baja, Rafael Amador y Hernández, ordered his priests to keep regular diaries. These diaries, called *libros de gobierno*, provide key insights into community histories, lay-clerical relations, quotidian religious practices, and individual priests and form the basis for the second half of this book.[77]

Despite this serendipitous discovery of the libros de gobierno, re-creating life in a provincial conservative region still remains tougher than outlining events in corresponding liberal or revolutionary areas. Nominally anticlerical coalitions ruled Mexico from 1857 to 2000. Although they often reneged on their most radical propositions, even more conservative regimes expected non-elite groups to couch their demands in the reformist language of the state and keep constitutional infractions off the radar. As James Scott argues, states often required the appearance of hegemony, if not strict compliance with the letter of the law.[78] As a result, finding evidence of prochurch or conservative practices is particularly hard. The discovery of cofradía properties disguised beneath agricultural societies during the 1870s or PAN councils hidden beneath juntas of civil administration in the 1950s requires the compilation and cross-checking of dozens of sources. Assuring that these were regional trends rather than chance exceptions necessitates the triangulation of even more. As a result, the book relies on nearly forty archives, from the ordered tranquility of locals' private collections through the bureaucratic muddle of the Oaxaca state archive to the carefully controlled chaos of Puebla's cathedral vaults.

The book is divided into six chapters. The first chapter outlines the web of socioeconomic, political, and religious relationships that formed the regional moral economy during the colonial period. Chapters 2 and 3 deal with the period 1821 to 1867; chapter 2 looks at socioeconomic, religious, and political developments, while chapter 3 formulates a narrative of provincial conservative political action. Chapter 4 focuses on religion, politics, and socioeconomic developments during the Porfiriato, including the creation of village agricultural societies and the establishment of the local diocese in 1903. Chapter 5 examines the revolutionary period from 1910 to 1940 and highlights religious and political responses to revolutionary violence and state anticlericalism. Finally, the last chapter looks at political shifts in the period 1940 to 1962 and concentrates on local mass support for the PAN.

The People of the Cross

The Mixteca Baja During the Colonial Period

+

O N APRIL 12, 1703, THE DOMINICAN PRIEST OF TONALÁ, ANTONIO Guerrero, wrote to the bishop of Puebla to ask permission to reform and expand the constitution of the cofradía of the Holy Cross. He explained that the cult of the Holy Cross possessed special significance for the inhabitants of Tonalá and the surrounding villages. On May 3, 1655, Mixtecs from the nearby village of Tindú had informed the Dominican friar that every year on the feast day of the Holy Cross they heard music emanating from a cave on the rock face above the village. In response, the Dominicans, the local Spanish administrator, and the villagers of Tonalá walked the six leagues to Tindú to investigate. When they arrived they found that the cave could not be entered easily from the valley below. Consequently, they decided that the only way to reach the entrance was to lower somebody from the rocky hilltop above. They eventually fixed on a local man condemned to death. As villagers collected the necessary ropes, the prisoner took Communion and gave confession with the Dominican friars. Then the assembled crowd attached him to the ropes and let him down "with much work and risk" toward the mouth of the cave. After struggling over a stone outcrop above the opening, the man "miraculously" reached the cave and clambered in. A few minutes later he returned holding a wooden cross and was hoisted up to the expectant throng. The Dominicans took the cross "with much reverence and veneration" and proceeded to parade it around the neighboring villages where it was received "with happiness and joy." Finally, the group arrived in Tonalá and placed the cross beside the altar of the monastery church, where it would remain. The friars immediately wrote to the Bishopric of Puebla and asked to establish a cofradía led by the region's indigenous nobles to celebrate the incredible find.[1] The discovery of the Holy Cross of Tonalá, its subsequent regional popularity, and its repetition in countless community Christ cults speaks not only to the profound influence of colonial Catholicism in the Mixteca Baja but also to the strong reciprocal links between indigenous elites, indigenous commoners, and the region's Dominican missionaries. This tale—of how pre-Hispanic Mixtecs became the "people of the cross"—is the story of this chapter.

After the Spanish Conquest, the regions of New Spain developed distinct local economies, interethnic relations, political systems, and religious cultures based on Spanish demands for raw materials and pre-Hispanic populations. In the north, intense waves of Spanish mining prospectors confronted dispersed, mobile indigenous groups. In the center of the country, commensurate levels of Spanish migrants interacted with a denser, sedentary indigenous population. Finally, in the south substantially fewer Spanish interlopers attempted to carve out a living among similarly dense indigenous settlements. However, divisions were much more complex than this rough cartography allows. In the south, varying physical geographies, pre-Hispanic population patterns and political systems, and regional market imperatives also had "enormous shaping power."[2] Over the three centuries of colonization, these differences combined to produce distinct local systems of economic interaction, political control, and religious identity. In some regions of the south, Spanish economic extraction, political domination, and religious intransigence generated sharp ethnic and cultural divisions that in turn caused high levels of political violence, especially during the eighteenth and nineteenth centuries. But in other regions, stable arrangements emerged that mitigated disagreements and encouraged political dialogue rather than insurrection.

During the colonial period, colonizers and colonized in the Mixteca Baja devised a social, economic, and political modus vivendi, elements of which survived into the nineteenth century and channeled popular support toward centralist and then conservative policies. Furthermore, they also constructed a regional language of religious devotion that allowed for, integrated, and eventually described the gradual changes wrought by the Bourbon Reforms and Independence. Limited Spanish immigration and sparse economic opportunities permitted the persistence of strongly hierarchical village organizations in which indigenous caciques and commoners engaged in paternalist relations of unequal but reciprocal exchange. Although migratory livestock haciendas and commerce drew these villages into the colonial economy, their internal relationships tended to be reinforced rather than undermined. This mutual interdependence of Spanish merchants, indigenous caciques, Mixtec peasants, and the environment was described in a series of regional cults both to the Cross and to Jesus Christ.

Although the demographic, economic, political, and cultural pressures of the eighteenth century strained this precarious compact, it survived. First, the political model of the hierarchical village was both decentralized and reproduced with the creation of numerous new *repúblicas de indios* with similar arrangements of social inequality. Second, intermarriage between Spanish and mixed-race merchants and indigenous caciques and migratory hacienda workers created a tier of socially prestigious and culturally bilingual *gente de razón* who would not only go on to form the post-Independence regional elite but who could also settle interethnic disputes. Third, although Bourbon ecclesiastical reforms threatened to open up a divide between native and non-native groups, the decentralization of the regional language of religious devotion stabilized possible conflicts. The regional paternalist pact that emerged during the eighteenth century and stressed hierarchy, reciprocity, decentralization, and common devotions would frame popular responses to the conflicts of the nineteenth century.

Geography, Pre-Hispanic Settlement, and the Conquest

The Mixteca is an extensive, geographically diverse region extending 270 kilometers from southern Puebla to the Pacific coast and around 180 kilometers from eastern Guerrero to the western edge of the valleys of Oaxaca and Tehuacán. At the end of the sixteenth century, the Spanish roughly adopted the indigenous division of the region into three distinct zones. The Mixteca Alta is the central highland area of the Mixteca located between 1,500 and 2,500 meters above sea level. The Mixteca de la Costa is the southern low-lying region with heights ranging from sea level to 750 meters, which stretches northward from the Pacific coast to Putla. Finally, the Mixteca Baja is the northwesterly region with altitudes predominantly between 750 and 1,650 meters.[3] This book will deal with the entire region of the Mixteca Baja, encompassing the modern political districts of Huajuapan and Silacayoapan and the northern sections of Juxtlahuaca and Teposcolula in Oaxaca as well as Acatlán in Puebla. But most of the historical data are taken from archives in the central district of Huajuapan.

These clear geographical divisions mask a host of complex microclimates. Although the Mixteca Baja is relatively low lying, it includes fertile valleys, sheer ravines, rolling hills, and towering mountains. The valleys follow the path of the Río Mixteco and its tributaries, which consist of short, seasonally fluctuating streams. At times the streams run through imposing gullies with rock sides as in San Sebastián del Monte or the Boquerón de Tonalá. Sometimes the streams open up into rivers and rich floodplains at places like Huajuapan, Juxtlahuaca, Atoyac, and Tonalá. The Dominican chronicler Francisco de Burgoa described the valley of Juxtlahuaca as very fertile, "with two beautiful rivers . . . which turned emerald in the sun." But regions of agricultural potential were divided by an extensive network of hills, mountains, and cliffs. Thus, Burgoa also claimed that Juxtlahuaca was "the most mountainous area of the country."[4] As the region ascends toward the Sierra Madre del Sur, mountains like La Soledad in Huajuapan, El Cerro del Venado in Juxtlahuaca, and El Cerro de Ihualtepec reach heights between 2,500 and 3,000 meters.[5] The contrast between the valleys and mountains is further accentuated by the differences in soil and temperature. While the valleys are covered by copious fluvial deposits, the hills and mountains are covered by a thin layer of dirt only 10 centimeters deep, extremely prone to erosion, and only amenable to hardy grasses, cacti like the nopal and bisnaga, and agaves like the maguey.[6] Moreover, whereas temperatures on the valley floors rarely fall below 10 degrees, thus avoiding the destructive frosts of the Mixteca Alta, temperatures in the mountains can dip below freezing. Low and irregular annual rainfall exacerbates the Mixteca Baja's environmental instability. Although the rainy season starts in May and lasts until September, monthly rainfall barely rises above 170 millimeters even in the wettest month of August.[7] As rains often come late or not at all, the region perpetually exists between the "danger of frost and the fear of drought."[8]

Sedentary peoples populated the Mixteca Baja over four thousand years ago, but not until AD 300 did complex settlement patterns start to emerge. From AD 300 to 800 the Nuiñe culture flourished at ceremonial centers like El Cerro de las Minas above the valley of Huajuapan. The Mixtec Baja stood at one end of a densely inhabited, commercially linked triangle of pre-Hispanic communities stretching from the Mixteca Baja in the south to Tehuacán in the east and Teotihuacán in the north. However, by the Late Classic period El Cerro de las Minas had been abandoned, and the Mixteca Alta became the hub of Mixtec culture.[9] "The Baja and Costa regions . . . were now regarded as . . . peripheral to the central zone."[10] Nevertheless they were still well populated and economically important. As complex centers declined, the Mixteca Baja became divided into numerous smaller "village-states" and resembled a "fragmented political panorama of de facto independent kingdoms."[11] The hills around Huajuapan supported Postclassic settlements like Ihualtepec, Tequixtepec, Chila, Acatlán, and Diquiyú as well as other small communities near the contemporary villages of Calihuala, Cuyotepeji, Huapanapan, Patlanalá, Tezoatlán, Tutla, Silacayoapan, Xochixtlapilco, and Suchitepec.[12]

Although many of these communities paid tribute to the Triple Alliance, they maintained a distinctly Mixtec political system. Individual village-states were highly stratified. At the apex of the pyramid was a class of royal lords (or *yya*) who held their position by right of inheritance. Below the lords was a class of nobles (or *toho*), often related to the royal family. They made up the administrators, warriors, and priests of these small city-states. Finally, at the bottom was a differentiated mass of commoners (*ñadehi*) and slaves who worked as servants, peasants, and artisans.[13] The nobility were "absolute masters and had full and complete jurisdiction" in their villages.[14] Furthermore, they also extracted labor and tribute from the commoners resident on their lands. In return, they offered physical protection and played important religious roles as priests and intermediaries between the earthly realm and the divine. As Kevin Terraciano argues, the Mixteca Baja was probably even more hierarchical than the Mixteca Alta.[15] But although individual communities were divided, the system itself was highly flexible and decentralized. Communities avoided internecine warfare through marriages between noble families. At the same time, supple bilinear inheritance patterns prevented the extreme concentration or fragmentation of territorial dominance.[16]

As Ronald Spores argues, the Spanish Conquest of the Mixteca was carried out with "little overt opposition from the natives." From 1520 to 1550 a handful of rebellions occurred along the coast around Tututepec, a few of which reached into the Mixteca Baja. But in general the response to mistreatment by the Spanish was flight rather than fight. When the population of Tamazulapan suffered the exorbitant assessments and excessive labor demands of a local Spanish landowner in 1535, the village went into hiding in the mountains.[17] Yet Spanish dominance did radically transform the region. Waves of disease hit the Mixteca on at least four occasions during the late sixteenth century.[18] According to Woodrow Borah and Sherbourne Cook, the population of the Mixteca Alta declined from a precolonial level of 700,000 to 57,000 by 1590 and 30,000 by 1670.[19] Although population decline may not have been quite this dramatic, the diseases were devastating.[20] A century later, Burgoa commented that there had been such a demographic drop "that some villages remain[ed] empty, without a person, and others . . . with eight or ten inhabitants."[21] By 1580, the Mixteca Baja had a population of around 6,500 Indian tributaries or around 23,500 inhabitants divided unevenly over the settlements. Whereas large towns like Acatlán and Silacayoapan possessed ample population, smaller villages like Petlalcingo and Tepeji listed less than two hundred tribute payers.[22] Within forty years the population had probably fallen by half again.[23]

As well as importing disease, the first generations of Spanish conquistadores also imposed a system of political governance on the region. At first they divided the territory into eleven encomiendas in which the Mixtecs were entrusted as laborers to individual conquistadores.[24] During the second half of the sixteenth century, the encomiendas were slowly phased out and replaced with another political organization that would endure until the late eighteenth century. Jurisdiction of indigenous settlements was now divided between *corregimientos* and *alcaldías* directed by appointed Spanish administrators. The Mixteca Baja had corregimientos with seats in Huajuapan, Ihualtepec, and Silacayoapan and two alcaldías with seats in Tonalá and Acatlán. This political geography changed little over the colonial period, although it appears that the small *corregimiento* of Ihualtepec was extinguished and the *alcaldía* of Tonalá shifted location to Huajuapan after a devastating earthquake in 1711.[25]

In addition to the establishment of Spanish jurisdictional seats during the late sixteenth century, the conquerors also instituted the process of *congregación*, attempting to concentrate the falling indigenous population into manageable units for reasons of political control and religious evangelization. These units were divided between a *cabecera*, or head town, and multiple smaller *sujeto* (subject) villages. The effects were distinctly mixed. On the one hand, some yya and toho families from outlying villages moved into the *cabeceras*, many of which had been established around the region's Dominican convents. In doing so, they effectively created new concentrations of noble power linked to the Spanish colonial regime. As late as 1770 14 percent of the missionary town of Tequixtepec claimed noble heritage.[26] On the other hand, other indigenous villages, including their noble families, stayed put. The attempted *congregaciones* of Zacatepec and Ihualtepec in 1603 left thirteen and twenty-seven subject villages, respectively. While some of these subject villages disappeared, others retained their lands and would become cabeceras during the eighteenth century.[27]

The geography, political system, and relatively pacific conquest of the Mixteca Baja shaped the region's subsequent history. The divergent, unbalanced semi-arid environment delineated the region's economy. In the fertile valleys, especially to the north around Atoyac, Spanish settlers struggled against entrenched Mixtec communities to establish small sugar plantations and mills. Yet the region's precipitous mountains also permitted the survival and adaption of other Mixtec villages. These tacked between developing their own intensive sheep- and goat-herding operations and renting pastoral lands to Spanish-owned mobile livestock estates or *haciendas volantes*. Moreover, precipitous geography and Postclassic patterns of political development not only delineated regions of agricultural expansion and pastoral enterprise, they also aided the survival of indigenous political organization.

The Colonial Moral Economy

Until recently, historians argued that indigenous groups survived the colonial period by reconstituting themselves as "closed, corporate communities." Building on the work of Woodrow Borah, Eric Wolf argued that the population decline of the sixteenth and seventeenth centuries caused a "century of depression." During this period indigenous villages retrenched, forming strong community structures that sought to meet Spanish demands for labor and resources without surrendering local autonomy to outsiders. These new communities possessed three distinct characteristics. First, by tenaciously enforcing corporate controls such as communal landholding, they were broadly egalitarian. Second, by encouraging endogamy and agricultural subsistence, they were closed to the outside world. Third, religion, and in particular the cult of village saints operating through religious confraternities, acted functionally to redistribute wealth.[28] Over the last two decades historians and ethnohistorians have started to question what John Chance calls this "anthropological invention of tradition," a "reified theory" that has acted as a substitute "for actual empirical inquiry."[29] Although the model of the closed corporate community may work for certain villages at certain times, it should not be imposed indiscriminately on the entirety of colonial Mexico.

In fact, many villages, including those of the Mixteca Baja, survived the colonial period as intensely hierarchical and open institutions within which religious organizations served not to redistribute wealth but instead described the uneven pact between indigenous lords, indigenous commoners, and the colonial regime. First, as numerous scholars have argued, the assertion that indigenous lords gradually became indistinguishable from the commoners they once dominated does not hold for huge swathes of New Spain.[30] In fact, indigenous lords, often directly descended from pre-Hispanic noble families, dominated villages in the valleys of Mexico, Puebla, and Toluca until the end of the eighteenth century. Indeed, the "supposedly egalitarian character of the indigenous community might not have existed in colonial" New Spain.[31] Second, most villages, even in the more peripheral regions of New Spain, were economically and socially open. Indigenous villagers voluntarily played a key role in commercial capitalism as producers, laborers, muleteers, and merchants.[32] At the same time, geographical mobility and consequently exogamy were extremely common.[33] Third, this system remained stable due to a series of reciprocal agreements between elites (both native and non-native) and commoners, or what E. P. Thompson and James Scott call a "moral economy.[34] Religion was so fundamental to these agreements, they might be better termed a spiritual economy and the community, as John Monaghan argues, a "congregation."[35] In return for produce, labor, obedience, and deference, commoners expected indigenous elites and the colonial church to provide the space, funds, and institutional backing for the local cults they believed to be essential to their subsistence. This moral economy, reconfigured and redrawn but not destroyed, became the foundation for regional conservatism during the nineteenth century.

Caciques and Commoners

During the sixteenth century the Spanish realized that in order to rule the colony without a large standing army, they needed to adopt the political patterns of the colonized. Particularly in regions of relatively pacific conquest, they allowed the continuation of noble, or what they termed "cacique," dominance. In 1558 the Council of the Indies demanded that Spanish administrators respect and treat justly "cacicazgos . . . caciques or their descendants that claim succession in them." If they had previously "unjustly deprived them of their cacicazgos," they were to be restituted "and judicial notice given to all concerned."[36] In some regions with a high Spanish presence, invasive haciendas, and a thin Indian population, the edict could not arrest the nobility's decline. But in others, like the Mixteca Baja, male and female members of yya or cacique families were exempted from tribute and taxes and were allowed to continue their social, economic, and political supremacy until the late eighteenth century in return for collecting tribute, keeping the peace, and taking a lead role in Christian evangelization,.

As in the pre-Hispanic period, cacique and *cacica* dominance was expressed in all facets of everyday life. Unlike their peasant counterparts who were baptized with two simple Spanish first names, they adopted the surnames of famous conquistadores, friars, and bishops, such as Alvarado and Villagómez, and were to be addressed with the noble Spanish prefix *don*.[37] In contrast to their dependants who inhabited one-room wooden shacks or jacales, most caciques continued to live in relative luxury in stone palaces in the centers of communities. These were large complexes with several rooms or groups of single-room houses arranged around sunken patios. Although earthquakes destroyed many of the stone palaces of the Mixteca Baja, they probably resembled those of the Mixteca Alta. Kevin Terraciano recounts that the complex at Yanhuitlán contained nine separate patios during the sixteenth century and that the main patio of the Teposcolula palace could fit over one hundred people.[38] The caciques also looked different. The men were permitted to dress in Spanish fabrics and styles, ride horses, and carry swords and guns. The women mixed European clothes with expensive indigenous jewelry.[39]

Caciques not only maintained the outward appearance of superiority, they backed up appearance with control of land, labor, commerce, and political power. Individual villages did petition for lands for the pasture of livestock during early colonial period, but caciques dominated the confirmations of landholdings from the Council of the Indies in the form of *mercedes*. For example, between 1593 and 1594 Juan de Velasco, the cacique of Huajuapan; Pedro de Alvarado, the cacique of Silacayoapan; Jeronimo de la Cruz, the cacique of Ihualtepec; and Diego Cortés, the cacique of Patlanalá all received permission to use sites for livestock pasture.[40] Between 1550 and 1620 caciques received sixteen plots. In comparison, individual communities gained eleven and Spanish settlers just three.[41] In addition to official confirmations, local Spanish administrators were also permitted to hand out mercedes to individual nobles.[42] Some families amassed enormous private landholding empires through perspicacious marriages and judicial persistence. In 1724 Domingo de la Cruz y Guzmán, the cacique of Tonalá, claimed to own lands in Atoyac, San Ildefonso Salinas, Santa María, Ayuquila, San Andrés, San Sebastián del Monte, Yuchío, Tindú, Huajuapan, and Tonalá.[43] When Narciso Villagómez Cortés de Velasco assumed the *cacicazgo* of Tequixtepec in 1790, he took over lands in the adjoining villages of Suchitepec, Cuyotepeji, Tequixtepec, Chila, and Miltepec.[44] His brother-in-law, Martín José Villagómez Pimentel de la Cruz Guzmán, had an even grander agrarian empire to the north around Acatlán and Petlalcingo and to the west in Tonalá and Silacayoapan. He even claimed huge properties to the south in Yanhuitlán, Teposcolula, and Chicahuaxtla.[45]

Caciques not only owned huge properties, they also laid claim to the labor of commoners resident on these properties. As a result, although the Spanish officially prohibited the ownership of *terrazgueros*, or serfs, by indigenous rulers in 1618, dependents in the Mixteca Baja continued to offer personal services to caciques well into the nineteenth century. The priest of Huajolotitlán certified that Narciso Villagómez Cortés de Velasco was the son of local nobles who "were attended by personal services and received as caciques."[46] In 1783 a peasant from Cuyotepeji claimed that the village traditionally supplied the local cacique with "two Indians for his house and a woman to grind the corn." They also handed over thirty bushels of maize, beans, and *chile* for his house and "two hens at Easter and during the other principal fiestas."[47] Other caciques were even more exacting. According to local villagers, Lucia de Terrazas Moctezuma, the cacica of Ihualtepec, demanded that four Indians work as textile weavers and domestic servants in her house each week without any recompense. She also forced other villagers to spend their own money on traveling "to distant lands with her merchandise." Another village complained that she had them give up half the salt they collected and half a bushel of maize per year.[48]

Finally, caciques also transposed their pre-Hispanic political dominance into the Spanish system of repúblicas de indios. As Arij Ouwenweel argues, "Caciques appropriated the [governorship of republics] in such a way that the terms [*governor* and *cacique*] were ... synonyms."[49] For example, members of the Cruz cacique family held the position of governor of Tonalá from 1715 to 1730 with only one interruption. Over the next century they shared the position with other caciques including members of the Mendoza, Guzmán, and Salazar families.[50] Caciques from the Villagómez and Bautista families monopolized political control of the villages of Tequixtepec, Suchitepec, and Miltepec during the 1730s and 1740s.[51] Martín Joseph de Villagómez

Guzmán y Mendoza held the position of governor of Silacayoapan from 1719 to 1723.[52] According to Margarita Menegus Bornemann, caciques ruled the villages of Tejupan, Chazumba, and Acaquizapan from 1757 to 1758.[53]

However, the relationship between caciques and indigenous commoners was not one sided. Rather, it was, as Ouwenweel argues, one of "reciprocal dominance."[54] In return for obedience, deference, and labor, Mixtec commoners demanded land use, justice, and protection. Lucia de Terrazas Moctezuma's dependents took her to court because they alleged that she refused to allow their "traditional rights" to build houses and collect palm, maguey flowers, copal, and wood on her lands. She retorted that she not only did this but also lent them lands to pasture cattle and goats.[55] Similarly, the commoners of Chazumba complained that in contrast to his predecessors, their present cacique no longer allowed them to "pasture their livestock on his mountainous lands, cultivate and sow on his fertile lands, and collect wood, palm, beehives, cacti, chiles, and clay from the forests."[56] Although arguments over the exact terms of this traditional contract between caciques and peasants became increasingly common during the late eighteenth century, most caciques still acknowledged their responsibilities. Esteban Jiménez, the cacique of Acaquizapan, defended the lands of his pueblo against the designs of the neighboring cacique, Gregorio Villagómez, during the 1780s.[57] Jacinto Jiménez de Esquivel, the cacique of Tequixtepec, claimed that he "loved the Indians without any [ulterior] motive."[58] In fact, so strong was the bond between nobles and peasants that villages often supported the more down-on-their-luck caciques. In 1705 the village of Tequixtepec claimed that their cacique had been "as a father to us" and asked whether the official house of the governor could be returned to him.[59] Although several villages accused Lucia de Terrazas Moctezuma of unjust exactions, other communities supported her case, acknowledging her possession of the lands they inhabited and claiming that they always gave to her "according to custom."[60]

The structure, if not the persistence, of cacique-commoner relations resembled that of many other villages of central New Spain, with one crucial difference. Unlike many other areas of the colony, noble rule in the Mixteca Baja was shared between male and female members of the noble house. Although the Spanish prohibited women from taking political roles in the villages and judicial roles in court, there was little decline in female status during the colonial era as *cacicas* could inherit, possess, and pass on titles like their male counterparts.[61] When nobles married, caciques and cacicas ruled property jointly, and if the man died first the woman took over the land and personal services of her husband. When she died, properties were split, often fairly evenly, between sons and daughters.[62] Bilinear inheritance patterns allowed the establishment of huge cacicazgos ruled over exclusively by women. Thus when her husband died, Lucia de Terrazas Moctezuma not only inherited a herd of over fifteen hundred cattle, "thousands of sheep," and a textile enterprise, but also the land and commoners of twenty-five separate villages. According to the litigants, their labor had provided her "with so much money" that she was one of the richest leaders in the Mixteca.[63] Similarly, in the early eighteenth century Teresa de la Cruz Villagómez Pimentel y Guzmán owned huge swathes of property around Yanhuitlán and Acatlán, which she inherited from her aunt in 1717.[64]

In some areas of New Spain, like Tarascan Michoacán, northern Yucatán, and the Sierra Norte de Puebla, caciques were in decline by the late sixteenth century.[65] In other areas, they survived, but only just. In these regions social relations were effectively reduced to an ethnic dyad as Spanish and mestizo interlopers confronted a fairly undifferentiated mass of Indian villagers. However, in the Mixteca Baja and other regions of central Mexico wealthy, powerful indigenous caciques not only survived the colonial rupture, but also prospered.[66] Furthermore, although commoners increasingly clashed with their noble lords, especially in the larger commercial villages of the region, the paternalist relationship of "reciprocal dominance" endured, was successfully replicated, and would provide a model for social and political relations during the late eighteenth and early nineteenth centuries. Finally, the strength of cacicas during colonial period and, as we shall see, up to the mid-nineteenth century suggests reasons for the ready acceptance of female religious leaders from the 1860s onward.

Religion and the Catholic Church

The relationship between caciques and commoners was not simply based on unequal economic exchange. As in the pre-Hispanic period, caciques were also expected to fulfill a religious role as key intermediaries between the divine and earthly spheres, thus ensuring regular rain and propitious harvests. In regions with limited or incipient church influence or declining cacique status, nobles sometimes reverted to unorthodox crypto-pagan methods of guaranteeing the economic stability of the community.[67] However, in regions like the Mixteca Baja where the missionary orders were well established by the end of the sixteenth century and caciques remained powerful throughout the period, the official church became a third actor in the moral economy. By framing a shared regional ideology and practice of religious devotion, the church legitimized the caciques' position. In return, caciques became the lay elite of the church and were expected to use their considerable power to bring commoners into the Catholic fold.

The Dominicans arrived in the Mixteca during the 1530s. After the shock of the Conquest, which precipitated a series of politically motivated trials for idolatry and culminated in the execution of several indigenous caciques, the friars started to establish huge monasteries throughout the region.[68] At first they concentrated their efforts in the more densely populated Mixteca Alta, erecting the magnificent complexes with their open-air chapels and large patios at Coixtlahuaca, Yanhuitlán, and Teposcolula. But by the end of the sixteenth century, they had moved into the Mixteca Baja and built monasteries in Chila, Tonalá, Tamazulapan, Tejupan, Huajuapan, Tequixtepec, Ihualtepec, Juxtlahuaca, and Tecomaxtlahuaca.[69] By the end of the sixteenth century the Mixteca monasteries accounted for eighteen of the sixty-four Dominican establishments in Mexico.[70] In 1596 the administration of the Dominican orders split. The Oaxaca City branch took control of the establishments in the Mixteca Alta, while the Mexico City branch continued to direct those of the Mixteca Baja.[71] In 1656 the Mexico City branch divided again, and the monasteries of the Mixteca Baja fell within the jurisdictional ambit of the new Puebla branch.[72] Although the Diocese of Puebla had occasionally attempted to replace the order with secular priests, by the mid-eighteenth century the Puebla Dominicans still possessed eleven monasteries in the region. They had even expanded during the period, constructing new complexes at Tamazola and Tezoatlán. In 1747 these employed forty-three friars, unevenly distributed over the different establishments. In the central region of the Mixteca Baja, roughly correspondent to the contemporary districts of Huajuapan and Silacayoapan, there were sixteen friars or one for every thousand indigenous inhabitants.[73] In addition, secular priests resided in the parishes of Tlapancingo and Silacayoapan.[74] Even in baroque New Spain, the concentration of priests in such a rural area was extraordinary. Outside the major cities, other regions of New Spain possessed around one priest per two thousand Indians.[75]

The concentration and longevity of the Dominican order in the Mixteca Baja allowed the development of an orthodox Catholic culture based on education, church construction, cofradías, and the regional cult of the Holy Cross. However, this relatively successful program of conversion depended on the adoption of the pre-Hispanic socioreligious system. Postclassic

nobles were not only political but also "religious rulers . . . intermediaries between the human community and the Other World, the domain of the Gods."[76] The term *yya* not only signified "lord" but also "god." As Maarten Jansen argues, nobles, through their allegedly divine heritage, were "depositaries of territorial sacrality," responsible for renewing the annual pact with the gods, which in turn ensured the survival and prosperity of the community.[77] Pre-Hispanic nobles in the Mixteca acted as priests, extracting blood "from their tongues and ears" to serve the spirits of the earth.[78] In the early post-Conquest period, before sustained evangelization had taken place, caciques continued these practices. In 1544 the Inquisition accused nobles from Yanhuitlán and Coatlán of continuing pre-Hispanic sacrifices to the old gods.[79] Despite these initial failures, over the next two centuries the co-option of nobles' roles as divine intermediaries would become the centerpiece of the conversion process. Discarding the less acceptable practices of blood sacrifice and direct mediation, caciques allied with the colonial church and became what Spores has termed "devices for directed acculturation." Thus, as church officers, church builders, and cofradía leaders they both "maintain[ed] an intimate tie to the past which justified and validated their position in the social hierarchy" and "made conscious efforts to embrace a new system of values and a new way of life."[80]

During the sixteenth century, Dominicans made their initial contact with the Mixtec nobility through a process of mutual education. The Dominicans learned Mixtec and, with the help of certain pious nobles, translated Christian texts into the indigenous language. From the 1550s onward Dominicans were expected to learn at least one indigenous language and were prohibited from preaching and administering confession before demonstrating their proficiency.[81] Burgoa's hagiography of the early Dominicans is replete with mentions of friars who studied and learned Mixtec.[82] Over two centuries later the obligation remained, and the Puebla branch still retained a Mixtec language teacher for the region's numerous friars.[83] During this period the Dominicans also produced numerous linguistic and religious texts, including dictionaries, catechisms, prayers, plays, spiritual tracts, and explanations of Christian doctrine. Especially initially, nobles had an important role in the production of these teaching aids. Jansen convincingly establishes that Benito Hernández's *Doctrina cristiana en lengua mixteca* was written with the cooperation of Mixtec nobles, not only adopting the noble Mixtec dialect but also native symbolism, with a heavy emphasis on gold, green plumes, and the sun.[84] Other nobles took a more direct role in the transmission of Christian knowledge. Diego Osorio was a cacique from the village of Achiutla and accepted the Dominican habit after he was widowed. As a friar he dedicated his remaining years to translating the prayers of saints and books of hymns into Mixtec.[85] Gabriel Valdiviesio was a noble "of such talent and so given to reading books that by his hand he translated and composed prayers and spiritual treatises that totaled 27 books . . . which many ministers have used."[86] The friars employed these materials to transmit the major tenets of Christianity to their Indian charges at schools established on the patios of the major monasteries. According to Burgoa, the monastery of Tecomaxtlahuaca possessed a music school and a school of Christian doctrine.[87] Although the general efficacy of these schools is uncertain, and many Mixtecs probably failed to attain the questionable benefits of a Christian education, they did manage to train many of the noble elite in the finer points of Catholicism. As the process of congregación had concentrated many elite families around the monasteries, the Dominicans forced them to send their children to the church schools. As a result, by the eighteenth century Mixtec nobles, living in their stone palaces surrounding the monastery complexes at Huajuapan, Tonalá, Tamazola, Tezoatlán, Ihualtepec, and Chila, formed an educated Christian elite. When the bishop of Puebla reached Tonalá in 1766, ten years after the Dominicans had left, he disparaged the educational level of the general Indian populace but admitted that the Mixtec nobles "knew Christian doctrine," could recite "the important prayers," "were very observant," and "went to church every Sunday for mass."[88]

As members of a lay elite, nobles not only reprised their pre-Hispanic religious roles, they also helped the church to establish the infrastructure of evangelization as patrons and church officers. In the Mixteca Alta, we have ample evidence that caciques organized labor for the construction of the enormous complexes and donated money and land to the Dominican order. Gabriel de Guzmán, the cacique of Yanhuitlán in the late sixteenth century, "actively collaborated in the building of [the monastery complex]." In exchange, the friars diverted some of the labor to build him a new stone palace beside the temple.[89] Evidence from the Mixteca Baja is sparser because so many of the monasteries collapsed during the region's periodic earthquakes. In 1555 the cacique of Tamazulapan donated a strip of fertile land to the institution.[90] Thirty years later the neighboring cacique of Tejupan allowed the friars of the nearby monastery to grow wheat on his fields.[91] The practice of collaboration continued into the eighteenth century. The cacique families of Tonalá pooled their resources to help reconstruct the temple of Tonalá after its collapse in 1711.[92] Caciques also funded the decoration of these massive churches. The nobles of Tamazulapan funded the painting of Our Lady of the Rosary in the church at Tamazulapan during the early 1700s. The painter immortalized their generosity by including them in the picture.[93]

Caciques also helped the process of evangelization as officers of the church, acting as *fiscales*, sacristans, *cantores*, and church notaries. These church officers assisted the Dominicans in their sacerdotal duties, maintained church buildings and ornaments, and policed the faith. The fiscales held the most controversial office. They collected church taxes, took roll at Sunday Mass, enforced the moral demands of the church, and administered corporal punishment to indigenous sinners. In contrast, sacristans were responsible for more mundane tasks including the cleanliness, security, and general care of the church buildings. Cantores led the choir in sung Masses, and church notaries helped the priest write down baptisms, marriages, and deaths.[94] Male members of the noble families dominated these positions throughout the colonial period. From 1689 to 1710, members of the Cruz, Velasco, Pacheco, and Bautista families were fiscales in Huajuapan and signed their names as marriage witnesses.[95] From 1720 to 1735 nobles from the Cruz, Guzmán, and Mendiola families in Tonalá held the role of *fiscal* and at least one of the sacristan positions every year.[96]

However, if ecclesiastical education, donation, and administration brought together the Dominican friars and the noble elite by overlaying the pre-Hispanic socioreligious order with Christian imperatives, three further innovations succeeded in drawing non-noble Mixtecs into the region's religious culture: cofradías, godparentage, and the cult of the Holy Cross. During the late seventeenth century the Dominicans started to establish cofradías throughout the Mixteca Baja. At first, the cofradías reflected the evangelical preoccupations of the friars and were chosen specifically to promote the central tenets of the new faith. So, like the other Dominican-controlled regions of New Spain, the Parish of Tonalá in 1752 possessed cofradías to the Holy Sacrament, the Holy Cross, Our Lady of the Rosary, Saint Dominic, the Souls in Purgatory, and Our Lady of Sorrows. As William Taylor argues, New World cofradías, like their Old World counterparts, played an important role in orthodox Christian practice and were intended as ways to "increase public devotion, maintain the [church] and make more secure the priests' income from masses and fiestas."[97] The cofradía of the Holy Sacrament of Tonalá was responsible for funding the weekly Mass throughout the year. Members paid for the regular supply of wafers, oil, sacramental wine, and flowers for these Masses. The organization also funded the parish's elaborate Corpus Christi celebrations in June.[98] Similarly, the cofradía of Our Lady of the Rosary in Chila possessed an image of the Virgin, two crowns, a dress, and a series of cloaks for the annual celebration in October. During the year they spent six pesos on monthly Masses, 12 pesos on Masses during the fiesta, and another 10 pesos on candles to light the image throughout the year.[99]

However, although cofradías were introduced by the Spanish to sustain religious cult, they were not simply another of the colony's imposed obligations. Throughout New Spain, indigenous groups took up, modified, and replicated these organizations according to regional political and economic circumstances. In some regions, they were adapted to the egalitarianism and gradual democratization of community life. But in the Mixteca Baja, they served to maintain the relationship of reciprocal dominance between caciques and commoners. From 1650 to 1750 caciques funded and administered most of the official cofradías in the Mixteca Baja. For example, according to the records for the cofradía of the Holy Sacrament of Tonalá in 1714, 150 of the organization's 286 goats were donated by the cacique, Domingo de la Cruz. The remaining livestock, including three bulls, thirty-two cows, and 136 goats, were handed over by individual villagers, but noble members of the Cruz, Velasco, and Navarrete families dominated. These families went on to monopolize control of the cofradía for the next three decades. Elections for the head, or mayordomo, of the organization, which were held every year after the celebration of Corpus Christi, happened "in the presence of the cacique and other nobles of the village." Almost invariably the voters chose a member of the cacique clans. Thus, Domingo de la Cruz, the cacique of Tonalá, was re-elected every year from 1718 to 1724. He then passed the post on to another cacique of Tonalá who held the position until his death in 1726. The electors then selected another cacique, Juan Bautista Cortés y Velasco, the cacique of Chila who was resident in Tonalá, to control the organization until 1738.[100] Nobles also funded and dominated the cofradía of Our Lady of the Rosary in Chila. Between 1741 and 1755 the mayordomos came exclusively from the noble Ximénez, Bautista, and Velasco clans. When the ecclesiastical authorities of Puebla arrived in 1754 and demanded money to pay the bishop, the cacique, Juan Bautista, made up the shortfall in the cofradía's accounts.[101] Although most church records only mention male members, records for the cofradía of the Holy Sacrament in Tequixtepec indicate that noble women replicated their economic dominance in the religious sphere. The list of the thirty members of the cofradía in 1740 lists fourteen nobles, including nine cacicas from the Velasco, Bautista, and Mendoza families.[102]

This noble pre-eminence in the religious sphere came with defined expectations. Although the cofradías were politically exclusive, they also served as forms of social security for the communities as a whole. On the one hand, cofradías performed distinct duties for members of the village. The cofradía of the Blessed Souls of Purgatory in Tonalá was in charge of shrouding, transporting, and burying the bodies of dead villagers. Members also paid for twelve candles to be lit atop the tomb. In addition, they were responsible for burying any bodies found unclaimed on the roads around the community and sending helpers to "give love and succor" to any of the villagers who fell ill.[103] On the other hand, cofradías also had a broad economic role in defending and distributing village wealth. At the most basic level, they placed the lands and goods of caciques and villagers under the protection of the church. During the eighteenth century, the various cofradías of Tonalá owned the lands of the Yetla ranch. At the beginning of the eighteenth century they pastured around five hundred goats and forty cattle and sowed a little corn. Over time they sold off the goats and bought up more cattle and horses. By 1754 the village's seven cofradías owned a total of 790 cows, 215 horses, and twenty-nine mules.[104] Other cofradías diversified further. The cofradía of Our Lady of the Rosary in Chila not only invested in fertile land but also maguey and wheat, which were then sold at the village market.[105] Cofradía ownership of land and property in Oaxaca prevented their usurpation or sale.[106] In the Mixteca Baja, where land was concentrated in the hands of a few noble families, the system was especially important. The moral economy of land ownership, whereby caciques were expected to permit villagers to use their lands for pasture and agriculture, was overlaid with a further religious imperative.

At the same time, as Danièle Dehouve argues, cofradías acted as the primary lenders for the incipient commercial economy.[107] During the eighteenth century, cofradías throughout the Mixteca Baja increased their cash capital by gradually selling off surplus livestock and agricultural produce. For example, between 1741 and 1747 the cofradía of Our Lady of the Rosary in Chila increased its cash capital from 100 to 260 pesos by selling maguey, cumin, palm, and wheat. By 1749 the mayordomo of the cofradía was not only responsible for the sowing and planting of the crops but also lending part of the capital to entrepreneurial villagers. After a year villagers were expected to pay back the loans together with 25 percent interest. By 1754 the organization was lending over four hundred pesos a year.[108] The system clearly had the potential to create serious economic divisions. However, in the Mixteca Baja they already existed. Here, cofradías, by offering credit to all, were more likely to smooth over the ruptures opened up by the introduction of a cash-based market economy. Cofradías also acted as important repositories of surplus food during times of crisis. During the seventeenth and eighteenth centuries, the Mixteca Baja suffered periodic droughts and consequent famines. In these years of shortage the cofradías distributed their goods among the starving villagers. For example, in 1754 the cofradía of Saint Dominic in Tonalá donated thirty cows to the "Indians and other members of the community" over the course of the year.[109] Lastly, cofradías defrayed the expenses of church construction, repair, and decoration. In 1745 the cofradía of Our Lady of the Rosary in Chila spent sixteen pesos on a curtain to cover the host. Two years later, it spent over one hundred pesos on restoring the church roof.[110]

If the economic role of cofradías fed easily into the system of reciprocal dominance, which characterized relations between caciques and the community, they also formalized and legitimized the spiritual demands made on the noble class. In the pre-Hispanic period caciques had maintained their status by annually confirming the covenant between the community and the gods through bloodletting and sacrifice. In the colonial world they adopted the same role as cofradía leaders. By funding and organizing annual feasts devoted to the new Christian gods, represented by the village saints, they once again worked to ensure climactic temperance, agricultural productivity, and community well-being. As Rodolfo Pastor argues and records from Tonalá, Chila, and Tequixtepec confirm, the fiestas that the Mixtecs accepted and celebrated closely followed the rhythm of the agricultural year. In particular, the feast of the Holy Cross, celebrated on May 3, heralded the beginning of the rainy season, and the feast of Our Lady of the Rosary on October 7 coincided with the harvest.[111] Furthermore, cofradía spending on these feasts testifies to their perceived importance. For example, the cofradía of the Holy Sacrament of Tonalá spent over thirty pesos per year on the Corpus Christi celebration during the eighteenth century. As well as paying for the Mass and butchering three to five cows, they also spent over twenty pesos on fireworks, musicians, singers, and other "goods" including, according to the bishop's representative, "many barrels of mescal and aguadiente."[112] As Taylor argues, cofradía outlay on these other "goods" points to the continuities between these Christian celebrations and their alcohol-fueled pre-Hispanic precedents.[113]

If the nobles' role as cofradía leaders placed the relationship between caciques and the community within an acceptable Christian framework, the system of godparentage, or *compadrazgo*, solidified the connection between caciques and individual commoners. In New Spain, godparents acted as the sponsors of important sacramental events including baptism, confirmation, and marriage. According to Catholic dogma, they also had a responsibility to "teach the child Christian doctrine." Finally, if the actual parents passed away, godparents were also responsible for the care and upkeep of their charges.[114] In a hierarchical society like that of the Mixteca Baja, the system of godparentage served to "structure individual or family relationships vertically between members of different classes."[115] For example, during the eighteenth century caciques dominated the position of godparents in the village of Tonalá. Between 1725 and 1735 Domingo de la Cruz was godfather at the baptism of twelve children from different indigenous families. His relation, María de la Cruz, was responsible for most of the children born on her lands. Between 1725 and 1730 Carlos de Salazar, the cacique of San Mateo, agreed to be godfather for six of the eight children born on his estates.[116]

These links between the church, caciques, and commoners were symbolized and strengthened by the regional devotion to the Holy Cross discovered by the dangling prisoner outside Tonalá in 1655. As Taylor argues, cults to the Cross were extremely common in New Spain. Although representations of the Virgin Mary "appear to dominate Mexico's devotional landscape," local representations of Christ and the Cross "often exceeded the popularity of celebrated images of the Virgin Mary during the colonial period." In fact, nearly 55 percent of the 480 shrines in the colony were Christocentric.[117] These cults and the stories that surrounded them were neither diluted Christian tales nor hastily masked fragments of pre-Hispanic beliefs. Although most contained elements of both, they also described the shifting relationships within New Spain's communities.[118] At times, Christ fables could appear radical and anti-authoritarian, thinly disguised reflections of local disgust with spiritual, political, or economic elites.[119] Yet at other times, they could also help explain shifting power relations in terms that were comprehensible and sanctioned by all groups.[120] Although Christ cults in the Mixteca Baja changed their meanings over time, during the colonial period the Holy Cross of Tonalá, by encapsulating and affirming both Mixtec and Christian beliefs, expressed the relationship between colonizers and colonized with exceptional force.

Figure 1: The Holy Cross of Tonalá. Serafín Sánchez Hernández.

Moreover, the creation of a mobile cofradía that wandered the mountains of the Mixteca Baja gave the cult of the Holy Cross a rare regional reach. By the end of the eighteenth century, the Cross had become the paradigmatic regional symbol of this reciprocal relationship throughout the Mixteca Baja. As a result, it was replicated in the creation of numerous similar cults in the region's new *repúblicas*.

Even in the Dominicans' pared-down story of the discovery of the Holy Cross, it is possible to perceive both Mixtec and European elements.

39

Throughout Mesoamerica, the cross was a common symbol. The first page of the Codex Fejérváry-Mayer shows the form of a cross and was designed for priestly meditation. According to Maarten Jansen and Gabina Pérez Jiménez, each branch represented a different subdivision of time and space associated with the "Gods of the Night" of the Mesoamerican pantheon.[121] At the same time, in Mixtec ritual the cross was used to symbolize the four winds.[122] Caves, like that of Tindú, also held multiple sacred meanings for pre-Hispanic groups as openings to the underworld, resting places of the noble dead, spaces of divinatory power, and locations for fertility rituals.[123] In the Mixteca, Burgoa mentions multiple sites of pre-Hispanic worship located around caves.[124] Here, they were primarily associated with the Mixtec rain god Dzahui, their damp, dripping interiors representative of pending precipitation.[125] As late as 1652 four caciques from Malinaltepec were accused of having entered a cave half a league from their community with wax candles and copal incense to pray for rain before a stone idol.[126] It seems no coincidence that the singing emanating from the cave of Tindú was heard on May 3, not only the feast day of the Holy Cross but also the date by which rains should start in the Mixteca. Finally, the position of the caciques in the story, as the inevitable leaders of the devotion to the Holy Cross, confirmed the Mixtec socioreligious hierarchy and the role of the local nobility in assuring favorable harvests.

Yet, if the discovery of the Holy Cross was a clever piece of what Serge Gruzinski has termed "spiritual piracy"—the usurpation of colonizing symbolism for colonized use—its transformation from potential local heterodoxy to regional orthodoxy owed as much to the belief system of the formal church.[127] In the story the Dominicans organized the prisoner's descent, authorized the cross as an authentic Christian symbol, managed its subsequent tour around the local villages, and established a cofradía with permission of the diocese. On the one hand, the discovery echoed European Catholic trends. As William Christian Jr. argues, seventeenth-century Spain was alive with Christocentric devotions surrounding shifting crucifixes and sweating, groaning, and bleeding Christs. Although these devotions often had roots in medieval traditions, they received new impetus following the Council of Trent's promotion of the liturgy of the Eucharist, the commemoration of Christ's Passion during Holy Week, the feast of the Holy Cross, and Corpus Christi. Furthermore, these devotions, based on verifiable discoveries or visions, were much less dangerous than individual apparitions. There were no "potentially heterodox divine messages, no human being elevated to the category of divine ambassador, nor was there even a threat to the existing organization of space." In fact, rather than threatening church authority, these miracles reinforced it. "They were controlled miracles, worthy of the Catholic Reformation."[128]

On the other hand, the discovery also meshed easily with the contemporary spiritual framework and political necessities of the Dominicans. Spanish spiritual entrepreneurialism did not automatically translate into a parallel movement in New Spain. Here, devotional innovation often inspired considerable skepticism.[129] Yet in the Mixteca Baja friars readily accepted the miraculous finding that proved the efficacy of their teachings, enhanced their sense of divine mission, and, as a result, defended the order against the growing threat of secularization. As Jansen and Pérez Jiménez argue, Dominican teachings in the Mixteca concentrated on devotion to the Cross. Hernández's *Doctrina* was replete with admonitions to worship "that piece of wood" and techniques to make the symbol comprehensible to Mixtec worshippers. He claimed that God had placed a symbol of the Cross in the sky, where it was represented by four stars, and argued that humans formed the shape of the Cross by extending their arms. At the center of the work was a prayer, allegedly spoken by Christ as he lay dying on the Cross, in which the Messiah affirmed to God that people now "believe that you are the true divine being."[130]

Yet the discovery of the Holy Cross did not simply confirm decades of missionary teaching, it also answered more immediate concerns. During the colonial period, numerous friars argued that the Americas had been Christianized long before the Conquest. They carefully constructed this fiction by extrapolating upon the *Acta tomae*, an apocryphal text that claimed that Saint Thomas had preached "beyond the Ganges." During the sixteenth century the myth of Saint Thomas wandering the world and preaching Christianity started to take root in Latin America. During the 1670s, the Mexican scholar Carlos de Sigüenza y Góngora synthesized the evidence for Saint Thomas's arrival in the New World. He argued that the failure of the apostles to evangelize the Indies would have been incompatible with Jesus's commandment to his followers to "teach all people." The only apostle who was known to have traveled widely and who consequently could have evangelized the region was Saint Thomas. Sigüenza y Góngora backed up his claim of Thomas's transatlantic missionary work with examples of indelible traces of feet, miraculous springs, and crosses discovered throughout Latin America, from Brazil to Huatulco in southern Oaxaca.[131] Thus, by discovering a cross in the Tindú cave local Dominican friars not only accommodated Christianity within a Mixtec cosmology but also tapped into an emerging creole belief in the New World's pristine evangelization, which "redeemed their American patria from the stigma of having lain in darkness for sixteen centuries, isolated from revelation."[132] By the mid-eighteenth century Tonalá was a key point on the imagined cartography of Thomas's travels and mentioned in Lorenzo Boturini Bernaducci's work on the pre-Hispanic Christianization of the Indies.[133]

Finally, the Dominicans' newfound position as the authorizers, discoverers, and custodians of a key part of New Spain's purported spiritual heritage offered the order substantial purchase in the ongoing struggle against secularization. In the decade before the discovery, the bishop of Puebla, Juan de Palafox y Mendoza, had initiated a campaign against the religious orders in the diocese. Although the movement focused on removing the Jesuits and Franciscans, Palafox also came into conflict with the Dominicans.[134] Furthermore, his profound Marianism and his support for the incipient cult of Our Lady of Ocotlán struck at the Dominican uncertainty over the Immaculate Conception.[135] The appearance of the Holy Cross, just two years after Palafox's exile, thus appeared as a strong counterclaim to secular religious superiority that could be wheeled out in subsequent conflicts. At the same time, the emergence of the Holy Cross in the 1650s may also have aided the Puebla branch of the Dominicans in their struggle to escape the tutelage of their Mexico City–based masters, which they eventually achieved in 1656.[136]

The parallel enthusiasm for the Holy Cross encouraged the popularity of the cult throughout the eighteenth century. In Tonalá the Holy Cross became the centerpiece of the Christian calendar. The cacique leaders of the cofradía would parade the cross throughout the streets on the first Friday of Lent, on May 3, and on Corpus Christi.[137] At the same time, numerous Mixtecs adopted the surname "de la Cruz." Between 1711 and 1712 14.4 percent of the 320 parents and godparents listed in baptismal records were named "de la Cruz," double those called by the next most common name, "del Rosario." Some, like Gabriel de la Cruz, who fathered a son in July 1712, were caciques. Others, like Petrona de la Cruz, who gave birth to a girl, Sebastiana, in December 1711, had no noble heritage.[138]

Furthermore, unlike other smaller Christocentric devotions that sprang up throughout Oaxaca during the late colonial era, the Holy Cross inspired equal commitment beyond Tonalá and its immediate environs, eventually extending its influence throughout the Mixteca Baja.[139] Although

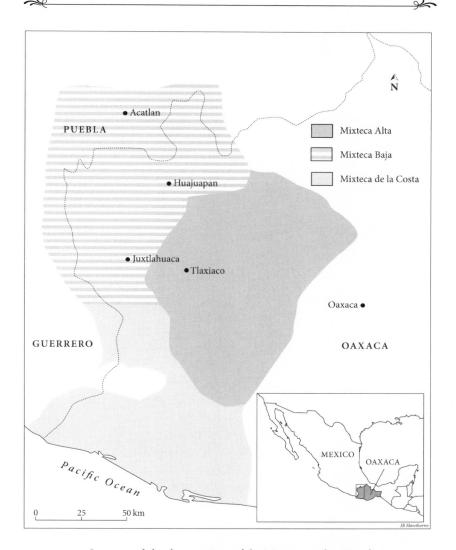

Map 1: Oaxaca and the three regions of the Mixteca. Jackie Hawthorne.

historians have tended to emphasize the attachment of communities to individual local saints, colonial New Spain also witnessed the establishment of strong panregional, intercommunity devotions.[140] During the 1740s, the Holy Cross's noble mayordomos, surrounded by musicians and singers, started to wander the region carrying the icon and demanding money

Map 2: Villages of the Mixteca Baja with contemporary district and state boundaries. Jackie Hawthorne.

from dispersed devotees. The records that survive cover the years 1786 and 1787. During these years the cofradía convoy visited seventy-one pueblos spanning the length of the Mixteca Baja, ranging from the mercantile centers of Huajuapan, Chila, Petlalcingo, and Tlapa to much smaller villages. Each village contained a small *hermandad*, or brotherhood, comprising an average of nine members. Followers were expected to give two reals "for the cult of the Cross." Although the lists rarely mentioned surnames, prefixes indicate that around 10 percent of the donors were from noble families, including doña María Teresa from San Miguel and don Manuel from Calihuala. Furthermore, women also played a central role in providing the mobile cofradía with financial support. They account for 40 percent of contributors and in many villages formed the majority. For example, eleven of the eighteen donors from Atoyac were women. Some members were cacicas and listed their names with the prefix *doña*.[141] Their contributions can be understood as logical extensions of their broad political and economic powers. But these far-reaching religious organizations, which were less bound to the exclusively male sphere of community politics, also seem to have offered space in which non-noble women could break down gendered divisions of religious devotion and prove their piety and fiscal influence; they were precursors of the more democratic cofradías and lay religious organizations that emerged in the nineteenth century.

At the same time, the Holy Cross also formed the root of multiple new community-level cults. Tonalá became an "exemplary center" of the Dominican-Indian pact as other indigenous villages started to imitate the devotion by erecting their own representations of Christ on the Cross. These cults originated in large population centers where a sizeable noble population surrounded the Dominican monasteries. For example, during the late seventeenth century the villagers of Ihualtepec started to worship the bloody image of Our Crucified Lord in a small chapel on one of the hills outside the village. Like the cross of Tonalá, the image of Our Crucified Lord was connected to expectations of precipitation. The chapel was built beside a spring, and celebrations were held on the first Friday of Lent and May 3. In 1717 the Dominican friars authorized the image by establishing a cofradía of local nobles with the diocese's permission.[142] Similarly, around the beginning of the eighteenth century the natives and non-natives of Huajuapan started to worship an even more sanguine image of Christ, Our Lord of Hearts.[143] Although the popularity of individual cults rose and fell, the images of the Cross and crucified Christ not only formed a common devotional language, but also would become the spiritual basis for the writing and rewriting of the relationship between elites and non-elites over the next two centuries. If, as Terraciano argues, the Indians of the Mixteca Alta maintained a kind of shadow identity as the "ñudzahui" or the "people of the rain," the people of the Mixteca Baja probably conceived of themselves as the "people of the Cross."[144]

By the eighteenth century religious devotion in the Mixteca Baja was both Indianized and deeply clerical. On the one hand, the religion resembled that of colonial Guatemala, Yucatán, or Chiapas, where noble control of church-building, godparentage, cofradías, and feasts affirmed the moral economy of communities and created a "harmonious, Indian-made synthesis."[145] On the other hand, the concentration and longevity of the Dominican project, the persistence of powerful cacique families, and the assumption of indigenous beliefs into an orthodox regional cult tied the religiosity of the Mixteca Baja closer to the colonial church. First, missionary continuity forestalled the arrival of less educated, less interested, and less committed secular priests. Second, as caciques remained so influential and unthreatened, they were less likely to confront colonizers by reverting to their previous role as the leaders of quasi-idolatrous cults. Third, by erecting a shared regional devotion that could be worshipped and if possible replicated in individual villages, they prevented the gradual atomization of religious beliefs into village-centered cults.[146] Of course, idolatry still existed, especially in villages outside the immediate ambit of the monastery complexes. Pre-Hispanic rituals were rumored to be practiced to the west around Tlapa, to the east around Tehuacán, and to the south around Tlaxiaco throughout the colonial period.[147] Furthermore, oral accounts testify to the continuation of small-scale fertility rituals and rain ceremonies in the Mixteca Baja during the nineteenth century.[148] But in most communities, social relations and the communal agrarian imperative were molded around acceptable, predominantly orthodox ceremonies authorized by the church. When the Spanish monk Francisco Ajofrín visited the region in the 1760s, his guide, a Mixtec Indian, accompanied Ajofrín's recitation of the Rosary in Mixtec. Unlike in other areas where Ajofrín dismissed indigenous religiosity as a pale impression of its European counterpart, in the Mixteca Baja he was impressed to witness the congregation of Chila singing in praise of San Antonio, whom he ascertained "they love very much."[149] Uniquely among the regions of Oaxaca, Joseph Antonio de Villaseñor y Sánchez, the author of the *Theatro americano*, described the region of Huajuapan as "very devout" and commented that its inhabitants "maintain[ed] temples with the greatest decency."[150] Although non-native immigration, the secularization of parishes, and periodic crackdowns on perceived indigenous heterodoxy would strain this compact, it still held well into the nineteenth century and became the basis of support for clerical conservative policies.

Commerce and the Haciendas Volantes

The persistence of indigenous caciques in the Mixteca should not mask the major changes caused by colonial rule. Spanish immigration, the arrival of a cash economy, and the demands of national and international markets undoubtedly caused disruptions throughout New Spain. In many regions, especially around Mexico City and the Bajío, market penetration broke up communities, dissolved old hierarchies, and created new ones.[151] As land became a valuable commodity, the peasantry tended to polarize as the upper stratum took "advantage of market opportunities, combat[ed] the egalitarian inhibitors of the community and embark[ed] on a course of profit-making and accumulation."[152] However, in other regions, the effects were much less disruptive. In the Mixteca Baja minimal Spanish immigration, poor quality land, shared (if unequal) commercial interests, and the rise of large mobile livestock haciendas, or haciendas volantes, served to cement rather than fracture village solidarity. Caciques and some villagers took advantage of the opportunities offered by the region's favorable commercial position and the passage of haciendas volantes. Yet neither they nor the limited numbers of Spanish settlers sought to usurp peasant lands or enforce commercial demands beyond those delineated "by custom" in the agreements between individual caciques and their communities. Consequently, at least until the mid-eighteenth century, Spanish cash, commerce, and haciendas volantes meshed easily with the moral economies of individual communities, avoiding land grabs and forced commercial exactions and protecting noble power.

During the mid-sixteenth century other settlers joined the handful of Spanish administrators and clergymen. Although the Spanish request to establish a town in Huajuapan was turned down in 1537, many ignored the crown's proviso and stayed anyway.[153] Over the colonial period, the Spanish presence increased. In the Mixteca Alta, successive waves of immigrants arrived from the 1590s onward and again during the 1650s.[154] Baptismal records indicate a similar pattern of settlement in the Mixteca Baja. By the late seventeenth century, Creoles accounted for around 5 percent of baptisms around Huajuapan and Tonalá.[155] By the 1740s the republic of Huajuapan contained three hundred Indian and three hundred Spanish, mestizo, and mulatto families. The population of Tonalá included twenty non-Indian families, Juxtlahuaca seventy, Acatlán twenty, and Piaxtla sixteen. There were also "some" Spanish families in Chila.[156] Together they formed 8 percent of the region's population. Although Spanish immigration never reached the levels of many central areas of the colony, and hence prevented the disintegration of indigenous traditions and forms of governance, Spanish influence was felt throughout the region through trade and livestock farming.

The region's lowland location and its position between the coast and central Mexico encouraged administrators and traders to establish three commercial arteries through the Mixteca Baja. One ran up from Guatemala through the Isthmus of Tehuantepec, Antequera, and the Mixteca Alta until it reached Huajuapan and Acatlán and headed for Puebla or Mexico City. The other two ran up from the Costa Chica. One traversed Putla, Juxtlahuaca, Tlacotepec, Huajuapan, and Acatlán before also proceeding to Puebla and Mexico City. The other followed the same route until Huajuapan where it deviated toward Tequixtepec, Chazumba, and Tehuacán.[157] Neither itinerary was particularly easy. In fact, Burgoa described the route down to the coast as a mix of "intractable risks" that included "the highest sierras, shaded by forests of pines and cedars" and "huge, steep-sided rivers." But these routes provided the only means to bring up cotton, sugar, livestock, and other products from the coast. In addition to these major roads, there were smaller and less amenable tracks that encouraged internal regional trade between Tlaxiaco and Juxtlahuaca, Tlaxiaco and Tezoatlán, and Silacayoapan and Tlapa. The road that ran through the village of Mixtepec was described by Burgoa as "four leagues of the roughest road, a footpath full of precipices, which still after so many years of travel inspires horror."[158] Despite the dangers, the Mixteca Baja's chance geographical location at the hub of New Spain's south-central trading axis changed political, economic, and social relations between colonizer and colonized.

During the seventeenth and eighteenth centuries Spaniards began to establish themselves, especially in Huajuapan, as large-scale merchants. María de Los Angeles Romero Frizzi has outlined the emergence of similar figures in Teposcolula and Yanhuitlán, individuals who received luxury goods, cloths, clothes, iron products, and other merchandise from the merchants of Puebla in exchange for cochineal, cotton, wool, and other livestock items produced by the local indigenous population.[159] Unfortunately, there are no judicial documents from the early colonial period for Juxtlahuaca, Huajuapan, or Tonalá. However, the few wills from the late eighteenth century point to a similar trading network in the Mixteca Baja. The will of the merchant Juan Acevedo, who died in Huajuapan in 1793, lists over seventy thousand pesos' worth of commercial goods. Some products, like the six thousand pesos of cotton or the thirty-two hundred pesos of wool, came from the south and were clearly destined for Puebla, Mexico City, or even Veracruz. Other goods, especially those of his shop, were designed for local sale and testify to the existence of a broad regional market; these included cloths, wines, oils, and soaps from Mexico City and Europe.[160] The differences from the lists of mercantile products of the average merchant from the Mixteca Alta are few but revealing. On the one hand, Acevedo possessed very little cochineal, which was at the time Oaxaca's most precious export. Although the small beetle, harvested to produce a rich dye, was produced in most of the state, few peasants in the Mixteca Baja were involved in the industry.[161] On the other hand, Acevedo's inventory includes mention of palm goods, especially *petates*, and the wool, dried meat, skins, and fat for candles from goats and sheep. These formed the region's major commercial products.[162] The priest of Chila claimed that local Indians produced petates as early as the 1580s.[163] Cofradías, communities, and individual villagers also owned flocks of livestock that they periodically slaughtered to consume and sell on the market.

However, although trade initiated the rise of a self-identified white elite in the Mixteca Baja's administrative centers, commerce failed to disrupt villages substantially. First, commercial interactions were unequal but not intrinsically divisive. As Jeremy Baskes has argued in his extensive work on *repartimiento* and the cochineal trade in Oaxaca, "While at times . . . market participation yielded undesired hardships, more often indigenous peasants benefited from economic exchange."[164] As the "Mixtecs had plenty of land but little cash or credit," the small amounts of money received for palm products, wool, and salted meat allowed indigenous villagers to purchase valued goods, especially those connected to religious worship, and acquire needed income with which to pay tribute.[165] Furthermore, repartimiento and other commercial interactions were rarely openly coerced. As a result interethnic trade failed to engender the same class and ethnic divisions stimulated by the imposition of mining or commercial agriculture. In fact, commerce often stimulated interethnic alliances. Small-time white and mestizo traders married into indigenous families, moved into indigenous villages, became godparents to their producers' children, and involved themselves in village religious rituals and fiestas. Also, the production of both livestock and petates failed to remove Mixtec men from their agrarian duties as women and children often did the jobs of shepherding and weaving.

Second, in the Mixteca Baja white elites rarely attempted to extend their wealth by buying up or commandeering indigenous lands. Most of the Mixteca Baja was mountainous, rocky, and generally unfit for commercial agriculture. The sparse fertile lands around villages were small; owned by caciques, cofradías, or communities; and rarely worth the legal and political headache caused by usurpation. As a result, clashes between white settlers and villages were infrequent. Between 1700 and 1810, the spotty records indicate only five in the alcaldía of Huajuapan compared with twenty-six struggles between villages and caciques or between caciques themselves. Furthermore, the tussles were extremely geographically limited, and most concerned the region's one area of potential sugar agriculture—the fertile floodplain around the village of Atoyac (see appendix A).[166]

Third, indigenous commercial enterprise balanced that of the white elite and prevented clear race-based inequalities. Caciques maintained their predominance, not simply through landholding and labor extraction, but also through developing some "entrepreneurial expertise."[167] They quickly became part of the colonial mercantile economy as livestock owners and merchants. Although few could compete with the Yanhuitlán cacique who left over one hundred thousand pesos of merchandise when he died in 1603, many took advantage of the Mixteca Baja's proximity to Puebla and its location on the royal road from Oaxaca to Mexico City to build up impressive commercial ventures.[168] As early as 1622 the cacique of Huajuapan, Feliciano de Velasco, requested permission to purchase twelve mules for his business operations.[169] When Diego Villagómez, the cacique of Acatlán, died he left two donkeys, four teams of oxen, 165 horses, twenty mules, 403 head of cattle, twenty-eight sheep, thirty-five hundred pounds of raw cotton, and five hundred pieces of tile made in Puebla. His relative, Lorenzo de Villagómez y Guzmán, the cacique of Miltepec, owned a shop in the commercial center of Huajuapan.[170] At the same time, other non-noble Indians also moved from agriculture to trade. Some worked as individual merchants.[171] In 1687 one indigenous merchant asked to sell salt, cotton, beans, fish, wheat, bread, and cloths throughout the region. He claimed to own twenty mules and employ four muleteers from his village to do the transportation.[172] Other villages operated as communal ventures. Thus, in 1696 the villagers of Tezoatlán asked permission to travel the markets of the region with their twelve mules, selling salt, maize, cotton, and chile.[173]

If commerce drew together colonizer and colonized in an unequal but not entirely unfavorable relationship, the emergence of haciendas volantes cemented these links, offering commoners work and caciques cash while preventing the exploitation of valuable fertile lands. The historiography of these huge, mobile flocks of sheep and goats that traversed lands from the Costa Chica to Puebla and supported a huge economy based on the sale of wool, meat, fat, and grease is relatively recent. As late as 1943 the anthropologist Roberto Weitlaner asserted that the Nahuatl-speaking villages of "Indian shepherds" he discovered in eastern Guerrero were actually forgotten outposts of the Aztec empire.[174] In fact, they were the descendents of the workers of these enormous itinerant herds. Until the 1970s studies of colonial landholding made no mention of these types of estate. In many ways, this is unsurprising. Not only did the haciendas disappear during the Revolution, but also, as the herds crossed three states and countless municipalities, the discovery of interconnected documentation was and still is extremely difficult. However, during the last three decades a few scholars have started to examine this phenomenon. Historians of Oaxaca like Rodolfo Pastor, María de los Angeles Romero Frizzi, and Andrew C. Mouat have argued that these haciendas were central to the economy of the Mixteca.[175] At the same time, scholars of Guerrero such as Danièle Dehouve and Roberto Cervantes Delgado have looked at the socioeconomic and cultural effects of the enterprises in the Guerrero montaña.[176] Finally, a handful of linguists have started to examine the "shepherd dialect" of Nahuatl spoken in many of the villages that dot the haciendas' former routes.[177]

Romero Frizzi argues that rich Spaniards started to pasture haciendas volantes in the Mixteca Alta during the early seventeenth century. Although similar institutions emerged in the Mixteca Baja slightly later, by 1700 they were well established. The twenty-four known haciendas operating in the area had a broad array of landlords. Five owners—José Mariano Maldonaldo, Manuel de León, Joseph de Guzmán, Diego de V., and Gerónimo Ramírez—established themselves in towns in the Mixteca Baja. Another two haciendas were owned by the Puebla-based Jesuit colleges of Espíritu Santo and San Ildefonso. The rest were probably owned by members of the Puebla elite like Agustín Obando, who traversed a hacienda of goats through the region in 1786.[178] The flocks were huge. In 1762 the Jesuit flocks alone totaled over sixty-one thousand sheep and sixty-seven thousand goats.[179] The hacienda of Manuel de León, which can be examined through his will of 1819, included 20,875 adult goats, 20,310 kids, 4,119 sheep, and thirty mules. Together the livestock was worth 39,865 pesos.[180]

Shepherds drove these flocks from the Costa Chica up to the Mixteca Baja each year. They would spend the rainy season from June to October in the mountainous scrublands of the region before arriving at the *haciendas de matanza* where they were slaughtered. Each hacienda took a different route. The debts of the hacienda of Manuel de León indicate that it was pastured on the lands around Pinotepa de Don Luis, Tlacamama, and Jamiltepec during the summer before moving over the Mixteca Baja through Teopan, Santa Catarina, and Camotlán.[181] In contrast, the Jesuits' Santo Rosario hacienda passed over the Sierra Madre del Sur in the winter, crossed the

Figure 2: "From the seventeenth century through to the present day workers have arrived from throughout the Mixteca Baja to work at the annual matanzas. This photograph was taken in 1966." Colección Bustamante Vasconcelos.

Mixteca Baja, and pastured in the Costa in spring before arriving back in the Mixteca Baja around June.[182] As Dehouve argues, "Most pueblos of the region were crossed by a hacienda at one time or another."[183] Although the haciendas were mobile, they possessed at least one stable piece of property in the Mixteca Baja on which the annual slaughter, or *matanza*, was performed in late October and early November. The Jesuits owned property near Santa Cruz Tlacotepec in Puebla, and Manuel de León owned the Rancho de San Francisco, probably outside Tezoatlán. *Matanzas* also took place around Huajuapan, Tehuacán, and Petlalcingo.[184]

The haciendas volantes played a fundamental role in the economic, social, and cultural life of the late colonial Mixteca. In the most prosaic terms, they employed hundreds of immigrant and local workers. The haciendas were usually run by a Spanish boss, or mayordomo, based in the main hacienda. On the move, control of the flocks was divided between Spanish-speaking mestizo and indigenous captains and a handful of indigenous shepherds. Scholars of Guerrero argue that many members of the mobile workforce were not locals but rather Nahuatl-speaking Indians from central Mexico.[185] But Mixtecs were involved in the trade in a host of other ways. Some learned Spanish, joined the herds, and became shepherds. Marriage records of hacienda employees from Huajuapan indicate that between 1739 and 1798 nearly 50 percent of the workers came from the Mixteca Baja. Only a handful came from Puebla. The rest came from the Mixteca Alta and the Mixteca de la Costa.[186] Others sold salt, corn, beans, and petates to the visiting shepherds as these workers traversed their lands.[187] Local Indians were also employed by the haciendas to sheer or castrate the livestock.

These regular transactions between local indigenous communities and the haciendas volantes reached a climax during the matanzas. Each year around October, the owners of the haciendas volantes ordered the butchering of their animals. When Manuel de León died he owned 4,809 goats, worth 11,786 pesos, ready for slaughter. All the animals' parts were processed and put up for sale. The fat, which was the principal product, was kept in large leather containers and sold to make candles and soaps. The skins were stripped, salted, and used to make leather. The wool was sheared, packed, and sent off to make garments. The flesh was carved up into a variety of products including *chito* (salted meat), cracklings, and intestines. Each item was directed at a different market. Some wool and fat was sold on the local market, but most was transported to industrialists in Puebla or Mexico City. Thus León's will demanded 11,778 pesos from a factory owner from Puebla for processed fat that was to be made into candles for sale in northern mines. The salted meat was purchased by large merchants and sold in the regional markets in Huajuapan, Acatlán, Teposcolula, and as far south as Oaxaca City. The cooked heads and cracklings were sold to small traveling merchants and nearby Mixtec villages. Finally, the intestines and blood were divided up among the butchers, workers, and shepherds to complement their pay.[188] The annual matanzas were huge operations that utilized considerable Indian labor. During the late nineteenth century the slaughter at the Hacienda del Rosario involved ninety-five workers. Eight operated the ovens, eleven processed the fat in the ovens, eight made the leather receptacles for the fat, thirteen were butchers, and fifty-five were general helpers. Some lived on the hacienda permanently, but most came from the surrounding villages. In fact, entire villages appear to have specialized in and lived off of this annual event.[189]

Haciendas volantes offered peasants valuable permanent and temporary employment, but they did not disrupt villages like traditional Spanish-owned landholdings, at least in the Mixteca Baja. First, the only properties belonging to the haciendas volantes were ranches for the annual matanzas. These were smaller than most haciendas, limited in number, and farmed or sharecropped by their resident workers for most of the year. Second, although the haciendas used village lands for pasture, they only used them for a few months and concentrated on unproductive, mountainous scrubland. Furthermore, in order to utilize these otherwise unusable lands for pasture, they also paid indigenous groups valuable cash rents. The debts of

Figure 3: "The annual matanza of goats in Huajuapan de León, 1960."
Colección Bustamante Vasconcelos.

Manuel de León's hacienda demonstrate the conspicuous interdependence of these enterprises and indigenous caciques and commoners. He rented Teopan from don Bonifacio Pimentel, Santa Catarina from doña Isidora Mendoza, and Cuyotepeji from don Mariano Villagómez. He also rented the communal lands of Camotlán, Chilapilla, and Diquiyú.[190] Although the rents seem to have started fairly low (around twenty pesos per year), they increased during the eighteenth century. By 1777 the rate paid by the haciendas was eighty-six pesos per year. [191]

Finally, the haciendas volantes also transformed the religious landscape of the Mixteca Baja. By traversing the mountainous extremes of the region, captains, shepherds, and their flocks gradually reduced the physical and imaginative distance between the low-lying institutional church and the mountainous preserves of indigenous idolatry. Crosses, shrines, and altars dot the region's hilly crests, wresting spaces of pre-Hispanic worship from indigenous practitioners and channeling them toward a hybrid, pastoral Catholicism. For example, the inhabitants of Tonalá recall that during the colonial period visiting shepherds left an icon of the Virgin Mary, allegedly brought over from Spain, in a small cave on the pastures above the town. According to the locals, the image was "very miraculous" and was visited by both resident Mixtecs and itinerant shepherds. Colonial church documents confirm that the local priests also visited the Virgin and her "sacred cave" on regular occasions to light candles and say Mass.[192]

Beyond these smaller shrines, the haciendas volantes also introduced a unifying regional cult based on the image of Our Lady of the Snows in the hilltop town of Ixpantepec. The legend surrounding the image, which is described in a colonial-era painting inside the church, claims that two Mixtec children who were working as shepherds on the hillside of Ixpantepec met an apparition of the Virgin Mary. The apparition demanded that the children build her a shrine. The children told their parents, who agreed to comply with the Virgin's wishes. But before they could construct the sanctuary, the bishop of Puebla started an investigation into the vision. At first, he was extremely dubious of the Mixtec shepherds' claims. However, he was eventually persuaded of their veracity after asking each child to pick out which version of Mary had appeared from a choice of hundreds. Both children immediately chose Our Lady of the Snows. The sanctuary was sanctioned in the early seventeenth century, and in 1636 the bishop of Puebla authorized a cofradía to the image. This authorization, in turn, helped fund the building of a large church that was eventually completed in 1761. Shepherds were not only the first legendary witnesses of the Virgin's apparition, they were also some of the principal pilgrims to the shrine, especially as the Virgin's feast day on August 5 coincided with the haciendas volantes' annual return to the Mixteca Baja. The cofradía books list donors from towns on the haciendas' various routes, including Tlapa, Jamiltepec, and Xicayan. During the 1740s these paid between ten and fifty pesos annually to the cult.[193] The acceptance of the apparition of Our Lady of the Snows is more difficult to explain than that of the Holy Cross. The echoes of the Guadalupe apparition are apparent, and the involvement of the bishop of Puebla perhaps indicates that, at least initially, the Marian shrine acted as a counterpoint to the Dominican stress on the Passion and the Cross. However, even if the sanctuaries emerged due to conflicts between the secular church and the orders, by the eighteenth century Our Lady of the Snows and the Holy Cross were acting in tandem as powerful regional cults. If the cult to the Cross overlay the old community compact between caciques, commoners, and the land, and through its peripatetic tour of Mixtec villages was imitated and repeated in numerous other Christocentric cults, the Marian devotion and its network of pilgrim followers symbolized the links between the church, the communities, and the new colonial economy.

The arrival of white merchants had a profound effect on the Mixteca Baja, drawing Mixtecs into the cash economy, delineating market imperatives, and creating a series of commercial centers. Yet colonial capitalism in the region was not as invasive as that of the valleys around Mexico City, the Bajío, or the thick sleeves of agricultural exploitation enclosing the roads from Acapulco or Veracruz to Mexico City. A mixture of commercial centrality and precipitous geography allowed merchants, caciques, and communities to forge an economic equilibrium or what John Tutino terms "relations of symbiotic exploitation" whereby cash, labor, and products were exchanged without the invasion of village lands or the heavy disruption of intravillage relations.[194] In fact, as Stephen Perkins has described for Tlacotepec, Puebla, poor lands, and consequently only moderate Spanish intrusion, permitted the social hierarchy of the Indian village to survive and even flourish during the colonial period.[195]

Threats to the Moral Economy and the Moral Economy Rewritten

During the second half of the eighteenth century, intertwining structural and political changes started to undermine the colonial moral economy and erode the carefully established internal and external pacts that dominated village life. On the one hand, the gradual recovery of indigenous birthrates combined with an increase in Spanish immigration to cause a rapid rise in population. As the competition for valuable resources grew, the system of reciprocal dominance waned as commoners saw their traditional expectations ignored by an increasingly acculturated and market-oriented noble class. Repúblicas sought political independence from cacique rule and confirmation of village lands. On the other hand, relations between colonizers and colonized also declined. During the 1750s the Dominican establishments were closed and secular priests introduced. At the same time, entrepreneurial Spaniards eyed villages' lands for exploitation. Finally, as the Bourbon monarchs imposed a series of administrative changes designed to monopolize revenues and undercut the political and cultural autonomy of all levels of colonial society, Spanish administrators increasingly interfered in village life. Yet despite these shifts, the region never experienced the escalating conflicts of the Bajío, the Huasteca, or even other regions of Oaxaca like Villa Alta or the Mixteca Alta.[196] As we shall see, despite considerable tensions the network of relationships between whites, the church, the caciques, and the commoners was redrawn but survived until the nineteenth century.

Although the Mixteca Baja had been entangled in the colonial economy since the sixteenth century, commercial involvement had strengthened rather than weakened the bonds between nobles and commoners. But from 1700 onward two things started to disrupt this compact. First, population growth and the corresponding rise in demand for basic products put increasing pressure on the region's limited resources. During the eighteenth century the population of the Mixteca Baja grew substantially. The *Theatro americano* of 1745 lists 3,975 indigenous and 320 Spanish, mestizo, and mulatto families in Huajuapan. Given that families averaged around four persons, the total population would have been about 15,900 Indians and 1,280 non-natives. By 1793 the population had increased by almost 50 percent to 30,770, of which 25,525 were indigenous, 483 Spanish, and 4,786 mestizo.[197] Second, increasingly acculturated caciques, tempted by the new market opportunities proffered by population growth and Spanish immigration, started to view their landholdings not as valuable elements of their relationship with their indigenous charges, but rather as potential sources of income.[198] As caciques started to rent out their lands to Spanish entrepreneurs, conflicts between nobles and commoners over land ownership increased. Between 1700 and 1810 the region of Huajuapan alone saw at least fourteen litigations over land that pitted villages against their former caciques.[199] Some were short-lived affairs. Others dragged on for over a century.

For example, in 1717 the Villagómez clan owned the lands of the villages of Tequixtepec, Miltepec, Suchitepec, and Cuyotepeji. As the century wore on, family members eschewed perspicacious noble alliances, started to marry into the regional Spanish elite, moved their residences out of villages and into commercial centers, and sacrificed their former roles as república governors. As they gradually lost local influence, they also started to rent their lands to outsiders. During the 1750s Bernardo Villagómez rented some of his lands to his brother-in-law and others to a Spaniard from Teposcolula. Forty years later his grandson Narciso Villagómez Cortés de Velasco rented pasture to seven Spaniards including a priest and the subdelegate of Huajuapan. In response, their indigenous charges engaged in increasingly virulent struggles inside and outside the courts to claim rights over the lands. In 1757 the villagers of Miltepec took advantage of colonial laws that banned personal service and assured repúblicas of minimum land ownership to overturn Bernardo Villagómez's claims and take possession of the village's communal property. The following year the pueblo managed to persuade the alcalde of Huajuapan to give them another two plots. Although the judicial conflict reached the Spanish courts, which decided in the cacique's favor, he died before the resolution, and the village kept the lands. Four years later, the neighboring village of Tequixtepec also attacked the cacique's demands for personal services and petitioned for the communal property they claimed was their due.[200] To the north other members of the Villagómez clan suffered similar problems. When Martín Carlos de Villagómez inherited the cacicazgo of Chila and Acatlán in the early eighteenth century, the "supremely ladino" cacique moved to Silacayoapan to concentrate on the wheat trade. Villagers took advantage of his political weakness and engaged in successive court cases. By the time his son took over the properties in 1761, Chance argues, he "lacked the funds to properly manage his assets because he was spending so much on litigation" and could probably only verify ownership of around half his former lands.[201]

As commercial imperatives increased, relationships between Spaniards and Mixtec peasants also started to disintegrate. In the region's scattered fertile valleys, sugar entrepreneurs increased the pressure on village lands. For example, in 1733 the viceroy conceded a license to Spaniard José Pérez de Vivas from Teposcolula to establish a sugar mill in Atoyac. This enterprise precipitated increasing conflicts with the local inhabitants, who argued that the lands were theirs and who would periodically invade the fields and tear up the crops. In 1782 the viceroy granted another license for sugar mills to Marcelo Antonio Vásquez in the same place, thus hastening another round of agrarian conflict. These regions, particularly the fertile river valley around Atoyac, would become isolated hubs of peasant rebellion and attempted agrarian reform.[202] However, the cadence of agrarian conflict in the more isolated, mountainous regions also escalated as Spanish livestock owners clashed with growing villages over pastoral lands. In 1751 the natives of San José complained that sheep and goats owned by the Spaniard José Martín de Gorospe, owner of the ranch of Ayuquila, were trampling and eating their crops. In 1762 the villagers of Ihualtepec demanded that the livestock of the widow Antonia Aranguti Aguayo stop trespassing on their lands.[203]

An increasing demand for indigenous goods also unbalanced the delicate commercial equilibrium between Spanish middlemen and indigenous producers. In 1794 the indigenous villagers of Huajuapan complained that the subdelegate ordered his agents to visit all the villages in the region, buy up livestock on the cheap, butcher the animals in an enormous matanza, and then sell the products in Puebla for inflated prices. If villagers refused to sell, the agents were instructed to beat them with whips and sticks. As the traditional system of trade declined, the villagers evoked this disappearing understanding between white traders and indigenous livestock owners: "We cannot deny that various Spanish subjects do their matanzas here, but they pay us legitimate prices for our livestock and we sell them as we wish, not through force like the subdelegate and his agents."[204]

Escalating economic conflicts between ethnic groups also bled into cultural divisions, precipitated by the secularization of the Dominican missions and changing policies around church education. By 1755 the Bishopric of Puebla had established secular parishes throughout the Mixteca Baja, and the city of Puebla's Dominican branch only controlled friars in three complexes in Teposcolula, Coixtlahuaca, and Tejupan.[205] In 1769 the new bishop of Puebla, Francisco Fabián y Fuero, compounded the profound dislocation caused by secularization by instructing priests to explain doctrine in Spanish rather than indigenous languages. A year later the Council of the Indies decided that priests would be assigned to native parishes even if they did not speak the Indian language, Spanish-language schools would be established in indigenous pueblos, and the role of minister of language would be abolished.[206] The policy had immediate effects in the Mixteca Baja, where the Dominican policy of learning indigenous languages had cemented the links between the church and the laity. In 1771 the priest of Huajuapan warned his successor, "For no reason should you talk to or deal with the Indians in their own language, as it is Castilian that has been ordered by the diocese."[207] During the same year, the policy precipitated a riot in Tezoatlán. The local priest, Manuel Ramírez Arellano, complained that the "men, women and children" from the neighboring repúblicas had encircled the church and demanded the release of Joseph Pasqual, whom he had recently imprisoned for being "very perverse and inclined to sedition." He claimed that the riot was led by Domingo Morales, the Indian cacique of Diquiyú, and Pedro Martín, the Indian governor of Yucuquimi. After Pasqual's imprisonment they had visited local villages and persuaded the Mixtec inhabitants to request his freedom. On the surface the case appears to be one of jurisdictional limits. However, the testimonies of a handful of residents demonstrate that the quarrel had deeper roots. One of the witnesses was married to the local schoolteacher. He claimed that the priest had recently established a series of schools in the parish's more remote villages. The teachers taught not only Catholic doctrine but also Spanish. According to his wife, the elders had forcibly banished the teachers, as "they did not wish to speak the Castilian language."[208]

Yet despite these strains on peasants' relations with caciques, Spaniards, and the church, the colonial moral economy did not disappear altogether. Mixtecs neither rebelled nor retreated into insular anomie. The colonial moral economy was never set in stone, but rather the "norms of reciprocity were constantly being negotiated between the two sides as conditions changed."[209] Although the last half of the eighteenth century introduced particularly difficult conditions, the various pacts between elites and non-elites were redrawn and still endured. Some caciques slipped into insolvency and irrelevance, but most still owned large quantities of land and played important roles in the communities. In spite of a handful of high profile conflicts, most relations between whites and indigenous villagers remained paternalist and exploitative but pacific. Finally, despite the Dominicans' departure and the bishop's increasing intolerance, a new generation of local priests took up where the missionaries had left off, embracing the regional religious culture and, together with their indigenous charges, redirecting it toward new demands.

Following the work of scholars on other regions of southern Mexico, Menegus Bornemann argues that by the final decades of the eighteenth century caciques in the Mixteca Baja were in terminal decline, shedding political prestige and locked in incessant cycles of litigation with indigenous villages.[210] Undoubtedly, in the large commercial centers of the Mixteca

Baja the caciques lost their control of town lands, which were now distributed by more pluralist república councils.[211] Furthermore, in the region's smaller villages many caciques also gave up their role as governors. Yet this pattern of blotchy economic decline and more comprehensive political debility masks the survival, maintenance, and even expansion of cacicazgos during the period. As John Monaghan, Arthur Joyce, and Ronald Spores argue, the cacicazgos of the region "had a much more lasting presence than students of the contemporary Mixteca have allowed."[212] In fact, as late as 1831 cacique families owned 60 percent of the district of Huajuapan's land, still expected personal services, and continued to hold religious (and some political) posts.[213] Furthermore, we should view these enduring caciques not as vestiges of a dying colonial order, a "problem of persistence" made flesh, but rather as powerful products of late colonial renegotiations of the nobles' role in Mixtec society.[214]

These renegotiations took two forms—economic and political. On the one hand, faced with the commercial opportunities of a putative land market, many caciques outside major market towns did not simply give in to Spanish demands. Rather, many maintained their relationships with their indigenous tenants, lowering expectations of personal service and charging very low rents. For example, in 1804 the cacique of Ihualtepec, Francisco de Mendoza, rented the lands of the Zoquiapan ranch to the cofradía of Our Lady of the Rosary for nine years for a mere 150 pesos or just over 15 pesos per year.[215] Similarly, in 1819 the village authorities of Yucuyachi agreed to pay the local cacique, Rafael Francisco de los Angeles, eighty pesos and half a bushel of maize for the use of his lands.[216]

On the other hand, caciques, especially those from less prestigious families, took advantage of conflicts between their more powerful relations and indigenous villages to forge independent spheres of influence. Between 1696 and 1745 the number of self-governing repúblicas in Huajuapan doubled from fourteen to twenty-eight. By 1800 the number had increased again to forty-nine. Most of these new villages were established during the 1740s and 1750s as formerly subject villages gained cabecera status.[217] Peter Gerhard notes that "the post-Conquest tendency of subject pueblos to break away from their cabecera, common in most parts of New Spain, was accentuated here."[218] Menegus Bornemann and others have assumed that this process demonstrates a gradual democratization of village politics as indigenous commoners in the subject villages successfully sought freedom from noble control in the cabeceras.[219] Undoubtedly, in some villages this was the case.

Yet as Ouwenweel finds for the valleys of central Mexico, low-level caciques were also instrumental to villages gaining this autonomy.²²⁰ The rapid establishment of new cabeceras did not indicate the rejection of a hierarchical system of governance but rather the decentralization of cacique rule. These caciques not only had the savvy to work the colonial system, but also the ready cash necessary to establish an independent república. For example, don Felipe de Guzmán not only funded the construction of the church at Chazumba, but also petitioned for and received the village's independence from Tequixtepec in 1715. These new caciques replicated the system of reciprocal dominance established by their predecessors. At the ceremony to inaugurate the new república the villagers agreed to "obey their cacique in everything relating to service to his majesty and to the divine cult," "not get drunk in public, not commit public sin, not sleep together if already married, and not live in the ravines."²²¹

Although the formal political role of the nobility undoubtedly diminished, caciques like those of the Guzmán family still dominated land ownership and religious appointments for over one hundred years.²²² In return, they were expected to use their power, wealth, and influence to defend village integrity in the increasingly tight competition over resources. Between 1700 and 1820, at least twelve land disputes pitched these new caciques and their pueblos against older caciques and their pueblos.²²³ In each case caciques conflated their own self-interest with that of the village. In 1818 don José Ramón Bautista y Guzmán, the inheritor of the Chazumba cacicazgo, defended his peasants' lands against the pretensions of don José Ximénez and his charges from Acaquizapan. He explained that "since time immemorial, [his] *causantes* [literally, the people from whom his rights were derived] had been in quiet and pacific possession of the lands belonging to [his] cacicazgo."²²⁴ Similarly, in 1781 don Sebastian Mariano de los Angeles Guzmán, cacique and governor of Yucuyachi, defended his village's lands against attempts by Martín Luna, cacique of Nuchita, to usurp the fertile valley of Yosotee for his charges.²²⁵

Unlike in the Mixteca Alta where by the late eighteenth century caciques were "simply well-to-do investors in Spanish-style enterprises who could make little claim to hereditary authority," caciques in the Mixteca Baja expanded their influence.²²⁶ Also unlike the Mixteca Alta, tensions between caciques and commoners over resources were resolved not through the outright destruction of the system of reciprocal dominance and the consequent polarization of society into an undifferentiated group of indigenous peasants and white elites, but rather through adaptation of the system to market conditions and decentralization into smaller administrative units. Although some cacique families like the empire-building Villagómez clan struggled to maintain control of their huge, interconnected landholdings, and caciques ceased to monopolize political positions in the village, more flexible caciques who owned less land actually flourished during the era. Furthermore, the system of paternalist control, with its expectations of mutual obligations, survived well into nineteenth century and formed the basis of village alliances with centralists and then conservatives.

Similarly, the relationship between native peasants and non-native elites was also renegotiated during the late colonial period. First, land in the Mixteca Baja was so poor that few whites wanted to risk protracted court cases just to acquire stony scrubland. Haciendas volantes, like the huge operation owned by Manuel de León, with their relatively uninvasive exchange of temporary pasture and cash rent, continued to be the central support of the region's economy. Although white renters and indigenous villages did clash during the period, these clashes never increased as they did in the Mixteca Alta. In fact, the available colonial documents seem to demonstrate that they actually declined during the eighteenth century, especially when compared to increasing conflicts between caciques and villages and between caciques themselves. Second, the increase in intermarriage between the indigenous elite and white Creoles created a regional class of village elites, or gente de razón, open to both Spanish and Mixtec traditions. Between 1745 and 1793 the number of non-natives in Huajuapan increased fourfold from 1,280 to over 5,000, of which over 90 percent were judged to be mestizo.[227] As such Huajuapan had the second-highest number of mestizos in the state, double the number in Oaxaca City. Historians like Pastor have often ascribed the huge increase in the Mixteca Baja's mestizo class to high levels of immigration.[228] However, this would be extremely surprising. The Indian population certainly grew much less in the same period, and we have little evidence that the mountainous region became an economic lodestone for rootless mestizos.

If the late colonial mestizos of Huajuapan were not immigrants, then who were they? Census records from Tonalá in 1818 seem to indicate that they consisted of racially mobile indigenous caciques and former workers from the haciendas volantes. The records, secreted in the Tonalá parish archive, list 95 *indios* and 245 gente de razón. Some of these gente de razón clearly self-identified as creole Spaniards. For example, according to the parish's baptism records every scion of the Ponce family was *español*. Others, however, lacked such clear, "untainted" roots. Don Juan Marcial de Luna, his wife, and their three children, presumably related to the Luna family of caciques from Nuchita, were included as gente de razón. Similarly, don Felipe Guzmán, don Anselmo Navarrete, don Mariano José de la Cruz, and don Felipe José de la Cruz were also listed as gente de razón despite their status as indigenous caciques. Others were identified as Indian shepherds from the region's transient haciendas volantes before they settled in Tonalá and shifted into the class of gente de razón. For example, the ancestors of the three members of the Solano family were described as *indios pastores* when they arrived in the village in the 1720s and took over day-to-day running of the village's cofradía livestock. Other families with noticeably indigenous surnames, like Pablo, Jorge, and Mariano, could trace their lineage back to these groups of shepherds.[229] Obviously, some of these indigenous elites became defined as gente de razón because they married into existing creole or mestizo families. For example, in 1772 don Juan Josef Reyes, son of Pasqual Reyes and Dorotea Mendoza, caciques of Tezoatlán, married Petrona María Baltasar, the daughter of two Spaniards from Huajuapan. In 1795 don Mariano Antonio Velasco, cacique of Diquiyú, married Crescencia Francisca, a mixed-race woman from Huajuapam.[230] But others seemed to have moved from indigenous to colonial elite simply by virtue of their superior wealth and knowledge of the Spanish colonial system. Working back through the genealogy of don Felipe Guzmán, cacique of Tonalá in 1818, there is no evidence that his forebears married outside the native elite.[231]

Having established that this mestizo group comprised members of the indigenous elite, we need to ask how this affected interethnic relations in the Mixteca Baja. Chance, in his work on late colonial nobles in the region, argues that the acculturation of indigenous caciques precipitated the group's decline.[232] As indigenous caciques moved to commercial centers, intermarried into non-native families, and aped Spanish customs, they gradually lost contact with their former charges and triggered conflicts over land and political power. In many instances this was undoubtedly the case. Yet Chance only looks at one side of the equation. If the upward mobility of indigenous elites fractured links to the indigenous peasantry, they also brought with them the necessary social capital and cultural insights for dealing with the Mixtec world. As Indian nobles adopted Spanish customs, so white elites also learned Mixtec ways. A comparison with other areas of late colonial New Spain is useful here. In most regions, social and economic forces actually precipitated a widening of the "cultural chasm" between natives and non-natives.[233] For example, in the southern states of Yucatán, Oaxaca, and Chiapas, where Spanish immigration was limited, the late colonial decline of the indigenous caciques precipitated a flat ethnic pyramid in which a narrow self-consciously white elite ruled a mass of undifferentiated Indians.[234] In the colony's cities and the commercial haciendas of the center and north, by comparison, many formerly indigenous peasants did shift racial categories to become mestizos. Yet only a very few breached the fiercely defensive upper echelons of the caste system to rub shoulders with the extensive Spanish elite.[235] The situation in the Mixteca Baja and, I would venture, other regions in the center that maintained powerful cacique families—like Tlacotepec, Cholula, and Tepeji in Puebla—was different.[236] Here, a limited and weak Spanish upper class confronted an upwardly mobile and numerous indigenous elite whose wealth and power encouraged cross-cultural learning. Here, the process of transculturation closely mirrored that of acculturation.

Obviously, this type of relative "cultural sensitivity" is difficult to pick up, especially during the increasingly paranoid late colonial period when efforts at proto-*indigenismo* were not only frowned upon but deemed positively traitorous.[237] They became much more apparent in the early republican period when links of kinship and culture established during the late eighteenth and early nineteenth centuries promoted close political ties between the regional elite and Mixtec peasants. However, by 1800 the religious aspects of this shared culture did start to surface. After the secularization of the Dominican monasteries during the 1750s, the Bishopric of Puebla divided the region of Huajuapan into secular parishes. By the 1790s there were at least thirteen, most of which were established in former Dominican seats. They comprised Huajuapan, Tamazola, Tezoatlán, Chazumba, Tequixtepec, Ihualtepec, Tlacotepec, Ixpantepec, Silacayoapan, Tonalá, Coicoyán, Tlapancingo, and Zacatepec.[238] By 1793 seventeen priests were divided between these parishes with a concentration of four in the commercial town of Huajuapan. Only the intendancies of Oaxaca City, Villa Alta, and Teposcolula had more, but they also contained much greater populations.[239] Many of these new priests came from the Mixteca Baja. In the seventeenth century the region's elite began a tradition of sending their sons to the seminary in Puebla. The student roll for the years 1649 to 1651 reveals that seven of the eighty-three prospective priests listed came from the area. Only the cities of Puebla and Veracruz proffered more sons for clerical employment. Furthermore, these students were all proficient in Mixtec and outnumbered those learning Otomi and Totonac.[240] A century later, this tradition of dispatching progeny to the Puebla seminary (now named the Palafox seminary) continued. As the new mixed-race elite provided the majority of the Mixteca Baja's priests, the region became what Timothy Tackett terms a "self-sufficient" ecclesiastical unit, which did not have to ship in unwilling clergy from remote regions, but rather employed its own.[241] Many were related to the indigenous nobility and seemed to bear out David Brading's tentative theory that one of the "unexpected effects of secularization" was "to accelerate the recruitment of Indians into the ranks of the Mexican clergy."[242] Thus, Joseph Rafael Oveda y Berdejo, the priest of Tequixtepec in 1796, was related to the Berdejo cacicazgo in charge of the nearby village of Ahuehuetitlan.[243] Pablo Sánchez Toscano, the priest of Ihualtepec, declared that before he took the cloth he was married to the cacica, Josefa Patricia Mendoza.[244] José Rafael Castillo y García, the priest of Coicoyán in 1805 and Zacatepec in 1817, was related to the Castillo noble family, who owned Chichihualtepec.[245] José Joaquín Guerrero, the priest of Tamazola in 1817, was the son of a member of the extended Villagómez clan, María Josefa Villagómez.[246] Others came from non-native local stock. Ignacio Amador, the priest of Coicoyán in 1797, was related to the Amador family of Chila, Puebla.[247] Vicente Alencaster, the priest of Huajuapan in 1810, was related to the Alencaster family, which had immigrated to the town from Veracruz in the late eighteenth century.[248]

But local birth did not necessitate sympathy with local religious tradition. Some of the priests just mentioned probably belittled indigenous practice, sought to downplay their rural roots, and yearned for employment in Puebla. Yet scattered documents seem to indicate that local priests tempered the religious changes enacted by Mexico's reformist ecclesiastical hierarchy and smoothed over the growing fissures between clerical opinion and popular religion. First, despite the bishop of Puebla's prohibition of indigenous language use, it seems unlikely that the mixed-race priests of the Mixteca Baja gave up communicating in their mother tongue completely. Just a decade before the ban, Miguel de Villavicencio, the priest of Silacayoapan, wrote a manuscript entitled *Prontuario del idioma mixteca*, which was divided into three parts on art, vocabulary, and Christian doctrine. Six years later his successor, Francisco Antonio Morales, wrote a similar manuscript on art and vocabulary in the dialect of the region.[249] Second, the handful of clerical wills from the period reveals a close link between these priests and their charges. In 1809 Pablo Sánchez Toscano, the priest of Ihualtepec, left twenty-five pesos and his collection of fifteen images to the church of Huajuapan, ten pesos to the poor, ten pesos to the Parish of Huajolotitlán, and his lands to the peasants of Ihualtepec.[250] José Joaquín Guerrero, the priest of Tamazola, also left one hundred pesos to the poor and a piece of land near San Mateo del Río to the parishioners of the region.[251]

Third, despite ecclesiastical pressures to limit and regulate village cofradías, the priests of the Mixteca Baja seem to have allowed the traditional cacique-led organizations to continue untouched. For example, in 1810 the priest of Chila still allowed the election for the leadership of the cofradía of Saint Ann of Tepejillo to take place "in the presence of the cacique, Narciso Jesús Velasco," who "ordered the election of the next mayordomo." Seven years later, his son, Andrés de Velasco, still orchestrated the voting procedure as "cacique and voice of the pueblo" and signed the account book to verify its completion.[252] Similarly, members of the Guzmán and Bautista cacique clans dominated the cofradía of Our Lord of the Holy Burial in Chazumba until the end of the colonial period. Jacinto Guzmán ran the cofradía from 1795 to 1800.[253] The cofradía of Our Lady of the Rosary of Chinango was run by the cacique, Manuel Lazaro de Rosas, during the 1770s.[254] Furthermore, we have no evidence that the local priests tried to cut back on cofradías or extract debilitating quantities of cash from parishioners. In fact, local priests attempted to defend their local organizations from ecclesiastical interference. In 1810 José Antonio Amador, the local priest of Chila, represented the devotees of the cofradía of Our Lady of the Rosary in front of an ecclesiastical commission. He argued that "since time immemorial our ancestors have worshipped this image with the greatest piety and devotion and following her example, and under her protection we have lived happily." He went on to explain that the cofradía not only paid for the priest, but also for the burial of poor members of the community. Consequently, he asked that the ecclesiastical powers not interfere in cofradía elections and continue to allow the cofradía to pay a lower price for burial than that designated by the official fees.[255] The alliance between local priests and cofradías seemed to have precipitated favorable results, and we have no evidence that the Mixteca Baja, as part of the Diocese of Puebla, suffered the co-option of cofradía funds by the Spanish state.[256] In fact, the late eighteenth century was the financial high point for the region's cofradías as their leaders diversified investments between livestock, agricultural production, candle production, and moneylending. For example, by 1800 the cofradía of the Holy Cross of Ixitlán possessed 493 pesos of capital, 327 goats, and 129 cattle. The organization was so successful that in 1802 it donated fifty pesos to construct an altar to the Virgin of Guadalupe, and in 1804 it handed over four hundred pesos to the government of the república.[257] Between 1799 and 1808 the cofradía of the Blessed Souls in Chila doubled its annual revenue by moving from goat farming to the growing of maize and cactus fruit.[258] Marcello Carmagnani estimates that around 131 cofradías thrived in the intendancy of Huajuapan, the third-highest total in Oaxaca.[259] However, even this figure may well be an underestimate. Most repúblicas seem to have possessed at least four or five organizations rather than the three Carmagnani proposes.

Fourth, local priests also embraced the region's Christocentric religious culture and helped establish new cults in the new repúblicas. Some of these cults became regional themselves, laying their own pilgrimage routes over the old paths trudged by followers of the Holy Cross. According to local legend, during the late eighteenth century merchants in the employ of a local cacique were transporting a bloody version of Christ from the Costa Chica toward Puebla. When they arrived in Miltepec, the statue became "extremely heavy," and despite their efforts it could not be moved. The authorities agreed that the saint "wished to stay in the village," paid off the merchants, and carried it with ease into the local chapel. By 1793 the local priest of Tequixtepec had authorized the establishment of a cofradía dedicated to what locals dubbed Our Lord of Wounds. Miracles, including the curing of a blind man and a paralytic, followed the image's official confirmation. Thus, less than a decade later the image was attracting pilgrims from nearby villages like Huajuapan, Chazumba, Chila, Petlalcingo, and Ayuquila and from more distant settlements like Acatlán, Chilac, and Coxcatlán. They in turn established *hermandades* to Our Lord of Wounds with which they funded extravagant celebrations on the first Friday of Lent.[260] Other devotions were more limited in influence but still demonstrate how local priests worked within the boundaries of local traditions and economic prerogatives. In 1792 the priest of Coicoyán, "having noticed the many and special miracles that the faithful had experienced from the miraculous image of Our Lord of the Holy Burial," invited villagers, shepherds from a neighboring hacienda volante, two local priests, and a cacique to establish a cofradía to the image. After agreeing to celebrate the image on the fifth Friday of Lent, they handed over money for the capital of the cofradía. The priest of Tamazola generously donated a coverlet, mattress, sheet, and a stained glass window. Priestly acceptance soon brought ecclesiastical confirmation, and two years later the bishop's representative visited the village and approved the cult.[261]

Population growth and administrative shifts changed socioeconomic and cultural relations throughout New Spain. In many economically dynamic regions, competition over resources combined with increasing Spanish interference in village life to produce an escalating rhythm of agrarian, political, and religious conflicts. Yet by ignoring the teleological pull of Independence, historians are starting to realize that these effects were not uniform but mediated both by relative Spanish influence and patterns of existing social relations. Robert Haskett argues that in Cuernavaca the effects of the Bourbon Reforms were negligible. Spanish administrators were so few that they barely influenced the indigenous elite's day-to-day running of the villages.[262] Peter Guardino claims that the effects in Villa Alta were ambivalent. Here, a more muscular Spanish state curbed the excesses of repartimiento but also attempted to crack down on indigenous ceremonies and take control of village funds.[263] In the Mixteca Baja, Spanish commercial imperatives and administrative changes strained the precarious equilibrium between indigenous elites, indigenous commoners, and the colonial power. Yet the moral economy, which regulated relations between these groups, failed to disintegrate completely. Rather, political devolution, poor lands, limited immigration, and the emergence of a new mixed-race elite precipitated new rules of the game. Although the new order was decentralized and diocesan, it maintained traditional paternalist bonds, answered peasants' expectations, and preserved similar religious rituals.

The War of Independence

Consequently, inhabitants of the Mixteca Baja had "little enthusiasm" for Independence from Spain.[264] Like successive radical mobilizations over the next century, the Independence movement arrived in the region from outside. Although it precipitated some ideological divisions among the elites and a handful of opportunist land grabs by indigenous villages, in general the region remained calm. There are no records of the kind of well-orchestrated hacienda invasions, *gachupín* killing, and ideological percolation (either constitutional or insurgent) that characterized events to the north and west.[265] Similarly, there is no evidence of the kind of vicious counterinsurgency enacted in other parts of New Spain.[266] If Independence was the "violent expression of previous tensions," it found little echo in a region that had already adapted to late colonial pressures by re-establishing relations between indigenous peasants, indigenous caciques, and white elites.[267]

As subsequent events demonstrated, certain Independence-era ideologies, including nationalism and the republican justification for self-rule, may have infiltrated popular thinking, but by the end of the decade, most indigenous villages still paid rents to their caciques, engaged in trade with white elites, and maintained clerically approved cofradías. If anything, events during the decade of Independence demonstrated a solidifying of ties between the different social groups, based on a shared religious culture.

On every occasion that the Mixteca Baja was dragged into the Independence conflict, this involvement was precipitated by outside forces. In late 1811 Nicolas Bravo and other troops from the future state of Guerrero entered the region, established themselves in sugar-growing regions around Atoyac to the north and Putla to the south, and made a succession of sniping raids on the region's major towns.[268] A year later Valerio Trujano, with troops from Tlapa and his hometown of Tepecoacuilco, again invaded the Mixteca Baja, moving up from Yanhuitlán to Huajuapan. Here they famously resisted a royalist siege for 111 days before they were relieved by the forces of José María Morelos.[269] After the insurgents' defeat in 1814, the same pattern of outside invasion continued. Ramón Sesma, originally from the Chalchicomula on the Veracruz-Puebla border, invaded in 1815, and Vicente Guerrero continued to harass royalists in the district from 1815 to 1817 from his base around Tlapa.[270] Yet although Sesma had family among the Huajuapan elite, both men failed to spark a wide-reaching insurrection. In short, the Mixteca Baja produced no Independence-era caudillos or large-scale rural revolts.

However, exterior pressures did precipitate divisions among the region's elite. In 1811 Huajuapan's upper class formed a cavalry militia of around sixty men led by the livestock owner Manuel de León. Most were members of the small group of creole Spaniards, but some, like the members of the Solano, Acevedo, and Reyes families, were of mixed descent.[271] The regiment provided some local knowledge for invading royalist forces but never established a large following. The priest of Huajuapan complained in late 1811 that the "cowardice" and "bad disposition" of the people caused frequent desertion.[272] Other elites chose the insurgent side. When Trujano arrived in Huajuapan in 1812, he was allegedly supported by José Manuel Herrera, a sugar magnate from Tlaxiaco, and Ignacio Navarro, a Huajuapan merchant. Together they locked down the market and forced the indigenous market sellers to defend the town. Although Carlos María de Bustamante wrote about the siege as an example of divinely inspired interethnic cooperation, and there is no doubt the story played a part in the Mixteca Baja's post-Independence regional

identity, we have no evidence that the besieged Indians, beyond the potentially mythical "Indian of Nuyoo," took any great part in the town's defense or were inspired by anything more than fear and coercion.[273] Without outside interference the town was overrun and occupied repeatedly by royalist forces and their Huajuapan allies in subsequent years. Furthermore, the San Lazaro regiment, which Trujano created out of the heroic defenders of Huajuapan, was hardly a huge popular force but rather a band of around forty members of the town's merchant elite.[274] At the same time the indigenous elites, who might have provided a link between choreographed creole enthusiasm and Indian mass insurrection, chose either lukewarm resistance or neutrality.[275] The cacique Mariano Villagómez declared royalist sympathies but only to denigrate his supposedly insurrectionary tenants in court.[276]

Undoubtedly, some indigenous villages took advantage of both Morelos's proto-*agrarista* propaganda and the relative administrative chaos of the Independence era to further their claims over cacique lands or delay rent payments. In 1812 the villagers of Cuyotepeji invaded the lands of the cacique, Mariano Villagómez, under the banner of Morelos. Five years later the villagers of Miltepec took over the lands of the same cacique.[277] Similarly, in 1818 Raymunda María Navarrete y Méndez complained that the villagers of Zacatepec had not handed over their rent.[278] The villagers of Tequixtepec especially seem to have adopted some of the radical, righteous, "quasi-millenarian" rhetoric of the decade, arguing in 1819 that the local caciques "under a tyrannical pretext" had prevented the peasants "from enjoying the property which the piety of the King gave them for sustenance and food."[279] No doubt Independence provided ample opportunity for villages to renegotiate or even slough off their obligations to the cacique class. But in general, the decade of civil war actually seems to have caused remarkably little disruption.

First, other villages seem to have continued to pay rent despite the insurrection's potentially liberating effects. In 1815 Navarrete y Mendez still rented out the Rancho de Pozo to the villagers of Simarrones for twenty-six pesos.[280] In 1818 the cacique of Ihualtepec rented out lands to the local cofradía for fifteen pesos a year.[281] Furthermore, most villages would go on to pay rents until the 1850s. Second, although default on an annual rent of twenty pesos may have grievously affected overlitigious, cash-strapped, empire-building caciques like the Villagómez clan, it hardly represented a radical break with the past or a descent into atavistic, localized bloodletting, as much of New Spain experienced. Most arguments between caciques and commoners, even the radicals of Tequixtepec, were still settled in court rather than through violence. Third, as a result and despite the threat of occasional guerrilla raids, the region's economy appears to have been barely affected. Haciendas volantes with their relatively unsupervised flocks would have made perfect targets, yet Manuel de León finished the decade with nearly twenty thousand animals.[282] Cofradía herds also seem to have suffered little loss during the period. For example, in 1815 the livestock of the cofradía of Our Lady of Guadalupe of Cuautepec had increased to number 525 goats, 144 sheep, and seventy-six cattle. Five years later the numbers had decreased, but only by around 10 percent.[283] During the revolutionary decade the annual profits of the cofradía of the Holy Sacrament of Suchitepec actually increased from eighteen to sixty-eight pesos from the sale of wheat.[284]

We can also perceive the limited enthusiasm for Independence in an 1817 list of rebel prisoners. Of the 122 men captured in the area between March and April 1817, only twenty-three came from the Mixteca Baja. Almost all came from the towns of Silacayoapan, Huajuapan, and Juxtlahuaca and appear to have been part of the mixed-race or creole commercial class. The two Herrera and the two Ramírez brothers were creole merchants from Huajuapan. José Guevara and Cristobal Letrada were non-native hat merchants from Silacayoapan. In fact, only three prisoners from the region listed their employment as *labrador*, or peasant laborer. Most of the men rounded up, then, came from outside the region. Around a third came from the coastal towns of Jamiltepec, Pinotepa, and Huazolotitlan. Another third came from regions of the Mixteca Alta badly affected by the expansion of the sugar industry, including Putla, Chalcatongo, Yosondua, and Tlaxiaco. The rest comprised a few strays from Juquila, Oaxaca City, and Puebla.[285]

As most inhabitants of the Mixteca Baja saw little advantage in throwing in their lot with either side, they instead sought a solution to incipient divisions by reasserting their communal relationship with the regional Christocentric cults. In 1819 Manuel Robles, a Creole from Huajuapan, made the second recorded entrance into the cave of the Holy Cross above Tindú to ask for peace. According to a villager who recounted the story in the mid-nineteenth century, Robles first called together the authorities of Tonalá and the neighboring pueblos to witness the event. The priest of Tonalá held Mass in the local church and gave Communion to Robles. The assembled crowd then proceeded to the hill above the cave, furnished Robles with ropes and a basket in which he sat, and slowly let him down. Robles was dressed in wide leather trousers known locally as *chapulinas*, bore a pistol and sword for defense, and wore sandals rather than shoes.

After negotiating the precipitous overhang, he swung himself into the cave where he stayed for "thirteen or fourteen minutes." He then pulled hard on the rope and was dragged up to the hilltop by the crowd. Over the next twenty days, Robles was bedridden, struck down by a fever that almost killed him, but he survived. The story, which was collected by the priest of Tonalá in the 1870s, is perhaps apocryphal. Yet it confirms the perceived ethnic and religious merger of the region's Spanish and indigenous inhabitants. Although a Spaniard entered the cave, he was married to an indigenous cacica, and he only went in after informing the local indigenous authorities. He wore a sword and pistol, the mark of Spanish descent, but also the sandals of a Mixtec peasant.[286] The pact between the Christian icon and its Mixtec roots, and by extension the white elite and their indigenous subjects, had been redrawn and reconfirmed.

The ambivalence of inhabitants of the Mixteca Baja toward Independence testifies to the successful rewriting of the region's moral economy during the late colonial period. Limited tensions brought limited violence, unless it was imposed from outside. The settlements of the Mixteca Baja resembled Juan Ortiz Escamilla's neutral villages, which sought to be free from interference rather than profess royalism or republicanism.[287] At the same time, the patterns of insurrection and compliance in the region anticipated the divisions of the next fifty years. In the Mixteca Baja radical movements from 1810 to 1857 only attracted an ideologically driven handful of urban true believers. Strong ties between local elite and non-elite groups meant that the believers were forced to look beyond local villagers and seek support from more disenfranchised groups in low-lying sugar regions to the west, south, and north. In contrast, most elites and most peasants from the region sought to defend or quietly renegotiate the status quo, often through reasserting their communal bond with regional cults. From the 1830s through to the 1850s the conflicts between the two groups would map onto Mexico's incipient political parties. While radicals and their extralocal supporters sought change through federalism and liberalism, the inhabitants of the Mixteca Baja sought certainty and stability through centralism and conservatism.

Conclusion

During the colonial period Spanish and indigenous inhabitants of the Mixteca Baja forged a moral economy. This moral economy entwined the region's four major groups—Mixtec peasants, Mixtec nobles, the church, and Spanish settlers—in a lattice of mutual obligations and expectations. Mixtec nobles expected land, labor, and deference from their indigenous charges. In return, Mixtec peasants demanded protection and religious service. The church played an important role in this paternalist system, legitimizing and guiding the nobles' religious role. In return, the Dominican friars required Mixtec caciques to act as a vanguard for the evangelizing project. Finally, although Spanish settlers demanded cheap palm and livestock products and the temporary rental of pastoral lands, Mixtecs expected merchants and livestock owners to limit land purchases, regulate commercial claims, and bolster the cash economy. This arrangement of reciprocal if unequal dependence was symbolized by the image of the cult of the Cross, either in its root form as the Holy Cross of Tonalá or in one of its derivative types as a representation of the crucified Christ.

During the eighteenth century, population growth, competition for resources, and increasing Spanish interference in local governance threatened to disrupt the connections between the region's social groups, yet through a process of modification they survived. Demands for self-rule were met as caciques stepped down from their political positions and subject villages were raised to the status of repúblicas. But nobles, many of whom helped establish these new repúblicas, still retained control of land and labor. In return, they were still expected to offer protection and religious service. At the same time, Spanish commercial imperatives were balanced by the poor quality of lands, the persistence of cacique power, and the emergence of a culturally bilingual mixed-race elite. Finally, although the secularization of Dominican parishes jeopardized church-lay relations, locally born priests protected the religious agreements between colonizers and colonized.

Although the system would be further modified, over the next half century this late colonial arrangement, which balanced decentralization and self-rule with paternalism and clerical religiosity, would guide popular politics in the Mixteca Baja. On the one hand, the desire to maintain devolved rule would encourage elite and non-elite inhabitants to support federalism and undermine the less democratic aspects of centralism. On the other hand, the bonds between these two groups, the shared religious culture, and the concern for order and stability shifted political support toward the centralists and then conservatives from the 1830s onward.

For "the peace and security of the pueblo"

The Roots of Provincial Conservatism, 1821–1867

⸽

D URING THE EARLY 1820S THE CONSERVATIVE HISTORIAN CARLOS
María de Bustamante wrote his version of Huajuapan's royalist siege. According to the account, the Independence leader Valerio Trujano arrived in Huajuapan with a small force on April 5, 1812. He was pursued by eleven hundred well-equipped royalist troops led by General Régules, which surrounded and besieged the town. As Trujano arrived on the day of the town fair, he immediately forced the visiting peasants to remain and created a defensive force of all the local residents. Meanwhile, the "immoral" royalists set up camp on the hill of the calvary to the north of the settlement, where they "profaned the church" and mockingly wore the priest's robes. Over the next three months Trujano resisted continuous royalist attacks with a series of imaginative military strategies. First he set up fake cannons that fooled the royalists into thinking he possessed substantial artillery. When this strategy no longer worked he forged three cannons from the local church's bells. The cannons lacked the necessary ammunition, so he used stones from the river, which spread out when fired, "causing the impression of cold air balanced with the heat of fire." The insurgent general also employed local indigenous sharpshooters, like the "Indian of Nuyoo," who not only declared that Christ "directed his bullet[s]," but also crawled through enemy lines

to aid the town's eventual rescue. At the same time, local religious rituals complemented Trujano's tactical innovations. During the siege, the town's inhabitants fervently prayed to the image of Our Lord of Hearts, "imploring his help," "shedding many tears," and "asking his intermission as he knew the rectitude of their intentions." In the nine days leading up to the icon's festival, the residents and Trujano's men held a "solemn novena" to the local Christ. On the last day, their prayers were answered, and the insurgent Morelos lifted the siege.[1] Bustamante clearly infused the tale with his own brand of insurgent, proto-*indigenista* republicanism.[2] Nevertheless, the story's principal themes of interethnic cooperation, defensive militarism, religious devotion, and providential favor were curiously prescient. Over the next four decades, these same factors shaped regional politics, pushing elites and non-elites toward support for centralist and conservative regimes. By the 1840s, Our Lord of Hearts had become a key regional icon, the Indian of Nuyoo a local hero, and Bustamante's narrative the uncontested, conclusive account.

When royalist and pro-Independence soldiers allied, marched into Mexico City, and declared Mexico independent in 1821, they had no clear plan for what type of republic they wished to create. No amount of choreographed cheering, loquacious speeches, and professions of patriotism could mask the country's deep divisions. Over the next half century, numerous politicians sought to restructure the country's political, economic, and social systems, debating issues of suffrage, church-state relations, economic growth, taxation, and citizenship. After Agustín de Iturbide's short rule most Mexican elites united in support of a restricted, democratic, federalist arrangement. However, over the following decades discord surfaced as emerging factions interpreted this arrangement in different ways. Shifting coalitions, broadly described as federalist and centralist between 1824 and 1848 and liberal and conservative between 1848 and 1867, sought national predominance. Mexican politics resembled an escalating war of position, as increasingly vituperative groups exchanged political control through coup and revolt. Federalists (1824–1836) ceded to moderate centralists (1836–1843), who succumbed to militant centralists (1843–1855), who in turn yielded to radical liberals (1855–1857). During the following decade the war of position transformed into an all-out civil war that pitted liberals against conservatives (the War of Reform, 1857–1861) and then liberals against a conservative-French alliance (the War of French Intervention, 1862–1867). Yet, even this account fails to encompass the sheer complexity of local, regional, and ideological alliances that accompanied these broad shifts. During this period of political experimentation, Mexico was also shaken by a series of foreign invasions and internal rebellions. Spanish, British, French, Austrian, and U.S. military forces all disrupted Mexico's development, while indigenous peasants in Yucatán, the Huasteca, the Sierra Gorda, and Guerrero took advantage of political openings and military limitations to engage in what alarmist contemporaries classed as regional "caste wars."[3]

Until recently, this period was "one of the least-studied and most-misrepresented periods of Mexican history," its historiography "a black hole."[4] Many early historians, following the victorious liberal propagandists, sought to mold the era's shifting politics to a Whiggish narrative of liberal ascendency. Federalist and liberal leaders were described as far-sighted, noble, nationalist progressives, while centralists and conservatives were portrayed as knee-jerk "reactionaries," "traitors," and *vendepatrias*, their followers "ignorant," "semi-savage" "barbarians" and "pseudo-Mexicans."[5] Although revisionist historians sought to correct this patriotic pastiche, they did so by minimizing the importance of unifying ideologies and thus severed the links between high and low political groups. The era was rewritten as one of "cacicazgos, caudillajes, despotisms, and revolutions," its protagonists a bewildering array of "self-serving dictators and military nabobs."[6] Following the instrumentalist appreciations of centralist politicians like José María Tornel, historians argued that people looked at these elite maneuvers "with cold indifference."[7] In fact, "for the landless rural masses and the urban proletariat . . . the daily struggle for survival took precedence and they watched events passively and without any visible interest."[8] If the popular classes occasionally fought, they did so either out of coercion or out of an instinctive rejection of any political or economic change. As Friedrich Katz argued, "The ideology of the regional caudillos was not of crucial importance." Rather, liberals and conservatives simply "tried to mobilize campesinos for their own benefit."[9]

However, over the past two decades a new generation of historians has started to chart a path between liberal cant and Manichean structuralism to trace "the intersection of ideology and constituency," if not yet to "delineate the full range of its complexities and contradictions."[10] As numerous scholars have argued, the imposition of a broadly liberal political system, introduced by the Cadiz Constitution of 1812, reaffirmed in 1820, and formalized in law in 1824, brought popular politics to Mexico. The rural and urban masses now took part in elections, read about and listened to political debates, and engaged with political theater.[11] In doing so, communities formed what Antonio Annino has described as "liberal political syncretisms," which emerged when they attempted to "incorporate the new political realities into their traditional practices."[12] As individual communities molded novel rituals and discourses to accommodate their divergent political, economic, and social necessities, they sought common ground with regional elites and formed distinct political groups. These groups "fully expected to participate in designing the state, shaping production, organizing social relations, and contesting cultural constructions."[13] And it was these cross-class, ideologically coherent regional factions, and not the righteous liberal dogmatists or mercenary caudillos and their posses of put-upon peasants, that generated political change.

In particular, historians have described the emergence of a radical federalist alliance that joined Independence-era anti-Spanish sentiment to the more emancipating aspects of liberalism, including broad political participation, decentralized municipal rule, and regional autonomy. As successive centralist governments tried to curtail these new rights, peasants and regional leaders defended them through mass electoral mobilization and, if necessary, armed force. Although Peter Guardino's path-breaking work focused on Guerrero, where a particularly virulent brand of centralism and Independence-era traditions of political literacy, interethnic association, and insurrection combined to produce large-scale revolts, historians have also started to outline similar radical federalist coalitions in Oaxaca, Mexico State, Yucatán, the Huasteca, Morelos, and Mexico City.[14] Thus, Alicia Hernández Chávez argues that the period's caste wars were "sociopolitical" uprisings that aimed to confront the "the attempts of the provincial elites to lessen the political role of the municipalities."[15] Furthermore, historians have also argued that radical federalism, with its stress on local peasant self-determination, formed the ideological basis of the "popular liberalism" of the succeeding decades. In the Sierra Norte de Puebla, the Sierra Juárez of Oaxaca, and Morelos, peasants formed national guard battalions, joined liberal armies, and fought the conservatives for over a decade, not to assure bans on church lands or the privatization of communal property, but to secure community independence through municipal rule.[16] Ironically, this popular, democratic liberalism even formed the underlying creed of putative dictator Porfirio Díaz's 1871 La Noria revolt.[17]

The delineation of these radical federalist coalitions and their popular liberal successors has been heralded as the single most important shift in recent Mexican historiography, and rightly so. By taking peasant politics seriously, scholars have started to add some ideological ballast to the tales of rakish caudillos, unscrupulous caciques, and what Bustamante described as their "suggestible, childlike supporters."[18] Yet, certain questions remain. As Erika Pani states, the idea of popular liberalism "both convinces and worries." First, there is the aching suspicion that the prioritizing of liberalism over any other political ideology may not necessarily reflect popular enthusiasm but rather "the seduction that liberalism exercised at all levels" during the late nineteenth century, restating rather than undermining the old orthodoxy of liberal ascendency.[19] Or worse, as Brian Hamnett argues, it may even reveal foreign scholars' greater sympathy for liberalism over the Catholic, anti-U.S. elements of conservatism.[20] Beyond methodological concerns, by conflating "the flexible, heterogeneous, contingent strategies of authorities and communities of peasants" with "popular liberalism," we can also overlook the "rural pragmatism" of nineteenth-century Mexicans. As Raymond Buve argues, peasants made rational calculations about conditions of security for their families and the village and the opportunities available on either side. Their pragmatism was expressed in "fluctuating alliances, and the utilization of opportune moments to better the interests of groups or individuals."[21] Finally, by setting federalism/liberalism and centralism/conservatism in stark opposition historians also overlook the complexity, reach, and force of the latter. If, as Guardino argues, conservatives simply comprised royalist army officers, ecclesiastical leaders, Mexico City merchants, and their provincial allies "united around a deep fear of . . . cross-class coalitions," what space is there to understand the dominance of and popular support for conservatism?[22] In fact, as this chapter demonstrates, provincial conservatives were as ready to make hard-nosed political compromises as their liberal counterparts. Furthermore, the conservative defense of clerical Catholicism, order and stability, gradual land reform, and even militarism found considerable echo in certain regions of indigenous Mexico. Only by explaining the links between regional social structures and political conservatism can we start to comprehend the apparently chaotic cartography of community politics, caste conflict, and civil war.

Although the peasants of the Mixteca Baja initially embraced the federalism encompassed by Oaxaca's 1825 Constitution, by the late 1820s they had shifted their support to what I have called "provincial conservatism." At first Mixtec peasants expressed this on a regional level, as opposition to neighboring radical federalists. However, by the late 1840s regional beliefs started to blend with national ideologies. Over the next decade, locals rose up against real or perceived liberal policies, especially those concerning the church. Although Porfirio Díaz's liberal army eventually succeeded in co-opting some of these peasants during the War of French Intervention, it did so only by adopting conservative alliances, agreements, and policies. The provincial conservatism that emerged in the Mixteca Baja and, I shall argue, in other regions with overlapping histories of social, economic, and political development contained four elements. First, effective provincial conservatism was politically pragmatic. As Manuel Payno argued, conservatism was "not always the same, but had distinct aspects depending on the epoch and political circumstances in which it was practiced."[23] Even the more reactionary national governments of the era were not instinctively for monarchy, military authoritarianism, or neo-absolutism, but rather a modified "corporative constitutionalism" that allowed a degree of local rule and limited suffrage.[24] In its provincial form, conservatism was even more flexible, permitting the continuation of federalist practices in return for consensus and stability. Second, provincial conservatism was not fundamentally opposed to socioeconomic change.[25] When threatened, its adherents were amenable to instituting changes like land reform as long as the common bonds of hierarchy and paternalism remained intact. Third, if provincial conservatism was, to an extent, a watered-down or gradualist version of federalism, it was also characterized by certain positive traits, including support for clerical Catholicism. Although national and provincial conservatives might debate the level of local rule or the pace of land reform, they were united by "a clear and defined ecclesiastical posture, based on guaranteeing Catholic unity, clerical dignity and Christian social values."[26] This posture not only fomented a process of re-Christianization that emphasized church education and morality, but also made regions of provincial conservatism hypersensitive to perceived anticlericalism. Fourth, if Catholicism provided provincial conservatism with its overarching ideology, concern for order and stability supplied its political impetus. In certain regions from the late 1820s onward, both elites and peasants voluntarily formed militia groups, formulated strong links with the national army, and allied with metropolitan conservatives in order to defend their communities from the violence of neighboring regions of radical federalism.

The sheer complexity of the changes enacted in Mexican society during the early republican period and the dialogue between national, state, and regional politics means that this chronological section, spanning the declaration of Independence to the defeat of Maximilian, is divided into two parts. Chapter 3 will examine the narrative of the Mixteca Baja's shift from federalism to centralism to conservatism and its comparative value in detail. Although the followers of "provincial conservatism" maintained a concern for gradual change and church support throughout the era, internal and external shifts generated dynamic state and national alliances. Provincial conservatism never mapped exactly over either metropolitan centralism or elite conservatism.

In contrast, this chapter, following the schema established previously, examines the political, socioeconomic, and cultural changes underlying the Mixteca Baja's emerging support for provincial conservatism. As such, it is divided into four sections. The first section points to the maintenance of highly decentralized political practice throughout the period, irrespective of shifts at the national or state levels. The second section looks at land tenure. Here I argue that non-native pressure on lands was relatively low. As a result, caciques continued to dominate ownership. When they started to go bankrupt, regional elites were uninterested in purchase. Instead, they encouraged the purchase of the lands by indigenous villages, initiating a process of land reform that would continue for the next fifty years. The third section looks at changes in religious practice. The church's residual institutional strength, a strong village-level education program, elite support for regional cults, and their non-interference in cofradías precipitated an adherence to the tenets of orthodox clerical Catholicism. The fourth section argues that the bonds between elites and non-elites established through political, economic, and cultural cooperation were reinforced by periodic radical federalist rebellions in neighboring regions. Auxiliary military forces, set up in order to deal with these revolts, created further connections. Together, this process of political, socioeconomic, and religious bargaining acted to redirect and politicize but not upend the region's moral economy, that dense network of reciprocal agreements established during the late colonial period.

Village Government Retained

The federalist system of government was introduced in Oaxaca with the 1825 Constitution. The Constitution, as will be discussed in the next chapter, established an extraordinary decentralized political system that permitted the continuation of village rule. Yet although the Constitution remained on the books over the next thirty years, centralist national elites imposed increasingly stringent laws governing popular political participation. In the

Mixteca Baja, as in much of Oaxaca, these changes had little effect. Regional elites were content to trade decentralization for stability. Government remained highly fragmented, and individual villages maintained a high degree of internal control.[27] As centralism had such a measured effect, the alternative—radical federalism—held little attraction. Conversely, as the concern to maintain local rule remained constant, the elites and non-elites of the Mixteca Baja were only ever selectively centralist.

In December 1836 national politicians introduced a new centralist Constitution dubbed the Seven Laws, which struck at the heart of radical federalism by calling for the replacement of elected councilmen with appointed officials in smaller municipalities. These new village leaders or *jueces de paz* would be "proposed by the subprefect, named by the prefect, and approved by the governor."[28] Following the national line, the government of Oaxaca suspended municipal and república elections and ordered prefects to choose the new village representatives. In many places, including Guerrero and Papantla, the centralist attempt caused mass insurrection as mestizo townspeople used the new laws to curtail village autonomy, carve up communal lands, and extract greater taxes.[29] Yet in most of Oaxaca, the shift passed without incident. In order to avoid discontent, subprefects simply appointed *jueces* who had been agreed upon by the village. Furthermore, they allowed the internal appointment of the cargo offices below the jueces to continue without interference. In essence, the decentralized system of governance, inherited from the late colonial period and replicated in the federal Constitution, continued unchanged.[30]

The deliberate sabotaging of this aspect of centralism can be clearly observed in the Mixteca Baja, where the Huajuapan elite and the Mixtec peasants effectively ignored national policy and maintained a highly decentralized system of indigenous rule. For example, in 1842 the *juez de paz* of Chichihualtepec reported to the subprefect, Juan Acevedo, that the village had "convened a meeting" and that the "pueblo" had decided on the juez de paz, his deputy, and his three assistants for the following year. All the appointees were indigenous, and only one spoke Spanish fluently. Acevedo wrote back with his full approval.[31] The choice of not only a *juez* but also a deputy and three assistants seems to indicate that despite centralist rules that limited village representatives, the inhabitants of the Mixteca Baja continued to appoint the five members who made up the república government. Chichihualtepec was a medium-sized village of around five hundred inhabitants, but even the smaller hamlets named their own officials. In the same year, the one hundred inhabitants of Joluxtla chose the local cacique, Juan Bautista de la Cruz, to represent their interests.[32] At the same time, during the centralist period these jueces and their numerous assistants performed exactly the same duties as their república predecessors. In 1838 the juez de paz of Chazumba presided over the division of communal lands, the spending of communal funds, small-scale judicial issues, and the enforcement of commercial contracts.[33] Perhaps most importantly, jueces continued to defend communal interests against those of neighboring villages or encroaching ranchers. In 1842 the juez de paz of Huapanapan issued writs against the people of Chazumba and a local livestock owner for pasturing their livestock on village land without permission.[34]

In 1843 the centralist government tightened controls on village autonomy even further by introducing the so-called Bases Orgánicas. These new laws only allowed cabeceras or head towns to appoint jueces de paz. Smaller villages were permitted to appoint their own leaders, known as *agentes de policía*, with severely curtailed roles. The change was designed to limit political representation to those with knowledge of Spanish.[35] In many regions the more centralized system precipitated another round of indigenous insurrection, another cycle of caste war.[36] Even in Oaxaca, many villages balked at the reduction of representation and the limiting of judicial and administrative roles.[37] Yet in the Mixteca Baja, there seems to have been no incentive for the local elites to implement the policy in any meaningful way. As a result, they simply allowed nearly all the old repúblicas to declare themselves cabeceras and possess jueces as before. By 1847 Huajuapan possessed thirty cabeceras. These each controlled around four pueblos and two thousand inhabitants, less than any other district in the state. In fact the average Oaxaca cabecera presided over around six villages and three thousand inhabitants.[38] These jueces de paz were chosen as before, not by imposition, but by village election. For example, in 1846 the leaders of Acaquizapan announced to the subprefect that the village had chosen three jueces de paz, two deputies, and three assistants. The subprefect, still Acevedo, acceded without question.[39] Again, the sheer number of appointments indicates that villages were basically running república administrations under new names. Furthermore, even in the smaller pueblos that had not attained cabecera status, the stringent laws that forbade agentes de policía to play judicial roles were conveniently ignored. In 1846 the agente de policía of Mixquixtlahuaca sorted out disagreements between two bickering couples, a couple of land-hungry peasants, and a merchant and his reluctant client. He even investigated the strange demise of a shepherd employed by the local cofradía who had fallen off a cliff in the middle of the night.[40]

Finally, in the Mixteca Baja even the hyperstrict laws of the country's most autocratic regime, which ruled Mexico between 1853 and 1855, ushered in only minimal changes in political practice. The regime, presided over by Antonio López de Santa Anna, effectively prohibited indigenous town government and replaced municipal councils with a single appointed juez de paz.[41] As in other mestizo-dominated towns in Oaxaca, where indigenous and non-indigenous inhabitants were accustomed to split political positions between both groups, in Tezoatlán and Chilapa de Díaz the move caused some discontent. Eventually it would precipitate the rise of a small liberal mestizo elite. But in most of the region, effects were extremely limited. In other large mestizo settlements like Huajuapan and Tonalá, the Mixtecs had already surrendered political power as early as 1825 in return for control of cofradía lands.[42] In the smaller villages decision-making remained under the control of groups of elders, communities continued to choose prospective appointments, and subprefects approved them accordingly. In Diquiyú, for example, villagers continued to elect a juez and four "assistants" throughout the early 1850s.[43]

Land and Politics

If the maintenance of indigenous self-rule in the face of restrictive national policy ensured limited tensions between native and non-native groups, decisions over land ownership drew the region's Mixtecs toward an alliance with the provincial conservative elite. The link between land tenure and political allegiance during the early nineteenth century still remains controversial. For some revisionists, liberal attempts to force indigenous villages to divide or give up communal lands was the sine qua non of pragmatic indigenous alliances with conservative leaders. In Jalisco, repeated liberal demands to dismember village properties precipitated the purchase of former communal lands in the northern district of Tepic. By 1856 dispossessed Cora and Huichol peasants, under the indigenous leader Manuel Lozada, rose up against further threats of liberal reforms and in favor of conservative rule.[44] Similarly, in Oaxaca Zapotec rebels under José Gregorio Melendez made a hurried alliance with Santa Anna's last conservative regime in order to save communal salt flats from liberal attempts at usurpation.[45] However, as other recent scholars have pointed out, this economistic division, which depicts liberals as a land-hungry agrarian bourgeoisie and conservatives as old-money paternalists, is hard to sustain throughout Mexico as a whole. First, as John Tutino argues, the early nineteenth century was actually a "period of agrarian decompression" during which poor ranchers and even indigenous villages reclaimed the lands they had lost during the previous century.[46] Second, centralist and conservative policies to reduce indigenous self-rule were often accompanied by parallel attempts to usurp village lands. In fact, in regions of the Sierra Norte de Puebla and the Huasteca, federalists and liberals, by defending municipal rule, actually acted to maintain village properties.[47] Some radicals even supported the kind of wholesale land reform later enacted by the Mexican revolutionaries.[48]

Yet to sever the relationship between structure and superstructure and to dismiss the link between land and politics completely seems to overstate the case.[49] Expansions and annexations of village lands precipitated strong political loyalties. But these were as dependent on regional histories of land tenure and economic relations as overarching national ideologies. The situation in the Mixteca Baja was particularly complex. Since the late colonial period, the region's economy had depended on commerce, haciendas volantes, cacique land ownership, and indigenous leasing of these lands for favorable prices. During the early postcolonial period, the regional elite struggled to maintain this system, both for reasons of stability and easy exploitation. However, by the 1830s legal changes, long court cases, and inheritance disputes had put many indigenous caciques under increasing financial strain. Faced with the disintegration of the system of "reciprocal dominance" that had characterized cacique-commoner relations for over three centuries, the regional elite was forced to act. Provincial conservatives, comprising former royalist soldiers close to the regional caudillo, Antonio de León, encouraged the gradual sale of cacique lands to indigenous villages. These sales alleviated caciques' cash flow crises, co-opted grateful peasants, ensured stability, and allowed the continuation of elite commercial activities.

During the late colonial period, caciques and commoners in the Mixteca Baja had come to a new arrangement. Caciques surrendered their rights to political rule but continued to demand limited services and low rents for the use of their lands. In return, Mixtecs expected religious service and protection. White elites, generally uninterested in the economic returns from the region's poor lands, supported this new status quo. After Independence, this system continued. Indigenous caciques and cacicas continued to dominate land tenure. In 1831 they still owned 171 livestock farms or 60 percent of the Mixteca Baja's land. Villages owned seventy-eight sites and private citizens thirty-six (see appendix B).[50] In 1826 the cacica of Chinango, Ignacia Antonia Zamora y Santiago, requested an inspection of her property's borders. Chinango and its attendant ranches were surrounded by seven other cacicazgos and only two independent villages.[51] Some cacique holdings were enormous. Favorable marriage alliances, financial perspicacity, and the absence of threats precipitated the concentration of multiple landholdings in one cacique's hands. Men like Mariano Villagómez, Bonifacio Pimentel, and José María Bautista and women like Petra Aja and Teresa Velasco owned upward of ten livestock farms each around 780 hectares in size.[52] Although the land was predominantly pastoral, such large tracts generated enormous combined wealth. Isabel de Mendoza, the cacica of Ihualtepec, had her lands evaluated in 1839. They comprised the pueblos of Tlachichilco, Ihualtepec, Tamazola, San Vicente del Palmar, Zapotitlán Lagunas, and three other properties and were worth 100,205 pesos.[53] In 1870 Mariano Villagómez's children inherited properties worth around 90,662 pesos. Yet other caciques were noticeably less prosperous. A third of the caciques only owned one or two livestock farms.[54] For example, when José María de Castro, the cacique of Yucuquimi, died in 1836, he could only prove ownership of a strip of land in San Sebastián del Monte.[55] According to Pastor, during this period non-native landholders started to buy up caciques' properties, create smaller ranches, and enter into disputes with the indigenous former tenants.[56] Yet although Juan Bautista Carriedo estimated that there were seventy ranches in Huajuapan in 1847, most were owned by caciques, inhabited by their extended families, or rented out to villages. Thus Villagómez owned eight ranches, Mendoza three, and Joaquín Antonio Bautista y Guzmán, cacique of Chazumba, at least two.[57]

These caciques continued to rent their lands to indigenous peasants in return for cash rents and services. Limited demand and the historic ties between lords and commoners kept rents extremely low. In 1825 Bautista y Guzmán rented pastoral lands to the village of Huastepec for only ten pesos per year.[58] In 1843 another cacique rented pastoral lands to the livestock of the cofradía of San Sebastián for five years for only twenty-five pesos annually.[59] In the villages, individual peasants paid a proportion of the overall rent depending on the amount of land they used. In Chazumba in 1837, each leaser paid one peso per animal and another peso if they sowed maize on the land.[60] Although rents were low, caciques were also flexible if their tenants were unable to make a payment. Thus, Lorenzo Alvarado, the cacique of Calihuala, rented a salt well to the inhabitants of San Ildefonso Salinas for seventy-five pesos a year. In 1834 he reduced the payment to fifty pesos and two bushels of maize as the "renters [were] very poor."[61] In 1839 Mariano Villagómez explained that he had let the rent for the lands of Mixquixtlahuaca drop from forty to thirty-five to twenty-five pesos per year.[62] In addition to cash rents, service to the lords continued. In 1863 the villagers of Cuyotepeji explained that Mariano Villagómez still obliged them to hand over chickens, wild turkeys, and maize if any of his children married. Widows were obliged to grind corn, make tortillas, and cook other foods for the fiesta.[63] In Acaquizapan, the villagers were accustomed to "contribute to the caciques a head of livestock and a silver peso each year."[64]

In return for rents, commoners continued to expect paternalism and protection from the caciques. Although scholars of the Mixteca Baja have emphasized the acculturation of the noble class, their marriage into the white elite, and their movement to the region's commercial centers, most caciques clearly remained close to their indigenous charges.[65] When neighboring villagers destroyed the house of Juan de la Cruz Mendoza, cacique of Chilixtlahuaca in 1841, he declared that he had lived in the house "since time immemorial."[66] In 1820 María Micaela Alvarado, the cacica of Tequixtepec, declared that she had been married three times, once to an elder from the village, once to a neighboring cacique, and once to a mestizo. She had lived in Tequixtepec all her life and demanded that when she died she was buried underneath the local church.[67] Also despite their relative wealth, most caciques still shared the humble living arrangements of their tenants. Thus, when María de la Concepción Zuniga y Velasco, the cacica of Tianguistengo, died in 1842, she left her children five livestock farms, but her house was described as "made of palm with a cornstalk floor."[68] Proximity, reciprocity, and shared values could engender strong bonds of affection. Francisca Xavier de los Reyes, cacica of Pueblo Viejo who died in 1826, declared that the villagers of Yucuná had always treated her as the "lady and owner of her lands, helping her with money, and all class of provisions." They had also provided her with a domestic servant and as many assistants as she needed for her business ventures. In order to reward their "good conduct and respect," she donated the lands of San Juan de las Cañas to the pueblo.[69] Even if caciques rarely expressed their mutual obligations in such tender terms, they regularly demonstrated their duties by protecting their village's lands. In 1844 Bonifacio Pimentel complained that villagers from Cuyotepeji had stopped his indigenous tenants from Silacayoapilla from harvesting magueys on his lands.[70] Some caciques even stood up to attempts by the non-native elite to usurp village lands. For example, in the same year Pedro Mendiola and his wife, Ignacia Antonia Zamora y Santiago, took the regional livestock owner Juan Matamoros to court for invading village lands and burning tenants' houses.[71]

This relationship of "reciprocal dominance" was reinforced and sustained by a similarly unequal but symbiotic relationship between villagers and the non-native elite. Some whites owned small ranches, and a few possessed small sugar plantations around Atoyac, Tonalá, and Huajuapan, but most remained employed in occupations that necessitated indigenous cooperation. The top tier of Mixteca Baja society as well as a handful of Puebla and Mexico City businessmen continued to own haciendas volantes. These haciendas were still enormous enterprises (see appendix C). In 1828 Juan de Osio bought the hacienda volante of Our Lady of the Rosary for 83,900 pesos.[72] In 1850 together they owned a total of 391,800 goats and sheep or nearly 90 percent of the livestock that pastured in the Mixteca Baja.[73] Despite their size, these operations, like their colonial predecessors, were not simply unobtrusive but actually cemented bonds between caciques, non-natives, and peasants. First, the huge flocks demanded limited lands. They spend most of the year around the Costa Chica and the Guerrero montaña. When they reached the Mixteca Baja, they either spent short periods on the sparse slopes of individual villages or waited at a series of relatively small ranches to be slaughtered. Second, the flocks contributed to the economic well-being of caciques and the handful of landowning villages as their owners paid cash for temporary land rental, salt, and spare maize. For example, in 1832 cacique Lorenzo Alvarado rented his mountainous lands to the hacienda volante of Manuel María Fagoaga.[74] Seven years later, Manuel Araos's hacienda volante signed an agreement with the juez de paz of Yolotepec to rent the mountainous lands of the village for sixty-five pesos per year.[75] Third, as the haciendas butchered select livestock at small ranches in the region every November, they offered nearby peasants temporary employment and cheap meat. Regional caudillo Antonio de León possessed two ranches in Diquiyú and Tezoatlán, which employed hundreds of Mixtecs to help with the annual slaughter.[76] Small butchering ranches also existed around Tehuacán, Petlalcingo, Chazumba, and Huajuapan. Describing these ranches in 1847, Juan Bautista Carriedo wrote, "They eat much goat meat, vulgarly called chito, and produce fat and skins at the matanzas they do annually in abundance."[77] Fourth, in the post-Independence world of mass mobilization, haciendas volantes also had a new political role in linking the regional elite to the peasant renters. Unlike most hacienda volante owners, who employed their regional managers to affirm rental agreements, Antonio and Manuel de León signed contracts with caciques and villagers in person. Furthermore, these were not toothless treaties but rather expressions of mutual responsibility. In 1822 Manuel de León signed an agreement with the council of Camotlán to rent the hills around the village for sixty pesos per year for nine years. He paid the full amount in advance and swore that the flocks would not touch village crops or houses.[78] Ten years later he signed an agreement with the cacica of Diquiyú, which promised that his flocks would keep to the hillsides, villagers could continue to sow the valley lands, and if his flocks inflicted any damage, his shepherds would pay.[79] When León became governor of Oaxaca during the 1840s, he used his position to increase legal support for these agreements, demanding that mayordomos of the haciendas "comply with the contracts that they [had] with the pueblos."[80]

The other major occupation of the regional elite was commerce. Like the owners of haciendas volantes, the Mixteca Baja's merchants relied on the cooperation of indigenous peasants. Many merchants owned shops in the region's main towns. For example, when Matias Galva died of cholera in 1861, he left a store and produce worth over eight hundred pesos, including clothes, coffee, shoes, knives, and, of course, palm.[81] Even top-tier elites with substantial livestock investments owned stores. When Antonio de León's brother, Manuel, died in 1835 he left a shop and 2,704 pesos' worth of stock including cotton, wine, chocolate, wax, chile, and again a plethora of palm products. The shops traded with all sectors of society. León's list of debts includes nearly two hundred people from villages throughout the Mixteca Baja.[82] Paulino González's two shops in Huajuapan and Chila sold to clients as far north as Puebla, west into Guerrero, and south toward Oaxaca.[83] If elites did not own shops, they bred and traded in livestock. In 1850 a few dozen livestock merchants owned around ten thousand sheep and goats, which they sold to indigenous farmers.[84] According to León's will, in 1834 he had sold over 1,370 sheep and goats to nearly one hundred farmers in eight separate villages.[85] As a result, indigenous villagers owned around twenty-five thousand head of livestock in 1850.[86]

As the Mixteca Baja's elites relied on a late colonial equilibrium between cacique ownership and indigenous land rental, which ensured cheap leases, political stability, and commercial relations, they sought to keep this system in place with a dual policy of defending indigenous caciques and mollifying indigenous villagers in their conflicts with non-native landowners. On the one hand, regional powerbrokers from the major towns of Huajuapan, Chila, and Silacayoapan often represented indigenous caciques in court. José Amador, a Chila mestizo, seemed to specialize in the defense of cacique lands against mestizo interlopers and encroaching villages during the period. In 1844 he defended Mariano Villagómez against the protestations of a handful of aspirant ranchers. The following year he defended the same cacique against Tequixtepec's demands for lands.[87] High-profile elites, like the long-standing prefect of Huajuapan, Juan Acevedo, even took time off from political duty to represent indigenous lords. In 1829 Acevedo argued that the village of Acaquizapan still owed Villagómez back rent for the use of his lands.[88] On the other hand, the elite also defended indigenous villages against infractions by white or mestizo landowners. For example, in late 1839 the council of Chichihualtepec complained to the Huajuapan judge that the cattle of Agustín Castillo had strayed onto their lands. In response the judge allowed the peasants to kill any of Castillo's livestock that inadvertently crossed the borders as compensation.[89] In fact, even political powerbrokers like Antonio de León got involved in small law cases and attempted to reach compromises that would minimize conflict and maintain the status quo. For example, in 1846 León wrote to the local judge about the ongoing struggle between Joaquín Bautista y Guzmán and the village of Chazumba over the cacique's lease of lands to a regional rancher. Although the rancher was one of his compadres, the three "indios" who had complained were also his "friends." Thus, he advised the judge to "avoid all conflict" and decide the case in a "rational and prudent manner." At the court session, the judge quoted León's advice, reduced the rancher's tenancy agreement, and ordered the cacique's children to continue renting most of the land to their peasant charges.[90]

Despite the regional elites' best attempts, by the mid-nineteenth century the region's caciques were in decline. During the colonial period, indigenous cacicazgos had been legally entailed estates. Entailment guaranteed the perpetuation of a family and its property by restricting inheritance to a single line of descent. In theory at least cacicazgos could not be divided up or sold. This system changed in 1821 when the new nation effectively prohibited the advantageous legal station of cacicazgos. Cacicazgos no longer existed as legal entities. Caciques were now simply indigenous citizens with large amounts of private land that could be sold and divided up among multiple heirs.[91] In the Mixteca Baja, the land-rich, cash-poor late colonial caciques, who often had been involved in protracted legal cases with neighboring caciques and villages for decades, saw their lands divided up and their debts increase. As a result, by the 1830s many were crippled not only by taxes and day-to-day expenses but also by legal commitments they were unable to pay. By 1836 Isabel de Mendoza owed over thirty-one hundred pesos to eighteen creditors from the main commercial towns. Some were small traders, some were village administrators, but the majority comprised the region's large merchants.[92] These non-native creditors repeatedly took indigenous caciques to court to extract the arrears. On June 6, 1837, José María Puga from Huajuapan demanded that Mendoza hand over the eighty pesos he was owed by the end of the month.[93] In April 1834 a Tequixtepec merchant claimed that the cacique of Chazumba, Juan Bautista y Guzmán, still owed him 117 pesos, which "he should have satisfied last year in May in the form of the livestock."[94] Many started to sell off their lands, citing debt as the principal cause.

As provincial conservatives like Antonio de León realized the financial predicament of their indigenous partners, they started to encourage land purchase by indigenous villages. This paternalist move had both economic and political motives. First, most of the lands were hilly, infertile, and simply not worth buying. Second, hacienda volante owners relied on low land rents, which they could better ensure from grateful peasants than aspirant mestizo ranchers. Third, by encouraging such land transfers, regional elites ensured stability, co-opted entire villages of peasants, and secured a support base for struggles against radical federalists in the neighboring regions around Putla, Copala, and into Guerrero. It was no coincidence that land sales peaked in the late 1830s and early 1840s when federalist bands roamed the region looking for other discontented peasant backers (see appendix D). As befitted the region's political arbiter, León seems to have been involved in most of the early sales. For example, in 1844 the cacica of Ihualtepec sold the lands of Ahuehuetitlan to the village council for ten thousand pesos. A year later the cacica's husband brought the villagers to court for an outstanding debt. During the proceedings a member of the village council explained in Mixtec why the village had purchased the land. Apparently, in early 1844 León sent to the juez de paz a letter that had "shown his well-known philanthropy and love for the well-being of the pueblos." In the letter the caudillo suggested that Ahuehuetitlan escape its state of "utter misery," "stop renting the cacica's lands," and "buy them by just acquisition." After the village's elders had discussed the offer, they decided to enter into a purchase agreement.[95] Furthermore, as the sales were desperate and uncompetitive attempts to pay off debt, prices were remarkably low. Even though the cacica of Ihualtepec had estimated that her lands in Zapotitlán Lagunas were worth thirty-three thousand pesos, she sold them to the village for only eighteen thousand in 1841.[96] The fee was payable over four or five years and eminently negotiable. In 1845 the husband of the cacica of Ihualtepec agreed to lower Ahuehuetitlan's annual payment from thirteen hundred to six hundred pesos per year.[97]

Although liberals gradually started to divide up cacique lands to attract peasant support, conservatives, as the originators of the scheme, continued to view the purchase of cacique lands by villages as key to social stability during the conflicts of the 1850s and 1860s. In May 1854 the prefect of Huajuapan, Santiago Rodríguez, lamented that he spent most of his days involved in "litigation between pueblos over borders and between pueblos and private citizens demanding rents." These legal processes not only cost money, they also involved long treks of "two or three days" to the seat of the prefecture. However, he claimed his heart "beat with feeling" when he observed the "suffering of the pueblos."[98] Consequently, in periods of regional conservative rule (1852–1854, 1859–1860, and 1864–1866), Huajuapan authorities also backed purchases.

Re-Christianization

If the basic maintenance of a late colonial moral economy, which involved political decentralization and economic symbiosis, ensured stability in the Mixteca Baja, as it did in much of Oaxaca, religious revival and the threat of violence drew the region's peasants toward support for centralism and conservatism. Brian Connaughton claims that historians have "left to one side the theme of religion in studying power in Mexico in the nineteenth century."[99] First, most scholars have emphasized the general decline in the influence of the church during the period. The papacy's long refusal to recognize Mexico's Independence left the hierarchy chronically understaffed. By 1831 no recognized bishops remained in the country. Insurrection, the expulsion of the Spaniards, the establishment of secular educational institutions, and lack of leadership precipitated a parallel reduction in the amount of clergy. Between 1810 and 1851 the number of priests in Mexico fell by over half to 3,232.[100] At the same time, the church no longer enjoyed its colonial status as a privileged corporation under royal protection, and as a result legal advantages like the ecclesiastical *fuero* were severely reduced.[101] Furthermore, the church's preeminent financial position, as landowner, tithe collector, and moneylender, also weakened. Tithes declined, land was sold, and new financial institutions vied for control of Mexico's investment capital.[102] Finally, divisions within the church, which had emerged during the War of Independence, hardened. Priests ignored the infrequent demands of the hierarchy and used their popular influence to support positions along the political spectrum. Some harked back to the colony, others embraced the republic, others still carved out distinct millenarian visions, like the Puebla priests who attempted to reintroduce an Aztec monarchy.[103] Second, most historians have argued that until the late 1840s the religious issue was not part of the debate and certainly cannot be used to explain the era's political schisms.[104] The federalist Constitution upheld the exclusive role of the Catholic Church, and most federalists, even Valentín Gómez Farias, vice president of Mexico during 1834's anticlerical reforms, were extremely pious individuals.[105] At the same time, many centralists, including Santa Anna, were not averse to curbing ecclesiastical privileges and co-opting church wealth.[106]

Both positions are valid. Overall the church did decline, and at the top tier of the political hierarchy the position of the church in independent Mexico only rarely engendered serious conflict. As evidence from the Mixteca Baja demonstrates, however, religion shaped and sustained everyday politics in the country's provinces. Throughout the period the "liturgical lines" dividing clerical and nonclerical religious cultures, sketched out during the reforms of late eighteenth century, were gradually engraved with greater force. In some regions, which I call regions of de-Christianization, the church's power declined precipitously. In these regions—like Papantla, the Mezquital Valley, Zitacuaro, the Guerrero montaña, and, as I shall argue, Putla and Copala to the south of the Mixteca Baja—elite and popular religious practices diverged, and heterodox, unsanctioned rituals increased. Priests became increasingly unnecessary for the fulfillment of regular religious customs. As a result, villagers held political autonomy over religious obedience, embraced anticlericalism, and supported radical federalism.[107] In other regions, like the Mixteca Baja, which I call regions of re-Christianization, numbers of priests remained constant, and church schools grew. Local and universal, popular and elite forms of worship aligned as frequent negotiations between the clergy, lay elite, and lay commoners precipitated the conscious reconstruction of a regional church orthodoxy. As priests and non-native merchants embraced local cults, cofradía autonomy, and the financial demands of the poor, so the region's indigenous peasants gravitated toward the church: building structures, paying tithes, adopting a clerical morality, and siding with order over insurrection. These twin processes of increasing orthodox practice and growing elite adoption of popular ritual put a premium on the involvement of local priests. As a result, in these regions that often surrounded provincial commercial centers like Zacapoaxtla, Chalpancingo, Tulancingo, and Huajuapan a "defensive clericalism," highly supportive of the clergy's status, emerged.[108] By the 1850s, as high politics divided over the position of the church, these oppositional rhythms of clerical-lay interaction broadly defined political allegiances as radical federalists sided with the liberals and centralists with the conservatives.

Around Huajuapan, secularization and the Bourbon Reforms had tested but not destroyed relations between the church and the indigenous communities. In fact, they may even have become stronger as a new generation of mixed-race priests, related to the Mixtec aristocracy, took over the secular parishes. As a result, the church retained its institutional strength during the early nineteenth century. Between 1790 and 1850, the number of parishes in the district of Huajuapan increased from thirteen to nineteen, or nearly 50 percent, as the small villages of Miltepec, Huapanapan, Chicahuaxtla, Huajolotitlán, Tlachichilco, and Huastepec acquired the necessary permissions.[109] In comparison, the number of parishes at the national level increased by barely 20 percent.[110] Furthermore, although clergy numbers declined slightly during the early 1820s, a decade later they had returned to pre-Independence levels. Few parishes remained vacant for long, clerics were keen to accept the region's favorable benefices, and interim priests remained for sustained periods.[111] Between 1835 and 1856 priests in the district of Huajuapan numbered between eighteen and twenty or one for every twenty-five hundred inhabitants. In comparison, the national average in 1850 was one priest for every four thousand laypersons.[112] As most priests favored urban living, the number in the countryside was probably even lower. The Mixteca Baja's preponderance of priests can be explained in part by the Diocese of Puebla's relative endurance. In the diocese as a whole numbers of priests declined during the period, but not at the same steep rate as in other areas. Furthermore, within the diocese some regions remained stronger than others. The Mixteca Baja's stability, piety, and commercial activity attracted some of Puebla's most ambitious and talented priests. Francisco Irigoyen, who would lead the diocese after Bishop Labastida's exile in 1857, was vicar general of Huajuapan from 1833 to 1845.[113] At the same time, the Mixteca Baja continued to generate its own clerical class. Many clerics were related to the region's white and mestizo elite.

Antonio de León's relative, Carlos Rueda de León, was priest of Silacayoapan during the early 1860s.[114] Another relative, José de Jesús de León, was priest in Tamazola in the 1850s. Ignacio Carrión, son of an important Huajuapan merchant, was interim priest of Tonalá during the same period.[115] Manuel Galva was priest of his hometown of Tezoatlán during the 1830s.[116] Others were the scions of cacique families, like Pedro Velasco y Villagómez, who was in charge of Chazumba during the 1840s, or Miguel Navarrete, who ran Tlachichilco during the 1860s, or José Antonio Sánchez Camacho, who was interim priest of Huajuapan in the 1820s.[117] Still others were the sons of aspirant indigenous elders. Eduardo Calixto de la Palma, who was priest of Tonalá from 1840 to 1854, was the son of a well-off indigenous couple from Teposcolula.[118] His successor, Felipe Martínez, would eventually lead Tonalá in rebellion against the Reform laws in 1856, was from the small indigenous village of Ixtlán on the Puebla-Oaxaca border.[119]

If the concentration of clergy offered the church considerable regional sway, especially in the parish seats, the expansion of church schools permitted the penetration of ecclesiastical doctrine into smaller villages. The ecclesiastical hierarchy and its conservative supporters believed that Catholic education, with its emphasis on doctrine, obedience, and a Christian morality, was essential to political stability.[120] As early as 1825 the diocese reminded priests that "one of their principal duties" was to "instruct the faithful about the dogmas of our beliefs and the principles of morality" and asked them to dedicate at least an hour a week to teaching "pure Indians."[121] Under centralist rule the ecclesiastical authorities were even more forceful. In 1840 Bishop Francisco Pablo Vázquez told political governors that their "first obligation" was "the care of the youth under principles of Christian morality."[122] In 1854 the new bishop, José María Luciano Becerra y Jiménez, supported Santa Anna's educational project and demanded that priests "instill education in the faithful and especially the children." In his opinion this education comprised "all the knowledge necessary for Catholics including the mechanics of our sacred religion." When the district governor received word of the instructions, he immediately wrote to all the jueces in the region, demanding their compliance.[123]

Countrywide results were questionable, and Anne Staples estimates that barely 1 percent of Mexico's population attended schools during the period. In many regions absenteeism was rife, and illiteracy actually increased.[124] But in other regions, like the Mixteca Baja, the programs seem to have generated considerable achievements. In 1832 the district of Huajuapan possessed

147 schools with 7,398 students. This figure made up a quarter of the state's total schools and a fifth of the state's pupils. Only one other district had over one hundred establishments.[125] A few years later, the governor claimed that schools in the region had increased to 158, and pupils totaled 9,441. This time, the next largest district only had thirty-seven schools and just under three thousand students.[126] Although the number of establishments declined, in 1840 Huajuapan still had the second-highest number of schools in the state.[127] Eight years later, the district still had over seventy schools with over thirty-five hundred students.[128] Even outside the region's commercial centers, indigenous boys and girls went to school throughout the period. In Chazumba, parents established a municipal school that ran without interruption, except during harvest time, from 1830 to 1861. Here they learned Christian doctrine by rote and were marked on their ability to memorize key texts like the Ten Commandments, the Apostles' Creed, and the Lord's Prayer. On average, around seventy boys and ninety girls attended the school each year.[129] Although further data are lacking, the preponderance of girls suggests one reason for the explosion in female pious organizations in the succeeding decades.

The success of the church's educational program in the region had its roots in the complex web of interethnic relations that this chapter tries to elucidate. However, two factors stand out. First, the regional authorities provided economic foundations for the schools. In 1832 the local prefect started handing out permissions to villages to hold weekly markets to pay for teachers, school buildings, and texts. Two years later, he decreed the establishment of over twenty markets in the region's smaller pueblos.[130] Over the succeeding decades, other villages successfully petitioned their local administrators for similar permissions designed to pay for the erection of educational establishments.[131] Moreover, in 1844 the governor of Oaxaca, Antonio de León, decreed that villages in the Mixteca Baja could collect a tax of two pesos per thousand goats from the haciendas volantes that crossed their lands. This money was to be used exclusively for the funding of primary schools.[132]

Second, the schooling program in the region benefited from the teaching of Christian doctrine in the area's diverse Mixtec dialects. Recent scholarship has played down the church's continued role in indigenous-language education and instead emphasized the introduction of so-called political catechisms, small guides to the rights and duties of Mexican citizens, redolent of the educational materials employed in postrevolutionary France.[133] However, in regions of putative Catholic revival, the Mexican church strengthened its focus on indigenous-language education. Clerical conservatives, fearful of indigenous insurrection, were essentially pragmatic and saw the production of dual-language catechisms and comprehensible guides as key to the drive to educate and discipline Mexico's illiterate masses. Thus, between 1810 and 1849 the church published twenty-eight Catholic texts in indigenous languages, well over double those released during the previous half century.[134] The Mixteca Baja was one of these regions of Catholic revival. Reneging on its Bourbon-era prohibitions, the Bishopric of Puebla published three religious texts in the language of the Mixteca Baja in the 1830s. These texts included a catechism published in 1834, another catechism printed in 1837, and a manual for the administration of the sacraments also published in 1837.[135] The first work was translated solely into the language of the Mixteca Baja, but the two subsequent pamphlets offered versions in the Mixtec "de la Mixteca Baja" (spoken around Huajuapan and Acatlán) and "de la Mixteca montañez" (spoken around Silacayoapan, Tonalá, and Tlapa). All three offered parallel versions of the text in Spanish and were clearly designed by local priests for village teachers under the auspices of the diocese. These small books formed the basis of peasant religiosity for the next half century. They were handed out to priests and pious parishioners and used in schools and in the confessional. The will of Eduardo Calixto de la Palma, the priest of Tonalá during the 1840s and 1850s, listed "many" copies of a "catechism in Mixtec."[136] As late as 1865, the prefect of Huajuapan mentioned that most schoolchildren still learned their Christian education "from a small catechism in Mixtec."[137]

Unfortunately, no copies of the 1834 catechism survive. However, the 1837 catechism and the 1837 manual do exist. Although the Spanish prologues to the texts reveal the ecclesiastical hierarchy's continued ambivalence toward indigenous-language teaching, the process of compiling the works revealed a genuine desire to teach doctrine, political obedience, and Christian morality effectively. On the most prosaic level, the ecclesiastical hierarchy overcame its obvious distaste for indigenous-language teaching and reverted to missionary methods, producing three religious texts for a language spoken in a handful of parishes at the remotest edge of the diocese. Furthermore, the texts were not simply reprints of colonial versions. These texts emerged from an intense period of negotiation between the bishopric, the local priests, and their parishioners. The priests clearly changed the catechism released in 1834 after realizing the differences between the Mixtec spoke in Acatlán and Huajuapan ("de la Mixteca Baja") and that spoken in Silacayoapan, Tonalá, and Tlapa ("de la Mixteca montañez"). In the 1837 version, the authors note that the first version "was released with very many errors which we have sought to correct and amend in this second edition."[138] The bishop of Puebla was so keen to avoid mistakes that after handing out the second version, he ordered priests to collect up and hand in any other printed or manuscript versions.[139] Although the second catechism and the manual contained mistakes, the writers were keen to make the text as functional as possible for subsequent priests. For example, the writers included a brief explanation of the tonal nature of Mixtec in order to prevent priests from reading out unaccented versions. Similarly, they included a long discussion explaining that the Mixtec word *zodonzute*, which had been translated as "to baptize," actually meant "to wet." Instead, they suggested using the word *necate*—"to wash"—in order to encapsulate the idea of purity and regeneration.[140] The process of ethnolinguistic investigation that preceded the second catechism and the manual is also suggested by the bishop's orders with regards to the production of a Mixtec dictionary, which unfortunately never saw the light of day. In June 1837 he asked local priests to collect "sufficient material" from their indigenous charges. This included "all the names and words in Mixtec, with emphasis on the proper orthography of the pueblo or respective pueblos."[141]

Furthermore, the contents of the works reveal the hierarchy's main interests. First, they emphasized liturgical orthodoxy. The second catechism, used for rote teaching in the classroom, was a fairly simple translation of certain key Christian texts, including the Sign of the Cross, the Our Father, the Apostles' Creed, the Ave Maria, the Ten Commandments, and the Seven Sacraments.[142] Second, they highlighted the importance of hierarchy, social stability, and political obedience. The manual, which was to be employed in classrooms, in confessionals, and in informal discussions with parishioners, was written in the form of a confession between a priest and an imagined Mixtec penitent. In one particularly revealing section, the peasant confessed that he had stolen livestock and heads of corn from a neighboring landowner, explaining that he had heard "it was not a sin to rob from the rich but only from the poor." The priest replied that these were still sins and ordered the man to return the stolen goods as soon as possible. Third, they drew attention to the significance of Christian morality. The manual in particular stressed the commandments that concerned the family, with large sections relating to filial piety, spousal unity, and sexual propriety.[143] These sections not only laid out the day-to-day responsibilities of the good

Christian, they also fed into the diocese's conservative political discourse, which viewed republican Mexico as a family linked by sacred ties of paternal and filial reciprocity.[144]

In the Mixteca Baja, the high concentration of priests, proliferation of church schools, and availability of indigenous-language teaching materials encouraged clerical obedience. Yet church orthodoxy was not simply imposed from the top down. The success of this re-Christianization also relied on what Edward Wright-Rios calls "the ongoing processes of interaction and negotiation within the church."[145] In order to institute a broad acceptance of liturgical orthodoxy, school attendance, regular worship, tithe payment, and Christian morality, lay and clerical elites were forced to make constant concessions to indigenous parishioners. These not only involved the reintroduction of Mixtec-language teaching but also support for local cults and backing for the village cofradías. Together, these parallel techniques of institutional imposition and local compromise gave the Mixteca Baja's religious orthodoxy a distinctly regional flavor, acting vertically to cement lay-clerical links and centripetally to draw together common regional devotions.

During the early nineteenth century priests and, increasingly, non-native elites encouraged the Christ cults, which formed the communal hubs of regional religiosity. On the one hand, they authorized and fast-tracked new village devotions. In Tamazulapan, indigenous peasants had worshipped the bloody, prostrate statue of Christ, dubbed Our Lord of Fainting, since the late eighteenth century. According to various devotees, they regularly visited his statue to ensure successful harvests. Yet the predominantly indigenous cult was poorly financed, the altar barely decorated, and the statue relegated to a corner of the parish church. But in 1845 things changed when two local merchants started to promote the devotion, persuading the local priest to move the statue to a more central altar, forming a cofradía, and appointing a local cacique as the first mayordomo.[146] Similarly, pious peasants in Chazumba had worshipped Our Lord of Hope since the early nineteenth century. But when the priest Antonio García arrived in 1850, he noted, "The altar, where the Sacred Image of Our Lord of Hope was placed, lacked ornamentation." He went to discuss the matter with the village council, and together they decided to ask the priest of Huajuapan to hold a Mass in honor of the image. At the end of the Mass the priest explained in Mixtec that it was the villagers' Christian duty to decorate the Lord's altar. He proposed the establishment of a cofradía, funded by donations of livestock or cash depending on the financial situation of each family. By 1854 most villagers had handed over between four reals and two pesos with which the priest established a cofradía and bought decorations for the altar.[147]

On the other hand, priests and elites also offered their support to existing devotions. The mayordomos of the Holy Cross of Tonalá continued to wander the region, demanding money from devotees. The account books from 1831 to 1832 reveal that devotees now included numerous non-natives, such as Francisco Irigoyen, the priest of Huajuapan; Juan Acevedo, long-time prefect of the region; and Antonio de León's brother, Manuel.[148] At the same time, Our Lord of Hearts, Huajuapan's own gory image of Christ, gradually replaced the root devotion and began to represent the region's new nationalist, interethnic religious fervor. Bustamante's narrative, which claimed that Morelos had liberated the city on the feast day of the image in 1812, became a popular regional myth repeated in sermons, celebrations, poems, and local histories.[149] And although indigenous peasants remained in charge of the image's cofradía lands, elites helped out with generous financial support. Few regional merchants died without donating money or property to the image.[150] Even the former royalist Antonio de León, who had fought against the miraculous image during the 1812 siege, agreed to buy up a run-down house left to the Christ for "the high sum" of two thousand pesos, which he paid directly to the cofradía.[151] Furthermore, elites also supported Our Lady of the Snows, the mountain-top apparition of Ixpantepec Nieves. The authors of the 1837 catechism even devoted their work to the saint, whom they implored to "take under her protection this small work so that it remains useful to the eternal salvation of the Mixtecs, and makes easier the work of its priests and ministers."[152]

Even in smaller towns, where one might have expected self-conscious gente de razón to dismiss local customs, pious elites embraced Christocentric indigenous devotions. In Saul Reyes Aguilar's biography of his rancher grandfather, Librado Aguilar y Cedeno, who lived in Tamazola during the mid-nineteenth century, the local author described how Aguilar, his family, and his extended household spent all Easter week at the festivities in honor of Our Crucified Lord, the image of Tlachichilco, and "gazed with devotion at his divine body hanging on the cross."[153]

Undoubtedly, growing elite support for previously indigenous devotions could cause arguments over conflicting customs. Yet by following a policy of compromise rather than confrontation, pragmatic authorities were quick to settle these encounters in favor of older devotees. For example, in

1854 indigenous followers of Our Lady of the Snows complained that the new priest was overcharging them, preventing them from marching in the celebration, and interfering in the business of the cofradía. The bishop's representative, in conjunction with the local prefect, ordered the priest to reduce costs and permit the indigenous mayordomos to lead the annual procession.[154] Similarly, in 1850 the liberal government of Benito Juárez, with the support of ecclesiastical authorities, introduced a tax on dancing at fiestas. Soon after the widely unpopular levy was introduced, both the prefect of Huajuapan and the local priest requested that dances at fiestas and weddings in the region be excluded from the charge, arguing that they were a "popular tradition" and a "form of solemnizing the marriage."[155]

Although elites embraced and backed regional devotions, they continued to concede the financial running of these devotions to traditional cofradías. Like their colonial predecessors, these early nineteenth-century sodalities elected annual representatives, paid for elaborate festivities, and controlled large amounts of communal land, property, and capital. Few priests interfered in the organizations except when communities demanded the sacking of a particularly corrupt or incompetent mayordomo. When the bishop asked the priest of Chazumba, Pedro Velasco y Villagómez, to send in cofradía accounts in 1845, he replied that he had "no rights" to the books, and would have to ask "permission" from the local leaders.[156] Even when priests did intercede, they usually had to accept at least partial defeat. When the priest of Trujapan attempted to stop the local cofradía from donating a third of its profits to the village government, he was forced to negotiate and back down. By 1831 he accepted that at least a fifth of the organization's "sacred money" would go to the secular institution.[157]

In large commercial towns like Huajuapan or Tonalá, where native groups had lost political control of the municipal council during the 1820s, continued indigenous control of sodalities was particularly important. Here the lands and properties of cofradías did not so much complement communal incomes as sustain entire indigenous minorities. In 1820 the six hundred inhabitants of Huajuapan's "indigenous barrios," who formed around a sixth of the city's population, lost control of their communal lands. However, they retained control of the lands, livestock, and properties of the cofradías of Our Father Jesus, Our Lady of the Rosary, Our Lady of Solitude, Saint Joseph, Our Lord of Hearts, and Our Lord of the Calvary. These eight "small pieces of land," their corn, livestock, magueys, and wheat not only provided for parish fees, church decorations, and annual fiestas, but also for their families.[158] Similarly, during the 1820s the two hundred indigenous peasants of Tonalá, or around a fifth of the town's population, relinquished control of communal lands but maintained control of cofradía properties in the nearby ranch of Yetla. In 1833 they eventually bought the land from the cacica, Petra Aja.[159]

As these semi-urban Mixtecs acted as mayordomos, organized fiestas, and controlled considerable cofradía property, they not only shaped regional devotions but also formed strong bonds with local priests. During the 1840s, a handful of Tonalá's aspirant mestizos attempted to take over the rich pasturelands of the Yetla ranch, demanding that the cofradías revert to non-native control. The priest, Eduardo Calixto de la Palma, refused. Between 1845 and 1850 the town's mestizos sent increasingly shrill complaints about the priest's "criminal conduct" to state and ecclesiastical authorities. Eventually, the diocese attempted to replace the stubborn cleric but to no avail. Palma decamped to the neighboring village of Atenango and then to San Sebastián del Monte. From here, he and the two hundred indigenous inhabitants of Tonalá continued to plant and pasture livestock on the cofradía lands.[160] Even after he died in 1854, his replacement, Felipe Martínez, continued the struggle. His cofradía followers would form one of the most resilient bands of conservative guerillas during the next decade.

As most regional elites left alone the internal running of cofradías, caciques still played important roles as mayordomos, renters, and donators. Members of the Villagómez family were regularly voted in as the heads of cofradías in various villages around their base in Suchitepec.[161] To the east, Joaquín Bautista y Guzmán and his brother, Francisco, rented their lands to the cofradías of Huastepec from 1825 through the 1840s.[162] Petra Aja, the cacica of Tonalá, not only sold her lands to the cofradías of Tonalá but also donated her father's image of Jesus of Nazareth to the church and set up a small cofradía with ten pesos of capital.[163] At the same time, peasants complemented cacique funds with increasingly diverse portfolios. Although mayordomos continued to care for cattle, sheep, and goats, they also invested in wax, wheat, corn, beans, chile, anise, cumin, and, increasingly, commercial loans and magueys.[164] By 1846 the Cofradía of the Holy Cross in Ayú was lending around 450 pesos to twenty-five small merchants each year.[165] At the same time, mayordomos also turned to the secure returns ensured by maguey farming. Magueys thrived on the region's barren slopes, survived drought easily, were difficult to steal, and allowed processors to profit from the fairly regular market in pulque and mescal. Between 1826 and 1830 the cofradía of Our Crucified Lord of Tejupan sold its cattle and invested in the crop. By 1830 they had over 120 plants.[166] A decade later, some cofradías had converted almost all their money into magueyes. By 1846 the cofradía of Our Lady of the Rosary in Chinango possessed over fourteen hundred plants and was pulling in seventy pesos a year.[167] A year later Bautista Carriedo commented that people in Huajuapan were accustomed to "drink very fine mescal."[168]

Strategic elite neutrality, cacique support, and peasant diversification allowed cofradías to thrive (see appendix E). Unlike many other regions of Mexico where the secular appropriation of religious funds, administrative changes, economic depression, and incessant warfare took their toll, few villages turned to funding fiestas through individual mayordomos.[169] Of the eight cofradías for which sustained records remain, all were managed communally, and seven retained fairly constant profits. Some, like the cofradía of the Holy Cross in Ayú or the cofradía of Our Lord of Wounds in Miltepec, were large regional operations, bringing in huge annual incomes. Others were considerably smaller and probably shared communal devotion with multiple other cults. Only one of the cofradías actually lost a large proportion of its income during the period, and this loss was due to individual mismanagement rather than systemic problems.

Pulpit propaganda, institutional strength, education, and elite flexibility over customs and cofradías triggered a regional religious orthodoxy. This orthodoxy was expressed in mass devotion to certain key images such as Our Lord of Hearts of Huajuapan, the Holy Cross of Tonalá, and Our Lady of the Snows of Ixpantepec, which became emblematic of the region's shared religious culture and were used to rally Catholics during the liberal-conservative conflicts of the midcentury. But it was also expressed in the acceptance of more mundane clerical demands. During the period, Mixtec worshippers continued to pay tithes, funnel devotional cash toward church-building, and comply, at least outwardly, with a Christian moral code. As threats from neighboring radicals grew, these everyday practices became increasingly politicized, their encouragement and acceptance part of a self-conscious regional statement of clerical efficacy and lay obedience.

In 1833 Mexico's anticlerical congress forbade civil authorities from enforcing the payment of tithes. Although centralist regimes attempted to resurrect some degree of coercion, from the 1830s onward tithes declined dramatically.[170] By 1845 the archbishop of Mexico estimated that they accounted for one-seventh of pre-Independence funds.[171] Without legal support, ecclesiastical authorities were now forced to emphasize Christians' moral duty to pay 10 percent of their income to the church. Soon after the congress's decision, Bishop Vázquez resorted to his customary familial metaphor and argued that "as good Catholics and faithful children" parishioners should continue to pay; if they did not, "their souls were in grave danger." He then ordered local priests to encourage payment in the pulpit and the confessionary.[172] In many regions, such moral admonitions failed to work. In the villages around Tlapa, local priests complained that most villagers had refused to pay a "single real" to the church since the 1810 insurrection.[173] The anticlerical measures simply sanctioned their refusal. However, in clerical regions, like the Mixteca Baja, Catholics continued to pay the church tax throughout the period. Undoubtedly, the church's appointment of Manuel and Antonio de León as the region's chief tithe collectors helped the effort. León's first move after rising up in support of the proclerical Plan of Cuernavaca in 1834 was to remind citizens that nonpayment of tithes would be punished by excommunication.[174] Yet volition rather than force ensured mass payment. In 1830 Manuel de León deposited sixty-four hundred pesos with the tithe administrators in the Puebla cathedral. The amount dwarfed other contributions, which averaged around five hundred pesos. Only the richer barrios of Puebla, Orizaba, and Veracruz handed over more.[175] Furthermore, in the Mixteca Baja all sectors of society footed the expense. Tithe records for Huajuapan reveal that merchants and livestock owners, like Felipe de León, Juan Acevedo, and Manuel Alencaster, turned over hundreds of pesos per year to the diocese.[176] According to Reyes Aguilar, his grandfather regularly paid his 10 percent.[177] At the same time, tithe records for Chazumba demonstrate that in the region's smaller villages over 90 percent of the inhabitants paid at least two reals a year. Only single men and women were exempt, and over half the widows made some type of contribution.[178]

As clerical influence inspired tithe payment, it also pushed Mixtecs toward orthodox expressions of communal piety. Many villages took advantage of regular cofradía incomes and, in agreement with local elites, channeled profits toward the construction of churches. In 1834 the villagers of Miltepec asked permission from the local priest to invest earnings from the shrine of Our Lord of Wounds in the construction of a village church. A year later, the local priest laid the first stone. For the next twenty years, the priest and the local authorities organized labor drafts to transport rocks, sand, and water and build the edifice until its completion in the late 1850s.[179] Other priests were involved even more directly. In 1834 the priest of Tlacotepec collected donations from all over the Mixteca Baja to aid in the construction of a new parish church.[180] Like their colonial predecessors, nineteenth-century caciques helped out. Joaquín Bautista y Guzmán continued his grandfather's work on the Chazumba temple, adding a small baptismal font. Local noble Ramón Antonio Ximénez y Enriquez de Alvarado paid for a new vault in Tequixtepec's church.[181] Provincial conservative authorities also encouraged such conspicuous Christian industry. In 1845 the juez of Miltepec argued that a decade of righteous labor on the new church had already benefitted the village in ways that the conservative authorities could admire, reducing criminality and "concentrating the will of the diverse classes." The combination of Christian work, morality, and unity certainly impressed. He asked for and received a year off from the head tax.[182] Similarly, in 1851 the elders of Tezoatlán, who had fought against the United States under Antonio de León, in a perfect echo of conservative propaganda conflated their patriotic and Catholic duties and announced, "Those arms that were exercised in the defense of the patria are now disposed to work on the house of God." They also received a year off from the tax.[183]

Elite encouragement and popular enthusiasm precipitated an extraordinary eruption of church construction. Between 1821 and 1867 twenty-seven, or around a third, of Huajuapan's villages built churches. At the same time, they also built thirteen sturdy houses for priests. Together these new buildings cost villagers seventy-five thousand pesos. Some, like the temple of Yutandú or the church of Amatitlán, were expensive constructions worth between four thousand and six thousand pesos. Others, like the small chapel to Guadalupe established in Santa Catarina Estancia, were smaller edifices worth barely one hundred pesos.[184] In any given year, there was more church-building in the Mixteca Baja than in any other region in the state. In 1852, for example, fifty-five villages were involved in the repair, construction, or decoration of their church. In Huajuapan itself laymen and laywomen were contributing to the erection of a chapel for prisoners, the decoration of the interior of the church, the repair of two images, and the purchase of a new organ and another two images. Smaller villages like Simarrones were involved in painting the church and erecting the roof of the Calvary temple. In comparison, villagers in Ejutla, the next most industrious district, were only involved in forty-one building projects, most of which were prisons and municipal palaces.[185] Even today, beneath the pimped-out exuberance of remittance-funded churches, evidence of the early nineteenth-century program and its intertwining of elite status-seeking and popular labor remains. The names of long-forgotten patrons from rich mercantile families are etched on the sides of churches and on the ornate bells of the hilltop church at Ixpantepec. At the same time, Mixtec symbols dot the outsides of temple walls in Suchitepec, Huajolotitlán, and Miltepec, symbolizing, at least for the historian, the Catholic revival's long pre-Hispanic roots.

Finally, the region's clerical orthodoxy was also expressed in a dramatic shift in parishioners' attitudes to basic issues of Christian morality. As scholars of gender and family have increasingly argued, nineteenth-century political divisions were as much expressions of competing subjective moralities as differing ideologies.[186] The War of Reform was as much a culture war as a political struggle. This connection between political obedience and moral comportment came from the top. As Connaughton argues, the bishops of Puebla constructed a particularly persuasive argument for social stability, which linked public and private spheres.[187] Threatened by foreign invaders, anticlerical activists, or caste war, diocesan leaders constantly reverted to the naturalizing metaphor of Catholic Mexico as a great family. When the French briefly landed on Mexican soil in 1838, Bishop Francisco Pablo Vázquez reminded a divided country that they formed "one family." Only together, "the young man with his courage and strength, the priest with his prayers, the old man and woman with their directing of opinions, and all with their obedience to the recognized authorities," could they overcome the foreign threat. At the Independence Day celebrations in Puebla in 1841 a clerical orator declared that Mexicans should not engage in rampant individualism but rather accept that they formed "a pueblo of brothers or a numerous family."[188]

The metaphor worked not only as political discourse but also as social admonition, politicizing everyday comportment. Before Independence, attitudes toward baptism, marriage, and burial were mediated by individual circumstance. Although priests harped on about the importance of the sacraments, the poor, the peripatetic, and the prurient often neglected to get married before having children, failed to find the money to get their children baptized, or slumped into a rough tomb before accepting the last rites. Illegitimacy rates, especially in the colony's cities, were extremely high, reaching nearly 50 percent in San Luis Potosí, Guadalajara, and Mexico City.[189] Although they dropped considerably in the countryside, they still averaged around 10 percent.[190]

However, after Independence, as the threat of social dissolution increased, the church made morality a matter of national concern, arguing that individual comportment at the microlevel of the family and the village and mass behavior at the macrolevel of the political sphere were innately linked, that the good Catholic was a good citizen and, by extension, that many good Catholics made a good country. This national "metaphysics" of sin, purification, and redemption, similar to that described by Raymond Jonas for France at the same time, was endlessly repeated in ecclesiastical pastorals and letters.[191] For example, in 1833 Bishop Vázquez declared that the congress's impious decrees were the result of God's anger at Mexicans' "lewd public depravities," "their mocking of chastity and virginity," and their "public drunkenness."[192] In 1847 the bishop of Puebla suggested that Mexicans needed to undergo a "deep reform of customs" if they were to repel the U.S. invasion.[193] A year later, the same bishop accused the leaders of the nation's caste wars of not only political but also moral dissolution as the "destroyers of moral and Christian principles that serve to keep together society and form the most tender links of individual families." He advised priests to "take every means to re-establish morality in the pueblos."[194]

In many regions the church's moral crusade fell flat. However, as Donald Stevens argues, in regions of high clerical influence like Puebla, social pressure forced all sectors of society to embrace the church's vision for a new moral order.[195] Even outside hyperpious provincial capitals, ecclesiastical admonitions still brought results. Elites and peasants in the Mixteca Baja accepted and followed clerical demands; the personal became political. At the most prosaic level, the number of illegitimate children fell. Between 1800 and 1810 priests recorded around 10 to 15 percent of children as belonging to "unknown parents." However, between 1830 and 1840 they accounted for only 2 percent of registered children.[196] Furthermore, the records also suggest that godparentage gained a new political imperative. Godparents, with their responsibilities to teach Christian doctrine, were no longer simply generators of pious individuals; they were the creators of new citizens. Between 1800 and 1810 non-native residents were godparents to only around 10 percent of Huajuapan's poorer residents. But from the 1830s onward, regional elites rushed to replace indigenous caciques and peasants as the godparents of the poor. Between 1830 and 1850 the members of the merchant elite were godparents to around 40 percent of the children from Huajuapan's outlying ranches. In these cases female elites played a particularly important role, acting as solitary godparents in at least a quarter of the cases. In doing so they not only lent social and financial support to clerical expectations but also foreshadowed their roles as lay leaders and clerical enforcers later in the century.

External Threats and Regional Militarism

In the Mixteca Baja the re-Christianization undergirding provincial conservatism did not develop in isolation. Elite and diocesan demands for
social stability, political obedience, and moral conduct gained popular
support because of the region's close proximity to other regions of de-
Christianization and radical federalism. Timothy Tackett has argued that a
similar process of localized retrenchment took place in areas of France that
neighbored Protestant or anticlerical strongholds.[197] From the late 1820s
until the 1850s the Mixteca Baja was threatened by insurrections to the
south in the Triqui village of Copala and the sugar plantations of Putla
and to the west around Tlapa. At first only regional elites took fright. As
the next chapter demonstrates, Antonio de León lost any sympathy he may
have had for radical federalism and became increasingly concerned with
the maintenance of hierarchy and order. However, during the 1830s elite
cant gained popular support. First, radical federalist insurgents started
to terrorize Mixtec communities, stealing livestock, targeting small merchants, and invading communities. Second, regional elites started to draft
Mixtecs into the regional militia, offering protection and cementing paternal bonds. For the next twenty years, regional elites and peasants, united
by their desire for stability and an accepted religious orthodoxy, fought
increasingly bloody conflicts against their federalist neighbors.

Before looking at the effects of these uprisings in the Mixteca Baja, we
need to examine their causes. This interlude attempts to offer a brief counterpoint to the situation in the Mixteca Baja, reinforces my assertion that
certain mercantile centers in Oaxaca were aggressively centralist, and ex-
pands on the idea of de-Christianization. Although the villagers of both
Copala and Putla experienced post-Independence policies in distinct ways,
they were linked by a firm rejection of centralism, agrarian encroachment,
and clerical Catholicism. The Triquis were a small indigenous group spread
over the highland villages of Itunyoso, Xochitlán, Chicahuaxtla, and Santo
Domingo del Estado and the lowland villages of San Miguel Copala and
San Juan Copala. The highland towns, with their thin soils and rocky hillsides, escaped non-native interference. But the fertile lowland areas around
San Miguel and San Juan Copala, which were suitable for fruit and cereal
crops and year-round pasture, had been coveted by predatory speculators
since the late eighteenth century. From the 1770s onward white and mestizo
merchants from the towns of Juxtlahuaca to the north and Putla to the

south sought to assert political dominance and usurp these lowland areas.[198] In response, Triquis took to the hills, organized themselves into clan-based barrios, and shunned settlement in the village's central plaza. These indigenous living arrangements reinforced racist regional stereotypes.[199] Like the Apaches of the north, the Triquis became the Mixteca's archetype of the untamed Indian and were described as "hill-dwelling barbarians," "tigers anxious to kill," "inhuman monsters," "criminals," and "bandits."[200] According to nineteenth-century historian José Antonio Gay, even the term *Triqui* was a racist epithet, a Mixtec term that mocked the Triqui language's allegedly incomprehensible repetition of consonants.[201] Although the peasants of Putla were predominantly Mixtec and not similarly despised, they shared with the Triquis the same disadvantageous geographical position. Flanked by the peaks of the Guerrero montaña to the west and the mountains of the Mixteca Alta to the east, the Putla valley with its confluence of four rivers was one of the region's rare fertile troughs. By the late colonial period whites and mestizos had flocked to the region in hopes of establishing wheat ranches and sugar haciendas.

Throughout the early nineteenth century, both regions' material attractions combined with the political opportunities offered by centralism to cause considerable tension between elite interlopers and indigenous groups. In the barren lands of the Mixteca Baja, centralist politics caused limited disquiet because non-natives had no interest in using the reforms to usurp village lands. They were content to leave the appointment of jueces to the communities' elders. However, Putla and Copala's fertile valleys precipitated an alternative response. Here, regional elites viewed political centralization as a means to dominate village government, undermine communal land use, and construct commercial haciendas. Antonio de León, defender of pueblo autonomy in his own patria chica, was quite happy to ride roughshod over such concerns in more profitable areas. From 1832 onward León shifted the dry-season base of his hacienda volante from the Costa Chica to the green valleys of Putla and Copala. In Putla he monopolized the rental of the local cacique's lands and ejected the former tenants. In Copala he did the same, pasturing his livestock where Triquis had grown corn and beans.[202] As a result, when Putla and Copala peasants rebelled in 1838 one of their first acts was to murder León's hacienda administrator with machetes.[203] Other regional elites employed tactics like León's to extend sugar cultivation. South of Putla, the huge sugar hacienda La Concepción, established by Spaniard Gabriel Esperón in the early nineteenth century, continued to expand.

By 1858 it produced around one hundred bushels of sugar and possessed over five hundred mules for transporting the product to the surrounding market towns.[204] Around Putla, local elites set up smaller but no less damaging enterprises like the sugar mills of San Vicente, Las Madres, and San Miguel. These became centers of insurrectionary activity. In 1831 the Putla rebel Manuel Medina established his base in the Hacienda La Concepción. After government forces attacked, he moved to neighboring San Miguel.[205]

If the Copala and Putla revolts were rooted in agrarian disputes, they were sparked, shaped, and sustained by radical federalism with its liberating ethos of popular suffrage, village rule, and political autonomy. In many ways, the rebels resembled those radical federalists described by Guardino in the neighboring state of Guerrero. First, many had fought in the wars of Independence. Hilario "Hilarion" Alonso, the leader of the Copala revolt from 1829 to 1834 and again from 1838 to his eventual public execution in 1841, was a former follower of Morelos and Guerrero. He led a small insurgent band in the region from 1812 onward and reached the rank of captain.[206] In his final, touching letter pleading for his life, he argued that he was a "liberator of [his] patria," that "inside [his] heart [he] was a good Mexican," and that his struggle had only been one of "independence from the Spanish yoke."[207] Like so many other former Independence fighters, he was animated by a deep hatred of the gachupín and suspicion of the merest hint of a Spanish reconquest. His first act of rebellion in 1829 was to decapitate Spanish landowner Tomás Esperón.[208] He later claimed he had verifiable intelligence that Esperón was going to lead a pro-Spanish rebellion in the Mixteca.[209] When Putla peasant Manuel Medina rebelled in 1830, one of his first acts was to execute the "gachupín" military commander José P. Quintana, "leaving his head attached only by the tendon."[210] Old rancor died hard, and as late as 1845 one of Hilario Alonso's successors, Feliciano Martín, signed his political plan with "Death to Ferdinand VII."[211] Second, like Guardino's radical federalists, the Copala and Putla rebels were often provoked to rebel by centralist assumption of village control. The Putla rebellion of 1844 was prompted by Antonio de León's decree extending Putla's municipal rule into neighboring, autonomous indigenous barrios.[212] The Copala uprising of the following year was instigated by the imposition of a non-Triqui juez in Copala.[213]

Third and as a result, Copala and Putla rebels consistently sought common cause with neighboring federalists. The Putla uprising of 1830 to 1831 was part of the War of the South and in direct support of Guerrero's presidential candidacy. When one of its leaders was defeated just outside

Huajuapan, government forces found a lance inscribed with the motto "Viva Guerrero 2nd President."[214] A decade later Putla and Copala rebels turned to Guerrero's successor, Juan Alvarez, for support, demanding his intervention in issues of state governance and ending their declarations with *vivas* to the federalist caudillo.[215] In 1845 and 1847 the prefect of Huajuapan speculated that Alvarez was encouraging the rebels, persuading them that payment of the *capitación*, or head tax, was optional and insurrection acceptable.[216] Fourth, as the last example suggests, the Putla and Copala rebels were linked by a militant refusal to pay the capitación—the monthly one real charge on indigenous heads of family, which Santa Anna introduced in 1842. For Guardino, this fiscal exaction was the fundamental cause of Guerrero's caste war, which ran from 1843 through 1848.[217] Furthermore, rejection of the tax provided a common cause that bound together disparate villages from Chilapa in the west to Tlapa in the east to Acapulco in the south. Putla and Copala were no different. In April 1843 the first act of the newly appointed non-native juez of Copala was to demand payment of the tax. When the villagers declined, he complained to the regional authorities and arrested a handful of refuseniks. The governor, Antonio de León, immediately sent one hundred troops to the village to shake down the inhabitants. At that point the Triquis rebelled.[218] In their 1845 plan, they denounced the "personal contribution exacted from the poor."[219] When Alvarez toured the region as part of his attempt to negotiate with the caste war leaders in 1845, he similarly claimed that one of the villagers' principal complaints was the charging of capitación "often in a cruel manner."[220]

If material conditions precipitated political sympathy, religious heterodoxy provided both additional motivation and a common discursive defense. During the early nineteenth century, Putla, Copala, and other neighboring areas of popular rebellion, as regions of de-Christianization, experienced a complete breakdown in lay-clerical relations as the polarizing effects of land loss and political imposition bled into the religious sphere. Catholic schools were scarce, church-building rare, and payment of tithes almost nonexistent.[221] The few priests in the area kept to the commercial centers, rarely visited their indigenous charges, and when they did often provoked confrontation. When Medina rose up in support of Guerrero in 1830, he chased the local priest out of Putla, who fled in fright to the safety of Huajuapan.[222] Martín's 1845 plan railed against the obligation to pay priests for baptisms, tithes, and local schools.[223] The deliberate targeting of priests accompanied their refusal to pay. When rebels attacked the parish seat of Juxtlahuaca, they invaded the temple and looked for the offending cleric, who only managed to escape by hiding behind a statue of Our Lady of Solitude.[224] In 1842 they shook down the priest of Coicoyán for one hundred pesos.[225] In 1844 they beat the priest of Tianguistengo over the head with a pistol butt.[226] Although the insurrections were infused with a popular anticlericalism, they were not inherently antireligious. Rather, rebels adopted a defiant religious heterodoxy, celebrating unauthorized devotions and defending their actions in terms of their reading of Catholic doctrine. According to the local military commander José de Jesús Maldonaldo, the Copala rebels believed that their "uprising and crimes" were just "as they were prescribed by the divine image" of Christ they kept in their temple. Revealing the self-conscious orthodoxy of a provincial conservative, the Huajuapan commander suggested that they remove the image of Jesus of Nazareth to a more pious community.[227] Although Maldonaldo's accusation revealed his own bias, it was probably correct. Over the next century Copala peasants jealously guarded what they called "Tata Chu" or "Uncle Saint," their image of Christ dressed in traditional Triqui garb.[228] The neighboring rebels in Tlapa, who periodically linked up with the Copala peasants, also rationalized their insurrection in religious terms. In their 1843 plan, they claimed that by rebelling they were only "serving Our God Lord Jesus Christ," who had blessed them with life and health but not the livestock ranches of the rich. Pulling apart the contradictions between republican rhetoric and everyday political practice, they asked why, if the Lord had given them freedom, they had to obey corrupt authorities. To encapsulate their rejection of the conservative appropriation of religious discourse, they ended their pronouncement, "Long live the freedom of the Indian, long live America, long live the Christian religion, we renounce obedience and what you want, long live God and the sacred mother Guadalupe."[229]

The interplay of agrarian discontent, political ideology, and radical religious language that characterized the Copala and Putla revolts deserves its own monograph. However, the long-running insurrection was important to the Mixteca Baja because it promoted the elite emphasis on order and stability and deepened the popular embrace of orthodox religiosity. As Michael Costeloe has argued, centralism arose from a fear of what contemporaries called "social dissolution." After the violence of the 1828 Parián riot, many members of the urban elite backed down from their initial support for the reforms of the 1824 federal Constitution.[230] Over the next two decades, the perceived prevalence of caste war, rural insurrection, and banditry reinforced elite anxieties. In Mexico City especially "reconciliation, continuity, and order" became the "leitmotivs of public discourse" and the rationale behind centralist government.[231] By the 1840s, centralists used the clamor for stability to crush federalist rebellions, limit suffrage, and decrease regional autonomy. By the 1850s issues of political practice as much as political ideology divided the two camps. Whereas liberals were prepared to harness popular revolt, conservatives argued that "destructive natural phenomena like earthquakes and volcanic eruptions" were not "models for human progress." As a result, they rejected "all forms of progress" that embraced "violent and revolutionary means."[232] Although the fear of "social dissolution" and the corresponding desire for stability were most clearly expressed in the alarmist editorials of the Mexico City press, provincial merchants and peasants were the ones who experienced the effects of endemic revolt up close. In the Mixteca Baja, rebels from Copala and Putla murdered political officials and small merchants, invaded mestizo towns and indigenous villages, and stole government funds and peasant supplies. As a result, both elites and non-elites embraced the conservative ideology of stability over reform, joined the military auxiliaries to combat their radical neighbors, and in doing so firmed up cross-class connections.

In the initial stages of each wave of indigenous revolt, Copala and Putla rebels acted like Eric Hobsbawm's social bandits and deliberately targeted non-native authorities, decapitating Spanish *hacendados*, chasing creole priests, and executing mestizo jueces.[233] These were terrifying acts of violence designed as part revenge, part performance. On September 25, 1843, Triqui forces executed the Juxtlahuaca juez and his scribe at the top of a hill overlooking the town. Together the officials suffered over thirty machete blows.[234] Yet as the revolts escalated from small-scale uprisings, redolent of colonial-era village riots, into full-scale guerrilla wars, things changed. Government troops fortified commercial centers, drove peasants from their villages, forced them into the mountains, and enforced their own terrifying pacification techniques. In response, the rebels started to resemble Anton Blok's robber thugs.[235] From 1830 onward government reports repeatedly stressed that neighboring rebels were attacking "cooperative Indians" and "peaceful pueblos."[236] By the mid-1840s, government reports reached an alarmist crescendo, decrying the rebels' "most atrocious disgraces" and claiming that "their robberies, assassinations and depredations [were] too scandalous" to enumerate.[237]

Although elites tended to exaggerate, examples of the rebels attacking indigenous communities are too numerous to dismiss. In late 1830 the Putla rebels under Medina had entered the town of Juxtlahuaca and shaken down a handful of rich merchants.[238] But within months they became desperate. In February 1831 the prefect of Huajuapan claimed that the Putla rebels had invaded the Mixtec villages of Tequixtepec, Amatitlán, and Chazumba and stolen corn and tax revenue.[239] By March they had fallen on Ayuquililla, Santiago del Río, Yutatio, and Nuchita.[240] And in April they entered Zacatepec, robbed the villagers, broke open the communal cash box, and lifted forty-seven pesos.[241] Hilario Alonso's uprising in 1837 was no different. After murdering León's hacienda administrator, the rebels increasingly preyed on defenseless villagers. In March 1840 they attacked Zapotitlán Lagunas and stole food, livestock, and cash.[242] In Hilario Alonso's final letter he confessed to "multitudes of murders committed in cold blood . . . as well as the assaults and robberies executed in the populations."[243] The 1843 uprising also terrorized the Mixteca Baja's indigenous villagers. After the very public murder of the Juxtlahuaca juez, rebels turned to softer targets. Later that year they robbed a small merchant from Zapotitlán Lagunas and sliced the council officer of the small Mixtec village of Santiago Naranja in the hand and chest.[244] In 1844 they attacked the cacique of Tianguistengo and stole over twenty pesos' worth of cloth.[245] In 1845 they killed Copala's imposed juez though he was no longer a mestizo interloper but rather a "faithful [Mixtec] Indian." At the same time, they also did away with five of his indigenous companions "in atrocious ways . . . so that they were unrecognizable."[246] A year later, the chief of police of Juxtlahuaca found the bloodstained bodies of two indigenous merchants on the road that led from the coast up to their village of Tecomaxtlahuaca. After a day of recuperation, one came around and explained that Copala rebels had attacked them with machetes in their sleep and stolen the money they had made selling livestock on the coast.[247]

In the Mixteca Baja the threat of a contiguous "caste war" "shifted ideas of solidarity" and reinforced bonds between the region's merchants and peasants in a kind of escalating dialectic.[248] Fearful Huajuapan elites compromised on political autonomy, land tenure, and religious practice. Equally fearful peasants gratefully accepted elite concessions; fulfilled elite expectations of obedience, piety, and moral comportment; and resisted violent confrontation. Mixtec indigenous groups increasingly described themselves as "loyal," "obedient," "faithful," and "pacific" in comparison with the "barbarians" of Copala and Putla.[249] In fact, the perceived division is still depicted in the village of Tecomaxtlahuaca's dance of the Mojigangas, which is performed every year at carnival. During the performance, some villagers dress up in elegant gear as gente de razón, and others dress in the traditional outfits of the Copala Triquis. The Triquis speak a mockingly garbled version of Spanish, gloat over their agricultural wealth, and (in an echo of the self-conscious moralism of the nineteenth century) boast about their numerous wives.

At the same time, the necessities of regional self-defense generated another connection between the region's ethnic groups—the army. From the 1830s onward many indigenous peasants from the Mixteca Baja voluntarily joined up as auxiliaries of the region's armed forces. As numerous historians have pointed out, military service was one of the most hated aspects of the Mexican citizen's new duties. Sent away from their homes, beaten by autocratic officers, employed as "beasts of burden," and used as cannon fodder, most peasants fled at the very mention of the *leva*.[250] In 1829 the governor of Oaxaca admitted that "to be a soldier in the concept of our Indians, is the worst ill that can threaten them." Twenty years later Governor Benito Juárez agreed—"Aversion to military service in the permanent army is almost general among the inhabitants of Oaxaca."[251] Yet in the Mixteca Baja, the very real threat of violence at the hands of neighboring radical federalists shored up elite demands. From 1831 onward, Antonio de León, as leader of the armed forces in the area, started to recruit permanent bodies of military auxiliaries to be called on in times of need. By 1833 he had gathered together at least two hundred men.[252] A year later there were auxiliary companies in Huajuapan and the smaller indigenous villages of Ihualtepec, Tezoatlán, Zacatepec, and Ayuquila.[253] Succeeding rebellions provoked similar responses. In 1838 León ordered auxiliary units established in Juxtlahuaca and Silacayoapan.[254] In 1843 the local prefect established more units in Juxtlahuaca, Tonalá, Tezoatlán, Tlachichilco, and Tamazola and called on local village leaders to send willing males to strengthen forces in Huajuapan.[255] When León called on these units to fight against the United States in 1847, they expanded their numbers even further. Tonalá's small unit of thirty men grew to nearly seventy members.[256] By 1849 the district possessed seven companies or over four hundred soldiers—nearly 20 percent of Oaxaca's total forces and more than any other rural district could muster.[257]

Undoubtedly, many Mixtecs were reluctant participants in this process of militarization, but their involvement in the regional auxiliaries of the early nineteenth century, like their involvement in the civic militia of the succeeding decades, failed to open up substantial divisions between elites and non-elites.[258] In general, military service cemented interethnic alliances. First, auxiliaries' principal tasks were to garrison their communities and to pursue local rebels. These duties not only kept Mixtec soldiers close to home but also dovetailed with their own aims to maintain village security. Second, the region's peculiarly localized military organization mitigated conflicts between officers and soldiers. Most high-ranking officers, in charge of the regular company of Huajuapan, were local livestock owners and merchants, like Antonio de León, Juan Acevedo, and Miguel Carrión.[259] Outside the regular forces, auxiliary companies were led by village leaders. Some, like Mariano Villagómez and José de Jesús Maldonado, were caciques or related to cacique families.[260] Other commanders, like Dionisio Rojas and Juan José Solano, who led the Tonalá force at the battle of Molino del Rey, or Pablo Martín, head of the auxiliaries in Tamazola, were village elders.[261] Third, self-preservation and paternalism motivated the regional elite to treat these local auxiliaries relatively well. In law cases, decrees, and personal letters, León and his brother, Manuel, show special care toward their indigenous companions in arms and often addressed them as "faithful friends" and even "compadres."[262] When León sent hundreds of Huajuapan auxiliaries to track down rebels in Tlapa, he reminded their new commanders that although they "lent their services with enthusiasm and loyalty," they were "simple peasants." Consequently, they should be paid on time and when possible "not be distracted from the work they do for their subsistence" because this would just make "more miserable the life of their families."[263]

Conclusion

For over thirty years cross-class factions in the Mixteca Baja backed centralist and conservative governments. Until now, explanations for such mass conservatism have been limited. As Hamnett argues, "So far, the historical literature has not been able to establish with regard to Conservatism similar linkages between national, provincial, and local levels to those which have emerged in the investigation of Liberalism."[264] Revisionists held that such support was the product of opportune and temporary pacts between peasants and elites, born of a shared but divergent distrust of liberalism. Whereas peasants recoiled from the gradual privatization of communal lands, elites balked at the introduction of free trade, the rise of a provincial political class, and the periodic attacks on their allies in the military and the clergy. Consequently, from the 1850s onward these two groups formed an awkward alliance against successive liberal administrations, following the rather precarious logic of "my enemy's enemy is my friend." During the 1860s politicians in Maximilian's government undergirded this arrangement with a series of concessions over peasant land tenure.[265] Although recent historians have moved on from such an economic reading of political allegiance, they have offered little in its place, reiterating that conservative support was sparse and fleeting but emphasizing that it was the result of the forced mobilization of peons and peasant clients by desperate elites.

In fact, as this chapter demonstrates, the cross-class alliances that promoted provincial conservatism emerged in the forty years leading up to the civil wars of the midcentury. Furthermore, they relied on four interconnecting factors—political decentralization, economic symbiosis, religious revival, and the immediate threat of radical federalist revolt. On the one hand, the continuation of community self-rule and an economic agreement that prioritized cooperation over conflict quelled any possible support for radical federalism. On the other hand, the escalating interplay of well-maintained church influence and nearby, often anticlerical, revolts drove elites and non-elites toward support for the conservative policies of order, stability, and Catholic orthodoxy. These close bonds were reinforced through the voluntary mass mobilization of regional militias. Together these changes reoriented but did not destroy the region's moral economy, that dense network of reciprocal agreements between elite and non-elite groups. Village politics stayed autonomous, and the economic system remained balanced between mercantile claims, noble needs, and indigenous necessities. Although local non-natives started to play an increasingly important political role—usurping town governments, extracting taxes, and demanding school attendance, clerical obedience, and military mobilization—in return they offered land redistribution, support for indigenous religious practice, and protection. In many ways, they gradually appropriated the caciques' political power and their communal roles as religious benefactors and economic and political arbiters, harnessing the colonial pact to new political necessities.

Although provincial conservatives shared the aims of many conservatives from the upper echelons of Mexico City, the two sets of beliefs were also qualitatively distinct.[266] Provincial conservatism, like popular liberalism,

was a menu à la carte.[267] Unlike their rather obdurate metropolitan counterparts, provincial conservatives were supremely politically pragmatic,
unwilling to risk regional disorder by imposing some of their leaders' more
extreme policies. Instead, they assured loyalty by deferring to late colonial
models of community rule and cofradía governance and took advantage
of cacique bankruptcies to offer peasants lands. Open-ended and reactive
provincial conservatism was, by its very nature, resistant to ideological
expression. Furthermore, conservative intellectuals were extremely keen to
downplay or ignore popular support. Yet traces of this ideology can be
observed in the positions of men like Carlos María de Bustamante, Faustino
Galicia Chimalpopoca, or Francisco de Paula Arrangoiz, who shared conservatism's support for Catholic mores, pragmatic republicanism, and social
stability, but resisted Lucas Alamán's dogmatic antidemocratic and pro-
Hispanic beliefs.[268] Instead, they saw Mexico's future in paternalist interethnic relations, church education, and the Catholic enthusiasm of the
indigenous classes. It seems no coincidence that Bustamante devoted his last
book, *El nuevo Bernal Díaz*, to the leader of the Mixteca Baja's provincial
conservatism, Antonio de León, whose name, he claimed, "was the correla-
tive of the peace and security of the pueblo."[269]

Beyond these public intellectuals, perhaps the best statement of this
brand of conservatism, with its blend of Catholicism, modified federalism,
and aversion to radical upheaval, comes from a small, anonymous 1863
pamphlet. The work, which claims to speak for "the conservatives of the
provinces" and is directed at the conservative politician and alleged son of
José María Morelos, Juan Nepomuceno Almonte, is no reactionary tract.
The author celebrates Mexican Independence, condemns liberals and conservatives as "small men protected by bastard interests," and views their
attempts at constitutional reform as both deliberately provocative and inca-
pable of striking the correct balance between central control and local independence. Echoing the work of Edmund Burke, he argues that the pueblos
are not "masses of wax" to be molded according to the desires of petty
politicians and utopian philosophers. Instead, constitutions should "be
accommodated to the nature of the country" and "should be an expression
of its social interests." According to the author, such an organic approach
demands that the constitution reflect the country's religious heritage and
its local power structures. Thus, he suggests that policy-makers "examine
the religious beliefs of the Mexican people," maintain Catholicism as the
nation's sole religion, and support the church's financial and educational

infrastructure. More provocatively, he also argues that conservative governments should eschew political elitism and dictatorship and embrace a modified federalist system wherein state governments are free to administer the "interests of their localities." At one level, the pamphlet reveals the growing disenchantment between metropolitan and provincial conservatives, the seeds, perhaps, of the movement's imminent demise. Yet at the same time, it also exposes provincial conservatives' continued efforts to balance their Catholic colonial past with their republican, and at least partially democratic, present.[270]

For a "government of Mexico, which protects our religion, our persons, and our families"

The Counternarrative of Provincial Conservatism, 1821–1867

ON AUGUST 20, 1859, THE VILLAGERS OF TEQUIXTEPEC MET IN THE community's municipal palace. Here they read out the liberal government's recent prohibition of cofradía properties. In response, the councilors condemned the decrees, claiming that they sought to "destroy cofradías . . . and brotherhoods and appropriate their capital." They argued that the policy was "a sacrilege against the Mexican church, an attack on the Catholic cult, and an atrocious blow to Mexican society." As a result they "denounce[d] the law and its authors and adhere[d] to the [conservative] government of Mexico, which protects our religion, our persons and our families." Ending on nationalist note, they claimed that the liberal statesmen were "traitors to our Independence," whereas the conservative leaders were "defenders of the interests of our beloved Patria." They concluded by pledging their allegiance to the conservative general José María Cobos.[1] Throughout the postcolonial period, in response to perceived or real anticlerical attacks, communities throughout the Mixteca Baja defended the status of the church, writing petitions, signing *pronunciamientos*, or plans, and mobilizing armed forces. As U.S. armies threatened and the liberals took power, defending what villagers termed "religion" or "cult" shifted from a regional to a national affair, pulling local parishioners into broad alliances with conservative leaders. The story of the emergence of this broad national coalition forms the basis of this chapter.

Between 1830 and 1867 provincial conservatives throughout Mexico's regions politicked, fought, and spilled blood for centralist and conservative causes. When radical federalists rose up to secure community autonomy, local land tenure, and low taxation in the Huasteca, Sierra Gorda, and Guerrero, provincial conservatives formed local military units, linked up with the regular army, and defended their towns and villages against incursion. When federalist governments attempted to pass anticlerical legislation in 1834 and 1847, provincial conservatives rushed to support diocesan demands, launched critical pronunciamientos, and took up arms. As the rhythm of caste war and foreign intervention quickened, they gradually moved along the political spectrum, shifting from selective support for centralism toward a more out-and-out backing for conservatism, which sacrificed political freedoms in the hope of securing stability, order, and a revival of Catholic morality. By the 1850s many were even prepared to support Santa Anna's last disastrous dictatorship and its fruitless promise of political permanence. Even when radical federalists forged a cross-party alliance under the Plan of Ayutla to unseat the faltering caudillo, many provincial conservatives held firm and refused to embrace the plan's liberating assurances. Finally, when radical liberals passed a raft of measures designed to curtail church power, alienate church property, and introduce religious tolerance three years later, provincial conservatives rebelled. Over the next decade, merchants, artisans, peasants, and peons from throughout Mexico formed regional battalions, volunteered for the conservative army, and fought a series of increasingly brutal battles against liberal forces. Even when metropolitan conservatives and a handful of moderate liberals allied with Napoleon III and his faintly ludicrous puppet emperor, Maximilian, provincial conservatives continued to seek to impose a stable, Catholic political system on Mexico.

Discerning and describing a conservative political narrative beneath the teleological pull of liberalism's eventual triumph is extremely hard. Political conservatism in a former colony smacks of treason, whereas the "liberal synthesis and its attendant heroes and holidays form the core of the Religion of the patria."[2] Until recently the telling of this story was left almost entirely to conservative apologists, whose hagiographies of individual leaders tended to dismiss liberal motives and play down the taint of mass support.[3] In Oaxaca, the *cuna del liberalismo,* the task is doubly difficult. The national predominance of men like Benito Juárez, Porfirio Díaz, Matías Romero, and Ignacio Mejía obscures regional variation and pockets of provincial conservative support. Instead, the allure of these liberal luminaries has driven generations of historians to scour Oaxaca's early nineteenth century in a search for the deep regional roots of liberalism in the classrooms of the state capital's secular university, in the haciendas and merchant houses of the region's aspirant bourgeoisie, and in streets, markets, and village squares frequented by the state's popular classes.[4] Although liberalism in Oaxaca did have a protracted heritage—reaching back to Independence, shaping the open-ended federalist Constitution of 1825, tempering centralist reforms, and culminating in both elite and non-elite support for the liberal insurgencies of 1857–1861 and 1862–1867—this pervasive narrative fails to explain political actions in the Mixteca Baja. Here, a strong counternarrative emerges. Here, liberalism assured the continuation of community autonomy but little else. Instead, the conjunction of gradual land reform and clerical Catholicism, compressed and shaped by the imminent threat of caste war, pushed elites and non-elites to favor, if not embrace, every aspect of centralist and then conservative rule. Although the example of the Mixteca Baja may represent an outlier for Oaxaca, the regional interplay of relative independence, gradual socioeconomic liberation, clerical religiosity, and political threat was common in Mexico as a whole. As a result, many cross-class groups sided with centralists and conservatives despite the well-publicized attractions of popular liberalism.

As the above outline suggests, political expressions of conservatism changed over time. In the early years of the post-Independence era, ideologies of provincial and elite conservatism never overlapped completely. At least initially, provincial conservatism was a shifting, pragmatic raft of beliefs, founded upon both the demand for internal stability and the perceived need to quash external dissent. Regional politics never synchronized entirely with national proscriptions. And, as a result, the local adoption of centralism was decidedly selective. In the Mixteca Baja, elites and non-elites never accepted national centralist attempts to curtail local autonomy. But they did embrace ecclesiastical edicts over church schooling, Catholic morality, and church-building. Furthermore, outside the Mixteca Baja, the Huajuapan cacique Antonio de León and his peasant followers harnessed new restrictive rules to regiment and dominate the neighboring regions of Copala and Putla. Even when Santa Anna appointed León as state governor during the 1840s, this process of "selective centralism" continued.[5] However, with the U.S. invasion and the rise of a more organized, aggressive liberal party, things changed. The cultural and political synchronization of provincial and elite conservatism gradually increased. The Mexican-American war, which pitted Protestant invaders against Catholic Mexicans, persuaded many Mixtec villagers to view their regional struggle for stability and "orthodox" Catholicism as part of a broader national struggle against both external and internal foes. For many, the fates of the "spiritual economy" of the Mixteca Baja and the nation aligned. As liberal attacks on the Catholic Church grew, local parishioners shifted from a selective centralism, which had accepted but not celebrated the last dictatorship of Santa Anna, toward out-and-out support for the conservatives of Mexico City. Under the elite conservative general José María Cobos, Mixtec merchants and peasants worked together to defeat liberal armies. After their defeat, the tensions between provincial and metropolitan conservatism arose once again. During Maximilian's empire, some locals remained conservative, fighting alongside French and Austrian campaigners. But many accepted modified liberal rule and channeled their incipient Catholic nationalism to defeat the foreign invaders.

This narrative of the links between provincial conservatism and broader national politics in the Mixteca Baja is divided into four sections. The first section examines the early 1820s. Independence and federalism were not intrinsically unpopular among the region's pueblos. The Constitution in particular confirmed the highly decentralized political arrangement introduced during the late colonial period and would remain key to Oaxaca's relative political stability in later years. Yet in the Mixteca Baja, both Independence and the federal Constitution were primarily the work of elites, imposed from the top down. The primary instigators were not the ragged remnants of the pro-Independence guerilla bands but rather former royalist soldiers. As a result, both movements failed to engender mass support or any greater degree of political freedom. If allegiances shifted, the shift was not to an imagined ideal of republican liberty, but rather to a regional caudillo, Antonio de León. The second section of the chapter looks at politics in the region from the late 1820s to the late 1840s. Although there was a federalist rebellion in Huajuapan in 1836, it comprised out-of-town military personnel, neglected to engage with regional interests, and failed to gather substantial elite or non-elite support. In fact, León and his regional supporters stepped back from their support for radical federalism during this period. At first they sought compromise, but when neighboring radical federalists took up arms, they turned to repression. Moreover, local centralists adopted a defensive clericalism extremely supportive of clerical status and as a result were often hypersensitive to any national anticlerical policies. The third section turns to the period of confrontation between conservatives and liberals from the late 1840s to the defeat of Maximilian in 1867. Here I argue that in the Mixteca Baja most elites and non-elites favored conservative rule, offering only lukewarm backing for the Plan of Ayutla and taking up arms against liberal reforms in 1856–1861 and 1862–1867. Only by embracing the initially conservative policy of gradual land reform were liberals able to secure regional support. Finally, the last sections looks at the Mixteca Baja in comparative perspective. Here I attempt to map out the local conditions, which pushed regions toward supporting provincial conservatism over Mexico as a whole.

Antonio de León, Independence, and Federalism, 1821–1826

The announcement of Independence and the introduction of a federalist Constitution in Oaxaca have elicited a broad range of historical opinions. For revisionists, the federalist Constitution, by eradicating legal distinctions between indigenous and nonindigenous groups, represented the "organization of creole power" and the "violent plundering of political prerogatives." The creation of municipalities, in particular, destroyed indigenous political autonomy.[6] For recent scholars, federalism embodied a delicate equilibrium between creole economic demands and the indigenous desire for political independence.[7] At the center of the debate stands the figure of the Huajuapan caudillo Antonio de León, who dominated state politics until his death fighting U.S. troops at the Battle of Molino del Rey in 1847. For revisionists, he was the monstrous, slippery creole face of the new republic, a political chameleon, ruthless oppressor of indigenous revolts, and "Santa Anna's proconsul in Oaxaca."[8] For recent historians, he was "a young mestizo cattleman," a mason, a gachupín killer, and Benito Juárez's patron, a shrewd yet principled negotiator who never gave up his adherence to radical federalism.[9] By examining León's role in bringing Independence and federalism to his patria chica of the Mixteca Baja, we can see that both arguments have some validity. Here, former royalist soldiers imposed Independence and federalism from the top down in order to assure regional elite rule. As a result, they engendered limited popular support. Yet neither Independence nor federalism was an inherently destructive force. The federalist Constitution was welcomed by communities throughout the region, not as a liberating agenda, but as the confirmation of the decentralized late colonial system. Moreover, León, like his Janus-faced cacique successors, embraced this ambiguity, playing the

Figure 4: A nineteenth-century portrait of Antonio de León, hero of the Mixteca Baja. Museo Regional de Huajuapan.

part of the ruthless radical to his federalist supporters in Oaxaca City and the domineering royalist caudillo to his power base in the Mixteca Baja.[10]

Antonio de León and his brother, Manuel de León, were the prime movers of both Independence and federalism in the Mixteca Baja. According to his most reliable biographer, Antonio de León was of creole stock. His family arrived from Spain in 1766, settled as landowners in Tepeaca, Puebla, and then moved to Huajuapan in the late 1780s. Here Manuel Mariano de León established a large hacienda volante and married a local creole woman, María de la Luz Loyola. In 1794 she bore a son, Antonio, who was baptized in the small church of Huajolotitlán, where her brother was the local priest.[11] Although León's political allegiances shifted depending on regional and

national circumstances, four links remained constant. First, although he routinely dabbled in state politics, his primary loyalty was to the elite of the Mixteca Baja. His first marriage to María Ignacia Niño de Rivera connected him to the powerful Niño de Rivera family of Huajuapan. His second marriage to Manuela Trinidad Orosia Torres, daughter of a Spanish family from Juxtlahuaca, broadened his ties to the Mixteca.[12] Family alliances were strengthened by compadrazgo. One compadre, Juan Acevedo, effectively ruled the Mixteca in periods of Antonio de León's absence. Another compadre, Manuel Alencaster, led the artillery regiment of Huajuapan and served as municipal president.[13] León and his family never aspired to the luxuries of Mexico City or the state capital but continued to live in Huajuapan throughout their lives. Their responses to national political agendas depended primarily on the situation in their patria chica. Second, León always maintained an attachment to the Mexican military. As a royalist soldier and then as a general of the new republic, he was a soldier first and a politician second. Like Santa Anna, "he felt a special affinity toward the army and his fellow soldiers," which would mark his career.[14] Third, León was part of a powerful economic elite. When his father died in 1819 he inherited the huge hacienda volante worth 72,731 pesos. When he died, the business comprised over fifty thousand head of livestock, four ranches, property in Putla and Oaxaca City, and hundreds of outstanding loans. His wealth totaled 110,794 pesos.[15] While the mechanics of running a successful hacienda volante brought León into a symbiotic relationship with indigenous villages, his appropriation of certain lands around Putla and Copala also precipitated indigenous revolt. Fourth, although on a personal level the caudillo may have quietly sympathized with the reformist urges of his more liberal counterparts, León never underestimated the political importance of the Catholic Church. At least two of his relations were priests, he and his brother were tithe collectors for the diocese, and he remained an important patron of local devotions until his death.[16]

At least two of these allegiances—to the local commercial class and to the church—kick-started his political career. Although some historians have interpreted León's switching sides as a kind of Pauline nationalist conversion, his motives were much more direct.[17] In 1820 the new liberal authorities of Spain had reintroduced the Cadiz Constitution of 1812, and Huajuapan had voted in its first municipal council. The council comprised the town's merchant class, many of whom were royalist soldiers. Antonio de León, by now a royalist captain, was made municipal president. During the council's first year, this royalist clique came into repeated conflict with the Spanish representative, the subdelegate Manuel María Leyton. First, he tried to close down the council because of infractions against the resurrected Constitution, and then he denied León's right to re-election.[18] In late February 1821 the bishop of Puebla wrote to León and other leading Huajuapan royalists and urged them to support the Plan of Iguala, citing the anticlerical measures brought in by Spain's new liberal government.[19] León and the Huajuapan elite, angered by the subdelegate's interference, needed little encouragement. In April León met the Independence fighter Nicolas Bravo and agreed to support the plan.[20] Initial elite backing was reflected in the plan's military supporters. When León declared Independence in the Mixteca Baja in June, he mobilized former royalists including members of Huajuapan's, Tezoatlán's, and Tonalá's royalist squadrons and a handful of soldiers from the battalion of Guanajuato stationed in the area. When they trekked down from Huajuapan toward Oaxaca City, they sought allies from royalist divisions rather than indigenous villagers or guerrilla bands. When the regional royalists eventually arrived in the state capital, they were greeted warmly by the city's elite. The bishop and the council sent out various certificates to certify León and his small army's good behavior.[21]

Similar concerns over regional elite power also motivated León's support for a break with Iturbide. Within days of announcing Independence in Oaxaca City, Iturbide ignored León's fairly reasonable expectations of high state office and appointed his godson as political chief and another close army colleague as military head of the state.[22] Furthermore, when León returned to Huajuapan in late 1821, he found the situation little better than under the Spaniards. National-level appointees like Vicente Castillejos, the local judge, and Cayetano Machado, the tax administrator, were interfering in municipal politics, overcharging merchants, and destabilizing the balance of forces between indigenous and nonindigenous residents. Although local residents brought charges, and León actually sacked both men, Iturbide had them reappointed.[23] Finally, in October 1822 Iturbide closed down the national congress, stripping León, an elected deputy, of his last remaining official influence.[24] Consequently, when anti-Iturbide forces edged nearer to the state, León declared his support, marched down to Oaxaca City, and declared himself military commander of the state. Although Iturbide sent more forces to the state in September 1823, León met them and signed a conciliatory agreement that ensured a degree of state sovereignty.[25]

Until late 1823 León had acted like other aspirant state caudillos, including Santa Anna, by mobilizing former royalist forces to ensure regional autonomy against invasive Spanish and imperial governments.[26] Yet over the next year, León appeared to radicalize profoundly. In early 1824 the Oaxaca governor refused to recognize Iturbide and declared himself for a federal system with the backing of the radical, cross-class *vinagre* party of Oaxaca City. León offered his full support. Rumors abounded that León's troops were about to revolt against the state's Spanish inhabitants. By April 17, 1824, he had ordered notices hung around the state capital that accused the Spanish of attempting to proclaim against the new republic. At the end of the month, his soldiers assaulted the shops of a well-to-do Spanish merchant. Finally, he marched off toward Huajuapan and demanded twenty-five thousand pesos from the state government for the payment of his troops. After receiving the money, he headed north. On the way, a couple of his troops murdered Huajuapan's unpopular Spanish tax collector, Machado. Oaxaca's fearful Spanish community was up in arms. Antonio and Manuel de León were accused of masterminding the crime and eventually sent to prison in Mexico City.[27]

For Guardino, León's alliance with Oaxaca City's vinagre party indicates his assumption of the ideology of radical federalism. According to Guardino, León, like the *vinagres*, was "fiercely suspicious" of the Spaniards and supportive of ideas of mass political involvement.[28] Undoubtedly, when forced to choose between the city's Spanish elite and a cross-class coalition of Creoles, mestizos, and Indians, León chose the latter. His demands for regional elite rule necessitated such a choice. Yet the alliance was one of convenience, precipitated by the state's increasingly polarized political scene.[29] León's anti-Spanish sentiment was temporary, politically astute, and deliberately targeted. The murder of Machado played to his Oaxaca City allies and ridded his patria chica of an unpopular tax collector. If León's momentary, tactical radicalism should not influence our assessment of his subsequent career, neither should his troops' involvement in the political effervescence of Oaxaca City indicate that they supported all the tenets of radical federalism. Although Bustamante portrayed León as "a capricious goat-herding Indian" and his troops as Mixtec rabble, he did so for political effect. León's soldiers were generally former royalists from Huajuapan's merchant class.[30] They, like their chief, wanted regional elite rule and had no interest in bringing the incipient class warfare of Oaxaca City back to the Mixteca Baja. As a result, when the state congress of Oaxaca passed the federalist Constitution in

January 1825, the inhabitants of the Mixteca Baja did not embrace the Constitution as a radical federalist agenda, a means of remaking society along democratic lines, but rather as a confirmation of the late colonial status quo.

The state deputies who introduced Oaxaca's federalist Constitution adapted Spain's Cadiz Constitution to local circumstances. They dictated that only towns with populations of over three thousand could elect municipalities. However, because elite wealth depended on the indigenous production of cochineal, textiles, and palm products, they also permitted considerable local rule. Villages with populations between five hundred and three thousand were allowed to elect repúblicas. These institutions were responsible for the same tasks as the municipalities, including education, resource management, tax collection, and guarding common funds.[31] Thus, in the Mixteca Baja the Constitution formalized two distinct political arrangements that would remain in place until the 1860s. In the region's large towns, like Huajuapan and Tonalá, inhabitants formed a bipartite system. The creole and mestizo mercantile elite formed municipal councils. These institutions started to take control of previously communal lands, carving them up into private ranches. But they never completely dominated resources. To do so would have risked riot or rebellion. Instead, they reached a compromise settlement. In return for performing religious services as sacristans, fiscales, and mayordomos, urban Mixtecs were allowed to maintain control of cofradía properties.[32] Meanwhile, in the region's rural villages federalist repúblicas simply overlaid late colonial repúblicas, aping the decentralized system that had emerged in the late colonial period. For example, in 1810 the district of Huajuapan comprised forty-two repúblicas. In 1829 the same district comprised forty-six.[33]

Mixtecs and merchants in the Mixteca Baja welcomed the establishment of this highly decentralized political system. As Karen Caplan argues, "Village autonomy was one area in which Oaxacan indígenas and non-indígenas could agree."[34] By permitting indigenous self-rule, the elite sidestepped many of the bloody interethnic conflicts of the early nineteenth century caused by the mestizo appropriation of indigenous political control. Even the arrangements in the large towns were not necessarily conflictive. In fact, urban Mixtecs, through control of cofradía lands, drew closer to the regional church. Furthermore, as chapter 2 delineated, to ensure stability the elite retained this decentralized aspect of federalist rule, even though they adhered to centralist national governments. However, to claim that the federalist Constitution radically altered how indigenous villagers viewed political relations, that "the overarching notion of subjecthood, with its implication of subordination" was replaced by "citizenship, backed up by the notion of liberty" would be going too far.[35] In the Mixteca Baja former royalist officers and not rebellious guerrillas had fought for the introduction of the federalist system. Consequently, the system inspired neither revelation nor liberation, but rather the maintenance of the status quo. Undoubtedly, some villages, involved in prolonged struggles with overweening caciques over land ownership, did invoke ideas of liberty and citizenship. In 1826 the notoriously bolshie authorities of Tequixtepec, who had been involved in litigation with the Villagómez, Velasco, and Aja cacicazgos for over fifty years, claimed their right as citizens to own what they termed a "patriotic land grant" and denigrated caciques' land rights as colonial impositions.[36]

But most villages maintained the hierarchical and paternalist political relations established during the late colonial era. Broad-based male suffrage and the institution of república elections did not precipitate the emergence of a young bilingual elite. Elders, who had completed the cargo ladder, continued to rule without opposition. In fact, although most caciques had surrendered their official political roles during the late eighteenth century, some local lords in the regions' smaller villages continued to dominate public office. In 1826 Ramón Antonio Ximénez y Enriquez de Alvarado was both mayor and cacique of Acaquizapan.[37] A year later the cacique Ignacio Velasco y Mendoza was voted in as representative of Magdalena.[38] Local cacique Juan Aguilar was a councilor of Diquiyú at least three times during the 1830s.[39] The cacique of Chazumba was municipal president of the village as late as 1856.[40] As we shall see, even when caciques neglected official roles they continued to exert considerable power in the villages as landowners, informal political backers, and lay religious leaders. Moreover, most villages continued to address regional and state leaders in supplicatory tones. In 1831 the villagers of Ahuehuetitlan asked that the judge defend them against mestizo imposters "as we are simple and naïve like children."[41] Two years later, the villagers of Ixitlán asked for protection as "poor Indians who know little better."[42]

The announcement of Independence and the introduction of a federalist Constitution affected the regions of Mexico in divergent ways. Political shifts at the national level were filtered through regional socioeconomic arrangements and histories of political mobilization. In regions where the War of Independence had opened up substantial political opportunities, like Guerrero or Oaxaca City, radical coalitions emerged that conflated demands for regional autonomy with political decentralization and mass suffrage.

In the cities the urban lower classes formed councils; in the countryside indigenous and Afro-Mexican peasants created municipalities. When centralist governments attempted to curtail these rights, these coalitions either attempted electoral mobilization (as in Oaxaca City) or armed insurrection (as in Guerrero).[43] Yet in many areas of Mexico regional elites, not cross-class coalitions, brought federalism to the masses. In some regions, like Yucatán or the Huasteca, these elites used the reforms to dominate municipal councils and appropriate indigenous lands.[44] But in other regions of limited agricultural value, like Oaxaca, elites modified the constitutional template and offered the continuation of indigenous rule.[45] In more egalitarian regions, like Villa Alta, a new generation of young bilingual Indians used electoral reforms to attack the communal gerontocracy.[46] However, in areas with established village hierarchies, like Huajuapan, federalism did little to alter political or social relations, except for raising the regional elites, like Antonio de León, from economic to political prominence. As a result, the Mixtecs of the Mixteca Baja refused to support radical federalist rebels during the 1830s and 1840s and sided instead with León and the mercantile elite.

From Federalism to Selective Centralism, 1826–1847

The same divisions that mark historical analysis of the early 1820s have influenced the examination of the succeeding two decades. For revisionists, the period witnessed the extension of creole power, the gradual takeover of communal lands, and the suppression of indigenous revolts, culminating in what Carmagnani has called "the second conquest of Oaxaca" in the late 1840s.[47] For more recent historians, the type of cross-class negotiations that marked the first decade after Independence continued, tempering indigenous responses to political changes, state exactions, and military mobilization. Compromise, not caste war, characterized the period.[48] Again, by examining political actions in the Mixteca Baja, which stood at the boundary between a region of relative calm and a region of almost perpetual insurrection, we can see that both interpretations possess a degree of validity. Federalism and centralism were never mutually exclusive. In the Mixteca Baja, internal demands and perceived external threats generated popular support for what I term "selective centralism." On the one hand, village rule continued despite centralist decrees. And in Oaxaca City, León still played to the federalist crowd. On the other hand, ecclesiastical demands for schooling, church-building, tithe payment, and Christian morality were met. At the same time, León and local militias united in order to repress neighboring radical federalists from Putla and Copala. These struggles not only encouraged cross-class alliances, but also provoked a hypersensitivity to conservative pronunciamientos. Although local confirmation of these national plans has often been viewed as coerced or perfunctory, responses in regions of provincial conservatism were not only more immediate and more enthusiastic than in other areas, they also often reveal grassroots interpretations of centralist doctrine.[49]

When Antonio de León returned to Oaxaca from his Mexico City prison in 1827, he was placed in charge of military forces in the Mixteca and stationed in Huajuapan. Upon arriving, he found that the state's political system was even more heavily polarized than before. On one side stood his former enemies: Oaxaca City's elites, *aceites*, members of the Scottish Rite masonic lodge, and supporters of the presidential candidacy of Manuel Gómez Pedraza. On the other side stood his former allies: Oaxaca City's poor, vinagres, members of the York Rite masonic lodge, and backers of the presidential candidacy of Vicente Guerrero. The first conflict between these two groups concerned the position of the Spanish.[50] While vinagres pushed for their expulsion, aceites argued that they should be allowed to remain. Although radical federalists automatically expected León and his regional supporters to back their campaign to expel the former colonizers, he was extremely hesitant to sanction such a wholesale purge. When faced with the logical extension of radical federalism's policies, León, like so many other members of the provincial elite, pulled away from unilateral support.[51] Thus, when Santiago García and other radicals who supported the expulsion rebelled in Oaxaca City in November 1827, León attempted to temper their enthusiasm, employing arguments for stability and order. On November 18 he wrote to one of García's co-conspirators, claiming that "order and peace" were his "true happiness" and arguing that the expulsion of the Spaniards would "cause a drop in confidence, paralyze commerce, drain resources and thus slow the march of the nation." Instead, he suggested that the congress only expel the Spaniards who endangered the state's "peace and tranquility." At the same time, he and his brother, Manuel, patrolled the Mixteca Baja persuading communities to resist rebellion and pursuing a handful of "bandits and thieves" that had heeded García's call to arms.[52] León continued to pursue this moderate federalist stance for the next two years. Although he established a York Rite lodge and was widely rumored to support Guerrero's presidential bid, he refused to join Santa Anna's 1828 rebellion in support of the candidate.[53] When Guerrero took power and started to push through various radical decrees, León resigned from his military command of the state, citing ill health.[54]

León's reluctance to support Guerrero's radical federalism became apparent during the War of the South (1830–1832). In December 1829 the so-called party of order, led by Antonio Bustamante and Santa Anna, called for Guerrero's resignation.[55] Soon after, Manuel de León, commander of Oaxaca's military, supported the *pronunciamiento*.[56] Ejected from elected office, Guerrero returned to his patria chica and started to foment revolt. By late 1829 the rebels had started to disrupt the Mixteca. In Copala, Hilario Alonso rose up in support, announcing his intentions by decapitating a local Spanish landowner.[57] At the same time, Juan Bruno and Manuel Medina rallied the peasants of Putla to Guerrero's cause.[58] Finally, José Mariano Narváez attempted to incite the sugar workers in the north of the Mixteca Baja around Atoyac. Although he was fairly unsuccessful, around fifteen men under Andres Abelino formed a small guerrilla band.[59] In February 1830 León returned to Huajuapan from Mexico City to find that "various groups of nonconformists threatened to alter the tranquility of the state."[60] In response, the regional caudillo started to establish village-based military auxiliaries throughout the region. Over the next two years, León, ex-royalist career soldiers from the regional elite, and these new Mixtec militias sought to quell the revolt. In January 1831 they defeated Narváez just north of Huajuapan.[61] In February auxiliaries from Juxtlahuaca helped defeat Medina's force of 130 men.[62] In June they chased and captured Abelino and his small force.[63] By early 1832, when Bishop Francisco Pablo Vázquez toured the region, he found the "people in the good sentiments of peace, order, and adhesion to the government." At the same time, Vázquez reminded Manuel de León of the importance of his peacekeeping role, urging him to pursue the remaining radicals. He reinforced his encouragement by threatening to remove the León brothers' valuable tithe concession if they refused.[64]

Clerical admonition and increasing rural violence turned León and his local supporters from moderate federalists to moderate or selective centralists, content to maintain federalist rule where it worked but concerned with order and stability where it appeared to generate dissent. Backed by the church, they sought to spread this ideal, brokering the first cacique land sale, establishing parish schools, and starting the campaign for classes in indigenous dialects. This new cross-class alliance faced its first test when the national congress under the vice president,

Valentín Gómez Farías, started to introduce a broad series of anticlerical reforms in 1833. Over the following year the Mexican government secularized missions, forced seminaries under state control, allowed religious tolerance, forbade government coercion of tithe payments, and placed ecclesiastical appointments under government supervision. In the Diocese of Puebla ecclesiastical intransigence provoked even more radical anticlerical measures. Bishop Vázquez decried the government's assumption of clerical appointments in November 1833. In response radical congressmen persuaded the state to force the church to hand over its properties to their secular renters. By March centralists had taken up arms against the move, begging for Santa Anna's return and signing the Plan of Cuernavaca.[65] For many recent historians, the reforms were the work of a small, desperate elite. The mass support for the Plan of Cuernavaca was so all-encompassing that it crossed political lines.[66] Again, this is only partly true. Most provincial capitals eventually signed off on the plan, and only a handful of radicals stood up in defense of the reforms. Yet as Brian Connaughton and Sonia Pérez Toledo argue, the immediacy and vigor of responses differed depending on regional political contexts. In regions of radical federalism, support was weak, tardy, or non-existent. In regions of incipient centralism, backing was popular and prompt. In Mexico City, alliances between elite council members and Catholic artisans provoked quick and vociferous endorsements for the plan, which were verified in community meetings throughout the metropolis. In Puebla, with its network of church institutions, clerical elites, and pious parishioners, support was equally strong.[67]

In the Mixteca Baja, with its system of church schools and high concentration of priests, the anticlerical reforms also precipitated rapid and widespread support for the institutional church similar to the reactive or defensive clericalism described in Europe at the time.[68] In February 1834 the council of Huajuapan sent one of the first letters to the national congress to demand the suspension of the reforms. Receiving no reply, the region's military auxiliaries decided to rebel.[69] On May 16, 1834, two local low-ranking officers from Huajuapan, Agustín Ruiz and Miguel Cisneros, "pronounced for religion" and encouraged the local garrison to follow. Although Antonio de León talked down the two rebels, within days the plan had spread.[70] By May 18 the council had called an extraordinary meeting of all the town's inhabitants. Here council members, military officers, militiamen, and citizens signed the plan in support, decrying the government's anticlerical attacks and its attempts to introduce religious tolerance. In the council's letter to the state congress, the signatories revealed the widespread fear that the raft of anticlerical policies would lead to a further breakdown of regional order, neatly summing up the rationale of provincial conservatism. According to the explanation of their decision, the Mexican government already had "thousands of enemies." By publishing these anticlerical decrees, the national congress was playing into their enemies' hands, undermining Catholic morality, exacerbating disobedience, and encouraging revolt.[71] Over the next few days, militiamen spread the plan throughout the region's communities. According to Antonio de León's nephew, Felipe, "All the head towns and villages of the department have the same opinion as that of the council and embrace the same feelings of religiosity."[72] Although the Huajuapan caudillo initially stood aloof, a few weeks later he threw his support behind the popular uprising, writing to the state congress that the Plan of Cuernavaca was "favored by public opinion." On June 17 he approved the Mixteca's support for the pronunciamiento, led a procession to the church to sing a Te Deum, and attended a Mass in which parishioners prayed for the "defense of religion, the constitution, and the union."[73] The next day he set off toward Oaxaca City with a force of over three hundred men. Stopping at Etla, he called together the region's soldiers and militiamen, including the smaller auxiliary garrisons of Ayuquila, Ihualtepec, and Zacatepec. Here they all agreed on the "cardinal point of sustaining the Catholic religion" before marching off to take the state capital.[74]

Between 1830 and 1834 the War of the South and the threat of anticlerical decrees had persuaded León and his supporters to surrender their initial support for federalism. But in June 1836, barely a year after they had entered Oaxaca City in the name of religion, soldiers from Huajuapan led a federalist revolt against the incipient centralist regime. A regular soldier, José María Payan, and a local auxiliary, Miguel Acevedo, led the movement. After surprising and defeating federal forces outside Chila, the rebels moved south, attacking Tlaxiaco and ransacking Oaxaca City before their eventual defeat at Etla on July 2.[75] How to account for this apparently dramatic volte-face? In fact, the explanation is fairly simple. Although Huajuapan lent its name to the revolt, very few of the actual rebels came from the region. None of the local leaders like Antonio de León, Juan Acevedo, or Miguel Carrión, who had backed the 1834 pronunciamiento, joined the movement. Beyond a handful of local militiamen like Miguel Acevedo and Francisco Herrera, around three-quarters of the sixty initial supporters were regular soldiers encamped in the city. According to the local prefect, only a few "restless youths" followed the rebels.[76] As they proceeded to march through the Mixteca, the federalists assembled a large force that totaled around seven hundred men by the time they reached Oaxaca City. But again, almost all were regular soldiers, stationed in the commercial centers of Acatlán, Tlaxiaco, or Teposcolula.[77] The plan itself basically reiterated the points of the federalist rebellion of Texas and failed to speak to local concerns.[78] As a result, the town and the surrounding villages remained unmoved. In fact, most of Huajuapan's citizens were so opposed to the uprising that they risked rebel retribution and refused to sign the pronunciamiento. When Payan asked the council to second the plan on June 7, the councilors and the local residents unanimously declined. Again their explanation invoked the specter of social dissolution as they argued that if they adhered they risked "disgraceful disorders."[79]

Despite this brief federalist insurrection, elites and non-elites continued to support this regional brand of selective centralism, which mixed decentralized village rule with church schooling and clerical obedience. During the late 1830s, successive federalist rebellions confirmed and strengthened the centralist elements of this hybrid raft of beliefs. In October 1838 Hilario Alonso again rose up against the usurpation of indigenous lands. On October 5 he entered the town of Putla with around two hundred Copala supporters and murdered León's hacienda manager and freed the prisoners from jail.[80] After persuading Putla peasants to join his rebellion, Alonso disappeared into the mountains. At first the regional military commander sent the small Huajuapan squadron after the rebels with orders to "totally exterminate" the band.[81] However, when the response was deemed insufficient, elites started another round of regional militarization. In late October, the prefect of Huajuapan demanded 240 pesos from the state government to establish a peacekeeping force in Juxtlahuaca, arguing that the local auxiliaries had "in other epochs, because of their topographic knowledge, lent important services to the persecution of the killer Hilario."[82] Antonio de León quickly agreed. In early November the prefect announced that he had given out arms to nearby Mixtec villages and had already established a small auxiliary detachment in Tequixtepec. At the same time, he had sent letters to the local communities explaining that Alonso was "a monster" accused of "horrendous crimes including robbery and the spilling of much blood."[83] Over the next two years the auxiliaries under the command of the Juxtlahuaca native Mariano Guzmán embarked on a campaign of brutal repression, targeting Hilario Alonso's peasant supporters around

Putla and Copala. In July 1839 Guzmán cornered and defeated the rebels outside Silacayoapan, hanging the prisoners for "disturbing the public peace." Although Alonso escaped, his forces now comprised barely twenty men.[84] Finally in March 1840, local troops from Juxtlahuaca captured the rebel. He was sent to Oaxaca City where he stood trial for multiple murders. He defended his acts as those of a patriot and federalist but was found guilty and hung. León, now military commander of the state, took credit for the arrest and execution.[85]

Over the next five years, this brand of selective centralism peaked as León became state governor. In late 1841 Santa Anna took power in Mexico City and proceeded to impose a centralist Constitution entitled the Bases Orgánicas. The new Constitution limited suffrage, reduced regional autonomy, and narrowed the freedom of the press.[86] In the Mixteca Baja, communities were quick to offer their support and orchestrated confirmations of Santa Anna's power in elaborate council ceremonies and church services.[87] At the same time, the regional caudillo's support for the Plan of Cuernavaca, his repression of federalist revolts, and his refusal to support the regional rebellion of 1836 received reward. In early 1842 Santa Anna appointed León state governor. Despite federalist attempts to discredit his regime, he held the position until late 1845 when he retired for reasons of ill health. During his governorship, León maintained his ambivalent position. Never a doctrinaire centralist, he made certain concessions to local federalists, appointing Benito Juárez as his minister of the interior and permitting the continuation of a degree of community autonomy despite national prescriptions.[88] But, at the same time, he also directed a prolonged counterinsurgency campaign against radical federalist rebellions and expressed ready support for conservative pronunciamientos.

In the mountains to the west of the Mixteca Baja the local caudillo's rule witnessed the continuation of centralist policy. Here, the region's military auxiliaries repressed neighboring federalist revolts throughout the 1840s. In 1843 peasants around Chilapa rose up against the imposition of the capitación. Within months the rebellion spread to the villages of the Guerrero montaña, where Dionisio Arriaga amassed forces of over eight hundred peasants from the indigenous villages.[89] Over the border in late September, three hundred neighboring Copala rebels followed suit, invading Juxtlahuaca, murdering the judge and their former persecutor, Mariano Guzmán, and stealing grain and taxes. Under their leaders, Bernadino José, Juan Santiago, and Feliciano Martín, they then proceeded to join Arriaga around Tlapa.[90] Following León's instructions, the Huajuapan captain, José de Jesús Maldonaldo, assembled a force of two hundred regular troops and auxiliaries (now dubbed *rurales*) from throughout the Mixteca Baja. They included men from Juxtlahuaca, Tlachichilco, Tamazola, Tezoatlán, Tonalá, and the villages and ranches around Huajuapan.[91] After a long forced march the Mixteca Baja forces caught up with the rebels. After six hours of combat that left eighty-seven rebels dead, the centralist troops were victorious. Arriaga fled mortally wounded, and the Copala rebels returned to the hills around their village. The commanding officer heaped the local soldiers with special praise, particularly the Huajuapan merchant Miguel Carrión (father of a local priest) and the Tezoatlán merchant Mariano Galvez (brother of another cleric).[92] After the victory, Maldonaldo started the mopping-up operation, invading Copala and forcing the remaining rebels to flee before marching back into Guerrero to combat Arriaga's diminishing band.[93]

Although the arrival of planting season brought temporary respite, Guerrero's federalists rebelled once more in September 1844, this time under the command of a mestizo militia captain from Chilapa, Miguel Casarrubias.[94] Again rebels complained about the continued enforcement of the capitación, and again Copala and Putla peasants joined the campaign. During late 1844 local troops were stationed around Tlapa, but in early 1845 they returned to pursue the rebels around the Mixteca Baja. In January Maldonaldo attacked Copala and arrested dozens of returning rebels.[95] Three months later, they captured Bernardino José in Chicahuaxtla after a tip-off from the local juez.[96] In August 1845 the Triquis rebelled once more. Led by Feliciano Martín, they murdered the imposed juez, José Anselmo, and his guards and took to the mountains on the border between Oaxaca and Guerrero.[97] Again local troops followed, beating Martín and his followers in a series of engagements. Although, the threat of U.S. invasion and the gradual decline of the Guerrero movement precipitated a rare peace in 1846, the following year Copala villagers took up arms. Yet by this point, the counterinsurgency campaign had taken its toll. The Triquis avoided orchestrated attacks on the region's town centers with their concentrations of militia forces and instead made occasional assaults on wandering merchants and isolated herds of goats and sheep.[98]

Despite the proximity of rural revolts and the constant pleas by rebels for local villagers to join the rebellion, the communities of the Mixteca Baja remained exceptionally pacific. Elite concessions and clerical influence cemented centralist support. The local prefect's reports, which span the period September 1843 to October 1846, frequently listed the "atrocities" and "disorders" committed by the neighboring rebels of Copala, Putla, and Tlapa but repeatedly assured León that "in all the pueblos" of the Mixteca Baja "public tranquility [was] enjoyed and the roads [were] safely guarded."[99] When a peasant murdered a local merchant outside Tonalá in April 1844, the prefect was quick to point out that it was an "extraordinary case."[100] Even when federalist leaders attempted to stir up local support, communities were unmoved. When Feliciano Martín published his 1845 plan, which included one article directly encouraging the region's peasants to stop paying cacique rents, villagers failed to follow.[101] After Juan Alvarez visited the region in March 1845 and told the peasants of Tlachichilco that "no divine law" ordered them to pay capitación, the local priest returned and countermanded the caudillo's claims, reminding villagers of their "divine obligations." Soon after, the local juez claimed that villagers were still "obedient and exact when complying with the orders of the authorities."[102] In fact, throughout the period Mixteca Baja peasants continued to pay capitación without fail, offering up around eight hundred to one thousand pesos per month to the prefect.[103]

León's political position and the three years of antifederalist campaigning not only intensified adherence to conservative expectations in the Mixteca Baja, but also acclimated local political leaders to national changes. Between 1845 and 1847, soldiers and citizens from the region acted as Oaxaca's bellwethers of conservative mobilization, voluntarily supporting conservative pronunciamientos without hesitation. In late 1845, military leaders and militiamen from the region met in León's house in Huajuapan and agreed to support Mariano Paredes's Plan de San Luis Potosí, an attempt to overturn the new national liberal administration.[104] Although the plan came to nothing, and Paredes was soon brought down, in early 1847 local groups tried again, protesting the liberal government's attempt to usurp ecclesiastical properties and use the money to pay for the struggle against the U.S. invaders.[105] On February 10 the inhabitants of Tamazulapan and the nearby villages met in the town's municipal palace. The hundreds of attendees were encouraged "not to be afraid to express their opinions." During the open discussions, many villagers spoke out against the move, aping clerical discourses that allied the fate of the church with the fate of the nation. For example, Hilario Segura argued that for three centuries nation and church had worked in tandem, "gathering wealth in the service of God," and questioned why any respectable national government would try to undermine the relationship especially at such a crucial time. At the same time, other speakers argued for the important role church properties played in maintaining indigenous piety. Gerardo Manzano pointed out that any expropriation threatened "to rob the churches of their gems and funds, which the unhappy indigenous [villagers] had acquired in order to see their temples well decorated and hear the hymns of God."[106] Two weeks later the militia and citizens of Huajuapan also met and berated the liberal state's attack on "the sacred cult and the faith with which we were born and still live."[107] Even outside the region's commercial centers, villagers drew up similar pronunciamientos. Conflating clerical and national interests, peasants from Ayuquililla and Chilixtlahuaca declared that they agreed with those "citizens who wished to save the goods consecrated to cult and to the Independence of the Republic." The following day the inhabitants of the neighboring villages of Ayuquila and Santa Catarina Estancia did the same.[108]

As the previous examples suggest, the U.S. invasion widened provincial conservatives' perspectives. Mixteca Baja inhabitants viewed clericalism not only as a means to secure regional stability, but also as a way to save the nation from Protestant takeover. Thus, despite scant sources, we have some evidence that elites and non-elites in the Mixteca Baja started to embrace the Catholic nationalism espoused by the diocesan authorities.[109] In January 1847 León emerged from retirement and agreed to collect supplies and forces and defend the country against invasion. In March regional elites established a committee in Huajuapan to coordinate regional efforts. Over the following month priests led parallel organizations in the parish seats. At the behest of the committees, peasants were asked to provide supplies, and women were instructed to make durable corn *totopos*. Many communities complied. On April 2 Tezoatlán sent ten bushels of totopos, twenty-one goats, twenty-nine chickens, and half a bushel of beans.[110] A week later, the villagers of Tlacotepec and Miltepec also sent the required amounts. At the same time, León attempted to mobilize the Mixteca Baja's militia. By August he had assembled a force of over 250 men.[111] In Tonalá, the local militia leader, Dionisio Rojas, claimed that he had recruited an extra thirty volunteers.[112] Sadly, such enthusiasm was in vain. On September 8 León led the Mixtec militia in the defense of a mill complex called Molino del Rey outside Mexico City. Despite what the official report on the battle called the Mixtecs' "heroic defense," the lack of coordination among Mexican forces brought León's defeat and death.[113] Whether the regional soldiers' heroism was born of fear, paternalist ties, or a new sense of Catholic nationalism is impossible to tell. Yet as years passed regional conservatives certainly interpreted the heroic defeat as proof of Huajuapan's providential patriotism.

Between 1826 and 1847, Mexico's political shifts played out in diverse ways across Oaxaca's regions. In general, as recent historians have argued, the quiet maintenance of a decentralized political system that ensured community autonomy and prevented the non-native takeover of lands brought order and stability. As Guardino argues for Villa Alta, this hands-off approach often circumscribed contact between indigenous communities and state politicians to a series of community-level negotiations over taxes, education, and military recruitment and, as a result, impeded the emergence of mass popular political mobilization, and slowed the arrival of regional political intermediaries.[114] In the Mixteca Baja, by contrast, the threat of continual caste war and the creation of a regional militia sealed links between elites and non-elites, regional *políticos*, and indigenous communities and encouraged the predominance of a regional caudillo, Antonio de León. Here, merchants and peasants adopted a selective reading of centralism, which mixed federalist respect for local rule with centralist tenets of clericalism, order, and stability. With the U.S. invasion, regional support for centralist policies alerted Mixtec citizens to the broader ramifications of political change, cementing alliances with national conservatives and generating a kind of incipient Catholic nationalism.

From Selective Centralism to Conservatism, 1847–1867

Between 1847 and 1867 the differences between political sympathies in the Mixteca Baja and the rest of Oaxaca, which the maintenance of community autonomy and León's astute politicking had managed to reconcile, started to open up. At the national level, the U.S. defeat and the loss of nearly half of Mexico's territory precipitated polarization. On the one side, liberals called for the wholesale reform of Mexican society, blending federalist policies of mass democracy with more radical schemes of land privatization and the complete separation of church and state. On the other side, conservatives, incorporated into a party under the leadership of Lucas Alamán, supported a limited franchise, the maintenance of ecclesiastical power, and conservation of the social hierarchy and its bonds of deference and obedience.[115] In Oaxaca, similar polarization occurred. Federalist elites like Benito Juárez and Porfirio Díaz, mollified by León's moderate governorship, now chose reform over stability. As national policies started to bite, they increasingly allied with peasant communities, wary of conservative attempts to limit local democracy. In 1854–1855, 1856–1861, and 1862–1867 peasants from the Oaxaca valleys, the Sierra Juárez, Juchitán, the Mixteca Alta, and Putla and Copala would mobilize in favor of the liberal cause.[116] In the Mixteca Baja, a thin tier of the region's young mestizo townsfolk, excluded from political power and eager to take over former cofradía lands, did adhere to the new order. But in general, most selective centralists, imbued with an appreciation of the import of church and hierarchy, sided with the conservatives, defending Santa Anna's final dictatorship, rising up against anticlerical reforms, and supporting (with less enthusiasm) the French Intervention.

Between 1847 and 1852, the future liberal statesman Benito Juárez governed Oaxaca. As Hamnett and Caplan argue, the new regime attempted to deepen popular allegiance to the civil authority, modernizing the state's antiquated transportation system, encouraging the expansion of state education, and promoting the creation of regional militias.[117] In the Mixteca Baja, state policies changed little. Provincial conservative elites, perhaps counting on León's previous patronage of the Zapotec politician, retained power. In fact, most municipal councillors of Huajuapan during the period, like Luciano Martínez, Alejandro Roldan, and Manuel Alencaster, would become the region's conservative leaders in the forthcoming civil wars.[118] At the same time, the tradition of church schools and the continued links between elites and the local clergy blunted state attempts to enforce lay education. In Huajuapan municipal presidents still relied on the local cleric to teach Christian doctrine, and in the villages church-appointed schoolmasters continued to use the Mixtec-language catechisms and manuals of the 1830s.[119] Finally, Juárez's attempt to rally local militias also had little effect. Those who had survived the bloody encounter at Molino del Rey simply became members of the new national guard. Furthermore, under the command of the regional elites they continued to perform the same task—suppressing radical federalism-turned-banditry in the neighboring districts.[120]

Whereas Juárez's brief reign failed to inspire a liberal following in the Mixteca Baja, the following regime was much more successful, albeit unintentionally. In late 1852 national politics transformed regional governance once again. Santa Anna returned, Juárez was exiled, and a new conservative administration ruled the state.[121] In the Mixteca Baja provincial conservatives ramped up cacique land sales and helped to establish new church schools.

However, although elite concessions in general brought stability, problems arose in some of the region's more mestizo towns. On the one hand, in Tezoatlán and Chilapa de Díaz new conservative rules that put a firm limit on the number of officials in the community caused considerable disquiet. Here, the slim majority of mestizo townsfolk faced off against their indigenous neighbors for a reduced number of elected positions. In the 1853 elections the self-declared gente de razón of Tezoatlán complained that the town's "indios" threatened revolt if they did not hold at least one of the positions.[122] As the delicate balance between indigenous and non-indigenous rule broke down, the town's mestizos turned against conservative rule. On the other hand, in Tonalá and Huajuapan, where local rule remained more simply divided between the secular and the religious spheres, some mestizos sought to extend their ranches and break the indigenous hold over cofradía properties. As the regional prefect allied with the local diocese to prevent the attempts, these men also turned against the conservative regime.[123] For the next two decades, this thin tier of young mestizos, excluded from political power or prevented from agrarian expansion, formed the small core of liberal supporters in the region. They included José Segura y Guzmán and Miguel Luna, mestizo ranchers from Chilapa de Díaz and Tezoatlán, respectively; Francisco Herrera and Casimiro Ramírez, ambitious hacendados from Huajuapan; Emigdio Olivera, a land lawyer repeatedly accused of overcharging indigenous clients, also from Huajuapan; and Mariano Rios, another landowner from Tonalá.

In many ways these new liberals resembled the "rustic individualists" of Guerrero, the Huasteca, or Michoacán who saw in liberalism "a means of social and economic advancement," a way to break down corporate controls on land and local politics.[124] Yet in the Mixteca Baja, they were an isolated minority. As a result, they were forced to look for support not only from friends, relatives, and Oaxaca City liberals, but also from neighboring radical federalists. Here, the rather exceptional figure of Francisco Herrera, a regular soldier, would prove crucial. Herrera was, to my knowledge, the only member of these new liberals who had sided with the radical federalists during the 1830s and 1840s. Described by his peers as "restless" and "difficult," he had joined the federalist rebellion in 1836 "while under the influence of a lot of liquor" and delivered the final blow to the juez of Juxtlahuaca during the Copala uprising of 1843.[125] Over the next decade, he would act as the intermediary between Copala and Putla's communalist popular radicals and Huajuapan's new ranchero bourgeoisie, part of a hybrid local liberalism that sought to mobilize one indigenous group to overcome another.

In late 1854 this new alliance came together to support the Plan de Ayutla, which aimed to end Santa Anna's rule and return a federalist regime to power. On December 19 Francisco Herrera invaded Huajuapan, defeated the local garrison, and called a meeting of the town's inhabitants.[126] During the meeting he attempted to persuade the assembled crowd of the plan's benefits, striking a self-interested note by arguing that the conservatives had taken "public positions and given them to ambitious men who [didn't] deserve them." Although locals initially raised their voices to disagree with Herrera's assertions, the written record of the meeting, which rather suspiciously lacks the wordy democratic feel of decisions over conservative manifestos, then promptly declares that all agreed with Herrera.[127] Perhaps sensing the popular disquiet, Herrera left the town almost immediately.[128] In response, the conservative government appointed a member of the regional elite, José Ramírez Acevedo, to undertake the pursuit "as he [wa]s from the town and count[ed] with the sympathies of the villages of the Mixtecas."[129] As the provincial conservatives collected regular military and regional volunteer forces, Herrera sought support in the neighboring sugar plantations to the north, especially around the former radical federalist hot spot of Atoyac.[130] Squeezed between Puebla and Oaxaca's troops, however, he became increasingly desperate. By early January his forces comprised barely eighty men including "many taken by the leva," and Herrera was forced to shake down communities, demanding contributions and committing "robberies and disgraces."[131] According to Ramírez Acevedo, the region's villages "looked on the revolution with horror."[132]

At the same time, Herrera's allies in Tezoatlán also faced popular disapproval. When Tezoatlán leaders Miguel Luna and José Segura y Guzmán attempted to take Tonalá in early 1855, forces led by the local priest, Felipe Martínez, soundly defeated them. They were defeated again in the neighboring village of Yucuyachi. Villagers stripped the skins from the feet of the captured Tezoatlán prisoners, forced them to march to Tonalá, then sent them to Yanhuitlán where they were shot.[133] Finally, although Herrera returned in early August accompanied by around eighty infantrymen and forty cavalrymen, he suffered another defeat. Ramírez Acevedo sent out two auxiliary companies from Huajuapan, including future conservative leader Luciano Martínez, who beat Herrera at Teotongo. Confirming the liberal leader's regional unpopularity, Martínez concluded that only four of the twenty prisoners had actually volunteered to join Herrera. The rest were "not part of that faction" but had been drafted from the surrounding villages.[134]

Despite Herrera's inability to secure widespread support, more successful uprisings in the rest of Oaxaca conspired against the Mixteca Baja's inhabitants. On August 18 liberal forces declared the plan in Oaxaca City, and less than a week later, goaded by liberal emissaries, provincial conservatives in Huajuapan followed suit.[135] Yet even when forced to confirm their backing for the plan, town councils throughout the region seemed extremely reluctant. In Huajuapan townsfolk made no mention of their support but rather thanked the local military commander for "avoiding an effusion of blood" during "difficult times."[136] In Tonalá the local leader refused point blank to second the plan, claiming (falsely) that he had already signed the manifesto in December 1854. In the small village of San Sebastián del Monte, villagers seemed equally recalcitrant. Many fled to the hills, and, despite the presence of a church school, the remaining villagers claimed they were "unable to write."[137] Well aware of the popular perception that the new liberal regime was inherently anticlerical, the minority of local liberals tried to prove that the new regime was what Herrera called "of a healthy and religious disposition." In September he encouraged the council to appoint the mayordomos, donate wax to the cofradías, and maintain the local priest in charge of the school.[138]

Yet over the following year national reforms undermined these local attempts to curry favor. In late November 1855 radical liberals passed the Ley Juárez, which prohibited military and clerical fueros. Barely two weeks later conservative cavalry officers in Puebla rose up in revolt. The government managed to quell the initial rebellion, but it soon spread to the Sierra Norte de Puebla where the priest of Zacapoaxtla also declared war on the liberal administration. In response, the state intensified its anticlerical policies and confiscated church property in the Diocese of Puebla on March 31, 1856. Although the bishop of Puebla attempted to distance the ecclesiastical hierarchy from the Sierra rebellion, a month later the government ordered his immediate exile. Finally, in June 1856 the liberal administration passed the Ley Lerdo, which demanded the privatization of communal properties, including village and cofradía lands.[139] As recent historians have argued, the liberal reforms were not inherently anti-Catholic. Rather, they represented an awkward blend of economic liberalism and the continuation of an attempt to rationalize and reform the church, reaching back to the Jansenist measures of the late eighteenth century.[140] As Anselmo de la Portilla argued, the oncoming conflict was not between Catholics and non-Catholics, but "a war for Catholicism and the signs it represented."[141] As a result, the reforms generated limited, regionally specific outrage. In regions of de-Christianization with long traditions of attempting to escape church control, liberal support took root.[142]

However, in regions of re-Christianization like the Mixteca Baja—with its small liberal cabal, its powerful community-led cofradías, and its close lay-clerical relations—peasants developed a profound clericalism that linked the church's fate to that of the region and increasingly the nation. They looked on the reforms "with fear" and "with horror."[143] Consequently, the popular response was widespread, rapid, and disruptive. In early May 1856 the liberal prefect discovered a plot to surprise the national guard battalion stationed in Huajuapan, masterminded by members of the formerly conservative council.[144] Although the first attempt was rapidly quashed, in July the provincial conservatives were more successful, mobilizing a mix of village priests, cofradía leaders, and pious parishioners and joining up with the insurrection to the north around Acatlán. In Silacayoapan local priest Andres Avelino, his nephew, and an "old Mixtec" in charge of the town's cofradías rose up in revolt.[145] In Ahuehuetitlan, villagers rang the bells of the local church, hung Mexican flags from the doorway, and announced that the reforms would be "the end of the church and the nation."[146] In Amatitlán, a local priest decried the government reforms from the pulpit and encouraged insurrection.[147] In Tonalá, Tiuxi, and Totoya, the local priest Felipe Martínez, who had helped maintain cofradía lands and defeated supporters of the Plan of Ayutla, also took to hills with over fifty indigenous cofradía members.[148] In Tlacotepec, the local priest and the scribe reiterated the popular conflation of church and state, claiming that the "current government [was] bound to fall as it [went] against religion."[149] The parish seats of Tezoatlán and Tequixtepec also saw smaller uprisings.[150] By September, conservative bands roamed the region. The largest, led by the Huajuapan merchant Luciano Martínez, comprised over one hundred men. In late October Martínez's band, armed with a handful of guns and sticks, defeated the garrison stationed in Mariscala.[151] In December it joined up with rebels from the Puebla towns of Chila and Izúcar de Matamoros and took the district seat of Acatlán.[152] In response, the region's liberal authorities appeared isolated, weak, and paranoid. The national guard comprised barely fifty men. Almost all were mestizos from Tezoatlán and Chilapa de Díaz.[153] Outside the major towns, the situation was even worse. The commander in Petalcingo claimed that he had around fifteen men, but "all were addicts of the reaction."[154] By December the local prefect, an outsider, had to call on forces from Mexico and

Oaxaca City to calm the revolt. Their methods included imposing a curfew in the region's major towns, imprisoning drunks and tramps "suspected of supporting the reaction," and starting to terrorize the region's villages. In what would become a familiar pattern, liberal forces stole the ornaments from the church of Petlalcingo in early 1857.[155]

Although the liberal forces managed to disperse conservatives around Acatlán in late January 1857, new reforms brought more uprisings. In February the national government ushered in the federalist Constitution, which introduced religious tolerance and confirmed the earlier measures.[156] In April, radicals prohibited the charging of parish dues, thus "liberating the poor," but undermining what had been a traditional mark of village piety.[157] In response, insurrections took place in Chila, Petlalcingo, and Tequixtepec in August. According to the local prefect, villagers collected over six thousand pesos to finance the rebellion.[158] A few months later rebels invaded Petlalcingo, handed round manifestos critical of the government, and robbed the shops of prominent liberals.[159] By late 1857, Mixteca Baja rebels joined up with regular conservative forces under the Puebla-based Spaniard José María Cobos. The conservative leader's message, that the liberal faction was a "destructive and turbulent, immoral and impious party" and that it threatened "social dissolution" by attacking the country's "strongest link . . . Religion," obviously chimed with local fears.[160]

Cobos's forces, including the two-hundred-strong "Luciano Martínez brigade" from the Mixteca Baja, took Huajuapan in early December and then moved south toward Oaxaca City.[161] Eventually, conservative units were forced to retreat, and liberal government was re-established soon after. But local rebellions continued throughout the following year. In May 1858 the liberal prefect sent troops to Tonalá where, it was rumored, he was holding covert Masses and "preaching against the government."[162] In December, a captured peasant recounted how the head of Nuchita's cofradías, because of his "more or less fanatic beliefs," had taken the cofradía funds and a band of local men and joined Tonalá's errant cleric.[163] Around Huajuapan, Ignacio Vázquez also organized a small band of about sixty men, formed of local peasants and a handful of deserters from the national guard that defeated Tezoatlán liberal José Segura y Guzmán's troops in Tonalá.[164] In response, the isolated liberal government employed increasingly savage pacification techniques, shaking down communities for taxes, combing the countryside for conservative spies, picking up and imprisoning wandering peasants, and even burning Nuchita to the ground.[165]

From 1856 to 1858 the conservative uprising in the Mixteca Baja was widespread but haphazard and disorganized, reliant on a handful of hard-nosed Huajuapan conservatives, individual rural priests, and their loyal local parishioners. But in 1859 sporadic uprisings coalesced into regional support for the conservative army. With conservative forces securely established in Mexico City, José María Cobos moved south again, linking up with Luciano Martínez's, Ignacio Vázquez's, and Felipe Martínez's irregular bands. By late 1859 Cobos's forces based in Tehuacán comprised around 1,150 infantrymen and 240 cavalrymen. Around 150 men and 100 cavalrymen came from Huajuapan.[166] Furthermore, according to the admittedly scant conservative records, most were volunteers, commanded by regional elites. According to one conservative observer, the fighting men knew "the state, were not forced to fight by leva . . . and were commanded by Luciano Martínez and other men from Huajuapan." In his opinion, "they ha[d] done many good services to the government."[167] In Tonalá at least thirty villagers joined up, commanded by a local peasant, Sebastian Solano.[168] In comparison, the liberals besieged inside the town of Huajuapan were forced to disband the national guard because of "a refusal to fight" and a high rate of desertion. The garrison now counted only eighty men, mostly from Oaxaca City, Tezoatlán, and Chilapa de Díaz.[169] In November 1859 the conservative forces captured Huajuapan, and two months later they defeated the last liberal forces at Tamazola, shooting prominent regional liberals like Emigdio Olivera and Miguel Luna.[170]

With conservative dominance of the region's countryside assured, Martínez toured the region's major pueblos, inciting opposition to Juárez's recent round of radical reforms that had been decreed in Veracruz just months before.[171] During the visits he read out a Oaxaca cleric's condemnation of the one of the decrees, which had declared goods "dedicated to cult" to be national property. If necessary, he translated the decree and the subsequent rebuke into Mixtec. The mandate, which attacked village ownership of cofradía property, struck at the heart of community clericalism—that mutual interdependence of priests and parishioners re-established during the late colonial period and continued throughout the early nineteenth century. As a result, most villages, instead of simply repeating the cleric's criticisms, added their own angry rebukes, revealing their genuine distaste for the liberal reforms and explaining their reinvigorated support for the conservative forces.

Most villages started their confirmations with extended personal condemnations of the liberal state's record. In Miltepec villagers complained that they could not "suffer more the oppression of the federal government whose laws are full of impiety." In Chila they lamented "the universal loss of our interests, our dead companions both in battle and by the impious hand of those that seek to destroy religion." In Tepeji they mocked the liberal triumvirate of "liberty, independence and progress," which simply sought to justify "disorder and sacrilege." As the examples suggest, villagers equated the raft of anticlerical measures, and especially the sale of communal cofradías, with an attack on religion itself. In Suchitepec villagers accused liberal authorities of "directly attacking our Catholic cult." In Ixitlán they argued that the government was "attacking in a direct manner and with premeditation our religion." Clearly, the subtleties of the liberal reforms—the thin line between the anticlerical and the antireligious— were lost in regions where elected cofradías, protected by the local clergy, still maintained village economies and shaped annual worship. Here, the defense of regional religion was all but indistinguishable from support for the institutional church.

The more loquacious peasants conflated this attack on religion with an attack on the patria and reiterated diocesan dictates that not only viewed Catholicism as Mexicans' unique bond but also saw Catholic observance and morality as key to the nation's success. In Tequixtepec they called the anticlerical reforms "an attack on our Independence" and claimed that the liberals wanted to "deprive us of all morality, the only bond of fraternity and the base of all society." Instead, they offered their support to the "defender of the great interests of our beloved Patria . . . a government which protects our religion, our persons, and our families." In San Sebastián del Monte villagers complained that the new laws would cause "disorder, immorality, and the destruction of the nation." Furthermore, they attempted to iron out the innate contradiction of the conservative insurrection, arguing that by fighting now, they guaranteed future peace. In Chila they claimed that they would "spill the last drop of blood" in support of the conservative cause in order to sustain "the peace and tranquility which we all wish to practice." In Tepeji they promised to ensure the "security of your lives and livelihoods" once victory was assured, ending their plea with "Long live the cause of order." Finally, in signing the agreements the provincial conservatives revealed the continuing importance of internal village hierarchies in which indigenous nobles still played formal religious and informal political roles. In at least a quarter of the responses, caciques—including Ignacio Bautista of Zapoquila, Francisco Ximénez of Acaquizapan, and Calixto Pimentel of Mixquixtlahuaca—declared their approval, often speaking for the village as a whole.[172]

Despite their control of the Mixteca Baja, over the next year U.S. support, popular national guard battalions, and liberal victories forced conservative troops to retreat. In August 1860 Porfirio Díaz and his Zapotec forces from the Sierra Juárez captured Oaxaca City and defeated Cobos and his heavily Mixtec army.[173] By September the conservative general and many of his allies had fled north. In the Mixteca Baja, some provincial conservatives fought on, mobilizing small bandit groups that harried liberal troops.[174] Yet most rejected the potential violence of guerrilla insurgency. When the Huajuapan merchant Miguel Moreno surrendered in January 1861, he defended his actions and those of other regional conservatives by claiming that they were "poor men, but honorable," who had simply committed a "political error." Reaching back to the conservative discourse of stability and order, he claimed that they had always acted "with morality, discipline and good faith, and never engaged in pillage, vandalism, or arson."[175] As a result, most conservatives returned to their towns and villages, ready to negotiate a working relationship with the triumphant liberals.

After the conservative defeat, politics in the Mixteca Baja changed. Provincial conservatives, cowed, demoralized, and perhaps less confident of the providential inevitability of conservative rule, drew back from confrontation. At the same time, ruling local liberals attempted, somewhat successfully, to secure regional support. Although they employed the laws privatizing cofradía properties to usurp fertile lands around the region's commercial towns, they also encouraged cacique land sales and allowed the continuation of tithes, church burials, and public religious ceremonies. This ambivalent position brought results. When the French arrived in the region in 1864, far fewer locals rallied to the conservative cause. In fact, the region split. Some supported the foreign invaders. But others, reassured of liberals' essentially pragmatic approach to issues of popular religiosity and communal landholding, backed the liberal rebels. By 1866 many had joined Porfirio Díaz's guerrilla insurrection, hoping to assure communal lands and cofradía properties through an alliance with their former enemies.

When the liberals returned to power in the Mixteca Baja in late 1860, they enforced the liberal Reform laws in a highly selective manner, making sure "policies if not always palatable were at least not so objectionable as to provoke a rebellious response."[176] Undoubtedly, the small liberal faction based in Huajuapan took control of the council and started to extend secular control over cofradía lands, destroying the forty-year pact between the town's indigenous and nonindigenous inhabitants. Following the state government's decrees, they claimed council control of the properties and started to sell them to interested parties. As a result, aspirant ranchers attempted to buy up the cofradías' most valuable lands. In January 1861 Rafael González, the owner of the Rancho de Jesús, claimed rights over the Rancho de Tano, where the town's cofradías used to pasture their sheep and goats.[177] But outside the region's rich central valleys, liberals permitted a less doctrinaire approach to the reforms. First, in a handful of villages they enhanced community control, continuing the conservative practice of cacique land sales. Between 1861 and 1864 liberals presided over the sale of ten thousand pesos' worth of cacique lands in six villages. Although liberal decrees expressly forbade villages from purchasing lands communally, the local authorities circumvented the issue by allowing individual peasants to buy the lands as shareholders in *sociedades agrícolas*, or agricultural societies.[178] (This legal evasion, which allowed communities to claim exclusive ownership over cacique lands and maintain cofradía properties, would be key to maintaining social stability and encouraging the regional adaption of provincial conservatism to the new economic dictates of the Porfiriato. It will be dealt with at length in the next chapter.) Second, they also allowed the continuation of orthodox religious practice in the region's rural villages. Priests continued to prohibit civil marriage, bury the dead inside churches, collect tithes, and preside over extravagant al fresco celebrations.[179] In late 1862 a visiting liberal complained to the state authorities that local communities remained "in complete ignorance of the laws of Reform."[180]

When the French invaded in 1862 to demand the repayment of Mexico's debt, the relatively lenient reality of local liberal governance persuaded many to support the country's national government. In 1862 the prefect of Huajuapan, José Segura y Guzmán, managed to mobilize over four hundred national guard members who joined up with the Army of the East.[181] Although many perished when a stray spark detonated a gunpowder store in Chalchicomula in March 1862, some survived to fight the French at the famous Battle of Puebla two months later.[182] Similarly, when the French-backed emperor Maximilian arrived in 1864, many inhabitants who had previously supported conservative regimes agreed to back the peripatetic liberal administration. Manuel de León, nephew of the former caudillo, led the resistance, announcing to the assembled citizens of Huajuapan that the conservatives were "traitors not Mexicans" and "traffickers in the liberty of our country."[183] Perhaps the patriotic rhetoric chimed with the Catholic nationalism that had inspired the Mixteca's battalion during the U.S.-Mexican war. Whatever the causes, the national guard, which had previously comprised a handful of mestizos from Chilapa de Díaz and Tezoatlán, now incorporated peasants from throughout the region.[184]

The French invasion and the arrival of Maximilian failed to inspire the kind of conservative support precipitated by the initial liberal reforms, but provincial support for a conservative administration did not disappear completely. From 1862 onward, local priests attempted to incite village rebellion. In April 1862 Miguel Navarrete, the local cleric of Tlachichilco, was reprimanded for "subverting the government" and preaching disobedience.[185] Three months later, the liberal authorities quashed attempted rebellions in Tequixtepec and Chila, both led by local priests.[186] In December the cleric of Huajolotitlán was accused of preaching insurrection, prosecuted, and ejected from the state.[187] In January liberal forces captured over two hundred lances hidden away under the priest of Chazumba's house.[188] At the same time, some former conservatives heeded the clerical call. In February 1863 Ignacio Vázquez and sixty members of the Huajuapan national guard deserted their barracks and declared for the empire.[189] By August they had assembled a force of nearly one hundred around Silacayoapan.[190] Yet without outside backing these anomalous rebellions gathered only limited support. When Vázquez briefly took Huajuapan in 1863 and demanded mass adherence to the conservative cause, most locals refused, and the rebels were forced to flee north toward Puebla.[191]

Although liberal moderation had undermined conservative support, in August 1864 the French army marched into the Mixteca Baja and captured Huajuapan. For the next two years provincial conservatives ran the region, matching the liberals for political initiative.[192] During the period, they attempted to reinvigorate their policies of Catholic education, devotional support, and cacique land sales, which had secured regional backing for the past half century. Barely a month after taking power, the new council of Huajuapan suggested the reopening of the town's Catholic school. They allowed the two local priests to devise a syllabus that would "destroy any anti-Catholic ideas that the children may have learned." They also agreed to pay the Catholic teacher a "decent" annual salary and collect funds for the purchase of a "religious painting" that would be hung at the back of the classroom to "inspire the children."[193] Outside the region's towns, rural priests also restored local schools. In early 1865 the priest of Chazumba offered the local council twenty pesos to fund "a teacher of Christian doctrine."[194] At the same time, provincial conservatives attempted to harness support for regional devotions. In late 1864 the priest of Tlacotepec encouraged the villagers of Ixpantepec to hold a "great celebration to the Virgin of the Mixteca" the following year and offered twenty-five pesos of his own money.[195] In the same year in Huajuapan the conservative council members each paid twenty reals toward an elaborate Mass for Our Lord of Hearts.[196] Finally, conservatives also continued to protect indigenous landholding. In December 1864 the Huajuapan council concluded that the repartition of town lands had been done "with much iniquity." As a result, it decreed that that the indigenous barrios no longer had to pay rent.[197] Furthermore, during his brief tenure the conservative prefect employed the same legal loophole as his liberal predecessor, allowing at least six local communities to purchase cacique lands as agricultural societies.[198]

Continued conservative concessions brought some results. When Porfirio Díaz escaped from prison in September 1865, fled to Guerrero, and started his campaign anew, only José Segura y Guzmán's Chilapa de Díaz reserves joined the future dictator's forces.[199] Over the following year, many locals risked liberal reprisals by refusing to offer food or money to the insurgent liberals.[200] Furthermore, when Díaz attacked Huajuapan on September 4, 1866, national forces and local troops defended the town successfully.[201] However, as the liberals gathered strength in the Mixteca Alta and the Sierra Juárez, the conservative coalition of Austrians, French, and national soldiers started to disintegrate, and Maximilian continued to support a liberal agenda, provincial conservatives in the Mixteca Baja began to switch sides.[202] In June 1866 Ignacio Vázquez's national guard deserters deserted again and linked up with Porfirio Díaz's Army of the East.[203] On October 18, 1866, they played a vital role in the liberal victory of La Carbonera, surprising the Austrian troops from the rear.[204] For the next six months they fought at Díaz's side, mopping up conservative stragglers in Puebla and around Mexico City.[205]

In much of Oaxaca, liberal anticlericalism made little negative impact. In fact, many peasants welcomed the elimination of tithes, the reduction of parish fees, and even the removal of cofradía properties from clerical control.[206] In Macuiltianguis in the Sierra Juárez villagers told a visiting French photographer that the flight of the local priest not only saved the community four thousand pesos per year, but also allowed local elders to give Mass instead.[207] As a result, few villages rallied to the alarmist declamations of the state's isolated rural preachers. Instead, liberal politicians harnessed popular support by adapting the federalist dictates of community autonomy to the necessities of mass mobilization. In the Sierra Juárez, Mixteca Alta, and the Isthmus of Tehuantepec, village leaders maintained municipal control, softened the implementation of liberal land laws, and marshaled local units of the national guard.[208] In contrast, in the Mixteca Baja provincial conservatives took the liberal threats to local priests, community cofradías, and even clerical charges extremely seriously. Here, over twenty years of confrontation with neighboring radical federalists had cemented relations between ethnic, class, and devotional groups and sharpened popular clericalism. As a result, between 1856 and 1860 and again between 1863 and 1866, elites and non-elites fought voluntarily for conservative governments. Only major liberal concessions, the dissolution of the conservative alliance, and the military success of Porfirio Díaz produced a late conversion to the winning side.

Comparison and Conclusion

In Oaxaca the provincial conservatism of the Mixteca Baja had little comparison. And from the 1830s onward, many peasant groups throughout Mexico made the same pragmatic decision as most of their southern compatriots, prioritizing the federalist aspects of liberalism over its threats to regional order and clerical power. In Guerrero, the Huasteca, and the Sierra Gorda, peasants fought against centralist elites to usurp municipal control and regain communal lands.[209] During the 1850s peasants from the Sierra Norte de Puebla, Morelos, eastern Michoacán, and Guerrero did the same, taking advantage of the political opportunity to mobilize armed groups and re-establish community control.[210] Although these insurgents did not share the programmatic, secularizing anticlericalism of their reformist liberal leaders, religion still played an important role. In these regions of de-Christianization limited church influence had encouraged the interplay of unauthorized religious practices and popular anticlericalism.[211] As in Copala, Putla, or Tlapa, these two factors worked together to motivate and provide allies for radical uprisings. As Elio Masferrer Kan argues, the Totonacs of Papantla had sustained conflictive relations with Catholic priests over church funds, education, and religious practices since the eighteenth century. When the bishop of Puebla prohibited the region's rowdy Easter week celebration in 1836, he precipitated a widespread federalist revolt.[212] Similarly, in the Yucatán declining clerical prominence weakened parish ties, ramped up popular anticlericalism, and eventually encouraged the outbreak of a radical insurgency that repeatedly targeted unpopular priests.[213] After the Reform laws of 1856, popular anti-clericalism and religious heterodoxy also acted to anaesthetize regional liberals to the alarmist clamor of the conservative clergy.[214] As Guy Thomson argues, in the Sierra Norte persistent arguments between a weak church and village Jacobins over parish fees and cofradía control preceded the liberal insurrection.[215] In the Sierra Gorda, popular liberals congregated around the former stronghold of the unsanctioned colonial devotion to the indigenous man-god the Cristo Viejo.[216]

However, in contrast to these areas of popular insurrection, in many regions elites and peasants supported conservative regimes. First, despite the increasingly autocratic dictates of metropolitan conservatives, many of their provincial allies allowed the continuation of indigenous self-rule. During the first post-Independence decades, regional centralism was often extremely selective. In the Valley of Mexico, municipal leaders simply permitted former repúblicas to appoint local officials as before.[217] In Sonora, the conservative leader Manuel Gandara brokered an agreement with the Yaquis, which allowed a degree of indigenous autonomy.[218] Second, in regions of economic stagnation elites were content to permit indigenous land tenure or even the peasant usurpation of hacienda lands.[219] Around Mexico City, conservative authorities established an office charged with the protection of the properties of the conurbation's indigenous barrios.[220] Even in more dynamic regions, like Michoacán, conservative leaders attempted to guard against the complete sell-off of indigenous communal lands.[221]

Third, if de-Christianization shaped federalist revolts, re-Christianization, or the firming up of relations between the laity and the clergy and the conflation of clerical expectations and popular rituals, marked mass backing for conservative regimes. Here, the church's institutional strength, inherited from the late colonial period, encouraged lay-clerical dialogue, shared interethnic devotions, church-building, and an acceptance of the political necessity of Christian morality. As a result, in these regions clerical influence remained strong, sharpening popular responses to perceived anticlericalism; persuading inhabitants of the conflation of communal, national, and ecclesiastical interests; and generating a popular, defensive clericalism. Most provincial conservative strongholds like Querétaro (Querétaro), Tepic (Nayarit), Zinapecuaro and Zamora (Michoacán), Tulancingo (Hidalgo), Chalpancingo (Guerrero), Huamantla (Tlaxcala), and Cholula,

Chignahuapan, Zacapoaxtla, and Chiautla (Puebla) had long histories of clerical predominance linked to prolonged missionary influence or the successful renegotiation of lay-clerical relations during the late colonial period.[222] For example, during the early nineteenth century secular priests in Tepic had sustained strong indigenous attachment to the church through the support of community cofradías. As a result, when liberals introduced anticlerical reforms targeting cofradía lands, mestizo merchants and indigenous peasants, under the leadership of Manuel Lozada, rose up in revolt.[223] In the late 1700s secular clergy in Zinapecuaro initiated a similar process of successful orthodox renewal, supporting local Christocentric cults and emphasizing sacramental devotion.[224] During the early nineteenth century local priests maintained church influence, establishing Catholic schools and encouraging the construction of village churches. During the 1850s and 1860s the region would become a center of conservative support.[225] Other conservative centers benefitted from very recent traditions of lay-clerical interaction. Between 1831 and 1853 the priest of Tlatlauqui (Puebla) donated seven new images to the parishes' churches. He also encouraged local devotions and funneled church collections toward the introduction of potable water and the provision of free meals and clothing for the poor. Although the priest left before the outbreak of hostilities, the town remained strongly proclerical throughout the civil war.[226]

Fourth, proximity to regions of radical federalist rebellion, "caste war," or endemic banditry also accentuated conservative backing. Community insecurity precipitated mass support for the conservative prioritization of order and stability and the clerical emphasis on Christian morality. Furthermore, the mobilization of local militias to combat federalist revolts cemented interethnic and cross-class ties. Tomás Mejía's extensive support network in the Sierra Gorda was founded on "loyal" indigenous militias who had fought with the caudillo against both "Apaches" and federalist rebels.[227] Lozada's initial supporters were indigenous and mixed-race peasants from armed frontier populations, well used to the interethnic co-operation that military service demanded.[228] There is even some evidence that Lozada and his Huichol allies were originally trained and employed as bandit hunters.[229]

Peasants were essentially pragmatic, and contingent factors, including rapid political concessions, sudden land grabs, and unpopular local clerics, could derail these general trends at the local level. But if we stand back from these regional rationales, a rough cartography of political sympathies emerges. Until now, historians have viewed political allegiances as fitting a fairly basic core-periphery model. For Richard Sinkin and David Brading, the Hispanicized colonial heartlands of Mexico City, Puebla, and the Bajío formed the conservative center, while the bordering states (Oaxaca, Guerrero, Michoacán, Jalisco, Zacatecas, San Luis Potosí, and Veracruz) formed a surrounding "liberal archipelago."[230] Although the system explains broad national cleavages, it fails to acknowledge the strong influence of rural conservative groups. In fact, conservative Mexico encompassed a tough core formed of doctrinaire, metropolitan conservatives and a series of extended, provincial conservative spokes. These spokes, which often followed traditional commercial routes, reached up into liberal areas. They were dotted with highly clerical mercantile towns and, if land tenure was uncontroversial, loyal indigenous and mestizo hinterlands. Periodic postcolonial conflicts between these outlying conservative regions and the surrounding liberal territories over municipal influence, agrarian development, and lay-clerical relations intensified liturgical and political divisions. By the 1850s, regional fissures dovetailed with national divisions. Metropolitan and provincial conservatives and metropolitan and popular liberals gradually aligned and engaged in the bloody conflicts of the succeeding decade.

Drawing parallels with the rest of Latin America is more problematic. In general, popular political mobilization was less commonplace than in Mexico, and most conservative regimes were top-down affairs redolent of Santa Anna's last disastrous dictatorship.[231] Yet certain similarities remain. Even the most authoritarian regimes were more pragmatic than much of their rhetoric suggested. Even Brazil's proslavery conservatives embraced a degree of constitutionalism.[232] Convinced of the unifying power of the Catholic religion, obsessed by stability and order, and by turns populist and patrician, many of the continent's conservative caudillos, such as Juan Manuel de Rosas in Argentina, Gabriel Garcia Moreno in Ecuador, or Rafael Carrera in Guatemala, seem like magnified versions of the Mixteca Baja's Antonio de León.[233] Further down the social hierarchy, symbiotic economic relations between elites and non-elites promoted cross-class support for broadly conservative movements. In the decades leading up to Peru's royalist revolt in Huanta (1825–1828), local hacendados and villagers established strong patron-client ties in the cattle-rustling business.[234] At the same time, the popular conservative assertion that radicals, by taking on the church, were threatening social stability, God's favor, and the nation's fate was key to fomenting the Huanta rebellion, Colombia's 1876–1877 civil war, and Carrera's popular support.[235] Finally, there is also evidence that military traditions, either emerging from communities' frontier status or the challenges of the wars of Independence, not only generated interethnic alliances but also aligned populations against the threat of radical change.[236]

In fact, decades of research and parallel traditions of popular mobilization make comparison with Europe much easier. During the period 1750 to 1850 in many Catholic countries, "regions of re-Christianization" developed alongside "regions of de-Christianization," delineating liturgical divides between more and less clerical areas. In France, Enlightenment Catholicism was most effective not where it crushed popular practices, but rather where the "clergy was able to impose its influence while maintaining a viable and flexible modus vivendi with popular expressions of religious sentiment."[237] These regions, including the Vendée, would become centers of popular clericalism and resist revolutionary anticlericalism through armed revolt. Fifty years later, comparable approaches to channeling popular piety achieved similarly favorable results.[238] In Germany, successful priests like those of Bavaria were equally pragmatic, resisting reformed Catholicism's rationalist impulses, embracing miracle and mystery, and meeting popular religion in the middle.[239] Again, these regions would become bastions of resistance to the *Kulturkampf* program of the 1860s. In Spain, successful clerics also balanced their encouragement of clerical obedience with some popular innovations.[240] Yet differences are also apparent. In France especially, the political expression of this particular brand of religiosity became intimately tied to reactionary politics, whereas in Germany, as in Mexico, popular clericalism included a degree of lay liberty and the acceptance of certain democratic ideals.[241]

CHAPTER 4

"The spirit of God . . . in the hearts of everybody"

Liberalism Modified and Catholicism Resurgent, 1867–1910

O N FEBRUARY 28, 1879, THE PRIEST OF ZAHUATLÁN, FELICIANO
Ramírez, visited the village of Amatitlán to hold Mass in honor of the
local image of Our Lord of Health. After the service, Ramírez noticed the
Christ had started to sweat. He mopped the statue, but by the time he had
called his fiscal to inspect the occurrence, the body was covered in globules
of water again. Over the next few hours the priest called together the entire
village population, who looked on the "miracle . . . in silence." According to
Ramírez, they interpreted the droplets falling from the statue as "eloquent
signs of the most tender affections of Christ's heart." Despite the sweating
Christ of Amatitlán's humble beginnings, the diocesan authorities, convinced by the priest and the municipal authorities' impassioned witness
statements, allowed the cult to continue. Over the next decade villagers from
around the region made regular pilgrimages to the site during the feast day
on the first Friday of Lent.[1] Although the empire's defeat concluded the political heyday of Mexican conservatism, local relations between merchants and
peasants and ecclesiastical authorities and lay worshippers shaped regional
responses to the new liberal state. In the Mixteca Baja, the authorization of
the sweating statue reveals the ongoing accord between priests and parishioners. Priests understood the true foci of popular devotion and did not

attempt to supplant these images with too many new foreign cults. At the same time, parishioners comprehended the limits of ecclesiastical patience and celebrated a distinctly orthodox and clerical miracle rather than a lay visionary or an indigenous healer. The story of these negotiations and how they affected the region's political, social, and economic development is the focus of this chapter.

Between 1867 and 1910 the victorious liberals held power in Mexico, first under the civil leaders Benito Juárez (1867–1872) and Sebastián Lerdo de Tejeda (1872–1876), and then under the military dictator Porfirio Díaz (1876–1880, 1884–1911). During the period, they attempted to impose a functional version of the liberal ideology, for which they had fought over a decade of civil war, on Mexico's expanding urban centers and recalcitrant rural hinterlands. On the one hand, in order to maintain social stability they retreated from their wartime support for radical liberalism, increasing central state power, curbing regional autonomy, and reducing municipal self-rule.[2] For the same reason, they also drew back from implementing the more controversial aspects of anticlerical legislation, forging pacts with conciliatory ecclesiastical leaders and ignoring all but the most egregious infringements of laws concerning public worship, church property, and Catholic education.[3] On the other hand, they also pursued an increasingly disruptive policy of agricultural modernization, building on Reform-era laws to divvy up communal village lands and cofradía properties. Although the move was originally designed to promote a vibrant land market and create a class of individual property holders, by the 1890s the laws were increasingly used to alienate peasant lands and augment large haciendas.[4] By 1910 the effects of what Charles Hale rather confusingly dubbed this "conservative liberalism" were felt. The disjunction between liberal political ideology on the one hand and centralizing practice and the "land grab" of village-owned properties on the other combined to precipitate an alliance of middle-class political reformers and land-hungry peasants and the outbreak of the first revolution of the twentieth century.[5]

This traditional narrative of the Restored Republic and the Porfiriato, most cogently restated by Alan Knight, is still extremely persuasive.[6] After four decades of uninterrupted rule, the top-down system of political appointment had become dogmatic and inflexible, its regional point men old, unresponsive, and authoritarian.[7] At the same time, the construction of roads, railways, and ports had opened up Mexico's agricultural base to foreign markets, stimulating the growth of commercial crops, raising land prices, and

escalating both legal and illegal assumptions of village lands in insurrection-
ist foci like Morelos and many other smaller towns and villages.[8] For good
reason the most oft-spoke battle cries of the Revolution were "Free election,
no boss rule!" and "Land and liberty!" Yet as numerous scholars have argued,
such a stark teleology of political despotism and economic extraction fails
to encompass the multiple ways in which local peasants, industrial workers,
and regional chiefs experienced the period and, by extension, the myriad
responses to the Revolution of 1910.[9] First, despite Juárez and Díaz's policies of political control and religious appeasement, old political allegiances
died hard. In particular, radical liberalism with its interlinking principles
of local rule, communal land tenure, and anticlericalism was robust, persistent, and influential. Up until the last years of the Porfiriato in the Sierra
Norte de Puebla, the Sierra Juárez, and even Morelos, peasant groups sought
to curb imperious *jefes políticos*, rogue rurales, electoral impositions, and
controversial land sales by invoking personal debts, wartime alliances, and
popular patriotism.[10] Although they achieved differing degrees of success,
this radical liberalism, retooled and redirected, undergirded many revolutionary insurgencies. Emiliano Zapata, agrarian rebel, author of the Plan
of Ayala, and son of a radical liberal insurgent, found no inspiration in the
anarchist pronouncements of Ricardo Flores Magón. Instead, echoing his
father's beliefs, he demanded the correct implementation of the Constitution
of 1857.[11]

Second, although infrastructure, market demand, and liberal laws
transformed national patterns of land tenure, at the regional level the effects
were distinctly mixed. Roads and railways only reached so far, and many
central agricultural areas still produced solely for regional markets. In some
areas, like Jalisco and Querétaro, haciendas "achieved a certain popular
legitimacy," providing temporary work, sharecropping opportunities, and a
limited threat.[12] In other areas, like Toluca, where "the change from communal to private property did not open the doors to speculation, monopoly and
large landholding," peasants embraced the shift, legalizing equitably divided
agricultural parcels and ring-fencing communal forests and pastures.[13]
Outside Mexico's central breadbasket, land tenure diverged even further.
In parallel strips along the sierras' foothills, mestizo and indigenous farmers used liberal laws to buy up unclaimed land and establish small family
ranches devoted to wheat, corn, and cattle production.[14] Meanwhile among
the sierras' more inhospitable peaks, indigenous villages simply ignored the
laws, maintaining communal lands free of outside interference until their

eventual confirmation by the postrevolutionary state.[15] During the revolutionary and postrevolutionary decades, these different systems of land tenure shaped regional political allegiances, delineating alternate responses to radical land reform programs.

Third, the covert pact between state and ecclesiastical authorities not only tempered civil war antagonisms, but also permitted a revival of the Catholic Church. While the ultramontane first generation of Porfirian bishops, imbued with the example of Pius IX's intransigence, publically refused to compromise on issues of ecclesiastical status and property, behind the scenes they quietly rebuilt and reoriented the Mexican church, attempting to create a "spiritual enclave or societas perfectas" replete with a well-trained and obedient clergy and a regimented and deferential laity.[16] Under the tutelage of these conservative veterans, the second generation of Porfirian prelates followed suit, gradually extending church influence into the gray area between private and public devotion. Yet they also went further. Many of the new bishops were educated at the Colegio Pío Latino Americano in Rome and were influenced by the currents of Social Catholicism that were sweeping the Vatican at the time.[17] When they returned to Mexico, they combined political belligerence with a new focus on the Christian solution to social inequality. During the first years of the new century, they held a series of conferences on the matter, established mutual aid societies and workers' circles, and attempted to extend church schools to the poor.[18] Although the effects of these ecclesiastical projects were mixed, in many regions they strengthened lay-clerical alliances and precipitated strong church support. Over the succeeding decades, especially when the postrevolutionary state sought to impose anticlerical policies, these new relations shaped political allegiances.

Building on these recent historiographical shifts, this chapter seeks to explain political, economic, and religious changes in the Mixteca Baja and to suggest reasons for the region's combative response to the Revolution and the revolutionary state. The chapter comprises four sections. In the first section, I examine the politics of local liberal governance. Although Porfirio Díaz relied on one of his former soldiers, Ignacio Vázquez, to rule the region for most of his reign, such a populist delegation failed to engender the maintenance of a radical liberal political culture, as it did in the Sierra Norte de Puebla or the Sierra Juárez. Vázquez and his supporters were former conservatives. Throughout their thirty-year rule, they sought to mold liberal policies to the region's existing social system, Catholicizing nationalist celebrations, encouraging church education, permitting the continuation of village rule, curbing the disruptive effects of mercantile capital, and promoting the maintenance of equitable landholding. In the second section I look at the economic effects of the Porfiriato. Although the arrival of a cabal of Spanish merchants and the growth of the sugar industry caused some discontent, deliberate political neutrality, the poor quality of lands, and peasant entrepreneurship combined to allow the expansion of communal landholdings in the form of *sociedades agrícolas*, or agricultural societies. Privately purchased but equitably divided and interspersed with illegal *cofradía* plots, these societies would prove to be bulwarks against the attractions of land distribution during the succeeding decades. The third and fourth sections examine the region's religious revival. Protected by a deeply Catholic political establishment, funded by the region's indigenous *cofradías*, and staffed by local elites, the church weathered the initial liberal reforms well. By the 1890s a new generation of aggressive, well-educated clerics headed by the vicar general, Rafael Amador y Hernández, sought to combine Roman regimentation and Social Catholicism with their sympathy for local traditions. The project, which culminated in the creation of the Diocese of the Mixtecas in 1903, was extremely successful, generating a mass of new local priests, urban and rural lay organizations, charity establishments, church schools, and regional cults.

Provincial Conservatism in a Liberal Nation

After the liberal victory, Oaxaca's major statesmen Benito Juárez, Porfirio Díaz, and Díaz's brother Felix divided up the state's regions among their wartime backers. Although Juárez and his moderate liberal supporters (dubbed the *borlados*) controlled most of the state, the Díaz brothers managed to appoint their own clients in certain key regions.[19] In the border districts of the Mixteca Baja, Díaz endorsed two former soldiers from the region: José Segura y Guzmán and Ignacio Vázquez. While Segura ruled the district of Huajuapan, Vázquez controlled the neighboring district of Silacayoapan.[20] Segura, a mestizo rancher originally from Chilapa de Díaz, had been a fervent liberal since 1854. He had supported the Plan of Ayutla and the liberal reforms and risen up against the French Intervention. Doctrinaire, radical, and anticlerical, he had gained fame for his heavy-handed fiscal policies, punitive political measures, and occasional iconoclasm.[21] He had been responsible for the burning of Nuchita and the sacking and destruction of the Chila church. In many ways, Segura exemplified the new breed of radical liberals on which Díaz relied but with one crucial difference: he possessed very little popular support. Thus, Díaz also appointed a conservative, Vázquez, as *jefe político* of the newly created district of Silacayoapan in order to ensure stability in a former conservative stronghold. Vázquez was born into a family of mestizo merchants in Huajuapan in 1839 and embodied the political tradition of provincial conservatism. Although he transferred loyalties to Díaz in 1866, as a young soldier he had combated the Plan of Ayutla, risen up against the liberal reforms, and joined the French-backed conservative government. Although Vázquez's economic status remained modest, kinship ties linked him to the local elite. His mother was a member of the Acevedo clan, and his brother's wife was former spouse of the last cacique of Chichihualtepec and owner of the indigenous leader's last remaining ranch.[22]

As Segura's and Vázquez's political affiliations stood in opposition, there were unspoken tensions between the two. Segura repeatedly complained that, following the advice of local clergymen, few parents sent their children to the new secular schools. In his 1870 report, he claimed that "continuing priestly influence" in the district made the residents "intractable" and "stubborn."[23] In contrast, Vázquez openly supported clerical foot-dragging over the implementation of the reforms by failing to impose the civil registry, permitting the continued teaching of church doctrine, and even helping to finance Silacayoapan's annual fiesta.[24] Despite these differences, both Segura and Vázquez were united by their reliance on Díaz's political patronage. When Juárez defeated Díaz in the 1871 presidential elections, both leaders rose up in support of their patron and signed the Plan of La Noria. Vázquez especially employed his local savvy to gather local support, promising villages that they would no longer have to hand over contributions for secular schools and gathering over 140 troops.[25] Despite Vázquez's endeavors, the Porfirian insurrection ended in defeat. Segura retired for reasons of ill health, and Vázquez was shunted from office. *Borlado* supporters of Juárez from outside the region took control. The imposition did not last for long. In 1876 Díaz rebelled against his failure to achieve the presidency again, this time under the Plan of Tuxtepec. In Huajuapan, Vázquez took the municipal palace, persuaded the garrison to support the Oaxaca caudillo, and helped to defeat Sebastián Lerdo de Tejeda's supporters at Yanhuitlán.[26] Loyalty brought rewards, and when Díaz became president in late 1876, he immediately made Vázquez a general and confirmed his election as local deputy for Huajuapan.[27] Vázquez's rise to prominence seems to offer local ballast to the oft-repeated argument that Díaz came to power with the support of former conservatives. There is some evidence for the assertion. Metropolitan Catholic newspapers and former religioneros from Michoacán supported Díaz's rebellion and sought respite from Lerdo's hard-nosed implementation of the Reform laws. Yet the Tuxtepec coup was no backdoor conservative insurgency.[28] Díaz was simply a supreme political pragmatist with the guerrilla fighter's nose for regional variation. Where initial conservative support caused public disenchantment, as in Mexico City, he backed liberal attacks. But in the Mixteca Baja, where provincial conservatives had long ruled, he allowed Vázquez and his band of conservative turncoats to rule with little interference.

Vázquez would lead the Mixteca Baja for the next twenty-five years as military commander, political chief, regional kingmaker, and Díaz's informal intermediary. From 1877 onward Vázquez took the monthly salary of a general.[29] As the region's leading military official, he continued to lead rurales against political rebels and bandits until the 1890s.[30] At the same time, he also took formal political positions as jefe político during the late 1870s, as police chief from 1884 to 1888, and as federal deputy from 1890 until his death in 1901.[31] Vázquez also used his influence with the president to ensure that members of his faction ruled other important regional posts. In 1881 he persuaded Díaz to appoint his cousin as the new jefe político, and in 1886 the same cousin was appointed federal deputy.[32] At the same time, municipal presidents of Huajuapan, like Zenón Acevedo (1881–1883), Luis Niño de Rivera (1883–1884, 1886–1888), and Aurelio García (1889–1892) were his relatives or compadres.[33] As we shall see, during Vázquez's long tenure as regional cacique he attempted to alleviate the economic and cultural effects of the liberal reforms, permitting the continuation of communal landholding and turning a blind eye toward infringements of laws prohibiting church schooling, church burials, public religious ceremonies, cofradía land ownership, and tithe collection. Furthermore, although he always attempted to appear as a loyal liberal warrior (his small autobiography in the archive of the Ministry of Defense is a master class in selective recall and deliberate obfuscation), this surreptitious continuation of provincial conservative policies periodically came to light in his attempts to manipulate political ceremony, his clashes with the region's small minority of radical liberals, and his perpetuation of decentralized village rule.

Throughout the Porfiriato statesmen, regional leaders, peasants, and workers, freed from the pressures of internecine warfare, started to celebrate a unifying national culture focused on a secular calendar of political events and military triumphs. As numerous historians have pointed out, these were negotiated events, standard texts interspersed with relevant regional, ethnic, and class motifs.[34] Thomson describes how indigenous radical liberals from the Sierra Norte de Puebla actively developed an anticlerical and anticonservative "patriotic liberalism" focused on the region's own martial experiences during the civil war. In order to do so, former guerrillas formed philharmonic bands and patriotic juntas; dutifully celebrated the anniversaries of the Plan of Ayutla, the victory at Puebla, and the publication of the Constitution; and even translated the Constitution into Nahuatl.[35] In former regions of provincial conservatism, like the Mixteca Baja, local leaders interpreted national history in a completely different way. Although they mirrored the radicals' regional focus, they ignored the most controversial liberal celebrations and Catholicized the more acceptable events. The liberal José Segura y Guzmán had attempted to start regional celebrations of the Constitution and the Battle of Puebla during his brief reign, but he claimed that the people had "little enthusiasm" for the events.[36] By the 1870s, Vázquez had dropped the celebrations completely. In 1889 a rival claimed that both anniversaries had "never been celebrated" in Huajuapan.[37] The lack of enthusiasm for celebrating the Constitution was hardly surprising given the region's historic animosity to the reforms. Throughout the Porfiriato, most of the region's municipal councils wrote to their local priests to ask for a pardon for swearing to the "atheist document" whenever they took charge.[38]

Instead, Vázquez and his supporters emphasized two local patriotic events, both of which they linked to the institutional church and portrayed as evidence of God's providential plans. First, they memorialized the lifting of the siege of Huajuapan in 1812 and held a celebration on July 23 each year. The occasion not only involved the usual bell-ringing, fireworks, military maneuvers, and other "expressions of pure patriotism," but also a Mass in the local church, a speech by the vicar general, and a special service in the chapel devoted to the town's alleged savior, Our Lord of Hearts.[39] Second, they commemorated the Battle of Molino del Rey, holding an annual ceremony on September 8, forming the "Patriotic Society Antonio de León," erecting a statue to the dead hero, and instigating elaborate funeral rites for the last of the battle's surviving soldiers. Again the celebrations were linked to the local church. Throughout the period, members of the patriotic society paid for a monthly Mass in honor of León on the eighth of each month.[40] At the fiftieth anniversary of his death, they organized a Mass, a speech by the vicar general, a parade of children to lay flowers on the caudillo's church tomb, and a series of speeches that lauded León's "Christian values" and "divine patriotism."[41] In so doing, they maintained the culture of Catholic nationalism, that sense of the intimate link between individual moral comportment, regional fate, and national success, which had imbued political conservatism for over two decades and would, after the Revolution, form the cultural carapace of regional clericalism and PAN support.

If Vázquez's cultural enterprises undermined local liberal enthusiasm, his regional predominance brought him into direct conflict with an unwieldy, opportunist, and ultimately doomed alliance of radical liberals, Spanish émigrés, and state politicians. The radical liberals were led by Segura's successor, Casimiro Ramírez, a rich Huajuapan rancher who had spent over a decade fighting for the liberals under Felix Díaz. When he returned to his hometown in the late 1870s he expected due political recompense but found his route blocked by Vázquez and his group of former conservatives.[42] The Spanish émigrés, led by the merchant, moneylender, and sugar hacendado José Gómez, were angered by Vázquez's failure to prosecute the murderer of one of their sons and his refusal to enforce their strict interpretation of property laws on indigenous villages.[43] Finally, the state governor, Albino Zertuche (1888–1890), was an old adversary of Vázquez from the civil war.[44] During the late 1880s, these adversaries came together to attempt to push the local cacique from power. At first they complained to Díaz of Vázquez's dubious political heritage, his failure to implement the Reform laws, and his open support for "murderers, bandits, and thieves."[45] Then in 1889 they attempted to overturn his recommendation for the municipal presidents of Huajuapan and Tonalá, claiming that the candidates were "old," "reactionary," and "perverse."[46] In response, Díaz played the mediator, supporting Ramírez's candidate in Tonalá and Vázquez's candidate in Huajuapan. The Solomonic gesture quickly ended the brief contretemps. Zertuche stood down soon afterward, and without state support the region's radicals were forced to accept Vázquez's rule.[47]

Outside the region's major towns, Vázquez's politics echoed those of his conservative forebears. In particular, he permitted the continuation of village self-rule. During the 1860s, liberal politicians in Oaxaca City had attempted to assert control over the former conservative stronghold by limiting the Mixteca Baja's municipalities, reducing the number to a paltry eighteen.[48] However, within a few decades a combination of popular pressure and Vázquez's support returned the region to pre-Reform levels of political decentralization. By 1895 the legislature had created around fifty new municipalities. Huajuapan, with seventy-four administrative units, had more than any other district.[49] Even when Vázquez was unable to engineer the creation of a new municipality, he suggested extralegal means to maintain village rule. For example, in 1888 the sixty Mixtec-speaking inhabitants of Guadalupe Olleras complained that the municipal council of Chazumba refused to recognize their lands, hassled them for taxes, corralled them into public service, and refused to allow them to appoint their own municipal agent. Although the liberal Constitution stated that all villages with under five hundred inhabitants were subject to a municipality's dominion, the jefe político ignored the law and told the burghers of Chazumba to leave Olleras alone. From now on the small ranch was in substance, if not in name, a municipality. The fifteen families that comprised the village were responsible for the division of pastoral lands, tax collection, their children's education, and the election of a municipal agent.[50]

Rural politics during the period not only witnessed the conflict between positivist, centralizing Porfirian emissaries and radical, liberal former guerrillas, but also the gradual recovery of the provincial conservatives. Don Porfirio's genius was not only his harnessing of radical liberal support but also his targeted delegation of power to former enemies. In Yucatán, Díaz supported Olegario Molina's clerical faction over the anticlerical clique led by Carlos Peón and helped usher in a resurgent Catholic Church, the expansion of rural clergy, and the reintroduction of tithes.[51] In Tulancingo, Tepic, Querétaro, Colima, and Campeche, don Porfirio did the same, allying with clerical strongmen and permitting the expansion of church governance and the creation of new dioceses.[52] Like Vázquez, these clerical caciques were distinctly two faced, maintaining the appearance of liberal orthodoxy while redirecting populist patriotism toward an old-fashioned Catholic nationalism.

Land and the Economy

According to the dominant narrative of the Porfiriato, land tenure during the period changed dramatically, concentrating land in the hands of a few hacendados at the expense of peasant communities. Even in a heavily indigenous state like Oaxaca, the general model has some validity. As Francie Chassen-López and Manuel Esparza argue, the expansion of the markets for rubber, coffee, bananas, timber, cattle, and more traditional crops led to an exponential rise in haciendas, fincas, and smaller ranches. By 1912 the government reported that the state had 450 large landholdings, a nearly sixfold increase since 1857.[53] Yet these broad economic changes percolated through to the regional level in different ways and at divergent paces. As Michael Ducey argues, "The results of the liberal legislation were more mixed than the inflexible articles of the laws suggest."[54] Oaxaca's precipitous geography, ethnic diversity, and alternate histories of indigenous landholding meant that many regions escaped or at least modified this process. Thus, although the few scholars of the Mixteca Baja argue that during the period there emerged a new Spanish-born landholding and commercial elite, they only tell part of the story.[55] As we shall see, the arrival of a cabal of Spanish merchants did precipitate some economic changes, including the expansion of the sugar industry and a rise in cash loans. Yet more importantly, the Porfiriato witnessed a huge redistribution of land toward the peasants. Between 1830 and 1890, indigenous villages bought up the vast majority of the region's properties as agricultural societies. As a result, relations between elites and non-elites were once again redrawn but not completely destroyed. The era of cacique rule ended, but in its place peasants received land, and merchants took advantage of this new, broader landholding class to extract interest and pasture their huge herds of sheep and goats.

During the mid-nineteenth century the pattern of land tenure in the Mixteca Baja shifted radically. Indigenous caciques, who had owned 60 percent of the region's land, bypassed the disinterested local elite and sold the vast majority of their properties to their indigenous former tenants. Between 1833 and 1867 thirty-six pieces of land were sold in the district of Huajuapan alone. Between 1867 and 1900 another thirty-seven were sold (see appendix F). Extrapolating from the sales for which figures remain, they were worth around two hundred thousand pesos. By 1900 the peasant share of regional landholding had jumped from around 27 percent in 1830 to around 80 percent.[56] The remaining lands comprised two haciendas, La Pradera and Santa Barbara, and a host of small ranches owned by former indigenous caciques, Spanish émigrés, and the Huajuapan elite.

At first, the region's peasants bought the land as entire villages, splitting the cost of purchase between each community member. However, soon they encountered a problem. The liberal reforms of the midcentury banned communal ownership. In 1856, 1859, and 1862 liberal governors passed laws that demanded the privatization of village lands. During the following decades, they upped the pressure on peasants to conform to the laws, complaining that the privatization "had not been practiced in many populations." In 1889 the dislocation between liberal legislation and rural reality came to a head.

State authorities demanded that municipalities declare all those lands privatized since 1862. The following year, they extended the law to include not only fertile agricultural lands, but also pastures and forests.[57] In order to get around the prohibitive legislation, Mixtec peasants, with the full knowledge of the local elites, used a clever legal sleight of hand. From 1862 onward they argued that they did not purchase the land as communities but rather as individual shareholders in legally constituted "agricultural societies." Here they citied Articles 2099 to 2117 of the state's civil code, which permitted the establishment of "societies of individuals" for exclusively commercial purposes. By extension, these societies could buy, hold, and sell land.[58]

As individual investors in these agricultural societies, the region's peasants started to become good liberal citizens at one level, fervent believers in the redemptive qualities of private property as "the basis for political peace and economic prosperity."[59] During conflicts with neighboring villages, indigenous communities often defended their properties by invoking the new laws, playing on the legal preference for privately owned over communal lands. For example, in 1881 the village of Cuyotepeji, which had purchased its lands from the Villagómez cacicazgo in 1861, came into conflict with Camotlán. The villagers' defense was couched in the language of liberalism: they explained that the lands had been "bought by the locals" and demanded that, at the very least, Camotlán should have its own properties divided because of the laws against civil bodies owning land.[60] Similarly, in 1890 the agricultural society of Chilixtlahuaca argued that the neighboring village was infringing upon "a great part of our exclusive private property," "secured by the law of 1856" and "assured by the recent regulations of 1890."[61] In fact, the idea that individuals within legally constituted societies still had private property rights penetrated so deeply that peasant women started to use the laws to assure their financial due. In 1902 Ricarda Martínez from Amatitlán invoked the same articles of the civil code used to defend agricultural societies to claim that by marrying her husband she had "celebrated a contract of society." When they married, they had effectively created a company in which she had invested one ox and twenty-five pesos. Over the years, this initial investment had produced returns totaling nearly eight hundred pesos. She now demanded her share of these returns as her husband had run off with another woman.[62]

Undoubtedly, in the few regions that lent themselves to commercial production, like Mariscala (on the edge of the sugar zone of Atoyac) or the old liberal stronghold of Tezoatlán, this celebration of individual property rights could cause the same problems that Emilio Kouri has described in Papantla and Aldo Lauria-Santiago has described in El Salvador.[63] As incentives grew, the rural middle class in both villages used the laws to usurp poorer peasants' properties and convert pastures and forests to private commercial use. Between 1883 and 1897 Tomás Osio, the head of Mariscala's agricultural society, brought recalcitrant members of society to court on at least three occasions, arguing that his superior investment gave him private rights over the village's hillside pastures, which he wished to rent out to a local livestock owner.[64] Similarly, in Tezoatlán richer community ranchers, keen to monopolize the village's extensive pastures, waged a low-level war against their poorer neighbors to usurp their hillside properties.[65] In both cases, the regional authorities sought compromise over legal rectitude, attempting to minimize rancher land grabs and leave some pasture for the other members of the societies. In both cases the attempts were not wholly successful, and both Mariscala and Tezoatlán would become centers of revolutionary land reform efforts in the succeeding decades as poorer villagers sought a more equitable division of lands.

But in most villages, the purchase of former cacicazgo lands and the establishment of agricultural societies brought security, relatively equal land distribution, and internal peace. The threat of the liberal reforms shifted ideas of solidarity once again. First, most societies were deliberately inclusive. In most villages, given that households comprised four to five individuals, the members of the agricultural society correlated almost exactly with number of households. For example, the total population of Yolotepec in 1900 was around 150 persons.[66] The number of members of the agricultural society was around forty. Similarly, the total population of Tetaltepec in 1900 was around 400. The number of members of the agricultural society was around eighty.[67] In fact, the buyers encouraged this inclusivity, this exact overlap of communities and societies, presumably to avoid internal divisions. Only around forty villagers from Chilixtlahuaca could afford the initial costs of the society's lands in 1875. But once the initial purchase was made, the members allowed their fellow villagers to join "as long as they agree[d] to pay for the lands and costs."[68] Furthermore, the societies were extremely flexible regarding changes in individual households. Single women and widows were allowed to inherit and buy shares in the societies and comprised 10 percent of the society of Miltepec and 18 percent of the society of Ayuquila.[69]

Second, if the societies were internally inclusive, they were also externally defensive. The regulations of the societies, which survive for Miltepec,

Ayuquila, Cuyotepeji, and Chilixtlahuaca, stipulated that individual share-holders were not allowed to sell their shares to people from outside the communities.[70] When outsiders tried to usurp societies' lands, members were quick to indicate these rules. In 1890 the agricultural society members of Silacayoapilla successfully complained that the mestizo newcomer Athenogenes González had not been a long-term member of the community or an investor in the society and, as a result, had no rights to their lands. Instead, land transfer within the societies was usually a matter of direct inheritance.[71] In most instances male heads of households took over the divided plots of their dead fathers. In 1905 the second generation of the Mixquixtlahuaca society handed over nearly a hundred baptism records to prove that they were the rightful inheritors of their parents' lands.[72]

Third, these societies were broadly democratic. Although an elected three-man *mesa directiva* or *junta menor* made the day-to-day decisions, represented the society in court, and collected rents, contributions, and taxes, there was little opportunity to construct an agrarian cacicazgo. The leaders' decisions were subject to the veto of a *junta general*, comprising all the members of the society. Cuyotepeji held an annual meeting of the junta general every January 8, which went over the society's accounts for the previous year.[73] Chilixtlahuaca forbade the junta menor to sign any contract without the junta general's mass support.[74] In Ayuquila, the junta menor was forbidden from "making any decision which was not agreed upon by the junta general."[75] Furthermore, this system of internal democracy was recognized in the region's courts. For example, in 1884 the junta general of Cuyotepeji successfully pleaded that a rental contract between the junta menor and a local rancher was invalid because "the society in common" had not agreed to it.[76] Similarly, in 1903 the majority of the society of Chilixtlahuaca complained that the junta menor was not distributing lands fairly. They held a meeting of the junta general, took the junta menor to court, pointed to the society's internal stipulations, and won the case.[77]

Fourth, and perhaps most importantly, the lands owned by these societies were equitably distributed among their members. According to the societies' rules, each member received a plot of land equivalent to the amount he or she invested. Thus in Cuyotepeji, as every villager had put down forty pesos for the purchase of the Villagómez cacicazgo, each society member received an equal plot of "around half a hectare of part-irrigated land, and one hectare of irrigated land."[78] Not all the societies were as balanced as Cuyotepeji's; most simply comprised the former tenants of indigenous caciques and thus avoided the concentration of lands in the hands of an incipient rural middle class (see appendix G). In six of the sixteen societies, all the members invested between zero and fifty pesos. In Yolotepec, only two members invested over ten pesos. Even the richer peasants of Tonalá, Zacatepec, Miltepec, and Camotlán, who had put more toward the purchase of the lands, were not noticeably wealthier than their fellow members, possessing only around two or three times more land than the others. Only in Tezoatlán, where liberal mestizos had attempted to usurp village lands for over a generation, was there a considerable gap between the rich and the poor members of the society. Here three rancheros owned over half the society's land.

The Reform laws in the Mixteca Baja produced a distinct attitude toward land ownership among the region's inhabitants. On the one hand, particularly when dealing with acquisitive or invasive outsiders, the members of the agricultural societies resembled the rancheros described by Luis González y González, Ian Jacobs, Jennie Purnell, and Frans Schryer and defended their territory by quoting liberal legislation, invoking the sacred right of private property, and celebrating their purchase of cacique land.[79] On the other hand, by maintaining the lands as agricultural societies, Mixtec communities also generated a version of the traditional closed corporate community, which was inclusive, defensive, democratic, and egalitarian. Villagers often conflated these two approaches, arguing that their lands were "private property employed by all the community" or "bought with our own money and planted since time immemorial."[80] Modern and traditional, rooted in private property and communal use, the hybrid agricultural societies of the Mixteca Baja fell somewhere between the defensive establishments described by Antonio Escobar Ohmstede and the commercial ventures depicted by Emilio Kouri. As such, they were uniquely resilient to revolutionary attempts at land reform.[81] Equal distribution united communities and prevented the emergence of radical landless factions. At the same time, in the postrevolutionary period the defense of private property generated an effortless alliance with the regional church, which not only shared the Mixtec landowners' ideology, but also shared a financial reliance on the region's agricultural societies.

Throughout the Porfiriato and well into the twentieth century, the Mixteca Baja's agricultural societies not only protected communal but also cofradía lands. In 1859 and again in 1862, the liberal authorities of Oaxaca ordered villages to distribute cofradía properties among the communities' inhabitants.[82] In many regions, peasants willingly complied with the new laws. As William Taylor, John Chance, James Greenberg, and Daniela

Traffano argue, villages shifted toward funding their annual fiestas through individual *mayordomías*.[83] But in the Mixteca Baja the regulations generated first active and then passive resistance. During the civil wars, clergymen and cofradía members took up arms to defend the properties. After their defeat, they sought to use more subtle means to ensure the existence of cofradía lands and disguised the lands beneath the new agricultural societies.[84] I shall examine the effects of the prolonged ownership of cofradía lands on church finances, clerical-lay relations, and religious culture in the next section. However, in economic terms the alliance served to cement the huge transfer of property from indigenous caciques to indigenous villages, ensuring that local-born priests, often related to the region's elite families, supported the shift.

As the alliance between the local church and the agricultural societies was both informal and illegal, discovering proof of the covert arrangement is extremely difficult. Yet scant, tangential references in parish, community, and state archives reveal a panorama of sustained cofradía property use. First, in many villages local priests helped to finance the purchase of the societies' lands. In 1879 the priest of Juxtlahuaca, Manuel Varela, offered 147 pesos of his own money to help agricultural society members buy the lands of Los Aguacates.[85] In 1877 and in 1879 the priest of Tonalá, Felipe Arenas, helped the society of Tonalá to purchase the lands of Arteaga and Peña Alumada.[86] In 1899 Marciano Eulogia García, the dying priest of Chazumba, declared in his will that he had invested seventy pesos in the local agricultural society's purchase of the local cacique's lands.[87] Second, although public summaries of cofradía properties often claimed that the properties only comprised a few pounds of wax, annual accounts reveal that in many cases the majority of the cofradías' incomes still came from the harvesting of church lands. For example, the accounts for the cofradía of Our Lady of the Rosary in Miltepec between 1881 and 1902 reveal that the establishment earned around forty to fifty pesos a year from the sale of maize and custard apples.[88] In the same village, the cofradía of Saint James the Apostle gained around forty pesos a year from the sale of maize, wheat, beans, and firewood.[89] The accounts for the cofradía of the Holy Sacrament in Tonalá demonstrate that from 1868 onward villagers funded the annual celebrations by selling maize grown and cattle pastured on the Yetla finca. The finca was an old cacique property, sold to the village cofradías in 1833 and legally reconstituted as an "agricultural society" during the late 1860s.[90]

Third, although relations between the church and the agricultural societies remained remarkably amicable throughout late nineteenth and early twentieth centuries, periodic squabbles revealed the nature of the alliance. For example, in 1896 the priest of Tonalá, Jesús Zamora, suggested that the cofradía of the Holy Sacrament sell the institution's cattle due to the diminishing quality of the pastureland. The members of the agricultural society, who officially owned the Yetla finca, declined the offer, claiming that recent rains would regenerate the finca's barren hills. During the discussion, local leader Francisco Castillo explained the Porfirian arrangement at length. In his opinion the priest had every right to interfere in the Yetla finca, as the lands "belonged to the cult." The priest could preside over the election of the annual mayordomo, wisely invest the funds generated by the sale of maize and cattle, buy ornaments for the church, and pay tithes. But Castillo also suggested that in order to help with this burdensome duty, the priest appoint a commission of agricultural society members to cope with the day-to-day running of the lands. Priest, parishioners, and the local vicar general agreed, and the pact was maintained.[91]

Fourth, although clergymen and villagers took great pains to disguise the continued existence of the properties, and agricultural society records remain well hidden, the parish archives contain the occasional impromptu mention, especially in priests' journals. In discussing the history of the village of Tequixtepec, for example, the local priest admitted that as the 1857 Constitution had failed to "protect" religion, villagers had formed a "society of individuals" to purchase the Rancho de Jesús to "sustain the Catholic cult."[92] Similarly, when the new priest of Miltepec went over cofradía holdings in early 1913 he revealed that together the six largest cofradías owned two houses and lands that produced forty-eight measures of maize.[93] According to contemporary government estimates, the church owned twenty hectares of irrigated land or a quarter of the village's total.[94] In the neighboring villages of Cuyotepeji and Suchitepec, cofradías produced thirty-four and thirty-eight measures, respectively. Fifth, the eventual dismantling of agricultural societies during the postrevolutionary period often revealed their church employment. I shall deal with this process at length in chapters 5 and 6, and one example will suffice here. When the government eventually transformed the agricultural society of Cuyotepeji's properties into communal lands in 1963, the local municipal president revealed that the society's territory included nineteen plots devoted to ten cofradías, which annually produced fifty-six measures of maize.[95]

Although the establishment of agricultural societies, the extension of community landholding, and the maintenance of cofradía properties drove regional politics for the succeeding decades, and perhaps lent the Mixteca Baja its unique resilience to revolutionary policies, other economic shifts were more in keeping with Porfirian patterns. As in many other regions of Mexico, political stability, improved infrastructure, and expanding urban markets allowed the growth of the sugar industry.[96] In the Mixteca Baja, the Spanish immigrant José Gómez, who had arrived in the region during the 1850s and built a small fortune on commerce and smuggling, led the way. Within a decade he had purchased the land around the old sugar mill at Atoyac and converted it into the Hacienda la Pradera.[97] Over the following years he succeeded in extending La Pradera's ambit in a series of bitter legal disputes with neighboring villages.[98] By 1882 the hacienda was worth fifty-two thousand pesos. By 1890 the hacienda produced one hundred thousand kilos of cane worth over twenty thousand pesos per year. Twenty years later, it comprised over eight thousand hectares, employed nearly fifty peons, and produced over a million kilos of cane.[99] At the same time, other interlopers also established much more limited sugar enterprises in the region. Around Huajuapan, a Spanish émigré family bought up three small ranches on which they produced sugar, cattle, and goats. In Tonalá the mestizo merchant Zeferino Romero bought up the ranches of San Juan de las Cañas and Los Arcos, planted cane, and built two sugar mills.[100] In Chazumba, Gabriel Mendiola purchased a small ranch and started to produce liquor from the harvested cane.[101] During the following revolutionary decades, La Pradera and this handful of smaller ranches would become centers of revolutionary land reform, generating the region's handful of radical agraristas from their peons, sharecroppers, and dispossessed villagers.

Yet these new commercial ventures, similar to those in the neighboring districts of Izúcar de Matamoros, Teotitlán, and Cuicatlán, were exceptions, beacons of ethnic and class conflict in an otherwise predominantly pacific zone. Outside these isolated sugar fincas, other market incursions were far less disruptive.[102] In fact, by maintaining the livestock economy, increasing moneylending, and encouraging seasonal migration to the tropical lowlands of Tuxtepec and Veracruz, elites not only built on previous arrangements but also helped indigenous villages purchase cacique lands. During the Porfiriato, the practice of goat, sheep, and cattle herding in the Mixteca Baja continued. Although dozens of haciendas volantes no longer traversed the region, Guillermo Acho, a Puebla-based businessman probably of French descent, continued the practice. During the late 1870s he bought up huge quantities of land around Putla, Jamiltepec, and into Guerrero and established three extensive haciendas: Santa Rosa, León, and Barragán.[103] As the name León suggests, he probably purchased at least one from the heirs of the Mixteca Baja caudillo. Every year, the three haciendas swept northward, like their predecessors, spending around three months in the Mixteca Baja before the slaughter around Tehuacán.[104] During these three months, Acho rented the lands of the new agricultural societies, offering valuable capital to the incipient organizations. In late 1880 his manager signed a contract with the society of Suchitepec for seventy pesos per year for seven years. The total of 490 pesos was paid up front and allowed the society to pay off its debts to the former cacique.[105] A week later, the same manager signed a similar contract with the agricultural society of Teopan, this time for only three years. Again the money was paid up front and was employed to pay off the society's debts.[106] Furthermore, as the villagers learned the value of their lands, they increased the rental price. By 1888 Cuyotepeji employed a local lawyer to secure the up-front payment of fourteen hundred pesos from Acho's organization.[107]

At the same time, the elite trade in livestock also continued. In particular, the arriviste Spanish elite, comprising the Gómez, Solana, and Peral families, used their ranches to breed sheep and goats. They then paid peasant farmers to fatten the animals so that they would be ready for slaughter the following year. By the end of the Porfiriato, the Solana brothers were killing five thousand to seven thousand livestock each year in their slaughterhouses around Huajuapan.[108] Like the commercial arrangements of the colonial period and early nineteenth century, the system was uneven and exploitative. Peasants were paid only a single peso to fatten up an animal that the owners would then sell for ten times that price.[109] However, like the previous arrangements it also injected much-needed capital into indigenous villages without damaging communal properties.

With the liberal prohibition of ecclesiastical mortgages, regional elites also turned to offering cash loans. Again Spanish émigrés led the way, forwarding money to indigenous communities in return for the promise of various products including petates, palm hats, and maize. In return, villages often put up their lands as collateral. Again, the system was deeply unbalanced. By the 1890s palm merchants in Huajuapan annually paid just twenty-five thousand pesos up front for petates and sombreros worth nearly five times that amount.[110] Furthermore, at times the trade could cause serious problems. In 1875 the Gómez sons lent the villagers of Atoyac eight thousand pesos in exchange for the future handover of eight hundred bushels of quicklime. When the community reneged on the deal, the Spanish entrepreneurs attempted to appropriate the village's fertile lands for the neighboring La Pradera hacienda.[111] Yet despite the iniquity of the exchange, the rise in moneylending was not heavily disruptive. First, it built on a tradition of unequal commercial transactions established since the colonial period. Second, it granted peasant villages valuable sources of cash at a time when they were desperately trying to pay off their recent land purchases. Third, the paternalist system was cemented by traditional links of godparentage. Palm buyers especially secured low rates by offering themselves as godparents to villagers' children.[112] Fourth, outside areas of viable sugar production, elites remained uninterested in the low returns from the region's barren lands and sold agrarian collateral as quickly as possible. For example, when Cuyotepeji's villagers bought lands from the Villagómez cacicazgo in 1861, they used a loan from the local merchant, Miguel Cantu. Unable to pay back the amount, they offered Cantu a piece of the agricultural society's land. In 1876 Cantu accepted, but a decade later he sold the land back to the society at two-thirds of the price it was worth.[113]

Finally, the Porfiriato also witnessed the beginnings of mass peasant migration. Mixtecs had been migrating in numbers since the late colonial period.[114] But at the end of the nineteenth century, the rhythm increased dramatically. Indebted by the purchase of cacique lands, overwhelmed by a series of harvest-wrecking droughts, and attracted by cash payments for temporary agrarian and industrial work, thousands of Mixtecs now spent at least half the year away from their villages.[115] In 1896 local authorities estimated that 912 peasants from just twenty-four villages had migrated over the past year. In Chinango, the local municipal president lamented that 107 villagers had left the community as "there [was] no maize and the livestock was suffering for lack of water and good pasture." Most went to work on the sugar, tobacco, tropical fruit, and rubber plantations in Tuxtepec, Matamoros, and Veracruz or in the textile factories of Córdoba and Orizaba. Furthermore, most migrants, perhaps as many as 80 percent, were men. Only in a few villages did whole families make the temporary shift.[116] Again, the region's commercial elite benefitted from the financial allure of nearby commercial ventures. Gómez's sons dabbled in contracting Mixtec labor for the lowland fincas of Tuxtepec, paying money up front (the so-called *enganche*, or hook) in return for the promise of harvest-time work. For example, in 1897 Gómez's sons gave thirty-four villagers from Cacaloxtepec a total of

830 pesos for three months' work in a Cuban tobacco farmer's hacienda in Tuxtepec. The pay was, of course, miserably low, around thirty cents per person per day. The work was extremely hard and the contractual promise of health care probably disingenuous.[117] But these were not John K. Turner's shanghaied hoards, semi-slaves loaded onto trains, deposited at El Hule railway station, and forced to work at gunpoint in the burning sun until they finally collapsed and were "ploughed back into the earth."[118] They were voluntary temporary workers, predecessors of the modern Mixtec migrants who, if they could avoid malaria, cholera, and exhaustion, returned to their hometowns marginally better off than when they had left.

During the Porfiriato the economy of the Mixteca Baja changed dramatically. Most importantly, a land distribution, equitable in scale to the land reforms of the postrevolutionary period, took place as peasant communities bought up the majority of the region as agricultural societies. *Socios* (as members of the agricultural societies called themselves) combined a ranchero pride in private property with more "traditional" village practices of closed membership, balanced distribution, and democratic rule. Historians of the Huasteca have discovered similar institutions, occasionally disguising cofradía lands, in Puebla, Veracruz, Hidalgo, and San Luis Potosí.[119] Edgar Mendoza García has examined the same organizations in the neighboring district of Coixtlahuaca, and Gloria Camacho Pichardo has come across sociedades agrícolas around Toluca.[120] Although limited research on the effects of liberal laws on land sales in the center and south of Mexico makes comparison difficult, most societies were located in a broad arc following the slopes of the Sierra Madre Oriental. Here, in regions of low productivity (*pace* Papantla) and limited commercial use, liberal reforms seem to have generated a more communitarian version of the ranchero land grab enacted in the Sierra Madre Occidental. At the same time, other less favorable changes did affect the Mixteca Baja. Sugar production increased, and Spanish finca owners attempted, only partly successfully, to buy up or usurp neighboring peasant lands. Livestock breeding, moneylending, large-scale commerce, and temporary migration also increased. Yet these activities, many of which simply built on traditions established by the colonial elite, served to buttress rather than undermine interethnic and interclass relations. In short, the moral economy with its paternalist relations and mutual expectations was reshaped and rewritten but remained largely intact. Peasants gained land and no longer served caciques nor paid caciques rent. In return, they now took part in a more unforgiving capitalist system, taking high-risk loans,

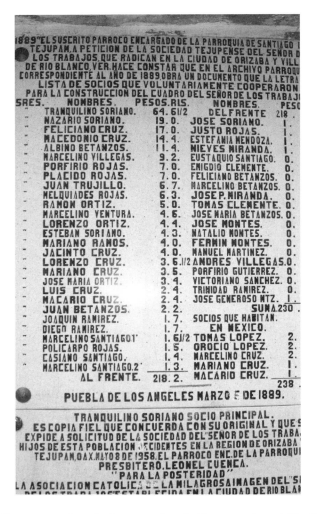

Figure 5: Commemoration of migrant workers in Veracruz who paid for the picture of Our Lord of Works in the church of Tejupan, 1889. Serafín Sánchez Hernández.

weaving countless palm hats, fattening up thousands of sheep and goats, and migrating every year to Mexico's agricultural and industrial heartlands. As in Querétaro, Guanajuato, and regions of Michoacán and Mexico State, a workable status quo was reached.[121] Revolutionary land reform would have to be imposed from outside.

The Church Resurgent, 1867–1903

During the late nineteenth century, the church experienced a rapid, transformative resurgence, comparable, according to François Xavier Guerra, to the sixteenth-century missionary effort.[122] In the first few decades after the Reform, the movement was "clericalist, Romanizing, and pietistic," an attempt to create an ordered spiritual hierarchy on earth.[123] Its methods were twofold. On the one hand, church authorities sought to improve internal bureaucracy, increasing the number of dioceses, establishing regional seminaries, and emphasizing clerical discipline. On the other hand, bishops and clerics also tried to regiment local religiosity, striving to redirect popular enthusiasm for drunken, rowdy fiestas and "crypto-pagan" practices toward sacramental rigor; clerically led, pious organizations; and authorized, acceptable cults, such as that of the Virgin of Guadalupe.[124] These reforms were top-down initiatives, designed to modernize, Europeanize, and purify Mexican Catholicism. Yet at the regional level, these changes, like their late eighteenth-century precedents, were always subject to reinterpretation and modification. In the Mixteca Baja, locally born priests implemented papal and diocesan efforts selectively. In short, they accepted moves that overlapped with the organic re-Christianization process of the preceding years, embracing initiatives to train up new priests, establish local seminaries, build chapels and churches, expand church education, and create new cults. Yet unlike many of their more ultramontane peers, they refrained from suppressing the region's indigenous religiosity and attempted instead to harness these beliefs, cults, and practices to a reinvigorated church. The local clergy's success was expressed in the establishment of the Diocese of the Mixtecas in 1903.

Reasons for the local church's less authoritarian approach to ecclesiastical renovation were both long and short term. First, priests and parishioners had experienced a sustained period of close cooperation during the early nineteenth century as part of the region's provincial conservative alliance. This partnership intensified as both clerics and cofradía networks took up arms and joined conservative forces during the civil wars of the 1850s and 1860s. This political allegiance, undergirded by mutual expectations and obligations, not only remained but also shaped future lay-clerical negotiations. Second, the Mixteca Baja's pre-existing social conventions facilitated the region's easy adjustment to certain Catholic innovations. In particular, the continued political prominence of indigenous caciques and, perhaps more importantly, indigenous cacicas lent itself to the establishment of lay elites and female-led pious organizations. Third, the region's conservative political elite, by deliberately turning a blind eye to continuing church practice, both permitted sustained public renewal and prevented the church from adopting an insular elitism.

Fourth, the regional church's new economic structure reinforced this ongoing process of collaboration. During the late 1850s a series of Reform laws had undermined the church's financial base by prohibiting church land holding and mortgage lending and banning the forced exaction of the tithe. Over the next half century, individual dioceses attempted to regain their financial position with differing degrees of success. In Guadalajara, ecclesiastical authorities emphasized the importance of voluntary tithes and established hundreds of *arreglos de conciencia* in which purchasers of church lands offered up discretionary contributions in return for forgiveness.[125] In contrast, in the Diocese of Oaxaca the Reforms "undercut the church's ability to compel parishes to sustain levels of pre-existing liturgical patronage."[126] Peasant contributions declined, and only a handful of wealthy hacendados paid tithes. As Ben Fallaw argues, these new arrangements reinforced regional inclinations as local clergy tended to ally with their principal paymasters.[127] Thus, in Guadalajara clerical interests dovetailed with those of repentant rancheros, and in Oaxaca priests were more sympathetic to the state's rural elite. In the Mixteca Baja, a more complex financial arrangement emerged. Here, cofradía lands, disguised beneath agricultural societies, not only bound priests and parishioners closer in a secretive act of collective defiance but also funded the regional church. As records for Miltepec, Tequixtepec, and Tonalá demonstrate, each year these organizations would devote 10 percent of their expenses to tithes and another 10 percent to the local priest.[128] As a result, the region's clergy often favored these indigenous villagers, placing their interests before those of the ecclesiastical elite.

Despite the Catholic resurgence's distinctly regional flavor, priests and parishioners in the Mixteca Baja incorporated some of the high church's suggested reforms. For example, both clerical and lay elites took advantage of the new emphasis on clerical schooling to produce a new generation of talented, well-trained, and well-connected local clergy. At first, Puebla, with its network of church schools and seminaries, remained the educational nexus. For example, in 1874 the priest of Chila sent his poor but promising nephew, Rafael Amador y Hernández, to the Palafox Seminary. After graduating, Amador received a scholarship to the Colegio Pío Latino Americano, the seminary for Latin American students in Rome. Here he became acquainted with the European Catholic resurgence, with its blend of neo-Thomism, Social Catholicism, and miraculous Marianism. Moreover, he established close relations with Mexico's up-and-coming ecclesiastical elite, men like Leopoldo Ruíz y Flores (future apostolic delegate), Martín Tritschler y Córdova (future bishop of Yucatán), and José Mora y del Río (future archbishop of Mexico). Finally, he took courses in theology in the Gregorian University and forged friendships with other European priests. When Amador returned to Mexico in the late 1880s, he was offered a permanent job at the Palafox Seminary. Instead, he opted to bring these new ideas and new connections back to the Mixteca Baja as the vicar general of Huajuapan.[129] Over the next decade, he would draw on his contacts to petition successfully for the creation of the region's diocese. Amador was clearly an exceptional student, but other more humble locals also received their initial priestly education in Puebla before returning to their patria chica. Concepción Barragán, who would become one of Amador's chief ecclesiastical leaders, was a Mixtec peasant from Tamazola who worked as a house servant for one of the village's wealthy families. In 1881 he visited Puebla for the first time. According to his own account, he was struck by the city's grandiose architecture and sense of spiritual pomp, and he vowed to return and attend the seminary. Less than ten years later he did just that, living on the floor of his wealthy master's Puebla house and funding his studies through continued housework. Finally, around 1900 he was consecrated a local priest.[130]

In 1889 the establishment of two branch seminaries in Huajuapan and Tezoatlán intensified this educational drive. The new institutions were part of a renewed effort to strengthen church teaching, an effort that saw the number of seminaries reach thirty-nine by 1910. The regional establishments offered courses on Spanish, Latin, philosophy, and theology. As student fees were predominantly funded by charitable donations, the schools were designed to "facilitate the studies of poorer youths inclined to careers as priests."[131] For example, in 1896 José María Hernández Cirigo, son of an agricultural society member from Tonalá, entered the Huajuapan institution. As he was too poor to pay for his monthly board, he often had to return to Tonalá to work on his uncle's farm. Yet priestly and charitable assistance eventually allowed the prospective cleric to complete his studies in 1903. He was rewarded for his perseverance with immediate appointment to one of the new diocese's most lucrative parishes. In the following years, his brother and two nephews followed suit, all attending the local seminary and becoming priests of the new diocese.[132] The local adoption of the ultramontane emphasis on clerical education produced a veritable boom in both elite and non-elite priests. During the early Porfiriato, numbers of priests in the Mixteca Baja had remained steady at their pre-Reform level of about one priest for every three thousand parishioners. In comparison, numbers of priests in Oaxaca had declined precipitously. Outside the state capital, pastoral care averaged around one priest per sixty-two hundred inhabitants.[133] With the establishment of the two branch seminaries, the region pressed its advantage. Throughout the 1890s the institutions pulled in between five and ten prospective priests per year. By 1900 the number of priests in the district of Huajuapan had reached twenty, or one cleric for every 2,250 parishioners. The figure was comparable to the center-west parishes of Jalisco and Michoacán.[134]

Local priests also followed ecclesiastical demands to increase the number of parishes, churches, and priests' houses. The policy was designed to diminish the distance between peasant communities and local places of worship and hence increase sacramental regularity. However, the top-down implementation again dovetailed well with the Mixteca Baja's pre-Reform traditions. Between 1867 and 1900 the number of parishes in Huajuapan rose from twelve to eighteen. Between 1865 and 1895 villagers in Huajuapan built fourteen new churches, ten chapels, and twenty parish houses. Together they were worth over seventy-five thousand pesos.[135] Two years later, when the local jefe político compiled a list of the region's ongoing building projects, he recounted that another eighteen villages were in the process of building or rebuilding village churches. In Huajuapan itself, pious private individuals were backing the construction of five new chapels and a tower for the main parish church.[136] This period of fevered activity, funded by cofradías, priests, and lay elites and driven forward by communal labor, resulted in a remarkable concentration of ecclesiastical infrastructure. By 1900 the district of Huajuapan possessed over one hundred churches and chapels or one place of worship per 450 inhabitants. In comparison, figures for Oaxaca were around one church per fourteen hundred faithful, and figures for Mexico overall were around one church for every twelve hundred people.[137] These unfussy new churches and chapels not only brought together priests and parishioners but also would provide the bricks-and-mortar basis for the expansion of ecclesiastical control after 1903.

The local church also adopted the ecclesiastical hierarchy's emerging emphasis on lay education.[138] In the region's larger towns private citizens established church-run private schools. Although they primarily catered to the scions of the urban elite, charitable donations permitted the attendance of those further down the economic scale. For example, in 1869 pious merchants in Acatlán formed a branch of the Sociedad Católica, a Mexican lay association established in the immediate post-Reform years to maintain Catholic unity. The association embraced the church's Roman direction, stressed rigorous public deportment, and was devoted to the Immaculate Conception, run by the local priest, and patronized by the bishop. At the same time the members' monthly dues contributed to a school for boys and a school for girls. Here, both rich and poor children from Acatlán and its surrounding barrios took classes in reading, writing, and arithmetic, as well as "Christian doctrine," "Christian morality," "Catholic history," and "The Dangers of Protestantism." Over the next two decades attendance increased, peaking at over three hundred students in 1888. Acatlán's private academies forged a new lay elite well versed in the demands of modern Catholicism. In a touching letter to the Sociedad Católica, one of the former students of the local girls' school thanked the pious organization for teaching her "first letters," "the fundamentals of Christianity," and "the importance of charity."[139] Outside Acatlán, pious citizens in league with Catholic ministers also established private schools in eleven other towns, more than any other district in the state.[140]

In the region's smaller villages, Catholics took advantage of the political elite's conservative sympathies to persuade local teachers to teach Christian doctrine. Like the cofradía cover-up, proof for the deliberate subversion of the laws is scarce. The school system lacked federal oversight, and teachers and local authorities kept understandably quiet about their infringement of the laws. Yet some evidence remains. In 1897 the municipal president of Ayuquililla thanked the state government for helping to establish a community school. He added that the priest supported the state's educational effort, forcing children to attend, buying school equipment and clothes, and "teaching classes on Christian doctrine."[141] Three years later the priest of Tequixtepec admitted that a laywoman taught catechism classes in the local secular school.[142] The covert inclusion of Catholic teaching and the consequent institutional support of the local church encouraged the region's relative educational success. In 1878 and 1885 Huajuapan possessed more schools than any other district in the state.[143] By 1900, 70 percent of villagers spoke Spanish, and nearly 20 percent of the population over twelve years old was functionally literate. In comparison, the average state literacy rate was around 10 percent.[144]

The local church also adopted many of the resurgent church's new associations and cults. At first the process was fairly organic as individual priests and their lay followers welded the new organizations to pre-existing cofradías. In Acatlán the association of San Vicente de Paul, a French organization devoted to caring for the sick, comprised of former members of the old cofradía of the Good Death, a colonial sodality established to fund Masses for the deceased. The new association's regulations maintained the same monthly payments and obligations but now extended its ambit over the dying as well as the dead.[145] Despite the rather haphazard establishment of these early organizations, by the 1890s priest and parishioners were making a concerted effort to introduce the Marian cults favored by the Roman hierarchy. Foremost among these was the devotion to Our Lady of Guadalupe, which ecclesiastical authorities had embraced since the 1870s.[146] The new vicar general of Huajuapan, Rafael Amador y Hernández, directed the shift, constructing a large church to the Virgin and leading the first pilgrimage to the Basílica de Guadalupe in the coronation year of 1895. Subsequent pilgrimages followed in 1897 and 1898. The last comprised over six hundred devotees and included men and women from throughout Huajuapan.[147] Individual parishes also embraced the new devotion. Before the 1890s only two or three cofradías to the Mexican Virgin were located in the region's major towns. By 1903 at least thirty such organizations existed in Huajuapan alone.[148] In the Parish of Tonalá, all seven outlying villages formed cofradías to Guadalupe.[149] At the same time, other Marian cults also gained ground. Organizations devoted to the Immaculate Conception abounded. In Petalcingo and Yosocuta, villagers even purchased statues of Our Lady of Lourdes, formed cofradías, and held annual celebrations.[150]

As numerous historians have demonstrated, the late nineteenth century witnessed a flowering of a supercharged female piety inspired by the ecclesiastical authorities' militant Marianism, necessitated by the fall-off in male church attendance, eagerly embraced by women excluded from the formal political sphere, and covertly welcomed by a state keen to farm off certain welfare obligations.[151] Even in rural Oaxaca, no bastion of Roman orthodoxy, Edward Wright-Rios has discovered a growth in clerically led female associations and a proliferation of village "*beatas.*"[152] The Mixteca Baja was no different. Pious women dominated the new organizations. Acatlán's cofradía of the Sacred Heart of Mary, formed in 1892, included thirty-four women and only sixteen men.[153] The Guadalupe Association of Tonalá, established in 1902, comprised forty women who each donated around two pesos per year.[154]

Yet some regions adapted to the church's profound gender shift more readily than others. In much of rural Mexico, tensions between male clerics and
female lay leaders remained and were expressed in conflicts over political
influence, financial control, and religious orthodoxy.[155] Furthermore, with
the economic crises of 1907 and the onset of revolutionary violence, many
of the cash-starved female organizations collapsed. But in the Mixteca
Baja, with its tradition of powerful indigenous cacicas, female-financed
cofradías, and girls' education, the move toward a more equitable division of church power was far smoother. Both sides already knew the rules
of the game. Local priests were used to harnessing the piety of relatively
rich, influential Mixtec women, and the region's female devotees were well
trained in the expectations of orthodoxy, deference, and obedience that
the close clerical connection demanded. Indigenous cacicas, stripped of
their role as regional landowners, now played prominent roles in the new
organizations. The female inheritors of the Aja, Villagómez, and Navarrete
cacicazgos all led Marian devotions in their respective villages.[156] In Tonalá,
female members of the Rios clan, mestizo heirs of the Guzmán cacicazgo,
represented nearly a third of the Guadalupe Association's members.[157]
These rural women would not only form the vanguard of the new diocese
but were also the primary obstacle to postrevolutionary anticlericalism.

Although priests and parishioners in the Mixteca Baja embraced
many aspects of the Porfirian church's new policies, they failed to adopt
the Mexican hierarchy's attempts to regiment popular religious practices. Instead, local priests authorized, encouraged, and commemorated
the region's indigenous devotions, drawing together old and new in an
increasingly conscious celebration of the region's deep spiritual past and
providential future. This continuing understanding was not only expressed
in occasional miracles like that of the sweating Christ of Amatitlán, but
also in the more formal celebration of local devotions. In Tonalá, the local
priest wrote a short history of the Holy Cross, linking the discovery to the
network of crosses discovered throughout Latin America during the early
missionary period. He even reiterated and regionalized the myth of Saint
Thomas's pre-Conquest evangelization, claiming that before Aztec dominance, Mixtecs had followed a version of early Christianity.[158] Huajuapan's
local elites also embraced the local devotion. In 1896 the local jefe político
led a group of regional notables to visit the cave of Tindú.[159] By the late
nineteenth century, the story had become a staple of regional historians,
repeated in the works of Manuel Martínez Gracida, Cayetano Esteva, and

José Antonio Gay, proof of the region's deep syncretic religiosity.[160] At the same time, priests also encouraged expansion of the geographical reach of the region's other Christocentric cults. Cofradías to Miltepec's Our Lord of Wounds and Huajuapan's Our Lord of Hearts now sprang up throughout the region in large towns like Petlalcingo and Tezoatlán and small villages like Tindú, Cuitito, and Camotlán.[161] In addition to supporting traditional village cults, local religious leaders also attempted to link the church's new stress on Marianism to local beliefs. In 1893 the priest of Tlacotepec persuaded the bishop of Puebla, Francisco Melitón Vargas, to authorize a prayer book devoted to Our Lady of the Snows in Ixpantepec.[162] The small tome reiterated the tale of the Virgin's miraculous appearance, again stressing the long period of mutual understanding between Mixtec peasants and the ecclesiastical hierarchy. Within a few years the vicar general of Huajuapan followed suit, advising local priests to lead pilgrimages to the hilltop shrine if their parishioners were unable to afford the more costly Guadalupe trail.[163] By 1903 cofradía and association members from throughout the region were obeying the vicar general's calls. In fact, pilgrimages to the small church increased so markedly at the turn of the century that the local cofradía's income doubled from 1898 to 1903, reaching a peak of 913 pesos and 95 kilos of wax.[164]

Finally, if local priests attempted to lend institutional support to regional icons and shrines, they also authorized indigenous beliefs about the devil, adding an acceptable Christian veneer to popular fears. Since pre-Hispanic times Mixtec villagers had believed that *tupas*, or spirits, resided in the region's caves and hills. The gradual process of evangelization had dampened popular enthusiasm for the rites needed to appease these spirits and persuaded many that the tupas were actually incarnations of the devil. However, many still believed that they haunted the region's isolated slopes.[165] By the late nineteenth century, local priests confronted these latent superstitions directly. In 1900 and again in 1901 the priest of Tequixtepec led elaborate processions of all the parish members to the peaks of the village's four surrounding hills. On each one he planted a cross, designed to keep the tupas, or devils, at bay. According to a pious villager, writing over a decade after the event, the crosses served to protect the community "from all ills." Tequixtepec's inhabitants still assert that the crosses keep the village's enemies at bay and have even replaced two of the more dilapidated crosses with more modern representations of Cristo Rey. Together they stand as testament to the power of this early twentieth-century effort.[166]

Figure 6: Felipe N. Arenas, originally from Zapotitlán Salinas, priest of Tonalá and author of the first text devoted to the miraculous Holy Cross of Tonalá, *Las cruces de Quetzalcoatl. Historia de Tonalá, Oaxaca coleccionada por el Sr. Pbro. D. Avelino de la T. Mora López para conmemorar el III centenario del hallazgo de La Santa Cruz en la gruta del Río de Santa María Tindú, Oax.*

Figure 7: Cross on the hillside above Tequixtepec. Crosses placed on hills were designed to ward off tupas, or devils. In the center of the photograph one can see the limestone inscription "Viva Cristo Rey." The inscription was placed during the 1950s. Serafín Sánchez Hernández.

The local church's careful blend of top-down regimentation and practical leniency, similar to the "clericalization of popular religiosity" described by Timothy Tackett in prerevolutionary France, was remarkably successful, ordering and cementing the re-Christianization of the early nineteenth century and creating a vibrant, emotive religious culture that fulfilled both high church demands for sacramental orthodoxy and the popular desire for devotional continuity.[167] Sadly, no figures on weekly church attendance exist. But visiting bishops repeatedly commented on the inhabitants' "regular taking of the sacraments," the "good condition" of the local churches, the "order and careful keeping" of ecclesiastical ornaments, and the general "enthusiasm" and "generosity" of the population.[168] Illegitimacy rates, which increased in much of the country, remained at pre-Reform levels.[169] At the same time, innumerable priests' letters, asking for the display of the Holy Sacrament at the request of local believers, indicate that even the new stress on Eucharistic devotion gained considerable ground.[170] When the Puebla bishop visited Tequixtepec in 1891, he noted "the inhabitants' customs" were "in harmony with the good practices of religious piety."[171] Six years later, before leaving Huajuapan, his comments were even more laudatory: "The piety here is well sustained and the frequency of the Holy Sacraments edifying. The moral and religious customs are exemplary and the priests' desire to teach them the small details is without comparison. Their attachment to virtue and their desire to hear the word of God is comparable with that of the earliest Christians."[172]

The Diocese of Huajuapam de León, 1903–1910

On May 10, 1903, Francisco Plancarte y Navarrete, the bishop of Cuernavaca, arrived in Huajuapan to considerable fanfare. He carried with him the papal bull "Apostolica sedes," which ordered the creation of the Diocese of the Mixtecas. The prospective diocese included over forty parishes, drawn from the neighboring dioceses of Puebla and Oaxaca, encompassing the whole of the Mixteca Baja from Acatlán in the north to Tejupan in the south and from Silacayoapan in the west to Coixtlahuaca in the east. Within two days thousands of parishioners from "all the villages" of the region assembled outside the Huajuapan church. The bells of the town's seven churches rang out, and the faithful set up triumphal arches covered with flowers and draped flags from the windows of their houses. At the same time, village bands from throughout the Mixteca struck up a selection of traditional tunes designed to welcome the visiting prelate. As Plancarte left the vicar general's residence, the crowd parted, and the Cuernavaca bishop slowly made his way to the temple. Here he entered, held a solemn Mass, and read out the bull. At the end of the ceremony, parishioners let off fireworks and started up their musical bands once more—"an expression of their genuine happiness" as one witness recounted. Plancarte then fixed the bull to the outside of the church, declaring that the building was now a cathedral. Over the next three weeks the festivities continued. According to contemporaries, "The spirit of God was felt in the hearts of everybody," and "the spending was excessive." Finally, in the cathedral of Huajuapan, the prelates of Oaxaca, Tulancingo, and Cuernavaca held a solemn ceremony in which they consecrated the former vicar general, Rafael Amador y Hernández, as the bishop of the newly erected diocese. The archbishop of Oaxaca, Eulogio Gillow, then gave a long speech in which he thanked both the pope and the Mexican president, whose "gift of political stability" had made the creation of the diocese possible.[173]

Figure 8: Rafael Amador y Hernández, first bishop of the Diocese of Huajuapam de León, 1903–1923. *Historia de Tonalá, Oaxaca coleccionada por el Sr. Pbro. D. Avelino de la T. Mora López para conmemorar el III centenario del hallazgo de La Santa Cruz en la gruta del Río de Santa María Tindú, Oax.*

The creation of the Diocese of the Mixtecas (renamed the Diocese of Huajuapam de León in late 1903) was part of the late nineteenth-century church's increasing bureaucratization, the attempt to create "an ecclesiastical counter-state—an episcopal pyramid, converging in papal absolutism."[174] Between 1863 and 1903, the papacy set up nineteen new dioceses in Mexico, making the country the most densely governed ecclesiastical area of Latin America.[175] The question remains, however, why create a diocese in the Mixteca Baja? For the first bishop, causation was clear: God's providential plan and his "divine kindness" had inspired the pope, Leo XIII, to permit the diocese's inception.[176] Yet beyond such theological musings, the underlying reasons more probably lay in the politics of the ecclesiastical establishment. As a graduate of the Colegio Pío Latino Americano and the Gregorian University, Amador had strong connections to Roman bureaucrats; young, foreign-educated prelates; and their older sympathizers. According to accounts written after the event, he drew on all these relations to ensure the diocese's creation, writing personal letters to Vatican ministers like Cardinals Emigdio Michetti and José de Calasanz Félix Santiago Vives y Tutó, leaning on former Pío Latino classmates like Bishops Ruíz y Flores and Tritschler, and gaining the support of the archbishop of Oaxaca. In 1889 he met Bishop Gillow in Tamazulapan and asked the prelate to take his petition outlining the benefits of a new diocese to Rome.

At the same time, Huajuapan's pious regional elites also promoted the creation of the diocese. They included Aurelio García Niño, who funded the construction of the San José church; Fiacro Torreblanca, the local tithe collector; Vicente Zamora, the principal of the Catholic school; and Juan de Dios Flores y León, a local lawyer and a relative of the former vicar general. This group of commercial, intellectual, and bureaucratic leaders formed a local junta to organize correspondence with Rome and wrote a series of letters delineating the church's recent improvements and "defending" the Mixteca Baja's unique religious culture.[177] The letters would have provided a unique insight into the developments of the Porfirian church but unfortunately remain under lock and key somewhere in the vaults of the Vatican archives.[178] Finally, the list of Mexico's new dioceses suggests that traditions of political conservatism also inspired and aided successful regional petitions. These histories could certainly explain the creation of dioceses in conservative strongholds like Tulancingo, Tepic, Cuernavaca, Aguascalientes, Saltillo, and Tehuantepec.

Figure 9: The secular petitioners for the creation of the diocese. Seated from left to right: Aurelio García Niño, Vicente Zamora, Felix Alonso, and Miguel López R. Standing: Fiacro Torreblanca and Juan de Dios Flores y León. Museo Regional de Huajuapan.

However, the new diocese not only rewarded past efforts, but also offered an opportunity to strengthen the contemporary church. As befitted a Pío Latino prelate, Amador started at the top, attempting to increase clerical discipline and intensify church governance. Almost immediately after his appointment he started a monthly series of obligatory conferences for local priests. The events were designed to ensure liturgical constancy and clerical deportment.[179] More importantly, he also followed the advice of the papal bull and made the improvement of the seminary a top priority. In 1903 he moved the institution into the house of the former jefe político, Ignacio Vázquez, who had left the building to the church. In 1904 he raised the branch institution to the status of a diocesan seminary, and a year later he drafted in an acquaintance from Rome, the Spanish theologian Guillermo López

García, to become the rector.[180] Both Amador and López García drew on their experience in Rome to forge a new, modern, Catholic syllabus with combined classes in Latin, theology, and the natural sciences. Echoing Leo XIII's neo-Thomist encyclicals, both reiterated the compatibility of church and scientific education, arguing that theology was not necessarily "retrograde and conservative" and that Catholics, like their secular peers, were bound to "the study of everything, to the last atom of creation."[181]

At the same time, Amador attempted to build on the efforts of the previous decade, to increase seminary attendance and train up a new generation of regional priests. At the 1906 diocesan synod he ordered priests to look out for promising, pious students to send to the institution.[182] The request had rapid results. By 1910 attendance had risen from around thirty to sixty, with fifteen to twenty students graduating per year. Many came from the local elite, including Ignacio Vázquez's nephew, José O. Vázquez; the Huajuapan merchant's son José Cantu Corro; and two Villagómez boys, Uriel and Zenón.[183] But others emerged from far humbler backgrounds. Tonalá, a village of around one thousand inhabitants, became a formidable generator of local priests, producing fourteen in the first few decades of the seminary, including the region's most forthright opponent of socialist education, Manuel Cubas Solano, and the future diocesan secretary Fidencio Rios.[184] Other smaller villages also sent their favored sons to the institution. Felix Huerta was the son of a "humble man" from Ayuquililla, while Daniel Ibarra was the son of a Tequixtepec laborer.[185]

A new influx of young, local graduates meant that by the end of the first decade of the twentieth century, the number of priests in the diocese had nearly doubled, rising from forty in 1900 to at least seventy in 1910. In comparison, overall priest numbers in Mexico increased by only 12.5 percent.[186] As a result, pastoral ratios (which had been quite high in the neighboring districts of Acatlán and Coixtlahuaca) dropped to the levels of the district of Huajuapan, or around one priest for every twenty-five hundred parishioners.[187] Governance also tightened as the bishop created dozens of new parishes. By 1910 these young, well-trained graduates and their reformed elders, ensconced in their new parish seats, formed a rural clerical vanguard ready to extend Amador's vision throughout the diocese.

In many ways diocesan policies simply built on those adopted over the past twenty years. Priests continued to promote Catholic education, introduce new associations, and establish Marian cults. But under Amador's careful guidance, these old arrangements gained new uniformity and intensity.

First, the new bishop attempted to regularize church funding, ordering each village to form a *sociedad católica agrícola*, or Catholic agricultural society. As their name suggests, these establishments were ecclesiastical versions of the organizations created during the early post-Reform period to purchase and run former cacique lands, encapsulating some kind of Homi Bhabha–esque "hybrid hybridity." The new institutions were instructed to take over communities' covert cofradía lands, which had previously been disguised beneath the secular organizations, and distribute funds according to diocesan instructions. In 1906 large towns like Huajuapan, Chila, Acatlán, and Tlacotepec formed these societies, and by 1910 even small villages like Ayú, Mariscala, Magdalena, and Ixitlán had concentrated their church wealth in the same way.[188] In many ways, the Catholic agricultural societies consolidated the day-to-day running of former cofradías. They organized the labor of church lands; collected the maize, beans, and other produce; and distributed the cash earned for various local ecclesiastical projects. In late 1910, members of the society of Magdalena agreed to spend the forty pesos they had gained during the recent blessing of the village's livestock on continued construction of the church tower.[189] In 1909 members of the society of Chila decided to lavish their recent income on brand new church ornaments.[190]

Yet these diocesan innovations were under closer clerical supervision than their cofradía forebears. As a result, local ecclesiastical authorities could now harness church wealth to improve church schooling and systematize the rather haphazard combination of exclusive private institutions and subverted secular schools. According to Amador's biographer, "a truly Christian instruction and formation was the slogan of his work for the humble classes."[191] His pastoral letters and circulars were replete with exhortations to the faithful to set up schools in response to what he saw as "pernicious doctrines that are divulged with such rapidity in the books, pamphlets and impious newspapers that penetrate the home" and "hurt the religious sentiments that should be inculcated in the children."[192] Again, the regional move paralleled broader national changes. The early twentieth century witnessed a huge expansion in confessional schooling. In 1910 private schools accounted for around 20 percent of educational establishments and taught around 18 percent of Mexican students.[193] The regional initiative was equally successful. By 1910 small private institutions, funded by Catholic societies, had been established in all but a handful of the Mixteca Baja's villages. For example, in 1910 the newly graduated priest José Cantu Corro claimed to have established schools in the parish seat of Tequixtepec and the outlying villages of Santa Gertrudis, Chinango, and Yolotepec.[194] Similarly, in 1909 the priest of Chila boasted that all the parish's villages except Simarrones possessed private educational institutions.[195] Furthermore, these new schools were not simply elite enterprises. Funded communally, like their secular counterparts, they attracted large numbers of local children. Cantu Corro revealed that around fifty children per year graduated from the Tequixtepec school. In comparison, the small secular school produced no more than ten graduates per year.[196] At the same time, Amador also instigated the widespread adoption of Sunday catechism classes. During the 1906 synod, the bishop complied with the instructions of the recent Latin American Plenary Council and ordered all priests to institute this basic teaching.[197] Again, the local clergy followed suit. In Tequixtepec Cantu Corro took the best female graduates from the village school and formed a group of school monitors to teach catechism classes after church. By 1911 monitors from the outlying village of Yolotepec were coercing children to make the five-kilometer walk to Tequixtepec to hear the religious tuition.[198]

The establishment of these new church-led institutions permitted high levels of ecclesiastical control over school syllabi, and Amador took great pains to inculcate students with modern Catholic values. In his carefully worded regulations for the diocese's Catholic schools, published in 1909, he laid out specific reading lists for each subject. Some were obvious choices: he recommended Pius X's *Primeros nociones del catecismo* for first-year classes on religion and Claudio Fleury's *Catecismo histórico* for older students.[199] Yet other choices reveal Amador's principal concerns. For instruction in Spanish he chose Querétaro priest Gabino Chávez's *El amigo católico de las niñas*. Although the tome was designed as an early reading aid, its principal narrative, which follows the story of an African orphan who is "rescued" and trained in a Piedmont nunnery, demonstrated the new ecclesiastical emphasis on female piety and social work. In a forthright introduction, Chávez laid out his argument that since the Reform laws had outlawed religious teaching, the position of Mexican women had decreased dramatically. In essence, liberal notions of female domesticity—the belief that the woman was only suitable as a "wife, mother and housekeeper"—prevented Catholic women from devoting themselves to more fulfilling occupations as nurses, teachers, and nuns. In particular, he attacked Dolores Correa Zapata's *La mujer en el hogar*, a liberal guide to "good domestic service" taught in upper-level secular schools. In contrast, he suggested that an education in Catholic morality, with its stress on individual piety and social duty, was not only emancipatory, but also would create a new generation of socially active pious women. The African orphan Josefina provided Mexican girls with the perfect role model, as she grew from a childish devotee into a young nurse.[200]

For national history, Amador chose José A. Reyes's 1895 *Nociones elementales de historia patria*. The brief book encapsulated the intellectual contortions of post-Reform Catholic nationalism. Like earlier Catholic historians, Reyes continued to condemn Aztec civilization and laud the redemptive qualities of the colonial church. The Aztecs were "not moral, wise, or rich" and "lacked all the necessary comforts for a civilized life." In contrast, the first missionaries were "good and humble priests" who brought the "gifts of God's word" to the ignorant masses. But unlike Lucas Alamán, whose multivolume history clearly underpinned the earlier chapters, Reyes tried to portray Independence as a broadly beneficial occurrence. Although he admitted that the initial uprising had generated "all types of excesses," including the massacre at the Guanajuato granary, he lauded Hidalgo's condemnation of the act and his subsequent disciplining of insurgency troops. Yet he reserved his fullest praise for Agustín de Iturbide, the Catholic Independence hero of choice. He called him the "father of the patria" and claimed that the Plan of Iguala was "an immortal monument to the political genius and patriotism of Independence." Reyes secured Independence as a broadly Catholic event, inspired by priests and shaped by a member of the conservative elite, but as he progressed further into the nineteenth century, his history became increasingly contradictory as he was torn between his allegiances to Catholic orthodoxy and martial patriotism. This ambivalence reached a climax during his portrayal of the midcentury civil wars. On the one hand, Reyes towed the resurgent church's line, arguing that the 1857 Constitution was "an insult to the religion of the majority of Mexicans," that the empire was a "noble idea," and that Miguel Miramón was "one of the country's greatest military generals." On the other hand, he admitted Juárez's "intelligence, talent, and his constancy" and advised Catholics to pray for his soul as a "great Mexican." Despite this relative leniency, his snappy conclusion summed up the basic position of the Catholic nationalism of the late nineteenth century—"Mexico: Hernán Cortés founded it, Agustín de Iturbide made it free, and Porfirio Díaz made it great."[201] The two books were used in schools throughout the Mixteca Baja well into the postrevolutionary period. They shaped the diocese's young Catholics, encouraging women's involvement in the religious, social, and political spheres and reinvigorating the narrative of Catholic nationalism and its distinct pantheon of heroes.

In addition to regimenting diocesan funding and improving church education, Amador, like his ultramontane colleagues, also put enormous emphasis on the fulfillment of the sacraments. Although the diocese's parishioners had taken baptism, marriage, and death rites extremely seriously since the ecclesiastical moralizing campaign of the 1830s, the new bishop encouraged an even greater sacramental orthodoxy. He demanded that priests teach the parents of newborns the exact responses to the baptismal questions, rather than letting church sacristans answer for them. He also forbade clerics from allowing "masons, concubines, or those only married in the civil registry office" to play the role of godparents.[202] By 1910 this comprehensive campaign was beginning to bear fruit. Baptisms increased, and in many villages illegitimacy almost disappeared. In Tequixtepec Cantu Corro scoured the parish's outlying villages for unmarried couples whom he would then persuade to wed. In February 1910 he persuaded eight couples from Yolotepec to tie the knot in the church, and by the end of the year he proudly boasted that only one couple in the parish was not formally united because the husband "had been working in Veracruz for the last two years."[203]

At the same time, echoing the European stress on regular Communion, he pressed the local clergy to encourage monthly or even weekly acts, "not just at Easter or near death." Priests adapted the rhythm of village fiestas to force regular Communion, or what Amador termed "the doorway to a Christian life."[204] For example, during Chila's celebration of its patron saint, the local clergyman persuaded four hundred locals to take Communion, ninety-five for the first time. A day later when another four hundred parishioners arrived from the neighboring Parish of Ayuquililla, they also accepted the rite.[205] Regular missions, led by Puebla's small Jesuit contingent, cemented the practice. In the last three weeks of January 1908, two missionaries enacted over eight thousand Communions in the Parishes of Acatlán, Petlalcingo, and Chila alone.[206]

Finally, Amador and his loyal priests augmented this offensive by developing a smattering of Social Catholic organizations. Few opportunities existed for the type of workers' circles and mutual aid societies introduced in the country's urban centers. Instead, Amador drew on diocesan traditions and redirected the handful of San Vicente de Paul organizations toward broader social aims. First, he placed diocesan control of the association in the hands of his most trusted priest, the Spanish Carmelite monk Antonio de Jesús Castillo, and a female member of the Huajuapan elite, Guadalupe Carrión de Solana. Then, he extended the organization beyond the female elite of the mestizo towns and into the diocese's smaller parishes.[207] By 1904 the original three associations had expanded to six, and by 1910 six had expanded to over twenty. These new organizations, predominantly staffed and funded by women, organized catechism classes and First Communions, visited the sick, funded at least five small hospitals, and collected money and food for the poor. In 1904 the Huajuapan institution alone made 635 visits to the sick, collected 1,388 pesos, and gathered together around 1,000 kilos of rice, 217 measures of beans, and 3,419 measures of maize. The food was handed out to prisoners on Thursdays and to the poor on Sundays at huge breakfasts that Amador would regularly attend.[208]

If the new diocese, with its emphasis on clerical discipline, church education, sacramental orthodoxy, and gentle social reform, followed the Roman route map established at the 1899 Latin American Plenary Council, the locally born bishop also continued the practice of encouraging certain acceptable local traditions. In particular, Amador took up Our Lady of the Snows at Ixpantepec as the patron of the new diocese. He ordered a painting of the Virgin to be hung to the right of the altar in the cathedral and inscribed with the words "The Mother of the Mixtecas." He also ordered local priests to organized parish pilgrimages to the icon.[209] By 1910 the community's cofradía was the richest in the region, pulling in nearly two thousand pesos a year in donations and in so doing outstripping the cults to the Holy Cross and Our Lord of Hearts.[210] At the same time, he also allowed the continuation of certain community rituals that were prohibited by the liberal state and had been long frowned upon by the modernizing Catholic Church. In Ayuquila a young priest and recent graduate of the local seminary bucked church opprobrium and reinvigorated the practice of public flagellation, encouraging the entirety of the Catholic society to engage in the act.[211] In Chila villagers dug up the grave containing Amador's patron and buried him with full honors under the church.[212] In Miltepec villagers gave a similarly illegal burial to the deceased local priest. Although five hundred mourners attended the event, including the bishop, three priests, and four municipal presidents, no one complained about the act.[213]

Amador's first seven years in charge of the diocese witnessed a quite remarkable religious fervor. Educated in the Vatican but born, raised, and trained in the Mixteca Baja, the bishop presided over the institutionalization and intensification of that delicate balance of Roman orthodoxy and local tradition that had marked regional church practice since the 1860s. The records of Amador's pastoral visits contain none of the overbearing snobbery, patent frustration, or ill-concealed disgust that mark Archbishop Gillow's works.[214] In fact, Amador seems perpetually delighted at not only the enthusiasm but also the soundness of his flock's faith. In November 1909 the bishop noted that the inhabitants of Ayuquila "continued to attend all the religious acts celebrated in the parish temple in huge numbers."[215] A year later in Tequixtepec, he lauded Cantu Corro's successful sacramental campaign, the establishment of the rural schools, and the general "good morality" of the people. "It seems that all of the parishioners, except one or two, take communion each month."[216]

Conclusion

How did the church's patent success in the Mixteca Baja compare to the rest of Mexico? Like those of previous evangelical efforts, the effects of Mexico's ecclesiastical revival were distinctly mixed, etching new "liturgical lines" over the old scars of Reform-era politics. Until recently, historians held that in the center and west the new priest-led orthodoxy dovetailed with local pious practices and that throughout Jalisco, Michoacán, Guanajuato, Aguascalientes, and Querétaro, local-born *curas de pueblo* forged highly sacramental, clerical religious cultures.[217] In the north, south, and east, this new ecclesiastical authoritarianism was less successful. Urban or foreign-born priests, parachuted into unfamiliar rural settings, proved less adept at harnessing communitarian indigenous practices to the new puritanical program. Underfunded, isolated, and without state support, priests alienated parishioners and struggled to eradicate popular devotions and encourage a new lay elite. At best, they created new devotional syncretisms: orthodox pious organizations awkwardly grafted onto traditional village cofradías. At worst, they pushed increasingly land-starved peasants toward anti-authoritarian devotions like those of Tomochic or Papantla.[218] The introduction of Social Catholicism complicated Mexico's spiritual geography still further. The establishment of mutual aid societies, workers' circles, and Catholic unions drew middle- and lower-class urban inhabitants toward the church, extending the Catholic restoration into commercial and industrial hubs throughout Mexico. Again, however, rural regions outside the center-west were poorly served. Priestly elites, often allied with local hacendados, were reluctant to introduce Social Catholic organizations, with their implicit criticism of Porfirian capitalism, into the increasingly polarized world that comprised much of the Mexican countryside.[219]

This cartographic exposition of Catholic revival is still extremely valid and provides an invaluable insight into the geography of the breakdown of church-state relations in the revolutionary period. For good reason, both Cristiadas reached their bloody zenith in the center-west. In contrast, northern, southern, and eastern states witnessed limited conflict outside a handful of pious towns. Yet this model of a clerical Catholic geopolitical core with its constellation of urban outliers does discount other regions of rural revival. Perhaps the Cristiadas' long shadow has led historians to overlook other, more self-contained, regions of Porfirian resurgence, where limited postrevolutionary anticlericalism precipitated less sanguinary clashes. In the Mixteca Baja Reform-era clerics and their Social Catholic successors forged flourishing local religious cultures by combining ultramontane concern for clerical obedience and church education with the quiet appropriation of local devotions. In doing so, they cemented and expanded the re-Christianization effort of the early nineteenth century, creating a new generation of locally born priests; a network of new parishes and churches; an educated, sacramental indigenous laity; and a series of powerful, authorized regional cults. Although evidence is extremely slight, many former areas of provincial conservatism, reluctant to surrender their popular base, seemed to have followed a similar policy. In the Diocese of Puebla priests combined clerical rigor with a renewed emphasis on indigenous-language catechisms and the embrace of local cults. By 1910 diocesan authorities had published new sacramental guides in Mixtec, Nahuatl, and Totonac and had green-lighted less orthodox devotions to Our Lady of Tlacuilac, the image of Quetzalcóatl/San Francisco, and, most surprisingly, a mushroom engraved with an image of Jesus Christ.[220] Similarly, in Querétaro former conservatives turned Porfirista loyalists allowed the new diocese's bishop, Ramón Camacho y García, to create an alternate system of private education and harness indigenous devotion to the conservative symbol Our Lady of the Village.[221] Finally, to the north in Nayarit, the bishop and priests of the new Diocese of Tepic attempted to channel civil war–era religious fervor toward a more pietistic orthodoxy, publishing a new catechism in Cora, celebrating festivals in honor of the grass cross of Tepic, and devoting the diocese to the popular pilgrimage route of Our Lady of Talpa.[222] Although they were dispersed, these pockets of provincial piety were not unique. During the next three decades they would generate isolated Cristiada violence, resistance to socialist education, and a strong Catholic or *"mocho"* electoral force.

The pattern of political neutrality, gradual economic change, and religious revival in the Mixteca Baja also paralleled shifts throughout the Catholic world. During the late nineteenth century, liberal regimes in Latin American and southern Europe attempted to reap the benefits of the second Industrial Revolution by softening their anticlerical policies and uniting with conservative elites to attain economic progress. The sanguine conflicts of the midcentury receded, and opposing factions limited their arguments to the pages of newspapers and journals and the classrooms of confessional schools.[223] Regionally, the differing tenors of economic reform and grudging co-existence precipitated the redrawing of political boundaries. In regions of rapid capitalist expansion, elites stuck with the bourgeois values of traditional liberalism, eschewing church attendance and turning toward new modern forms of association including business organizations, Masonic lodges, and sport clubs.[224] Here, priest numbers and church infrastructure declined. Non-elites accepted the liberal nationalism of their employers or turned toward the more radical anticlerical doctrines of anarchism, socialism, or communism. In contrast, in regions of gradual change, where new market imperatives meshed more easily with traditional forms of peasant or artisanal production, a hybrid modern Catholicism, imbued with what one scholar has termed the "paradoxes of orthodoxy," emerged: traditional but modern, bureaucratic but inclusive, hierarchical but democratic, nominally ruled by men but actually run by women.[225] Although this modernist Catholicism was designed in Rome and often aimed at harnessing the urban working class, it often had its most powerful effects in the Catholic and economic semi-periphery. From Finistère, France, through Santander, Spain, to Medellín, Colombia, down to Santiago, Chile, bishops, priests, and rich and poor parishioners united to forge new regional churches that successfully interwove customary rituals and charitable practices with modern associational methods and devotional emphases.[226] In these new regions landlords, industrialists, peasants, and workers created "dense networks of sociability" that not only assuaged class tensions but also formed the building blocks of the political Catholicism of the succeeding decades.[227] The Mixteca Baja would be no different.

CHAPTER 5

"No leaf of the tree moves without the will of God"

Regional Catholicism During the Revolution, 1910–1940

O N AUGUST 19, 1919, TRANQUILINO PACHECO, A FORMER PRIEST OF Tequixtepec, wrote to his "beloved friend" and municipal president, Luis Niño Pacheco. After recounting his day-to-day affairs he turned to the fate of the village, suggesting both the cause of and the solution to the Zapatista raids, harvest failures, and epidemics that had afflicted the village for nearly ten years. He reminded his compadre that two decades ago the priest and parishioners of Tequixtepec had placed crosses on the surrounding hills to ward off "demons" and "devils." But now, "Who remember[ed] the devotion to these crosses? Who remember[ed] the processions? Who remember[ed] these signs of redemption?" He concluded that the villagers of Tequixtepec "no longer ha[d] faith in the holy cross to free them from the evil enemy." As a result, "so many bad things ha[d] befallen the village." To remedy the situation he suggested the revival of devotion to these community icons, the reinvigoration of the cofradía of the Holy Cross, the celebration of regular hilltop Masses, and the inception of a regular festival in honor of the Cross on September 14. Starting with the situation in his own village, he pondered the fate of Mexico as a whole, speculating that without such communal acts "the Americans will intervene . . . what is worse they are all protestants!"[1] During the armed phase of the Mexican Revolution,

203

Tranquilino Pacheco was not alone in his lamentation and spiritual solution. Throughout Mexico, priests and parishioners saw the regular rhythm of violence, pestilence, and hunger as God's punishment for the citizens' declining faith. To survive, they suggested a mass of devotional innovations ranging from the hierarchy's consecration of the Mexican church to the Sacred Heart to the establishment of new apparition cults and messianic sects. In regions like the Mixteca Baja where Porfirian evangelization had worked and revolutionary reforms offered few gains, these devotional innovations highlighted the importance of the sacraments, intensified lay-clerical relations, and aligned the interests of the community and the parish. As a result, in these regions successive governments' anticlerical policies gained few adherents and pushed most villagers into an intense distrust of the postrevolutionary state.

Between 1910 and 1940, Mexico underwent a widespread, popular, and transformative uprising that replaced Díaz's dictatorial regime with a revolutionary state. During the armed phase of the Revolution (1910–1920), peasants, workers, and disgruntled members of the middle class, combined into huge unwieldy armies or operating as small irregular bands, roamed Mexico, attempting to gain regional superiority and implementing formal and impromptu agrarian, labor, and political reforms. At first, revolutionaries worked together against the Porfirian regime. But with the defeat of don Porfirio and the election of the Coahuila rebel Francisco Madero, the alliance fell apart. In late 1911 radical peasants and workers, dissatisfied with the pace of reform, rose up in revolt. In 1913 right-wing remnants of the Porfirian party followed suit, murdering Madero and imposing a militarist regime. For the next two years, General Victoriano Huerta and his battalions of the conscripted poor faced off against northern rebels under Venustiano Carranza and Pancho Villa and southern insurgents under Emiliano Zapata. Despite Huerta's defeat, victory brought limited respite. From 1915 to 1920 Carranza's so-called Constitutionalists wore down and eventually subjugated Villa and Zapata's more radical plebian armies. Yet military superiority was not enough to achieve national control. To pacify Mexico's dissident masses, the Constitutionalists had to push through a radical platform of their own. On the one hand, they borrowed from the defeated radicals and instituted Article 27 of the Constitution, which encouraged the redistribution of land in the form of ejidos. On the other hand, they also reiterated the virulent anticlericalism of their liberal predecessors, asserting state control of the church, banning ecclesiastical properties, and prohibiting confessional education.

For the next twenty years these twin policies, often operating "in tandem," acted to undergird the developing policy of reconstruction. Successive governments combined the *pan* of land grants with the *palo* of cultural reform to placate land-starved peasants, undermine clerical authority, and engender a broad loyalty to the state.[2]

As numerous historians have argued, the effects of revolutionary violence and postrevolutionary state formation percolated through Mexico's divergent regional economies, social hierarchies, and political arrangements in myriad ways, precipitating enthusiasm and horror, collusion and revolt. In the hacienda hubs of Morelos, Mexicali, Tlaxcala, La Laguna, the Yaqui valley, and Veracruz, peasants sided with radical revolutionaries, pressed for the implementation of agrarian reform, and embraced the state's cultural diktats.[3] In the ranchero foothills of Michoacán, Jalisco, and Guanajuato, in contrast, small landowners resisted revolutionary incursion, refused government inducements, and combated state anticlericalism in the first and second Cristero revolts.[4] Although the Mixteca Baja lay hundreds of miles to the south of these Cristero heartlands, parallel histories of Porfirian land distribution, political decentralization, and Catholic revival provoked similar political reactions to the revolutionary and postrevolutionary campaigns. From 1910 to 1920 only a few footloose regional radicals showed any enthusiasm for Madero's political reform, Zapata's land distribution, or Carranza's new constitutional order. Urban elites liquidated their moveable wealth and made their way to the cities or hunkered down and negotiated cash-backed pacts with the transitory armed bands. Rural peasants fled to the hills, bribed visiting insurgents, or took up arms and formed village-based defense forces. From 1920 to 1940, regional convictions were similarly limited. Hacienda-owning sugar magnates and the peasant members of the *sociedades agrícolas* united against land reform and in defense of private property. At the same time, both groups bitterly opposed the anticlerical reforms, heading a strike against the official school from 1934 onward.

Pre-revolutionary developments triggered a defensive reaction to external changes. This reaction, in turn, fed into the modernizing state's presumptions about the country's peasants—their social deference, clerical reverence, and economic apathy.[5] Yet although the Mixteca Baja's inhabitants failed to follow the revolutionary road map of social change, the threat of violence, state incentives, and cultural programs induced substantial transformations in their lives all the same. Extempore and organized land reform forced local elites—keen to maintain the unifying ideology of private property—to sell off their ranches and small haciendas to the few peasants uninvolved in agricultural societies. At the same time, the state's growing presence pressured elites and rural peasants to shape their paternalist social relations into more formal political alliances, first cross-class parents' associations, then confessional organizations, and then political parties. Finally, and perhaps most importantly, the specters of both disorder and coerced change intensified and reshaped lay-clerical relations. As Matthew Butler argues, the Revolution was a period of "genuine religious ferment as well as social upheaval." Radicalization and violence "were accompanied by innovative, often improvised response in the religious sphere."[6] From the under-churched north to the indigenous south, these responses were often radically anti-authoritarian, conscious rebuttals of clerical control. But in regions of recent and effective evangelization, priests often managed to harness people's heightened sense of Providence to serve orthodox Catholic goals. Like their early nineteenth-century predecessors, Rafael Amador y Hernández's seminary vanguard recognized and even encouraged large-scale penitential rites, regional pilgrimages, and beliefs in miraculous intervention. Yet at the same time, the region's parishioners searched for succor in the official church's prescribed remedies, including the Virgin of Guadalupe, the Rosary, and church education. Surrounded by Protestants, "communist" land reformers, and socialist teachers—a region of re-Christianization in a sea of perceived heterodoxy and impiety—the region's subtle balance of clerical flexibility and lay orthodoxy again proved extremely politically powerful, reinforcing popular responses to the state's rural policies for the next forty years.

This chapter is divided into three sections. In the first section, I examine the effects of the armed Revolution on the Mixteca Baja. Here, equitable land distribution, limited political discontent, and stable interclass relations precipitated little support for either Maderista or Zapatista groups. Instead, communities turned toward self-defense, establishing village forces to protect village borders from marauding revolutionaries. At the same time, outside threats brought a renegotiation of religious practice as both priests and parishioners sought divine help for earthly injustices. The second section looks at the political effects of postrevolutionary agrarismo, or land reform, in the region. Because most villages owned lands as sociedades agrícolas, land reform offered few benefits. Instead, regional elites manipulated the state project to avoid their own landholdings and create a political clientele. In so doing, they divided villages in two between a majority of society shareholders and a minority of *ejidatarios*. Consequently, they managed to destabilize the carefully managed moral economy that, reconstituted and rewritten, had governed relations between elites and non-elites up to this point. In the third section of the chapter, I show the effects of state anti-clericalism on the Mixteca Baja. Far from the Cristero heartlands and protected up to a point by the Oaxaca state government's laissez faire attitude to national pronouncements, the region saw little violence during the 1920s. However, with the introduction of socialist education in 1934, priests and parishioners, united by a common regional religious culture, started to protest against the state. As the battlefield shifted from the sociedad agrícola to the local school, cross-class opposition to the postrevolutionary government hardened and broadened, provoking a long-term and widespread adherence to the PAN.

Revolution and Re-Christianization, 1910–1920

In other regions of Oaxaca, excluded politicians and land-hungry peasants welcomed the disintegration of the Porfirian regime, using the opportunity to slough off unpopular jefes políticos and invade hacienda plots.[7] But in the Mixteca Baja political stability and equitable land distribution dampened any incipient uprisings. Although both Maderistas and Zapatistas invaded the region during the early years of the civil war, elites and non-elites alike showed little enthusiasm for political reordering or agrarian radicalism. Forced to survive among disinterested or hostile communities, these invading bands, like their federalist predecessors, took to banditry and theft. As a result, like Luis González y González's *revolucionados*, most peasants experienced the decade as one of "savage crimes, robbery, kidnappings, hanging corpses, ravished women, and religious images stripped of their Milagros."[8] In response communities attempted both political and spiritual solutions. Many established village-based defense forces or *defensas sociales* to combat roaming bands. Still more turned to the regional church, reading each revolutionary encroachment as providential punishment, each near escape as divine reward. In an attempt to restrain God's wrath, priests and parishioners sought complex religious remedies, hastily blended devotional drafts combining Roman, Mexican, and local elements.

On November 20, 1910, the defeated presidential candidate Francisco Madero declared an uprising against Díaz's sclerotic regime. Although the announcement of revolt inspired waves of insurrection throughout the northern sierras and the sugar-farming south, in the Mixteca Baja no one moved. According to Saul Reyes Aguilar's Revolution-era memoir, his father (a hacienda owner) and a few other excluded members of the mestizo elite met up with Puebla revolutionaries, collected arms, and took to the hills in late 1910.[9] If they did, they made little impression on the local jefe político, who reported "complete tranquility" in the region.[10] Instead, Maderismo arrived from outside. In February 1911, the Maderista army arrived in Silacayoapan before making its way to Huajuapan.[11] Undoubtedly, some locals joined up. Yet according to Reyes Aguilar, most were well-off merchants, recently arrived in the Mixteca Baja and keen to take advantage of the movement to scale the political ladder. In fact, most Mixtecs probably reacted more like Reyes Aguilar's devout mother, who locked herself inside her house and prostrated herself before an image of the Sacred Heart of Jesus, only opening the door to the local priest, who joined her in prayer.[12]

Despite Madero's victory, the Mixteca Baja had little respite from the revolutionary violence. In November 1911 Emiliano Zapata, frustrated at the slow pace of agrarian reform, took up arms against his former chief. Gradually, military forces pushed the Zapatistas out of their Morelos base and toward southern Puebla, eastern Guerrero, and northern Oaxaca.[13] In early 1912 around four hundred rebels under Eufemio Zapata and the Ayutla cantina owner Jesús "El Tuerto" Morales invaded the region, besieging Acatlán and then Huajuapan.[14] The following year, former federal soldiers turned fair-weather Zapatistas Higinio Aguilar, Juan Andreu Almazán, and Benjamín Argumedo also moved into the Mixteca Baja.[15] These repeated incursions generated some valuable local converts. By 1915 there were Zapatista bases in Acatlán under Ricardo Reyes Márquez, in Tonalá under Miguel Salas, in the Hacienda la Pradera under Isidro Vargas, and around Suchitepec under Iñes Villagómez.[16] Yet these local leaders were not land-starved villagers. Most were ranchers, lured by the promise of political and military control by the increasingly desperate Zapatista high command.[17] Reyes Márquez was a former teacher and scribe for the jefe político of Acatlán. José Larios was a "rancher" and owner of "very many livestock" who joined the Zapatistas to protect his sheep and goats from raiding bands. Iñes Villagómez was a scion of the Villagómez clan, who established a small livestock ranch just south of Petlalcingo. He only joined the Zapatistas because the widow of a man his son had murdered accused his entire family of sympathizing with the rebels.[18] Linked neither by kinship, common provenance, nor ideology, these ambitious leaders came into regular conflict. In 1915 Miguel Salas murdered Isidro Vargas. A few months later Aguilar, Almazán, and Argumedo killed a group of Reyes Márquez's men and forced the Acatlán rebel to flee to the Carrancista camp.[19]

Apart from these opportunist caciques, some made efforts to conquer the hearts and minds of the local Mixtec peasants. Salas, probably the most savvy of the local Zapatista leaders, claimed that he was trying to "inculcate and develop in the Mixteca Baja the revolutionary ideas we have been sustaining for so long."[20] When the Guerrero revolutionary leader Encarnación Díaz arrived, he also ordered his lieutenants to travel to the region's pueblos, discover the major landholders, and distribute their lands among the landless.[21] In the villages around Hacienda la Pradera such incentives worked. In 1912 hacienda peons burned down the buildings, forced the manager to flee, and squatted on the lands. Over the next four years, La Pradera and the neighboring pueblos of Tacache de Mina, Mariscala, and San Nicolas Hidalgo would become safe havens for the region's disparate Zapatista groups.[22] Yet most Zapatista groups were not comprised of dispossessed peasants, but rather extended familial groups. The mainstays of Iñes Villagómez's forces consisted of his five sons and two daughters.

In fact, outside Morelos, the sugar zone of southern Puebla, and the ethnically divided Guerrero montaña, Zapatista relations with contiguous villages were often tense.[23] And in the Mixteca Baja, with its history of recent land reform, Zapatistas from outside the region not only struggled to engage local communities but also often seriously misunderstood local land tenure arrangements. For example, on November 20, 1915, the municipal president of Zapotitlán Lagunas wrote to Zapata to explain that the village had bought their lands as part of a *sociedad agrícola* during the mid-nineteenth century. Each villager was a shareholder in the society, and the junta menor of the society divided lands equitably. With the arrival of the Zapatistas, however, the land arrangement started to fall apart. Calixto Quintero, a mestizo merchant, sent his nephew to fight on behalf of Salas's forces. He then proceeded to use his nephew's connections to claim that the "authorities" had "stolen" his lands. In early November, Zapatistas arrived and handed out a large proportion of the society's terrain to the interloper.[24] Similarly, in November 1915 the authorities of San Mateo del Río explained to Zapata that they had purchased their lands from the local cacique. But when Zapatistas arrived in the neighboring community of Santiago del Río, villagers persuaded the rebels to support their attempt to take over San Mateo's lands. Backed by the Zapatista forces, they entered the pueblo,

Figure 10: Zapatistas entering the town of Huajuapan
during the Revolution. Museo Regional de Huajuapan.

stole over 783 pesos' worth of livestock, and proceeded to destroy the village's crops. Mocking the Zapatista slogan, the villagers asked whether this orchestrated robbery and land grab was what the rebel leader meant by "land and justice."[25]

Isolated, unable to harness support through social reform, and desperate, Zapatista bands increasingly turned to robbery and extortion to fund their campaign. In January 1915 the Guerrero Zapatista Anselmo Guzmán attacked Zapotitlán Lagunas, sacked the houses, robbed the merchants, raped the women, and mocked their husbands and fathers.[26] In June 1915 Salas's force stole fifty-nine measures of maize that the peasants of Atoyac had just harvested from their lands, leaving "their wives weeping and their children starving."[27] Zapotitlán Lagunas and Atoyac got off relatively lightly. Zapatista forces descended on Tequixtepec three times from 1913 to 1914. During the last assault, three hundred rebels forced the villagers to take to the hills, stole the church ornaments, and burned down the town. When the new priest arrived four months later, he found "nothing except ruins, mountains of ashes, burned trees and desolation without any kind of animals." The villagers, fearful of further retribution, still cowered in the hills.[28] These community attacks often precipitated extended blood feuds between villagers and rebels. Between 1916 and 1919 Iñes Villagómez and his clan made repeated attempts on Chazumba, blaming the villagers for betraying them to the Carrancistas. Even in 1919, after Iñes and four of his sons had been killed, the youngest, nineteen-year-old Castulo, invaded the village and attempted to burn it to the ground.[29]

At the same time, their ongoing need for funds also tied these local rebels (like Anton Blok's robber thugs) to the regional elite, alienating communities even further. The manager of the Hacienda la Pradera returned to the region after paying Aguilar a large bribe. Almazán, perhaps the most opportunist of all the Mixteca's Zapatistas, placed his base in Huajuapan and spent his time cavorting with the daughters of the town's Spanish landowners.[30] In a poignant note written in June 1918, the priest of Ayuquila wrote that the Revolution simply consisted of "constant invasions, the stealing of food, pasture land and money, and the sowing of panic in the communities." He recounted the deaths of at least five villagers at the hands of roaming Zapatista bands over the past year.[31] In fact, Reyes Aguilar's conclusion that most local Zapatistas "operated without any revolutionary plan" and that their "only mission was to rob and destroy whatever was in their path" seems close to the mark.[32]

In response to Zapatista incursions, villagers marshaled both military and spiritual defenses. Many spontaneously collected arms and formed *defensas sociales*. When Zapatistas invaded Tequixtepec in February 1913, they took the municipal palace and demanded payments of cash, food, and livestock. In response, villagers tricked the bandits into believing they were collecting funds, picked up a few scattered rifles and machetes, and turned on the imposters, killing at least three. A year later they formed a more formal defense force and repelled Zapatista invaders on the edge of the town.[33] During the same year other neighboring villages like Chazumba, Trujapan, and Acaquizapan followed suit.[34] These were not simply armed appendages of a desperate elite, like the famed Spanish-dominated *defensa social* of

Durango, but cross-class popular organizations, like those established in the Bajío to combat Chavistas or those one thousand "armed ranchers" drafted into pacification duty in upstate Veracruz.[35] Although these community groups started off as broadly neutral organizations, established organically to fight off specific threats, as Zapatista attacks increased communities gravitated toward national groups that promised the return of stability and order. At first they begged the Huerta government for arms, federal troops, and support. In early 1914 the municipal authorities of Tequixtepec wrote directly to Huerta to request the installation of a federal garrison in the village.[36] But as Huerta's regime fell, villages turned to Carranza's troops to fulfill the same role. In 1916 Carrancista forces in Tehuacán and Acatlán organized defensas sociales throughout the Mixteca Baja. Selected members of these defensas sociales were given food, money, guns, and military training on the surrounding hills.[37] Over the next three years, formal Carrancista forces would call on these community organizations to help pursue the remaining Zapatistas. In fact, as Knight argues, "it was only by enlisting such local support that the army . . . could undertake offensives in the remote country districts."[38] For example, in August 1919 Reyes Márquez combined 150 federal troops with the defensas of Acaquizapan, Cosolotepec, and Chazumba. On August 16 they encountered the Villagómez forces outside Cosolotepec, killed Iñes's son Friolán, and forced the rest to flee.[39]

Beyond these military and political solutions, priests and parishioners also sought divine aid, precipitating a process of re-Christianization similar to that of the mid-nineteenth century. For the ecclesiastical hierarchy, the disciplined clerical vanguard, and the orthodox lay devotees, the Revolution was God's punishment. This providential rationale came from the top. During the first years of civil war, the Mexican ecclesiastical hierarchy issued repeated warnings, arguing that impiety, the perversion of customs, and the ignorance of sacramental duties were the causes of the increase in violence, sacrilege, and disorder. In particular, many prelates viewed the Revolution as "divine punishment" for the laicization of Mexican society after the Reform wars of the nineteenth century. In response, the ecclesiastical hierarchy suggested mass repentance and an increase in penitential acts, heartfelt prayers, and the performing of the sacraments. This ecclesiastical rationale reached its height in early 1914 when the ecclesiastical hierarchy organized the consecration of the Mexican nation to the Sacred Heart of Jesus. The celebration was designed as "the greatest guarantee of the salvation of the country," the processions, penitential acts, and Masses "the symbol of a repentant Catholic people."[40] As an obedient Roman prelate, Amador followed suit. Immediately after the first Zapatista incursion in 1912, he issued a letter arguing that the "present problems" were divine retribution for earthly sins. Similarly, when he visited his hometown, Chila, in early 1913 he reminded the thousands of listeners that "the Revolution [wa]s God's vengeance on the impious."[41]

In much of Mexico, this official "providential economy of transgression, repentance and atonement" fell flat.[42] In these regions of de-Christianization, where the clerical presence was weak, revolutionaries like Villa and Carranza attempted to harness the popular distrust of priests and engaged in a series of anticlerical campaigns.[43] At the same time, underpoliced devotees invented their own economies, mixing Protestant, spiritist, millenarian, and unauthorized indigenous rituals with Catholic acts.[44] Yet in regions of re-Christianization that had recent histories of harmonious lay-clerical relations and little revolutionary enthusiasm, the providential economy, reformed and reinterpreted at the village level, became the dominant framework for understanding day-to-day suffering. In the Mixteca Baja priests and parishioners understood each Zapatista incursion, each violent *quemazón*, as divine revenge and each *defensa social* victory as evidence of good practice and God's consequent favor. For example, when villagers defeated invading Zapatistas in Santa Gertrudis in December 1913, the local priest described the victory as a "miracle of the Eucharist." When the neighboring village of Tequixtepec fought off the same band on May 3, 1914, the priest affirmed that this event was a "miracle postulated by God and Our Lady of Perpetual Succor that protected the village in its hour of danger."

Individual examples cemented this belief. When revolutionaries eventually burned the village to the ground, the only house left standing belonged to a man "whose good Christian life" had ensured his survival.[45] In 1919 Tranquilino Pacheco, the former priest of Tequixtepec, explained to the community that God "directs the revolution with his providence, punishing the pueblos that lack his superior government." Or in simple terms, "No leaf of the tree moves without the will of God." Revealing the efficacy of Amador's seminary education program, he even backed his claims by referencing Jacques-Bénigne Bossuet, the seventeenth-century French theologian who had argued that God's Providence guided all historical occurrences. He suggested that the only way to alleviate God's anger was to perform "good works like acts of piety, public actions, processions, pilgrimages and masses repeated many times."[46] Priests, as the official interpreters of these repeated auguries, were the most vocal advocates of these providential explanations, but parishioners were also believers. Pacheco's friend, the municipal president of Tequixtepec, Luis Niño Pacheco, clearly understood Providence the same way. In 1914 he told the priest that he had escaped the Zapatistas because of the intervention of Our Lady of Perpetual Succor and the Holy Cross. Twenty years later he wrote that he felt as if "a supernatural force" had moved him out of the way of the rebels' bullets.[47]

This heightened sense of Providence, this hardening of the link between the temporal and the spiritual spheres, provoked a kind of escalating devotional free-for-all as both priests and parishioners desperately employed international, national, regional, communal, and personal rituals to quell God's ire. Initially, Amador favored diocesan worship of the Virgin, the Sacred Heart of Jesus, and the Rosary. In doing so, he consciously covered the three strains of regional Catholicism: the Mexican, the modern European, and the colonial Dominican. Throughout the last months of 1911, he organized repeated pilgrimages to the recently constructed shrine to the Virgin of Guadalupe in Huajuapan. Although the harvest was in full swing, on November 12 five hundred devotees from Miltepec "full of fervor and confidence" made the short journey "to ask for peace." The celebrations culminated in the diocesan capital's "glorious celebration" of the image on the image's feast day of December 12. Throughout the diocese, smaller parishes held their own fiestas. On the same day in Ayuquila, three hundred faithful received the Eucharist "with the intention of asking God for peace in the Patria." The pilgrimages continued well into the next year. On March 12, 1913, the priest of Tequixtepec led six hundred parishioners and three local bands to the Huajuapan church.[48]

At the same time, the bishop also promoted the redemptive qualities of the Sacred Heart of Jesus. During his early tenure as vicar general of Huajuapan, Amador had attempted to establish parish associations in honor of the icon but with limited success. With the consecration of the Mexican church to the Sacred Heart in early 1914, however, the cult gained considerable purchase. The devotion, popularized in France as a means to counter radical European anticlericalism and replete with a series of penitential rites, provided a ready-made solution to Mexican impiety.[49] In 1914 and 1915 Amador reminded local priests of their duty to establish devotions to the Sacred Heart. He even attempted to localize the cult by adorning the wrist of Huajuapan's Our Lord of Hearts with the Sacred Heart cult's symbol of Christ's five wounds. Throughout the civil war, clerics and lay Catholics enthusiastically embraced the devotion. Associations arose in Tonalá, Miltepec, Tequixtepec, Chila, Chazumba, Tlacotepec, and most of their outlying pueblos during the period. Priests in the same villages successfully organized month-long celebrations of the icon, including the exposition of the Eucharist, every June. By 1925 the priest of Huajuapan claimed that nearly every diocesan home possessed an icon of "the Sacred Heart of Jesus" and named a committee of the most devout female followers to ensure the devotion's dominance.[50] At the same time, branches of the Apostolado de la Oración, an association connected to the cult, which encouraged weekly prayers, monthly Masses, and the maintenance of the church icon, sprang up throughout the region, forming a hard core of both male and female believers. Over the next half century, Apostolado members would form a clericalized lay vanguard, eagerly involve themselves in disputes between church and state, and eventually coalesce into the village branches of Acción Católica and the PAN.

Finally, diocesan authorities also encouraged the regular use of the Rosary. The Dominicans introduced the devotion to the Mixteca Baja during the colonial period, and during the late nineteenth century "the Rosary pope," Leo XIII, revived the practice, issuing twelve encyclicals in which he established the Rosary as a public devotion and linked its regular use to the defense of the church against impious secular forces. According to Leo XIII, by "recalling the mysteries of salvation in succession," the Rosary was to act as a "balm for the wounds of society."[51] During the revolutionary period, the counting of beads and the repetition of Hail Marys and Our Fathers became a kind of penitential addendum to all religious ceremonies. Easter week celebrations, Guadalupe Masses, and pilgrimages all now included "prayers to the rosary" designed, as the priest of Miltepec claimed, to "calm the present calamities." At the same time, individual priests also established daily devotions to the Rosary. In Ayuquila the priest introduced regular prayers in August 1915. Within months he reported that this "daily nocturnal act" was now "extremely popular" and that hundreds of devotees attended the ritual, which culminated in a month of prayer in November of that year.[52]

These broad, orthodox devotions, often initiated at the suggestion of the Mexican hierarchy, were influential. Yet as Zapatista incursions and the threat of violence increased, diocesan authorities also turned to regional devotions to atone for local sins. In particular, Amador pushed regular pilgrimages to the image of Our Lady of the Snows in Ixpantepec. Diocesan-level pilgrimages were organized in 1914, 1915, and 1916. They included thousands of worshippers from individual parishes. In fact, the cofradía of the image became so wealthy during the Revolution that it could spend over two thousand pesos on church reconstruction and still retain a capital of fifteen hundred pesos. Events at the 1916 celebration cemented the image's perceived powers. During the festivities, the Tlacotepec priest gained permission from the cofradía leaders to lead a procession of the image throughout the village in order to ask for rain. When they arrived in the Ixpantepec cemetery, the clouds opened, and it started to pour. Over the next ten days, the rains never stopped. According to the cleric, the event "filled the devotees with faith."[53]

Beyond these top-down celebrations, village priests also imbued local images, especially the popular images of crucified Christ, with penitential and redemptive qualities. In 1913 and 1914 the priest of Ayuquila reported that he had devoted the celebrations of the fourth Friday of Lent, in honor of the local Christ, to "an end to the endless conflicts," not only preaching on the subject but also getting parishioners to engage in prayer and penitential acts. In 1914 seven hundred faithful—the entire village except a handful of men—turned up for confession and Communion.[54] In 1916 the priest of Ayuquila visited the Easter week celebrations in honor of Our Lord of Pities in the nearby village of Tamazola. Expectant parishioners had not only paid for a Mass by three priests, but also invited the Christ cofradías of Ayuquila, Chilixtlahuaca, Santa Catarina Estancia, and Chapultepec to attend. During the Friday celebrations, all five villages carried their respective Christs in procession through the village. The celebrations included acts of penitence, a Communion of thousands, and much "weeping." According to the Ayuquila priest, the performance "moved people so much that many said they had never witnessed such elaborate festivities."[55] As this example suggests, certain community devotions gained fame for their protective qualities as village fates diverged. As neighboring parishioners desperately sought divine help, small extempore pilgrimage circuits emerged. Around Miltepec, local villages risked revolutionary shakedowns to attend the annual festivities of Our Lord of Wounds. By 1921 the priest claimed that all the villages from Huajuapan to Tehuacán came to the celebrations and that they brought "a prodigy of offerings and gifts." In that year alone, three new villages attended the event, and the communities of Coxcatlán and Miahuatlán, "despite their poverty," donated two angels and two vases to the church.[56]

Finally, revolutionary violence not only encouraged the recycling and revamping of existing traditions but also considerable devotional innovation. As Edward Wright-Rios argues, parishioners in the Archdiocese of Oaxaca sculpted these new rites from both indigenous traditions and modern Catholic practice. East of the Mixteca Baja, in the valley of Tehuacán, an indigenous woman from Tlacoxcolco claimed that Miltepec's Our Lord of Wounds appeared to her, spoke in Nahuatl, administered the sacraments, and delivered a sermon to the devotees. Unsurprisingly, ecclesiastical authorities and local priests looked on the apparition with a mixture of resignation and hostility, proof of their illiterate, unschooled parishioners' borderline paganism.[57] In regions of Mexico with limited histories of lay-clerical interaction, similar outré devotions emerged, exposing the tensions between the new, pushy seminary-trained priests and their less orthodox followers. Devils, Moseses, Marías, and mad Messiahs stalked the land. In 1912 outside Guadalajara, a "mysterious celestial figure" appeared, claimed to be the Messiah, and announced that the end of the world was nigh. Seven years later in Tequisistlan, Oaxaca, parishioners attempted to crucify a deranged Italian man who also claimed to be the second coming of Jesus Christ.[58]

Although these idiosyncratic cults and popular apparitions gained substantial publicity, most devotional innovations were much more orthodox. In regions with long traditions of lay-clerical negotiation and successful church education programs, priests and parishioners designed divine solutions together, producing a series of icons and practices with limited or no disagreement. In the Mixteca Baja, these remedies took two forms. On the one hand, ecclesiastical authorities, local clerics, and the faithful started an intensive campaign of erecting crosses on hills at the borders of individual villages. The practice, designed to keep the devil from the community, had been resurrected during the early 1900s. But with the devil now roaming the region in the form of Zapatista bandits and predatory troops, the practice gained immediate political import, and villagers throughout the region adopted the ritual. In 1914 the bishop and the priest of Tlacotepec led a huge procession of villagers up to the hill of Yucuquimi. Here they placed an image of the Holy Cross, celebrated Mass on a makeshift altar, and handed out wine and wafers to over one thousand penitent guests. According to the priest, the ritual was designed to "keep Satan" from the parish.[59] In 1916 the residents of Tonalá erected a similar cross "with much enthusiasm" on a hill overlooking the town. Three years later, the villagers of Paxtlahuaca did the same, dutifully singing hymns to the Sacred Heart and praying to the Rosary.[60] In 1921 the bishop, a constant advocate of the power of this hilltop variant of the cross cult, expanded the community ritual into a diocesan practice. On April 5, 1921, he announced that he was going to "combat Satan using the instrument of redemption, the Holy Cross." He called together over twenty priests from throughout the western part of the diocese and asked them to bring their flocks to the foot of the Cerro Verde. After assembling over five thousand devotees, they made their way up the hill, constructed an altar, held Communion, and prayed for peace. The act, described by one priest as "one of the most remarkable in the history of the diocese," not only reflected continuing popular religiosity but also demonstrated the two-way nature of these devotional negotiations. Just as parishioners had taken up devotions to Guadalupe and the Sacred Heart, so Amador was prepared to authorize community practices.[61]

On the other hand, priests and parishioners also worked together to create more effective intermediaries between the communities and a wrathful God. Despite privations, villagers throughout the diocese spent thousands of pesos on new church icons. In Tequixtepec, cofradía members bought new images of Our Lady of Perpetual Succor, Our Lord of the Sepulcher, Saint Joseph, Saint Peter, and Our Lady of the Rosary during the first five years of the Revolution alone.[62] When funds were short, the clergy and the lay inhabitants also experimented with changing the names of ineffective icons. In 1914 the priest of Tequixtepec changed the name of one of the pueblo's images of the crucified Christ from Our Lord of the Sanctuary to Our Lord of Clemency, hoping that more apposite nomenclature would glean better results.[63] Hard-pressed communities also sought to change their devotional practices aimed at these divine intermediaries, believing that by asking for succor in a different manner, they might better harness the image's power. In Juxtlahuaca in 1915, the priest and members of the predominantly indigenous barrio of Santo Domingo took the old image of Saint James from the town's main church and placed it in their own chapel. They then formed a cofradía, bought up several cattle, and pastured them on the sociedad agrícola's lands. The same year the priest reported that "they held a much bigger festival than that of the center" and, as a result, managed to avert Zapatista invasion.[64]

Finally, communities also attempted to change the physical form of their existing images. In 1919 Virginia Perpetua, the head of Tequixtepec's Daughters of Mary association and a famed local *beata*, had a vision. She claimed that if the villagers lifted the reclining figure of Our Lord of the Holy Burial to his feet, placed him on a cross in the central altar of the local church, and implored him to forgive their sins, God would end the village's suffering. The vision, similar in many ways to the Tlacoxcolco apparition described by Edward Wright-Rios, was radical. By voicing the vision, doña Virginia threatened both clerical and gender hierarchies. Yet Tequixtepec's visionary, unlike her Tlacoxcolco peer, understood the rules of the game and pushed the limits of orthodox behavior sufficiently to ensure divine appeasement but not too much to offend diocesan norms. As a result, the local priest quickly accepted the innovation, nailing the Christ to a hastily constructed cross and institutionalizing a celebration of the new saint on the second Friday of Lent. Ecclesiastical authorization soon followed. In 1921 the bishop agreed to bless the image, organized a Mass by three priests, and named godparents for the ceremony. Devotees arrived from villages along the Huajuapan-Tehuacán valley, and the local priest claimed that he witnessed "much piety." Summing up the local belief in the efficacy of the providential economy, the villages called the icon Our Lord of Forgiveness.[65]

The establishment of this providential economy had profound and long-lasting effects. Amador's young priests were forced to put the diocese's philosophy of devotional flexibility to the test and engage in dynamic negotiations with their desperate indigenous parishioners over communal security. The threat of violence upped the stakes: success delivered obedience and sacramental orthodoxy; failure brought the erosion of clerical authority. Thus, when the seminary graduate Daniel Ibáñez Soriano arrived in Tequixtepec in 1913, he immediately had to engage in his parishioners' pragmatic "whatever works" approach to village Catholicism, celebrating the protective powers of the Eucharist and the Virgin of Guadalupe (1913); then those of Saint Catherine (1914), patron of the outlying pueblo of Chinango; then those of Our Lady of Perpetual Succor (1914); and finally those of Our Lord of Forgiveness (1919).[66] This experience of devotional dialogue prepared lay-clerical relations for the difficult upcoming decades, drawing priests closer to their charges and ridding them of their residual prejudices over indigenous religiosity.

This shift along the spectrum from wary paternalism to something approaching grateful respect can be best viewed in the speech delivered by José Cantu Corro at celebrations of the Day of Race in Huajuapan on October 12, 1919. The young priest was a local merchant's son, had graduated from the local seminary in 1909, had worked in Tequixtepec and Tezoatlán during the Revolution, and was the perfect product of Amador's diocesan vision. His speech, eventually published in 1924, not only repeated the familiar tropes of Catholic nationalism, Social Catholicism, and sacramental orthodoxy, but also added a new confidence in the power of Mexico's racial heritage. As one might expect, Cantu Corro lauded the qualities of European Catholics, or what he described as "the Latin race," lifting entire lists of composers, artists, writers, and pugilists from Reyes's 1895 *Nociones elementales de historia patria*. Yet he also celebrated the qualities of the country's indigenous groups, inverting nineteenth-century discourses and praising their "tenacity," their "loyalty," and their "religious and civic virtues." Pre-empting the work of anthropologists like Manuel Gamio and Moisés Sáenz, he blamed their drunkenness not on innate character flaws, but on "the poor examples of the Europeans." At the same time, he revealed his own revolutionary-era experiences, encouraging listeners to "talk to the Indians as brother in their own dialect" and claiming that he "loved the Indians and was a compadre to them." Finally, he also concluded that Mexicans, as "the descendents of Spaniards and Indians," blessed and brought together by the providential presence of the Virgin of Guadalupe, encapsulated the best qualities of both groups. In so doing, they formed a Catholic bulwark against the "cold, calculating," "impious," and "destructive" Anglo Saxons. In many ways, the Cantu Corro speech, with its celebration of indigenous values, reached back to the colonial-era utopianism of the early missionaries. But in other ways, the priest's celebration of Mexicans' mixed heritage offered a new Catholic version of racial politics, born from the necessities of Revolution-era survival. As such, the text resembled a kind of ecclesiastical version of José Vasconcelos's *La raza cosmica*; the Mexicans portrayed within embodied a divinely inspired hybrid vigor.[67]

If devotional dialogue offered local priests quick lessons in rural pragmatism, the same negotiations also affected lay parishioners. Just as mid-nineteenth-century Catholics embraced the ecclesiastical call for a rigid Catholic morality, so the repeated need for divine intercession increased the sacramental rhythm for Revolution-era Catholics. Although no exact figures

Figure 11: José Cantu Corro, one of the first graduates of the new seminary and one of the leading intellectuals of the diocese for the next thirty years. *Historia de Tonalá, Oaxaca coleccionada por el Sr. Pbro. D. Avelino de la T. Mora López para conmemorar el III centenario del hallazgo de La Santa Cruz en la gruta del Río de Santa María Tindú, Oax.*

exist, priests' diaries suggest that regular Communion became extremely common during the period. Between April 1915 and April 1916 the priest of Ayuquila reported huge Communions of more than three hundred residents on at least twenty occasions. In July 1915 the priest claimed that "the faithful" had "not lost their faith or their piety." In fact, "they celebrat[ed] fiestas and [attended] the sacraments with greater frequency." Most surprisingly, the "vice of drunkenness" had "almost vanished," "dances happen[ed] very little," and "other public vices ha[d] been disappearing." In all, he concluded, "the priest [wa]s very well-respected and the faithful [we]re very obedient."[68] Even assuming that Ayuquila's regular attendees were the same, this description indicates a Communion rate of at least 15 percent. In comparison, Edward Wright-Rios estimates that Communion rates in Oaxaca only reached around 4 percent, and Matthew Butler argues that Communion rates in the Archbishopric of Mexico at the 1914 Sacred Heart celebrations were little over 12 percent.[69] The parishioners of Tequixtepec embraced a similar orthodoxy. In 1911 the local priest claimed that during the Lent celebrations, his "affability and paternal kindness" persuaded fourteen hundred parishioners to confess and take Communion.[70]

Even as villagers sought to quell revolutionary violence through penitential acts, they also sought to extend these rites to cope with other natural phenomena. Priests and parishioners had always engaged in elaborate festivities on the day of the Holy Cross (May 3) to call for rain. Yet when rain failed to appear, parishioners were often left to their own devices and held priest-free rain ceremonies in mountain caves.[71] But by the end of the revolutionary period, clerics and lay faithful regularly came together to end droughts. In 1917 Amador encouraged his priests to use the special Mass "Ad petendam pluviam" if rains were not forthcoming.[72] Four years later, worshippers in Petlalcingo persuaded their local priests to organize a penitential procession to call for rain. After carrying the image of Our Lord of the Calvary through the streets, they held a sung Mass, prayed, wept, and took Communion. On the last day of the weeklong entreaties, "a notable thing happened." "Christ covered the sky with clouds and water fell on all the pueblos. All the devotees recognized that it was the protection of God, obtained by Our Lord of the Calvary."[73] Other priests tapped into local traditions even more directly. In the same year, the priest of Tlacotepec heard that villagers believed that the burial of the image of Saint Peter the Apostle under the walls of the local church was causing the prolonged drought. As a result, he persuaded his parishioners to dig up the image, dust it off, and establish a new cofradía. After he blessed the restored statue, the rains eventually fell.[74]

In the Mixteca Baja, an earlier program of land distribution and the consequent rise of an indigenous landowning class dissuaded most inhabitants from supporting Maderista or Zapatista revolutionaries. Instead, communities sought sanctuary both through the creation of defensas sociales and through rituals of prayer, repentance, pilgrimage, and devotion. Some of these rituals were diocesan dictates, others were revamped community traditions, and still others were imaginative innovations. By engaging in this devotional debate, the clergy tested their seminary instruction, adapting their late nineteenth-century training to a new, more violent age. In most cases, long histories of good lay-clerical relations combined with Amador's quiet acceptance of local traditions to aid the priests' task. Whereas in much of the country elite and popular forms of Christianity diverged, the Mixteca Baja again became a region of re-Christianization. Despite a decade of revolutionary violence, drought, hunger, and influenza, by 1920 most communities were engaged in a modern hypersacramental Catholicism with a smattering of regional variations, and priests and parishioners were perhaps closer than they had ever been before. In effect, the Revolution cemented what the Porfirian evangelization had only half achieved: a true community of Catholic believers. Over the next four decades this regional Catholic culture would prove extremely resilient to state-led change.

The Failure of Postrevolutionary Land Reform, 1920–1940

By 1920 an uneasy peace had descended upon the Mixteca Baja. Most local Zapatistas had been murdered, paid off, or co-opted. The coup against Venustiano Carranza had, for the time being, quelled fears of incipient government anticlericalism. Yet over the next twenty years, state policies opened up new regional rifts. In particular, the introduction of official land reform caused prolonged local conflicts, institutionalizing the isolated misunderstandings of the revolutionary era. As historians have argued, state agrarismo was designed specifically to appease regions of revolutionary insurgency. At the same time, it only offered "unitary solutions" to Mexico's diverse rural problems.[75] Agrarian legislation only recognized two forms of unequal land tenure. First, Article 27 of the 1917 Constitution envisaged the Mexican countryside as essentially divided between encroaching, if poorly funded, haciendas and independent villages.[76] Second, although the 1934 Agrarian Code adapted the legislation slightly, it basically acknowledged that some regions of hacienda predominance lacked independent villages and thus allowed rural workers living on haciendas the opportunity to acquire land. Between 1920 and 1940 these two models of land tenure circumscribed rural reforms. In regions that approximated these models, agrarismo was fairly successful. In fertile central areas (like Oaxaca's central valleys) where landholding remained divided between invasive haciendas and independent villages, communities gratefully accepted state largesse and ruined local estates.[77] In others areas (like Mexicali, La Laguna, the Yaqui valleys, and Tuxtepec) where well-funded fincas had effectively usurped communal lands and now employed a relatively rootless proletariat, peasants also supported state reforms.[78]

But as scholars have increasingly shown, these models failed to encompass the wide variation in regional economies and landholding patterns established during the Porfiriato. In particular, Porfirian changes had not only enlarged local haciendas, but also provoked an expansion of individual farms along the foothills of the two sierras. Here state agrarismo was a disaster. To the west in Jalisco, Michoacán, and the Bajío, ranchers, who were keen to retain their lands and imbued with a strong belief in the sanctity of private property, bitterly opposed the reforms, conflating what they perceived as a communist land grab with state anticlericalism and rising up in the First (1926–1929) and Second (1934–1938) Cristiada revolts.[79] To the east, in regions of restrained state anticlericalism and limited clerical force (like San Luis Potosí and Hidalgo), ranchers simply harnessed reforms to extend their political, economic, and social control over neighboring indigenous groups.[80]

In the Mixteca Baja, state reforms precipitated even more contradictory results. During the nineteenth century, the region's elites and peasants had established an economic pact in which the peasants accepted increasing commercial exploitation in return for the right to buy up former caciques' lands. Despite Zapatista incursions, this pact remained intact. Regional elites still bought local produce at criminally low prices. In Huajuapan around twenty local merchants amassed considerable fortunes forcing peasants to sell their palm hats on the cheap. Just outside the district capital, Antonio García Peral continued his father's trade, forwarding money to hard-up villagers so they could fatten up goats and sheep.[81] But in exchange most villagers still owned their lands as shareholders in sociedades agrícolas. In 1936 the state treasury estimated that over forty villages in Huajuapan managed properties in this way.[82] In this context, the state was utterly ill equipped to deal with its redistributive role. Rather than attacking commercial monopolists and attempting to build a popular peasant-state alliance, uncomprehending federal officials created small agrarista groups around the region's major towns. Presuming that village assertions of widespread land ownership were elaborate elite ruses to protect large estates, they directed land reform at the society properties. By doing so, they created violent interclass conflict, cleaving apart closed corporate communities as elite-backed society shareholders faced off against state-backed agrarista alliances.

Despite this rather bleak overview, there were some regions of the Mixteca Baja, around the major sugar haciendas, that benefitted from the government's agrarian program. Here, in the isolated Zapatista strongholds, the official land tenure model of encroaching haciendas and defensive villages closely paralleled local circumstances. As a result, reform in these scattered pueblos generated substantial popular support. Just months after the publication of the Constitution, for example, the inhabitants of Tacache de Mina, on the edge of Hacienda la Pradera, petitioned for an ejido. The Gómez family had abandoned the property during the early revolutionary incursions, so redistribution was relatively swift. By 1921 new president Álvaro Obregón, keen to pacify former Zapatista regions, had signed over 846 hectares of Gómez's lands to the community. Nine years later, the state governor, wanting to shore up regions of agrarista support in a Cristero-sympathizing zone, increased the grant by another six hundred hectares.[83] Soon other villages on the boundaries of the plantation followed suit. In 1931 agrarian engineers divided the remaining La Pradera lands between San Nicolas Hidalgo (1,724 hectares), Atoyac (3,326 hectares), and Guadalupe la Huertilla (999 hectares). In fact, although hacienda peons were still legally unable to petition for lands, here they simply changed the name of their community from Hacienda la Pradera to San José la Pradera and successfully gained a grant of 995 hectares. By 1931 most of the Gómez family was back in Spain, the huge Porfirian finca in ruins, and the fertile lands returned to their former owners.[84] In other smaller sugar zones redistribution also had limited support.[85] Over the next few decades, the ejidos of western Huajuapan would become secluded centers of state support where inhabitants built schools, backed teachers, joined peasant unions, voted PRI, and spoke an increasingly orchestrated "language of the state."

Outside the isolated sugar regions, few agrarista groups enjoyed such general community-wide support. First, they were thinly scattered. Only peasants in Huajuapan, San Francisco del Progreso (in the municipality of Huajuapan), Yucuquimi (Tezoatlán), San Francisco El Chico (Huajolotitlán), Santa Catarina Estancia (Ayuquililla), Amatitlán, Suchitepec, Mariscala, and Tonalá petitioned for land during the postrevolutionary period.[86] Second, they were often extremely small. In 1921 the priest of Tonalá claimed to know of only nine vocal agraristas, and three had recently confessed they wished to leave the movement. Even a visiting agrarian engineer who arrived at the scene of a massive anti-agrarista rally in 1927 admitted that the opponents of land reform made up "the vast majority of the village." A decade later, another engineer estimated that anti-agraristas outnumbered agraristas ten to one.[87] In Huajuapan numbers were similarly low. In 1934 the agrarian engineer estimated that only 40 out of the 4,772 families wanted land. Two years later the local agrarian official reported that only seven peasants worked the ejido.[88] Third, the agrarista groups comprised uneasy cross-class alliances. Many members were politically ambitious ranchers, keen to employ land reform to make links with the government or expand existing properties. Thus Eduardo Castillo, the leader of the Tonalá agraristas, was the scion of a local cacique family, a doctor, and a local landowner who had only returned to the village from Mexico City the year before. His eight accomplices included his brother, a Mexico City lawyer, and three brothers from the wealthy Solano family.[89] Similarly, Vicente Ramírez Pacheco, the leader of the regional peasant union throughout most of the 1930s, was from a fairly well-off Huajuapan family.[90] Others were disgruntled sociedad members, men like José María Duran of Tonalá, who already had a piece of land but now claimed that he wanted the society's lands "distributed more equally."[91] Still others were from the Mixteca Baja's thin tier of sharecroppers and landless peasants, recent arrivals, or extremely poor villagers who were unable to take advantage of the nineteenth-century purchases. As chapter 4 demonstrates, outside a few mestizo hubs like Tezoatlán or Huajuapan, these groups were either small or non-existent.

Despite their fairly limited numbers, the Mixteca Baja's agraristas caused considerable disruption by allying with aspirant politicians. At first, mestizo leaders bypassed conservative local authorities and approached state officials directly. In 1921 Tonalá agraristas contacted the governor, the local military commander, and the local tax collector and claimed that the society's properties—comprising a small sugar mill, two "huge" swathes of fertile valley, and four hundred cattle, which together were worth around sixty thousand pesos—were actually illegally owned by the church. Over the next year, the pueblo divided, with Castillo, his small group of Tonalá reformers, and state military forces confronting the increasingly virulent majority. In late 1926 tensions came to a head. The chief of the local defensa social murdered one agrarista, apprehended the rest, and locked them in the local jail. When the agrarian engineer arrived on May 13, 1927, he reported that the rumor that the state was going to redivide the society lands had caused "considerable ill-feeling." And at the village meeting the following day, over three hundred society members assembled to demonstrate against the planned distribution. A few days later, tempers flared again, and the two groups fought with machetes out on the streets. The municipal president was forced to imprison the agraristas for their own safety and call on the local military battalion to calm the situation. In what would become a repetitive refrain, the engineer explained in his detailed report that the state's agrarian program, with its limited understanding of Porfirian landholding practices, was utterly unsuitable for this sort of situation. As he pointed out, in many ways the reformers were correct. The society, by using lands to fund fiestas and support the local church, was in violation of constitutional laws prohibiting ecclesiastical landholding. Yet at the same time, the majority anti-agraristas, with their individual strips of society land, were in line with the egalitarian spirit of state reform. In this instance the engineer advised a policy of inaction.[92] But as the state upped the pace of agrarian reform, agrarian authorities backed by local landowners were far less perspicacious.

Until 1926 most local landowners had brazenly opposed land reform, forming a natural alliance with the region's agricultural societies. In Mariscala, Amatitlán, and Huajolotitlán landowners even sold their lands to newly created sociedades agrícolas in an effort to cement popular support for private property.[93] According to angry ejidatarios, the church authorities, like Luis González y González's *cura de pueblo*, helped broker the sales to ensure a unified front.[94] However, with the threat of Cristero revolt looming, pressure on the region's thin tier of hacendados increased. Although Calles's conservative land policy (1930–1932) offered a brief respite, the creation of a national peasant union, the election of agrarista president Lázaro Cárdenas, and the introduction of the new Agrarian Code in 1934 upped tensions again. Rather than risk political alienation during these successive periods of state reform, the landowners played a devious double game, publically supporting land reform but redirecting agrarista efforts away from their own properties and toward those of the agricultural societies. To do so, they formed a new alliance with the local peasant union boss, Vicente Ramírez Pacheco. Acting out of a commitment to political advancement rather than socioeconomic reform and eager to secure some kind of mass support, Ramírez Pacheco followed along, harnessing the state's incomprehension to avoid breaking up large estates and instead target equitably distributed societies. The policy, motivated by political ambition and distorted by local strongmen, was a disaster as Ramírez Pacheco guided small minorities of agraristas to apply for the redistribution of society lands. In 1926 the state donated over eight hundred hectares of land to the small community of San Francisco El Chico, Huajolotitlán. Persuaded by local elites to avoid their properties, agrarian authorities handed over the lands of the village agricultural society instead.[95] Over the next fifteen years the situation in San Francisco El Chico was repeated again and again. In 1936 the state offered some Amatitlán peasants nearly five hundred hectares from the village's agricultural society. In 1937 Mariscala agraristas gained 3,226 hectares of land from the local society instead of from two landowners' five-hundred-hectare estates. In 1938 Suchitepec's small reformist contingent demanded and received 2,511 hectares from the local sociedad agrícola. Also in 1938, the twenty families of Corral de Piedra requested and received the neighboring society of Cacaloxtepec's lands. In 1940 even the small group of Tonalá radicals gained control of 1,478 hectares of society land.[96]

At first the society members defended their lands by wheeling out the discourse of private property ownership, stating that their ancestors had bought the lands with their own money. In 1927 in Tonalá, the anti-agrarista majority explained to the agrarian engineer that they had bought the Yetla hacienda from the former cacica in 1838. Since then, they had split the huge estate between the village's three hundred families, paying one real a year to the village's principal cofradías.[97] Eight years later, the municipal president of Chazumba attempted to stop the takeover of local society lands by arguing that villagers had "acquired the lands in which they live by buying them from the cacique via sociedades."[98] In 1937 the sociedad agrícola of Cacaloxtepec explained that the society comprised thirteen hundred members or over three hundred families. Although they had purchased the land "as a private property," they possessed the land "in common." In contrast, the twenty agraristas of Corral de Piedra were shepherds from one of the region's haciendas volantes. During the late nineteenth century the society had permitted the recent arrivals to establish a small community on their lands in exchange for minimal rent. "In order to take revenge," this new community now wanted to take the society's lands.[99]

In fact, this ideology of private property, similar to that delineated by Jennie Purnell for Michoacán, was so powerful that ejidatarios even tried to justify their land ownership in similar ways.[100] The agraristas of Tacache de Mina defended their new ejido to the local priests by claiming that they "believe[d] that the land was legally acquired . . . but from the government not from the owner."[101] Despite the rhetoric's regional force, in most cases these explanations failed to stick. In general, official emissaries not only saw landholding in Mexico in binary terms but also were suspicious of peasant capabilities and convinced of the redemptive power of state reforms. As a result, they usually viewed the peasant justifications as carefully constructed fictions designed to disguise continued elite landholding. Time and time again, agrarian engineers, local politicians, and federal teachers describe the societies' lands as "owned by the clergy," "actually owned by the local landowner," and "pseudo-purchases." Moreover, they described peasant resistance to the planned reforms as instigated and manipulated by a shadowy cabal of high clergy and rich elites.[102]

As these detailed letters explaining the villages' landholding situations were misunderstood or ignored, most former society members turned to intimidation and violence. In February 1926, in what would become a familiar trend, socios armed with rifles, machetes, and sticks entered San Francisco El Chico, arrested the head of the ejido association, and announced that prospective ejidatarios were "fucked." They then proceeded to invade the neighboring houses, drag out the women and children, and threaten to kill their men if they continued to petition for lands.[103] Between 1927 and 1931 anti-agraristas murdered four aspirant ejidatarios in Tonalá.[104] In 1935 Amatitlán ejidatarios complained that former society members had burned their crops, invaded their lands, murdered two agraristas, and wounded another two.[105] In 1936 and 1940 Suchitepec peasants complained that anti-agrarista forces had attacked their houses, beaten them up, and threatened their wives and children.[106] In 1938 two hundred members of the agricultural society of Cacaloxtepec attacked visiting agrarian engineers and their federal escort, forcing them to flee.[107] In 1939 anti-agraristas shot another San Francisco El Chico ejidatario, precipitating another round of intravillage violence.[108]

The paradoxical effects of land reform efforts in the Mixteca Baja have few direct parallels. In some ways, they resemble those of the Bajío and the center-west, which pitched rancher communities against indigenous villages.[109] However, even here indigenous agraristas enjoyed substantial support and could, if they survived Cristero and white guard attacks, forge insulated ejido communities. However, in the Mixteca Baja the establishment of these small, unpopular ejidos effectively and perpetually divided communities in two, punishing the prescient and rewarding the ambitious, the arriviste, and the very poor. Or to put it another way, by targeting sociedades agrícolas, regional elites and state officials jeopardized the Mixteca Baja's moral economy, riding roughshod over the reciprocal system set up during the late nineteenth century. While labor exploitation, in the form of commercial monopolies of palm products and livestock, continued, state agrarismo now threatened the established palliative—land. As a result, Mixteca Baja peasants saw the agraristas and not the regional merchants as their principal opponents. This unbalancing of the moral economy shaped future political allegiances. Despite continued mercantile profiteering, counter-revolutionary discourses, which condemned land reform and exalted private property rights, generated mass support. The region's scattered ejidos became cautionary exemplars of the power, insensitivity, and political chicanery of the revolutionary state. Over the succeeding decades alarmist right-wing tirades against "communism," "socialism," and state control gained popular credibility. This credibility, in turn, hardened peasant opposition to the revolutionary state, not only precipitating the election of PAN municipal councils but also an attack on the Huajuapan barracks in 1962.

State Anticlericalism, Education, and Regional Religion, 1920–1940

Between 1920 and 1940, successive revolutionary governments not only sought to placate land-starved peasants, harness popular support, and change socioeconomic relations, but also, like so many other radical states, to create "new men." Brought up within a tradition of Enlightenment anticlericalism and embittered by ecclesiastical involvement in the Huerta coup of 1913, northern revolutionaries especially saw the elimination of the church's rural power as a central tenet of this "veritable cultural revolution."[110] These anticlerical campaigns were instigated from the top in two broad waves. In June 1926 the Sonora caudillo, President Plutarco Elías Calles, signed the Law for Reforming the Penal Code, which laid out a series of harsh penalties for priests who did not adhere to the anticlerical provisions of the 1917 Constitution. In retaliation, the Mexican episcopacy suspended public worship. As churches closed and priests fled, devout parishioners from the center-west states of Jalisco, Michoacán, Guanajuato, Zacatecas, and Colima rose up in revolt. Although church-state negotiations brought the so-called Cristero War to a close in 1929, within a few years conflicts over religious practice and church education divided Mexico again. From 1932 onward priests were closely monitored, churches forcibly closed, sacred festivals prohibited, and worshippers intimidated.[111] Most importantly, the government attempted to remove religion from the sphere of education. Although Mexico's minister of education Narciso Bassols had enacted some anticlerical reforms in the early 1930s, the project reached a crescendo in December 1934 when the government changed Article 3 of the Constitution.[112] It now read that education should be "socialist . . . and exclude all religious doctrine" and "combat fanaticism and prejudices" so that children would be given a "rational and exact concept of the universe and social life."[113]

Anticlericalism in the Mixteca Baja

As these national policies filtered down to Mexico's state governments, they developed distinct regional hues. In some states, radical *comecura* revolutionaries, what visiting U.S. priest Wilfred Parsons called the "wild men of the party," persecuted clerics, humiliated the devout, sacked churches, and burned saints.[114] In Tabasco, the regional strongman Tomás Garrido Canabal boarded up temples, ordered priests to marry, encouraged widespread iconoclasm, and established paramilitary "Red Shirt" organizations to persecute local priests. At the same time, he publicly mocked Catholic beliefs, decreeing the compulsory consumption of meat on feast days and naming his own son Lucifer. In other regions, by contrast, less virulent state governors, like Saturnino Cedillo in San Luis Potosí, Bartolomé García Correa in Yucatán, and Carlos Riva Palacio in Mexico State, tempered national laws, turned a blind eye toward cult practice, and effectively cut a deal of noninterference with the ecclesiastical hierarchy—a kind of decentralized, sub-rosa version of the Porfirian agreement.[115]

In Oaxaca, state policy hardened over time, shifting from an under-the-table understanding to outright hostility. During the Cristero revolt, Governor Genaro V. Vázquez (1925–1928) effectively ignored federal anticlerical prescriptions and made a covert pact with the local church. Priests and parishioners were allowed to continue formal worship, run catechism classes, and use churches. In return, the ecclesiastical hierarchy agreed to avoid egregious demonstrations of religious liberty and pull support from Cristero insurgencies. As one outraged teacher complained two years after the official implementation of the Calles law, "ignorance and fanaticism" still reined in Oaxaca. Here, "priests continue[d] to infringe the laws relating to cult and perform[ed] antipatriotic, anti-human, and erroneous acts."[116] With the election of Francisco López Cortes as state governor in 1928, however, this cautious administrative approach changed. Indebted to his political godfather, Calles; surrounded by radical teachers and bureaucrats; and without a popular base, López Cortes moved against the Catholic Church. In 1931 he decreed the reduction of priests to one for every ten thousand inhabitants. At the same time he ordered the establishment of Committees for the Fight Against Fanaticism in each municipality.[117] These organizations were designed to enforce a four-part campaign of observation, dissemination, education, and secularization. Members were instructed to watch over the municipal and educational authorities to ensure their ideological integrity and to introduce the civic calendar, cultural Sundays, and night schools into their communities. They were to act also as adjuncts to the lay schools of the area, holding talks on historical topics such as the Conquest, Independence, the Reform, and the Revolution. Finally, López Cortés demanded that the committees attempt to replace the dominant Catholic culture and practices with the rituals of the modernizing revolution, ordering that religious festivals be replaced by "fairs, open-air dances and popular fiestas" dedicated "to promote agricultural, industrial, commercial and school activities."[118]

In 1934 this increase in anticlerical rhetoric dovetailed with the re-emergence of a more aggressive national project. Pressured by Calles's increasingly vocal Jacobinism and the growing influence of radical teachers organized into groups like the Confederation of Socialist Teachers of Oaxaca or the Defanaticization Committee of the Normal School of Oaxaca, López Cortés's successor, Anastasio García Toledo (1932–1936), was obliged to enforce even more stringent limits on the church, moving from "constructive" to "destructive" anticlerical measures.[119] In September 1934 he limited the ratio of priests per inhabitant to one per sixty thousand, leaving eighteen priests in the state and only three in the Diocese of Huajuapam de León.[120] Furthermore, with the congressional acceptance of socialist education the following month, he backed the national campaign, attempting to mold Oaxaca's teachers into a tightly bound anticlerical vanguard. Private schools were banned, suspicious teachers fired, and federal school inspectors instructed to disseminate the new version of Article 3 throughout the state.

In the Mixteca Baja, this shift in state policy had powerful effects. As in the rest of Oaxaca between 1926 and 1929, national laws were only occasionally enforced. Although a handful of visiting federal officials precipitated small-scale village riots, priests and local administrators successfully tempered popular outrage and effectively allowed religious practices to continue as before.[121] With the introduction of socialist education in 1934, however, state authorities increased the pressure for local change. In Huajuapan the federal school inspectors Arcadio Lozano and Ernesto Zarate López led the charge. Both were radical Jacobins, educated at the state teacher-training college and indoctrinated in Oaxaca City's Masonic lodge.[122] Over the next four years, they attempted to instill the revolutionary, anticlerical culture in the region, executing constitutional laws, demanding the strict enforcement of the federal syllabus, giving talks on socialist education, and handing out books on "Marxism, the Paris Commune, and the Illness of Capitalism."[123] By 1935 a handful of anticlerical federal teachers joined the campaign. Like their federal overseers, they were born outside the region, trained in distant colleges, and imbued with a distinct distrust of the church. As they took the reins of the local schools, they brought state policies to the region's communities, fining priests, disrupting fiestas, closing private schools, petitioning for the removal of "fanatical" municipal authorities, and teaching deliberately inflammatory lessons on "Scientific Socialism," "God's real plans for humankind," and "the role of the clergy in class war."[124]

As elites sought to safeguard their political power, some made the pragmatic choice to back the federal campaign. In the district capital of Huajuapan, regional landowners like José Peral Martínez united with ambitious peasant leaders like Vicente Ramírez Pacheco to form defanaticization committees, decry clerical intrigue, and secure regional dominance.[125] In the region's agrarista hubs, prospective ejidatarios did the same, demanding municipal control and the handover of society lands in return for regular school attendance, anticlerical demonstrations, and the defense of local teachers.[126] Yet even where the stakes were lower, where communities had escaped divisions over land reform, out-of-favor or recently arrived politicians also allied with federal teachers to guarantee local rule. In Tequixtepec, Luis Niño Pacheco, who had confessed his belief in the providential powers of Our Lady of Perpetual Succor during the Revolution, fell out of favor with the ruling group, joined the government party, and started to support the official school.[127] In Mariscala the state postal official and the tax collector also backed the federal teacher, shifting from community outsiders to municipal officials through this practical alliance with the state.[128] Just over the Puebla border in the village of San Pablo Anciano, backers of the local school included Cipriano Rivera, "the husband of the communist teacher," and Gabriel Vega, "the brother of a Methodist teacher and also a communist."[129] Other federal school supporters came from the village but were educated outside. In Tequixtepec the "communist" minority included Geronimo Gaspar Niño, who had gone to school in Oaxaca City, and Pedro Morales, who had spent most of his adult life in the federal army.[130] By 1940 these state-backed leaders formed the region's political elite, dominating federal, local, and municipal elections. Yet they remained an isolated and unpopular group. Collusion brought national but not local support, and the region would remain divided between this alliance of elite chancers, small-town politicians, and true believers and their clerical opponents for the next two decades.

Resistance to the Socialist School

In fact, most Mixteca Baja peasants rejected the introduction of socialist education and its penumbra of associated anticlerical measures and formed an alliance with the local church. On the one hand, most communities opposed the teachers' promotion of land reform, fearing that agrarismo threatened their sociedad agrícola lands. Without the offer of land distribution offering forward momentum, "the organizational tandem" of agrarismo and socialist education was at best underpowered and at worst static.[131] On the other hand, the regional religious culture also militated against the acceptance of the state campaign.[132] In regions of weak ecclesiastical power, divergent spiritual practices, and popular anticlericalism, teachers' attacks on provincial priests confirmed prejudices and often freed young men from tiresome religious duties. In the Sierra Juárez where priests were scarce and religious practices often grated against clerical expectations, peasants joined teachers in their attacks on the local priests.[133]

In contrast, in regions of re-Christianization like the Mixteca Baja, where Porfirian evangelization and revolutionary violence had strengthened links between the clergy and the laity and where popular religion was effectively clericalized, defanaticization campaigns, secular education, and the assaults on priests struck at communities' spiritual economies. First, statutory limits on the number of priests threatened both the regular rhythm of Masses, festivals, prayer months, and penitential rites and the one-off, priest-led attempts to ensure rain, counter disease, or guarantee village security. As one querulous petition bluntly stated, "Without a priest, the villagers [we]re unable to fulfill their sacred duties."[134] Second, verbal and physical attacks on individual clerics were not only assaults on the villages' chosen divine intermediaries, but also on a distinct class of powerful friends, compadres, and patrons who had not only grown up in the region but also, through their offices, devoted their wealth, time, and effort to community well-being. According to the villagers of Ayuquila, the local priest was not only "a son of the community" but had also "baptized thousands of our children," "built a local school," and "helped to construct the church tower."[135] Third, the imposition of secular teaching threatened the future of this diocesan system. Without the network of Catholic schools and catechism classes, priests and parishioners feared that local youths would grow up "without moral-ity," "without obedience," and "without God," unaware of the importance of these reciprocal links between the church and the local communities.[136] Fourth, locals also feared that the association of agrarismo and anticlerical-ism would unmask the continued existence of cofradía properties, robbing the community of its regular funding and slicing through the Gordian knot of self-interest that had bound priests and parishioners since the Porfiriato.

As befitted a regional alliance designed to protect priestly interests, resis-tance to state anticlericalism was designed and orchestrated at the top. Both of Amador's successors, Luis María Altamirano y Bulnes (1923–1933) and Jenaro Méndez del Río (1933–1952), shaped popular strategies, admonish-ing armed insurgencies and encouraging passive resistance, school strikes, and the continuation of private education. In so doing both prelates harked back to the Porfirian system of mutual noninterference, repeated the ecclesi-astical hierarchy's post-1929 position, and guarded the region against heavy state reprisals. For example, in 1932 Bishop Altamirano responded to a failed regional uprising against Governor López Cortés's initial anticlerical decrees by warning parishioners against violent insurrection and declaring that all Mexicans who took up arms would be "disobedient to the supreme Pontiff." At the same time, he recommended a course of acceptable action to counter the "tribulations and difficulties" of the present, including prayer, the prac-tice of a religious life, and Catholic education.[137] With Altamirano's move to Tulancingo in 1933, Méndez del Río took over the diocese and retained a similar policy of virulent but nonviolent opposition to state plans. Thus, with the reduction of priests to one for every sixty thousand inhabitants Méndez del Río ordered all priests to refrain from seeking registration or abandon-ing their parishes. Rather, he demanded that "in all cases they conserve the divine cult in the temples" or, if this was not possible, "move the parish ser-vices to private houses." Although ecclesiastical authorities claimed to vis-iting journalists that the diocese had limited priests to the state minimum, in fact the bishop maintained around sixty priests in the diocese during the entire period of persecution.[138] In December 1934 the vicar general, Rafael Gutiérrez Maza, boasted that "in all parishes of the state of Oaxaca the priests continue in their places, with more or less difficulties; in the state of Puebla there is general suffering but they have not had the kind of treatment that they have had to leave their posts."[139]

In order to combat the state campaign, priests harnessed two overlap-ping groups—family members and lay religious organizations. On the one

Figure 12: Jenaro
Méndez del Río, third
bishop of the Diocese
of Huajuapam de León,
1933–1952. *Historia
de Tonalá, Oaxaca
coleccionada por el Sr.
Pbro. D. Avelino de la
T. Mora López para
conmemorar el III
centenario del hallazgo
de La Santa Cruz en la
gruta del Río de Santa
María Tindú, Oax.*

hand, most priests came from the Mixteca Baja and still possessed extended
kin networks in local villages. These often formed the village vanguard of
antistate protest. José Cubas Solano, brother of the rector of Huajuapan, led
the "fanatics" in Tonalá, while the "Catholic caciques" of Miltepec, Cipriano
Cruz and Felipe Suárez, were both fathers of priests.[140] In Chila, Bishop
Amador's influential family, related by marriage to the Villagómez clan,
repeatedly offered local support to under-fire clerics and even invited seminary students to hide in their nearby ranch. On the other hand, priests also
relied on cofradías and church organizations established during the early
twentieth century. In Miltepec the "Catholic Agricultural Society" instigated
repeated protests against the socialist school, and in Tequixtepec members
of the Daughters of Maria group harangued the teacher and visiting school
inspector. In Amatitlán the priest Rufilio Flores Ayala described how he

welded together the congregations of the Vela Perpetua and the Apostolado de la Oración into the female branch of the parents' group. All "swore against the diabolical teaching" of the regime.[141] These networks, linked by blood, compadrazgo, mutual interest, and now common experience, would form the basis of opposition to the state for the next three decades.

Beneath the gaze of an increasingly intrusive state but protected by networks of sympathetic family members, compadres, and pious villagers, these priests practiced a kind of guerrilla clerical orthodoxy, shifting from temple to temple, private house to private house before announcing their presence with a deliberately threatening piece of popular religious theater. In 1935 the Secretaría de Educación Pública (SEP) inspector for Huajuapan complained, "From five in the morning to ten at night the liturgical songs that the voices sing in chorus are heard even in the park, while the bells and the fireworks ring out and explode in the air and bands of music are stationed in front of the atrium of the church, mocking the precepts of the constitution."[142] The following year the federal teacher of Suchitepec complained that the local cleric and the faithful had held a covert Mass in honor of the village saint early in the morning in a chapel outside the town. By the time the federal teacher went to complain about the infringement of the laws, the priest had disappeared, but the several hundred drunk revelers remained and proceeded to harangue the state employee. Yet these continued religious practices were designed not only for show, but also in order to retain traditional links between priests and parishioners. Méndez del Río's 1935 New Year message to the clergy reminded them of the "serious obligation that each one of us has of attending at least the most urgent spiritual needs of the faithful with whom we live, even at the cost of certain sacrifices."[143] Government archives are replete with accusations of "clandestine marriages and baptisms" and priests practicing "despite the removal of their license."[144]

If the continued clerical presence scuppered federal attempts to cut everyday church-lay ties, priests also used these extended familial and religious networks to mold popular resistance to the secular school to diocesan expectations. Following the norms laid down by the Mexican episcopate, Bishop Méndez del Río ordered the priests to instruct their parishioners not to send their children to the schools, as "there they will inculcate atheism." They were to threaten excommunication for noncompliance.[145] This message was repeated time and time again from the pulpit as priests like Manuel Cubas Solano in Huajuapan, Avelino Mora in Tezoatlán, and Vicente Arroyo in Mixquixtlahuaca "denigrated the principles of the revolution" and "advised the parents not to send their children to the official schools."[146] One priest explained to his flock that socialism was "hatred against Our Lord God and the Catholic church, destruction of paternal authority and the right of property and the complete dissolution of society."[147] Cubas Solano actually read from a textbook of socialist education in order to forewarn the citizens of Huajuapan of the potential dangers.[148] The priests also handed out the printed propaganda of the church, which the bishop often sent down from Mexico City with his chauffeur. This included magazines like *La Lucha* and *Christus* as well as printed fly sheets.[149] The posters were designed to instill fear and intransigence in the *padres de familia*. One warned that socialist education would "tear religion and the existence of God from the soul of the child."[150] They proved to be extremely popular, and Cubas Solano demanded up to four thousand per month.[151] Not only were they read in private, they were plastered over municipal palaces at night and read out at community meetings and in private homes.[152] The propaganda effort caused one SEP inspector to remark that the Indians only knew of the socialist schools "through the opaque prism of the viperous preaching of the priests."[153]

Priests not only spread propaganda against state education, they also organized mass nonattendance. At the end of December 1934, the local canon suggested to the bishop that they start to arrange a strike against the official schools.[154] Bishop Méndez del Río approved of the idea, and the next six months saw priests and seminary students traveling the diocese attempting to instigate this organized truancy.[155] For example, in April 1935 Cubas Solano walked north out of Huajuapan toward Chazumba, visiting villages one by one and ordering parents' groups to keep their children out of the official schools.[156] Over the next four years, the effects of the priest-led school strike were dramatic. Outside a few small agrarista enclaves, attendance from 1934 to 1938 was effectively nil. Although over five hundred children were listed on the school census, attendance in the city of Huajuapan never rose above sixty according to the state or thirty according to the church. Both agreed that the only children to attend were those of federal employees and their servants.[157] In Mixquixtlahuaca only five or six children attended out of the sixty on the census. In May 1936 the subinspector of schools, Isidro Velasco, wrote exasperatedly to the director general of federal education of the "utter lack of support for the socialist school" in the area. In the past month he had traversed the northern part of the district. He found that in Cuyotepeji, Suchitepec, Miltepec, La Luz, El Espinal, and Llano Grande the parents "did not accept the new school, refused to support the teacher or enroll their children." In Guadalupe the school was open, but the locals refused to pay the teacher. Even in the ejido of Tacache de Mina the teacher had to close the school, as the authorities gave no guarantees and offered no payment. In Ayuquililla the school proved impossible to run as the municipal president had to pay for it out of his own pocket. Only in Las Piñas was the school functioning; however, the inspector's enthusiasm was dampened by the news that the teacher was only being paid eight pesos and continued to teach "fanaticism."[158] Time after time state and SEP representatives singled out the Mixteca Baja as uniquely resistant to socialist education in Oaxaca. The director of federal education wrote to the SEP director in 1935 to complain that Huajuapan was the "most difficult zone in the state." His only suggested solution was the removal of all the priests and all the municipal authorities.[159]

Beyond the school strike, diocesan authorities, keen to avoid armed conflict, also green-lighted other forms of popular resistance. Foremost among these was the petition. These written complaints, often compiled by committees of parents and priests and presented to federal employees, highlighted the problems with any negotiated settlement. For example, on March 5, 1935, the municipal president of Huajuapan, José Peral Martínez, and the tax collector, Manuel Díaz Chavez, met with two hundred parents to discuss the problem of school attendance. The parents were represented by a group of eleven, four of whom were women. They agreed to send their children to school if there was liberty of teaching, the teachers appointed were trusted by the pueblo, and there was absolute liberty for the establishment of private schools. Given government policy, none of the demands could be met, and the strike continued.[160]

Other informal means of disrupting the official school system were also encouraged. Both priests and parishioners understood the boundaries of official tolerance, the point at which noncompliance became insurrection, and pushed these boundaries to the limit by employing a series of "weapons of the weak" including foot-dragging, feigned incomprehension, drunkenness, mockery, laughter, and minor acts of vandalism.[161] In particular, many villages refused to contribute the monthly payment of twenty-four centavos for the municipal teacher's wage. In November 1936 the school inspector informed the state government that four teachers had passed through Dinicuiti since May that year. They all complained that the municipal authorities declined to pay their salaries. But when the inspector interviewed the municipal president about the nonpayment, he claimed no knowledge of the

Figure 13: Gender-segregated demonstrations against Article 3 of the Constitution in Huajuapan, 1937–1938. Archivo General del Poder Ejecutivo del Estado de Oaxaca.

matter.[162] Fiestas, especially the annual carnivals, offered an excellent opportunity to ridicule and intimidate the socialist schooling system. Not only were most residents fortified by alcohol, they were often disguised and customarily had used the festivals—like European peasants had used the early modern carnival—to mock the richer members of the village with impunity.[163] In April 1938 the rural teacher of Dinicuiti complained that the municipal authorities permitted the carnival procession. The villagers, dressed in traditional masks, shouted, "Long live religion, death to the government, death to the state governor and death to the bad president of the republic," before banging on the school doors and declaiming, "Death to the masons, long live religion," only then to descend into various distasteful speculations about the teacher's mother.[164]

Finally, priests also undermined the official schools by maintaining confessional education. Again, the tactic came from the top. Both Altimirano and Méndez del Río repeatedly ordered local clerics to "open catechism classes to counter the secularist ideas of the official schools" or to "offset the labor of the government" by "establishing private colleges and other centers of instruction."[165] To comply, priests improvised widely, paying for schools out of their own pockets, arranging for local branches of the San Vicente de Paul to give "cereals and other materials for life" to the struggling teachers, and employing previous students, compadres, and relatives as private teachers.[166] This covert schooling was a resounding success. In the smaller pueblos some schools remained permanently under the radar, appearing in priestly records but not in state investigations. Others continued regardless of denunciation and closure, merely relocating and reopening in a different place. The director of the Morelos private school moved the school from private house to private house throughout the 1930s.[167] Still others disguised themselves as "art schools." The Academia de Corte, Costura y Música run by Rosario Sandoval was condemned as merely the new incarnation of Leona Vicario school for girls.[168] By 1936, at the height of the anticlerical campaign, Bishop Méndez del Río could boast of over one hundred schools for boys and one hundred schools for girls in the diocese. Together they catered to ten thousand children. As a result, and despite the complete failure of the socialist education project, literacy levels in the Mixteca Baja remained remarkably high at 46.02 percent of the population in 1950 or 10 percent above the state average.

The predominance of these confessional schools not only dissuaded ambitious parents from sending their children to the state establishments but also ensured a new generation of politicized Catholics. The link between church education and party allegiance will be dealt with more fully in the next chapter, but clearly the politicization of Catholic students started in the clandestine schools of the 1930s. Private classes allowed a continuation of the diocesan education program that was developed during the early twentieth century. Schools continued to teach basic Catholic dogma, prescribe Reyes's *Nociones elementales*, celebrate colonial evangelization, and laud Iturbide's peaceful road to Independence. Nationalism was still "an expression of our unity under the Catholic religion." Yet the syllabi also changed to suit new necessities. In contrast to their Porfirian forebears, teachers and clerics, keen to vote out imposed anticlerical councils and agrarista cabals, now emphasized citizens' democratic rights. In lessons on citizenship, teachers talked of the responsibility of the state—as the "representative of the interests of society"—to its citizens. Under the title "Politics," teachers at the Ignacio Rayón school taught the "importance of popular suffrage" and the "independence of the municipality and its council."[169] Over the next three decades, this discourse of electoral involvement, redolent of Christian Democrat parties, would become the ideological basis of local PAN support.

Although diocesan authorities and priests led the campaign against the socialist school, they were forced to make some concessions in order to maintain popular support. In general these were not over liturgical practice. Local clerics briefly and unsuccessfully attempted to authorize and control Copala's image of Tata Chu, but there is no evidence of the "white masses" or female-led services that Butler has described in Michoacán.[170] Amador had already instituted so many compromises during the first decades of the century that few indigenous demands remained. At the same time, the maintenance of such a high number of priests prevented these kinds of lay innovations. Instead, local priests were forced to negotiate over issues outside their circumscribed sphere of influence. One of the key issues was the age of marriage. Although Bishop Amador had tacitly accepted the practice of underage marriage, the postrevolutionary church was less lenient.[171] In 1927 Rufilio Flores Ayala, the priest of Amatitlán, enraged his parish by annulling thirty-eight marriages between men in their thirties and girls between the ages of thirteen and fifteen. By 1935 the confrontation between the cleric and certain pueblos had become critical. The municipal agent of the small satellite village Concepción Porfirio Díaz complained that Flores Ayala was obliging the children to go to the socialist school and refusing to come to the village to marry couples or baptize children. They asked their village to be moved from the Parish of Amatitlán to the Parish of Ayuquililla. According to the vicar general, however, behind the request and mendacious accusations was the pueblo's desire to maintain the practice of marriage between older men and younger girls. Apparently the priest and municipal authorities of Ayuquililla were more lenient in the matter. Despite Flores Ayala's protestations, Concepción Porfirio Díaz (now called Concepción Buenavista) was allowed to move parishes.[172]

Somewhat paradoxically, the other principal concession was over female political participation. During the late nineteenth century, women came to form the core of the region's new bureaucratic, clerical Catholicism by forming sodalities and lay associations and teaching in local schools. Yet few if any played any formal role in municipal politics. During the 1930s, things changed. As the state started to interfere in traditionally female concerns, including the education of children, the provision of charity, and the organization of religious festivities, pious women gradually became involved in the political sphere. In an effort to mold the "new man," the state inadvertently created the "new woman." Women now wrote petitions, represented communities before the local authorities, led marches, and formed a vituperative vanguard of stone-throwers, name-callers, and satirists. In April 1936 the federal teacher of Amatitlán complained that the local Guadalupe organization, "formed entirely of women," had approached and berated him in the street, threatening to "fuck him up" if he didn't return to Oaxaca City.[173] Later that year, one of Huajuapan's pragmatic anticlericals complained that "women and children" had thrown stones through the windows of his house, threatened his wife, and announced that he was "going to hell."[174] These women not only saw state anticlericalism as a threat to their traditional roles, but also viewed involvement in the resistance effort as a welcome opportunity for political participation and a means to gain greater community status. Writing to a local cleric to ask for his approval of a new cofradía in 1939, one Tequixtepec woman claimed that she had "always been at the forefront of the political struggle against the atheist state."[175] In addition, these women also took advantage of the patriarchal political system, escaped accusations of violent assault, and often only suffered a stern reprimand and a warning to their husband or father to take more care of them next time. In response to this radical politicization, local clerics, either convinced of the efficacy of female-led demonstrations or out of sheer desperation, offered their full support. The vicar general of Huajuapan boasted that women had "never faltered in their support for Catholic education" and that he took particular pleasure when they "mock[ed] and jeer[ed]" his opponents.[176] In Ayuquila the priest was equally laudatory, praising "the open and sustained work of the female faithful against the socialist school."[177] Although women would not receive the vote until the early 1950s, this alliance of local clerics and pious female parishioners would become key to the PAN electoral campaigns of the next twenty years.

In the Mixteca Baja, the persecution of priests and the introduction of socialist education formalized regional ambivalence about the revolutionary project and generalized the isolated complaints of dispossessed agricultural society members. Here, government policies brought priests and parishioners into a vociferous and truculent antistate alliance. As Ben Fallaw argues, despite Cárdenas's offer of economic redistribution, these broad, organized, and often priest-led political movements against state cultural policy were remarkably common throughout the 1930s, ruining federal education plans and mobilizing what he terms the "mocho" electorate in clerical hotbeds like Guanajuato and Aguascalientes but also in less churched areas like Campeche, Coahuila, and Guerrero.[178] In other ways, the regional alliance resembled the provincial conservative alliance of the mid-nineteenth century, but with one crucial difference. Whereas the earlier coalition had been an organic, bottom-up movement with only pragmatic ties to the ecclesiastical hierarchy, this new partnership, which emerged from a period of intense church bureaucratization and was cemented during the Revolution, was initiated and directed from the top. Clericalism was no longer defensive, village centered, and ad hoc but aggressive, regionally based, and well organized. Throughout the period ecclesiastical authorities shaped local resistance, instigating school strikes and nonviolent protests but discouraging direct, armed confrontation with the state. Moreover, unlike its conservative predecessor this organized movement outlasted immediate state demands. Even after 1938 when the national government started to retreat from its anticlerical campaign, regional animosity lived on. Shaped by historical memory, sustained by Catholic schools, and occasionally invigorated by the threat of agrarian reform, this prolonged resistance to state intrusion eventually became institutionalized in support for the PAN.

Conclusion

In many ways, the effects of the Revolution on the Mixteca Baja demonstrate what Orlando Figes has termed "pervasive counter-productivity of state mobilization."[179] Here, land redistribution failed to harness peasant support, disrupt vertical regional alliances, or engender a growing loyalty to the state. Instead, agrarismo targeted smallholders, boosting discourses of private property ownership, forcing peasants into an alliance with regional elites, and fomenting widespread, community-based antistate groups. At the same time, a combination of violence and anticlerical reforms actually solidified lay-clerical links. Together priests and parishioners forged an alternative Catholic nationalist culture that would remain highly resilient to state interference until at least the 1960s. In many ways, these counter-revolutionary reactions mirrored those of the center-west. Yet there were also some crucial differences. First, agrarian reform did not cleave apart regions but split small closed corporate communities in two. Second, the timing and nature of the state of Oaxaca's anticlerical campaign marginalized the Mixteca Baja from the Cristiada. Cristero organizations, like the Liga Nacional Defensora de la Libertad Religiosa, made little or no headway; Cristero practices like armed insurrection and lay-led religiosity gained little purchase; and heavy state persecution failed to materialize. Third and consequently, resistance to the state project remained priest led: channeled through diocesan organizations and materializing in orthodox practices. Over the next two decades, these differences would become manifest. Rather than supporting Sinarquismo, Mixteca Baja Catholics would transfer their loyalties to the PAN.

Yet if in some ways the ramifications of the Revolution divided the Mixteca Baja from the mass of insurgent Mexicans, more generally the region's pious inhabitants shared experiences with many of their Christian peers. Around the globe revolutionary insurrection tested the reformed, modern church in new ways, sugarcoating cultural change with the offer of social reform. In many regions, state policies broke down lay-clerical relations, revealing the atmosphere of prolonged distrust between the nineteenth-century ecclesiastical reformers and their lay followers. In Russia and Spain (and outside the Christian world in China and North Korea), radical leaders, following their French revolutionary forebears, channeled popular religiosity uncoupled from clerical control toward new state religions, taking down orthodox saints and placing secular ones on the wall.[180] Yet in other regions, violent uprisings and state cultural policies strengthened sacramental orthodoxy and hardened lay-clerical links. Here, revolutions and radical anticlericalism acted as quenching tanks, hardening the molten metal of ultramontane Catholicism into a cohesive form. During Spain's Second Republic (1931–1936), reformers encountered "a more resilient foundation for resistance than that available to the clergy struggling against nineteenth-century liberalism."[181] In cities of limited industry and rural smallholding areas, the expansion of the number of priests, the revival of the mission orders, and, perhaps less importantly, the proliferation of Catholic associations pushed devout parishioners toward an aggressive clericalism.[182] When republicans passed a raft of anticlerical bills and failed to prevent successive waves of popular anticlerical violence, priests and parishioners nodded at the ecclesiastical hierarchy's condemnations and joined to overturn the regime.[183] In Argentina, Juan Perón's controversial 1954 secular education law generated an alliance between the Catholic hierarchy, the military, and middle- and lower-class Catholics. The following year thousands of worshippers heeded the hierarchy's demands, attended a massive antistate rally during the celebration of Corpus Christi, and even attempted an armed coup.[184] Even in distant Vietnam, fear of communist violence drove nearly a million Catholics into the arms of local clerics who led a mass migration to the south in 1954.[185]

CHAPTER 6

"En el nombre de Dios, adelante"

From Resistance to Revolt, 1940–1962

A T 11:00 P.M. ON NOVEMBER 17, 1962, THREE LOUD EXPLOSIONS followed by the rat-a-tat of gunfire awoke Huajuapan's residents. A group of young Catholic activists led by the local PAN politician Manuel del Refugio Herrera Ponce and armed with rifles, grenades, and machetes had assaulted the town's army barracks. After killing one soldier and injuring another two, the rebels captured the base, secured the bleeding men, stole the weapons, and fled. On their way out of the town, they pinned a series of manifestos to the walls of the municipal palace, which berated the state's electoral monopoly, accused the government of attempting to "take the nation toward communism," and ended with the call to arms "en el nombre de Dios, adelante." They also broke into the local tax collector's house and stole an estimated six thousand pesos. Over the next week, soldiers and secret service agents descended on the Mixteca Baja, arresting, interviewing, and often beating Catholic activists, Panistas, and priests. By early December, they had fanned out to the surrounding villages, hassling priests and picking up suspected "ringleaders," "terrorists," and "fanatics." At the same time, planes circled overhead, searching out signs of the "guerrilla insurgents" holed up in the region's rugged mountains.[1] Journalists also arrived and linked the attack to recent plots in Ciudad Hidalgo, Michoacán, and Matamoros, Tamaulipas, and wrote of the "serious worry that this [wa]s just the beginning of further violence."[2] Further violence, at least on the part of the Catholics, never came. And within a month, government agents had concluded that despite these initial alarmist accounts, the attack was little more than a "simple local scandal."[3] Official estimates of the number of rebels involved declined from around two hundred to barely twenty. Yet this *"pueblerino"* revolt, what later journalists termed "the last Cristiada," revealed the depth, virulence, and longevity of divisions between the postrevolutionary state and the region's religious activists. Despite over two decades of official rapprochement, the Mixteca Baja's lay and clerical Catholics maintained a staunch opposition to the state's policies, not only launching occasional poorly planned insurrections but also combating agrarian reforms, federal schools, state-sponsored cultural events, and electoral impositions.

In many regions of Mexico, tensions between church and state declined during the late 1930s. As both parties toned down their confrontational rhetoric, they established a modus vivendi that has lasted with only minor modification up to the present day. On the one hand, the state retreated from its twin policies of aggressive anticlericalism and socialist education. As early as February 1936 Cárdenas declared that his government did not seek to "combat religious beliefs."[4] His successor, Manuel Avila Camacho, went even further, declaring himself a believer, burying his mother with full Catholic rites, and even visiting the Cristero heartlands of Los Altos de Jalisco to widespread local acclaim.[5] Public declarations soon led to administrative reform. Avila Camacho appointed a well-known conservative, Octavio Vejar Vázquez, as minister of education, and in 1941 he proposed the reform of Article 3, arguing that "the misinterpretation of socialism" had "caused lamentable results for the peace of the nation, and for the development of educational action."[6] Although Vejar Vázquez resigned, by late 1945 the congress passed a new version of the article, which removed the Marxist rhetoric and now emphasized education's role in "fomenting love for the country."[7] At the same time, the president and the new education minister, Jaime Torres Bodet, brought teachers into line, persuading their leaders to form a centralized, more regimented union, the Sindicato Nacional de Trabajadores de la Educación (SNTE).[8] From this point on, PRI bureaucrats viewed education, leeched of its reformist content, as a means of calming class animosity, generating patriotic fervor, and engendering loyalty to the state.[9] To reflect this pragmatic shift, in 1951 President Miguel Alemán and the SEP produced a pamphlet entitled *Pro-México* to be used in all state schools. The missive directed teachers to instruct their pupils in "the importance of hard work," "the moral greatness of the nation," and the "essential democracy" of the Mexican state.[10]

On the other hand, the church hierarchy also shifted toward a more reconciliatory stance, welcoming Cárdenas's offer of a détente and rallying support for oil expropriation in 1938.[11] Over the next decade less intransigent prelates, like Luis María Martínez, the archbishop of Mexico, and José Garibi Rivera, the archbishop of Guadalajara, came to the fore. Like their early Porfirian forebears they limited the mission of the church to purely spiritual matters, distanced the institution from party politics, and echoed government calls for national unity.[12] By 1955 Martínez was described as "the archbishop of prudence, the leader of the reconciliation between church and state."[13] In practical terms, the hierarchy forsook popular political activism, scaling down worker organizations like the National Catholic Confederation of Work and severing its ties to the more intransigent rank-and-file extremists like the Sinarquistas.[14] At the same time, prelates and priests also attempted to regiment their lay followers by incorporating them into Acción Católica Mexicana (ACM). The organization, which emerged in 1929 as a product of the post-Cristiada arrangement, was designed to control lay religiosity and instill clerical obedience in the faithful. A central board with close connections to the ecclesiastical hierarchy spat out reams of doctrinaire propaganda, including the flagship publications *Christus* and the *Boletín de la ACM*. These organs stressed members' obligations to "the pope, the clergy, and the central board."[15] In the localities, prelates appointed priests to head local branches. Here, they were directed to monitor regional religiosity, steer groups away from political conflict, and focus members on exclusively spiritual issues such as prayer, personal morality, family, work, and good reading.[16] In Aguascalientes, the organization was so insipid and nonconfrontational that it was dubbed "Acción Castrada."[17]

At the regional level these elite shifts encouraged considerable demobilization on both left and right. Many caciques, no longer forced to display their anticlerical credentials, negotiated deals with local priests, built ejido churches, and gradually reincorporated saints' day celebrations and Sunday Masses into village life.[18] Even in notoriously Jacobin areas, like La Laguna, Campeche, or Tabasco, where teachers and ejidatarios had indulged in priest-baiting, iconoclasm, and the open mockery of religion, they pulled back from confrontation, put away their copies of *Candide*, and were reduced to mumbled insults and the principled nonattendance of church.[19] At the same time, in the Cristero hotbeds of the center-west, ecclesiastical and state pressure also brought conciliation. Most Catholic rebels put down their arms, descended the mountains to their homes, and negotiated an agreement with government officials. At the apex of Guadalajara society, pious elites pulled their support from Catholic workers' circles, embraced the new drive for industrialization, and took jobs in the state administration.[20] Further down the social hierarchy, Catholic immigrants negotiated deals with urban authorities to buy lands, establish new churches, and set up hospitals and private schools.[21] In the countryside, things were little different. In Coalcomán, Michoacán, former rebels Gregorio Guillén and Ezequiel Mendoza brokered a pact with Cárdenas himself, molded state policy to fit local religious sensibilities, and redefined themselves as "socially conservative economic modernizers," ranchero chiefs of the new PRI state.[22] To the north, San José de Gracia's cura de pueblo stifled his antistate preaching, allied with Cárdenas's brother Damaso, and tried to harness government aid to build the town's new road.[23] In fact, as many political scientists pointed out, so successful was this process of conciliation that by the late 1970s devout Catholics were more supportive of the PRI regime than their more secular counterparts.[24]

This narrative of post-1940 church-state compromise is extremely persuasive. Particularly in the center-west, former Cristeros bartered state support for economic aid and political power and united over a common understanding of Mexican nationalism. Avila Camacho's famous expression "Soy creyente" often translated into regional exclamations of "Soy cacique." Yet this narrative fails to explain why devout Catholics in the Mixteca Baja and other regions of Mexico continued to combat state initiatives in the fields, in the polls, and on the streets. Despite state violence, internal divisions, and the withdrawal of church support, Sinarquistas flourished in the Bajío until the late 1940s.[25] At the same time, urban movements in León, Aguascalientes, Tapachula, Oaxaca City, and Mexico City ignored the apolitical diktats of the ACM and harnessed the group's organizational structure to pressure the government for social reforms, operating what Roberto Blancarte has termed a "double militancy."[26] Even the "loyal opposition" of the PAN—long viewed as the political escape valve for middle- and upper-class fanatics— was not as elitist, as supine, or as "loyal" as historians have claimed.[27] During the 1950s a new generation of militant activists coupled the party's federalist agenda to growing Catholic anticommunism and gained broad support, not only in Mexico City (where the PAN regularly received between 40 to 50 percent of the vote) but also in provincial towns and villages.[28] During the 1940s and 1950s Catholic opposition in the Mixteca Baja paralleled and fed off these larger movements. Here, tensions over land tenure, municipal politics, education, and even Mexican nationalism remained well into the period of the Pax Priísta and kept the region divided between devout Catholics and secularist PRI supporters until the state followed up the 1962 rebellion with interlinking policies of irrigation (pan) and military repression (palo).

In order to explain the continuation of Catholic opposition in the Mixteca Baja, this chapter is divided into four sections. In the first section I examine regional land tenure. Although the government shifted away from large-scale land reform, old tensions between ejidos and sociedades agrícolas and new, allegedly neutral, attempts to confirm the communal ownership of lands caused repeated confrontations. Without the legal apparatus or the political will to solve these conflicts, villagers often became involved in cycles of intense intracommunity violence. The second section looks at the region's ongoing cultural conflicts. Despite the church hierarchy's conciliatory recommendations, priests and parishioners refused to accept either watered-down federal schooling or the state rhetoric of national unity. Parent associations and preachers continued to run state teachers out of town, establish private institutions, and prioritize their own version of national, regional, and local history. The third section examines regional politics. Popular agrarian and cultural opposition combined with divisions among the regional elite to produce a strong regional variant of the PAN. Emboldened by the combative rhetoric of the party's militant leadership, municipal PAN organizations fought PRI slates throughout the 1950s, often gaining electoral victories despite state violence. The final section looks at the 1962 barracks attack. Here I argue that although the assault was a one-off, the PRI response, which employed elite fears of peasant rebellion to re-establish the regional church-state pact, was a common one throughout Mexico during the period.

"An epoch of terror and banditry": Land Tenure and Agrarian Conflict

After 1940, national authorities retreated from the policy of land reform that had marked the earlier decades. The central aim of agrarian policy shifted from redistribution to productivity. Successive governments funneled scarce funds toward infrastructural megaprojects, like the Alvaro Obregón, Papaloapan, and Falcón dams, designed to aid large-scale commercial agriculture.[29] At the same time, ejido grants decreased dramatically. Whereas Cárdenas handed out over 18 million hectares of land, his successors, Avila

Camacho and Alemán, donated 5.9 million and 4.8 million hectares, respectively.[30] At the same time, the state offered certificates of exemption to an increasingly broad category of small-property owners. In February 1947 the congress passed a series of amendments to Article 27 of the Constitution. The government now upped its designation of a small property from fifty to one hundred hectares. Further exemptions were offered to sugar plantations, forestry enterprises, and cattle stations.[31] During the Alemán presidency alone, the government signed off on over one hundred thousand such certificates.[32] Reforms brought results, and between 1940 and 1950 the proportion of agricultural lands in the form of ejidos dropped from over 48 to 44 percent.[33] In Oaxaca, successive governors followed suit, limiting ejido grants and offering coffee farmers, pineapple *finqueros*, and ranchers increasingly generous exemptions.[34]

One might have expected the state's shift in emphasis from land distribution to small-property ownership to calm community conflicts in Mixteca Baja. But the reverse occurred. Most villages still owned their lands as sociedades agrícolas. Although members tried to register their shares as individual "small properties," local authorities lacked both the legal framework and the political will to protect society lands. As a result, conflicts between ejidatarios and socios, established during the Cárdenas era, continued as before. At the same time, local peasant leaders also managed to expand these intracommunity divisions into new villages. Using new legislation on communal land ownership, they attempted to reclassify society lands as *bienes comunales*. In doing so, they sought to remove control of the lands from the elected society authorities and replace these authorities with government-approved *comisariados de bienes comunales*. The venture initiated the same splits as the earlier land reform program. Only this time small factions of *comisariado* supporters (or *comuneros*) rather than ejidatarios faced off against large groups of village socios. As it became clear that local authorities favored the loyal minorities over the increasingly antistate majorities, conflicts turned violent, precipitating what one socio member described as "an epoch of terror and banditry."[35]

Ejidatarios versus Socios

During the early postrevolutionary period, the government created twenty-four ejidos in the district of Huajuapan and ten in the neighboring districts of Coixtlahuaca and Silacayoapan, carving at least seven out of former sociedad agrícola lands.[36] In these villages conflicts between ejidos and sociedades agrícolas lasted well into the 1960s. The pattern of small state-backed pockets of ejidatarios confronting larger church-supported groups of former socios, described in chapter 5, continued.[37] In most villages the agraristas remained a minority. In 1942 a visiting engineer in Tonalá concluded that society members outnumbered ejidatarios six to one.[38] As late as 1959, another engineer claimed that only thirteen peasants worked the ejido in Huajuapan.[39] Furthermore, many ejidatarios were village newcomers. Society members in Ayuquila claimed that they comprised 270 families, "each with around three hectares of land." In contrast, the agraristas numbered four landowners (with properties of between ten and twenty hectares) and around fifty supporters from neighboring villages.[40] As ambitious arrivistes, these ejidatarios now defended their property rights not through plaintive explanations of long-term ownership or unfashionable statements of socialist purpose, but rather by pointing out that society members were disobeying the law and the state. In 1942 the local head of the Confederación Nacional Campesina (CNC) complained that Tonalá's society members, by refusing to allow ejidatarios to plant on their lands, were not only "ignoring the government decree" but also "refusing to obey the president of Mexico and the governor of Oaxaca." He concluded that they had "turned into criminals."[41] Similarly, Ayuquila ejidatarios declared that socios' land invasions "infringed on the authority of the agrarian authorities and the national government."[42]

In contrast to the small groups of legalistic agraristas, society members sought to recuperate their lands by harnessing the new government emphasis on small-property ownership and portraying themselves as disenfranchised rancheros. Emphasizing private ownership came easy. Socios had used a similar rhetoric during the liberal era and were taught the sanctity of property in private church schools. Thus, in 1943 the sociedad agrícola of Ayuquila, now pertinently renamed the "Society of Small Property Owners 'Antonio de León,'" argued that their ancestors had purchased the community's lands during the 1880s.[43] Ten years later the society members of Guadalupe Morelos did the same, arguing that the prospective ejidatarios threatened the lands "we purchased many generations ago."[44] Yet despite the broad national shift toward supporting small landowners and the Mixtecs' genuine belief in private property, the argument was as unsuccessful as it had been during the Cárdenas period. Again, both law and politics conspired against the socios. On the one hand, villagers had purchased the lands as societies. They had no legal proof of individual ownership, except a few tax documents showing how the societies were split. As a result, they were unable to petition for one of the thousands of "certificates of exemptions" that served to ensure the maintenance of small-property ownership in other areas of the country. On the other hand, the local authorities, keen to create loyal community clienteles, were also unwilling to allow societies to take advantage of potential legal loopholes. By creating local agrarista groups, the local CNC head, Vicente Ramírez Pacheco, was not interested in "distributing land," but in using the ejido committees "to usurp control of the councils of the district."[45]

Legal inflexibility and a lack of political will forced society members to return to the tried and tested methods employed during the 1930s—church opprobrium and violence. Again and again ejidatarios complained that local priests tried to dissuade them from occupying their lands. In 1942 the priest of Tonalá praised the "good work" of the society members and declared that the agraristas dissidents were "condemned to hell."[46] In 1956 the priest of Miltepec refused to baptize the ejidatarios of Suchitepec "for taking the lands of the church."[47] The following year, the priest of Ayuquila declared the local ejido owners "followers of Satan."[48] When clerical reproaches failed, socios turned to violence. In November 1942 socios attacked ejidatarios in Tonalá, stealing their crops and preventing them from tending their fields. A month later they killed the head of the ejido.[49] By 1949 "repeated threats of death and murder" had forced so many ejidatarios to leave Guadalupe Morelos that a woman, María Arias Fuentes, reluctantly accepted the role of head of the ejido administration. Seven years later socios shot her dead as well.[50] In 1957 Ayuquila's ejidatarios complained that society members had recently invaded their fields, stolen twelve cattle, and beaten up three members.[51] Socios even targeted high-up peasant leaders. In 1948 unnamed assassins invaded the head of the district branch of the CNC's Huajuapan house and shot him three times through the chest and head.[52]

In response, ejidatarios also employed violence. At times, they called on nearby garrisons to send soldiers for protection, but generally they used similar means as their opponents. In 1942 the socios of Tonalá countered accusations of beating, theft, and murder by claiming that the agraristas had brought in a "professional killer" to target society members.[53] In Ayuquila socios listed over twenty murders committed by the ejidatarios between 1935 and 1956. They noted two high points in 1948 and 1951. On the first occasion, the ejido head, Bibiano Bello, had brought "friends and relations" from the neighboring town of Chila, who engaged socios in "the bloody battle of Pitalla Verde." On the second occasion, Bello had been elected municipal president "through fraudulent means" and preceded to fill the local police force with his own "*pistoleros*."[54] The government official who visited the village in the following year affirmed the tally, claiming that there had been as many as sixteen deaths between 1950 and 1956 as "both bands ran around committing crimes yet no one intervenes."[55]

Comuneros versus Ejidatarios

If the ejido's legacy in the Mixteca Baja was inequality, division, and violence, new agrarian policies made matters worse. From the 1940s onward, regions that had maintained communal lands throughout the Porfiriato (like the Nayarit Sierra, the Sierra P'urhépecha, the Chiapas highlands, and the Sierra Juárez) were forced to reclassify these lands as bienes comunales and appoint comisariados de bienes comunales to deal with state officials. On the surface the policy was designed to quell intercommunity border disputes, ensure the fair distribution of communal lands, and provide villages with an official spokesman in agrarian matters. In some areas the policy worked, and the comisariados were smoothly subsumed into village political hierarchies and made real gains.[56] Yet in practice, in most regions mestizo or bilingual comisariados often used their new state contacts to create independent power bases, usurping municipal power, concentrating land in the hands of loyal clients, and funneling state funds into their private coffers.[57] These new *caciques de bienes comunales* caused ample resentment but proved vital to state control, particularly in the mountainous, predominantly indigenous sierras.

Between 1945 and 1970 the state classified the lands of the vast majority of villages of the Mixteca Baja as bienes comunales.[58] As in other regions, administrators defended the policy by claiming it would put an end to intercommunal struggles.[59] But in the Mixteca Baja, attempts to reclassify lands as bienes comunales proved particularly divisive. Like the earlier ejido distribution, the new legislation failed to fit local circumstances. When small groups of progovernment villagers attempted to use the legislation to take control of village lands, they rode roughshod over communities' economic interests, existing political structures, and local appreciations of land tenure. As a result, they faced ample opposition. First, most villages owned lands not as communal properties, vestiges of colonial-era donations, but as private purchases bought during the late nineteenth century by sociedades agrícolas. As society members from Zapoquila argued, their lands "were not communal, but private properties bought generations ago."[60]

Second, societies already had a clear administrative structure with an elected council and a fairly equitable system of land distribution. What right did these new government appointees have to redistribute their fields, whose quality and extent depended on their parents' perspicacity and their own hard work? Third, society properties not only encompassed individual villagers' strips but also cofradía and church lands that were designed for to pay for tithes, the celebration of saints' days, church repairs, and private schools. As a result, societies had an easy ally in the local church establishment, which feared a drastic loss of parish income.

This escalation of violence and the interplay of economic, political, and cultural interests can be seen by taking the example of Cuyotepeji. During the nineteenth century the village had purchased over six thousand hectares of land from the Villagómez cacicazgo as a sociedad agrícola. The lands had been split between individual family use, cofradía properties, and communal pasture. As late as 1961 the lands remained fairly equally divided. Of the 192 heads of family, 175 possessed half a hectare of irrigated land and one hectare of less fertile property. However, when government representatives arrived in 1947 and offered to classify the society lands as bienes comunales, the village started to fracture. A handful of aspirant politicians led by Lauro Solano and the small group of villagers who were not members of the society saw that the legislation provided an opportunity to wrestle control of the community's lands from the society. For about a decade Solano's group, who called themselves the "comuneros," and the old socios exchanged allegations. Both claimed the right to be the legally constituted "comisariado" of Cuyotepeji's lands. But in 1955 the government decided in the comuneros' favor and appointed Solano head of the comisariado. In response, the socios attacked, beating up two of the new administrators and stabbing another. Two years later they contracted a Mexico City hit man to kill Solano, but he managed to escape. The violence brought some results, and by 1959 the socios had taken back the comisariado. But two years later agrarian authorities arrived again and returned control to the comuneros. In league with the authorities, Solano now used his position to attempt to redistribute the cofradía plots among his supporters. Finally, on June 14, 1963, the day before the celebration of the village's patron saint, a handful of cofradía leaders visited Solano and demanded the money from the church plots. When Solano refused, they entered, beat his mother-in-law with sticks, announced that they were looking for this "*hijo de la chingada*," found him, and shot him dead.[61]

The case of Cuyotepeji stands out. Solano's death so soon after the garrison attack generated considerable government interest and administrative ink. Yet evidence of similar tensions in other villages dots the archival records. In 1953 in Silacayoapilla, the state-backed comisariado complained that the former socios refused to pay taxes on their lands, arguing that "they had already paid quite enough for lands that were already theirs." When the local agrarian inspectors arrived, the socios claimed that they wanted "nothing to do with agrarian authorities in Huajuapan or anywhere else."[62] In 1962 the comuneros of Camotlán blamed "former members of the sociedad agrícola" for the public assassination of their leader.[63] Throughout the 1950s the comuneros of the small village of Tutitlán alleged that the socios of Tequixtepec crushed their crops, robbed them of their livestock, and administered the occasional beating.[64]

The agrarian situation in the Mixteca Baja was distinct. Few other regions maintained sociedades agrícolas well into the second half of the twentieth century. In some ways, the divisions between pro–private property socios and groups of state-backed comuneros and ejidatarios resembled the struggles between the center-west rancheros and agraristas of the earlier postrevolutionary decades.[65] Yet by the 1940s government support for small-property ownership had, in general, quelled these conflicts. Local caciques kept the agraristas in check while a resurgent rancher class now dominated in the west "from Colima to Chiapas."[66] In other ways, the attempt to insert loyal comisariados into village administrations approximated the agrarian policies enacted in other indigenous sierras. But the popular response, which involved a consistent campaign of mass church-backed violence, was very different. Few other indigenous zones possessed the administrative counterweight of the democratically elected sociedad agrícola council or the institutional ecclesiastical presence. However, if the Mixteca Baja lacked an exact comparison, the pattern of government intervention, escalating violence, and widespread anti-agrarian sentiment did resemble some zones of the Bajío. Here, sharecroppers and peons had been the primary losers in government agrarian reform. But like the socios, they reacted to their economic loss by turning against the state and embracing right-wing political organizations.[67]

"Muchos maestros, mucha mierda": The Continuing Struggle over Education

In much of Mexico, the tensions between church and state over public education receded after 1940. State bureaucrats and rural teachers stopped their vitriolic attacks, and bishops and priests halted their pulpit critiques. Presidents and papal representatives, clerics and educators united beneath a powerful revolutionary nationalism stripped of its explicit anticlericalism. In the Mixteca Baja, ecclesiastical and political elites also attempted to calm Cardenista conflicts. In 1941 the archbishop of Mexico wrote to the bishop of Huajuapam de León and discussed a "long and cordial" meeting with Avila Camacho, which had concluded in "favorable results." During the meeting, Avila Camacho offered to allow the diocese's private schools to remain outside the federal ambit. If any problems arose, he recommended the archbishop talk "to him in secret."[68] The under-the-table agreement, redolent of the pacts Peter L. Reich has claimed started in the 1930s, was paralleled by reconciliatory state policies.[69] The following year the new federal schoolteacher of Tequixtepec told the municipal president that he did not care if children attended the local private school. "What is important is that children do not waste the best time of their life."[70] Six years later when a federal cultural mission arrived, the teachers explained to the villagers that they did not intend to "attack the church," but rather "teach the children necessary skills."[71] In the local education colleges, prospective rural teachers now received instructions to avoid conflict at all costs. When the novice teacher Eloy David Morales Jiménez turned up in Zapotitlán Lagunas in 1955 and was asked whether he could take his pupils to Mass each Sunday, he followed the new state line and claimed that he would be willing but had to fulfill certain administrative duties in the local town.[72]

If both state and church elites embraced conciliation, why was the region racked by another twenty years of intense, often violent confrontation over village schooling and regional culture, which generated ample popular support for the PAN and culminated in the barracks attack of 1962? Continuing agrarian conflicts undoubtedly played their part. State-backed ejidatarios and comuneros still supported federal schools and denigrated private establishments in an effort to slander their opponents and gain state support. At the same time, priests and socios, linked by their joint reliance on society lands, continued to view federal schools as pernicious institutions that were often supportive of agrarian reform. And even in villages that had not undergone such divisive changes in land tenure, neighboring ejidos remained permanent reminders of the dangers of state influence. Yet divisions over schooling were not simply the cultural manifestations of economic malaise, small ideological cracks branching out from broader agrarian splits. The priests, private teachers, and parents who beat rural teachers and declaimed the federal school were not simply projecting their fears of economic disinheritance on a convenient target. They genuinely believed that the state establishment was "the school of the devil" and that its teachers, by neglecting to teach Christian doctrine, were undermining the religious culture of the region and, by extension, the nation. The reasons for these extended conflicts lay as much in the nature of local church institutions as in the ripples of economic strife.

During the 1930s, priests, private-school teachers, and parishioners had created a strong, oppositional culture to state schooling. In the subsequent decades, isolated from the broader process of church-state appeasement in the center-west, these groups struggled to lay aside the training and the experiences of the earlier decades and reorient this culture to the new political realities. The Mixteca Baja's Catholic activists believed that by neglecting to teach religious matters, federal schools still threatened to turn children against the church, their parents, and communities' religious traditions. In response to this insistence on the dangers of public schooling, the diocesan authorities could do little. Successive bishops, born outside the region, relied entirely on these groups to preach, to educate, and to form lay organizations. Furthermore, they were unable to replace this combative generation with more compliant, conciliatory leaders. Now, the institutional strength of the regional church—the seminaries, private schools, and lay organizations—created during the early twentieth century worked against them. As local militant Catholics controlled these establishments, they were able to reproduce this critical culture through the training of local priests, schools, church organizations, and, increasingly, public historical commemorations, thus imbuing a new generation with a profound distrust of the state. Ironically, institutions designed to instill order and obedience were being used to promote a local religious culture that ran contrary to the elite's new political aims. And neither ecclesiastical nor state elites were able to apply the handbrake to habitus. Disruptive provincial conservatism, now uncoupled from its elite leaders, returned again.

Both bishops who ruled the diocese during this period were born outside the region. Jenaro Méndez del Río (1933–1952) was born in Pajacuarán, Michoacán, in 1867. His successor, Celestino Fernández y Fernández (1952–1967), was born nearby in Jiquilpan, Michoacán, in 1890.[73] Both formed part of the center-west's emerging domination of the ecclesiastical hierarchy during the post-1940 period.[74] However, unlike their pragmatic peers they were unable to implement the ecclesiastical modus vivendi with any degree of efficacy. Although Méndez del Río had formulated the strategy against socialist schooling from Mexico City, in order to implement his plan he was forced to delegate the day-to-day running of the diocese to local priests and particularly the Tonalá-born vicar general Manuel Cubas Solano. When he returned in 1937, the bishop's health problems compounded the situation, and the system stayed in place. Thus while the ailing bishop advised caution and placed his faith in his ecclesiastical and political contacts in the capital, diocesan priests who had cut their teeth during the conflicts of the 1930s took a more combative view. For example, in early February 1948 Méndez del Río directed the priest of Juxtlahuaca to avoid confrontation with the parish's federal teachers and instead "remain confident . . . in the good faith of the prominent persons resident in Mexico City."[75] Although the local priest acknowledged the prelate's advice, he ignored it completely, haranguing the state educators from the pulpit in a series of inflammatory sermons.[76] The following year, the bishop ordered the Tequixtepec priest to follow similar placatory tactics. Again, his missive was politely received and then ignored.[77] The next bishop, Fernández y Fernández, was less frail than his predecessor but no less reliant on more aggressive local priests. Cubas Solano still remained his key adviser, and local seminary graduates dominated the higher echelons of the diocese. When Fernández y Fernández urged priests to stay out of politics during the late 1950s, many refused, continuing to preach against the government's "slide toward communism."[78]

Furthermore, and despite the state's and the bishops' conciliatory aims, local priests replicated this confrontational approach through the continued production of local priests and young Catholic activists. The Diocese of Huajuapam de León's educational infrastructure had remained in place throughout the 1930s. As government pressures relaxed, both seminaries and private schools expanded. At the regional ACM meeting of 1941, the visiting speaker, the bishop of Tulancingo, encouraged Catholics to found a feeder school for the local seminary "as so many children wish to be priests but lack basic primary education." The following year, the local bishop opened the diocese's apostolic school. A decade later, the school was converted into the diocese's official lower seminary. Local clerical intellectuals directed both upper and lower seminaries.[79] With the educational establishments in place, priests were instructed to search out prospective "pious and intelligent candidates" from their local congregations. Clerics, rich merchants, and devoted widows also offered scholarships for boys from poorer backgrounds. A small group of local nuns also ran an equivalent establishment for girls, the "Teresa Martín" school. As one local author explained, the girls' school, the seminary, and its prep school were the only institutions available for those of modest means who wished to continue education beyond fifth or sixth grade. There was a small federal secondary school in Huajuapan, dubbed "the communist school," but teachers were scarce and often transitory, and attendance involved severe social stigma. Beyond this school, state universities in Oaxaca, Puebla, or Mexico City were simply too expensive and too far away.[80]

The church's virtual monopoly over secondary and higher education ensured the constant production of local priests and members of the religious orders. In 1960 the diocese maintained 109 priests. Despite the region's population increase, there was still one cleric per three thousand lay devotees. The national average was around one cleric per seven thousand, and only a handful of center-west dioceses (Zamora, Guadalajara, Aguascalientes, Colima, Querétaro, and Tacambaro) had greater concentrations of priests.[81] At the same time, although no direct figures exist, between 1940 and 1960 the village of Tonalá alone produced six nuns and the town of Huajuapan at least ten.[82] Some of these priests and nuns came from the region's commercial elite, but many were poor but pious men and women from the region's smaller villages. Pedro Gómez Ayala, the scourge of Tequixtepec's federal teachers, was the son of a laborer from Amatitlán.[83] The neighboring priest of Miltepec, Juan Barragán González, was son of a palm weaver from one of Huajuapan's ranches.[84] Two of the priests involved in encouraging the 1962 barracks attack, Narciso Villa Hernández and Arnulfo de Jesús Barragán Ramírez, were also seminary graduates from poor Huajuapan families.[85] These young priests, brought up in villages and ranches during high point of the conflicts over socialist education and trained in seminaries and schools to believe that federal education was "atheist" and "diabolical" and that the state was a cabinet reshuffle away from communism, were key to the perpetuation of these divisions in later decades.

Beyond the seminary, private church education also remained strong. In 1960 the ACM reported that the diocese possessed forty-nine private schools and that devout parents' groups controlled the curricula in four other federal institutions. On average each parish had at least one private school.[86] Many, like Petlalcingo, operated one in the parish center and another one or two in far-off ranches.[87] These schools were well attended. In 1950 the priest of Tequixtepec boasted that over two hundred boys and girls had finished the school year.[88] In Ayuquila the priest reported similar numbers.[89] Furthermore, although the schools were private institutions, they were not socially exclusive. Even at Huajuapan's flagship Pio XI school, clerics and rich parents paid the one-peso-a-month fee for poorer students. As a result, hundreds of poor laborers' sons "walked kilometers barefoot from the surrounding ranches" to attend each day.[90] Although priests often acted as nominal directors of these institutions, the teachers were generally loyal Catholic activists. Maríana de León, head of the private school in Las Peñas, was also head of the local female branch of the ACM. María Herrera, a teacher at the private school in Cuyotepeji, was the niece of the local priest.[91] The leader of the 1962 revolt, Manuel del Refugio Herrera Ponce, had been head of a private art school established by the diocese's vicar general. His fellow rebel, Felix Moran Rios, was headmaster of Tamazulapan's private institute.[92] Numerous, well attended, socially inclusive, and controlled by local priests and lay devotees, these private institutions continued to produce radical antistate activists long beyond the supposed rapprochement of 1940. For good reason, the security service agents who patrolled the region in the wake of the barracks attack focused their attention on the region's numerous private schools, or what one federal teacher called "the root of all fanaticism."[93]

Priests also instilled political opposition in the weekly meetings of the ACM. Between 1940 and 1960 membership of the ACM increased until every parish contained at least one or two of the four branches. The senior female branch was particularly strong. In 1959 seventy-eight committees were spread over the diocese's parishes.[94] Although the ecclesiastical hierarchy had designed the organization to keep lay activists in check, in the Mixteca Baja clerical directors hijacked and politicized the parish committees, using them to preach against the state and the dangers of federal education.[95] During the first meeting of the ACM in Huajuapan in 1938, priests allowed the future head of the PAN, Miguel Niño de Rivera, to give a speech in which he lamented the "lack of civic spirit among the men of Mexico" and encouraged each listener to "be a good citizen as well as a good Catholic."[96] In what Cubas Solano described as the most popular speech, another lay leader attacked secular schooling and argued that failure to teach "the norms of Catholicism" led to "sacrilegious local customs ... filled with dancing and drunkenness and all sorts of acts against morality."[97] Ten years later at an ACM meeting in Tezoatlán, the clerical head of the diocese's female branch continued to encourage the organization's combative role, ordering members to "defend the faith" and "fight secular education in homes and private schools."[98] By the late 1950s, ACM rallies were even more explicitly political. In 1959 diocesan directors instructed their members to "fight anti-Catholic celebrations" and "watch for any signs of communism."[99] Guided by their clerical directors, the ACM activists remained key opponents of federal schooling during the 1940s and by the 1950s formed the base of the regional branch of the PAN. According to the head of the ACM, the two organizations were interchangeable and often held combined meetings.[100] In 1962 ACM members formed the core of the rebels while the clerical advisers, with their tales of imminent communist takeover, were the intellectual instigators.

Finally, priests and lay leaders buttressed the church's institutional efforts with increasingly public commemorations of regional religious culture. By funding celebrations, building monuments, and publishing small monographs, they attempted to expand confessional education beyond the classroom and into village squares. This propaganda effort was designed to teach parishioners a distinct narrative of local history. This narrative built on the cultural efforts of the preceding century and placed the church at the center of regional development by lauding the region's colonial heritage, praising its early evangelizers, and portraying local religiosity as an easy blend of both Spanish and Mixtec traits. For example, in May 1955 the Tonalá priest Avelino Mora celebrated the three hundredth anniversary of the discovery of the Holy Cross. Thousands of the diocese's inhabitants attended, and many returned from their new homes in Mexico City, Puebla, and Veracruz for the event. Parishioners clubbed together to construct a statue devoted to the "distinguished evangelizing order of the Dominicans" and "the greater glory of God." The statue portrayed a benevolent monk staring upward, his hand resting gently on a genuflecting, penitent Indian. The short book that accompanied the celebration repeated the myth of Saint Thomas's evangelization and echoed Cantu Corro's Catholic hybridization theory, arguing that regional Christianity emerged from a distinct mixture of "Mixtec greatness and pride" and "the faith of the early missionaries."[101] In 1949 the priest of Tlacotepec published a similar work, in honor of Our Lady of the Snows of Ixpantepec, that also lauded both Mixtec and Spanish devotion. According to the text, the Virgin was both the "fruit of the apostolic work of the Dominican missionaries" and the "humble Mixtec shepherds" who first witnessed the apparition.[102]

Although few other commemorations left such explicit explanations, the sheer prevalence of plaques, statues, and murals erected during the 1940s

Figure 14:
Statue commemorating the three hundredth anniversary of the discovery of the Holy Cross of Tonalá, 1955. A Dominican friar rests his hand on a repentant indigenous sinner. Serafín Sánchez Hernández.

Figure 15: Frontispiece of the book commemorating the three hundredth anniversary of the discovery of the Holy Cross. Note the illustration of the prisoner hanging from a rock and attempting to enter the cave of Tindú. *Historia de Tonalá, Oaxaca coleccionada por el Sr. Pbro. D. Avelino de la T. Mora López para conmemorar el III centenario del hallazgo de La Santa Cruz en la gruta del Río de Santa María Tindú, Oax.*

and 1950s demonstrates a deliberate church program to teach this understanding of regional history. In Petlalcingo, priests and lay activists placed a plaque commemorating the dogma of the Immaculate Conception on the other side of a monument in honor of dead Zapatistas. In Tequixtepec priests and parishioners painted the words "Viva Cristo Rey" on the hill overlooking the state-funded Tehuacán-Huajuapan road. In Chila devotees paid for the construction of a monument to the first bishop, Rafael Amador y Hernández. In Acatlán the priest inscribed the history of the town, replete with laudatory commentaries on local priests, on the inside of the new bell tower. And in 1960 the priest of Tonalá engraved a brief chronology of the town on the side of the church atrium. The public history, predominantly gleaned from the work of the nineteenth-century Dominican scholar José Antonio Gay, repeated the stories of early evangelization and even claimed that "in 1505, on the coronation of Moctezuma II, there still existed the vestiges of Christianity in Tonalá."

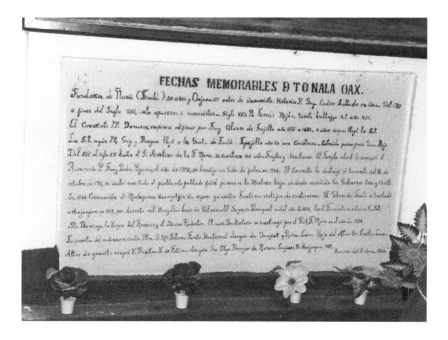

Figure 16: Inscription of memorable dates in Tonalá's history, written on the wall of the atrium of the Tonalá church. Serafín Sánchez Hernández.

Figure 17: Plaque in Petlalcingo commemorating the one hundredth anniversary of the pope's acceptance of the Immaculate Conception as part of Catholic dogma, 1954. Serafín Sánchez Hernández.

Most of these cultural efforts failed to critique the state directly. Nonetheless, they served to support local animosity for the state in two ways. First, they provided a regional rationale for contemporary support of the church by popularizing a cogent myth of continuous religious and ethnic cooperation. When a Tequixtepec teacher asked one of his pupils why his parents obeyed the priest, the boy replied that "the church ha[d] always helped the people of Tequixtepec since the days of the Dominicans."[103] Second, these cultural efforts also carried an implicit criticism of the state's nationalist propaganda. Although post-1940 Mexican nationalism was anodyne and deliberately non-confrontational, it still carried the flotsam of the postrevolutionary cultural campaigns. Spanish influence was downplayed, the role of the Catholic Church was ignored, heroes remained predominantly secular, and the overall narrative was one of gradual emancipation.[104] The PRI, by portraying itself as both revolutionary and modernizing, appeared to be the logical conclusion of this national narrative, Mexico's inevitable leader. In the Mixteca Baja, by contrast, local Catholics sought to portray regional history as one of continuous post-Conquest harmony, solidified by Spanish evangelization and ensured by generations of pious parishioners and priests. Here, activists viewed the

Figure 18: Painting of the Virgin of Guadalupe on the side of the church in Petlalcingo. Catholics commemorated the region's religious heritage in murals, inscriptions, statues, and public events during the 1940s and 1950s. In doing so, they attempted to impose a religious narrative of local history. Serafín Sánchez Hernández.

church as the region's natural guardian. As a result, state calls for national unity, patriotism, and the celebration of secular cults, which provided the PRI with its ideological support, not only failed to function, but often appeared as a direct affront to regional historical understandings.

The grassroots strength of the church, its prolonged, aggressive anti-state stance, and its public cultural program generated considerable conflict throughout the region. Struggles focused on village schools and state-run cultural events. Despite official reconciliation, priests continued to use the pulpit to preach against federal education. In 1951 the priest of Tequixtepec attacked the school as "atheist" and "contrary to the will of God."[105] In 1950 the PRI president complained that the priest of Ayuquililla was claiming that the local schoolteachers "had forged a pact with the devil."[106] In 1957 the municipal president of the fairly liberal town of Chazumba complained that the local priest "used the pulpit microphone to attack the local teachers, call them communists, and forbade parishioners to send their children to the local school."[107] When state investigators scoured the region following the 1962 attack, they found that the priest of Cuyotepeji had claimed that those parents who sent their children to the federal school were the "children of the devil" and that the neighboring priest of Miltepec had claimed that these parents were "brutes that w[ould] be condemned."[108] In order to emphasize their point, priests employed a variety of threats. The priest of Tequixtepec established a two-tier system of punishments. For parents of state-school children, he threatened to withdraw absolution. For parents who simply neglected to send their children to the private school, he refused to administer Communion.[109] Outside the confines of the church, priests employed other strategies. Some priests took to writing persuasive letters to village leaders. In 1947 the local cleric explained to the new municipal president of Tequixtepec that "whoever supports the socialist school is damned by God . . . for the socialist school attacks God and his precepts, human rights and society itself."[110] Others chose more public means of remonstration. In 1953 the priest of Tezoatlán pointed to the cultural mission teachers exercising in the town square and shouted, "muchos maestros, mucha mierda," to the general amusement of the surrounding crowd. Summing up the situation in 1963, a visiting university student concluded: "The priests indicate to the parents that they should not send their children to the schools of the government; because they are the schools of the devil; and because they should instead send them to Catholic schools, which the population has always sustained behind the government's back."[111]

Catholic activists supported local priests in this continuing campaign. When the SEP inspector visited Coicoyán in 1944, "the Indians that made up the village authorities" refused to hand over the building for the federal school, and the religious organizations shouted that state instruction taught "ignoble, immoral, anti-social and anti-Christian ideas." One activist argued that he would "accept any punishment of the government before accepting their school," and another warned that the "federal school was a slippery danger for the children."[112] Sometimes confrontations turned violent. In 1957 the tax collector and ACM leader in Chazumba attempted to shoot the local schoolmaster.[113] In 1948 villagers beat the cultural mission's carpentry teacher senseless.

As during the 1930s, female Catholics played a dominant role. In Coicoyán the head of the senior female branch of the ACM convoked the members of the organization before the arrival of the SEP representative. In a very public display of prayer, or what one local teacher called "feminine hypocrisy," she collapsed on her knees in front of the altar, started to cry, and asked God to hear her entreaties that "the parents do not send their children into the hands of the government and our enemies."[114] Others took an active role in buttressing church propaganda. The young head of the female branch of the ACM in Tequixtepec, Angela Morales de Moran, not only helped build the village's new private school, she also composed the following paean to the importance of religious education:

> The youth is the hope
> For my idolatrous patria chica
> A well-instructed and educated youth
> Will be the stamp of pride for my race
> The redemption of the village, is the school
> The book, and also work[115]

Still others organized more aggressive demonstrations against the school. In March 1949 the authorities of Tequixtepec asked for military support when a group of "46 women" "armed with sticks and knives" attempted to storm the municipal palace and release a single woman arrested for refusing to send her son to the federal school. One hit the unpopular state-backed municipal president on the head with a rock.[116]

This consistent church-backed pressure yielded impressive results. In 1950 the visiting Mexican economist Moisés T. de la Peña lamented that the "weak attempts to establish schools" had "failed because of the resistance of the indigenous [villagers] . . . and the influence of the clergy."

Of the sixty schools officially established in the district of Huajuapan, fourteen had no teachers and were effectively closed. The neighboring district of Silacayoapan was even worse, and twenty of the thirty-four federal establishments had shut their doors. Even when schools were open they failed to attract students in large numbers. In Ahuehuetitlan only 46 of the 310 children on the educational roll went to the local school.[117] Similarly, in 1950 in Tequixtepec only 45 of the 245 prospective students attended the federal institution.[118] Although the Alemán administration jettisoned all mention of the explicitly social role of education, a decade later the panorama had hardly changed. In 1963 in Cuyotepeji and Tequixtepec the majority of children attended the private rather than the public school, and in Ayuquililla the municipal president claimed that church-educated children outnumbered state students six to one.[119]

Beyond the conflicts over federal schooling, priests and church organizations also challenged the state over its understanding of national culture. Following the template laid out by the national government, local state representatives attempted to ease regional tensions by holding deliberately inoffensive celebrations. Although bureaucrats and politicians were careful to avoid divisive events and dotted their speeches with pleas for unity and harmony, local Catholic activists, imbued with a religious vision of regional development, often undermined or disrupted the festivities. In doing so, they demonstrated their hostility not only to the government's old agrarian and educational policies, but also the new nationalist ideology of the post-1940 state. For example on September 8, 1947, locals assembled to celebrate the centennial of Antonio de León's death. Both PRI administrators and prochurch dignitaries took part in the planning of the event. Over the course of the speeches and festivities, however, it became clear that both sides were celebrating different ideas of patriotic consensus. While the local PRI chief's speech was restrained and secular, those of the prochurch group were steeped in religious imagery. One speaker described León's attachment to the Virgin of Guadalupe, Huajuapan's churches, and God; another claimed that the "Angel of Mexico" was celebrating the Immaculate Conception the day León died and thus neglected to care for one of his chosen sons. The tonal disjuncture between the speeches was reinforced during the subsequent re-enactment of the 1812 royalist siege. During the event Catholic peasants from the ranches around the town beat up the PRI-backed actors, turning an event designed to demonstrate regional accord into a running street battle.[120]

The pattern of conflict in Huajuapan was repeated in the region's smaller villages throughout the period. In July 1948 cultural missionaries in Tequixtepec attempted to organize a commemoration of Benito Juárez's death. The municipal authorities politely explained that the villagers "refused to celebrate anything to do with that man."[121] Two months later they tried again, this time endeavoring to organize a community celebration of Independence. They invited public- and private-school children to take part and publicized the event as a "demonstration of Mexican unity." Yet both groups failed to find common ground. The public-school children used the opportunity to expound upon the evils of Spanish colonialism, condemn "the opposition of the [nineteenth-century] Conservative party and its treasonous attitude to our freedom," and argue that present-day conservatives were still "bathed in blood." In opposition, the private-school orator lauded the "Catholic values" of "Mexico's priest heroes" Hidalgo and Morelos, claimed that conservatives had tried to protect Mexico from "the radical liberal ideas of the Europeans," and lauded contemporary Catholics for continuing the tradition. After the antagonistic speeches, the festivities descended into a drunken brawl with the village Catholics chasing cultural missionaries, teachers, and the handful of public-school supporters into the municipal palace.[122] Ten years later in Ayuquililla, a similar cultural conflict occurred when the local teacher attempted to celebrate the anniversary of Benito Juárez's death. According to the head of the local PRI, the students of the Catholic school "scoffed at our Fatherland's hero" during the ceremony. He claimed the incident was "irreverent and highly embarrassing."[123]

Maybe it is unwise to draw too many conclusions from the maintenance of strong opposition to federal schooling in the Mixteca Baja. Perhaps few other areas shared the region's strange constellation of agrarian conflict, isolation, weak bishops, and strong local Catholic institutions. Most state records, national newspapers, and ecclesiastical reports certainly claimed their followers had reached an easy concordat. Yet I suspect that further research in municipal archives and parish diaries will reveal that beneath these tales of national unity lies an alternate narrative of continued priest-led community opposition to the federal school. Sometimes this combative stance was localized in a single church, the product of one disobedient cleric and his pious followers. The Mexico City Jesuit José Aurelio Jiménez preached against the "atheist" state throughout the 1940s and was supported by hundreds of former Cristeros.[124] In 1947 Oaxaca City priests encouraged members of the ACM to take on and eventually force out the state governor,

Edmundo Sánchez Cano.[125] Up in the Sierra P'urhépecha, the priest of Tarecuato continued to criticize state policies and run off-the-book private schools well into the 1960s with the support of local ACM members.[126] Yet on other occasions, as in the Mixteca Baja, bands of local clerics linked by common education, experience, and ideology may have formulated widespread and long-lasting opposition movements. Although the church played down its support for the Sinarquistas, local priests continued to denigrate the state and support the organization in the pulpit and on the streets.[127] Despite the co-option of Cristero caciques, priests and lay groups still led virulent opposition to Article 3 of the Constitution in Jalisco and Zacatecas throughout the 1940s and 1950s.[128] Around Ciudad Hidalgo, Michoacán priests were accused of encouraging the murder of the old Cardenista cacique Aquiles de la Peña as late as 1959.[129] Furthermore, if this sustained opposition was more commonplace than previously observed, can we start to question the assertion that negotiations between teachers and parents over the local implementation of socialist education generated "a hegemonic consensus" that in turn served to buttress the power of the emerging one-party state?[130] In the Mixteca Baja, the church, not the state, was the most powerful institution in town. In 1950 priests still outnumbered schoolteachers in the districts of Huajuapan and Silacayoapan. Thus, even the watered-down nationalist education program of the 1940s failed to engender dialogue, unless one counts beating, stone-hurling, and name-calling. As a result, meaningful consensus over key issues like land reform, school syllabi, national culture, or, as we shall see, political allegiance failed to emerge.

"The party of God, the party of the Pope's blessing, and the party of the Catholic religion": Politics and the PAN

Taking their cue from government propaganda, scholars of Mexico's so-called Golden Age have always assumed that elections were "safe and predictable," barely contested patriotic rituals designed to sanction party appointees and, by extension, the PRI regime.[131] According to this account, from the 1930s onward the governing party employed its powerful corporatist machinery, control of electoral laws, media might, and financial sway to marginalize antagonistic groups and regiment the vast majority of Mexicans to accept elite nominations. For many, Mexico was an electoral authoritarian regime that merely "play[ed] the game of multiparty elections" and yet "violat[ed] the liberal-democratic principles of freedom and fairness so profoundly and systematically as to render elections instruments of authoritarian rule"[132] Historians of the principal opposition party, the PAN, have corroborated this view, arguing that the organization's strategy of putting forward candidates for what were mere formalities simply legitimized an increasingly authoritarian state. For Soledad Loaeza, the PAN was the "loyal opposition," the elitist instrument of an antidemocratic regime.[133]

Yet as recent scholars have pointed out, few contemporary Mexicans viewed elections in such inconsequential terms. First, during the 1940s PRI primaries acted as what Paul Gillingham has described as "unseen elections" and "sites for intense, contestatory mobilizations," the results of which often reflected local balances of power more than elite manipulation.[134] Second, even after the end of primaries in 1950 municipal, if not presidential, senatorial, and congressional, elections remained important. Opposition factions, whether grouped together into official parties or masquerading as spin-off factions of the PRI, used the opportunities to gain concessions and, if they made enough noise, a slice of local power. Third, provincial Panistas influenced by European Christian Democratic ideals, U.S. Progressive Era politics, and (perhaps more importantly) local traditions of municipal struggle played a key role in these conflictive votes. As Kevin Middlebrook argues, this focus on municipal elections "facilitated the PAN's efforts to build a multiclass constituency" that occasionally gained power but more frequently forced the PRI to accept elements of their agenda.[135] The following account of electoral politics in the Mixteca Baja confirms this view. Here, municipal elections were highly contested until the 1962 barracks attack. Furthermore, the local branch of the PAN played an important role, providing an institutional base for consistent and virulent opposition to the ruling party.

Between 1940 and 1962, political competition in the Mixteca Baja took place in two distinct stages. At first, community divisions over land tenure and federal education played out in municipal PRI primaries. As local PRI organizations were weak or divided, church-backed groups often won. However, with the abolition of primaries in 1950 and the growth in the regional strength of the PAN, things changed. Some clerical groups continued to work from within, forming independent community-based parties that claimed PRI affiliation, despite overtly opposing the official slate. Others opted to side with the PAN, forming strong municipal committees. During the next decade overwhelming grassroots support for both approaches forced the PRI's hand. Despite repression, and numerous instances of patent fraud, Panista and opposition groups won some elections outright. Even when the state party refused to admit an out-and-out victory, local leaders were often forced to establish PAN-dominated juntas of civil administration. When PRI officials rejected these options, PAN slates established completely separate administrative operations in alternative municipal palaces or local private schools.

PRI Primaries, 1946–1950

In 1946 the national party changed its name to the Partido Revolucionario Institucional. At the same time, party officials changed party voting procedures. PRI candidates were no longer nominated in sectoral assemblies, but rather in inclusive municipal primaries.[136] The move paralleled democratic openings in other Latin American countries.[137] The shift was also an ad hoc attempt to calm political divisions after the bloody conclusion of municipal elections in León, Guanajuato.[138] In some regions, the change worked as government officials used the public primaries to monitor popular allegiances and construct stable, consensual local councils.[139] In the divided communities of the Mixteca Baja, however, the opening up of the nomination procedure generated fierce competition. Here, both pro- and antistate groups viewed primaries as effective elections and struggled to prove that they made up a majority in an effort to gain the official nomination of the state branch of the national party. For example, during the municipal elections of 1948 agraristas and socios held fierce primary contests in Tonalá, Ayuquila, Huajolotitlán, Amatitlán, and Atenango. Those for and against federal schooling also clashed in Tequixtepec, Camotlán, and Zapotitlán Lagunas. In almost all the cases, both groups claimed allegiance to the national party, although only the supporters of ejidos or public schools were members of party organizations or could support their claim with any verifiable proof.[140] Furthermore, these contests often turned violent. In Amatitlán the socio faction beat two agraristas with sticks. In Ayuquila socios shot at least two aspirant agraristas.[141]

The new electoral primaries not only caused considerable confrontation, they also favored prochurch groups. Between 1946 and 1950, the organizational structure of the governing party in the Mixteca Baja was embarrassingly weak. Corporatist organizations were almost non-existent. The CNC only encompassed a handful of agraristas, and the Confederación de Trabajadores de México (CTM) and the Confederación Nacional de Organizaciones Populares (CNOP) presence was nil. Most CNC supporters were concentrated in regions around the former sugar plantations. In 1942 the local deputy reported that only seven of the municipalities in the districts of Huajuapan, Silacayoapan, and Teposcolula possessed CNC groups.[142] Ten years later at a meeting of the regional branch of the peasant union, opposition politicians mocked the "small group of confused campesinos" bussed in to attend.[143] Municipal PRI committees were similarly sparse. Most overlapped almost exactly with village's small ejidatario or *comunero* groups. According to the disenfranchised socios of Cuyotepeji, the PRI committee and the comisariado de bienes comunales were exactly the same. The chief comunero, Lauro Solano, ran both.[144] Federal teachers, keen to gain some official support, ran the rest. In 1952 in Arteaga, the local teacher was head of the PRI, head of the local teachers' union, and municipal president.[145] Moreover, factional divides compounded organizational weakness. From 1944 onward two aspirant caciques from the town's merchant elite, Rodolfo Solana Carrión and Trinidad Sosa Niño de Rivera, ran separate PRI campaigns. The division undermined party legitimacy, encouraged the emergence of rival parties, and offered considerable opportunities for exacting concessions.[146]

Without a functioning administrative structure or mass support, regional Priístas were unable to ensure victory for their small groups of village clients. Although they backed agraristas and those who sent their children to the federal schools, socios and prochurch groups often far outnumbered these groups. And as Gillingham argues, during this period state party leaders allowed most municipal primaries to be decided by majority vote. The PRI nomination simply acted as "booty, a title the party conceded to unstoppable local candidates in *de jure* recognition of *de facto* grassroots power."[147] As the more conservative groups made up the majority of the Mixteca Baja's villagers, on most occasions they won. In Ayuquila members of the sociedad agrícola became municipal authorities in 1946 and 1948. Every time the local agraristas complained, arguing that the authorities were "subservient to the priest" and "against the principles of the revolution."[148] Yet the local party could do little. An investigation by the local deputy in 1947 summed up the government position: "The municipal authorities oppose the federal school and agrarian reform, yet they are always in the majority so can dominate the authorities."[149] In Amatitlán the chief of the sociedad agrícola and future head of the village branch of the PAN, José E. Beltran, won the municipal presidency in 1946. Two years later he had a compadre and fellow socio elected. Again agraristas complained, but to no avail.[150]

A Bi-party System, 1950–1962

In 1950 this conflictive electoral system, which saw both groups fighting it out for primary victories and PRI nominations, ended. At the end of the year the PRI changed its statutes, replacing primaries with sectoral assemblies again. The shift was designed to bring tighter centralized control to what had become a chaotic, if broadly democratic, electoral regime. Local party officials were to monitor these assemblies closely, and at these meetings only members of the party's three branches were allowed to vote.[151] The change suddenly swung elections in the Mixteca Baja in favor of the small minorities of agraristas and federal school supporters who had become members of the CNC or CNOP. As Mexico's democratic opening swung shut, socio and prochurch groups were forced outside the ambit of the national party. They turned to the only alternative, the rapidly expanding local branch of the PAN.

In 1939 democratic reformists and Catholic activists had allied to form the PAN. At first the party was limited to certain sectors of the elite—bankers, industrialists, lawyers, intellectuals, and Catholic students who feared that the continuation of Cardenista policies threatened to undermine Mexico's economic and political stability as well as its religious culture.[152] Early provincial committees, like those of the Mixteca Baja, followed this social profile.[153] In Huajuapan Miguel Niño de Rivera, a former Catholic student, a land lawyer, and a member of one of the region's most important commercial families, started the organization.[154] In the neighboring district of Silacayoapan, Manuel Aguilar y Salazar, another lawyer and son of one of the area's few hacendados, founded the first regional committee.[155] At first this limited, elitist party struggled to make headway. Niño de Rivera was often away in Puebla on business, and Aguilar y Salazar lived most of the time in Oaxaca City. Both lacked the time or the inclination to travel mountainous roads and search out allies in the region's far-flung pueblos. According to a local historian of the PAN, both leaders demonstrated a marked distaste for the kind of organizational legwork and community demagogy that political power necessitated.[156] In 1942 a report on the Huajuapan regional committee pointed to "a lack of propaganda, a lack of collaborators . . . and difficulties due to the economic situation of the area."[157] In 1943 Niño de Rivera admitted that even his urban allies "were disoriented" and "did not understand the principles of the party."[158] Four years later, he had yet to form a female branch of the party.[159]

However, in the late 1940s the PAN started to transform from a patrician into a populist party. First, in 1947 and 1952 Niño de Rivera and the local party gained recognition by leading local opposition to two unpopular state governors.[160] The governors' swift dismissals and the appointment of conservative-leaning replacements offered local supporters the hope, however illusory, of future electoral victories.[161] Second, the national PAN changed orientation. Until then, Manuel Gómez Morin, who encapsulated the secular reformist branch of the original alliance, had led the party. In late 1949 he stepped down, and a succession of religious activists took his place. The move ushered in what Donald Mabry has described as the "Catholic decade" of PAN politics. As former members of Catholic student organizations and contemporary heads of the ACM, this new generation of PAN politicians changed the emphasis of the party from one of intellectual critique and limited action to one of aggressive electoral engagement.[162] From 1949 to 1956, the party put up 177 candidates for local councils, compared to only a handful in the previous decade.[163] At the same time, they used their contacts within official Catholic organizations to attempt to harness animosity over the state's historical anticlericalism and the ongoing disquiet over public schooling.[164] By the early 1950s, these new leaders had even secured a pact with the remaining Sinarquista organizations.[165] Third, this national shift brought regional results. Niño de Rivera also resigned, and Angel Mora, a dentist, brother of a local priest, and head of the local branch of the ACM, took over control of the party. Like the new leaders of the PAN, the young, energetic politician attempted to extend party support beyond the few urban ultra-conservatives and toward the broad mass of Catholic activists.[166]

In order to popularize the PAN, Mora attempted to exploit the network of priests, private-school teachers, and religious organizations that had opposed federal schooling for the past twenty years. For example, in 1952 Mora sent the local PAN activist Procopio Martínez Vásquez to drum up support for the upcoming elections. In every village he first visited the house of the local priest. After explaining the "civic importance of the official party," he asked the priest to help to establish the party's municipal committee. In San Juan Trujano, Narciso Villa Hernández gathered together churchgoers and encouraged them to join the PAN. He then traveled with Martínez Vásquez to help set up committees in the parish's outlying villages. In Ihualtepec the local cleric translated the Panista propaganda into Mixtec and helped set up another organization. In Zapotitlán Lagunas another priest called together parishioners and asked them to support PAN candidates.[167] Throughout the 1950s these village priests became unofficial propagandists of the PAN. In Ayuquililla the local cleric was "the active director of the PAN" and regularly claimed that the organization was the "party of God, the party of the Pope's blessing, and the party of the Catholic religion." When PAN candidates lost, he "made direct accusations against the political system from the pulpit." He also condemned local members of the PRI, claiming that they had "made a pact with the devil."[168]

Where priests were absent, Mora used the influence of the private-school teachers. In the tiny village of San Luis Morelia, Martínez Vásquez gained the support of the local master, who gathered together villagers, translated party propaganda, and headed the village committee. In San Ildefonso Salinas a similarly enthusiastic private-school teacher founded the party.[169] Finally, Mora also harnessed the voting power of the region's Catholic organizations. As head of the region's ACM, he often handed out PAN propaganda after religious rallies. His wife, who led the female branch of the institution, used weekly meetings to interweave church and party messages. In fact, Mora acknowledged that the "ACM and the PAN in Huajuapan" were "effectively the same."[170] Beyond the ACM, Mora also gained supporters from other Catholic organizations, including Adoración Nocturna, San Vicente de Paul, and various community cofradías. In Tlachichilco the local priest established a PAN committee that comprised all the mayordomos of the local Christ cult.[171] In 1952 Panistas hijacked the diocese's Christmas celebrations, "grabbed the microphone and in an open and aggressive way encouraged the listeners to vote for the PAN."[172]

The direct overlap of church organization and party affiliation was, if not illegal, at least contrary to the spirit of the church-state accords of the late 1930s. Yet local PAN members often flaunted these close ties. In *Huajuapan, Seminario de Orientación y Cultura*, a magazine directed at local Panistas, one activist admitted that most associates were "seminary students, priests' relatives, ACM members, and regular attendees of mass." He even confessed that the party "often asked the seminary and the church for help." Yet he claimed that this strategy did not infringe upon the law, but simply reflected Huajuapan society.[173]

As the latter example suggests, the local PAN complemented its organizational effort with increasingly sophisticated propaganda. Whereas early advocates carried earnest, centrally produced pamphlets over the region's rugged terrain by donkey, by the 1950s party organizers in Huajuapan had motorized transport, megaphones, and plenty of locally written party publicity.[174] These materials were explicitly tailored to fit local concerns. PAN supporters followed up the monthly *Huajuapan, Seminario de Orientación y*

Cultura with a weekly newspaper, *Verbo*, in 1956. The new paper was put together by Senén Martínez Rodríguez, a former seminary student, and included tales of political corruption, PRI incompetence, and left-wing infiltration. In September 1958 the newspaper led with a story that accused federal teachers of channeling the celebration of Antonio de León's death toward "communist ends." The paper also included articles on "agrarian caciques" attempting to take over socio lands and PRI cadres manipulating federal elections. An editorial stated, "A Catholic can never be a Priísta," described the Constitution as atheist, and railed against the proliferation of "schools without God."[175] Beyond local newspapers, PAN supporters also produced corridos designed to advertise specific election campaigns. During the 1947 local deputy elections, they handed out copies of the "Himno del PAN," which drew a direct parallel between León's martial patriotism and that of the region's new conservative party members.[176] Ten years later, a wit produced the "Corrido de Sadismo," a pun on the local PRI candidate Enrique Sada's name. The song claimed that to "Place Sada in congress / With such disgusting cynicism / Is the definition of Sadism."[177] Finally, PAN propagandists also produced fly sheets on particular issues of local corruption. These contained strong stuff, often written by individual citizens who were carrying the PAN badge. In 1957 the party published "Esta es la justicia para el indio," which accused the municipal president of Tezoatlán of charging the relatives of dead Mixtecs three hundred pesos for pointless autopsies and forcing small communities to pay for a telephone line that went directly to his house. The same year, another fly sheet entitled "Tezoatlán: Sin ley y sin justicia" revealed that the municipal president's brother was a convicted child killer, a thief, an alcohol monopolist, and an immoral man "who lives with young girls from poor families who offer him their virginity with which he satisfies his instincts."[178]

Founded upon the institutional strength of local Catholic groups and encouraged by a combative local media, Mora's new aggressive PAN had permanent committees in most communities by the early 1950s. Over the next decade these organizations faced off against PRI minorities in a series of fiercely contested elections. In 1952 there were electoral conflicts in twelve of Huajuapan's twenty-seven municipalities. Four years later, there were sixteen. Between 1952 and 1961 the party also ran four campaigns for federal deputy. In most competitions, PRI slates clearly confronted PAN groups. Members of both parties voted and claimed electoral majorities. However, in the larger towns of Tequixtepec, Huajuapan, and Mariscala local Panistas tried another tactic. Here, they ditched official PAN support and instead ran campaigns as independent local parties. In 1952 Panistas in Huajuapan called themselves Voto Libre Huajuapeño. In the same year, Panistas in Tequixtepec rebranded their organization (with a good deal of deliberate irony given the village's recent history) the Frente Zapatista de Tequixtepec. Four years later Mariscala PAN supporters called their party the Partido Independiente Cívico Progresista. Although these parties claimed no affiliation, they comprised PAN members and put forward manifestos that smacked of local PAN concerns.[179] Voto Libre Huajuapeño's proposals included "liberty of religion," "the liberty of parents to send children to any school they choose," and "the preservation of traditional festivities and the explanation of their spiritual, social, and historic bases."[180] The Mariscala plan was even more explicit and extolled the virtues of "the Catholic religion," "private schools," and the "rebuilding of the church tower . . . as it is the principal building in our village."[181]

Whether brazen or covert, these PAN organizations encountered a more muscular state electoral machine that was less willing to accommodate dissident groups. PRI officials now regularly employed electoral fraud in order to secure regional power. At the local level, fraud entailed three stages. The first stage was capture of the town's voting booths. Again and again local Panistas complained that Priístas "monopolized control of the voting booths," "took the voting booths by force," or filled them with compliant local officials. Some scheming party officials even set up the booths in the middle of the night and closed them early in the morning. Others hid them at the back of local houses or in the fields to prevent a large turnout.[182] Once voting booths were secured, Priístas set about minimizing numbers of possible PAN voters. Known PAN members were struck from the electoral roll or were refused electoral credentials.[183] Where PAN support was highly prevalent, PRI officials enforced blanket bans. In Camotlán in 1952, they refused to allow women, "most of whom [we]re members of the ACM," to vote.[184] In the same year, they barred an entire ranch of PAN supporters in Huajuapan from taking part in the elections.[185] Four years later they jailed sixty PAN supporters in Cuyotepeji during the week of the municipal contest.[186] The third stage was ballot stuffing. If Panistas voted and elections were close, PRI officials, or what one local termed "electoral raccoons," manipulated the results, filling the boxes with voting slips that had already been filled out.[187] At times PRI exuberance outstripped reality. In December 1956 Panistas pointed out that the PRI had received 298 votes in Ayú, although the village only comprised 170 adults. Four years later in Tetaltepec the PRI gained 502 out of a possible 200 votes.[188]

If Priístas failed to secure a majority by direct manipulation, they increasingly resorted to violence. At times, they even called on the local garrison. In late 1955 the local deputy, accompanied by federal troops, arrived in villages with PAN councils. On each occasion he threatened to shoot up the municipal palace if the Panistas refused to leave. In Amatitlán they did, and the troops stormed the building at night, killing at least one council member and wounding another two.[189] The following year, troops monitored elections in all of Huajuapan's major towns. In 1959 a new deputy, again accompanied by soldiers, overturned the council in Ayuquililla in the same way.[190] But in general, local Priístas employed less blunt displays of force, using extraregional pistoleros to rub out key PAN activists and then covering up subsequent investigations. In 1952 PRI hit men shot the PAN candidate for federal deputy, dumped his body in an unmarked grave, and then persuaded authorities to claim he had been run over. Six years later, a band of unknown gunmen ambushed another PAN candidate outside Zapotitlán Lagunas. Ignoring the wounded victim's statement, local authorities asserted that the community's PAN representative had attempted to murder his own candidate.[191] Beyond these high-profile cases, intravillage disputes between PAN and PRI supporters were also decided by force. Although specific figures are scant, the sheer number of homicides committed between 1940 and 1960 indicates that political murder was on the up. In 1957 one local military commander asked to investigate disturbances in Ayuquila said that the region was "at war."[192]

The end of primaries, electoral fraud, and violence all served to strengthen the official vote. Yet having dominated municipal elections for decades, prochurch factions were unwilling to give up power so easily. Their strategies were twofold. Like PRI officials, PAN supporters realized that in order to assure election, they needed to secure individual voting booths. Mora's cry after the end of each campaign was, "Now the campaign has ended, let us defend the voting booths."[193] In 1959 he told a local PAN representative, "He who takes the voting booths is always the winner."[194] In 1950 Panistas secured the voting booths in Silacayoapan and faced down the local judge (whose "face resembled that of a killer more than a respectable society lawyer"), the police, and out-of-town pistoleros. In 1952 PAN supporters in Huajuapan did the same. Mora entrusted two market women, Juana Corro and Juana Ceballos, to defend the booths "at all costs," which they

Figure 19: PAN municipal government in Amatitlán following expulsion by PRI forces, 1951. Archivo General del Poder Ejecutivo del Estado de Oaxaca.

did, punching police and throwing chili powder in the face of PRI officials.[195] Throughout the villages, PAN committees aped the PRI, capturing booths and preventing rival factions from voting.[196] As Mora anticipated, the tactic sometimes worked. Particularly in smaller villages, massive electoral majorities, publicized in local rags and national PAN papers, forced the PRI to cede local control.

However, in larger towns the official party was less willing to give up authority. After the PAN gained 1,804 votes to the PRI's 157 in the 1952 Huajuapan elections, the state governor simply sent troops to hand over the municipal palace to the losing slate.[197] In response, local Panistas tried another strategy—establishing alternative municipal councils. In early 1953 Voto Libre Huajuapeño set up council premises in the house of a well-known PAN lawyer. Here, they appointed representatives to outlying ranches and ordered their supporters to give taxes, market permissions, and livestock certificates to the unofficial authorities. By late January, the PRI council described the situation as "ungovernable." The state governor was forced to hand over power to the PAN front, covering up the loss by appointing Voto Libre Huajuapeño members to a junta of civil administration.[198] Over the next few months, other losing PAN committees followed suit, often rioting and assaulting PRI offices to press home their numerical superiority. In March 1953 PAN members in Camotlán set up an alternative government, broke into the municipal palace at night, and nailed the door shut.[199] In Tequixtepec, Suchitepec, Nochixtlán, and Dinicuiti villagers did the same, and in Amatitlán the old PAN leader José E. Beltran led "all the villagers" in an assault on the palace, shouting, "Death to bad government and up with the PAN."[200]

As these examples suggest, PAN tactics yielded results. In 1952 PAN slates won outright victories in Suchitepec, Cuyotepeji, Ayuquila, and San Vicente Nuñu. In 1955 a PAN candidate became federal deputy of the region, and the following year the organization triumphed in Amatitlán, Suchitepec, and Ayuquililla.[201] Beyond these clear-cut victories, electoral pressure and bargaining by riot forced PRI authorities to form juntas of civil administration.[202] Although these were rarely counted as official electoral successes, PAN slates dominated these juntas in Amatitlán and Camotlán. In Huajuapan members of Voto Libre Huajuapeño formed the organization, and in Tequixtepec members of the Frente Zapatista de Tequixtepec ruled the town.[203] Finally, in the region's smallest municipalities PAN members outnumbered PRI supporters so greatly that they often took control of council offices irrespective of government instructions. In Dinicuiti and Ihualtepec PAN authorities ran local affairs from 1953 through 1956, despite the state governor's orders.[204] Even in villages where the PRI had attained municipal power, opposition groups simply ran their own administrative structures. In 1958 the municipal president of Zahuatlán complained that the priest and "the women of the village" had established alternative offices in the parish residence. They established their own private school, cut communal wood without asking permission from the proper authorities, refused to record their children's births in the civil register, denied the burial of Priístas in the local graveyard, and claimed that their government was "that of the PAN" and that the official school was "the school of the devil."[205] In municipalities' small dependent ranches, this abject refusal to accept PRI rule was commonplace. In Ayú the federal teacher protested that villagers had ignored his official appointment as municipal representative and instead "continued to obey their own authorities," maintaining control of communal lands, neglecting to hand over the requisite parcel to the federal school, and refusing to send their children to the state institution.[206]

Between 1940 and 1962 prochurch groups in the Mixteca Baja eagerly took part in municipal elections, despite growing PRI control. At first, they took advantage of the party's democratic opening to assert large majorities in PRI primaries and gain official recognition. However, during the 1950s electoral procedure changed. Prochurch groups now allied with an increasingly aggressive branch of the PAN and sought to undermine PRI electoral control through electoral campaigning, mass voting, and, if necessary, rioting. In many cases they were successful, either gaining a clear victory or running a PAN council under the government radar. The emergence of electoral competition despite increasing PRI authoritarianism mirrors events throughout the country. In Guerrero and Veracruz, opposing factions competed for municipal rule throughout the period.[207] And on many occasions, state and national authorities were forced to accept the electoral victories of less pliant groups. In southern Oaxaca, railway workers, conservatives, and supporters of the local cacique all vied for municipal control.[208] Even in San Luis Potosí, the pistol-wielding Priísta autocrat Gonzalo Santos was unable to regiment electoral politics effectively.[209]

Where the Mixteca Baja perhaps differed was in the relative strength and combativeness of the local PAN. Despite the influence of the party's new generation of young Catholic activist leaders, most local branches remained firmly oriented toward the interests of the urban middle class. As a result, official municipal victories were still rare. Between 1950 and 1960 the PRI only recognized a total of thirteen PAN triumphs, seven of which were in the Mixteca Baja.[210] Yet the prevalence of unauthorized PAN councils in the Mixteca Baja suggests that these figures only reveal part of the story. The national party was always keen to assert dominance even where very little existed. For Beatriz Magaloni the PRI elites' "image of invincibility" was a key tool for survival.[211] Beneath this veneer, how many other municipal elections were resolved by the appointment of PAN-dominated juntas of civil administration? How many PAN-affiliated organizations ran under independent banners? Finally, how many other small villages ignored PRI stipulations and simply appointed their local PAN representative as municipal agent? For example, the continuation of electoral violence, the accusations of widespread Sinarquista support, and the smattering of PAN victories in the Sierra P'urhépecha indicate that here indigenous prochurch groups also allied with the opposition party to establish more autonomous councils.[212]

The Cold War in the Mixteca Baja

During the late 1950s, political divisions within the Mixteca Baja became more pronounced. During this period, international, national, and local developments acted in concert to heighten tensions between prochurch and prostate groups. On all three levels, left-wing and right-wing campaigns acted dialectically to increase political allegiance and amplify the threat of opposition groups. In the Mixteca Baja, national conflicts combined with existing political divisions, increasing electoral control, and Cárdenas's involvement in local irrigation works to persuade a handful of Catholic militants that only armed insurgency would save the nation from communist takeover. Such alarmist responses paralleled other right-wing uprisings in Michoacán and Nuevo León. Yet the long-term importance of the garrison attack was not in its execution but rather its aftermath. Growing extremism on the right, like its counterpart on the left, allowed the PRI to regiment opponents and retake the middle ground. In the Mixteca Baja party officials persuaded PAN leaders to retreat from electoral competition and discipline or expel difficult cadres. Church leaders were forced to do the same, toning down pulpit propaganda and finally assuming the modus vivendi of many of their peers. The church-state pact, which had failed to take hold in the late 1930s, was finally put in place.

In early 1959 Fidel Castro and his ragtag band of guerrilla fighters and peasant radicals finally took control of Cuba. After two years of provocations by U.S.-backed exiles, Castro declared the revolution "socialist," started to implement far-reaching land distribution, and brokered a series of commercial treaties with the Soviet Union. The emergence of a communist state a short boat ride from the Americas' east coast amplified anticommunist propaganda throughout the continent. In Mexico, Cuban émigré groups and small factions of right-wing extremists established organizations like the Regional Anti-Communist Crusade to distribute anti-Castro propaganda, list the country's dead, claim that the new government had "killed Christmas," and try to prove that "communism [wa]s not simply something nebulous and intangible that appeared long ago in Russia." David Mayagoita's shrill 1951 opus *Definámonos! O Católico o Comunista* sold out a print run of 360,000 copies. The new introduction warned that "Soviet barbarity which had covered with blood and ruins entire peoples, like Poland, Hungary, and most recently Cuba, has been launched into our country as well."[213]

Yet Mexican anticommunism was not simply a knee-jerk response to overseas events. At home, declining wages, rising prices, the return of large-scale commercial agriculture, and growing political exclusion had precipitated a series of union conflicts and peasant land seizures throughout the late 1950s, culminating in the railway workers' strike of 1959.[214] Despite the movement's repression, over the next three years the brio of the Cuban Revolution combined with these internal factors to sustain the left. After the Bay of Pigs, students in Morelia attacked and set fire to the Instituto Cultural México-Norteamericano. Similar pro-Cuban demonstrations took place in Puebla, Guadalajara, and other provincial cities.[215] Former president Lázaro Cárdenas became the figurehead of these new campaigns, celebrating Cuban liberation with Castro in Havana in 1959 and organizing the pro-Cuban Latin American Conference for Sovereignty, Economic Independence, and Peace in March 1961. In the same year he created the Movement of National Liberation (MLN), a civic organization designed to bring together the disparate efforts of the Mexican left under one umbrella. The MLN was a classic Cardenista organization: well meaning, inclusive, and ramshackle, its rhetoric "written within the vocabulary of reformist movements."[216] Yet in the increasingly polarized world of Mexican politics, the involvement of Communist Party members and Cárdenas's close links to the Cuban regime generated the assumption that the organization was, in the words of the Central Intelligence Agency, "a rabidly anti–United States, pro-Cuba Communist front."[217] Outside the MLN other old Cardenistas took a more confrontational approach. In September 1961 a branch of former Henriquistas under General Celestino Gasca led a series of concerted assaults on military posts, police installations, and municipal palaces throughout Mexico's southern states.[218]

The escalating rhythm of radical protests forced the government to wheel out its dual strategy of reward and repression, popularly known as *pan o palo*. Often PRI operatives decapitated social movements by removing their leaders. Paramilitaries murdered Rubén Jaramillo, Zapata's agrarista heir, and state forces imprisoned Sonoran land invaders, the communist chiefs of the railway strike, and over two hundred of Gasca's Henriquista followers.[219] Yet more worryingly for the right, they also frequently followed up force with favor. The nomination of union broker Adolfo López Mateos for president, rather than candidates close to former president Miguel Alemán, signified a slight reformist shift, rather overstated by his campaign slogan "extreme left within the constitution."[220] Once in power, the new president sought to placate Mexican radicals by denigrating U.S. hemispheric power and offering revolutionary Cuba diplomatic support.[221] At the same time, he also initiated some internal reforms, increasing land distribution, upping the budget devoted to social welfare, and nationalizing U.S.-owned electricity companies.[222] Two policies in particular concerned the right. In February 1959 López Mateos created the National Commission of Free Textbooks, which was entrusted with distributing free tomes to the country's schoolchildren.[223] Two years later, he persuaded the increasingly high-profile figure of Lázaro Cárdenas to head the Río Balsas project.[224] The scheme aimed, through the construction of a series of dams, to offer power and irrigation to some of the poorest regions of the country, from the Mixteca in the south through Guerrero's Tierra Caliente and into Michoacán.

The emergence of homegrown radicals merged with the perceived moderation of the PRI to intensify Mexican anticommunism, broadening the red scare beyond scattered Cuban exiles and paranoid fanatics to include more mainstream groups. Employing the biomedical metaphors so prevalent at the time, many believed that communism had "infected" the state, that the PRI's leftward shift was not simply a realpolitik response designed to co-opt key constituencies, but rather more proof of the party's communist-addled hierarchy. In Mayagoita's mind, communist "agents live[d] in the cities, tr[ied] to pervert our children, and wr[o]te the books that our kids are forced to study in their schools."[225] Abandoning the policy of political nonintervention, prelates, priests, and parishioners led the way, reviving the anticommunism of the Cárdenas era. In Puebla the archbishop responded to the cries of "Cuba sí! Yanquis no!" with a diocesan circular that declared that communists "threatened both Christian and Mexican civilization with total destruction."[226] In May 1961 over fifty thousand Catholics assembled to celebrate the anniversary of the encyclical "Rerum novarum." Church and lay leaders told the crowd that communism was now "victorious in Cuba and open and unmasked in our own country."[227] Even model followers of the modus vivendi like José Garibi Rivera, recently appointed as Mexico's cardinal, now exclaimed that communism sought to "destroy all religion and rub out the idea of God from the world."[228] The PAN, under the leadership of the Catholic militant José González Torres, followed suit, conflating external and internal threats. For Panistas the free textbook campaign smacked of socialist education. Cárdenas's public prominence not only proved the point, but also warned of a parallel revival of "collective agriculture . . . and union control." Reviving memories of the 1930s and linking them to contemporary threats, the PAN's organ, *La Nación*, argued that Mexican "socialism" was as pernicious as communism and that the country's "extreme left" was "allying with the positions of international communism."[229] In October 1962 the same newspaper announced that new teacher-training colleges had been established to "indoctrinate" educators with "the theories and tactics of international communism."[230]

For Soledad Loaeza, the confrontations "were strictly limited to . . . the middle class" and culminated in business-backed protests in Monterrey.[231] Yet the struggle went beyond urban demonstrations, broadsheet exchanges, and high-church denunciations. As the PAN's editorial suggested, the ripples from the Cuban Revolution threatened to reopen discussion on Mexico's revolutionary trajectory, to upend the church-state pact, and to revive the widespread clashes of the immediate postrevolutionary era. In the Mixteca Baja the national debates had particular resonance. Accusations that the state was "lurching toward communism" confirmed existing convictions. But they also dovetailed with recent developments. First, the biparty political system, which had offered a degree of local control to antistate groups, ended. During the 1959 municipal elections and the 1961 federal deputy elections, state officials ordered soldiers to defend the voting booths throughout the region's major towns. Military patrols also prevented the parties from taking any municipal palace by force.[232] From 1959 to 1962 the PAN registered no electoral victories. During the federal elections of 1961, military control and multiple instances of ballot box fraud culminated in a landslide victory for the PRI. The official party candidate gained over 27,000 votes to the PAN's 7,362. Although the PAN candidate protested to the electoral college of "many anomalies" in the voting process, his complaints were ignored.[233] Confrontations turned increasingly violent. In early November 1962 forty women "affiliated with the PAN" stormed the municipal palace of Cacaloxtepec and beat the authorities with sticks and rocks. In response, the PRI gunmen shot up a local PAN meeting, shooting three activists in the legs and one in the back.[234] The PAN's frustration with these more authoritarian rules of the electoral game was clearly visible in the following heated exchange between local leaders and PRI representatives in Silacayoapan during the local deputy elections in August 1962:

> The voting booth had began to function normally on 19 August at 9am when Lic. Jorge Jiménez Ruiz arrived from Oaxaca as the representative of the PRI. He immediately ordered that the voting slips not be counted.

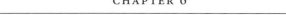

He then said, "I am going to say with all frankness that those of the PAN who are trying to defend this voting booth, will not succeed as you do not have enough people. The people voted for us as they understand that we are bringing progress."

PAN: Lic. to prove you are lying, I invite you to a plebiscite wherever you want, and you will see who has more people.

PRI: That is because you threaten and deceive them and clearly the poor people have to follow you.

PAN: Yes, you are right, we have the prisons, the judges, the agents of the public ministry, the comisariados, the rural commanders, the caciques and the federal teachers. And we quit parcels of land from peasants who don't toe the PRI line on pointless pretexts.

PRI: Maybe if you choose Silacayoapan, you may win. Why don't we choose another village?

PAN: We told you that you could choose any pueblo you want, for example San Marcos where everyone votes for us. There, you claimed that 475 people voted for you and only 30 for us. We could hold a plebiscite here and prove that you are stepping on the dignity of those people in whose name you claim to speak. If you did this in any of the pueblos around, you would find that the majority supports the National Action Party, which is concerned with the salvation of Mexico.

PRI: Sir, don't get angry, you could only do this as your people are blind and fanatic.

PAN: No, they are defending their rights and the rights of others, they are defending their children from communism, and their brothers from hunger, misery and injustice.[235]

Second, if growing political marginalization persuaded some local Panistas of the futility of electoral competition, Cárdenas's tour of the region, as part of the Río Balsas commission, confirmed the state's growing affiliation with communist groups. In October 1962 Cárdenas visited the districts of Silacayoapan and Huajuapan to inspect viable irrigation projects. On the advice of the commission's engineers, he suggested solving the problem of the region's chronic droughts by building reservoirs in Huajolotitlán, Tezoatlán, Tonalá, and Mariscala.[236] According to secret service agents who scoured the region after the garrison assault, the former president's arrival had "initiated rumors that he was going to impose communist doctrine on the people."[237] Priests and lay leaders now increased anticommunist propaganda, drawing a direct connection between top-down propaganda and bottom-up electoral frustration and fears of Cardenismo's imminent return. One cleric claimed that "the government was influenced by communism, and for that reason did not allow the people to vote." Another argued, "Communists had many positions in Mexico's government" and "by taking away lands . . . were responsible for the misery of the people."[238] They also distributed anticommunist propaganda, like the tract "On Mexican Atheism" found in the house of one of the rebels. The pamphlet warned that "the communist menace and the Masonic conspiracy" obliged all Catholics "to be on their guard" and concluded that the "communist threat [was] not far from us."[239] Lay followers like the leader of the garrison attack, Manuel del Refugio Herrera Ponce, repeated the clerical line, arguing that "good Catholics and those that believe in God" had to "defend religion" as the "communists [we]re preparing a coup d'état."[240] Members of the female branch of the ACM joined in, railing against the government's "ties to communism" and "socialist tendencies."[241]

As national anticommunist campaigns, narrowing local political opportunities, and regional clerical propaganda collided, some militant Catholics chose to confront the government through armed insurrection. According to Herrera Ponce, during the late 1950s a disenchanted military major from Jalisco, Jesús Barragán Leñero, brought together around four hundred religious activists, including Catholic journalists, PAN politicians, and ACM leaders, from throughout Mexico to plan military revolt under the banner of the National Liberation Army. In 1959 the recruits assembled above the village of Amecameca in the foothills of Popocatépetl and held a Mass to consecrate the movement. For three years the conspirators regularly traveled to Mexico City, where they would circle the cathedral talking in hushed tones about the country's descent into communist tyranny. Finally, in July 1962 they decided to act. Barragán Leñero sent Herrera Ponce back to the Mixteca Baja to gather support. At the same time, he dispatched other rebels to Michoacán, Chihuahua, Tamaulipas, Zacatecas, and Jalisco to establish similar insurrectionary foci.[242] In the end, the uprising was a disaster. Chihuahua rebels, originally inspired by the defeat of the PAN candidate during the last gubernatorial elections, stayed in their homes.[243] Prospective rebels from Jalisco and Zacatecas did the same. The handful of homemade bombs tossed into the Cuban embassy failed to explode.[244] In Matamoros secret service agents captured the prospective rebels and their small armory without incident. Only rebels from Huajuapan and Ciudad Hidalgo enacted the plan, causing minimal damage before fleeing to the hills.[245] In both cases, militants had failed to harness sufficient support, despite increased local tensions. In Huajuapan rebels comprised only a handful of PAN politicians, like Herrera Ponce; a group of disenfranchised socios from Amatitlán; and a smattering of private-school teachers and other Catholic militants.[246]

The abject failure of "the last Cristiada" has condemned the uprising to historical obscurity. Nonetheless, the statements and documents collected by secret service agents in the succeeding months point to the continuing lack of consensus between the state and militant Catholics. Priests and lay leaders imprisoned after the rebellion maintained that the government was "full of communists," that "the PRI was influenced by communist ideas," and that "if there was a free vote, the president of Mexico would be a priest."[247] Herrera Ponce's manifesto, which was pinned to the municipal palace after the assault, summed up both the political marginalization and sense of impending doom shared by many Catholic activists. The tract claimed that "the call of effective suffrage" had been "trampled by fraud, corruption, and brute force," declared that the government had "shut off the pacific roads to re-establishing order," and added that the rebel government's first act would be to hold "a national vote which represented the common good." It also contained condemnations of the "lack of liberty of the press," "the perversion of justice," and "the political control of unions". There were also calls for "municipal autonomy . . . according to the constitution." Reflecting increasing military involvement in local elections, the poster reserved special opprobrium for soldiers' "crimes and injustices, abuses and robberies" and called for citizens to "break the chains and recognize [their] rights and liberties." At the same time, Herrera Ponce argued that the "present faction of the government" intended to "drag the nation to communism, and thereby destroy all the values of our culture." Linking the rebellion to international events, the manifesto ended with a rejection of "any settlement with the red beast" and a statement of sympathy with "the disgrace felt by our brothers in China, Russia, Hungary, and Poland."[248]

If the failed rebellion highlighted the continuing differences between the national party and a minority of radical Catholics, the subsequent clean-up operation brought to light broader processes of state control. The garrison attack proved a political windfall for the PRI. In fact, subsequent events as well as Barragán Leñero's easy escape from government forces convinced many local PAN officials that the plot was a deliberate setup.[249] First, local officials used the assault to justify higher levels of repression. Although secret service agents concluded that only a few Panistas had joined the insurrection, hundreds were rounded up, beaten, tortured, and thrown in jail.[250] Some were released after a month, but other key regional linkmen like Procopio Martínez Vásquez spent years behind bars.[251] When Herrera Ponce eventually walked free, he was left deaf and crippled from his severe beating at the hands of soldiers and PRI investigators.[252] Another two suspects were beaten so badly that they had to spend two months in hospital.[253] Furthermore, in the years following the rebellion the military presence in the region increased. Military units protected voting booths at elections, guarded municipal palaces, and hassled and intimidated priests and PAN activists.[254] At the same time, opposition politics became increasingly criminalized as individual municipalities introduced harsh new police codes. In January 1963 the council of Huajuapan forbade citizens from "disobeying the municipal authorities" or "destroying the regulations or announcements of the authorities" and upped the fine for nonattendance at the federal school to one hundred pesos.[255] Meanwhile, secret service agents patrolled the region, picking up Panistas suspected of breaches of the peace. In January 1963 they caught Manuel Zaragoza Acevedo with a small tract condemning the government's education policy. According to the report he threatened officers with a knife. Although Zaragoza Acevedo replied that he simply carried the knife to cut palm, he was thrown in jail.[256] In July 1963 agents arrested five Panistas accused of murdering the head of the Cuyotepeji comisariado, Lauro Solano.[257] Six months later they rounded up another five PAN activists, including two women, accused of insulting Huajuapan's authorities. All received jail terms.[258]

Second, the specter of armed right-wing revolt also forced ambivalent elites into line. In the months following the revolt, the PAN's new, more amenable leader, Adolfo Christlieb Ibarrola, desperately distanced the party from the Huajuapan "fanatics," arguing that the revolt was the "work of private individuals and not the party."[259] In December he ordered local activists to withdraw candidates from the upcoming municipal elections, and he warned female party members "to discipline themselves or leave the party."[260] At the same time, national and regional ecclesiastical authorities used the opportunity to regiment wayward local clerics, scolding many and banishing the ringleaders to Mexico City.[261] Third, the insurrection persuaded the left to take a less confrontational approach. Over the next year, Cárdenas met regularly with the region's ecclesiastical authorities in an effort to dissuade them of his supposed communist affiliations and promote the irrigation program's benefits. For the most part, the public relations exercise was a success. In 1964 the "entire village" of Tonalá, split for over forty years between prochurch and prostate groups, inaugurated a statue in Cárdenas's honor. Even the priest attended, saying he believed that Cárdenas "had changed."[262] Although it would not last for long, some kind of stable consensus had arrived in the Mixteca Baja.[263]

Conclusion

Although the garrison attack was a one-off, this model of revolt, repression, and moderation paralleled events throughout Mexico during postwar period. Furthermore, this pattern suggests how a state with limited military capability, a weak bureaucratic structure, and limited cultural hegemony managed to ride out crisis after crisis without enormous upheaval. In fact, extremely disenfranchised groups prone to armed confrontation, from the peasant radicals of Morelos and Ciudad Madera to the Sinarquistas of the Bajío and the Catholic activists of the Mixteca Baja, were key to PRI rule. Small-scale, poorly organized revolts acted as local warning beacons, revealing to the state where to concentrate military force and bureaucratic effort. At the same time, the irregular cadence of peasant insurrection regimented potential allies on the left and right. Just as Herrera Ponce's revolt inspired church and PAN leaders to pull local backing, so Jaramillo's militancy alienated Cardenistas, and Sinarquista conflicts provoked the withdrawal of ecclesiastical support. In each case, the PRI took advantage of serious discontent to restate the pact with more pliable out-of-favor groups. As the Cold War heated up, the PRI's strategy of dealing with both right-wing and left-wing groups proved extremely effective. Initial political polarization pushed activists on both sides into confrontation with the state. Extremists surfaced, and the state had them murdered or jailed. In response, left-wing and right-wing organizations, fearful of large-scale revolt, gradually moved toward the center. Cárdenas took state employ and directed the MLN toward less confrontational ends, militant Catholics decreased the tenor of their anticommunist propaganda, and Panistas under Christlieb accepted limited electoral reforms.[264]

Outside Mexico the church's political involvement in the Mixteca Baja paralleled two developing strands of Catholic activism. On the one hand, the church's open support for the PAN and some degree of electoral democracy resembled attempts in Europe and South America to create popular parties. Here, Catholic anticommunism had spiked during the 1930s, and during succeeding decades prelates and priests sought alliances with center and center-right groups. In Germany, Italy, and Chile, they backed the creation of Christian Democrat parties, and in France they supported Charles de Gaulle.[265] Although these factions were formed to counter Russian influence, forward-thinking members were willing to countenance and even work with certain center-left or socialist groups. Despite pressure from Rome, some French Catholics sought a dialogue with the left throughout the 1950s and 1960s, culminating in the Christian-Marxist movement of the succeeding decade.[266] At the same time, despite goading from U.S. and Vatican emissaries, the ecclesiastical establishment in Chile remained neutral toward the left-wing regime of Salvador Allende.[267] On the other hand, the Mixteca Baja's virulent anticommunism matched that of more reactionary church leaderships in North and Central America. In the United States, many prelates supported Joseph R. McCarthy's witch hunt. And in Guatemala bishops claimed that the government was "completely Communistic" and threatened to establish an "agrarian dictatorship."[268] In comparative terms, political opportunity appears to have shaped postwar political Catholicism in the Mixteca Baja as much as ideological position. During the late 1940s and early 1950s the church (like its counterpart in Germany, Italy, or Chile) had a stake in the democratic process as PAN committees won a series of electoral victories. When the PRI restricted this possibility in the late 1950s, however, priests and parishioners (like their counterparts in Guatemala) upped their alarmist rhetoric and turned to more radical political action.[269]

Conclusion

✝

A FEW KILOMETERS OUTSIDE HUAJUAPAN ON THE ROAD BACK TO Oaxaca City there was a piece of political graffiti that read, "Ulises, God knows you are a murderer, you are going to hell." The sign referred to the last governor of Oaxaca, Ulises Ruíz, who was almost ousted by a cross-class coalition in late 2006. During the following year, the signposts and walls of Oaxaca were plastered with accusations of the governor's complicity in various political assassinations, but the slogan in Huajuapan was differ-ent. Rather than list the deceased, denigrate the party, or urge the people to revolt, the sign contained a clear religious message. An omniscient God was going to condemn the governor to eternal damnation for his crimes: if political intrigues saved the governor in this life, they would not save him in the next. Although the graffiti may have been the work of a lone mal-content or a piece of opportune political propaganda in the seat of the local diocese, it seemed (or at least it seemed to the historian) to make a more profound point. The growth in communications, large-scale socioeconomic change, mass migration, and political horse-trading may have all but wiped out the region's tradition of provincial conservatism. Nonetheless, an echo of the link between religion and politics still remained.

Until very recently, religion, politics, and socioeconomic relations in the Mixteca Baja were closely intertwined, coalescing into a set of agreed-upon expectations between elite and non-elite groups. During the early colonial period, indigenous caciques dominated the region, laying claim to community lands, political appointments, and peasant labor. In exchange, villagers demanded land use, physical and legal protection, and the proper fulfillment of religious practices. Although Hispanic colonists gradually established haciendas volantes and mercantile networks, they did not undermine this arrangement. In many ways both enterprises served to cement community relations, not only failing to take over village properties, but in fact offering small cash and labor incentives to both noble and non-noble groups. The Catholic Church, through the Dominican friars, solidified this arrangement even further, offering rituals, legitimacy, and ideological backing to indigenous caciques in exchange for their support for the missionary effort. During the eighteenth century, population growth, increasing commercial opportunities, and bureaucratic changes strained these relationships. In fertile valley regions, interlopers usurped village lands, planted sugarcane, and built small mills. Even up in the hills, some caciques sought to build upon their quasi-feudal status and attempted to rent out community pasture to nonlocal ranchers. At the same time, the secularization of the missions created tensions between the new priests and their parishioners, especially over issues of schooling and language. Yet despite these pressures, the agreements between the region's diverse groups endured. The poor quality of the region's lands limited outside investment, and a new faction of populist indigenous caciques replicated the old colonial hierarchy in a series of decentralized repúblicas. Finally, these indigenous caciques or their mestizo children took over control of the local church, refining the reformist urges of their superiors and tailoring them to traditional arrangements. In turn, this gradual, predominantly pacific rewriting of the moral economy stemmed enthusiasm for Mexican Independence.

During the post-Independence period, the decline of the noble class, the threat of neighboring radicals, and the polarization of Mexican national politics also brought change. However, elites and non-elites again mixed tradition and innovation to forge a new status quo. On the one hand, elites allowed communities to maintain decentralized village rule and take advantage of the decline of noble status to purchase their own lands. Only in a handful of cases did white elites start to dominate municipal government, and even here they continued to allow indigenous groups to maintain control of religious practice. At the same time, between 1830 and 1890 around half of the region's land was transferred from the indigenous noble class to their previous tenants. On the other hand, elites also demanded more, including political loyalty and service in the militia. Antonio de León's approach to regional politics highlighted this gradual exchange. During the period, he encouraged cacique land sales and protected village integrity. But at the same time, he demanded political acquiescence and forced hundreds of Mixtecs to confront rebellious Triquis on the Oaxaca-Guerrero border. In doing so, he consciously modernized the old arrangement between noble and non-nobles groups, ridding the region of old feudal duties but widening political loyalty to include armed service. Finally, local church leaders overlay this arrangement with a new religious imperative that expected greater sacramental orthodoxy and clerical support in return for the authorization of local devotions and ritual practices.

The stability of the Porfiriato encouraged increasing commercial opportunities, nonindigenous immigration, and, at least on the surface, political control. Nonetheless the new politicized moral economy, established in the early nineteenth century, endured. Undoubtedly, economic exploitation, in the form of high-interest cash loans, elite-run migration programs, and haciendas volantes, increased. But at the same time, certain bottom-up demands were met. Land, this time in the form of agricultural societies, remained in the hands of the peasants, and villagers sustained control over municipal politics. Local clerical policies again reflected and molded this dynamic. The reinvigorated, increasingly Romanized church expected the establishment of new pious organizations, the construction of growing numbers of churches and chapels, and the continued financing of ecclesiastical institutions. Yet these same priests concurrently authorized and formalized the celebration of traditional local devotions. The everyday running of cofradías exemplified the parameters of the transaction with their mixture of autonomy and authority. In exchange for allowing communities to continue controlling the institutions and their lands, priests expected the regular income from tithes and the ability to channel some funds toward schools and new cult projects. During the twentieth century, this social, economic, and cultural arrangement stayed in place. Communities, constituted in the form of broad-based agricultural societies, continued to dominate the region's lands and municipal politics. But while commercial transactions remained exploitative and unequal, they failed to threaten either of these gains. Clerical-lay relations both aped and shaped the ongoing agreement as church leaders demanded clerical piety and loyalty to the church in exchange for allowing a degree of ritual and devotional innovation.

The shifting stages of this regional moral economy, with their multiple moving parts, resist easy definition. Perhaps they could be defined according to their dominant elements, as "hierarchical" (during the colonial period), "decentralized" (from 1750 to 1830), "politicized" (from 1830 to 1870), "institutionalized" (during the Porfiriato), and "sub rosa" (during the difficult revolutionary years). Yet taken together, they do explain why elites and non-elites in the Mixteca Baja repeatedly opted to follow a political ideology of "provincial conservatism." In the most prosaic terms, both groups resisted sudden exterior threats to the various elements of these mutual arrangements. At times, these exterior threats comprised rebellious outside groups. During the 1830s and 1840s radical federalists from the Oaxaca-Guerrero border brought violence, economic disruption, and dangerous doctrines of political liberation. In response, both nonindigenous and indigenous villagers formed militia groups, allied with the centralist authorities, and sought to put down the rebellions. During the 1910s, revolutionaries from Puebla, Morelos, and Guerrero played the same role, threatening the carefully negotiated agreements between commercial and peasant groups. Again, both factions joined together to resist outside interference, forming village defense units, calling on popular icons and local saints to provide redemption, and allying with national groups that promised to bring order and stability. At other times, these exterior threats were directed by the state. During the 1850s liberal politicians attempted to undermine clerical authority and usurp cofradía lands. During the 1930s and 1940s revolutionary anticlericals did the same, while during the 1950s PRI leaders tried to wrest political control from municipal governments. In each case, merchants and peasants resisted, either through armed force, ballot box contests, or manifold weapons of the weak.

Throughout this book I have been at pains to draw similarities between the interwoven moral economy of the Mixteca Baja and comparable situations in Latin America and Europe. Yet at its core, this regional narrative questions some fairly basic assumptions about rural economic relations, indigenous religiosity, and peasant politics in Mexico. The history of land tenure, in particular, runs counter to most historical appreciations. The longevity of noble land ownership challenges presumptions about eighteenth-century noble decline, growing Hispanic and mestizo agrarian domination, and peasant impoverishment. The large-scale land distribution of the following century and the establishment of long-lasting, fairly equitable agricultural societies questions understandings of increasing agrarian commercialization and community land loss. Finally, popular support for the maintenance of agricultural societies as private properties and the consequent bitter conflicts over postrevolutionary agrarian reform unsettle, if not wholly undermine, simplistic narratives of revolutionary redemption. Clearly, the arid, mountainous geography and the resilient social hierarchy of the Mixteca Baja make the place rather exceptional. Yet perhaps the region's situation is not quite as unprecedented as agrarian historiography might lead us to believe. As Emilio Kourí argues, historical arguments about nineteenth-century privatization's deleterious effects may have some validity. But in general, they have emerged not from empirical inquiry but rather from revolutionary-era presumptions and proposed political solutions.[1] Even the most recent historians of the Mixteca Baja have tailored their investigations to fit the standard model, portraying the elites as rapacious land-grabbers and the peasants as landless victims who were occasionally cajoled into compliance by force or sudden bouts of false consciousness.[2] Perhaps, as a handful of contemporary agrarian historians have started to suggest, it is time to stop loading the prevalent agrarian narrative with provisos, map out a new agrarian cartography, and dismiss these old assumptions altogether.[3]

In addition, the narrative of close religious cooperation, especially in such an indigenous area, questions Mexico's assumed religious geography. Historians have assumed that clerical Catholicism was most powerful in what Manuel Ceballos Ramírez has termed the "Catholic geo-political axis," a predominantly mestizo zone stretching between Zacatecas and Puebla.[4] In contrast, the Catholicisms of the indigenous north, south, and southeast have been held to be a heady and unorthodox mix of overliteral doctrinal interpretations and quasi-pagan continuities. However, the Mixteca Baja's strong, authorized devotions not only indicate that the Indian-made synthesis of the colonial period and the clerical religiosity of the nineteenth century were compatible, but also that pockets of provincial piety, under the right circumstances, could exist far outside Mexico's traditional conservative hubs. At the same time, the tales of lay-clerical negotiations, the stories of locally born clergy, and the narratives of mutual protection have started to suggest ways in which regional socioeconomic structures and institutional forces served to integrate many of Mexico's indigenous groups into colonizing rituals and practices in a way that did not simply generate outward resistance or resigned compliance. Power relationships were deeply unequal, but discourses and demonstrations of obedience and deference could bring results. And over time Mixtec worshippers managed to transform the region's rituals to serve local necessities.[5]

Finally, the narrative of continued conservative support also refines recent understandings of peasant politics. Over the past twenty years, political historians of Mexico, keen to escape condescending Marxist interpretations, reflect the prevalence of contemporary rural discontent, and move

beyond simplistic economistic readings, have started to take peasant discourses seriously, scouring the archives for evidence of ideological percolation and complex alliance formation in Mexico's communities. As
most villagers were, at least until recently, illiterate, the search is not only
extremely difficult but also often determines the results. In order to assure
discovery of the documents, contemporary historians have gravitated
toward regions of famed, predominantly radical, revolt. State archival practices have cemented this tendency. In particular, the origins of the Porfirian
and postrevolutionary regimes in popular uprisings regimented subsequent
peasant entreaties to the state, forcing even the unenthused to adopt the
tropes of the party in power. Gazing back over two decades of Mexican historiography, we can easily imagine that the country comprised a handful of
metropolitan conservatives and a vast rebellious mass drifting from federalism to liberalism to revolutionary socialism with each shift of its amenable
mid-tier leadership. Undoubtedly, many peasants did follow this pattern,
embracing the liberating facets of modern political ideologies and reformu-
lating their more constraining elements to suit local circumstances. But at
the same time, many, including the inhabitants of the Mixteca Baja, did not.
Early nineteenth-century caste wars generated indigenous support for order
and stability even in racially divided Yucatán.[6] Conservative-supporting
peasants probably outnumbered their liberal counterparts during the War
of Reform.[7] Despite the late Porfiriato's disruptive policies, González y
González's poor defensive "revolucionados" played an important role in the
Revolution of 1910.[8] Finally, the growth of popular right-wing organizations
paralleled that of left-wing groups during the Cold War. Conservatism, perhaps as much as its radical equivalents, had a profound provincial echo.

Appendices

Appendix A

Land Disputes in the Eighteenth Century in Huajuapan

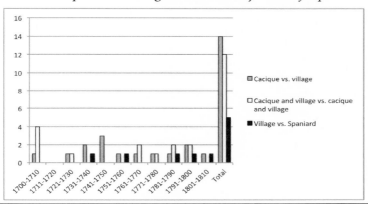

Source: The table is based on the conflicts listed in AGN, Tierras.

Appendix B

Land Ownership in the District of Huajuapan, 1831
(One *sitio de ganado menor*, or livestock farm, was around 780 hectares in size.)

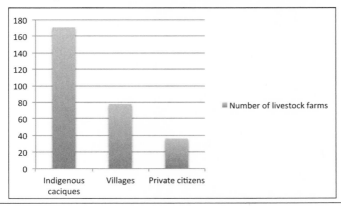

Source: AGPEO, Gobierno de los Distritos, Siglo XIX, Huajuapan, legajo 23, exp. 24, Informe of Juan Acevedo, March 21, 1850. The report claimed to refer back to an earlier report done in 1831.

Appendix C

Haciendas Volantes Traversing the Mixteca Baja During the First Half of the Nineteenth Century

DATE	OWNER	AMOUNT OF LIVESTOCK
1828	Juan de Osio	
1840	Manuel José de Araoz	
1843	José María Maldonaldo	
1847	Antonio de León	50,000
1850	Señor Olaragati [*sic*]	80,000
1850	Señor Fernando Pardo	65,000
1850	Señor Pardo	80,000
1850	Señor Lic. Mariano	28,000
1850	Señor Joaquín Pacheco	73,000
1850	Manuel María Fagoaga	65,800
1861	Manuel García Fernal	

Source: AGPEO, Gobierno de los Distritos, Siglo XIX, Huajuapan, legajo 23, exp. 24, Informe of Juan Acevedo, March 21, 1850; AGNEO, Huajuapan, Juan de Osio and Juan Manuel Eguren, November 13, 1828; AJO, Huajuapan, Civil, legajo 13, Mauricio Martinez Salaman and Toribio Mora, October 20, 1840; AGNEO, Huajuapan, Manuel García Fernal and Felipe Canas, April 2, 1861.

Appendix D

Cacique Land Sales Under Conservative Rule in the Mixteca Baja, 1833–1867

DATE	CACIQUE	BUYER	COST IN PESOS
1833	Petra Aja, cacica of Tonala	Cofradías of Tonalá	2,190
1833	Bonifacio Pimentel, cacique of Tepejillo	Ixitlán	
1835	Bonifacio Pimentel	Santiago Plumas	
1836	Bonifacio Pimentel	Ixitlán	
1838	Petra Aja	Tianguistengo	
1839	Isabel de Mendoza, cacica of Ihualtepec	Ihualtepec	
1839	Isabel de Mendoza	Cofradías of Nejapa	

Appendix D continued on following page

Appendix D continued

DATE	CACIQUE	BUYER	COST IN PESOS
1839	Isabel de Mendoza	San Martín Peras	
1840	Bonifacio Pimentel	San Miguel de las Cuevas	800
1841	Isabel de Mendoza	Zapotitlán Lagunas	18,000
1841	Isabel de Mendoza	Atenango	3,800
1841	Isabel de Mendoza	Tamazola	10,000
1841	Bonifacio Pimentel	Camotlán	
1843	Francisco Santamaría	Mariscala	
1843	Rafael Francisco de los Angeles	Tecomaxtlahuaca	
1844	Isabel de Mendoza	Ahuehuetitlan	10,000
1852	Mariano Villagomez, cacique of Suchitepec	Tonalá	
1853	Francisco Santamaría	Mariscala	1,000
1854	Petra de Aja	Ayú	
1854	Bonifacio Pimentel	Tilapa	
1854	José Isidro Rivera, cacique of Tlalixtaquilla	La Libertad	1,400
1854	Franquilina Galindo	Cofradía of Rancho Rosario	
1854	Petra Aja	Tetaltepec	
1855	José María Bautista y Guzmán, cacique of Chazumba	Zapoquila	
1860	José María Bautista y Guzmán	Chazumba	1,000
1865	Leandro Alvarado	Nuchita	1,600
1865	Andrés Mendiola	Mixquixtlahuaca	3,300
1865	Leónardo Aja	Tindú	1,000
1865	Petra Aja	Cuitito	800
1866	Petra Aja	Santiago del Río	
1866	Petra Aja	Yodoyuxi	
1866	Juan de la Cruz Mendoza	Yutatio	
1866	Isabel Navarrete	Mariscala	
1866	Petra Aja	Dinicuiti	

Source: Data from AMHL, Tierras, as well as notarial and judicial cases in AJO and AGNEO, 1830–1867.

Appendix E

Capital of Cofradías, 1821–1857 (in Pesos)

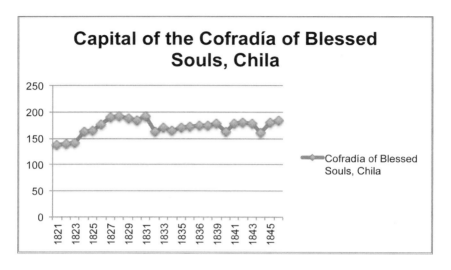

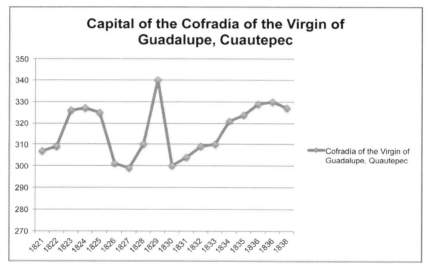

Appendix E continued

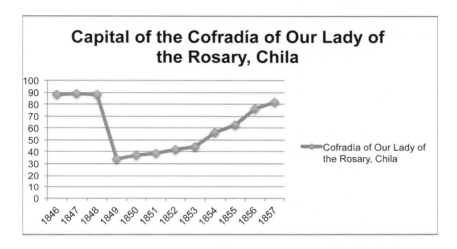

Capital of the Cofradía of Our Lady of the Rosary, Chila

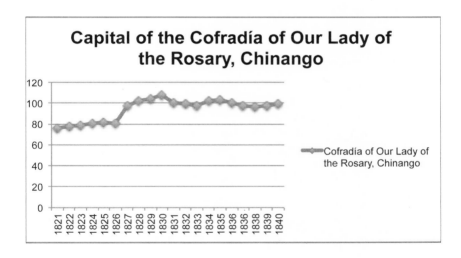

Capital of the Cofradía of Our Lady of the Rosary, Chinango

Appendix E continued

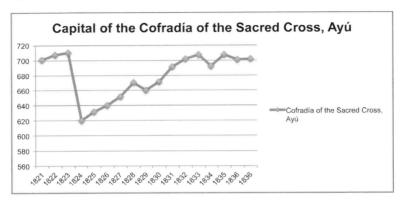

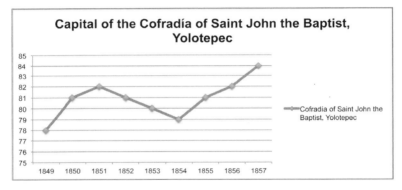

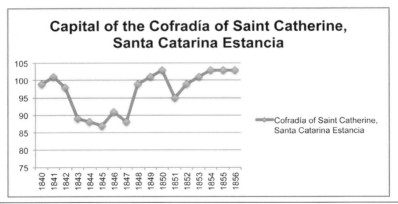

Source: Data from APSDT, caja 50, vol. 2, Cofradías; Church of Jesus Christ of Latter-day Saints, Tequixtepec, Cofradías, 1738–1893, vault INTL, film 676938; APAC, caja 43, vol. 2, Cofradía de Santo Rosario, 1741–1880.

Appendix F

Cacique Land Sales During the Liberal Period, 1867–1897

DATE	CACIQUE	BUYER	COST IN PESOS
1867	Guadalupe de la Cruz Velasco	Tianguistengo	1,220
1867	José Mariano Alvarado	Calihuala	5,130
1867	José Mariano Alvarado	Atenango	
1867	Alvino Luna	Nuchita	800
1867	Marcelo de Castro	Yucuquimi	3,000
1867	Andres Villagómez	Miltepec	400
1868	Concepción Zuñiga de Velasco	Tianguistengo	
1868	Carmen Bazan del Castillo	Chichihualtepec	
1868		Cacaloxtepec	
1868		Huastepec	
1868		Atoyac	
1868	Juan Bautista	Acaquizapan	
1870	Andres Villagómez	Suchitepec	2,651
1871	María de Jesus Villagómez	Ixtapan	
1873	Andres Villagómez	Chinango	600
1875	Isabel Navarrete	Santa Catarina Estancia	3,000
1875	José María Bautista	Ayuquila	
1875	José María Bautista	Ayuquila	3,000
1877	Nicolas González	Cuitito	120
1877	Alejandro Roldan	Yucuná	825
1879	Isabel Navarrete	Santa Catarina Estancia	
1879	Calixto Mendoza	Yutandú	1,750
1881	Ignacia Antonia Zamora y Santiago Viuda de Mendiola	Mixquixtlahuaca	960
1885	Juan Bautista	Olleras	
1889	Benita Delgada de Marín	Chazumba	1,730
1890	Andres Mendiola	Mixquixtlahuaca	960
1892	Manuela Payan	Yucuñuti	3,000
1897	María Concepción Camacho de Cisneros	Tequixtepec	300

Source: Data from AMHL, Tierras, as well as notarial and judicial cases in AJO and AGNEO, 1867–1900.

Appendix G

*Land Distribution in Agricultural Societies of the Mixteca Baja
(According to Amount Invested in Societies in 1892)*

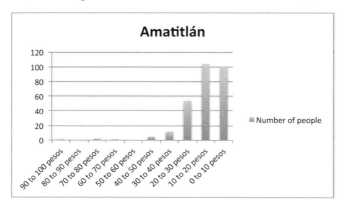

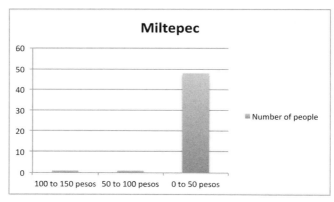

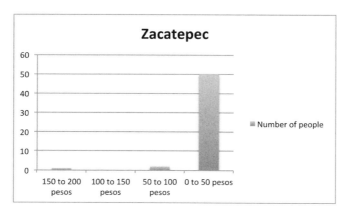

Appendix G continued

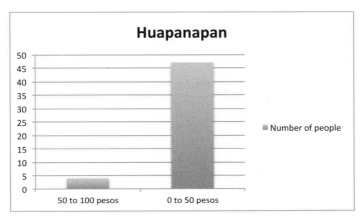

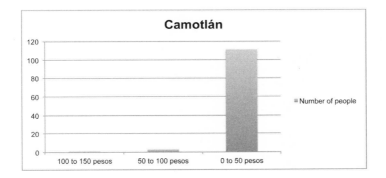

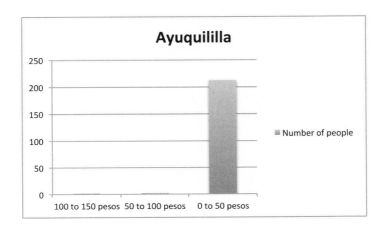

Appendix G continued

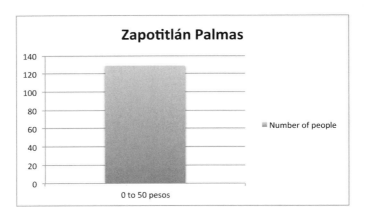

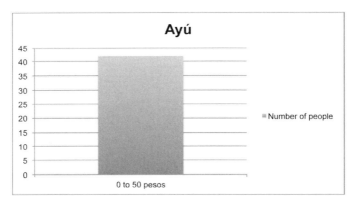

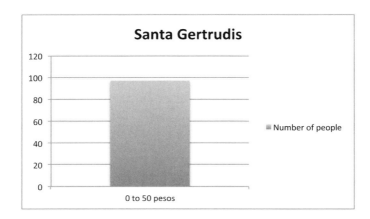

Appendix G continued

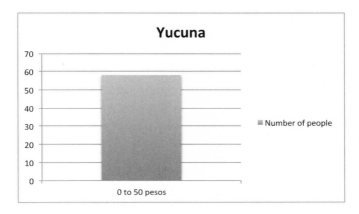

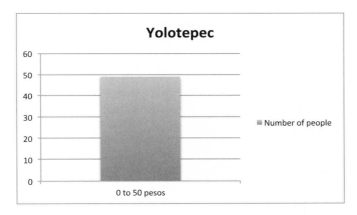

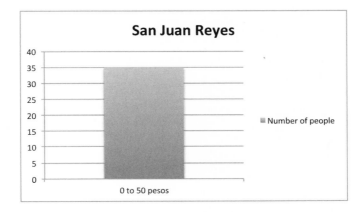

Appendix G continued

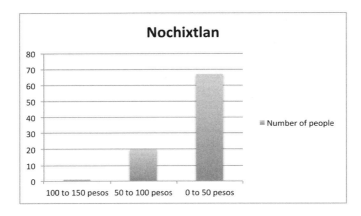

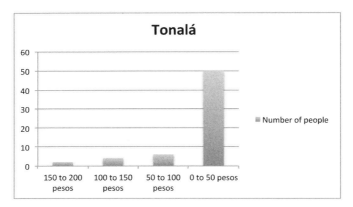

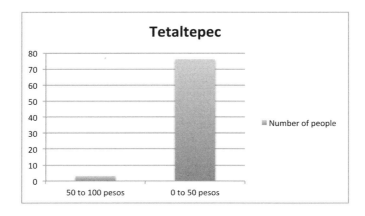

Appendix G continued

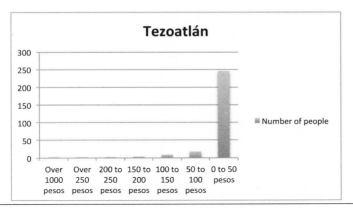

Source: Data from AMHL, Tierras.

Notes

🕇

INTRODUCTION

1. Lázaro Cárdenas quoted in Benjamin, *La revolución*, 165.

2. Benjamin, *La revolución*; O'Malley, *The Myth of the Revolution*; Brunk, *The Posthumous Career*.

3. González y González, *Pueblo en vilo*. For the utility of local and regional history, see Carr, "Recent Regional Studies"; Fowler-Salamini, "The Boom in Regional Studies"; Serrano Alvarez, "Historiografía regional mexicana"; Martínez Assad, "Dos versiones"; Van Young, ed., *Mexico's Regions*. For some excellent recent médian durée approaches, see Jacobsen, *Mirages of Transition*; Larson, *Cochabamba*; Radding, *Landscapes of Power*.

4. Pani, *El segundo imperio*, 55–71.

5. Olavarria y Ferrari, *México*, 338.

6. Sierra, *Juárez*, 162–63.

7. Ceballos, *Aurora y ocaso*, 1:269.

8. Vigil, *México*, 274.

9. Toro, *La iglesia*, 347.

10. Portes Gil, *La lucha*; Larin, *La rebelión*; Barba González, *La rebelión*.

11. Classic works include Womack, *Zapata and the Mexican Revolution*; Reed, *The Caste War*; Cockcroft, *Intellectual Precursors*; Cordova, *La revolución*; Katz, ed., *Riot, Rebellion, and Revolution*. The term *heroé agachado* comes from Bartra, *La jaula de la melancolía*, 91–97.

12. Examples include Hale, *Mexican Liberalism*; Wilkie, "The Meaning"; Quirk, *The Mexican Revolution*; Brown, "Mexican Church-State Relations."

13. Aldana Rendón, *La rebelión agraria*, 34; Azuela, *Precusores*.

14. Tutino, *From Insurrection to Revolution*, 345–46; Shadow and Rodríguez-Shadow, "Religión, economía y política"; Betanzos Piñon, "Las raíces agrarias"; Cordova, *Los maestros rurales*.

15. The point is also made by Bantjes, "Religion and the Mexican Revolution"; Vanderwood, "Religion"; ibid., "The Millennium," 172; Butler, *Popular Piety*, 7–9; Blancarte, *Historia de la Iglesia Católica*, 11–15.

16. Guardino, *Peasants*, 98.

17. Mallon, *Peasant and Nation*, 92–96.

18. Vaughan, *Cultural Politics*, 109–14; ibid., "El papel político," 175; ibid., "The Educational Project," 117, 120.

19. Meyer, *La Cristiada*, 1:385.

20. Meyer, *El conflito religioso*; ibid., *El catolicismo social*; ibid., *Esperando a Lozada*; ibid., *El Sinarquismo*; ibid., *La tierra de Manuel Lozada*.

21. Butler, *Popular Piety*, 8.

22. Meyer, *La Cristiada*, 1:9.

23. Thompson, "The Moral Economy," 79.

24. Thompson, "The Moral Economy."

25. Scott, *Moral Economy*, 23.

26. Examples include Stern, "The Struggle for Solidarity"; Wickam-Crowley, *Guerillas and Revolution*, 231–62; Roseberry, "Peasants, Proletarians, and Politics."

27. Thompson, "Patrician Society," 389.

28. Diacon, *Millenarian Vision*, 56–78.

29. Gosner, *Soldiers of the Virgin*, 10.

30. Scott, *The Moral Economy*, 85.

31. Rugeley, *Yucatán's Maya Peasantry*, 114; Hart, *Bitter Harvest*, 7.

32. Scott, *The Moral Economy*, 173.

33. Moore, *Injustice*, 18, 77–80; Thompson, "Patrician Society," 388–90.

34. Scott, *The Moral Economy*, 180.

35. For classic works highlighting this binary division, see Nutini, *Todos Santos*; Bonfil Batalla, *Mexico Profundo*, 79.

36. Lewis, *Hall of Mirrors*, 6–7.

37. Van Young, "In the Gloomy Caverns," 41–43.

38. Vanderwood, *The Power of God*, 175, 189.

39. Brown, *The Cult of Saints*; Davis, "Some Tasks and Themes"; Kselman, "Ambivalence and Assumption," 27–28; Davis, "From 'Popular Religion'"; Christian, *Local Religion*, 8.

40. Taylor, *Magistrates of the Sacred*, 5, 67.

41. Butler, *Popular Piety*, 11; Butler, "Keeping the Faith," 12.

42. Wright-Rios, *Revolutions in Mexican Catholicism*, 7.

43. Davis, "Some Tasks and Themes," 314.

44. Joseph, "The Challenge of Writing"; Viotta Da Costa, "New Publics"; Bonnell and Hunt, "Introduction."

45. Bantjes termed these two methods "Children of the Enlightenment" and "millenarian" approaches, and he and Knight have asked for a suitable rapprochement between the two. Bantjes, "Religion and the Mexican Revolution," 192; Knight, "Review."

46. Wallace, *The Long European Reformation*, 7; Taylor, *Magistrates of the Sacred*, 5.

47. Asad, *Genealogies of Religion*, 35.

48. Atkin and Tallett, *Priests, Prelates, and People*, 131–41; Clark, "The New Catholicism," 17–18; Anderson, "The Kulturkamf," 109; ibid., "The Limits of Secularization," 666.

49. Tackett, *Religion, Revolution*, 229–33; for an example in Mexico, see Butler, "Revolution and the Ritual Year," 489.

50. Taylor, *Magistrates of the Sacred*, 12–13.

51. Ibid., 180–206.

52. Tackett, *Religion, Revolution*, 235.
53. For example, the Archdiocese of Oaxaca, Wright-Rios, *Revolutions in Mexican Catholicism*, 226.
54. Tackett, *Religion, Revolution*, 234; ibid., *Priest and Parish*, 46.
55. Lannon, *Privilege, Persecution, and Prophecy*, 9–35; Zeldin, *France*, 989–92.
56. Knight, "Popular Culture," 438.
57. Underdown, *Revel, Riot, and Rebellion*, 4–5; Butler, *Popular Piety*, 10; Knight, "Popular Culture," 438.
58. One could argue that this process happened in the Bajío during the late eighteenth century, generating the divisions between priests and parishioners discussed by Van Young (*The Other Rebellion*, 205–6).
59. For popular concern with orthodoxy and "boundary maintenance," see Cannell, "Introduction," 25–27; Toren, "The Effectiveness of Ritual."
60. Subaltern studies scholars have examined this rapid creation of cross-class alliances in the face of external threats for over thirty years. See Pandey, "'Encounters and Calamities'"; Hardiman, "The Bhils and Shahukars"; Chakrabarty, *Rethinking Working-Class History*.
61. Rugeley, *Of Wonders*, 169.
62. For example, Warren, "Elections"; Guerra, *Las revoluciones hispánicas*; Di Tella, *National Popular Politics*; Guardino, *Peasants*; Rugeley, *Rebellion Now and Forever*, 10–57.
63. For example, Mcnamara, *Sons of the Sierra*; Thomson, "Bulwarks of Patriotic Liberalism"; Thomson, "Popular Aspects"; Knight, "El liberalismo mexicano."
64. Padilla, *Rural Resistance*, 85–108; Zolov, "Cuba sí"; Blacker, "Cold War."
65. Knight, "Popular Culture," 438; ibid., "El liberalismo mexicano," 63; ibid., *The Mexican Revolution*, 1:312.
66. Padilla, *Rural Resistance*, 85–108.
67. For introductions to the basic stages of Mexican conservative thought, see Noriega, *El pensamiento*; Pani, *Para mexicanizar*; Sherman, *The Mexican Right*; Goddard, *El pensamiento político*; Torre, García Ugarte, and Ramírez Saíz, eds., *Los rostros*; Pani, ed., *Conservadurismo y derechas*.
68. For a good starting definition of clericalism, see López Villaverde and Cueva Merino, "A modo de introducción," 20–23.
69. Balandier, *Political Anthropology*, 173.
70. Sanders, *Contentious Republicans*, 42.
71. Tilly, *The Vendée*; Jonas, *France and the Cult*, 54–117; Lewis, *The Second Vendée*.
72. Mendez G., *The Plebian Republic*; Sanders, *Contentious Republicans*, 39–42; Sullivan-González, *Piety, Power, and Politics*.
73. Meyer, *La tierra*; Alvis, *Religion and the Rise of Nationalism*, 76–111, 145–84; Clark and Kaiser, eds., *Culture Wars*; Anderson, "The Limits of Secularization"; Lannon, "1898 and the Politics of Catholic Identity."
74. Anderson, "The Limits of Secularization," 662.

75. Butler, *Popular Piety*, 12.
76. Over the past seven years, ADABI has organized countless parish and municipal archives and published hundreds of guides to these archives. See http://www. adabi.org.mx/. Sadly, few historians have taken advantage of the opportunities this work provides.
77. The tradition of priests keeping journals seems to have been widespread during the late nineteenth century in the Diocese of Puebla (Torre Villar, *Diario de un cura*).
78. Scott, *Domination*, xii.

CHAPTER 1

1. Archivo Parroquial de Santo Domingo, Tonalá (APSDT), box 51, vol. 1, Cofradía de la Santa Cruz, 1752–1958.
2. Lockhart, "Introduction," 3.
3. Spores, *The Mixtecs*, 11; Romero Frizzi, *Economia y vida*, 8.
4. Burgoa, *Geográfica descripción*, 167–71.
5. Alvarez, *Geografía general*, 32–39.
6. Ibid., 70–78.
7. Instituto Nacional de Estadística y Geografía, http://mapserver.inegi.gob.mx/ geografia/español/estados/oax/precip_tot_mes.cfm?c=1214&e=20&CFID=18782 89&CFTOKEN=23351445, accessed September 5, 2009.
8. Alvarez, *Geografía general*, 90.
9. Winter, *Cerro de las Minas*, 83–102.
10. Spores, *The Mixtecs*, 3.
11. Jansen and Pérez Jiménez, *Encounter with the Plumed Serpent*, 9.
12. Gerhard, *A Guide*, 128. The relation between the larger settlements and the smaller settlements has yet to be established. See Menegus Bornemann, *La Mixteca Baja*, 20–22; Dahlgren, *La Mixteca*, 142–44; Spores, "Postclassic Mixtec Kingdoms," 255–60.
13. Terraciano, *The Mixtecs*, 134–45.
14. Paso y Troncoso, *Papeles de Nueva España*, 71.
15. Terraciano, *The Mixtecs*, 142.
16. Spores, "Marital Alliance."
17. Ibid., "Differential Response," 33.
18. Acuña, *Relaciones geográficas*, 2:296.
19. Cook and Borah, *The Population*, 32, 57.
20. Spores, *The Mixtecs*, 95–96, 123, 150–53.
21. Burgoa, *Geográfica descripción*, 390.
22. García Pimentel, *Relación de los obispados*, 18–21.
23. Gerhard, *A Guide*, 129.
24. García Pimentel, *Relación de los obispados*, 18–21
25. Gerhard, *A Guide*, 42–44, 128–32.
26. Chance, "Los Villagómez."

27. Archivo General de la Nación (AGN), Tierras, vol. 2809, exp. 22; ibid., Congregaciones, vol. 1, fol. 7; Menegus Bornemann, *La Mixteca Baja*, 36-41.

28. Wolf, "Closed Corporate Peasant Communities"; ibid., "Aspects of Group Relations"; ibid., *Sons of the Shaking Earth*, 202-32.

29. Chance, "Mesoamerica's Ethnographic Past," 391-92. Wolf has also sought to reform his earlier model ("The Vicissitudes").

30. Gibson, *The Aztecs*, 156-213.

31. Ouwenweel, "From 'Tlahtocayotl,'" 756; Chance, "The Caciques of Tecali"; ibid., "The Mixtec Nobility"; ibid., "The Noble House"; ibid., "Descendencia"; Castillo Palma and Hermosillo Adams, "Familias, linajes"; Menegus, "La territorialidad"; Perkins, "Corporate Community."

32. Amith, *The Mobius Strip*, 292-385; Ouwenweel and Torales Pacheco, eds., *Expresarios, indios y estado.*

33. Farriss, "Nucleation versus Dispersal"; Amith, *The Mobius Strip*, 217-54.

34. Ouwenweel, "Altepeme"; Scott, *The Moral Economy.*

35. Gosner, *Soldiers of the Virgin*, 9-10; Monaghan, *The Covenants*, 9; Carmagnani, *El regreso*, 21-51.

36. Spores, *The Mixtec Kings*, 112.

37. Terraciano, *The Mixtecs*, 151-54.

38. Ibid., 160-65.

39. Ibid., 202-3; Ceballos Soto, *Historia de Santiago Chazumba*, 175-76.

40. AGN, Mercedes, vol. 18, fol. 228; ibid., fol. 285; ibid., fol. 228.

41. Spores and Saldaña, *Documentos.*

42. Pastor, *Campesinos y reformas*, 143.

43. AGN, Tierras, vol. 494, exp. 5, fs. 155.

44. Chance, "Los Villagómez," 13.

45. Ibid., "Marriage Alliances," 110.

46. Menegus Bornemann, *La Mixteca Baja*, 61.

47. Peralta Hernández, *Cuyotepeji*, 18. A Mexican bushel, or fanega, was around 1.5 U.S. bushels or fifty-five liters. See Gibson, *The Aztecs*, 552-53.

48. AGN, Tierras, vol. 494, exp. 5, fs. 155.

49. Ouwenweel, "From 'Tlahtocayotl,'" 779.

50. APSDT, box 50, vol. 1, Cofradía del Santisimo Sacramento, 1702-1940; ibid., vol. 2, Cofradía de la Señora del Rosario, 1702-1940.

51. Chance, "Los Villagómez," 13.

52. Ibid., "Marriage Alliances," 116.

53. Menegus Bornemann, *La Mixteca Baja*, 76.

54. Ouwenweel, "Altepeme," 26-30.

55. AGN, Tierras, vol. 494, exp. 5, fs. 155.

56. Menegus Bornemann, *La Mixteca Baja*, 59-60.

57. AGN, Tierras, vol. 1220, exp. 2, fs. 162.

58. Menegus Bornemann, *La Mixteca Baja*, 60.

59. Archivo Judicial de Oaxaca (AJO), Teposcolula, Civil, legajo 74, exp. 4.

60. AGN, Tierras, vol. 494, exp. 5, fs. 155.

61. Compare this to the conclusions of Stern, *The Secret History*; Kellogg, *Weaving the Past*; Silverblatt, *Moon, Sun and Witches*.

62. Spores, "Mixteca Cacicas."

63. AGN, Tierras, vol. 494, exp. 5, fs. 155.

64. Chance, "Marriage Alliances," 104.

65. Farriss, *Maya Society*; García Martínez, *Los pueblos*; Castro Gutiérrez, *Los tarascos*, 346.

66. Ouwenweel, "From 'Tlahtocayotl,'" 784–85.

67. Gruzinski, *Man-Gods*; Gosner, *Soldiers of the Virgin*, 122–59.

68. Terraciano "The People."

69. Medina, *Los Dominicos*, 90–92; Jiménez Moreno and Mateos Higuera, eds., *Codice de Yanhuitlán*, 12–14.

70. Mullen, *Dominican Architecture*, 12. This figure is based on the low estimate of Agustín Dávila Padilla for 1591. Mullen actually estimates twenty establishments in the Mixteca.

71. Pita Moreda, "El nacimiento."

72. Medina, *Los Dominicos*, 94.

73. Acta provincialia.

74. Gerhard, *A Guide*, 130.

75. Taylor, *Magistrates of the Sacred*, 79, 548.

76. Jansen and Pérez Jiménez, *Encounter*, 9.

77. Jansen, *Huisi Tacu*, 292–94.

78. Antonio de Herrera quoted in Jansen, *Tnuhu niquidza iya*, 7.

79. Terraciano, "The People."

80. Spores, *The Mixtec Kings*, 180.

81. Terraciano, *The Mixtecs*, 67.

82. For example, Burgoa, *Geográfica descripción*, 14; see also Arroyo, *Los Dominicos*.

83. Acta provincialia.

84. Jansen and Pérez Jiménez, *La lengua señorial*, 149–76.

85. Arroyo, *Los Dominicos*, lv.

86. Jansen and Perez Jiménez, *Voces del Dzaha Dzavui*, x.

87. Burgoa, *Geográfica descripción*, 174.

88. APSDT, box 1, vol. 4, Bautismos, 1711–1766.

89. Spores, *The Mixtec Kings*, 112.

90. Terraciano, *The Mixtecs*, 226.

91. Ibid., 227.

92. APSDT, box 50, vol. 1, Cofradía del Santisimo Sacramento, 1702–1940.

93. "Nuestra Señora del Rosario," 12–13.

94. Taylor, *Magistrates of the Sacred*, 324–44; Terraciano, *The Mixtecs*, 285–86.

95. Archivo Parroquial, El Sagrario, Huajuapan de León (APSHL), box 13, vol. 2, Matrimonios, 1712–1792.

96. APSDT, box 1, vols. 2–3, Bautismos, 1711–1766.

97. Taylor, *Magistrates of the Sacred*, 305.

98. APSDT, box 50, vol. 1, Cofradía del Santisimo Sacramento, 1702–1940.

99. Archivo Parroquial de Santa María de la Asunción, Chila (APSMAC), box 43, vol. 2, Cofradía del Santo Rosario, 1741–1880.

100. APSDT, box 50, vol. 1, Cofradía del Santisimo Sacramento, 1702–1940. See also Menegus Bornemann, La Mixteca Baja, 58–59.

101. APSMAC, box 43, vol. 2, Cofradía de Santo Rosario, 1741–1880.

102. Church of Jesus Christ of Latter-day Saints, Tequixtepec, Cofradías, 1738–1893, vault INTL, film 676938. See also Chowning, "La feminización"; Guardino, The Time of Liberty, 33; Gosner, Soldiers of the Virgin, 89.

103. APSMAC, box 42, vol. 1, Cofradía de las Benditas Animas del Purgatorio, 1698–1889.

104. APSDT, box 50, vol. 4, Cofradía de Santo Domingo, 1702–1940.

105. APSMAC, box 43, vol. 2, Cofradía de Santo Rosario, 1741–1880.

106. Carmagnani, *El regreso*, 132–44; Pastor, *Campesinos y reformas*, 181; Romero Frizzi, *Economía y vida*, 190–91.

107. Dehouve, *Cuando los banqueros*, 178–83.

108. APSMAC, box 43, vol. 2, Cofradía de Santo Rosario, 1741–1880.

109. APSDT, box 50, vol. 4, Cofradía de Santo Domingo, 1702–1940.

110. APSMAC, box 43, vol. 2, Cofradía de Santo Rosario, 1741–1880.

111. Pastor, *Campesinos y reformas*, 219–23.

112. APSDT, box 50, vol. 1, Cofradía del Santisimo Sacramento, 1702–1940.

113. Taylor, *Drinking, Homicide, and Rebellion*, 28–44.

114. Nutini and Bell, *Ritual Kinship*, 8–14.

115. Mintz and Wolf, "Analysis of Ritual Co-parenthood," 341.

116. APSDT, box 1, vol. 1, Bautismos, 1711–1766.

117. Taylor, "Two Shrines," 945; Weckmann, *The Medieval Heritage*, 289–92.

118. Monaghan, *The Covenants*, 307–55; Scheper Hughes, *Biography*.

119. Sau Witte and Sau, "Quetzalcóatl"; Jansen and Pérez Jiménez, *La lengua señorial*, 465–66.

120. Monaghan, *The Covenants*, 307–55.

121. Jansen and Pérez Jiménez, *La lengua señorial*, 25–26.

122. Ibid., *Encounter*, 295.

123. Kimball Romney and Ravicz, "The Mixtec," 373, 394; Byland and Pohl, *In the Realm*, 87–88, 169, 171; Monaghan, *The Covenants*, 105–7.

124. For example, Burgoa, Geográfica descripción, 129, 132, 159–61, 170.

125. Terraciano, *The Mixtecs*, 265–67.

126. Tarvaez, *The Invisible War*, 111.

127. Gruzinski, *Man-Gods*, 102.

128. Christian, *Moving Crucifixes*, 7–8.

129. Gosner, *Soldiers of the Virgin*, 116.

130. Jansen and Pérez Jiménez, *La lengua señorial*, 173.

131. Brading, *The First America*, 365–72; Lafaye, *Quetzalcóatl and Guadalupe*, 177–207.
132. LaFaye, *Quetzalcóatl*, 182.
133. Boturini Benaducci, *Catálogo del Museo Indiano.*
134. Alvarez de Toledo, *Politics and Reform*, 64–95.
135. Gruzinski, *Man-Gods*, 97–98; Melvin, "Urban Religions."
136. Medina, *Los Dominicos*, 94.
137. APSDT, box 51, vol. 1, Cofradía de la Santa Cruz, 1752–1958.
138. APSDT, box 1, vol. 1, Bautismos, 1711–1766.
139. Barabas, "Los santuarios."
140. Gruzinski, "Indian Confraternities," 212–15; Taylor, *Magistrates of the Sacred*, 265–70; Gosner, *Soldiers of the Virgin*, 87–88.
141. APSDT, box 1, vol. 4, Cuentas de Cofradías, 1752–1958.
142. Josefat Herrera Sánchez, interview with author, June 2007; Diario Dispertar de Oaxaca, March 13, 2010.
143. Fraile, *Cristo*, 20–41.
144. Terraciano, *The Mixtecs*, 327–29.
145. Taylor, *Magistrates of the Sacred*, 58; Farris, *Maya Society*, 286–354; Gosner, *Soldiers of the Virgin*, 83–95; Van Oss, *Catholic Colonialism.*
146. Nutini, *Todos Santos.*
147. Spores, *The Mixtecs*, 152–53; Taylor, *Magistrates of the Sacred*, 68; Tavarez, *The Invisible War*, 164.
148. González Huerta, *El Tupa*; Santos Soriano, *Santos Reyes Tepejillo*, 135–46.
149. Ajofrin, *Diario del viaje*, 45.
150. Villaseñor y Sánchez, *Theatro americano*, 2:329.
151. Tutino, *From Insurrection*, 41–98.
152. Knight, *Mexico*, 91.
153. Fraile, *Cristo*, 5.
154. Romero Frizzi, *Economía y vida*, 132.
155. APSHL, box 1, vols. 4–7, Bautismos, 1638–1739; APSDT, box 2, vols. 1–4, Bautismos, 1766–1812.
156. Villaseñor y Sánchez, *Theatro americano*, 1:325–29.
157. Romero Frizzi, *Economía y vida*, 28–30.
158. Ibid.
159. Ibid., 177–205.
160. APSHL, box 56, vol. 4, Padrones, 1807–1892.
161. Baskes, *Indians, Merchants and Markets*, 15.
162. APSHL, box 67, vol. 4, Cofradía del Santisimo Sacramento, 1696–1888.
163. Paso y Troncoso, *Papeles de Nueva España*, 68.
164. Baskes, *Indians, Merchants and Markets*, 2.
165. Terraciano, *The Mixtecs*, 227.
166. The statistics come from an evaluation of documents in the AGN, Tierras, and are displayed in appendix A.
167. Gosner, *Soldiers of the Virgin*, 76.

168. Spores, *The Mixtec Kings*, 164–70.

169. AGN, Indios, vol. 9, exp. 371, fs. 4.

170. Chance, "Marital Alliances," 101.

171. Romero Frizzi, *Economía y vida*, 102.

172. AGN, Indios, vol. 27, exp. 161, fs. 77v; ibid., vol. 30, exp. 48, fs. 37r–37v.

173. Ibid., vol. 33, exp. 92, fs. 55r–55v.

174. Weitlaner, "Chilacapa y Tetecingo."

175. Mouat, "Los Chiveros"; Romero Frizzi, *Economía y vida*, 324–54; Pastor, *Campesinos y reformas*, 230–35.

176. Dehouve, *Cervantes Delgado*, and Hvilshøj, eds., *La vida volante*; Dehouve, *Entre el caimán*, 98–99; ibid., *Cuando los banqueros*, 63–66.

177. Hvilshøj, "El dialecto pastor." Here, I would particularly like to thank Michael Swanton, who invited me on a wonderful outing to track down many of these Nahuatl-speaking communities, often buried deep within the Mixteca Baja.

178. These twenty-four were compiled by splicing the list produced by Dehouve with those listed in the baptism records of Huajuapan and Tonalá from 1700 to 1800 (Dehouve, "Las haciendas volantes," 83; APSHL, box 2, vols. 1–4, Bautismos, 1739–1798; APSDT, box 2, vols. 1–4, Bautismos, 1766–1812).

179. Ewald, *Estudios*, 128.

180. AJO, Huajuapan, Civil, June 6, 1834 (copy of document from April 1819), Will of Manuel de León, 1819.

181. Ibid.

182. Dehouve, "Las hacienda volantes," 86–87.

183. Ibid., 84.

184. Ewald, *Estudios*, 111, 129; Dehouve, "Las haciendas volantes," 82; AGN, Subdelegados, vol. 28, exp. 6, fs. 86–426.

185. For example, Cervantes Delgado, "Los Nahuas."

186. APSHL, box 2, vols. 1–4, Bautismos, 1739–1798. Presumably this estimate is on the high side, and many hacienda employees would have returned to their homes to get married.

187. Ewald, *Estudios*, 124.

188. AJO, Huajuapan, Civil, June 6, 1834 (copy of document from April 1819), Will of Manuel de León, 1819.

189. Dehouve, "Las haciendas volantes," 90; see also Paredes Colín, El distrito, 178–80; Sante Croix, Onze mois, 116–19.

190. AJO, Huajuapan, Civil, June 6, 1834 (copy of document from April 1819), Will of Manuel de León, 1819.

191. Dehouve, "Las haciendas volantes," 88.

192. Sebastian Reyes, interview with author, May 2007; El Imparcial, March 4, 2002; APSDT, box 1, vol. 4, Bautismos, 1702–1766.

193. Archivo Parroquial de Tlacotepec de las Nieves (APTN), Cofradías, La Virgen de las Nieves.

194. Tutino, *From Insurrection*, 144.

195. Perkins, "Corporate Community," 34.

196. Van Young, *Hacienda and Market*, 271–342; Escobar Ohmstede, *De la costa*; Ducey, *A Nation of Villages*, 23–59; Pastor, *Campesinos y reformas*, 163–358; Taylor, *Drinking, Homicide, and Rebellion*, 113–52; Guardino, *The Time of Liberty*, 91–122.

197. Villaseñor y Sánchez, *Theatro americano*, 2:325–29; AGN, Historia, 523, Censo de Revillagigedo, 1793.

198. Pastor, *campesinos y reformas*, 169–71.

199. See appendix A.

200. Chance, "Los Villagómez."

201. Ibid., "Marriage Alliances," 111.

202. AGN, Tierras, 1740, vol. 5, exp. 1, fs. 98.

203. Ibid., 1762, vol. 2967, exp. 107, fs. 2.

204. Ibid., Subdelegados, vol. 28, exp. 6, fs. 86–426.

205. Acta provincialia.

206. Bono López, "La política linguistica"; Yannayakis, *The Art*, 173–77.

207. APSHL, box 79, vol. 1, Gobierno, 1764–1901.

208. Archivo Parroquial de Tezoatlán (APTez), Cofradías Varios.

209. Gosner, *Soldiers of the Virgin*, 9.

210. Menegus Bornemann, *La Mixteca Baja*, 66–71; see also Guardino, *The Time of Liberty*, 57, Romero Frizzi, *El sol*, 125–33; Terraciano, *The Mixtecs*, 182–86.

211. AGN, Tierras, vol. 229, exp. 3, fs. 6.

212. Monaghan, Joyce, and Spores, "Transformations," 132.

213. Archivo General del Poder Ejecutivo del Estado de Oaxaca (AGPEO); Gobierno de los Distritos, Siglo XIX, Huajuapan, 23.24, Informe of Juan Acevedo, March 21, 1850. The report claimed to refer to an earlier report done in 1831.

214. Adelman, *Colonial Legacies*.

215. Archivo General de Notarías del Estado de Oaxaca (AGNEO), Huajuapan, June 4, 1818.

216. Ibid., May 15, 1819.

217. Miranda, "La población indígena"; Villaseñor y Sánchez, *Theatro americano*, 1:325–29; Gerhard, *A Guide*, 131.

218. Gerhard, *A Guide*, 131.

219. Menegus Bornemann, *La Mixteca Baja*, 69–72.

220. Ouwenweel, "From 'Tlahtocayotl,'" 780.

221. Archivo del Municipio de Chazumba (AMC), Documentos Inéditos, Fundación del Pueblo de Chazumba.

222. A member of the Guzmán y Bautista family was municipal president as late as 1856.

223. See appendix A.

224. AGN, Tierras, Año: 1788–1820, vol. 1220, exp. 2, fs. 162.

225. Ibid., Año: 1769–1782, vol. 1057, exp. 2, fs. 88.

226. Terraciano, *The Mixtecs*, 197; Pastor, *Campesinos y reformas*, 307–14.

227. Villaseñor y Sánchez, *Theatro americano*, 2:325–29; AGN, Historia, Censo de Revillagigedo, 1793.

228. Pastor, *Campesinos y reformas*, 411.

229. APSDT, box 52, vol. 4, Padrón.

230. APSHL, box 3, vols. 1–4, Bautismos, 1770–1815.

231. APSDT, box 2, vols. 1–5, Bautismos, 1766–1817.

232. Chance, "Los Villagómez"; ibid., "Marriage Alliances"; ibid., "The Mixtec Nobility."

233. Van Young, "In the Gloomy Caverns," 43.

234. Farriss, *Maya Society*, 355–74; Pastor, *Campesinos y reformas*, 410; Yannayakis, *The Art*, 161–219; Gosner, *Soldiers of the Virgin*, 67.

235. Chance, *Race and Class*; Chance and Taylor, "Estate and Class."

236. Perkins, "Corporate Community"; Cruz Pazos, "Los caciques"; ibid., "La nobleza indígena"; Castillo Palma and Hermosillo Adams, "Familias, Linajes."

237. Van Young, *The Other Rebellion*, 524.

238. Gerhard, *A Guide*, 131.

239. AGN, Historia, 523, Censo de Revillagigedo, 1793.

240. Torre Villar, "Seminario Palafoxiana," 241–47.

241. Tackett, *Priest and Parish*, 46.

242. Brading, *Church and State*, 68.

243. Archivo Parroquial de Tequixtepec (APTeq), Libro de Bautismos.

244. AJO, Civil, Huajuapan, legajo 3, October 10, 1809, Will of Pablo Sánchez Toscano.

245. Villavicencio Rojas, Donde se canta y se baila, 66; AGPEO, Gobierno de los Distritos, Siglo XIX, Huajuapan, legajo 6, exp. 24.

246. AGNEO, Huajuapan, Will of José Joaquín Guerrero, October 4, 1817.

247. Villavicencio Rojas, *Donde se canta y se baila*, 66; APSMAC, box 43, vol. 6, Cofradía de la Santisima Trinidad, 1741–1880.

248. APSHL, box 3, vol. 4, Bautismos, 1770–1815; AGNEO, Will of Manuel Alencaster, June 14, 1842.

249. Manuel en Lengua Mixteca. Another priest of Silacayoapan wrote the introduction to the 1755 Mixtec edition of the Ripalda catechism (González, Catecismo).

250. AJO, Huajuapan, Civil, legajo 3, October, 10, 1809, Will of Pablo Sánchez Toscano.

251. AGNEO, Huajuapan, Will of José Joaquín Guerrero, October 4, 1817.

252. APSMAC, box 45, vol. 1, Cofradía de Santa Ana, 1744–1893.

253. Private archive of Ricardo Ceballos Soto, Libro de Cuentas de la Cofradía del Santo Entierro de Chazumba.

254. APTeq, Cofradías, La Señora del Rosario, Chinango, 1767–1843.

255. APSMAC, box 43, vol. 2, Cofradía del Rosario, 1747–1891.

256. Pastor, *Campesinos y reformas*, 308.

257. APSMAC, box 44, vol. 4, Cofradía de la Santa Cruz de Ixitlán, 1747–1891.

258. Ibid., box 42, vol. 3, Cofradía de las Benditas Almas de Purgatorio, 1698–1889.

259. Carmagnani, *El regreso*, 131.

260. Archivo Parroquial de Miltepec (APM), Libro de Gobierno, vol. 1, Relación de la parroquia.

261. Villavicencio Rojas, *Donde se canta y se baila*, 61–67.

262. Haskett, *Indigenous Rulers*, 221–23.

263. Guardino, *The Time of Liberty*, 91–122.

264. Pastor, *Campesinos y reformas*, 417.

265. Van Young, *The Other Rebellion*, 471–74; Landavazo, "El asesinato"; Ducey, "Village, Nation and Constitution"; Guardino, *Peasants*; Guedea, *La insurgencia*.

266. Archer, "Years of Decision"; Hamnett, "Royalist Counterinsurgency."

267. Taylor, *Magistrates of the Sacred*, 23; Hamnett, *Roots of Insurgency*, 8.

268. AGN, Indiferente Virreinal, Operaciones de Guerra, 2471–034, fs. 3; ibid., 4420–047, fs. 3; ibid., 6661–013, fs. 3; ibid., 6661–070, fs 3.

269. Alamán, *Historia de México*, 3:155–56.

270. AGN, Operaciones de Guerra, vol. 53, fs. 199–214; ibid., vol. 77, fs. 333–35; Méndez Aquino, "La Batalla"; Alamán, *Historia de México*, 4:425–26.

271. AGN, Operaciones de Guerra, vol. 103, fs. 168–74.

272. Ibid., *Indiferente Virreinal*, Operaciones de Guerra, 3720–012, fs. 10.

273. Bustamante, *Cuadro histórico*, 2:87–91.

274. AGN, Indiferente Virreinal, Operaciones de Guerra, 6710–1, fs. 4.

275. Van Young, *The Other Rebellion*, 381.

276. AJO, Huajuapan, Civil, legajo 4, Mariano Villagómez, April 4, 1818.

277. Chance, "Los Villagómez"; Menegus Bornemann, La Mixteca Baja, 92–93.

278. Menegus Bornemann, *La Mixteca Baja*, 93.

279. AJO, Huajuapan, Civil, legajo 4, exp. 7, Principales of Tequixtepec.

280. AGNEO, Huajuapan, Raymunda María Navarrete y Méndez and Simarrones, June 27, 1815.

281. Ibid., Cofradía del Santisimo Sacramento de Ihualtepec, December 6, 1818.

282. AJO, Huajuapan, Civil, legajo 8, June 6, 1834 (copy of document from April 1819), Will of Manuel de León, 1819.

283. APTeq, Cofradías, Nuestra Señora de Guadalupe, Cuautepec, 1802–1839.

284. Ibid., *Santisimo Sacramento*, 1783–1850.

285. AGN, Indiferente Virreinal, Operaciones de Guerra, 1380–32, fs. 7. The concentration of rebels from these areas of sugar capitalism echoes Brian Hamnett's reading of the effects of the insurrection in the region (Hamnett, *The Roots*, 149).

286. *Historia de Tonalá*, Oaxaca, 60–63.

287. Ortiz Escamilla, *Guerra y gobierno*, 111–13.

CHAPTER 2

1. Bustamante, *Cuadro histórico*, 2:87–91.

2. Fowler, "Carlos María de Bustamante."

3. For an excellent overview of the period, see Zoraida Vázquez, "Los primeros tropiezos."

4. Anna, "Demystifying," 119; Fowler, *Mexico*, 1.

5. Vigil, *México*, 274; Olavarria y Ferrari, *México*, 338; Toro, *La iglesia*, 347; Sierra, *Juárez*, 162–63; Altamirano, *Historia y política*. For an overview, see Pani, *El segundo imperio*, 55–71.

6. Anna, "Demystifying," 119.
7. Quoted in Fowler, "Mexican Political Thought," 302.
8. Costeloe, *The Central Republic*, 26.
9. Katz, "Introduction," 10; Reina, *Las rebeliónes*; Baum, "Retórica y realidad"; Ferrer Muñoz, ed., *Los pueblos*; Meyer, *Problemas campesinos*; ibid., *La tierra*; Hart, "Mexico Peasants' War"; Meyer, *Esperando a Lozada*; Coatsworth, "Patterns of Rural Rebellion"; Tutino, *From Insurrection*, 249–57.
10. Brading, "Creole Nationalism," 145.
11. Warren, "Elections"; ibid., *Vagrants and Citizens*; Palacios, ed., *Ensayos*; Guerra, *Las revoluciones*; ibid., *Modernidad y independencia*; Lempérière, *Los espacios públicos*; Di Telia, *National Popular Politics*; Ortiz Escamilla y Serrano Ortega, eds., *Ayuntamientos*; Annino, "Nuevas perspectivas."
12. Annino, "The Two-Faced Janus," 74; Ducey, *A Nation of Villages*, 95.
13. Tutino, "The Revolution," 371.
14. Guardino, *Peasants*; Ducey, *A Nation of Villages*; Caplan, *Indigenous Citizens*; Rugeley, *Rebellion*.
15. Hernández Chávez, *La tradición*, 41.
16. Guardino, *Peasants*, 178–210; Mallon, *Peasant and Nation*, 316; Mcnamara, *Sons of the Sierra*, 20–68.
17. Mallon, *Peasant and Nation*, 129–32.
18. Quoted in Di Telia, *National Popular Politics*, 6.
19. Pani, "La nueva historia," 71.
20. Hamnett, "El Partido Conservador," 214.
21. Buve, "Pueblos indígenas," 97; Di Tella, "The Dangerous Classes," 104; Chevalier, "Conservateurs et liberaux," 459.
22. Guardino, *Peasants*, 5.
23. Quoted in Hernández, "El efecto," 78.
24. Hamnett, "Liberales y conservadores," 195.
25. Pani, *Para mexicanizar*; Fowler and Morales Moreno, "Introducción," 17–18.
26. Torre and García Ugarte, "Introducción," 20.
27. Mendoza García, *Los bienes*, 91; Mendoza García, "El ganado comunal," 756–57.
28. Caplan, *Indigenous Citizens*, 89.
29. Guardino, *Peasants*, 139–40; Ducey, *A Nation of Villages*, 126–28; Flores, *La revolución*, 24–30, 35, 76.
30. Guardino, *The Time of Liberty*, 229–49; Caplan, *Indigenous Citizens*, 89–101.
31. AMC, Presidencia, 1843, Manuel Ambrosio Sánchez to Juan Acevedo, January 2, 1843.
32. Ibid., Juan Bautista de la Cruz, July 5, 1842.
33. Ibid., Mariano Mendiola to Juan Acevedo, November 18, 1838.
34. Ibid., Justicia, José Mariano Cruz Rosas to Andres Avelino, April 6, 1842.
35. Caplan, *Indigenous Citizens*, 94.
36. Ducey, *A Nation of Villages*, 142–70; Guardino, *Peasants*, 147–76.

37. Caplan, *Indigenous Citizens*, 95–99.

38. Bautista Carriedo, *Estudios históricos*, 2:116.

39. AMC, Presidencia, Principales of Acaquizapan to Juan Acedevo, January 7, 1846.

40. Ibid., José Clemente to Juan Morelos, October 11, 1846.

41. Caplan, *Indigenous Citizens*, 164–70.

42. APTez, Cordilleras, Tomás Rios to José María Masas López Gamboa, March 28, 1842; AGPEO, Gobierno, Siglo XIX, legajo 17, exp. 23, Pedro Ortiz, Juan Ortiz, and Pablo Hernández to Prefect of Huajuapan, March 16, 1865.

43. Archivo del Municipio de Huajuapan de León (AMHL), Presidencia, Juan Martin to Santiago Rodríguez, December 8, 1853.

44. Aldana Rendón, *Proyectos agrarios*, 61–120; Meyer, *La tierra*, 37–41; Meyer, *Esperando a Lozada*, 120–30, 145–60, 202–5; Knowlton, "La individualización."

45. Tutino, "Rebelión indígena."

46. Ibid., *From Insurrection*, 215–421.

47. Reina, *Las rebeliónes*, 325–40; Escobar Ohmstede, "El movimiento"; Ducey, *A Nation of Villages*, 120–41; Mallon, *Peasant and Nation*, 320; Ducey, "Liberal Theory," 79.

48. Guardino, *Peasants*, 194–200.

49. The point is made with regard to Guardino's work in Guerrero by Kyle, "Land, Labor."

50. AGPEO, Gobierno de los Distritos, Siglo XIX, Huajuapan, legajo 23, exp. 24, Informe of Juan Acevedo, March 21, 1850. The report claimed to refer back to an earlier report done in 1831.

51. AJO, Huajuapan, Civil, legajo 4, October 17, 1826, Border Inspection of Ignacia Antonia Zamora y Santiago.

52. AGPEO, Gobierno de los Distritos, Siglo XIX, Huajuapan, legajo 23, exp. 24, Informe of Juan Acevedo, March 21, 1850; Galván Rivera, *Ordenanzas*, 72–73.

53. AGPEO, Gobierno de los Distritos, Siglo XIX, Huajuapan, legajo 54, exp. 2, Juan Acevedo, Informe, March 5, 1839.

54. AGNEO, Will of Isabel de Mendoza, March 21, 1850.

55. Ibid., Will of José María de Castro, April 1843.

56. Pastor, *Campesinos y reformas*, 460.

57. Bautista Carriedo, *Estudios históricos*, 2:116; AGNEO, Will of Mariano Villagómez, May 6, 1861; ibid., Will of Isabel de Mendoza, March 21, 1850; ibid., Will of Joaquín Bautista y Guzmán, September 3, 1845.

58. AJO, Huajuapan, Civil, legajo 8, Francisco Juan and Joaquín Bautista y Guzmán, March 20, 1834.

59. Ibid., legajo 15, José María Castro and Principales of San Sebastián, July 8, 1843.

60. AMC, Presidencia, Contrato del Pastor de Ganado, January 6, 1837.

61. AGNEO, Huajuapan, Lorenzo Alvarado, April 5, 1834.

62. AJO, Huajuapan, Civil, legajo 12, José Amador and Principales of Mixquixtlahuaca, March 2, 1839.

63. AGPEO, Reparto y Ajudicaciónes del Siglo XIX, legajo 12, exp. 6, Tomás Rojas et al., October 19, 1869.

64. Menegus Bornemann, *La Mixteca Baja*, 97.
65. Ibid., "La desvinculación"; ibid., "La territorialidad"; Chance, "The Caciques"; ibid., "The Mixtec Nobility"; ibid., "The Noble House"; ibid., "Descendencia."
66. AJO, Huajuapan, Civil, legajo 14, Juan de la Cruz Mendoza, September 11, 1841.
67. AGNEO, Huajuapan, Will of María Micaela Alvarado, February 20, 1820.
68. Ibid., Will of María de la Concepción Zuniga y Velasco, July 7, 1842.
69. Ibid., Will of Francisca Xavier de los Reyes, December 29, 1826.
70. AJO, Huajuapan, Civil, legajo 15, Bonifacio Pimentel, February 14, 1844.
71. Ibid., Pedro Mendiola and Juan Matamoros, August 6, 1843.
72. AGNEO, Huajuapan, Juan de Osio and Juan Manuel Eguren, November 13, 1828.
73. AGPEO, Gobierno de los Distritos, Siglo XIX, Huajuapan, legajo 23, exp. 24, Juan Acevedo, Informe, March 21, 1850.
74. AGNEO, Huajuapan, Lorenzo Alvarado and Mariano Ignacio Osorio, July 23, 1832.
75. Ibid., Principales of Santo Domingo Yolotepec and Bruno Valladolid, October 29, 1839.
76. Montesinos Cruz, *Monografía*, 6; Mendoza García, "La matanza," 56; Rangel Rojas, *General Antonio de León*, 34.
77. AMHL, Tierras, Impuestos, January 3, 1844; Paredes Colín, *El distrito*, 178–80.
78. AGNEO, Huajuapan, Juan Benito and Manuel de León, January 2, 1822.
79. Ibid., María de Jesus Sánchez and Antonio de León, June 12, 1838.
80. AGPEO, *Memoria del gobierno del estado de Oaxaca, 1844*.
81. AGNEO, Huajuapan, Will of Matias Galva, December 7, 1861.
82. AJO, Huajuapan, Civil, legajo 9, Will of Manuel de León, January 2, 1835.
83. Ibid., legajo 14, Will of Paulino González, April 8, 1841.
84. AGPEO, Gobierno de los Distritos, Siglo XIX, Huajuapan, legajo 23, exp. 24, Juan Acevedo, Informe, March 21, 1850.
85. AJO, Huajuapan, Civil, legajo 9, Will of Manuel de León, January 2, 1835.
86. AGPEO, Gobierno de los Distritos, Siglo XIX, Huajuapan, legajo 23, exp. 24, Juan Acevedo, Informe, March 21, 1850.
87. AJO, Huajuapan, Civil, José Amador and Juan Matamoros, January 8, 1844; ibid., legajo 16, José Amador and Council of Tequixtepec, September 26, 1845.
88. Ibid., legajo 4, Juan Acevedo and Principales of Acaquizapan, May 8, 1829.
89. Ibid., legajo 13, Agustín Castillo and Vecinos of Chichihualtepec, November 5, 1839.
90. Ibid., legajo 17, Agustín Castillo and Vecinos of Chazumba, April 17, 1846.
91. Monaghan, Joyce, and Spores, "Transformations," 132; Ladd, *The Mexican Nobility*, 78.
92. AGNEO, Huajuapan, Isabel de Mendoza and Pueblo of Ihualtepec, March 30, 1841.
93. AJO, Huajuapan, Civil, legajo 11, José María Puga and Isabel de Mendoza, July 6, 1837.
94. Ibid., legajo 8, José Patricio de Santiago and Juan Bautista Guzmán, April 28, 1834.
95. Ibid., legajo 16, Gaspar Tamayo and Pueblo of Ahuehuetitlan, April 3, 1845.
96. AGNEO, Huajuapan, Inventory of Lands of Isabel de Mendoza, March 6, 1839; ibid., José Rafael Torija and Vecinos of Zapotitlán de las Lagunas, March 3, 1841.
97. AJO, Huajuapan, Civil, legajo 16, Gaspar Tamayo and Pueblo of Ahuehuetitlan, April 3, 1845.

98. AGPEO, Gobierno de los Distritos, Siglo XIX, Huajuapan, legajo 17, exp. 11, Santiago Rodríguez, May 16, 1854.

99. Connaughton, "1856–1857," 395.

100. For a broad overview of the decline, see Staples, *La iglesia*; Costeloe, *Church Wealth*; ibid., *Church and State*; Connaughton, *Clerical Ideology*; González Ramírez, *La iglesia*, 75; García Ugarte, *Liberalismo*, 23–32; Matute, Trejo, and Connaughton, eds., *Estado, iglesia y sociedad*; Rugeley, *Of Wonders*, 45–78.

101. Costeloe, *The Central Republic*, 108–12. The ecclesiastical fuero was the right of the clergy to be tried in ecclesiastical and not civil courts.

102. Cervantes Bello, "De la impunidad"; Connaughton, "La iglesia mexicana," 308; Staples, *La iglesia*, 121–22.

103. Connaughton, "Clérigos federalistas"; ibid., *Clerical Ideology*, 259–309; Staples, "Clerics as Politicians"; Connaughton, "A Most Delicate Balance," 58–59.

104. Guardino, *Peasants*, 98; Stevens, *Origins of Instability*, 4; Zoraida Vázquez, "Iglesia, ejercito, y centralismo."

105. Fowler, "Valentín Gómez Farias."

106. Fowler, *Santa Anna*, 220–21.

107. Connaughton, "Los curas"; Butler, *Popular Piety*, 29–34; O'Hara, *A Flock Divided*, 178–82.

108. For comparisons in Europe, see Cueva, "The Assault," 197; López Villacerde and Cueva Merino, "A modo de introducción," 16; Anderson, "The Kulturkamf"; ibid., "The Limits," 666; López Villaverde and Cueva Merino, "A modo de introducción," 20–23.

109. Church of Jesus Christ of Latter-day Saints, Tequixtepec, Cordilleras, 1839–1905, Vault INTL, film 0676469, List of Parishes; Archivo Parroquial Santiago Apostol, Petalcingo (APSAP), box 67, vol. 4, Cofradía del Señor de Calvario, 1757–1870; AMC, Presidencia, Division of State, May 9, 1837.

110. González Ramírez, *La iglesia mexicana*, 76.

111. The average priest's wages in the Mixteca Baja in 1838 were a fairly respectable thirteen hundred pesos annually (APSL, box 83, vol. 11, Padrones, December 29, 1838).

112. Thomson, "La contrarreforma," 242.

113. APSHL, box 77, vol. 5, Edictos, 1789–1901, Francisco Irigoyen to Priests, August 8, 1839; Peña Espinosa, "Desacralización de espacios," 172.

114. APSAP, box 69, vol. 3, Cordilleras, 1765–1888, Carlos María Colina y Rubio, April 4, 1864; Reyes Aguilar, *Bodas paralelas*, 299.

115. AMHL, Presidencia, Manuel Niño y Celis to Ignacio Carrión, October 29, 1855.

116. AGNEO, Huajuapan, Will of Matias Galva, November 20, 1866,

117. Ibid., Will of José Sánchez Toscano, March 14, 1837; ibid., Pedro Velasco y Villagómez to Ignacio Antonio Velasquez, December 27, 1834; APHL, Cordillera, Bishop of Puebla to Miguel Navarrete, April 28, 1862; AMHL, Presidencia, Actas del Ayuntamiento, July 2, 1820.

118. AGNEO, Huajuapan, Will of Eduardo Calixto de la Palma, November 7, 1854.

119. Ibid., Will of Felipe Martínez, October 5, 1871.

120. Tanck de Estrada, "La alfabetización," 120–22; Staples, *Recuento*, 227; Fowler, "The Compañia Lancastriana"; Lira, *Comunidades indígenas*, 128–32; Staples, "La educación."

121. APSHL, box 77, vol. 3, Edictos, 1789–1901, Decree of Bishopric of Puebla, April 16, 1825.

122. Ibid., vol. 4, Edictos, 1789–1901, Francisco Pablo Vázquez to Priests of the Diocese, December 7, 1840.

123. Ibid., José María Luciano Becerra y Jiménez to Priests of Diocese, February 14, 1854; AMHL, Presidencia, Santiago Rodríguez to Jueces, March 4, 1854.

124. Staples, *Recuento*, 231–33.

125. AGPEO, *Exposición del tercer gobernador del estado, 2 julio 1832*.

126. Ibid., *Memoria del gobernador constitucional a la sesta legislatura en sus siguentes sesiones ordinarias el mes de Julio de 1835*.

127. Ibid., *Exposición que en cumplimento del articulo 83 de la constitución del estado hace el gobernador del mismo al soberano congreso al abrir sus sesiones el 2 de Julio de año 1840*.

128. Colección Manuel Martínez Gracida (CMMG), vol. 56, Informe of Juan Acevedo, April 12, 1848.

129. AMC, Presidencia, Educación, 1830–1861.

130. Ibid., Felipe de León to Alcaldes of Huajuapan, July 28, 1834.

131. AGPEO, Educación, exp. 14, Felipe Soriano to Juan Acevedo, December 18, 1851.

132. *El Regenerador*, December 16, 1844.

133. Bono López, "La política lingüística"; Traffano, "Educación, civismo"; Weber, *Peasants into Frenchmen*, 332–33.

134. Luque Alcaide, "Catecismos mexicanos."

135. *Doctrina cristiana en el idioma mixteco*; *Catecismo en el idioma mixteco*; *Manual de administrar los sacramentos*.

136. AGNEO, Huajuapan, Will of Eduardo Calixto de la Palma, November 7, 1854.

137. CMMG, vol. 54, Informe of José Acevedo, May 2, 1865.

138. *Catecismo en el idioma mixteco*, 4.

139. APTN, Cordilleras, Francisco Pablo Vázquez to Priests of Diocese, November 7, 1837.

140. *Catecismo en el idioma mixteco*, 7.

141. APTez, box 67, vol. 3, Cordilleras, 1755–1888, Francisco Pablo Vázquez to Priests of Diocese, December 13, 1837.

142. *Catecismo en el idioma mixteco*, 10–23.

143. *Manual de administrar los sacramentos*, 23–25, 31–35.

144. Connaughton, "Conjuring the Body Politic"; ibid., "La familia"; ibid., "La sacralización."

145. Wright-Rios, *Revolutions*, 7.

146. Archivo Parroquial de Santa María de la Natividad, Tamazulapan (APSMNT), box 40, vol. 4, Cofradía del Señor del Desmayo.

147. AMC, Presidencia, Invitación para Participar en la Bendición del Collateral, August 19, 1855; Acevedo Carrasco, *Chazumba 2000*, 30.

148. APSDT, box 51, vol. 1, Cofradía de la Santa Cruz, 1752–1958.

149. Bustamante, *Cuadro histórico*, 2:87–91; AMHL, Historia, El Sitio de Huajuapan; CMMG, vol. 24, Sitio de Huajuapan, 180–85; ibid., box 38, Manuscript Concerning Valerio Trujano.
150. AGNEO, Huajuapan, Will of Juan Acevedo, March 25, 1854; ibid., Will of Manuel Alencaster, August 7, 1843; CMMG, vol. 18, Will of Antonio de León, October 11, 1847; AGNEO, Huajuapan, Will of Francisco Gutierrez de la Madrid, July 9, 1828.
151. APSHL, box 70, vol. 7, Cofradía Cuentas, 1772–1914, Escritura de Compra, March 6, 1842.
152. *Catecismo en el idioma mixteco*, 4.
153. Saul, *Bodas paralelas*, 28–39, 33.
154. APTN, Cordilleras, Santiago Rodríguez and Principales of Ixpantepec Nieves, June 3, 1854; AGPEO, Gobierno de los Distritos, Siglo XIX, Huajuapan, legajo 10, exp. 16, Santiago Rodríguez and Tomás Cuerto, May 24, 1854.
155. Guardino, *The Time of Liberty*, 78; AGPEO, 2.20, Juan Acevedo to Benito Juárez, March 10, 1850.
156. AMC, Presidencia, Pedro Velasco y Villagómez to Vicar General of Huajuapan, April 5, 1845.
157. AGNEO, Huajuapan, Justo Pastor Arellano and Antonio García, December 14, 1831.
158. AMHL, Presidencia, Informe of Justo González, April 8, 1848.
159. Ibid., Tomás Rios to Santiago Rodríguez, February 19, 1853.
160. AGPEO, Gobierno de los Distritos, Siglo XIX, Huajuapan, legajo 10, exp. 19, Santiago Rodríguez, February 17, 1854; ibid., 10.15, Mariano Rios to Santiago Rodríguez, November 19, 1853; ibid., 10.2, Juan Acevedo, November 29, 1851.
161. AJO, Huajuapan, Civil, legajo 9, María Manuel Villagómez, May 19, 1835.
162. AGNEO, Huajuapan, Joaquín Bautista y Guzmán and Principales of Huastepec, December 4, 1825; ibid., Francisco Bautista and Mayordomos of Huastepec, May 2, 1834.
163. *Historia de Tonalá, Oaxaca*, 36.
164. APSMAC, box 42, vol. 6, Cofradía de las Benditas Almas de Purgatorio, 1698–1889; APSHL, box 71, vol. 1, Cofradía de San Jose, 1801–1894.
165. APSMAC, box 44, vol. 1, Cofradía de la Santa Cruz, 1747–1880.
166. Ibid., box 46, vol. 2, Cofradía del Señor Crucificado, 1807–1890.
167. Church of Jesus Christ of Latter-day Saints, Tequixtepec, Cofradías, 1802–1902, Vault INTL, film 676939, Cofradía de Nuestra Señora del Rosario, Chinango.
168. Bautista Carriedo, *Estudios históricos*, 155.
169. Chance and Taylor, "Cofradías and Cargos"; Silva Prada, "Las manifestaciónes"; Castillo, "Cambios y continuidades"; O'Hara, *A Flock Divided*, 208–17.
170. Staples, *La iglesia*, 105; Costeloe, *The Central Republic*, 43.
171. Connaughton, "El ocaso del proyecto," 255.
172. APSHL, box 77, vol. 5, Edictos, 1789–1901, Francisco Pablo Vázquez to Priests of Diocese, January 18, 1835.

173. Archivo del Cabildo de la Catedral de Puebla (ACCP), Cartas de Francisco Pablo Vázquez, Guillermo López to Francisco Pablo Vázquez, June 3, 1841; *Carta pastoral del exmo. el ilmo. señor Obispo de Puebla.*

174. AMC, Presidencia, Circular of Antonio de León, July 23, 1834.

175. ACCP, Libro de Diezmos, 1828–1845.

176. APSHL, box 83, vol. 1, Padrones, 1793–1895.

177. Saul, *Bodas paralelas*, 78.

178. AMC, Presidencia, Lista de Contribuciones, 1843.

179. APM, Libro de Gobierno, vol. 1.

180. AGPEO, Gobierno de Distritos, Siglo XIX, Huajuapan, legajo 21, exp. 5, José Salazar y Rocha to Felipe de León, June 9, 1840.

181. AGNEQ, Huajuapan, Will of Roman Antonio Ximénez y Enriquez de Alvarado, May 1, 1843.

182. AGPEO, Gobierno de Distritos, Siglo XIX, Huajuapan, legajo 10, exp. 5, Francisco Iglesias, March 26, 1845.

183. Ibid., 15.15, Manuel Cisneros to Governor Juárez, April 26, 1852.

184. Martínez Gracida, *Cuadros sinópticos*, 27–44.

185. AGPEO, *Memoria del gobierno del estado de Oaxaca, 1852.*

186. Varley, "Women and the Home"; Dore, "One Step Forward."

187. Connaughton, "Conjuring the Body Politic"; ibid., "La familia"; see similar argument in Pottash-Jutkeit, "La moral pública."

188. Connaughton, "La familia," 472.

189. Calvo, "The Warmth of the Hearth," 295; Carmagnani, "Demografía y sociedad," 444; Valdés, "The Decline," 33; Pescador, *De bautizados*, 147–49.

190. Morin, *Santa Inés Zacatelco*, 73–74.

191. Jonas, *France*, 163.

192. Stevens, "Temerse la ira," 95.

193. Church of Jesus Christ of Latter-day Saints, Tequixtepec, Cofradías, 1708–1847, Vault INTL, film 0676469, Bishop of Puebla to Priests of Diocese, May 5, 1847.

194. Ibid., June 9, 1848.

195. Stevens, "Lo revelado," 225.

196. In comparison, children of unknown parents accounted for around 20 percent in San Luis Potosí, 17 percent in Mexico City, and 41 percent in Oaxaca City (Stevens, "Lo revelado," 224). Church of Jesus Christ of Latter-day Saints, Tequixtepec, Bautismos, 1826–1850, Vault INTL, film 674961; ibid., Huajuapam [*sic*] de León, Bautismos, 1835–1846, FHL INTL, film 603767.

197. Tackett, *Religion, Revolution*, 167.

198. AGN, Acaldes Mayores, vol. 3, fs. 199–202; García Alcaraz, *Tinujei*, 279–85.

199. Huerta Rios, *Organización Socio-política*, 132–33.

200. CMMG, vol. 58, Informe of José Carrasquedo, October 17, 1843; ibid., box 37, José María Muñoz to Juan Acevedo, October 12, 1844; Archivo Histórico de la Secretaria de

la Defensa Naciónal (AHSDN), XI, 481.3/1962, Informe of Subprefect of Juxtlahuaca, September 29, 1843; ibid., XI, 481.3/1964, Informe of José de Jesús Maldonaldo, October 18, 1843.

201. Gay, *Historia de Oaxaca*, 1:52.

202. AGNEO, Huajuapan, Antonio de León and José de la Cruz, December 1, 1837; CMMG, vol. 58, Informe of José Salazar y Rocha, October 6, 1838; Martínez Gracida, *Cuadros sinópticos*, 69. León probably took over the lands of the former Jesuit livestock hacienda in Putla.

203. CMMG, vol. 58, Informe of José Salazar y Rocha, October 9, 1838.

204. Pastor, *Campesinos*, 461.

205. CMMG, vol. 71, Informe of Juan Acevedo, April 24, 1831; ibid., Informe of José María Santaella, August 18, 1829; ibid., box 49, Informe of Prefect of Teposcolula, December 17, 1830.

206. *Correo Americano del Sur*, February 25, 1813; CMMG, vol. 58, Anonymous Letter, ca. March 1841.

207. CMMG, vol. 58, Hilario Alonso, March 14, 1841.

208. AGN, Siglo XIX, Justicia, vol. 176, fs. 140–50; Alamán, *Historia de México*, 5:629.

209. CMMG, vol. 58, Hilario Alonso, March 14, 1841.

210. Ibid., box 49, Informe of Prefect of Teposcolula, December 17, 1830.

211. AHSDN, XI, 481.3/2124, Plan of Feliciano Martín, August 2, 1845.

212. *El Regenerador*, September 2, 1844.

213. AHSDN, XI, 481.3/2128, Informe of Juan Acevedo, September 5, 1845.

214. AGN, Gobernación, vol. 143, exp. 2, fs. 1–57.

215. AHSDN, XI, 481.3/2124, Plan of Feliciano Martín, August 2, 1845.

216. Ibid., 481.3/2128, Informe of Juan Acevedo, August 13, 1845; AGPEO, Gobierno de los Distritos, Siglo XIX, Huajuapan, legajo 2, exp. 20, Informe of Juan Acevedo, June 23, 1847.

217. Guardino, *Peasants*, 147–77.

218. Abardia M. and Reina, "Cien años," 446.

219. AHSDN, XI, 481.3/2124, Plan of Feliciano Martín, August 2, 1845.

220. Ibid., 481.3/2128, Informe of Juan Alvarez, September 5, 1845.

221. Archivo Parroquial de Chazumba (APC), Cartas de Pablo Fracisco Vázquez, Manuel Gamboa to Pablo Francisco Vázquez, April 2, 1842; ibid., Libro de Diezmos, 1828–1845; *El Regenerador*, February 9, 1844; CMMG, vol. 40, Informe of J. Segura, April 8, 1862. For the Tierra Caliente, see Fisher, "Relaciones entre fieles," 335–43.

222. CMMG, vol. 71, Informe of Juan Acevedo, February 1, 1831.

223. AHSDN, XI, 481.3/2124, Plan of Feliciano Martín, August 2, 1845.

224. Beristain Romero, "*Yosocuiya*," 145; Martínez Gracida, *Cuadros sinópticos*, 68.

225. *El Regenerador*, February 9, 1844.

226. Ibid., May 27, 1844.

227. AHSDN, XI, 481.3/1964, Informe of José de Jesus Maldonaldo, October 18, 1843.

228. Barabas, *Dones, duenos*, 86.

229. AHSDN, XI, 481.3/2055, Plan del Campo, October 15, 1843.

230. Costeloe, *The Central Republic*, 22–23.

231. Warren, *Vagrants and Citizens*, 105.

232. Hale, *Mexican Liberalism*, 17.

233. Hobsbawm, *Primitive Rebels*, 33–45.

234. AHSDN, XI, 481.3/1964, Manuel Ruiz to Antonio de León, 1843; ibid., Informe of Prefect of Huajuapan, October 3, 1843.

235. Blok, *Honor and Violence*, 14–28.

236. AGPEO, Gobierno de los Distritos, Siglo XIX, Huajuapan, legajo 33, exp. 11, Informe of Juan Acevedo, May 30, 1848.

237. AHSDN, XI, 481.3/2129, Informe of José Ibáñez, October 20, 1845; ibid., Informe of Manuel Andrade, January 25, 1845.

238. AGN, Justicia Eclesiastica, exp. 95, fs. 38–43.

239. AGPEO, Memorias, *Memoria de gobierno del estado de Oaxaca, 1831*, 16.

240. Ibid., Gobierno de los Distritos, Huajuapan, 33.1, Informe of Juan Acevedo, March 16, 1831.

241. CMMG, vol. 71, Informe of Juan Acevedo, January 12, 1831.

242. AGN, Justicia, vol. 176, fs. 140–50.

243. CMMG, vol. 58, Hilario Alonso, March 14, 1841.

244. AHSDN, XI, 481.3/1964, Informe of Prefect of Huajuapan, September 28, 1843.

245. *El Regenerador*, May 27, 1844.

246. AHSDN, exp. XI, 481.3/2128, Informe of Manuel López, August 26, 1845.

247. AGPEO, Gobierno de los Distritos, Siglo XIX, Huajuapan, legajo 38, exp. 1, Informe of Juan Acevedo, February 6, 1846.

248. Pandey, "Encounters and Calamities"; Hardiman, "The Bhils and Shahukars"; Chakrabarty, *Rethinking Working-Class History*.

249. AHSDN, exp. XI, 481.3/2128, Principales of Calihuala to Antonio de León, n.d.; AGPEO, Gobierno de los Distritos, Siglo XIX, Huajuapan, legajo 56, exp. 3, Juez of Acaquizapan to Prefect of Huajuapan, September 6, 1846.

250. Otero, *Consideraciones*; Santoni, "A Fear of the People"; Caplan, *Indigenous Citizens*, 81–88; Hamnett, *Juárez*, 54–55; Thomson, "Los indios"; Falcón, "Indígenas y justicia"; Rugeley, *Rebellion Now and Forever*, 38–40; Lira, *Comunidades indígenas*, 148.

251. Quoted in Hamnett, "Los pueblos indios," 193.

252. AGN, Gobernación, 166.8, Governor of Oaxaca, June 4, 1833.

253. CMMG, vol. 39, Acta de Pronunciamiento, June 19, 1834.

254. AGN, Justicia, vol. 176, fs. 140–50, Antonio de León to Juan Acevedo, October 29, 1838.

255. AGPEO, Gobierno de los Distritos, Siglo XIX, Huajuapan, legajo 1, exp. 17, Informe of Juan Acevedo, November 4, 1843.

256. AMHL, Presidencia, Informe of Antonio de León, August 24, 1847.

257. AGPEO, *Exposición que en cumplimento del articulo 83 de la constitución del estado hace el gobernador del mismo al soberano congreso al abrir sus sesiones el 2 de julio de ano 1849*.

258. Thomson, "Bulwarks of Patriotic Liberalism"; ibid., "Popular Aspects"; Mallon, *Peasant and Nation*; Mcnamara, *Sons of the Sierra*, 65–89; Hernández Chavez, *La tradición republicana*, 55–57; Thomson, "Cabecillas indígenas"; Rugeley, *Rebellion Now and Forever*, 43; Radding, "Etnia, tierra y estado."

259. AGPEO, Gobierno de los Distritos, Siglo XIX, Huajuapan, legajo 1, exp. 15, Informe of Juan Acevedo, November 1, 1842.

260. AJO, Huajuapan, Civil, legajo 15, Principales of Tequixtepec, April 3, 1844; AHSDN, Informe of José de Jesus Maldonaldo, November 4, 1843.

261. AGPEO, Gobierno de los Distritos, Siglo XIX, Huajuapan, legajo 1, exp. 25, Pronunciamiento of Plan of San Luis Potosí, December 20, 1845.

262. AMHL, Presidencia, Informe of Antonio de León, August 24, 1847; AJO, Huajuapan, Civil, legajo 15, Principales of Acaquizapan, June 5, 1843.

263. AHSDN, XI, 481.3/2124, Informe of Antonio de León, August 16, 1845.

264. Hamnett, "Mexican Conservatives," 190.

265. Pani, "'Verdaderas figuras de Cooper'"; Meyer, "La junta"; González y González, "El indigenismo de Maximiliano"; González Navarro, "Instituciones indígenas"; Zavala, "Victor Considerant"; Arenal, "La protección indígena"; Duncan, "Legitimation"; Hernández Rodríguez, "Los indios"; Falcón, "Subterfugios, armas y deferncias."

266. Hamnett, "Mexican Conservatives," 188.

267. Thomson, "Popular Aspects," 273.

268. Lira, *Comunidades indígenas*, 202–4; Paula de Arrangoiz, *Apuntes*; García-Gutierrez, "La experiencia cultural"; Fowler, "Carlos María Bustamante," 59–85.

269. Bustamante, *El nuevo Bernal Díaz del Castillo*, 1.

270. *Esposición que los conservadores.*

CHAPTER 3

1. CMMG, vol. 50, Principales of Tequixtepec, August 20, 1859.

2. Brading, "Creole Nationalism," 154.

3. Niceto de Zamacois, *Historia de Méjico*; Díaz R., *La vida heroica*; Paula de Arrangoiz, *Apuntes*; Cuevas, *Historia de la iglesia*, vol. 5; Abascal, *La revolución.*

4. Sierra, *Juárez*, 47–52; Martínez Vásquez, *Historia de la educación*, 54–59; Reina, "De las reformas," 1:238–43; Pastor, *Campesinos y reformas*, 453–56; Carmagnani, "Local Governments"; ibid., *El regreso*, 231–36; Sánchez Silva, *Indios, comerciantes*, 191–200; Guardino, *The Time of Liberty*, 156–222; Caplan, *Indigenous Citizens*, 63–101.

5. I would like to thank Erika Pani for her close reading of this section. As she and Will Fowler have argued, binary divisions between centralism and federal or liberalism and conservatism may form useful organizing terms but rarely capture the messy nature of regional political alliance formation or ideological standpoint. Pani, *Para mexicanizar*; Fowler, *Mexico in the Age of Proposals.*

6. Pastor, *Campesinos y reformas*, 420–25; Carmagnani, *El regreso*, 231–36.

7. Caplan, *Indigenous Citizens*, 67–73; Guardino, *The Time of Liberty*, 156–222; Mendoza García, "El ganado comunal," 756–57.

8. Abardia M. and Reina, "Cien años," 448–52; Reina, "De las reformas," 246–51; Pastor, *Campesinos y reformas*, 503–4. The term is taken from Bulnes, *Juárez y las revoluciones*, 104.

9. Hamnett, "Benito Juárez," 8; Guardino, *The Time of Liberty*, 153, 168, 184–85; Hamnett, *Juárez*, 29–30. The debate reaches back to the postrevolutionary period. Whereas revisionists lift much of their evidence from Iturribarria, *Historia de Oaxaca*, more recent historians lift theirs from Tamayo, *El general Antonio de León*.

10. Wolf, "Aspects of Group Relations"; Peña, "Poder local."

11. Legaria Corro and Legaria Guzmán, *Vida, pasión*, 16; AJO, Huajuapan, Civil, legajo 8, June 6, 1834 (copy of document from April 1819), Will of Manuel de León, 1819.

12. Legaria Corro and Legaria Guzmán, *Vida, pasión*, 28, 54; CMMG, vol. 18, Will of Antonio de León, October 11, 1847.

13. AJO, Huajuapan, Civil, legajo 17, Antonio de León to Alejandro Roldan, April 18, 1846; AMHL, Presidencia, Manuel Alencaster to Antonio de León, September 6, 1833.

14. Will Fowler, *Santa Anna*, 219–20.

15. AJO, Huajuapan, Civil, legajo 8, June 6, 1834 (copy of document from April 1819), Will of Manuel de León, 1819; CMMG, vol. 18, Will of Antonio de León, October 11, 1847.

16. APSAP, Cofradía del Calvario; Reyes Aguilar, *Bodas paralelas*, 299; APSHL, Cofradías, Escritura de Compra, March 6, 1842; ACCP, Libro de Diezmos, 1828–1845.

17. Tamayo, *El general Antonio de León*, 12.

18. Martínez, *Los primeros ayuntamientos*, 40–45.

19. Legaria Corro and Legaria Guzmán, *Vida, pasión*, 29; ACCP, Cartas del Obispo José Antonio Joaquín Pérez Martínez y Robles, José Antonio Joaquín Pérez Martínez y Robles to Manuel de León, February 23, 1821.

20. Legaria Corro and Legaria Guzmán, *Vida, pasión*, 29–30; Bustamante, *Diario histórico*, vol. 1.

21. AHSDN, Cancelados, Antonio de León, vol. 1; ibid., Timoteo Reyes Ramírez; "Ejercito imperial mejicano," 4:401.

22. Iturribarria, *Historia de Oaxaca, 1821–1854*, 11.

23. Martínez, *Los primeros ayuntamientos*, 86–91.

24. Anna, *The Mexican Empire*, 118.

25. Bustamante, *Diario histórico*, vol. 1.

26. Fowler, *Santa Anna*, 43–70.

27. Guardino, *The Time of Liberty*, 184–85; AHSDN, Cancelados, Antonio de León, vol. 1; Bustamante, *Diario histórico*, vol. 1; AGN, Siglo XIX, Justicia, vol. 218, exp. 8, fs. 93, Trial of Antonio and Manuel de León.

28. Guardino, *The Time of Liberty*, 184.

29. The point is made for Oaxaca as a whole by Hamnett, "Oaxaca," 64; Sánchez Silva, "El establecimiento del federalismo"; and ibid., "La consumación."

30. Bustamante, *Diario histórico*, vol. 1; Archivo de Luis Castañeda Guzmán, Biblioteca Burgoa, C17 195, Compañia Nacional de Huajuapan, August 1, 1822.

31. Caplan, "The Legal Revolution," 272–74.

32. Martínez, *Los primeros ayuntamientos*, 58–59; AMHL, Presidencia, Tomás Rios to Santiago Rodríguez, February 19, 1853.

33. Gerhard, *A Guide*, 131; AMC, Juan Acevedo to Alcaldes of Huajuapan, December 2, 1829.

34. Caplan, *Indigenous Citizens*, 26.

35. Ibid., 5.

36. AJO, Huajuapan, Civil, legajo 4, Mariano Villagómez and Council of Tequixtepec, January 13, 1823; ibid., October 22, 1823.

37. Ibid., exp. 21, Ramon Antonio Ximénez, February 3, 1826.

38. Ibid., Criminal, legajo 4, exp. 17, Ignacio Velasco y Mendoza, August 7, 1827.

39. Ibid., Civil, legajo 12, Juan Aguilar, May 6, 1838.

40. AMC, Presidencia, Joaquín Bautista y Guzmán to Luis Mejía, January 7, 1856.

41. AJO, Huajuapan, Civil, legajo 5, Juez of Ahuehuetitlan, March 5, 1831.

42. Ibid., legajo 7, Juez of Ixitlán, June 25, 1833.

43. Guardino, *Peasants*, 147–77; ibid., *The Time of Liberty*, 156–222.

44. Escobar Ohmstede, "Del gobierno indígena"; Rugeley, *Rebellion*, 106–51.

45. Caplan, *Indigenous Citizens*, 45–52.

46. Guardino, *The Time of Liberty*, 240–41.

47. Reina, *Las rebeliones campesinas*, 233–39; Pastor, *Campesinos*, 529–35; Carmagnani, *El regreso*, 230.

48. Caplan, *Indigenous Citizens*, 73–101; Chassen-López, *From Liberal to Revolutionary*, 337.

49. Guardino, *Peasants*, 159, 206; Fowler, "El pronunciamiento mexicano"; Zoraida Vázquez, "Political Plans."

50. Guardino, *The Time of Liberty*, 185–86; Iturribarria, *Historia de Oaxaca*, 89–90.

51. Chowning, *Wealth and Power*, 117–21, 141–42.

52. AHSDN, XI, 481.3 398, Informe of Antonio de León, November 18, 1827.

53. Bustamante, *Diario histórico*, vol. 1; Legaria Corro and Legaria Guzmán, *Vida, pasión*, 105; Iturribarria, *Historia de Oaxaca*, 130–31.

54. AHSDN, Cancelados, Antonio de León, vol. 1.

55. Fowler, *Santa Anna*, 126–27.

56. Bustamante, *Diario histórico*, vol. 1.

57. CMMG, vol. 72, Informe of José María Santaella, August 18, 1829.

58. AGN, Gobernación, s/s vol. 143, exp. 2, fs. 1–57; CMMG, vol. 49, Informe of Juan Acevedo, August 20, 1830.

59. CMMG, vol. 49, Informe of Juan Acevedo, December 14, 1830; ibid., vol. 71, Informe of Juan Acevedo, June 29, 1831.

60. AHSDN, Cancelados, Antonio de León, vol. 1.

61. AGN, Gobernación, s/s vol. 143, exp. 2, fs. 1–57.

62. CMMG, vol. 49, Informe of Juan Acevedo, February 1, 1831.

63. Ibid., June 29, 1831.

64. Lucas Alamán Papers, Nettie Lee Benson Latin American Collection, University of Texas, Austin, document 202, Francisco Pablo Vázquez to Lucas Alamán, February 21, 1832. The link between clerical control and these financial concessions given to important regional families is suggested in Cervantes Bello, "El dilema."

65. Costeloe, *The Central Republic*, 101; García Uguarte, "La jerarquia católica"; Costeloe, *Church and State*, 45–46.

66. Guardino, *Peasants*, 136.

67. Connaughton, "La sacralización"; Pérez Toledo, "Movilización social."

68. Anderson, "The Kulturkamf," 86–87.

69. *Respetuosa representación.*

70. CMMG, vol. 39, Informe of Felipe Paz, May 16, 1834.

71. AGPEO, Gobierno de los Distitos, Siglo XIX, Huajuapan, legajo 5, exp. 58, Ayuntamiento de Huajuapan, May 18, 1834.

72. Ibid., Felipe de León, May 20, 1834.

73. CMMG, vol. 39, Acta de Pronunciamiento in Huajuapan, June 18, 1834.

74. CMMG, vol. 39, Discurso of Antonio de León, June 22, 1834; Iturribarria, *Historia de Oaxaca*, 206–8.

75. Iturribarria, *Historia de Oaxaca*, 218–19; CMMG, vol. 39; AHSDN, XI, 481.3/7841, Informe of Luis Quintanar, June 23, 1836.

76. CMMG, vol. 39, Informe of Rafael Pimentel, June 12, 1836.

77. AHSDN, XI, 481.3/7841, Informe of Luis Quintanar, June 23, 1836.

78. Jiménez Codinach, ed., *Planes en la nación*, 1:82–84.

79. CMMG, vol. 57, Informe of Manuel González, August 11, 1836.

80. AHSDN, XI, 481.3/1274; CMMG, vol. 58, Informe of José Salazar y Rocha, October 10, 1839.

81. Ibid., Informe of José María Castillo, November 2, 1838.

82. AGN, Siglo XIX, Justicia, Informe of José Salazar y Rocha, October 11, 1838.

83. AHSDN, XI, 481.3/1274, Informe of Juan Acevedo, October 13, 1838.

84. CMMG, vol. 58, Informe of Mariano Guzmán, May 27, 1839; AGN, Siglo XIX, Justicia, Informe of Mariano Guzmán, March 20, 1840.

85. CMMG, vol. 58, Hilario Alonso, March 14, 1841; AGN, Archivo de la Guerra, vol. 210, exp. 2122, fs. 76–106, Informe of Antonio de León, September 6, 1841.

86. Fowler, *Santa Anna*, 213–37; Costeloe, *The Central Republic*, 145–54.

87. AGPEO, Gobierno de los Distritos, Siglo XIX, Huajuapan, legajo 38, exp. 7, Informe of Marcelino Martínez, December 31, 1841; ibid., Informe of Juan Pablo, October 27, 1841.

88. Hamnett, *Juárez*, 29–30.

89. Hernández Jaimes, "Actores indios."

90. AHSDN, XI, 481.3/2055, Prefect of Huajuapan, September 28, 1843; Iturribarria, *Historia de Oaxaca*, 294–95.

91. AGPEO, Gobierno de los Distritos, Siglo XIX, Huajuapan, legajo 1, exp. 17, Informe of Juan Acevedo, November 4, 1843; Church of Jesus Christ of Latter-day Saints, Oaxaca Military Records, Vault INTL, film 1152896; AGPEO, Gobierno de los Distritos, Siglo XIX, Huajuapan, legajo 2, exp. 14, Informe of Manuel Andrade, December 18, 1843.

92. AHSDN, XI, 481.3/2055, Informe of Isidro Reyes, October 2, 1843.

93. Ibid., Informe of Juan Maldonaldo, October 16, 1843.

94. Hernández Jaimes, "Actores indios."

95. AGPEO, Gobierno de los Distritos, Siglo XIX, Huajuapan, legajo 35, exp. 11, Informe of Juan Acevedo, February 12, 1845.

96. AHSDN, XI, 481.3/ 2124, Informe of Vicente Tamayo, April 21, 1845.

97. Ibid., 481.3/2128, Informe of Manuel Pelaez, August 26, 1845.

98. AGPEO, Gobierno de los Distritos, Siglo XIX, Huajuapan, legajo 38, exp. 1, Informe of Juan Acevedo, February 6, 1846; ibid., legajo 35, exp. 14; ibid., legajo 35, exp. 15; ibid., legajo 35, exp. 16.

99. Ibid., legajo 35, exp. 15.

100. *El Regenerador*, April 18, 1844.

101. AHSDN, XI, 481.3/2124, Plan of Feliciano Martin, August 2, 1845.

102. Ibid., 481.3/2116, Informe of Juan Alvarez, September 3, 1845.

103. *El Regenerador*, April 18, 1846.

104. CMMG, vol. 37, Comisión de la Asemblea de Oaxaca, January 5, 1846; AGPEO, Gobierno de los Distritos, Siglo XIX, Huajuapan, legajo 1, exp. 25, Acta de Pronunciamiento, December 29, 1845; Esparza, "El difícil camino," 503–4.

105. Knowlton, "La iglesia mexicana," 517–18.

106. AGPEO, Gobierno de los Distritos, Siglo XIX, Huajuapan, legajo 38, exp. 8, José Basilio Herrera, February 10, 1847.

107. Ibid., legajo 38, exp. 3, Acta de Pronunciamiento, February 24, 1847.

108. Ibid., legajo 8, exp. 14, Juan Francisco, February 27, 1847.

109. See also Connaughton, *Dimensiones*, 73–99.

110. Legaria Corro and Legaria Guzmán, *Vida, pasión*, 212–34.

111. AGPEO, Gobierno de los Distritos, Siglo XIX, Huajuapan, legajo 21, exp. 38, Documentos acerca de la Guerra.

112. Martínez Gracida, *Cuadros sinópticos*, 39.

113. Olavarria y Ferrari, *México*, 686–87; Magnum, "Battle of Molino del Rey," 268.

114. Guardino, *The Time of Liberty*, 264–67.

115. Hale, *Mexican Liberalism*, 15–22; Reyes Heroles, *El liberalismo mexicano*, 2:350–53; Connaughton, "1856–1857."

116. Berry, *The Reform*, 69–74; Hamnett, *Juárez*, 49–70; Mcnamara, *Sons of the Sierra*, 28–66; Molino, *Historia de Tehuantepec*; Méndez Aquino, *Historia de Tlaxiaco*, 194.

117. Hamnett, *Juárez*, 89–101; Caplan, *Indigenous Citizens*, 150–64.

118. AMHL, Presidencia, Inauguración del Ayuntamiento de 1849; ibid., Inauguración del Ayuntamiento de 1850; ibid., Inauguración del Ayuntamiento de 1851.

119. AGPEO, Gobierno de los Distritos, Siglo XIX, Huajuapan, legajo 36, exp. 9, March 25, 1850; AMC, Presidencia, Libros de la Escuela, 1849–1852.

120. AGPEO, Gobierno de los Distritos, Siglo XIX, Huajuapan, legajo 37, exp. 16.

121. Fowler, *Santa Anna*, 292–316; Johnson, *The Mexican Revolution*, 1–20.

122. AMHL, Presidencia, Miguel Luna to Salvador Rodríguez, September 18, 1851.

123. AGPEO, Gobierno de los Distritos, Siglo XIX, Huajuapan, legajo 10, exp. 35, Informe of San Andrés Sabinillo, September 27, 1853; ibid., legajo 10, exp. 1, Tomás de Aquino Melo to Prefect, December 23, 1852; ibid., legajo 20, exp. 15, Mariano Rios, November 19, 1853; ibid., legajo 21, exp. 12, Informe of Juan Acevedo, November 29, 1851.

124. Butler, "The 'Liberal' Cristero," 648; Jacobs, *Ranchero Revolt*, 48–53; Schryer, *The Rancheros*, 6–9, 27–29, 33–36; Knight, "El liberalismo mexicano," 78–79.

125. CMMG, vol. 39, Informe of José Salazar y Rocha, August 12, 1836; AHSDN, XI, 481.3/2129, Informe of Antonio de León, April 24, 1845; ibid., 481.3.1274, Informe of José María Castillo, November 2, 1838.

126. Iturribarria, *Historia de Oaxaca*, 434–35.

127. CMMG, vol. 49, Pronunciamiento of Francisco Herrera, December 19, 1854.

128. Ibid., Informe of Manuel Sandoval, December 22, 1854.

129. Ibid., Minister of War to Prefect of Huajuapan, December 22, 1854.

130. Ibid., vol. 43, Manuel Mora to Manuel Martínez Gracida, February 13, 1892.

131. Ibid., vol. 49, Informe of Pedro Noriega, January 24, 1855.

132. AGPEO, Gobierno de los Distritos, Siglo XIX, Huajuapan, legajo 44, exp. 52, Informe of José Ramírez y Acevedo, January 3, 1855.

133. Sebastian Reyes, interview with the author, May 2007.

134. AHSDN, XI, 481.3/3365, Informe of Rafael Espinosa, August 4, 1855.

135. Hamnett, *Juárez*, 105.

136. CMMG, vol. 49, Acta de Huajuapan, August 22, 1855.

137. AGPEO, Gobierno de los Distritos, Siglo XIX, Huajuapan, legajo 10, exp. 39, Acta de Tonalá, August 24, 1855; ibid., Acta de San Sebastián del Monte, August 27, 1855.

138. AMHL, Presidencia, Actas del Ayuntamiento, September 1855.

139. García Uguarte, "Church and State"; Hamnett, "El partido conservador," 218–19; Thomson, "La contrarreforma," 249–51.

140. Voekel, "Liberal Religion"; Connaughton, "1856–1857," 458.

141. Portilla, *México*, 261.

142. Powell, "Priests and Peasants"; Thomson, "La contrarreforma," 241–42.

143. AHSDN, XI, 481.3/3775, Informe of Subprefect of Acatlán, March 3, 1857; AGPEO, Gobierno de los Distritos, Siglo XIX, Huajuapan, legajo 21, exp. 21, Informe of Luis Mejía, July 18, 1856.

144. AJO, Huajuapan, Criminal, legajo 61, Informe of Luis Mejía, May 2, 1856.

145. AGPEO, Gobierno de los Distritos, Siglo XIX, Huajuapan, legajo 21, exp. 21, Informe of Luis Mejía, July 18, 1856.

146. AHSDN, XI, 481.3/5592, Informe of Marcial Camano, July 14, 1856.

147. Ibid., 481.3/5522, Informe of Luis Mejía, August 4, 1856.

148. AGPEO, Gobierno de los Distritos, Siglo XIX, Huajuapan, legajo 23, exp 4. Informe of Luis Mejía, June 18, 1858.

149. AJO, Huajuapan, Criminal, legajo 5, Interview with José Reyes, July 16, 1856.

150. Ibid., legajo 6, Interview with José Reyes, July 16, 1856; AGPEO, Gobierno de los Distritos, Siglo XIX, Huajuapan, legajo 1, exp. 44, Informe of Luis Mejía, July 25, 1856.

151. CMMG, vol. 74, Informe of Luis Mejía, October 30, 1856.

152. Ibid., December 17, 1856.

153. AJO, Huajuapan, Criminal, legajo 6, Informe of Luis Mejía, May 2, 1856.

154. AHSDN, XI, 481.3/3775, Commander of Petlalcingo, September 6, 1856.

155. APSAP, Libro de Gobierno 1. For others acts of iconoclasm, see Rivera, *Anales mexicanos*, 66; Paula de Arrangoiz, *México desde 1808*, 2:361; Thomson, "La contrarreforma," 243.

156. Hamnett, "The Comonfort Presidency."

157. *Ley sobre derechos.*

158. AGPEO, Gobierno de los Distritos, Siglo XIX, Huajuapan, legajo 44, exp. 50, Informe of Emigdio Olivera, August 2, 1857.

159. AHSDN, XI, 481/3/6858, Informe of Prefect of Huajuapan, November 12, 1857.

160. José Maria Cobos quoted in Hernández López, "La 'reacción a sangre y fuego,'" 284.

161. Iturribarria, *Historia de Oaxaca*, 119–56.

162. AGPEO, Gobierno de los Distritos, Siglo XIX, Huajuapan, legajo 1, exp. 46, Informe of Luis Mejía, June 18, 1858; ibid., May 14, 1858.

163. AJO, Huajuapan, Criminal, legajo 66, Case against Antonio Santiago, December 21, 1858.

164. CMMG, vol. 54, Informe of Luis Mejía, September 18, 1859; AGPEO, Gobierno de los Distritos, Siglo XIX, Huajuapan, legajo 44, exp. 49, October 15, 1858; Manuel Martínez Gracida, *Efemerides oaxaqueñas*, 56.

165. AJO, Huajuapan, Criminal, legajo 71, Manuel Reyes to José Segura y Guzmán, February 18, 1859.

166. Church of Jesus Christ of Latter-day Saints, Documentos Militares, Oaxaca, Vault INTL, film 1153146; AHSDN, XI, 481.3/7943, Informe of Luciano Martínez, March 4, 1860.

167. AHSDN, XI, 481.3.7943, Informe of Unknown, February 6, 1860.

168. CMMG, vol. 50, Pronunciamiento de Tonalá, August 3, 1859.

169. AMHL, Presidencia, Informe of Luis Mejía, January 10, 1859.

170. Galindo y Galindo, *La gran década*, 2:315; Martínez Gracida, *Efemerides oaxaqueñas*, 89.

171. Hamnett, *Juárez*, 188.

172. CMMG, vol. 50.

173. Berry, *The Reform*, 196, 233; Mcnamara, *Sons of the Sierra*, 47–48.

174. AGPEO, Gobierno de los Distritos, Siglo XIX, Huajuapan, legajo 1, exp. 47, Informe de Francisco Enriquez, December 21, 1860.

175. AJO, Huajuapan, Criminal, legajo 78, Vicente Moreno, July 8, 1862.
176. Thomson and LaFrance, *Patriotism, Politics*, 9.
177. AGPEO, Gobierno de los Distritos, Siglo XIX, Huajuapan, legajo 20, exp. 23, Pleito de Tierras; ibid., legajo 20, exp. 22, Pleito de Tierras. The same happened in Atoyac (ibid., legajo 4, exp. 33, Informe of J. Segura, July 30, 1863).
178. AMHL, Presidencia, Informe of Bernadino Castro, December 28, 1867; ibid., Informe of Joaquín Gordillo, February 15, 1870; AJO, Huajuapan, Civil, legajo 45, Cuyotepeji, March 25, 1867; ibid., legajo 77, Acaquizapan, September 3, 1894.
179. AMC, Presidencia, Luis Medrano to J. Segura, March 28, 1862; ibid., Lista de Diezmos, September 30, 1863.
180. AGPEO, Gobierno de los Distritos, Siglo XIX, Huajuapan, legajo 45, exp. 4, Informe of T., December 1862.
181. Martínez Gracida, *Efemerides oaxaqueñas*, 134.
182. Mcnamara, *Sons of the Sierra*, 51–55; Loyola Jiménez, "El problema," 31; Ortiz Castro, *Apuntes históricos*, 49.
183. AMHL, Presidencia, Council Meeting, June 20, 1864.
184. Ibid., Guardia Nacional, July 3, 1865; Church of Jesus Christ of Latter-day Saints, Oaxaca, Military Records, Vault INTL, film 1153149; AGPEO, Gobierno de los Distritos, Siglo XIX, Huajuapan, legajo 2, exp. 48, Informe of J. Segura, May 23, 1863. This point is suggested in Connaughton, "1856–1857," 455.
185. CMMG, vol. 52, Informe of Jefe Político of Silacayoapan, October 14, 1863.
186. AGPEO, Gobierno de los Distritos, Siglo XIX, Huajuapan, legajo 27, exp. 28, Informe of J. Segura, September 17, 1862.
187. Ibid., legajo 27, exp. 29, Informe of J. Segura, May 8, 1863.
188. Martínez Gracida, *Efemerides oaxaqueñas*, 145.
189. AGPEO, Gobierno de los Distritos, Siglo XIX, Huajuapan, legajo 2, exp. 51, Informe of J. Segura, February 13, 1863.
190. CMMG, vol. 52, Informe of Jefe Político of Silacayoapan, September 21, 1863.
191. AMHL, Presidencia, Council Meeting, April 7, 1863.
192. Iturribarria, *Historia de Oaxaca*, 105; Thomson and LaFrance, *Patriotism, Politics*, 70.
193. AMHL, Presidencia, Actas del Ayuntamiento, September 1864.
194. AMC, Presidencia, Actas del Ayuntamiento, January 26, 1865.
195. ATN, Libro de Gobierno, December 2, 1864.
196. AMHL, Presidencia, Actas del Ayuntamiento, December 1864.
197. AGPEO, Gobierno de los Distritos, Siglo XIX, Huajuapan, legajo 20, exp. 23, Pleito de Tierras; ibid., legajo 20, exp. 22, Pleito de Tierras.
198. See the sales in AMHL, Presidencia, 1865–1867; LaFrance and Thomson, *Patriotism, Politics*, 102.
199. *Archivo del general Porfirio Díaz*, 2:98–102; Hernández Rodríguez, "Las Campañas"; Iturribarria, *Historia de Oaxaca*, 190–91.
200. *Archivo del general Porfirio Díaz*, 2:112.
201. Ibid., 2:140; Zamacois, *Historia de Méjico*, 18:557.

202. Mcnamara, *Sons of the Sierra*, 56–63; Berry, *The Reform*, 105–9; Dabbs, *The French Army*, 156–76.

203. Iturribarria, *Historia de Oaxaca*, 198; CMMG, vol. 52, Informe of Antonio Herrera, July 1, 1866.

204. *Archivo del general Porfirio Díaz*, 2:162–68.

205. Santibáñez, *Reseña histórica*, 2:203.

206. Hamnett, "Liberales y conservadores," 205–6.

207. Charnay, *Ciudades y ruinas*, 135–36.

208. Mcnamara, *Sons of the Sierra*, 56–66; Chassen-López, *From Liberal to Revolutionary*, 315–48, 394.

209. Guardino, *Peasants*, 147–77; Ducey, *A Nation*, 142–70; ibid., "Indian Communities"; Tutino, *From Insurrection*, 242–58; Reina, "The Sierra Gorda."

210. Mallon, *Peasant and Nation*, 23–62, 137–75; LaFrance and Thomson, *Patriotism, Politics*, 55–126; Hart, *Bitter Harvest*, 77–118; Ruiz, *Historia de la guerra*, 301–78.

211. A similar pragmatic conflation of elite and popular anticlericalism was also occurring in areas of Europe (Mcmillan, "'Priest hits girl,'" 90).

212. Masferrer Kan, "Los factores étnicos"; ibid., "Los totonacos"; Flores, *La revolución*, 37–38.

213. Rugeley, *Of Wonders*, 169–202; Morrison, "José Canuto Vela," 180; Rugeley, "From Santa Iglesia."

214. Powell, "Priests and Peasants," 296–313; ibid., "Los liberales," 653–67.

215. Thomson, "La contrarreforma," 241–42.

216. Cypher, "Reconstituting Community," 145; Lara Cisneros, "Aculturación religiosa." In contrast, the Sierra Gorda's conservative caudillo, Tomás Mejía, celebrated the authorized devotion to the Virgen del Pueblito (Hamnett, "The Formation," 124–27).

217. Guarisco, "Indios, cultura"; The point is also made with regards to the Huasteca by Ducey, *A Nation*, 100–101.

218. Hu-Dehart, *Yaqui Resistance*, 59–71.

219. Tutino, *From Insurrection*, 215–41.

220. Lira, *Comunidades indígenas*, 90–111.

221. Chowning, *Wealth and Power*, 87–191.

222. Connaughton, "1856–1857"; Hamnett, "Mexican Conservatives," 191–92; Butler, *Popular Piety*, 30–32; Hamnett, "El partido conservador," 214; Ruiz, *Historia de la guerra*, 277–78; Thomson, "La contrarreforma," 248–51; Buve, "Pueblos indígenas," 67.

223. Meyer, *Esperando a Lozada*, 50–51, 158; Brittsan, "In Faith or Fear," 154.

224. Butler, *Popular Piety*, 25–26.

225. Ibid., 32.

226. Torre Villar, *Diario*, 124–25; Mallon, *Peasant and Nation*, 335.

227. Hamnett, "The Formation," 127–36; Reed Torres, *El general*, 6, 23–24.

228. Meyer, *Esperando a Lozada*, 41.

229. Ibid., *La tierra*, 151; ibid., *Esperando a Lozada*, 73.

230. Sinkin, *The Mexican Reform*, 37–39; Brading, "Creole Nationalism," 185.

231. Collier, *Chile*, 20; Mallon, "Entre utopia."

232. Needell, *The Party of Order*, 30–116; for Colombia, see Sanders, *Contentious Republicans*, 70–71.

233. Lynch, *Argentine Caudillo*, 44–52; Henderson, *Gabriel García Moreno*, 79–83, 117–18; Woodward, *Rafael Carrera*, 57–61, 127–47.

234. Mendez G., *The Plebian Republic*, 145–46.

235. Ibid., 91–94; Sanders, *Contentious Republicans*, 154–55; Sullivan-González, *Piety, Power*.

236. Mendez, *The Plebian Republic*, 19, 23, 74.

237. Tackett, *Religion, Revolution*, 233.

238. Gibson, *A Social History*, 136–45.

239. Anderson, "Piety and Politics," 692; Blessing, *Staat und Kirche*.

240. Callahan, *Church, Politics*, 209–47.

241. Anderson, "The Kulturkampf," 109.

CHAPTER 4

1. Bonilla Duran, *Un municipio*, 56; Archivo Parroquial de San Simón Zahuatlán, Documentos Inéditos, Feliciano Ramírez, March 3, 1879.

2. Hamnett, "Liberalism Divided."

3. Schmitt, "The Evolution"; ibid., "Catholic Adjustment"; Septién Torres, *La educación privada*, 53–84.

4. Tutino, *From Insurrection*, 277–325.

5. Hale, *The Transformation*.

6. Knight, *The Mexican Revolution*, 1:78–170.

7. Falcón, "Poderes y razones"; ibid., "Force and the Search"; Camarena, "El jefe político"; Delgado Aguilar, *Jefaturas políticas*; Perry, *Juárez y Díaz*, 290; Carmagnani, "El federalismo."

8. The best overviews are Knight, *The Mexican Revolution*, 1:78–170; Katz, *The Life and Times of Pancho Villa*, 11–56; Coatsworth, *Growth against Development*; Hart, *Empire and Revolution*, 71–268.

9. For a good introduction, see González y González, *Pueblo en vilo*; Benjamin and MacNellie, eds., *Other Mexicos*; Brading, "Review."

10. Thomson, "Bulwarks of Patriotic Liberalism"; ibid., "Popular Aspects"; Mcnamara, *Sons of the Sierra*, 93–121.

11. Knight, *The Mexican Revolution*, 1:309.

12. Miller, *Landlords and Haciendas*, 143.

13. Knight, "El liberalismo," 181; Menegus, "La venta," 88.

14. González y González, *Pueblo en vilo*, 89–101; Schryer, *The Rancheros of Pisaflores*, 34–55; Jacobs, *Ranchero Revolt*, 41–59; Barragán López, ed., *Rancheros y sociedades*; García Uguarte, *Hacendados y rancheros*, 201–22; Barragán López, *Más allá*; Baisnée, *De vacas y rancheros*, 15–20; Brading, *Haciendas and Ranchos*, 178–201.

15. Hoffman, *Tierras y territorio*, 56; Chassen-López, *From Liberal to Revolutionary*, 119.

16. Butler, "Religious Developments"; Staples, *El estado*, 15–55.

17. O'Doherty, "El ascenso"; Vera Soto, *La formación*, 89–198; Bautista García, "Hacia la romanización."

18. Ceballos Ramírez, ed., *Catolicismo Social*; Ceballos Ramírez and Garza Rangel, eds., *Catolicismo Social*; Ceballos Ramírez, *El Catolicismo Social*; Overmyer-Velazquez, *Visions of the Emerald City*, 70–97; Díaz Patino, "Catolicismo Social"; Salmeron Sangines, "Catolicismo Social"; Weiner, "Trinidad Sánchez Santos."

19. Berry, *The Reform*, 110–27; Falcone, "Federal-State Relations," 104–24.

20. AGPEO, Gobierno de los Distritos, Siglo XIX, Huajuapan, legajo 20, exp. 29, Ignacio Vázquez to Rafael González, February 15, 1868.

21. For a extremely favorable local history of José Segura y Guzmán, see Ortiz Castro, *Apuntes históricos*, 49–59, 109–12.

22. AHSDN, Cancelados, X, III/2–753, Ignacio Vázquez; AGNEO, Huajuapan, María Acevedo, January 18, 1868.

23. AGPEO, Memorias, José Segura y Guzmán, September 2, 1870.

24. CMMG, vol. 40, Informe of Ignacio Vázquez, September 2, 1868; ibid., Informe of Head of Militia, August 3, 1875; APHL, Negativas, Ignacio Vázquez to Vicar General, May 3, 1869.

25. Juárez, *Documentos, discursos*, 6:67.

26. AHSDN, Cancelados, X, III/2–753, Ignacio Vázquez; AGPEO, Gobierno de los Distritos, Siglo XIX, Huajuapan, legajo 1, exp. 60, José María Ramírez, February 1, 1876.

27. AHSDN, Cancelados, X, III/2–753, Ignacio Vázquez.

28. Case, "El resurgimiento"; Beals, *Porfirio Díaz*, 78–93; Soto Correa, *Movimientos campesinos*, 282–96, 355; Ochoa Serrano, "Religioneros en Michoacán."

29. AHSDN, Cancelados, X, III/2–753, Ignacio Vázquez.

30. Ramírez Rancano, *El patriarca Pérez*, 30–31; AGPEO, Gobierno de los Distritos, Siglo XIX, Huajuapan, legajo 16, exp. 46, J. Ramírez, May 13, 1885.

31. Archivo de Porfirio Díaz (APD), L11 11215, December 12, 1885; ibid., L6 1953, September 14, 1881; *Diario de los debates*, 1:13; Camp, *Mexican political biographies*, 290.

32. APD, L6 1953, Ignacio Vázquez to Porfirio Diáz, September 14, 1881; ibid., L11 5705, Ignacio Vázquez to Porfirio Diáz, June 7, 1886.

33. AMHL, Presidencia, Acta de Elección, January 1, 1881; ibid., January 5, 1883; ibid., January 1, 1886; ibid., Correspondencia, J. Ramírez to Luis Niño de Rivera, July 6, 1886.

34. Beezley, *Judas at the Jockey Club*; ibid., "New Celebrations"; Pérez-Rayon "The Capital Commemorates"; Beezley, *Mexican National Identity*; Morgan, "Proletarians, Políticos"; Vaughan, "The Construction."

35. Thomson, "Bulwarks of Patriotic Liberalism"; ibid., "Popular Aspects"; ibid., "The Ceremonial."

36. AGPEO, Memorias, José Segura y Guzmán, September 2, 1870.

37. AMHL, Correspondencia, Casimiro Ramírez to J. Ramírez, October 4, 1889.

38. APSHL, box 77, vol. 7, Edictos, 1789–1901.

39. AMHL, Presidencia, Celebraciones, Act of July 21, 1886.

40. APSHL, box 70, vol. 8, Misas, 1772–1914.

41. AGPEO, Gobierno de los Distritos, Siglo XIX, Huajuapan, legajo 51, exp. 3, Informe of Juan de Dios Flores y León, April 16, 1887; ibid., legajo 51, exp. 5, Informe of Aurelio García, November 18, 1894; ibid., legajo 51, exp. 12, Informe of Luis Niño de Rivera, April 10, 1894; ibid., legajo 51, exp. 16, Informe of Luis Niño de Rivera, October 10, 1895.

42. Mendoza Guerrero, *Ciudad de Huajuapan*, 43; APD, L14 13642, J. Ramírez to Porfirio Díaz, December 4, 1889.

43. AMHL, Presidencia, José Gómez to Ignacio Vázquez, March 17, 1880; *Revista Huajuapan*, June 1975; APD, L12 03927, José Gómez to Porfirio Díaz, November 6, 1880; ibid., L9 12842 Francisco Meixueiro to Porfirio Díaz, July 6, 1880.

44. APD, L14 848, Ignacio Vázquez to Porfirio Díaz, January 2, 1889.

45. Ibid., L14 13645, Governor Zertuche to J. Ramírez, July 12, 1889.

46. Ibid., L14 13642, J. Ramírez to Porfirio Díaz, December 4, 1889.

47. Ibid., L14 848, Porfirio Díaz to J. Ramírez, January 17, 1890.

48. AGPEO, Gobierno de los Distritos, Siglo XIX, Huajuapan, legajo 23, exp. 31, Informe of J. Segura, March 7, 1862.

49. Ibid., legajo 17, exp. 32, Alcaldes de Huajuapan, December 26, 1895.

50. AMHL, Tierras, Informe of Aurelio Sánchez, October 1, 1888.

51. Menéndez Rodríguez, "The Resurgence"; Menéndez Rodríguez, *Iglesia y poder*, 107.

52. Fallaw, "An Uncivil Society"; García Uguarte, "Proyecto pastoral"; Romero de Solís, *El aguijón*, 53–54.

53. Chassen-López, *From Liberal to Revolutionary*, 77–186; Esparza, "Los proyectos," 288–311.

54. Ducey, "Liberal Theory," 75.

55. Steffen Riedemann, *Los comerciantes*, 23–45; Menegus Bornemann, *La Mixteca Baja*, 148, 150–56.

56. Data on land transactions collected in the AMHL, AJO, AGNEO, and AGPEO.

57. Esparza, "Los proyectos," 282.

58. *Codigo civil del estado de Oaxaca*, 228–29.

59. Hale, *Mexican Liberalism*, 99.

60. AGPEO, Ajudicaciones, legajo 12, exp. 7, Men of Cuyotepeji to Governor of State, July 5, 1882.

61. AJO, Huajuapan, Civil, legajo 70, Chilixtlahuaca, June 3, 1890.

62. Ibid., legajo 90, Ricarda Martínez, January 18, 1902.

63. Kouri, *A Pueblo Divided*; Lauria-Santiago, *An Agrarian Republic*, 163–94.

64. AJO, Civil, Huajuapan, legajo 64, Tomás Osio and Men of Mariscala, April 12, 1883; ibid., legajo 66, Tomás Osio and Men of Mariscala, June 5, 1885; AMHL, Tierras, Adolfo Arellano to Jefe Político, August 2, 1897.

65. AMHL, Tierras, Pedro Zuniga to Jefe Político, October 29, 1880; AGPEO, Gobierno de los Distritos, Siglo XIX, Huajuapan, legajo 20, exp. 41, Informe of Luis Niño de Rivera, September 26, 1891.

66. AGNEO, Huajuapan, Sociedad Agrícola de Yolotepec, February 4, 1878; *Censo de 1900*.

67. *Censo de 1900*.

68. AGNEO, Huajuapan, Sociedad Agrícola de Chilixtlahuaca, May 13, 1875.

69. AJO, Huajuapan, Civil, legajo 98, Sociedad Agrícola de Miltepec, August 4, 1902; AGPEO, Ajudicaciones, legajo 12, exp. 5, Sociedad Agrícola de Ayuquila, December 15, 1891.

70. AJO, Huajuapan, Civil, legajo 98, Sociedad Agrícola de Miltepec, August 4, 1902; AGNEO, Huajuapan, Sociedad Agrícola de Ayuquila, September 20, 1889; AGN, Archivo de Buscas, Cuyotepeji, October 31, 1895; AJO, Huajuapan, Civil, legajo 100, Sociedad Agrícola de Chilixtlahuaca, September 22, 1903.

71. AJO, Huajuapan, Civil, legajo 70, Sociedad Agrícola de Silacayoapilla, October 1, 1890.

72. Ibid., legajo 105, Sociedad Agrícola de Mixquixtlahuaca, October 8, 1905.

73. AGN, Archivo de Buscas, Cuyotepeji, October 31, 1895.

74. AJO, Huajuapan, Civil, legajo 100, Sociedad Agrícola de Chilixtlahuaca, September 22, 1903.

75. AGNEO, Huajuapan, Sociedad Agrícola de Ayuquila, September 20, 1889.

76. AGN, Archivo de Buscas, Cuyotepeji, October 31, 1895.

77. AJO, Huajuapan, Civil, legajo 100, Sociedad Agrícola de Chilixtlahuaca, September 22, 1903.

78. Peralta Hernández, *Cuyotepeji*, 43.

79. González y González, *Pueblo en vilo*, 54–67; Jacobs, *Ranchero Revolt*, 45–48; Purnell, *Popular Movements*, 23–31; Schryer, *Rancheros of Pisaflores*, 78–89.

80. AJO, Huajuapan, Civil, legajo 54, Sociedad Agrícola de Cuyotepeji, June 12, 1875; ibid., legajo 96, Sociedad Agrícola de Amatitlán, June 4, 1901.

81. Escobar Ohmstede and Schryer, "Las sociedades agrarias"; Escobar Ohmstede, "La estructura agraria"; ibid., "Los condueñazgos indigenas"; Kouri, *A Pueblo Divided*, 157–86.

82. Mendoza García, "El ganado comunal," 767.

83. Chance and Taylor, "Cofradías and Cargos"; Greenberg, *Santiago's Sword*, 76–92; Traffano, *Indios*, 178–96.

84. See Mendoza García, "Las cofradías," on the neighboring district of Coixtlahuaca for a similar process occurring in Suchixtlahuaca.

85. Beristain Romero, "*Yosocuiya*," 407.

86. AJO, Huajuapan, Civil, legajo 73, Sociedad Agrícola de Tonalá, October 3, 1892.

87. Ibid., legajo 86, Marciano Eulogia García, March 3, 1899.

88. APM, Cofradía de Nuestra Señora del Rosario, 1787–1934.

89. Ibid., Cofradía de Santiago Apostol, 1876–1923.

90. APSDT, box 50, vol. 11, Cofradía del Santisimo Sacramento, 1702–1940.

91. AGPEO, Gobierno de los Distritos, Siglo XIX, Huajuapan, legajo 10, exp. 48, Sociedad Agrícola de Tonalá, November 8, 1896.

92. APTeq, Libro de Gobierno 1.

93. APM, Libro de Gobierno 1.

94. Secretaría de Fomento, *Boletín de agricultura*, 128.

95. Peralta Hernández, *Cuyotepeji*, 65.

96. Hart, *Bitter Harvest*, 145–92.

97. AJO, Huajuapan, Criminal, legajo 56, José Gomez, September 5, 1860; AGPEO, Memorias, *Memoria, 1879*.

98. AJO, Huajuapan, Civil, legajo 98, José Gomez and Pueblo of Atoyac, December 26, 1902; ibid., legajo 54, José Gomez and Pueblo of Atoyac, December 13, 1875.

99. Ibid., legajo 63, Will of José Gómez Maza, July 25, 1882; AGPEO, Memorias, *Memoria del gobierno del estado de Oaxaca 1890*; Esteva, *Nociones elementales*, 151.

100. Martínez Gracida, *Cuadros sinópticos*, 27–44.

101. AMHL, Presidencia, Informe of Emigdio Carvajal, October 5, 1872.

102. Chassen-López, *From Liberal to Revolutionary*, 166–70; Gómez Carpinteiro, *Gente de azúcar*, 93–134.

103. Dehouve, "Las haciendas volantes," 94–98; Valdes, *Ethnicity, class*, 58.

104. Paredes Colín, *El distrito de Tehuacán*, 178–80.

105. AJO, Huajuapan, Civil, legajo 62, Sociedad Agrícola de Suchitepec, January 1, 1881.

106. AGNEO, Huajuapan, Sociedad Agrícola de Teopan, October 30, 1880.

107. Ibid., Sociedad Agrícola de Cuyotepeji, October 12, 1888.

108. AGPEO, Gobierno de los Distritos, Siglo XIX, Huajuapan, legajo 81, exp. 30, Jefe Político to Governor, January 7, 1901.

109. For example, AJO, Huajuapan, Civil, legajo 65, Benito Gómez, May 7, 1884; ibid., legajo 66, José Martínez, December 8, 1885.

110. AGPEO, Memorias, *Memoria del gobierno de Oaxaca, 1889*; *Memoria administrativa presentada por el C. General Martin González*.

111. AJO, Huajuapan, Civil, legajo 54, José Gómez, December 13, 1875.

112. Church of Jesus Christ of Latter-day Saints, Tequixtepec, Bautismos, 1889–1968, Vault INTL, film 674968.

113. Peralta Hernández, *Cuyotepeji*, 56; AGPEO, Ajudicaciones, legajo 12, exp. 6, Men of Cuyopeji, October 19, 1869; AGN, Archivo de Buscas, Cuyotepeji, October 31, 1895.

114. Gruzinski, "Indian Confraternities," 210.

115. Escobar Ohmstede, *Desastres agrícolas*, 154–58.

116. AGPEO, Gobierno de los Distritos, Siglo XIX, Huajuapan, legajo 57, exp. 1, Varios Pueblos, August–September 1895.

117. AJO, Huajuapan, Civil, legajo 85, Men of Cacaloxtepec, February 18, 1899.

118. Turner, *Barbarous Mexico*, 54–67; Chassen-López, *From Liberal to Revolutionary*, 149–64.

119. Escobar Ohmstede and Schryer, "Las sociedades agrarias"; Escobar Ohmstede, "La estructura agrarian"; ibid., "Los condueñazgos indigenas"; Kouri, *A Pueblo Divided*; Chevalier and Buckles, *A Land without Gods*, 24–27; Jacklein, *Un pueblo popoluca*, 187–88.

120. Mendoza García, "Las cofradías"; ibid., "Poder político"; Camacho Pichardo, "Las sociedades agrícolas."

121. Miller, *Landlords and Haciendas*, 178; Brading, *Haciendas and Ranchos*, 190; García Ugarte, "Estabilidad de Querétaro," 321.

122. Guerra, *Le mexique*, 1:199–206; Alcala Alvarado, "La iglesia"; Gutiérrez Casillas, *Historia de la iglesia*, 326–57; Meyer, *La Cristiada*, 2:43–53.

123. Butler, "Religious Developments."

124. Ibid.; Fallaw, "An Uncivil Society"; Wright-Rios, *Revolutions*, 82–90; Brading, *Mexican Phoenix*, 289–90.

125. Juárez, *Reclaiming Church Wealth*.

126. Traffano, *Indios*, 99–108; Wright-Rios, *Revolutions*, 58.

127. Fallaw, "An Uncivil Society."

128. APM, Cofradía de Nuestra Señora del Rosario, 1787–1934; ibid., Cofradía del Señor de las Llagas, 1792–1967; APSDT, box 50, vol. 11, Cofradía del Santisimo Sacramento, 1702–1940; Church of Jesus Christ of Latter-day Saints, Tequixtepec, Cofradías, 1802–1902, Vault INTL, film 676939.

129. Vera Soto, *La formación*, 90–92; APSMAC, Libro de Gobierno, vol. 1; *Album conmemorativo que la junta organizadora*; Cantu Corro, *In memoriam*; *El Tiempo*, July 20, 1903.

130. Reyes Aguilar, *Mi madre*, 210–14.

131. Vera Soto, *La formación*, 89; *La Voz de Mexico*, December 22, 1897; *Rafaga*, May 1952.

132. *Historia de Tonalá, Oaxaca*, 97–98.

133. Martínez Gracida, "El estado," 58.

134. Purnell, *Popular Movements*, 95.

135. AGPEO, Gobierno de los Distritos, Siglo XIX, Huajuapan, legajo 23, exp. 46, Informe of Luis Niño de Rivera, 1895.

136. Ibid., legajo 23, exp. 40, Informe of Luis Niño de Rivera, July 20, 1897.

137. *Censo de 1900*; González Ramírez, *La iglesia mexicana*, 62.

138. Schmitt, "Catholic Adjustment"; ibid., "The Evolution"; Septién Torres, *La educación privada*, 53–84.

139. Archivo Parroquial de San Juan Bautista, Acatlán de Osorio (APSJBAO), box 143, vol. 1, Sociedad Católica, 1884–1927.

140. Velasco, *Geografía y estadística*, 9; Archivo Parroquial Santa María de la Natividad, Tamazulapan (APSMNT), box 46, vol. 1, Libro de Gobierno 1.

141. AMHL, Estadística, Informe of Feliciano A Osorio, July 24, 1897.

142. APTeq, Libro de Gobierno 1.

143. AGPEO, Memorias, *Memoria del gobierno del estado de Oaxaca, 1878*; ibid., *Memoria del gobierno del estado de Oaxaca, 1885*.

144. *Censo de 1900*.

145. APSJBAO, box 137, vol. 1, San Vicente de Paul. For the history of the organization in Mexico, see Arrom, "Mexican Laywomen."

146. Murillo, "The Politics," 180–234.

147. Cantu Corro, *In Memoriam*; Herrera Sánchez, "Bodas de oro."

148. *Informe de las actividades*, 4.

149. APSDT, box 56, vol. 2, Libro de Gobierno 1, Memoria of Jesus Zamora, January 1, 1898.
150. *El Imparcial*, May 21, 1994.
151. For example, Welter, "The Feminization"; Ford, *Divided Houses*.
152. Wright-Rios, "Visions of Women."
153. APSJBAO, box 142, vol. 7, Asociaciones, Asociación de la Sagrada Corazón de Maria.
154. APSDT, box 53, vol. 4, Cofradías, Asociación Guadalupana.
155. Wright-Rios, *Revolutions*, 242–70.
156. APSJBAO, box 137, vol. 1, San Vicente de Paul; Church of Jesus Christ of Latter-day Saints, Tequixtepec, Cofradías, 1738–1893, Vault INTL, film 676938, Suchitepec, Cofradía del Patron.
157. APSDT, box 142, vol. 7, Cofradías, Asociación Guadalupana.
158. Arenas, *Las cruces*.
159. *Historia de Tonalá, Oaxaca*, 60.
160. Martínez Gracida, *Cuadros sinópticos*, 39; Esteva, *Nociones elementales*, 161; Gay, *Historia de Oaxaca*, 1:94.
161. Church of Jesus Christ of Latter-day Saints, Tequixtepec, Cofradías; APSDT, box 56, vol. 2, Libro de Gobierno 1, Memoria of Jesus Zamora, January 1, 1898.
162. Rivera S., *Novenario a la Virgen*.
163. APSDT, box 142, vol. 7, Cofradías, Asociación Guadalupana.
164. APTN, Cofradía de la Señora de las Nieves, 1902–1924.
165. González Huerta, *El Tupa*, 15.
166. Archivo del Municipio de Tequixtepec (AMT), Presidencia, Tranquilino Pacheco to Luis Nino, August 19, 1919.
167. Tackett, *Religion, Revolution, and Regional Culture*, 229–33.
168. APM, Libro de Gobierno 1, Santa Visita, February 18, 1890; APT, Libro de Gobierno, Santa Visita, February 9, 1891.
169. Church of Jesus Christ of Latter-day Saints, Tequixtepec, Bautismos de Hijos Naturales, 1889–1968, Vault INTL, film 674968; Fallaw, "An Uncivil Society."
170. APSJBAO, box 145, vol. 5, Cofradía Nuestra Señora del Rosario, Miguel Paneda, October 23, 1883.
171. APTeq, Libro de Gobierno 1, Santa Visita, January 5, 1891.
172. APSHL, box 79, vol. 1, Libro de Gobierno 1, Santa Visita, May 18, 1896.
173. *Album conmemorativo que la junta organizadora*; *El País*, July 8, 1903; Archivo de la Diócesis de Huajuapan de León (ADHL), Circulares, circular 1; ADHL, Bula de la Diócesis; *Rafaga*, August 1952; ibid., June 1952.
174. Butler, "Religious Developments."
175. González Ramírez, *La iglesia mexicana*, 40–41.
176. *Primera carta pastoral*.
177. *Huajuapan*, May 1978; Cantu Corro, *In memoriam*.
178. My efforts to find these documents were unfortunately hampered by the death of the pope and the closure of the Vatican archives in 2005.
179. *Instalación y reglamento*.

180. *Rafaga*, July 1952.
181. *Discurso leido por el Sr. Canonigo D. Guillermo López García*; Smith and Van Oosterhout, "The Limits."
182. *Primer sinodo diocesano de Huajuapam.*
183. *Rafaga*, July 1952.
184. *Historia de Tonalá, Oaxaca*, 45–46.
185. Archivo Parroquial de Ayuquila (APA), Libro de Gobierno 1; APTeq, Libro de Gobierno 1.
186. González Ramírez, *La iglesia mexicana*, 93.
187. ADHL, circular 13, December 3, 1910.
188. APTN, Libro de Gobierno, Santa Visita, May 24, 1910; Archivo Parroquial de Mariscala, Libro de Gobierno 1; APC, Libro de Gobierno 1.
189. APSMAC, box 52, vol. 1, Libro de Gobierno 1.
190. Ibid.
191. Cantu Córro, *In memoriam*, 40.
192. *Quinta carta pastoral*, 5. This is typical of Porfirian Catholic reactions to positivist lay education (Septién Torres, "La unión nacional").
193. Vera Soto, *La formación*, 154.
194. APTeq, Libro de Gobierno 1.
195. APSMAC, box 52, vol. 1, Libro de Gobierno 1.
196. APTeq, Libro de Gobierno 1.
197. *Quinta carta pastoral.*
198. APTeq, Libro de Gobierno 1.
199. *Reglamento de instrucción.*
200. Chávez, *El amigo católico.*
201. Reyes, *Nociones elementales.*
202. *Primer sinodo diocesano de Huajuapam.*
203. APTeq, Libro de Gobierno 1.
204. Anderson, "The Divisions," 32.
205. APSMAC, box 52, vol. 1, Libro de Gobierno 1.
206. Ibid.
207. Arrom, "Las Señoras de la Caridad."
208. *Apuntes biográficos of Rafael Amador*; Cantu Corro, *In memoriam.*
209. ADHL, Circulares, circular 12, September 6, 1906.
210. APTN, Cofradías de la Señora de las Nieves, 1903–1924.
211. APA, Libro de Gobierno 1; Trexler, *Reliving Golgotha*, 9–23.
212. APSMAC, box 52, vol. 1, Libro de Gobierno 1.
213. APM, Libro de Gobierno 1.
214. Esparza, *Gillow*, 40–57.
215. APA, Libro de Gobierno 1.
216. APTeq, Libro de Gobierno 1.
217. González y González, *Historia moderna*, 363–69; ibid., "Un cura de pueblo"; Butler, "Religious Developments."

218. Wright-Rios, *Revolutions*, 141–63; Vanderwood, *The Power of God*; Kouri, *A Pueblo Divided*, 206–10.

219. Ceballos Ramírez, *El Catolicismo Social*, 130–35; Wright-Rios, *Revolutions*, 65–66.

220. *Sexta carta pastoral*; Ripalda, *Catecismo*; *Catecismo en el idioma mixteco*; Smith and Van Oosterhout, "The Limits"; Thomson, "La contrarreforma," 263; Schneider, *Cristos, Santos*, 45–46.

221. García Uguarte, "Proyecto pastoral," 67

222. Nájera Espinoza, *La Virgen de Talpa*, 85–87.

223. Clark and Kaiser, eds., *Culture Wars*.

224. The literature on these new forms of organization is immense. For masons, see Legrand, "Living in Macondo," 346; Bastian, "Protestants, Freemasons." For sports clubs, see Goldblatt, *The Ball Is Round*, 40–134; Beezley, *Judas at the Jockey Club*, 13–66; Chassen-López, *From Liberal to Revolutionary*, 254–56; González Navarro, "The Hours of Leisure," 123–28.

225. Blasco, *Paradojas de la ortodoxia*; Cueva Merino, "Clericalismo," 49.

226. Ford, *Creating the Nation*; Cueva, "Inventing Catholic Identities"; ibid., "The Assault"; Londoño-Vega, *Religion, Culture*; Anderson, "The Divisions"; Valenzuela and Maza Valenzuela, "The Politics."

227. Londoño-Vega, *Religion, Culture*, 183.

CHAPTER 5

1. AMT, Presidencia, Tranquilino Pacheco to Luis Niño Pacheco, August 19, 1919.

2. The best introductions to this narrative of revolutionary reform are Knight, *The Mexican Revolution*; ibid., "Cardenismo"; ibid., "Popular Culture."

3. Womack, *Zapata*; Buve, *El movimiento revoluciónario*; Fowler-Salamini, *Agrarian Radicalism*; Dwyer, *The Agrarian Dispute*, 44–76, 103–37.

4. The most important works are Meyer, *La Cristiada*; Butler, *Popular Piety*.

5. Palacios, "Postrevolutionary Intellectuals"; Becker, "Black and White."

6. Butler, "Introduction," 2; Bantjes, "Religion," 309.

7. Chassen-López, *From Liberal to Revolutionary*, 495–538; Martínez Vásquez, ed., *La revolución*; Garner, *La revolución*.

8. González y González, "La Revolución Mexicana."

9. Reyes Aguilar, *Mi madre*, 33–47.

10. AGPEO, Revolución, legajo 23, exp. 12, Informe of Jefe Político, January 2, 1911.

11. *Huajuapan*, May 5, 1975.

12. Reyes Aguilar, *Mi madre*, 35.

13. LaFrance, *Revolution*, 34–38; Womack, *Zapata*, 118–19.

14. AGPEO, Revolución, legajo 2, exp. 23, Informe, March 5, 1912; Rojas, *Efemerides oaxaqueñas 1912*, 47.

15. *El Universal*, May 11, 1958; Magaña, *Emiliano Zapata*, 4:159–60.

16. Ruiz Cervantes, "Movimientos zapatistas."

17. Aguilar Reyes, *Mi madre*, 174, 321, 331–32.

18. Ibid., 174, 338–51; Villagómez, *Memorias*, 15; Ceballos Soto, *Historia*, 143–45.

19. González Escamilla, *Memoria de Acatlán*, 12–23; AGN, Archivo de Emiliano Zapata, Gabino Lozano Sánchez to Emiliano Zapata, June 26, 1915.

20. AGN, Archivo de Emiliano Zapata, Miguel Salas to Emiliano Zapata, August 14, 1916.

21. Ibid., Encarnación Dìaz to Angel Barrios, March 3, 1916.

22. Ibid., Miguel Salas to Emiliano Zapata, November 8, 1914.

23. Brunk, "The Sad Situation."

24. AGN, Archivo de Emiliano Zapata, Municipal President of Zapotitlán Lagunas to Emiliano Zapata, November 20, 1915.

25. Ibid., Feliciano López to Emiliano Zapata, November 16, 1915.

26. Ibid., Nicolas Vidal to Emiliano Zapata, January 23, 1915.

27. Ibid., Brigido García to Emiliano Zapata, June 14, 1915.

28. APTeq, Libro de Gobierno 1; Archivo Particular de Luis Niño Pacheco, Luis Niño Pacheco, "Incendio."

29. Ceballos Soto, *Historia*, 156–59.

30. AGN, Archivo de Emiliano Zapata, Higenio Aguilar to Emiliano Zapata, November 8, 1914; *El Imparcial*, January 24, 1963; *Huajuapan*, October 1, 1976.

31. APA, Libro de Gobierno 1.

32. Reyes Aguilar, *Mi madre*, 92

33. APTeq, Libro de Gobierno 1.

34. Ceballos Soto, *Historia*, 145–48.

35. Knight, *The Mexican Revolution*, 2:437.

36. AMT, Municipal President to Victoriano Huerta, May 8, 1913.

37. Ceballos Soto, *Historia*, 147–48; González Escamilla, *Memoria de Acatlán*, 41.

38. Knight, *The Mexican Revolution*, 2:438.

39. Ceballos Soto, *Historia*, 152–56; Villagómez, *Memorias*, 67; Martínez Soriano, *Monografía de Cosolotepec*, 170–72.

40. Butler, "El Sagrado Corazón."

41. ADHL, circular 12, March 4, 1912; APSMAC, box 59, vol. 1, 1909–1992, Libro de Gobierno 1.

42. Butler, "Introduction," 12.

43. Katz, *The Life and Times*, 447, 532; Knight, *The Mexican Revolution*, 2:499–505; ibid., "The Mentality," 31–32.

44. Wright-Rios, *Revolutions*, 164–205; Brewster and Brewster, "Ethereal Allies"; Bastian, "Protestants, Freemasons"; Garza Quiros, *El Niño Fidencio*; Smith, "El Señor del Perdon."

45. APTeq, Libro de Gobierno 1.

46. AMT, Presidencia, Tranquilino Pacheco to Luis Niño Pacheco, August 19, 1919.

47. Archivo Particular de Luis Niño Pacheco, Luis Niño Pacheco, "Incendio"; APTeq, Libro de Gobierno 1.

48. ADHL, circular 23, September 3, 1911; APM, Libro de Gobierno 1; APA, Libro de Gobierno 1; APTeq, Libro de Gobierno 1.

49. Jonas, *France*, 54–90.

50. APSDT, box 56, vol. 1, Libro de Gobierno 1; APM, Libro de Gobierno 1; APTeq, Libro de Gobierno 1; APSMAC, Libro de Gobierno 1; APTN, Libro de Gobierno 1.

51. Miller, *Beads and Prayers*, 177–80.

52. APM, Libro de Gobierno 1; APA, Libro de Gobierno 1.

53. ADHL, circular 34, July 4, 1913; APTN, Libro de Gobierno 1; ibid., Cofradía de la Señora de las Nieves.

54. APA, Libro de Gobierno 1.

55. Ibid.

56. APM, Libro de Gobierno 1.

57. Wright-Rios, *Revolutions*, 164–206.

58. Butler, "Introduction," 11–12; Meyer, *La Cristiada*, 3:287–88; Rodríguez, ed., *José Guadalupe Posada*, 60; Smith, "El Señor del Perdon"; Smith and Van Oosterhoot, "The Limits," 59.

59. APTN, Libro de Gobierno 1.

60. APSDT, box 56, vol. 1, 1921–1942, Libro de Gobierno 1.

61. APSAP, box 72, vol. 1, 1904–1990, Libro de Gobierno 1.

62. APTeq, Libro de Gobierno 1.

63. Ibid.

64. Beristain Romero, "*Yosocuiya*," 138–39.

65. APTeq, Libro de Gobierno 1; Gregorio Eduardo Rivera, interview with author, March 2008.

66. APTeq, Libro de Gobierno 1.

67. Cantu Corro, *Patria y raza*. The approach echoed the clerical Slavophilism George Freeze has described emerging among priests in Russia during preceding century (Freeze, *The Parish Clergy*, 35).

68. APA, Libro de Gobierno 1.

69. Butler, "El Sagrado Corazón."

70. APTeq, Libro de Gobierno 1.

71. González Huerta, *El Tupa*.

72. ADHL, circular 43, June 2, 1917.

73. APSAP, box 72, vol. 1, 1904–1990, Libro de Gobierno 1.

74. APTN, Libro de Gobierno 1.

75. Butler, *Popular Piety*, 52.

76. Kouri, "Interpreting the Expropriation."

77. Margolies, *Princes of the Earth*, 37–54; Smith, *Pistoleros*, 216–25; Butler, *Popular Piety*, 80–105.

78. Dwyer, *The Agrarian Dispute*, 44–76, 103–37; Bantjes, *As if Jesus*, 123–516; Knight, "Mexico," 35–36; Smith, *Pistoleros*, 210–16; Fallaw, *Cárdenas Compromised*, 80–96; Lewis, *The Ambivalent Revolution*, 157–80; Ashby, *Organized Labor*, 103–4.

79. Butler, *Popular Piety*, 179–212; Guerra Manzo, "El fuego sagrado"; González Navarro, *Cristeros y agraristas*, 4; Sosa Elízaga, *Los códigos ocultos*, 99–103; Meyer, "La Segunda Cristiada."

80. Schryer, *Ethnicity and Class*, 67–134; Lomnitz-Adler, *Exits from the Labyrinth*, 188–204.

81. Steffen Riedemann, *Los comerciantes*, 33–56.

82. AGPEO, Gobernación, 1936, List of Properties Greater than 100 Hectares.

83. Archivo del Registro Agrario Nacional (ARAN), Oaxaca, 20/557/1/01, Tlacache de Mina.

84. Ibid., 253, San José La Pradera, Ramon Placencia to CAN, November 28, 1931; ibid., 335, Guadalupe la Huertilla, Informe of Benjamín Patino, May 23, 1929.

85. AGPEO, Asuntos Agrarios, legajo 28, exp. 14, Solicitud of El Higo, Chazumba, August 17, 1931.

86. *Periodico Oficial*, 1920–1940.

87. APSDT, box 56, vol. 1, Libro de Gobierno 1; ARAN, 193, vol. 1, Tonalá, Informe of Ramón Placencia, May 13, 1927; ibid., 193, vol. 1, Enrique Ochoa to Departamento Agrario, November 2, 1939.

88. ARAN, 20/084/1/01, Informe of Castillo Chacón, August 28, 1934; ibid., Gumesindo Tapia to Arturo Calderón, June 25, 1926.

89. APSDT, box 56, vol. 1, Libro de Gobierno 1.

90. AMHL, Presidencia, Cirilio Méndez to Municipal President, April 3, 1937; Martínez Vásquez, *Relatos y vivencias*, 28–29.

91. ARAN, 193, vol. 1, Tonalá, Informe of Ramon Placencia, May 13, 1927.

92. AGPEO, Asuntos Agrarios, legajo 27, exp. 1, Solicitud de Tonalá, April 18, 1923; ibid., Samuel Solano to Governor Vázquez, May 18, 1927; ARAN, 193, vol. 1, Tonalá; AGPEO, Gobernación, Comité Agraria of Tonalá to Departamento Agrario, August 3, 1939; ADHL, Fidencio Rios to Bishop Altamirano, September 4, 1929.

93. AGPEO, Asuntos Agrarios, legajo 29, exp. 4, Sociedad Agrícola de Huajolotitlán, March 3, 1933; ibid., Enrique Robles to Comité Local Agraria, April 1, 1933; ibid., legajo 26, exp. 3, Men of Mariscala to Departamento Agrario, July 1, 1936; ARAN, 210–00T, Mariscala de Juárez, Piquinto Guerrero to Comité Local Agraria, December 2, 1933.

94. González, "Un cura de pueblo," 172; AGPEO, Asuntos Agrarios, legajo 29, exp. 4, Enrique Robles to Comité Local Agraria, April 1, 1933.

95. AGPEO, Asuntos Agrarios, legajo 28, exp. 5, Florentino A. Hernandez, October 2, 1930; ARAN, 23/61, Santiago Huajolotitlán, Ambrosio Montano, April 7, 1926.

96. *Periodico Oficial*, 1930–1943; AGPEO, Asuntos Agrarios, legajo 29, exp. 13, Comité Agrario of Amatitlán, August 29, 1935; ibid., legajo 26, exp. 3, Procurador de Pueblos, November 4, 1937; ARAN, 23/694, San Juan Bautista Suchitepec, Comité Ejidal to Departamento Agrario, November 19, 1936; AGPEO, X, legajo 983, exp. 25, Vecinos of Corral de Piedra to Departamento Agrario, March 4, 1937; ibid., Asuntos Agrarios, legajo 30, exp. 1, Confederación Campesina Mexicana to Governor García Toledo, September 17, 1936; ARAN, 193, tomo 1, Dario Meixueiro to Departamento Agrario, November 22, 1939.

97. ARAN, 193, vol. 1, Tonalá, Informe of Ramon Placencia, May 13, 1927.

98. AGPEO, X, legajo 983, exp. 23 1935, Municipal President of Chazumba to Departamento Agrario, September 7, 1935.

99. Ibid., legajo 983, exp. 25, Vecinos of Corral de Piedra to Departamento Agrario, March 4, 1937.

100. Purnell, *Popular Movements*, 192–93.

101. ADHL, Parish Documents of Mariscala, Narciso Villa to Bishop Altamirano, February 25, 1926.

102. AGPEO, legajo 30, exp. 1, Confederación Campesina Mexicana to Governor García Toledo, September 17, 1936; ibid., Asuntos Agrarios, legajo 27, exp. 2, Carlos Belleza to Departamento Agrario, November 21, 1935; ARAN, 1.335, Guadalupe la Huertilla, Informe of Adan Ramírez López, May 11, 1938.

103. AGPEO, Asuntos Agrarios, legajo 26, exp. 5, Men of Huajolotitlán to Governor Vázquez, April 28, 1926.

104. ARAN, 193, vol. 1; AGPEO, Asuntos Agrarios, legajo 27, exp. 1; AMHL, Presidencia, Vicente Castillo to Municipal President of Huajuapan, November 2, 1926.

105. AGN, Ramo Lázaro Cárdenas, Jose. F. Urube to Departamento Agrario, December 5, 1935.

106. AGPEO, Asuntos Agrarios, legajo 29, exp. 1, Liga Central de Comunidades Agrarias de la República to Governor Constantino Chapital, December 16, 1936; Archivo Histórico de la Secretaría de Educación Pública (AHSEP), C4, Comité Ejidal de Suchitepec to SEP, April 3, 1940.

107. AGPEO, legajo 30, exp. 1, Vicente Ramírez Pacheco to Governor Chapital, May 4, 1938.

108. Ibid., Gobernación, Justicia, Rafael Castro to Departamento Agrario, January 24, 1939.

109. González y González, *Village in Transition*, 181–216.

110. Bantjes, *As if Jesus*, 7.

111. For an overview of anticlericalism in Mexico, see Bantjes, *As if Jesus*, 6–20; Bantjes, "Idolatry and Iconoclasm"; ibid., "The Eighth Sacrament"; Knight, "The Mentality"; Fallaw, "Varieties."

112. Britton, *Educación y radicalismo*, 1:30–45.

113. Zoraida Vázquez de Knauth, "La educación socialista," 413.

114. This disaggregation of state anticlericalism is described extremely well in Knight, "The Mentality"; Fallaw, "An Uncivil Society"; ibid., "Varieties"; Parson, *Mexican Martyrdom*, 134.

115. Kirshner, "Tomás Garrido Canabal"; Martínez Assad, *El laboratorio*, 15–55; Fallaw, "Varieties," 506.

116. Meyer, *El conflito religioso*, 76.

117. AGN, Ramo Dirección General de Gobierno, 2.340 (17) 62, 10566, Governor García Toledo to Secretaría de Gobierno, March 22, 1934.

118. *La Voz del Sur*, February 5, 1932; AGN, Ramo Abelardo Rodríguez, 514.1/2–84, circular 2, October 12, 1932.

119. *El Oaxaqueño*, June 5, 1934; ibid., June 14, 1934; ibid., September 30, 1934.

120. Archivo Histórico de la Arquidiócesis de Oaxaca (AHAO), Diócesis, Gobernación, Autoridades Civiles, article 213; *Periodico Oficial*, September 1, 1934; *Revista Huajuapam*, September 1, 1934; *Periodico Oficial*, October 27, 1934.

121. The principal riot occurred in Huajuapan in late June 1926 when a government agent closed one of the town's private schools and locked up the head of the seminary (AMHL, Presidencia, Miguel Aguilar Melgarejo to Governor Vázquez, June 30, 1926; *Revista Huajuapam*, July 1, 1974; *Rafaega*, November 12, 1952).

122. Both applied to and joined the city's Masonic lodge during the early 1930s (Archivo de la Gran Logia "Benito Juárez" de Oaxaca [AGLBJO], GLD 48-58, 1926-1934).

123. AHSEP, 178, Informe of Arcadio Lozano, August 30, 1936; ibid., Informe of Arcadio Lozano, September 6, 1936.

124. AHSEP, 178, Esteban García to Secretaría de Gobernación, September 4, 1936; ibid., Informe of Luis G. Ramírez, April 16, 1936; ibid., Antonio Neri, "Plan de Trabajo," January 2, 1937; AGLBJO, Jeronimo Salazar Canedo to Benito Juárez lodge," September 20, 1937; AGPEO, Luis G. Ramírez to Governor Chapital, July 25, 1939.

125. AMHL, Presidencia, José Peral Martínez to Governor Chapital, January 4, 1937; ibid., José Peral Martínez to SEP, April 17, 1937; ibid., Vicente Ramírez Pacheco to Luis G. Ramírez, September 5, 1936.

126. For example, AGPEO, Pedro Romero Vásquez, Secretario General of Liga de Comités Agrarias, to Governor Chapital, September 25, 1940.

127. Rivera, "Resistance among Mixtec Indians," 27.

128. ADHL, Narciso Villa to Bishop Méndez del Río, March 16, 1938.

129. Ibid., Lucio Leónard to Bishop Méndez del Río, August 29, 1936.

130. Rivera, "Resistance among Mixtec Indians," 181.

131. Knight, "Popular Culture," 427. This was not always the case. In former regions of popular liberalism like the Sierra Juárez or Juchitan, where a well-educated, underchurched indigenous elite realized that support for socialist education could lead to a degree of political autonomy, the policy was successful (Smith, *Pistoleros*, 115-34, 138-46).

132. Few scholars of socialist education have examined the influence of the institutional force of the church and popular religious culture on the acceptance of the state campaign, preferring to lend greater causal value to issues of community autonomy, gender, and local histories of state interaction. Exceptions include Romero, "De la religión jacobina"; Guerra Manzo, "The Resistance"; ibid., "Entre el modus vivendi"; Septién Torres, "Guanajuato"; Camacho Sandoval, *Controversia educativa*, 113-87; Fallaw, "An Uncivil Society."

133. AHSEP, box 4, Luis G Ramírez, Informe on Sierra Juárez, September 3, 1936; Fallaw, "An Uncivil Society."

134. AGPEO, Gobernación, Sociedad Católica de Amatitlán to Governor Chapital, April 5, 1938.

135. Ibid., Men of Ayuquila to Secretaría de Gobierno, September 13, 1936.

136. AMHL, Presidencia, "Women of Huajuapan de León" to Arcadio Lozano, December 23, 1936.

137. ADHL, Carta Pastoral of Bishop Altamirano, November 26, 1932.

138. Ibid., Bishop Méndez del Río to Dr. Guillermo Piani, June 23, 1935. Another of his letters reveals why such low estimates of numbers of priests have been made throughout the period. Rafael Gutiérrez Maza confessed to the bishop that when the *Washington Post* correspondent Mr. Murray asked how many priests remained in the diocese, he lied and claimed that there were only four, as per government regulations (ADHL, Rafael Gutiérrez Maza to Bishop Méndez del Río, May 20, 1936).

139. Ibid., Informe of Rafael Gutiérrez Maza, November 20, 1934.

140. AGPEO, Asuntos Agrarios, legajo 27, exp. 1, Juan Flores to Secretario del Despacho, February 5, 1927; AHSEP, box 8, Juan I. Flores to Governor Vázquez, January 27, 1927.

141. ADHL, Parish records, San Miguel Amatitlán, Rufilio Flores Ayala to Bishop Méndez del Río, March 7, 1934.

142. AHSEP, 180 240.11, Arcadio Lozano to SEP, May 11, 1935.

143. ADHL, Bishop Méndez del Río to Clergy of Huajuapam, January 1, 1935.

144. AGPEO, Gobernación, 1934, Secretario de Gobierno to Governor García Toledo, October 26, 1935; ibid., Gobernación, O. Rodríguez, Manuel M. León, Honorario Cruz Flores, and Sidonio G. Suarez to Governor García Toledo, February 5, 1935; ibid., 1934, Men of Cosolotepec to Governor García Toledo, May 29, 1935.

145. ADHL, Bishop Méndez del Río, Instrucciones al Clero, December 20, 1934.

146. AGPEO, Gobernación, 1937, School Inspector to Governor Chapital, May 19, 1937; ibid., 1934, Rosendo Mendoza to Governor García Toledo, September 10, 1934; ibid., Eloy Bautista to Governor García Toledo, May 14, 1935.

147. ADHL, Porfirio López Alavez to Bishop Méndez del Río, August 12, 1935.

148. AMHL, Presidencia, Honorio Cruz to Governor Chapital, February 2, 1937.

149. ADHL, Bishop Méndez del Río to Gutiérrez Maza, October 18, 1935; ibid., Cubas to Bishop Méndez del Río, April 9, 1936; Sherman, "Reassessing Cardenismo," 362–63.

150. AGPEO, Gobernación, 1934, Aviso Importante.

151. ADHL, Manuel Cubas Solano to Bishop Méndez del Río, April 9, 1936.

152. AGPEO, Gobernación, Luis Ramírez to Director of Federal Education in Oaxaca, May 23, 1936; ADHL, Manuel Cubas Solano to Bishop Méndez del Río, April 23, 1936.

153. AHSEP, 176.10, Arcadio Lonzano to Ramírez, November 4, 1935.

154. ADHL, Jesús Villagómez to Bishop Méndez del Río, December 26, 1934.

155. Ibid., Bishop Méndez del Río to Gutiérrez Maza, January 23, 1935.

156. Ibid., Manuel Cubas Solano to Bishop Méndez del Río, April 25, 1935.

157. Ibid., April 24, 1936; AHSEP 180, 240.11, Arcadio Lonzano to Director of Federal Education in Oaxaca, May 21, 1935.

158. AGPEO, Gobernación, 1937, Isidro Velásco to Director of the SEP, May 16, 1936.

159. Ibid., Educación, Luis G. Ramírez to Director of the SEP, March 4, 1936.

160. Ibid., Gobernación, 1937, José Peral Martínez to Governor García Toledo, March 5, 1935. Also see petition from parents in Suchixtlahuaca, Coixtlahuaca, regarding mixed education (AHSEP, box 8, Parents of Suchixtlahuaca to Governor García Toledo, September 17, 1935).

161. Scott, *Weapons of the Weak*.

162. AMHL, Arcadio Lozano to Manuel Díaz Chavez, November 12, 1936.

163. Burke, *Popular Culture*, 178–204. For carnivals in a Mexican context, see Beezley, *Judas at the Jockey Club*, 97–108; Rugeley, *Of Wonders*, 85–86.

164. AGPEO, Asuntos Católicos, 1940, Justo Ramírez to Luis G. Ramírez, April 16, 1938.

165. ADHL, circular 14, April 5, 1925; ibid., Instrucciones al Clero, January 12, 1937.

166. Ibid., Zenón Villagómez to Bishop Méndez del Río, July 23, 1936.

167. AMHL, Director de la Escuela Primera Antonio de León to Director of Federal Education in Oaxaca, February 7, 1935.

168. Ibid., Ernesto Zárate López to Director of Federal Education in Oaxaca, November 6, 1936; Torres Septién, *La educación privada*, 150–52.

169. AMHL, Reports of the Ignacio Rayón School. For a comparison, see Torres Septién, *La educación privada*, 72, 142.

170. ADHL, Porfirio López to Bishop Méndez del Río, August 6, 1937; Butler, "Revolution and the Ritual Year," 475–78.

171. ADHL, Bishop Amador to Jesús Martínez, July 2, 1909.

172. Ibid., Parish Records, San Miguel Amatitlán, Rufilio Flores Ayala to Bishop Méndez del Río, November 27, 1927; ibid., April 4, 1933; ibid., Men of Concepción Porfirio Díaz to Bishop Méndez del Río, August 24, 1934; ibid., Bishop Méndez del Río to Narciso Villa, December 20, 1935.

173. AGPEO, box 46, Isidro Méndez del Río to SEP, December 3, 1936.

174. Ibid., Asuntos Católicos, 1936, Ignacio Cruz to Arcadio Lonzano, March 13, 1936; AMHL, Presidencia, José Peral Martínez to Director of Federal Education in Oaxaca, November 23, 1935; ibid., Arcadio Lozano to Director of Federal Education in Oaxaca, December 12, 1936.

175. ADHL, Patricia López to Bishop Méndez del Río, December 6, 1939.

176. Ibid., Manuel Cubas Solano to Bishop Méndez del Río, September 12, 1936.

177. APA, Libro de Gobierno 1.

178. Fallaw, "An Uncivil Society"; Blanco, "El Tabasco garridista"; Padilla Rangel, *Despues de la tempestad*.

179. Figes, "Stalin's Oblomov."

180. Young, *Power and the Sacred*; Priestland, *The Red Flag*, 366–68, 302–3.

181. Callahan, *The Catholic Church*, 306.

182. Lannon, *Privilege, persecution*, 189–96.

183. Ibid., 201–11.

184. Burdick, *For God*, 65–76.

185. Hansen, "Bac Di Cu."

CHAPTER 6

1. The above story is taken from AGN, Dirección Federal de Seguridad (DFS), 100–8–1–62; ibid., 100–18–8–1–62 H25; ibid.; ibid., H88; ibid., 100–18–1H 57; *Excelsior*, November 18–23, 1962; *La Prensa*, November 18–29, 1962; *El Imparcial*, November 28–December 14, 1962; *Oaxaca Gráfico*, November 19–December 9, 1962.

2. *El Imparcial*, November 30, 1962.

3. *La Prensa*, November 21, 1962.

4. Reich, *Mexico's Hidden Revolution*, 57.

5. Knight, "Cardenismo," 101.

6. Niblo, *Mexico*, 95–96.

7. Medina, *Historia de la revolución*, 399.

8. Raby, "Teacher Unionization," 688.

9. Segovia, *La politización*, 15–16.

10. Niblo, *Mexico*, 223–24.

11. Knight, "Cardenismo," 100.

12. Blancarte, "El arzobispado"; Valles, "José Garibi Rivera"; Padilla Rangel, *Después de la tempestad.*

13. Loaeza, *Clases medias*, 160.

14. Blancarte, *Historia*, 90, 92–95.

15. Archivo de Acción Católica Mexicana (AACM), Instrucciones para Aspirantes y Miembros de la AJCM, October 7, 1959.

16. Aspe Armella, *La formación social*; Barranco, "Posiciones políticas"; Loaeza, "Notas."

17. Padilla Rangel, *Después de la tempestad*, 71.

18. Friedrich, *The Princes of Naranja*, 68; AGPEO, Asuntos Católicos, 1940, Ignacio Regalado to Governor González Fernández, February 8, 1941.

19. Wilkie, *San Miguel*, 104–9.

20. Gauss, *Made in Mexico*, 89–92.

21. Peña and Torre, "Microhistoria," 126.

22. Butler, "God's Caciques"; Contreras Valdés, *Reparto de tierras*, 130–35; Martínez Saldaña and Gándara Mendoza, *Política y sociedad*, 5–47; Guerra Manzo, "Entre el modus vivendi," 35–50.

23. González y González, "Un cura de pueblo," 178.

24. Davis, "Religion and Partisan Loyalty"; Loaeza "La Iglesia Católica"; Camp, *Crossing Swords*, 121–22.

25. Serrano Alvarez, *La batalla*, vol. 2; Meyer, *Sinarquismo*, 78–121; Whetton, *Rural Mexico*, 482–522.

26. Smith, *Pistoleros*, 335–37, 393; AGN, Investigaciones Politicas y Sociales (IPS), 102.9, Eduardo Negri Baeza to Secretaria de Gobierno, October 29, 1947; Martínez Assad, *Los sentimientos*, 182–84; Serrano Alvarez, *La batalla*, 2:193, 233–50; Medina, *Historia de la revolución*, 98–108; Blancarte, *Historia*, 94; ibid., "Intransigence, Anticommunism."

27. Lujambio, *Democratización via federalismo*; ibid., "Democratization through Federalism?"; Middlebrook, "Party Politics"; Mabry, *Mexico's Acción Nacional*, 50–70.

28. Davis, *Urban Leviathan*, 330, appendix C.

29. Torres Ramírez, *Historia*, 57–86; Hewitt de Alcantara, *La modernización*, 56–98.

30. Medina, *Historia*, 63.

31. Niblo, *Mexico*, 183–88.

32. Medin, *El sexenio alemanista*, 129.

33. Hewitt de Alcantara, *La modernización*, 33.

34. Smith, *Pistoleros*, 335–40; Segura "Los indígenas."

35. AGPEO, Gobernación, 173 6–7 56, Melitón Ramírez to Governor Pérez Gasca, December 6, 1956.

36. Peña, *Problemas sociales*, 37.

37. Ibid., 42.

38. ARAN, 193, tomo 1, Tonalá, Fidencio Hernández to Manuel Castanos, July 16, 1942.

39. Ibid., 232, tomo 2, Huajuapan de León, J. Mexueiro Bonola Informe, August 25, 1959.

40. AGPEO, Gobernación, 2/080 (7) 1443, Donicio Cortes Conteras to Governaor Vasconcelos, February 4, 1957.

41. ARAN, 193, tomo 1, Tonalá, Carlos Belleza to Governor González Fernández, May 6, 1942.

42. AGPEO, Gobernación, 2/080 (7) 1443, Bibiano Bello to Governor Cabrera Carrasqueado, March 3, 1953.

43. Ibid., 173 6–7 56, Donocio Cortes Contreras to Governor Pérez Gasca, October 15, 1957.

44. ARAN, 840 DOT, Guadalupe de Morelos, Basilio Salazar to Secretario General del Despacho, March 4, 1953.

45. AGPEO, Gobernación, Miguel Bennets to Secretario General del Despacho, April 16, 1947.

46. ARAN, 193, tomo 1, Pedro Romero Vásquez to Governor González Fernández, June 15, 1942.

47. APM, Libro de Gobierno 3, May 4, 1956.

48. AGPEO, Gobernación, Bello to Governor Vasconcelos, December 2, 1949.

49. ARAN, 193, tomo 1, Pedro Romero Vásquez to Governor González Fernández, December 11, 1942.

50. Ibid., 840 DOT, Guadalupe de Morelos, José Caballero Bolivar to Confederación Nacional Campesina, February 28, 1949.

51. AGPEO, 173 6–7 56, Salomon Ramírez Martínez to Governor Cabrera Carrasqueado, January 5, 1955.

52. AJO, Huajuapan, Criminal, July 7, 1948.

53. AGPEO, Gobernación, Victoria Hernández to Governor González Fernández, January 15, 1943.

54. Ibid., 173 6–7 56, Melíton Ramírez to Governor Pérez Gasca, December 6, 1956.

55. Ibid., Moisés López Guzmán to Governor Pérez Gasca, December 4, 1957.

56. Harvey, *The Chiapas Rebellion*, 59.

57. Zárate Hernández, *Los señores*, 165–73; Benitez, *Los indios*, 2:511–12; Escalona Victoria, *Etúcuaro*, 229; Ventura Patiño, *Disputas*, 52.

58. Between 1940 and 1964, government engineers measured out over 135,000 hectares in the district of Huajuapan alone. Only one other district received more lands as bienes comunales during the same period (Segura, "Los indígenas," 243).

59. Peña, *Problemas sociales*, 109.

60. ARAN, 276.1 439, Santa Catarina Zapoquila, Castulo Villaseñor to Departmanto Agrario, August 25, 1950.

61. Ibid., 276.1/502, Cuyotepeji, Leogario Sandoval to Departamento Agrario, September 13, 1947; ibid., Eutamio Díaz to Departamento Agrario, September 11, 1951; ibid., Juan Solano Reyes to Departamento Agrario, September 25, 1957; ibid., Inspector Davis to Departamento Agrario, July 19, 1960; ibid., Comuneros of Cuyotepeji to Director General de Tierras y Aguas, January 29, 1961; ibid., Canuto Muñoz Mares to Departamento de Asuntos Agrarios y Colonización, April 15, 1961; ibid., Manuel Hernández Solano to Departamento de Asuntos Agrarios y Colonización, March 8, 1964; AJO, Huajuapan, Criminal, June 20, 1963.

62. ARAN, 172-TC, San Jeronimo Silacayoapilla, Abraham Cedillo Reyes to Departamento Agrario, January 8, 1953.

63. AGPEO, Gobernación, 615 140 161 "62," Sadot García León to Governor Pérez Gazga, November 1, 1962.

64. AMT, Moisés López to Secretario del Despacho, September 8, 1958.

65. Purnell, *Popular Movements*, 163–78; Butler, *Popular Piety*, 78–89; González y González, *Pueblo en vilo*, 181–216.

66. Peña, *El pueblo*, 371–72.

67. Gutierrez Alvarez, "Sinarquismo."

68. Archivo Histórico del Arzobispado de México (AHAM), Luis Maria Martínez, Carpeta Episcopada, Huajuapam, Luis Maria Martínez to Bishop Méndez del Río, December 15, 1942.

69. Reich, *Mexico's Hidden Revolution*.

70. AMT, Bonifacio Cruz Informe, August 1941.

71. Rivera, "Resistance," 133.

72. David Eloy Morales Jiménez, interview with author, September 2008.

73. ADHL, Biografía de Jenaro Méndez del Río, 1952; *Rafaega*, September 1952; ibid., August 1952.

74. Blancarte, "El arzobispado."

75. ADHL, Bishop Méndez del Río to Porfirio López, February 21, 1948.

76. Ibid., Manuel López to Bishop Méndez del Río, January 4, 1949.

77. Ibid., Bishop Méndez del Río to Pedro Gómez, January 30, 1948.

78. For example, ADHL, Celestino Fernández y Fernández to Narciso Villa Hernández, November 6, 1958.

79. *Rafaega*, July 1952.

80. González Orea, *El Huajuapan*.

81. González Ramírez, *La iglesia mexicana*, 105–9.
82. *Historia de Tonalá, Oaxaca*, 45–46; *Huajuapan* (revista), September 1977.
83. AGPEO, Gobernación, Bibiano Bello to Governor Vasconcelos, April 6, 1947.
84. APM, Libro de Gobierno 2.
85. Josefat Herrera, interview with author, September 2007; Procopio Martínez Vásquez, interview with author, August 2005.
86. AACM, Informe of Acción Católica Mexicana, Huajuapan de León, 1960.
87. APSAP, box 72, vol. 3, 1904–1990, Libro de Gobierno 3.
88. APTeq, Libro de Gobierno 3
89. APA, Libro de Gobierno 3.
90. González Orea, *El Huajuapan*, 78.
91. AGN, DFS, 242–4, Informe, November 19, 1962; ibid., 242–4, Informe, September 5, 1963.
92. Ibid., 210–19, Informe, December 10, 1962.
93. Ibid., 232–5, Informe, September 4, 1963; *Verbo*, May 1, 1962.
94. AACM, Assembleia Plenetaria de Huajuapan, 1959.
95. For a parallel, see Septién Torres, "Guanajuato," 115–16.
96. AACM, Informe of Manuel Cubas, July 14, 1939.
97. Ibid., Informe of Manuel Cubas, November 23, 1938.
98. *Album conmemorativo del congreso eucaristico parroquial.*
99. AACM, Informe of AJCM, September 18, 1959.
100. Angel Mora, interview with author, August 2004.
101. *Historia de Tonalá, Oaxaca*, 1–7.
102. Rivera S., *Novenario a la Virgen.*
103. AHSEP, 102.4, Bonifacio Cruz to SEP, December 9, 1942.
104. Benjamin, *La revolución*, 125–26.
105. AMT, Anacleto C. Vivas to Vicente Pacheco, December 12, 1951; see also AMT, Rafael Morales to Pedro Gómez, October 1, 1948.
106. AGPEO, Gobernación, 1/082 (7) 1012, Juan Arellano Martínez to Governor Vasconcelos, June 19, 1950.
107. Ibid., Juan Alvarez Martínez to Governor Perez García, 140 161.1 "57" Cultos, October 10, 1957.
108. AGN, DFS, 242–4 , Informe, September 5, 1963.
109. Ibid., Dirección General de Gobierno, 2.347, box 11, 15716, Felipe Hernández to Secretario de Gobierno, March 19, 1949; ibid., Manuel Avila Camacho, 542.2/476, Higenio Rojas to President Avila Camacho, April 17, 1944.
110. AMT, Gregorio Villavicencio to Rafael Morales, March 27, 1947.
111. Salazar Paz, "Problemas sociales," 71.
112. Villavicencio Rojas, *Donde se canta*, 7–9.
113. Rivera, "Resistance," 130.
114. Villavicencio Rojas, *Donde se canta*, 13.
115. *Tequix* (revista), April 7, 1994.
116. AMT, Presidencia, Luis Aragon to Governor Vasconcleos, March 17, 1949.

117. Peña, *Problemas*, 143–44.

118. Rivera, "Resistance," 155.

119. AGN, DFS, 242–4, Informe, September 5, 1963; ibid., 232–4, Informe, September 4, 1963.

120. *La Voz de Oaxaca*, September 10, 1947; ADHL, speech, Manuel López y López, September 8, 1947; ibid., Rodolfo Solana Cruz, September 8, 1947; Procopio Martínez Vásquez, interview with author, August 2005; Martínez, *La lucha electoral*, 227–28.

121. Rivera, "Resistance," 140.

122. AMT, Informe Rafael Morales, September 18, 1948.

123. AGPEO, Gobernación, 173 6–7 56, Narciso Vargas Guzmán to Secretario del Despacho, August 27, 1958; see also ibid., 259 500–537 "53," Elpidio Arias to Governor, November 29, 1954.

124. Ram Garmabella, *El criminologo*, 201.

125. Smith, *Pistoleros*, 338.

126. Ventura Patiño, *Disputas*, 55–59; Rivera Farfán, *Vida nueva*, 136.

127. "Entrevista con Salvador Abascal," 108; Zermeño and Aguilar, "Ensayo introductorio," 22.

128. AGN, IPS, 2–1/131/770, Informe on Damas Católicas of Zacatecas, 1943; ibid., 2–1/131/655, tomo 4, Informe on Article 3 in Jalisco, 1949.

129. Pérez Escutia, *Taximaroa*, 389–97.

130. Vaughan, *Cultural Politics*, 20.

131. Levy and Bruhn, *Mexico*, 87–88.

132. Andreas Schedler quoted in Gillingham, "Mexican Elections."

133. Loaeza, "El Partido Acción Nacional."

134. Gillingham, "Force and Consent," 202.

135. Lujambio, *Democratización via federalismo*, 29–50; Middlebrook, "Party Politics," 25; Mabry, *Mexico's Acción Nacional*, 50–70.

136. Gillingham, "Mexican Elections."

137. Grandin, *The Last Colonial Massacre*, 37; Niblo, *Mexico*, 96; see the essays in Rock, ed., *Latin America*; Bethell and Roxborough, eds., *Latin America*.

138. Newcomer, *Reconciling Modernity*, 143–76.

139. Smith, *Pistoleros*, 326.

140. AGPEO, Gobernación, Emigdio Gómez to Governor Vasconcelos, December 4, 1948; ibid., Jeronimo Herrera to Governor Vasconcelos, December 9, 1948; ibid., Alejandro Arando to Governor Vasconcelos, January 10, 1950.

141. Ibid., José E. Beltran to Secretario del Despacho, February 14, 1949; ibid., Salomon Ramírez, March 6, 1949.

142. AGN, Dirección General de Gobierno, 2/311 M (17), Carlos Belleza to Secretario de Gobierno, December 15, 1942; AGPEO, Gobernación, Alberto H. Von-Thaden Arias to Secretario del Despacho, December 7, 1944.

143. Centro de Documentación e Investigación del Partido Acción Nacional (CEDISPAN), Oaxaca, 1952–1960, Angel Mora to Comité Ejecutivo, April 15, 1952.

144. ARAN, 276.1/502, Cuyotepeji.

145. AGN, Dirección General de Gobierno, 2311 DF 17 5, box 43, Informe of Celerino Ramírez, January 30, 1952.

146. AGPEO, Gobernación, Guillermo Solana Carrión to Secretario del Despacho, June 15, 1946; ibid., Dr. Ubaldo Luna Paz to Secretario del Despacho, June 11, 1945.

147. Gillingham, "Mexican Elections."

148. AGPEO, Gobernación, Bibiano Bello to Secretario del Despacho, January 4, 1947; ibid., Emigdio Bello to Secretario del Despacho, December 13, 1949.

149. AJO, Huajuapan, Criminal, Informe of Lucretia Hernández, June 20, 1963.

150. Bonilla Duran, *Un municipio*, 56; AGPEO, Gobernación, Antonio Martínez to Secretario del Despacho, June 5, 1949.

151. Gillingham, "Mexican Elections."

152. Mabry, *Mexican Catholic Action*, 34.

153. Almada, *El vestido azul*, 73–78.

154. CEDISPAN, Oaxaca, 1939–1948, Miguel Niño de Rivera to Comité Ejecutivo, June 29, 1939.

155. Ibid., Manuel Aguilar y Salazar to Comité Ejecutivo, December 1, 1939; Martínez, *La lucha electoral*, 19–35.

156. Martínez, *La lucha electoral*, 19–20, 510.

157. CEDISPAN, Oaxaca, 1939–1948, Informe on Huajuapan de León Regional Committee, Clicero Cardoso, May 12, 1942.

158. Archivo Manuel Gómez Morin (AMGM), vol. 169, exp. 510, Miguel Niño de Rivera to Manuel Gómez Morin, May 31, 1943.

159. Ibid., Manuel Gómez Morin to Miguel Niño de Rivera, January 22, 1947.

160. The PAN produced fly sheets publicizing the campaign and held marches of over five thousand people (private Archive of José Antonio Velasco, Huajuapan de León).

161. Smith, *Pistoleros*, 354.

162. Mabry, *Mexico's Catholic Action*, 50–70.

163. Lujambio, *Democratización via federalismo*, 67–68.

164. According to some political theorists, the church hierarchy and the PAN allied from 1955 onward, with local clergy instructed to tell parishioners to vote for the party. While this seems to be the case in Huajuapan, I doubt the assertion can be extended over the rest of Mexico (Camp, *Crossing Swords*, 55).

165. Serrano Alvarez, *La batalla del espíritu*, 2:304–7.

166. Martínez, *La lucha electoral*, 507–17; Angel Mora, interview with author, September 2004. The move was not without controversy. Niño de Rivera was adamant that the people of Huajuapan were not ready for populist politics (AMGM, Manuel Aguilar Salazar to Manuel Gómez Morin, July 7, 1949).

167. Martínez, *La lucha electoral*, 87–102.

168. AGPEO, Gobernación, 1/082 (7) 1012, Efren Davila Sánchez to Eduardo Vasconcelos, May 14, 1950.

169. Martínez, *La lucha electoral*, 95–96.

170. Angel Mora, interview with author, September 2004.

171. AGPEO, Gobernación, Informe of Maurilio Pavila Gil, October 28, 1950.

172. Ibid., Miguel Niño de Rivera to Governor, December 23, 1952. In fact, Miguel Niño de Rivera's rather worried letter to the governor seems to indicate that he had reservations over Mora's more aggressive stance.

173. *Huajuapan, Seminario de Orientación y Cultura*, July 19, 1953.

174. Procopio Martínez Vásquez, interview with author, September 2005; CEDISPAN, Oaxaca, 1939–1948, List of Propaganda Sent to Huajuapan, May 18, 1945. For a comparison note the preparation for the arrival of Luis M. Alvarez on January 10, 1958, which included two trucks, a meal for one hundred supporters, a ceremonial crowning of Antonio de León, PAN balloons, and a group of cyclists to follow the candidate's car. Mora had over ten thousand copies of the state's electoral law (CEDISPAN, Oaxaca, 1952–1960, Informe, January 10, 1958).

175. *Verbo*, September 28, 1958.

176. Ibid., October 5, 1958.

177. Ibid., September 28, 1958.

178. AGPEO, Gobernación, "Tezoatlán, Sin ley y sin justicia," July 12, 1957; ibid., "Esta es la justicia para el indio," July 29, 1957.

179. Archivo Particular de José Antonio Velasco, Alvaro Vásquez Romero to Emlio Herrera Ramírez, January 1, 1953; AGPEO, Gobernación, 219–3 173 (7) "52," Cirilo Luna to Manuel Monjardin, January 6, 1953; ibid., Frente Zapatista de Tequixtepec to Secretario del Despacho, January 4, 1953.

180. Archivo Particular de José Antonio Velasco, fly sheets of Voto Libre Huajuapeño.

181. AGPEO, Gobernación, 173 6–7 56, Pedro Gómez to Secretario del Despacho, December 4, 1956.

182. CEDISPAN, Oaxaca, 1952–1960, Memorandum on Elections in Huajuapan de León, July 6, 1952; ibid., 1948–1952, Guillermo López Guerrero to PAN, July 12, 1949; ibid., Informe, January 2, 1956.

183. Ibid., Memorandum on Elections in Huajuapan de León, July 6, 1952.

184. AGPEO, Gobernación, 219–3 173 (7) "52," Genaro Carrasco to Governor Carrasquedo, December 14, 1952.

185. CEDISPAN, Oaxaca, 1952–1960, Memorandum on Elections in Huajuapan de León, July 6, 1952.

186. AGPEO, Gobernación, 210–2 327 "56," Marcelino López to Governor, December 4, 1956.

187. Martínez, *La lucha electoral*, 434.

188. CEDISPAN, Oaxaca, 1952–1960, Memorandum on Huajuapan Elections, December 14, 1956.

189. AGPEO, Gobernación, 219–3 173 (7) "52," José Moral to Secretario del Despacho, March 18, 1955; ibid., Secretario del Despacho to Secretario de Gobierno, March 23, 1956; AJO, Huajuapan, Criminal, January 3, 1956.

190. AGPEO, Gobernación, 485–17 173 "59," Ismael Zambrano Gordillo to Secretario del Despacho, December 5, 1959.

191. Calderon Vega, *Memorias del PAN*, 3:261–62; Martínez, *La lucha electoral*, 123.

192. AGPEO, Gobernación, 275 171 220 "54," Informe of Manuel Ponce Ambrosio, February 5, 1955.

193. Martínez, *La lucha electoral*, 205.

194. CEDISPAN, Oaxaca, 1952–1960, Angel Mora to José González Torres, November 13, 1959.

195. AGPEO, 219–3 173 (7) "52," List of PAN Supporters, November 3, 1952; Martínez, *La lucha electoral*, 513; AGN, Dirreción General de Gobierno, 1.173 (7) 1730, Comité Regional del PRI de Oaxaca to Governor Carrasquedo, December 9, 1952.

196. AGPEO, 219–3 173 (7) "52," Isidro Mendiola to Governor, December 9, 1952; ibid., Guadalupe Martínez to Governor Carrasquedo, December 4, 1952.

197. *La Nación*, January 11, 1953.

198. AGPEO, 219–3 173 (7) "52," Voto Libre Huajupeno to Governor Carrasquedo, January 3, 1953; ibid., Emigdio Flores to Governor Carrasquedo, January 23, 1953.

199. Ibid., Gobernación, Mauricio González to Secretario del Despacho, March 5, 1953.

200. Ibid., Moisés Francisco Bello to Secretario del Despacho, June 6, 1953.

201. Reveles Vázquez, *Partido Acción Nacional*, 497–98.

202. The term is borrowed from Hobsbawm, "The Machine Breakers," 58–59. Gillingham has used the term to describe the situation in post-1940 Mexico. See Gillingham, "Maximino's Bulls."

203. AGPEO, Gobernación, 219–3 173 (7) "52," Frente Zapatista de Tequixtepec to Governor Carrasquedo, March 19, 1953; ibid., Rafael Barragán López to Governor Carrasaquedo, January 23, 1953.

204. Ibid., Secretario General del Despacho to Silvestre González, December 31, 1952; ibid., Efren Michael Guzmán to Secretario del Despacho, February 4, 1954; CEDISPAN, Oaxaca, 1952–1960, Informe of Manuel Bautista, January 19, 1957.

205. AGPEO, Gobernación, 173 6–7 56, Municipal Authorities of Zahuatlán to Procurador de Justicia, April 14, 1958.

206. Ibid., Mauricio López to Governor Pérez Gasca, July 4, 1957.

207. Gillingham, "Force and Consent," 166–204.

208. Rubin, *Decentering the Regime*, 45–46; Smith, *Pistoleros and Popular Movements*, 333–34.

209. Pansters, "Tropical Passion."

210. Reveles Vázquez, *Partido Acción Nacional*, 493–500.

211. Magaloni, *Voting for Autocracy*, 9, 26, 52.

212. Reveles Vázquez, *Partido Acción Nacional*, 496; Pérez Escutia, *Taximaroa*, 389–97.

213. White, *Creating a Third World*, 68–75.

214. Bassols Batalla, *El noreste*, 548–51; Eckstein, *El ejido colectivo*, 165–68; Gil, *Los ferrocarrileros*; Alonso, *Movimiento ferrocarrilero*.

215. Zolov, "Cuba sí, Yanquis no"; Dávila Peralta, *Las santas batallas*; Pansters, *Politics and Power*, 113.

216. Pellicer de Brody, *México*, 107.

217. Doyle, "After the Revolution."

218. Servin, "Hacia el levantamiento armado."

219. Padilla, *Rural Resistance*, 134–39; Servin, "Hacia el levantamiento," 325; Alonso, *Movimiento ferrocarrilero*.

220. Zolov, *Refried Elvis*, 53; Pellicer de Brody and Luis Reyna, *Historia*, 215–18.

221. White, *Creating a Third World*, 82.

222. Sandstrom, *Agrarian Populism*, 157; Moguel, "La cuestión agraria," 141–56.

223. Loaeza, *Clases medias*; Villaseñor, *Estado e iglesia*; Septién Torres, *La educación*, 170–76; Villa Lever, *Los libros*.

224. Barkin and King, *Regional Economic Development*, 107–9.

225. Quoted in White, *Creating a Third World*, 74.

226. Dávila Peralta, *Las santas batallas*, 50–60; Loaeza, *Clases medias*, 322–30.

227. Loaeza, *Clases medias*, 308.

228. Pacheco, "Cristianismo sí!"

229. Mabry, *Mexico's National Action*, 68; *La Nación*, July 3, 1960.

230. *La Nación*, October 4, 1962.

231. Loaeza, *Clases medias*, 56.

232. CEDISPAN, Oaxaca, 1952–1960, Angel Mora to Jefe del PAN, July 6, 1961; ibid., Informe of Manuel Bautista, February 3, 1960.

233. *La Nación*, July 9, 1961; Martínez, *La lucha electoral*, 124–29.

234. AJO, Huajuapan, Criminal, Juvencio Reyes, November 5, 1962.

235. CEDISPAN, Oaxaca, 1962–1965, Angel Mora to Lic. González Torres, August 25, 1962.

236. *Oaxaca en México*, November 1962.

237. AGN, DFS, 100–18–8–1–62, Memorandum, November 20, 1962; ibid., 100–18–8–1–62 H25, Manuel Rangel Escamilla, November 21, 1962.

238. Ibid., 100–18–8–1–62 H88, Informe, November 23, 1962.

239. Ibid., 100–8–1–62, Informe, November 21, 1962.

240. Ibid., 100–8–14–8, Informe, November 21, 1962.

241. Ibid., 100–8–1–63, Informe, January 2, 1963.

242. Martínez, *La lucha electoral*, 370–409; AGN, DFS, 100–8–62–8, November 30, 1962.

243. Mabry, *Mexico's National Action*, 65.

244. *Excelsior*, November 19, 1962.

245. Ibid., November 20, 1962; *Oaxaca Gráfico*, November 27, 1962. The latter mentions similar attacks in Hidalgo and Tuxtla Gutiérrez. I have found no other evidence of these attacks.

246. AGN, DFS, 210–19 December 10, 1962. The DFS concluded that twenty-eight men took part in the attack and described them as "all ignorant religious fanatics."

247. Ibid., 100–18–8–1–62 H88, November 23, 1962.

248. Ibid., 100–8–14–8, Informe, November 19, 1962. Interestingly, the manifesto published by the press made no mention of political rights or municipal autonomy. Only the religious demands were included (*La Prensa*, November 23, 1962).

249. José Antonio Velasco, interview with author, July 2007.

250. AGN, DFS, 100-8-1-62, Informe, November 21, 1962.

251. Martínez Vásquez, *Relatos y vivencias*, 47–48; Martínez, *La lucha electoral*, 476–81.

252. Martínez, *La lucha electoral*, 464–75.

253. *El Imparcial*, November 29, 1962.

254. AGN, DFS, 100-18-8-1-63 H223, Informe of Manuel Rangel Escamilla, August 31, 1963.

255. AMH, Presidencia, Codigo Municipal of Ramon Pérez Castillo, January 2, 1963.

256. AJO, Huajuapan, Criminal, Informe of Manuel Zaragoza Acevedo, January 10, 1963.

257. Ibid., Informe of Lucretia Hernández, June 20, 1963.

258. Ibid., Paquete 1964 1–28, January 22, 1964.

259. AGN, DFS, 100-18-16-62, Informe, November 26, 1962; *La Nación*, November 25, 1962.

260. AGN, DFS, 100-1-18 H26 MRE, Informe of Manuel Rangel Escamilla, November 30, 1962. Adolfo Christlieb Ibarrola (head of the PAN from 1962 to 1968) represented the Gómez Morin branch of the PAN and led a general move away from the Christian Democratic efforts of the preceding decade. See Meyer, "La Iglesia Católica," 2:637.

261. ADHL, Presidencia, Celestino Fernández y Fernández to Narciso Villa Hernández, January 2, 1963; ibid., Celestino Fernández y Fernandez to Virgilio Leyva Chavez, January 4, 1963; APM, Libro de Gobierno 3.

262. APSDT, box 45, vol. 1, Libro de Gobierno 3.

263. Cárdenas's reconciliation with regional Catholics was paralleled by a shift at the national level where Gustavo Díaz Ordaz, a rabid anticommunist and a friend of the Vatican delegate, was chosen as the presidential candidate (Camp, *Crossing Swords*, 43).

264. Loaeza, *Clases medias*, 392–94; Doyle, "After the Revolution."

265. Dunn, *The Catholic Church*, 146–49.

266. Kelly, "Catholicism and the Left," 154–62.

267. Smith, *The Church and Politics*, 106–282.

268. Crosby, *God, Church*; Grandin, *The Last Colonial Massacre*, 78–82.

269. I deliberately finish this history in 1962 not only because this year marks the end of antistate provincial conservatism in the Mixteca Baja but also because it heralds the beginning of a sea change in Catholic theology as announced at the Second Vatican Council. First, limited historical studies make any sort of comparison extremely difficult. Second, limits on archive access circumscribe available primary documents. Third, the complexity of other factors, including democratization, shifts in PAN ideology and electoral policy, and the emergence of cross-class social movements and left-wing parties make any sort of short, simple epilogue that would draw a parallel between the Catholic activism of the postwar period and the 1990s rather pointless. However, the division between the moderate, modernizing political Catholicism of the 1950s and the paranoid anticommunism of the early 1960s, which we can see emerging in the Mixteca Baja, clearly shaped local reactions to the raft of reforms. In essence, the clergy and laity in the region split. Many were influenced by their close links to indigenous communities and became advocates of "the option for the poor," drifting gradually to the left, leaving the PAN, and embracing the radical

indigenous politics of the last decades. Others attempted to fashion a populist PAN, while others, most notably Bishop Felipe Padilla Cardona (1992–1996), still adhered to the reactionary anticommunism of the 1960s. The divisions came to a head during the late 1990s when the archbishop of Mexico, tipped off by a handful of local priests, closed down the Huajuapan seminary, claiming that the institution taught Marxism to its students (Reveles Vázquez, *Partido Acción Nacional*, 497–99; Mora Paz, *Luis Guevara Camacho*; Guzmán Navarro, "Perspectivas," 112).

CONCLUSION

1. Kouri, "Interpreting the Expropriation."
2. Menegus, *La Mixteca Baja*; Steffen Riedemann, *Los comerciantes.*
3. Brading, "Introduction," 13; Escobar Ohmstede, "Review"; Kouri, "Los pueblos."
4. Ceballos Ramírez, *El Catolicismo Social*, 16.
5. Taylor, "Two Shrines"; Nandy, *The Intimate Enemy*, 107–8.
6. Rugeley, *Rebellion Now and Forever*, 163.
7. Quoted in Thomson, "La contrarreforma," 244.
8. González y González, "La Revolución Mexicana."

Bibliography

ARCHIVES

Mexico City

Archivo de Acción Católica Mexicana (AACM), Universidad Iberoamericana
Archivo de Porfirio Díaz (APD), Universidad Iberoamericana
Archivo General de la Nación (AGN)
Archivo Histórico del Arzobispado de México (AHAM)
Archivo Histórico de la Secretaría de Educación Pública (AHSEP)
Archivo Histórico de la Secretaría de la Defensa Nacional (AHSDN)
Archivo Manuel Gómez Morin (AMGM)
Centro de Documentación e Investigación del Partido Acción Nacional (CEDISPAN)
Hemeroteca Nacional

Mixteca Baja

Archivo de la Diócesis de Huajuapam de León (ADHL)
Archivo del Municipio de Chazumba (AMC)
Archivo del Municipio de Huajuapan de León (AMHL)
Archivo del Municipio de Tequixtepec (AMT)
Archivo Parroquial de Ayuquila (APA)
Archivo Parroquial de Chazumba (APC)
Archivo Parroquial de Mariscala
Archivo Parroquial de Mixtepec (APM)
Archivo Parroquial de San Juan Bautista, Acatlán de Osorio (APSJBAO)
Archivo Parroquial de San Simón Zahuatlán
Archivo Parroquial de Santa María de la Asunción, Chila (APSMAC)
Archivo Parroquial de Santa María de la Natividad, Tamazulapan (APSMNT)
Archivo Parroquial de Santiago Apostol, Petlalcingo (APSAP)
Archivo Parroquial de Santo Domingo, Tonalá (APSDT)
Archivo Parroquial de Tequixtepec (APTeq)
Archivo Parroquial de Tezoatlán (APTez)
Archivo Parroquial de Tlacotepec de las Nieves (APTN)
Archivo Parroquial, El Sagrario, Huajuapan de León (APSHL)
Archivo Particular de José Antonio Velasco, Huajuapan

Archivo Particular de Luis Niño Pacheco, Tequixtepec
Archivo Particular de Ricardo Ceballos Soto, Chazumba

Oaxaca City

Archivo de la Gran Logia "Benito Juárez" de Oaxaca (AGLBJO)
Archivo del Registro Agrario Nacional (ARAN)
Archivo de Luis Castañeda Guzmán, Biblioteca Burgoa
Archivo General del Poder Ejecutivo del Estado de Oaxaca (AGPEO)
Archivo General de Notarías del Estado de Oaxaca (AGNEO)
Archivo Histórico de la Arquidiócesis de Oaxaca (AHAO)
Archivo Judicial de Oaxaca (AJO)
Colección Manuel Martínez Gracida (CMMG), Biblioteca del Estado de Oaxaca

Puebla

Archivo del Cabildo de la Catedral de Puebla (ACCP)

United States

Church of Jesus Christ of Latter-day Saints Microfilm Library
Lucas Alamán Papers, Nettie Lee Benson Latin American Collection, University of
    Texas, Austin

NEWSPAPERS

El Imparcial (1962–1963)
El Oaxaqueño (1934)
El Regenerador (1844–1846)
Excelsior (1962–1963)
Huajuapan, Seminario de Oritentación y Cultura (1953)
La Prensa (1962–1963)
Oaxaca Gráfico (1962–1963)
País (1903)
Rafaega (1952)
Revista Huajuapam (1974–1975)
Verbo (1958)

PRIMARY SOURCES

Acta provincialia sancti Michaelis Archangeli sanctorum angelorum provinciae ordinis
    praedicatorum commitijis habitis in Conventu S.P.N. Dominici Angelopolitano die VI
    menfis maij anni MDCCXLVII, Pro natis in Hispania. Puebla de los Angeles, 1747.

Acuña, René. *Relaciones geográficas del siglo XVI: Antequera*. 4 vols. Mexico City: UNAM, 1984.

Ajofrin, Francisco. *Diario del viaje que por orden de la sagrada congregación de propaganda fide hizo a la América septentrional en el siglo XVIII*. Madrid: Maestre, 1958.

Album conmemorativo del congreso eucarístico parroquial en Tezoatlán. Huajuapan de León, 1940.

Album conmemorativo que la junta organizadora dedica a su dignisimo prelado el Ilmo. y Rmo. Ser Obispo Dr. D. Rafael Amador y Hernández en sus bodas de plata. Huajuapan de León, 1910.

Apuntes biográficos de Rafael Amador y Hernández, obispo de Huajuapam de Leon. Huajuapan de León, n.d.

Archivo del general Porfirio Díaz, memorias y documentos. 30 vols. Mexico City: UNAM, Instituto de Historia, 1947–1961.

Arenas, Felipe N. *Las cruces de Quetzalcóatl*. Puebla: Imprenta de M. Corona Cervantes, 1895.

Boturini Benaducci, Lorenzo. *Catálogo del Museo Indiano*. Mexico City, 1871.

Burgoa, Francisco de. *Geográfica descripción de la parte septentrional del polo ártico de la América y nueva iglesia de las Indias Occidentales y sitio astronómico de esta provincia de predicadores de antequera, valle de Oaxaca*. Oaxaca de Juárez: Editorial Porrua, 1997.

Bustamante, Carlos María de. *Cuadro histórico de la Revolución Mejicana*. Mexico City: Imprenta de Juan R. Navarro, 1854.

———. *Diario histórico de México (1822–1848)*. 2 CDs. Mexico City: Colegio de México, 2001.

———. *El nuevo Bernal Díaz del Castillo o sea historia de la invasión de los Anglo-Americanos en México*. Mexico City: Imprenta de Vicente García Torres, 1847.

Cantu Corro, José. *In memoriam Ilmo. y Rmo. Sr. Dr. D. Rafael Amador y Hernández, primer obispo de Huajuapam de León*. Huajuapan de León, n.d.

———. *Patria y raza*. Mexico City: Escuela Tipografica Salesiana, 1924.

Carta pastoral del exmo. el ilmo. señor obispo de Puebla a sus diocesanos labradores sobre el pago de diezmos. Mexico City: Impresa en la oficina de Galvan, 1841.

Catecismo en el idioma mixteco, según se habla en los curatos de la Mixteca Baja y de la Mixteca montañez por una commisión de curas. Puebla: Imp. Del Hospital de San Pedro, 1837.

Catecismo en el idioma mixteco, según se habla en los curatos de la Mixteca Baja y de la Montañez, que pertenecen al obispado de Puebla. Puebla: Tip. Y Lit. de P. Alarcon, 1892.

Censo de 1900: Resultados del censo de habitantes que se verificó el 28 de octubre de 1900. Mexico City: Oficina de la Secretaría de Fomento, 1901.

Chávez, Gabino. *El amigo católico de las niñas, lecciones instructivas y edificantes, morales doctrinales, y recreativas para el uso de las escuelas católicas*. Queretaro: Luciano Frias y Soto, 1893.

Codigo civil del estado de Oaxaca. Oaxaca: Imprenta del Estado, 1887.

Discurso leido por el Sr. Canonigo D. Guillermo López García, rector del seminario conciliar de Huajuapam en la solemne apertura del curso académico que tuvo verificativo en la Santa Iglesia Catedral. Huajuapan de León, 1906.

Doctrina cristiana en el idioma mixteco, conforme al método con que actualmente se habla en la Mixteca Baja, por un cura del obispado de Puebla. Puebla: Imp. Del Hospital de San Pedro de Manuel Buen-Abad, 1834.

"Ejercito imperial mejicano de las tres garentias, papel volante no. 11, 13 Jul. 1821." In *Documentos históricos mexicanos,* edited by Genaro García, 4 vols. Mexico City: Comisión Nacional para las Celebraciones del 175 Aniversario de la Independencia Nacional y 75 Aniversario de la Revolución Mexicana, 1975.

Esposición que los conservadores de las provincias dirigen al Sr. General Almonte a sus correligionarios y propietarios de la capital sobre las bases de la futura organización politica del país. Mexico City: J. M. Lara, 1863.

Galván Rivera, Mariano. *Ordenanzas de tierras y aguas.* Mexico City: Leandro J. Valdes, 1844.

García Pimentel, Luis. *Relación de los obispados de Tlaxcala, Michoacán, Oaxaca y otros lugares.* Paris: Real Academia de Historia, 1904.

González, Antonio. *Catecismo y explicación de la doctrina cristiana compuesto por el P. Geronymo de Ripalda de la sagrada compania de Jesús y traducido en lengua mixteca por el M.R.P. Antonio González.* Puebla: Viuda de Miguel de Ortega, 1755.

Historia de Tonalá, Oaxaca coleccionada por el Sr. Pbro. D. Avelino de la T. Mora López para conmemorar el III centenario del hallazgo de la Santa Cruz en la gruta del Río de Santa María Tindú, Oax. Santo Domingo Tonalá, 1957.

Informe de las actividades de las organizaciones de San Vicente de Paul. Huajuapan de León, 1903.

Instalación y reglamento de conferencia liturgicos-morales de la Diócesis de las Mixtecas. Huajuapan de León, 1903.

Juárez, Benito. *Documentos, discursos y correspondencia.* Selection and notes by Jorge L. Tamayo. CD-ROM. Azcapotzalco: Universidad Autónoma Metropolitana, 2006.

Ley sobre derechos y observaciones. Oaxaca: Gobierno del Estado, 1857.

Manual de administrar los sacramentos en lengua mixteca de ambos dialectos bajo y montañés para los curatos de Puebla. Puebla: Imp. del Hospital de San Pedro, 1837.

Martínez Gracida, Manuel. *Cuadros sinópticos de los pueblos, haciendas y ranchos del estado libre y soberano de Oaxaca.* Oaxaca: Imprenta del Estado de Oaxaca, 1883.

———. *Efemerides oaxaqueñas, 1853–1892.* Mexico City: Tip. del Siglo XIX, 1892.

———. "El estado de Oaxaca y su estadística del culto católico." *Boletín de la Sociedad Mexicana de Geografía y Estadística* (1882): 57–66.

Memoria administrativa presentada por el C. General Martin González gobernador constitucional del estado de Oaxaca a la legislatura del mismo, en cumplimiento de lo prevenido en la Fraccion X del Articulo 61 de la Constitución política el 17 de septiembre de 1900. Oaxaca: Impresión Oficial, 1900.

Memoria del consejo central de Señoras de la Caridad de Huajuapam. Huajuapan de León, 1904.

Paso y Troncoso, Francisco del. *Papeles de Nueva España*. Vol. 5, *Relaciones geográficas de la Diócesis de Tlaxcala*. Madrid: Suesores de Rivadeneyra, 1905.

Primera carta pastoral que dirige al venerable clero el primer obispo de Huajuapam, Doctor Rafael Amador con motivo de su consegración episcopal. Huajuapan de León, 1903.

Primer sinodo diocesano de Huajuapam celebrado por el Ilmo. y Rmo. Sr. Obispo Dr. D. Rafael Amador y Hernández en la S.I.C. en los dias 3, 4 y 5 del me de diciembre de 1906. Huajuapan de León, 1907.

Quinta carta pastoral del ilmo. y rmo. señor obispo de Huajuapam, por la que convoca al clero de la diócesis a la celebración del primer sinodo diocesano. Huajuapan de León, 1906.

Reglamento de instrucción primaría para las escuelas católicas de la Diócesis de Huajuapam. Huajuapan de León: Tipografia de José G. Velasco, 1909.

Respetuosa representación que hace el ayuntamiento de Huajuapan á la honorable legislatura de Oajaca, para que no se derogue el Artículo 30. de la Constitución general. Huajuapan de León, 1834.

Reyes, José A. *Nociones elementales de historia patria, escritos conforme al programa de la vigente ley de instrucción*. Mexico City: Talleres de la Librería Religiosa, 1895.

Reyes Aguilar, Saul. *Bodas paralelas*. Mexico City, 1949.

———. *Mi madre y yo; Sucesos históricos en la Mixteca*. Mexico City: Botas, 1972.

Ripalda, Geronimo de. *Catecismo de la doctrina cristiana*. Puebla: Imprenta de M. Corona, 1886.

Rivera S., Basilio. *Novenario a la Virgen de las Nieves, Ixpantepec*. Puebla: 1949.

Secretaría de Fomento, Colonización e Industria. *Boletín de Agricultura, Mineria e Industrias* 8, no. 2 (1895).

Villaseñor y Sánchez, Joseph Antonio de. *Theatro americano, descripción general de los reinos y provincias de la Nueva España y sus jurisdicciones*. 2 vols. Mexico City: Editorial Notaria, 1952.

SECONDARY SOURCES

Abardia M., Francisco, and Leticia Reina. "Cien años de rebelión." In *Lecturas históricas del estado de Oaxaca*. Vol. 3, *Siglo XIX*, edited by Ma. de los Angeles Romero Frizzi, 435–92. Mexico City: INAH, 1990.

Abascal, Salvador. *La revolución de la reforma de 1833 a 1848; Gómez Farías-Santa Anna*. Mexico City: Editorial Tradición, 1983.

Acevedo Carrasco, Gelasio. *Chazumba 2000. 150 aniversario de las festividades del Señor de la Esperanza*. Mexico City, 2000.

Adelman, Jeremy, ed. *Colonial Legacies: The Problem of Persistence in Latin American History*. London: Routledge, 1999.

Alamán, Lucas. *Historia de México*. 5 vols. Mexico City: Editorial Jus, 1942.

Alcala Alvarado, Alfonso. "La iglesia camina por nuevos senderos (1873–1900)." In *Historia general de la iglesia en América Latina*. Vol. 5, *México*, edited by Enrique Dussel, 264–88. Mexico City: Sigueme, 1984.

Aldana Rendón, Mario A. *La rebelión agraria de Manuel Lozada, 1873*. Mexico City: Fondo de Cultura Económica, 1983.

———. *Proyectos agrarios y lucha por la tierra en Jalisco, 1810–1866*. Guadalajara: Gobierno del Estado de Jalisco, 1986.

Almada, Rossana. *El vestido azul de la sultana: La construcción del PAN en Zamora, 1940–1995*. Zamora: Colegio de Michoacán, 2001.

Alonso, Antonio. *Movimiento ferrocarrilero en México, 1958–1959: De la conciliación a la lucha de clases*. Mexico City: Era, 1979.

Altamirano, Ignacio. *Historia y política de Mexico, 1821–1882*. Mexico City: Empresas Editoriales, 1947.

Altman, Ida, and James Lockhart, eds. *Provinces of Early Mexico: Variants of Spanish American Regional Evolution*. Los Angeles: UCLA Latin American Center Publications, 1976.

Alvarez, Luis Rodrigo. *Geografía general del estado de Oaxaca*. Mexico City: Sociedad Geográfica de México, 1981.

Alvarez de Toledo, Cayetana. *Politics and Reform in Spain and Viceregal Mexico: The Life and Thought of Juan de Palafox, 1600–1659*. Oxford: Clarendon Press, 2004.

Alvis, Robert E. *Religion and the Rise of Nationalism: A Profile of an East-Central European City*. Syracuse, NY: Syracuse University Press, 2005.

Amith, Jonathan D. *The Mobius Strip: A Spatial History of a Colonial Society in Guerrero, Mexico*. Stanford, CA: Stanford University Press, 2001.

Anderson, Margaret Lavinia. "The Divisions of the Pope: The Catholic Revival and Europe's Transition to Democracy." In *The Politics of Religion in an Age of Revival: Studies in Nineteenth-Century Europe and Latin America*, edited by Austen Ivereigh, 22–42. London: ILAS, 2000.

———. "The Kulturkamf and the Course of German History." *Central European History* 19, no. 1 (1986): 82–115.

———. "The Limits of Secularization: On the Problem of the Catholic Revival in Nineteenth-Century Germany." *Historical Journal* 38, no. 3 (1995): 647–70.

———. "Piety and Politics: Recent Work on German Catholicism." *Journal of Modern History* 63 (1991): 681–716.

Anna, Timothy E. "Demystifying Early Nineteenth-Century Mexico." *Mexican Studies/ Estudios Mexicanos* 9, no. 1 (1993): 119–33.

———. *The Mexican Empire of Iturbide*. Lincoln: University of Nebraska Press, 1990.

Annino, Antonio. "Nuevas perspectivas y una vieja pregunta." In *El primer liberalismo mexicano 1808–1855*, edited by Josefina Zoraida Vázquez and Antonio Annino, 43–91. Mexico City: INAH, 1995.

———. "The Two-Faced Janus: The Pueblos and the Origins of Mexican Liberalism." In *Cycles of Conflict, Centuries of Change: Crisis, Reform, Reform and Revolution in Mexico*, edited by Elisa Servin, Leticia Reina, and John Tutino, 60–90. Durham, NC: Duke University Press, 2007.

Archer, Christon I., ed. *The Birth of Modern Mexico, 1780–1824*. Lanham, MD: Rowman & Littlefield, 2003.

———. "Years of Decision: Felix Caileja and the Strategy to End the Revolution of New Spain." In *The Birth of Modern Mexico, 1780–1824*, edited by Christon I. Archer, 125–50. Wilmington, DE: Scholarly Resources, 2003.

Arenal, Jaime del. "La protección indígena en el segundo imperio mexicano: La junta protectaora de clases menesterosas." *Ars Juris* 6 (1991): 1–35.

Arrom, Silvia Marina. "Las Señoras de la Caridad: Pioneras olvidadas de la asistencia social en México, 1863–1910." *Historia Mexicana* 57, no. 2 (2007): 445–90.

———. "Mexican Laywomen Spearhead a Catholic Revival: The Ladies of Charity, 1863–1910." In *Religious Culture in Modern Mexico*, edited by Martin Austin Nesvig, 50–77. Lanham, MD: Rowman & Littlefield, 2007.

Arroyo, Esteban. *Los Dominicos, forjadores de la civilización oajaqueña*. Vol. 1, *Los misioneros*. Oaxaca, 1958.

Asad, Talal. *Genealogies of Religion: Discipline and Reasons of Power in Christianity and Islam*. Baltimore, MD: Johns Hopkins, 1993.

Ashby, Joe C. *Organized Labor and the Mexican Revolution under Lázaro Cárdenas*. Chapel Hill: University of North Carolina Press, 1967.

Aspe Armella, Maria Luisa. *La formación social y política de los Católicos mexicanos*. Mexico City: Instituto Mexicano de Doctrina Social Cristiana, 2008.

Atkin, Nicolas, and Frank Tallett. *Priests, Prelates, and People: A History of European Catholicism since 1750*. Oxford: Oxford University Press, 2003.

Azuela, Mariano. *Precusores*. Santiago: Editorial Ercilla, 1935.

Baisnée, Pierre-Francois. *De vacas y rancheros*. Mexico City: Centre d'études mexicaines et centraméricaines, 1989.

Balandier, Georges. *Political Anthropology*. New York: Allen Lane, 1970.

Bantjes, Adrian. *As if Jesus Walked the Earth: Cardenismo, Sonora, and the Mexican Revolution*. Wilmington, DE: Scholarly Resources, 1998.

———. "The Eighth Sacrament: Nationalism and Revolutionary Political Culture in Mexico." In *Citizens of the Pyramid: Essays on Mexican Political Culture*, edited by Wil G. Pansters, 131–46. Amsterdam: CEDLA, 1997.

———. "Idolatry and Iconoclasm in Revolutionary Mexico: The De-Christianization Campaigns, 1929–1940." *Mexican Studies/Estudios Mexicanos* 13, no. 1 (1997): 87–120.

———. "Religion and the Mexican Revolution: Towards a New Historiography." In *Religious Culture in Modern Mexico*, edited by Martin Austin Nesvig, 223–54. Albuquerque: University of New Mexico Press, 2007.

Barabas, Alicia. *Dones, duenos y santos: Ensayo sobre religiones en Oaxaca*. Mexico City: INAH, 2003.

———. "Los santuarios de vírgenes y santos aperecidos en Oaxaca." *Cuicuilco* 13, no. 36 (2006): 225–58.

Barba González, Silvano. *La rebelión de los Cristeros*. Mexico City: Talleres de Manuel Casas, 1967.

Barkin, David, and Timothy King. *Regional Economic Development: The River Basin Approach in Mexico*. Cambridge: Cambridge University Press, 1970.

Barragán López, Esteban. *Más allá de los caminos: Los rancheros del portrero de Herrera*. Zamora: Colegio de Michoacán, 1990.

———, ed. *Rancheros y sociedades rancheras*. Zamora: Colegio de Michoacán, 1994.

Barranco, Bernardo. "Posiciónes politicas en la historia de la Acción Católica Mexicana." In *El pensamiento social de los Católicos mexicanos*, edited by Roberto Blancarte. Mexico City: Fondo de la Cultura Economica, 1996.

Bartra, Roger. *La jaula de la melancolía*. Mexico City: Grijalbo, 1996.

Baskes, Jeremy. *Indians, Merchants and Markets: A Reinterpretation of the Repartimiento and Spanish-Indian Economic Relations in Colonial Oaxaca, 1750–1821*. Stanford, CA: Stanford University Press, 2000.

Bastian, Jean Pierre. "Protestants, Freemasons, and Spiritists: Non-Catholic Religious Sociabilities and Mexico's Revolutionary Movement, 1910–1920." In *Faith and Impiety in Revolutionary Mexico*, edited by Matthew Butler, 75–92. London: Palgrave, 2007.

Baum, Dale. "Retórica y realidad en el México decimonico: Ensayo de interpretación de su historia política." *Historia Mexicana* 27, no. 1 (1977): 79–102.

Bautista Carriedo, Juan. *Estudios históricos y estadísticos del estado libre de Oaxaca*. 2 vols. Mexico City: Talleres gráficos de Adrian Morales, 1949.

Bautista García, Cecilia Adriana. "Hacia la romanización de la iglesia mexicana a fines del siglo XIX." *Historia Mexicana* 55, no. 1 (2005): 99–144.

Beals, Carleton. *Porfirio Díaz, Dictator of Mexico*. New York: J. P. Lippincott, 1932.

Becker, Marjorie. "Black and White and Color: Cardenismo and the Search for a Campesino Ideology." *Comparative Study of Society and History* 29, no. 3 (1987): 453–65.

Beezley, William. *Judas at the Jockey Club and Other Episodes of Porfirian Mexico*. Lincoln: University of Nebraska Press, 1989.

———. *Mexican National Identity: Memory, Innuendo, and Popular Culture*. Tucson: University of Arizona Press, 2008.

———. "New Celebrations of Independence, Puebla (1869) and Mexico City (1883)." In *Viva Mexico! Viva la Independencia! Celebrations of September 16*, edited by William Beezley and David E. Lorey, 131–40. Wilmington, DE: Scholarly Resources, 2001.

———, and David E. Lorey, eds. *Viva Mexico! Viva la Independencia! Celebrations of Sept. 16*. Wilmington, DE: Scholarly Resources, 2001.

———, Cheryl English Martin, and William E. French, eds. *Rituals of Rule, Rituals of Resistance: Public Celebrations and Popular Culture in Mexico*. Wilmington, DE: Scholarly Resources, 1994.

Benitez, Fernando. *Los indios de México*. 4 vols. Mexico City: Ediciónes Era, 1967–1972.

Benjamin, Thomas. *La Revolución: Mexico's Great Revolution as Memory, Myth, and History*. Austin: University of Texas Press, 2000.

———, and William MacNellie, eds. *Other Mexicos: Essays on Regional Mexican History, 1876–1911*. Albuquerque: University of New Mexico Press, 1984.

Beristain Romero, Candido. *"Yosocuiya," Juxtlahuaca a través de su historia*. Mexico City: 2002.

Berry, Charles. *The Reform in Oaxaca, 1856–1876: A Microhistory of the Liberal Revolution*. Lincoln: University of Nebraska Press, 1981.

Betanzos Piñon, Oscar. "Las raíces agrarias del movimiento cristero." In *Historia de la cuestión agraria mexicana: Modernización, lucha agraria y poder político 1920–1934*, edited by Enrique Montalvo, 150–206. Mexico City: Siglo XXI, 1988.

Bethell, Leslie, and Ian Roxborough, eds. *Latin America between the Second World War and the Cold War, 1944–1948*. Cambridge: Cambridge University Press, 1992.

Blacker, O'Neill. "Cold War in the Countryside: Conflict in Guerrero, Mexico." *Americas* 66, no. 2 (2009): 181–210.

Blancarte, Roberto. "El arzobispado Luis María Martínez, prelado pragmático o traidor a la iglesia." In *A Dios lo que es de Dios*, edited by Carlos Martínez Assad, 255–66. Mexico City: Aguilar, 1995.

———. *Historia de la Iglesia Católica en México*. Mexico City: Fondo de Cultura Económica, 2004.

———. "Intransigence, Anticommunism and Reconciliation: Church/State Relations in Transition." In "La Dictablanda: Soft Authoritarianism in Mexico, 1938–1968," edited by Paul Gillingham and Benjamin Smith. Unpublished manuscript, on file with author, Michigan State University.

Blanco, Isabel. "El Tabasco garridista y la movilización de los Católicos por la reanudación del culto en 1938." In *Religión, política y sociedad: El Sinarquismo y la iglesia en México (nueve ensayos)*, edited by Guillermo Zermeño P., 117–67. Mexico City: Universidad Iberoamericana, 1992.

Blasco, Inmaculada. *Paradojas de la ortodoxia: Política de masas y militancia católica femenina en España, 1919–1939*. Zaragoza: Prensa Universitarias de Zaragoza, 2003.

Blessing, Werner K. *Staat und Kirche in der Gesellschaft: Institutionelle Autorität und mentaler Wandel in Bayern während des 19. Jahrhunderts*. Göttingen: Vandenhoeck & Ruprecht, 1982.

Blok, Anton. *Honor and Violence*. Oxford: Blackwell, 2001.

Bonfil Batalla, Guillermo. *Mexico Profundo: Reclaiming a Civilization*. Austin: University of Texas Press, 1996.

Bonilla Duran, Juan Carlos. *Un municipio de la Mixteca Oaxaqueña: San Miguel Amatitlán*. Mexico City: CONACULTA, 2000.

Bonnell, Victoria E., and Lynn Hunt. "Introduction." In *Beyond the Cultural Turn: New Directions in the Study of Society and Culture*, edited by Victoria E. Bonnell and Lynn Hunt, 1–34. Berkeley: University of California Press, 1999.

Bono López, María. "La política lingüística y los comienzos de la formación de un estado nacional en México." In *Los pueblos indios y el parteaguas de la Independencia de México*, edited by Manuel Ferrer Muñoz, 13–42. Mexico City: UNAM, 1999.

Brading, D. A. *Church and State in Bourbon Mexico, the Diocese of Michoacán, 1749–1810*. Cambridge: Cambridge University Press, 1994.

———. "Creole Nationalism and Mexican Liberalism." *Journal of Interamerican Studies and World Affairs* 15, no. 2 (1973): 139–90.

———. *The First America: The Spanish Monarchy, Creole Patriots, and the Liberal State, 1492–1867*. Cambridge: Cambridge University Press, 1991.

———. *Haciendas and Ranchos in the Mexican Bajío, León, 1700–1860*. Cambridge: Cambridge University Press, 1978.

———. "Introduction." In *Caudillo and Peasant in the Mexican Revolution*, edited by David Brading, 1–20. Cambridge: Cambridge University Press, 1980.

———. *Mexican Phoenix: Our Lady of Guadalupe; Image and Tradition across Five Centuries*. Cambridge: Cambridge University Press, 2001.

———. "Review of Alan Knight, *The Mexican Revolution*." *Journal of Latin American Studies* 19, no. 2 (1997): 442–46.

Brewster, Keith, and Claire Brewster. "Ethereal Allies: Spiritism and the Revolutionary Struggle in Hidalgo." In *Faith and Impiety in Revolutionary Mexico*, edited by Matthew Butler, 93–110. London: Palgrave, 2007.

Britton, John A. *Educación y radicalismo en México*. 2 vols. Mexico City: SEP, 1976.

———. *Molding the Hearts and Minds: Education, Communications, and Social Change in Latin America*. Wilmington, DE: Scholarly Resources, 1994.

Brittsan, Zachary A. "In Faith or Fear: Fighting with Lozada." PhD diss., University of California, San Diego, 2009.

Brown, Lyle C. "Mexican Church-State Relations, 1933–1940." *Journal of Church and State* 6, no. 2 (1964): 202–22.

Brown, Peter. *The Cult of Saints: Its Rise and Function in Latin Christianity*. Chicago: University of Chicago Press, 1981.

Brunk, Samuel. *The Posthumous Career of Emiliano Zapata: Myth, Memory, and Mexico's Twentieth Century*. Austin: University of Texas Press, 2008.

———. "The Sad Situation of Civilians and Soldiers: The Banditry of Zapatismo in the Mexican Revolution." *American Historical Review* 101, no. 2 (1996): 331–53.

Bulnes, Francisco. *Juárez y las revoluciones de Ayutla y de la reforma*. Mexico City: Editorial Nacional, 1972.

Burdick, Michael A. *For God and the Fatherland: Religion and Politics in Argentina*. Albany: State University of New York Press, 1996.

Burke, Peter. *Popular Culture in Early Modern Europe*. Cambridge: Cambridge University Press, 1996.

Butler, Matthew. "El Sagrado Corazón de Jesús." Unpublished manuscript, on file with author, Michigan State University.

———, ed. *Faith and Impiety in Revolutionary Mexico*. London: Palgrave, 2007.

———. "God's Caciques: Caciquismo and the Cristero Revolt in Coalcomán." In *Caciquismo in Twentieth-Century Mexico*, edited by Alan Knight and Wil Pansters, 94–112. London: ILAS, 2005.

———. "Introduction: A Revolution in Spirit, 1910–1940." In *Faith and Impiety in Revolutionary Mexico*, edited by Matthew Butler, 1–20. London: Palgrave, 2007.

———. "Keeping the Faith in Revolutionary Mexico: Clerical and Lay Resistance to Religious Persecution, East Michoacán, 1926–1929." *Americas* 59, no. 1 (2002): 9–32.

———. "The 'Liberal' Cristero: Ladislao Molina and the Cristero Rebellion in Michoacán, 1927–9." *Journal of Latin American Studies* 31, no. 3 (1999): 645–71.

———. *Popular Piety and Political Identity in Mexico's Cristero Rebellion, Michoacan, 1927–29.* Oxford: Oxford University Press, 2004.

———. "Religious Developments in Mexico, 1865–1945." Unpublished manuscript, on file with author, Michigan State University.

———. "Revolution and the Ritual Year: Religious Conflict and Innovation in Cristero Mexico." *Journal of Latin American Studies* 38, no. 3 (2006): 456–90.

Buve, Raymond. *El movimiento revoluciónario en Tlaxcala.* Tlaxcala: Universidad Autónoma de Tlaxcala, 1994.

———. "Pueblos indígenas de Tlaxcala, las leyes liberales juaristas y la Guerra de Reforma: Una perspectiva desde abajo, 1855–1861." In *Los pueblos indios en los tiempos de Benito Juárez (1847–1872)*, edited by Antonio Escobar Ohmstede, 91–121. Mexico City: UAM, 2007.

Byland, Bruce E., and John M. D. Pohl. *In the Realm of 8 Deer: The Archeology of the Mixtec Codices.* Norman: University of Oklahoma Press, 1994.

Calderon Vega, Luis. *Memorias del PAN.* 4 vols. Mexico City: Jus, 1978.

Callahan, Charles William. *The Catholic Church in Spain, 1875–1998.* Washington, D.C.: Catholic University of America Press, 2000.

Callahan, William J. *Church, Politics, and Society in Spain, 1750–1874.* Cambridge, MA: Harvard University Press, 1984.

Calvo, Thomas. "The Warmth of the Hearth: Seventeenth-Century Guadalajara Families." In *Sexuality and Marriage in Colonial Latin America*, edited by A. Lavrin, 287–312. Lincoln: University of Nebraska Press, 1989.

Camacho Pichardo, Gloria. "Las sociedades agrícolas en los pueblos del sur del valle de Toluca y la desamortización (1856–1900)." In *La vida, el trabajo y la propiedad en el estado de México: Los primeros juicios de amparo en la segunda mitad del siglo XIX*, edited by César de Jesús Molina Suárez, René García Castro, and Ana Lidia García Peña, 249–94. Mexico City: Suprema Corte de Justicia de la Nación, 2007.

Camacho Sandoval, Salvador. *Controversia educativa entre la ideología y la fe. La educación socialista en la historia de Aguascalientes, 1876–1940.* Mexico City: Consejo Nacional para la Cultura y las Artes, 1991.

Camarena, María Iñes. "El jefe político y el orden institucional en la formación del estado. El caso de los Altos de Jalisco." *Estudios Jaliscenses* 3 (1991): 25–40.

Camp, Roderic Ai. *Crossing Swords: Politics and Religion in Mexico.* Oxford: Oxford University Press, 1997.

———. *Mexican Political Biographies, 1884–1935.* Austin: University of Texas Press, 1991.

Cannell, Fenella, ed. *The Anthropology of Christianity.* Durham, NC: Duke University Press, 2006.

———. "Introduction." In *The Anthropology of Christianity*, edited by Fenella Cannell, 1–50. Durham, NC: Duke University Press, 2006.

Caplan, Karen D. *Indigenous Citizens: Local Liberalism in Early National Oaxaca and Yucatán*. Stanford, CA: Stanford University Press, 2009.

———. "The Legal Revolution in Town Politics, Oaxaca and Yucatán, 1812–1825." *Hispanic American Historical Review* 83, no. 2 (2003): 255–93.

Carmagnani, Marcello. "Demografía y sociedad: La estructura social de los centros mineros del norte de México, 1600–1720." *Historia Mexicana* 21, no. 3 (1972): 419–59.

———. "El federalismo liberal mexicano." In *Federalismos latinoamericanos: Mexico/Brazil/Argentina*, edited by Marcello Carmagnani, 135–79. Mexico City: Fondo de Cultura Económica, 1993.

———. *El regreso de los dioses: El proceso de reconstitución de la identidad étnica en Oaxaca, siglos XVII y XVIII*. Mexico City: Fondo de Cultura Económica, 1988.

———. "Local Governments and Ethnic Governments in Oaxaca." In *Essays in the Political, Economic, and Social History of Colonial Latin America*, edited by Karen Spalding, 107–24. Newark: University of Delaware Press, 1982.

Carr, Barry. "Recent Regional Studies of the Mexican Revolution." *Latin American Research Review* 15, no. 1 (1980): 3–14.

Case, Robert. "El resurgimiento de los conservadores en México, 1876–1877." *Historia Mexicana* 25, no. 2 (1975): 204–31.

Castillo, Norma Angelica. "Cambios y continuidades entre las repúblicas indias y los ayuntamientos constucionales de Cholula, 1768–1865." In *Poder y legitimidad en México en el siglo XIX*, edited by Brian Connaughton, 137–79. Mexico City: UAM, 2003.

Castillo Palma, Norma Angelica, and Francisco González Hermosillo Adams. "Familias, linajes y poder político en la ciudad de Cholula y sus barrios." In *Practicas populares, cultura política, y poder en México, siglo XIX*, edited by Brian F. Connaughton, 39–95. Mexico City: Casa Juan Pablos, 2008.

Castro Gutiérrez, Felipe. *Los Tarascos y el imperio español 1600–1740*. Mexico City: UNAM, 2004.

Ceballos, Ciro B. *Aurora y ocaso, 1867–1906: Gobierno de lerdo*. 2 vols. Mexico City: Talleres Tipográficos, 1919.

Ceballos Ramírez, Manuel, ed. *Catolicismo Social en México*. Vol. 2, *Las instituciones*. Mexico City: Instituto Mexicano de Doctrina Social Cristiana, 2005.

———. *El Catolicismo Social: Un tercero en discordia Rerum Novarum, la cuestión social y la mobilización de los Católicos mexicanos, 1891–1911*. Mexico City: Colegio de México, 1991.

———, and Alejandro Garza Rangel, eds. *Catolicismo Social en México, teoria, fuentes e historiografía*. Monterrey: Academia de Investigación Humanística, 2000.

Ceballos Soto, Ricardo. *Historia de Santiago Chazumba, 1900–1920*. Oaxaca: PACMY, 2007.

Cervantes Bello, Francisco Javier. "De la impunidad a la usura: Los capitales eclesiásticos y el crédito (1825–1863)." PhD diss., Colegio de México, 1993.

———. "El dilema de las rentas eclesiásticas en una era de cambio: Puebla ca. 1765–1847." In *Religión, política e identidad en la independencia de México*, edited by Brian Connaughton, 99–130. Mexico City: UAM, 2010.

Cervantes Delgado, Roberto. "Los Nahuas que la etnografía olvidó." In *La vida volante: Pastoreo trashumante en la Sierra Madre del Sur, ayer y hoy*, edited by Danièle Dehouve, Roberto Cervantes Delgado, and Ulrik Hvilshøj, 19–39. Mexico City: Joral, 2004.

Chakrabarty, Dipesh. *Rethinking Working-Class History: Bengal, 1890–1940*. Princeton, NJ: Princeton University Press, 1989.

Chance, John K. "The Caciques of Tecali: Class and Ethnic Identity in Late Colonial Mexico." *Hispanic American Historical Review* 76, no. 3 (1996): 475–502.

———. "Descendencia y casa noble nahua. La experiencia de Santiago Tecali de finales del siglo XVI a 1821." In *Gobierno y economía en los pueblos indios del México colonial*, edited by Francisco González Hermosillo Adams, 29–48. Mexico City: INAH, 2001.

———. "Los Villagómez de Suchitepec, Oaxaca: Un cacicazgo mixteco, 1704–1860." Unpublished manuscript, on file with author, Michigan State University.

———. "Marriage Alliances among Colonial Mixtec Elites: The Villagómez Caciques of Acatlan-Petlalcingo." *Ethnohistory* 56, no. 1 (2009): 96–123.

———. "Mesoamerica's Ethnographic Past." *Ethnohistory* 43, no. 3 (1996): 379–403.

———. "The Mixtec Nobility under Colonial Rule." In *Codices, caciques y comunidades*, edited by Maarten Jansen and Luis Reyes García, 161–78. Leiden: Asociación de Historiadores Latinoamericanistas Europeos, 1996.

———. "The Noble House in Colonial Puebla, Mexico: Descent, Inheritance, and the Nahua Tradition." *American Anthropologist* 102, no. 3 (2000): 485–502.

———. *Race and Class in Colonial Oaxaca*. Stanford, CA: Stanford University Press, 1978.

———, and William B. Taylor. "Cofradías and Cargos: An Historical Perspective of the Mesoamerican Civil-Religious Hierarchy." *American Ethnologist* 12, no. 1 (1986): 1–26.

———. "Estate and Class in a Colonial City: Oaxaca in 1792." *Comparative Studies in Society and History* 19, no. 4 (1977): 454–87.

Charnay, D. *Ciudades y ruinas americanas*. Mexico City: CONACULTA, 1994.

Chassen-López, Francie R. *From Liberal to Revolutionary Oaxaca: The View from the South, Mexico, 1867–1911*. University Park: Pennsylvania State University Press, 2004.

Chevalier, François. "Conservateurs et liberaux au Mexique—Essai de sociologie et geographie politiques de l'independence a l'intervención francaise." *Cahiers d'Histoire Mondiale* 8, no. 3 (1965): 457–74.

Chevalier, Jacques, and Daniel Buckles. *A Land without Gods: Process, Theory, Maldevelopment, and the Mexican Nahuas*. Atlantic Highlands, NJ: Zed Books, 1995.

Chowning, Margaret. "La feminización de la piedad en México: Género y piedad en las cofradías de Españoles. Tendencias colonias y poscoloniales en los arzobispados de Michoacán y Guadalajara." In *Religión, política e identidad en la Independencia de México*, edited by Brian Connaughton, 475–514. Mexico City: UAM, 2010.

———. *Wealth and Power in Provincial Mexico: Michoacán from the Late Colony to the Revolution*. Stanford, CA: Stanford University Press, 1999.

Christian, William A., Jr. *Local Religion in Sixteenth-Century Spain*. Princeton, NJ: Princeton University Press, 1981.

———. *Moving Crucifixes in Modern Spain*. Princeton, NJ: Princeton University Press, 1982.

Clark, Christopher. "The New Catholicisim and the European Culture Wars." In *Culture Wars: Secular-Catholic Conflict in Nineteenth-Century Europe*, edited by Christopher Clark and Wolfram Kaiser, 11–46. Cambridge: Cambridge University Press, 2003.

———, and Wolfram Kaiser, eds. *Culture Wars: Secular-Catholic Conflict in Nineteenth-Century Europe*. Cambridge: Cambridge University Press, 2003.

Coatsworth, John. *Growth against Development: The Economic Impact of Railroads in Porfirian Mexico*. Princeton, NJ: Princeton University Press, 1988.

———. "Patterns of Rural Rebellion in Latin America: Mexico in Comparative Perspective." In *Riot, Rebellion, and Revolution: Rural Social Conflict in Mexico*, edited by Friedrich Katz, 21–62. Princeton, NJ: Princeton University Press, 1988.

Cockcroft, James D. *Intellectual Precursors of the Mexican Revolution, 1900–1913*. Austin: University of Texas Press, 1968.

Connaughton, Brian F. "A Most Delicate Balance: Representative Government, Public Opinion, and Priests in Mexico, 1821–1834." *Mexican Studies/Estudios Mexicanos* 17, no. 1 (2001): 41–69.

———. *Clerical Ideology in a Revolutionary Age: The Guadalajara Church and the Idea of the Mexican Nation, 1788–1853*. Translated by Mark Alan Healey. Calgary: University of Calgary Press, 2003.

———. "Clérigos federalistas: ¿Fenómeno de afinidad ideológica en la crisis de dos potestades?" In *Raices del federalismo mexicano*, edited by Manuel Mino Grijalva et al., 71–88. Zacatecas: UAZ, 2005.

———. "Conjuring the Body Politic from the Corpus Mysticum: The Post-Independence Pursuit of Public Opinion in Mexico, 1821–1854." *Americas* 55, no. 3 (1999): 459–79.

———, ed. *Dimensiones de la identidad patriótica: Religión, política, y regiones, siglo XIX*. Mexico City: UNAM, 2001.

———. "1856–1857: Conciencia religiosa y controversia ciudadana. La conciencia como poder político en 'Un pueblo eminentemente católico.'" In *Practicas populares, cultura política y poder en México, siglo XIX*, edited by Brian Connaughton, 395–464. Mexico City: Casa Juan Pablos, 2008.

———. "La familia como tropo de la oración civica mexicana. Puebla (1828–1907)." In *Familia y vida privada en la historia de Iberoamerica*, edited by Pilar Gonzalbo Aispuru and Cecilia Rabell Romero, 471–88. Mexico City: UNAM, 1996.

———. "La iglesia mexicana, 1821–1856." In *El nacimiento de Mexico, 1750–1856; De las reformas borbónicas a la reforma*, edited by Josefina Zoraida Vázquez, 301–20. Mexico City: Planeta, 2001.

———. "La sacralización de lo cívico: La imagen religiosa en el discurso cívico-patriótico del México independiente. Puebla (1827–1853)." In *Estado, iglesia y sociedad en México, siglo XIX*, edited by Alvaro Matute, Evelia Trejo, and Brian Connaughton, 223–50. Mexico City: Porrua, 1995.

———. "Los curas y la feligresia ciudadana en México, siglo XIX." In *Las nuevas naciones. España y México, 1800–1850*, edited by Jaime E. Rodríguez O., 241–72. Madrid: Fundación MAPFRE, 2008.

———. *Practicas populares, cultura política y poder en México, siglo XIX*. Mexico City: Casa Juan Pablos, 2008.

———, ed. *Religión, política e identidad en la Independencia de México*. Mexico City: UAM, 2010.

Contreras Valdés, José Mario. *Reparto de tierras en Nayarit, 1916–1940: Un proceso de ruptura y continuidad*. Mexico City: INEHRM, 2001.

Cook, Sherbourne, and Woodroh Borah. *The Population of the Mixteca Alta, 1520–1960*. Berkeley and Los Angeles: University of California Press, 1968.

Cordova, Arnaldo. *La revolución y el estado en México*. Mexico City: Ediciones Era, 1989.

———. *Los maestros rurales como agentes del sistema político en el Cardenismo*. Mexico City: UNAM, 1974.

Costeloe, Michael. *The Central Republic in Mexico, 1835–1846: "Hombres de bien" in the Age of Santa Anna*. Cambridge: Cambridge University Press 1993.

———. *Church and State in Independent Mexico: A Study of the Patronage Debate, 1821–1857*. London: Royal Historical Society, 1978.

———. *Church Wealth in Mexico: A Study of the Juzgado de Capellanias in the Archbishopric of Mexico, 1800–1856*. Cambridge: Cambridge University Press, 1967.

Crosby, Donald F. *God, Church, and Flag: Senator Joseph R. McCarthy and the Catholic Church, 1950–1957*. Chapel Hill: University of North Carolina Press, 1978.

Cruz Pazos, Patricia. "La nobleza indígena de Tepexi de la Seda durante el siglo XVIII. La cabecera y sus sujetos, 1700–1786." PhD diss., Fundación Universitaria Española, 2008.

———. "Los caciques de Tepexi de la Seda y sus descendientes a través de los testamentos (1798–1799)." *Tiempos Modernos* 19 (2009): 1–18.

Cueva, Julio de la. "The Assault on the City of the Levites: Spain." In *Culture Wars: Secular-Catholic Conflict in Nineteenth-Century Europe*, edited by Christopher M. Clark and Wolfram Kaiser, 181–201. Cambridge: Cambridge University Press, 2003.

———. "Inventing Catholic Identities in Twentieth-Century Spain: The Virgin Bien-Aperecida, 1904–1910." *Catholic Historical Review* 87, no. 4 (2001): 624–48.

Cueva Merino, Julio de la. "Clericalismo y movilización católica en la España de la restauración." In *Clericalismo y asociacionismo católico en España: De la restauración a la transición*, edited by Angel Luis López Villaverde and Julio de la Cueva Merino, 27–50. Cuenca: Centro de Estudios de Castilla–La Mancha, 2005.

Cuevas, Mariano. *Historia de la iglesia en México*. 5 vols. Tlalpam: Impr. del Asilo "Patricio Sanz," 1921–1928.

Cypher, James. "Reconstituting Community: Local Religion, Political Culture, and Rebellion in Mexico's Sierra Gorda, 1846–1880." PhD diss., Indiana University, 2007.

Dabbs, Jack Autrey. *The French Army in Mexico, 1861–1867.* The Hague: Mouton, 1963.

Dahlgren, Babro. *La Mixteca: Su cultura e historia prehispánicas.* Mexico City: UNAM, 1990.

Dávila Peralta, Nicolás. *Las santas batallas: El anticomunismo en Puebla.* Puebla: Gobierno del estado de Puebla, 1978.

Davis, Charles L. "Religion and Partisan Loyalty: The Case of Catholic Workers in Mexico." *Western Political Quarterly* 45, no. 1 (1992): 275–97.

Davis, Diane. *Urban Leviathan: Mexico City in the Twentieth Century.* Philadelphia: Temple University Press, 1994.

Davis, N. Z. "From 'Popular Religion' to Religious Cultures." In *Reformation Europe: A Guide to Research,* edited by Steven Ozment, 56–67. Saint Louis, MO: Center for Reformation Research, 1982.

———. "Some Tasks and Themes in the Study of Popular Religion." In *The Pursuit of Holiness in Late Medieval and Renaissance Religion,* edited by C. Trinkaus and H. Oberman, 307–36. Leiden: Brill, 1974.

Dehouve, Danièle. *Cuando los banqueros eran santos. Historia económica y social de la provincia de Tlapa, Guerrero.* Translated by Bertha Chavelas Vázquez. Chilpancigo: Universidad Autónoma de Guerrero, 2002.

———. *Entre el caimán y el jaguar: Los pueblos indios de Guerrero.* Mexico City: INI, 1994.

———. "Las haciendas volantes de la Sierra de Tlapa: Origen e historia." In *La vida volante: Pastoreo trashumante en la Sierra Madre del Sur, ayer y hoy,* edited by Danièle Dehouve, Roberto Cervantes Delgado, and Ulrik Hvilshøj, 81–102. Mexico City: Joral, 2004.

———, Roberto Cervantes Delgado, and Ulrik Hvilshøj, eds. *La vida volante: Pastoreo trashumante en la Sierra Madre del Sur, ayer y hoy.* Mexico City: Joral, 2004.

Delgado Aguilar, Francisco Javier. *Jefaturas políticas: Dinámica política y control social en Aguascalientes, 1867–1911.* Aguascalientes: Universidad Autónoma de Aguascalientes, 2000.

Diacon, Todd A. *Millenarian Vision, Capitalist Reality: Brazil's Contestado Rebellion, 1912–1916.* Durham, NC: Duke University Press, 1991.

Díaz Patino, Gabriela. "Catolicismo Social en la Arquidiócesis de Morelia, Michoacán (1897–1913)." *Tzintzun, Revista de Estudios Históricos* 38 (2003): 97–134.

Díaz R., Fernando. *La vida heroica del general Tomás Mejía.* Mexico City: Editorial Jus, 1970.

Di Tella, Torcuarto S. "The Dangerous Classes in Early Nineteenth-Century Mexico." *Journal of Latin American Studies* 1, no. 1 (1973): 79–105.

———. *National Popular Politics in Early Independent Mexico, 1820–1847.* Albuquerque: University of New Mexico Press, 1996.

Dore, Elizabeth. "One Step Forward, Two Steps Back: Gender and the State in the Long Nineteenth Century." In *Hidden Histories of Gender and the State in Latin America,* edited by Elizabeth Dore and Maxine Molyneux, 3–32. Durham, NC: Duke University Press, 2000.

Doyle, Kate. "After the Revolution: Lázaro Cárdenas and the Movimiento de Liberación Nacional." National Security Archive Electronic Briefing Book 124. http://www.gwu.edu/~nsarchiv/NSAEBB/NSAEBB124/index.htm#article, accessed January 4, 2011.

Ducey, Michael T. "Indian Communities and Ayuntamientos in the Mexican Huasteca: Sujeto Revolts, Pronuciamentos, and Caste War." *Americas* 57, no. 4 (2001): 525–50.

———. "Liberal Theory and Peasant Practice: Land and Power in Northern Veracruz, Mexico, 1826–1900." In *Liberals, the Church, and Indian Peasants: Corporate Lands and the Challenge of Reform in Nineteenth-Century Spanish America*, edited by Robert H. Jackson, 65–90. Albuquerque: University of New Mexico Press, 1997.

———. *A Nation of Villages: Riot and Rebellion in the Mexican Huasteca, 1750–1850*. Tucson: University of Arizona Press, 2004.

———. "Village, Nation and Constitution: Insurgent Politics in Papantla, Veracruz, 1810–1821." *Hispanic American Historical Review* 79, no. 3 (1999): 463–93.

Duncan, Robert H. "Legitimation and Maxmiliano's Second Empire in Mexico, 1864–1867." *Mexican Studies/Estudios Mexicanos* 12, no. 1 (1996): 27–66.

Dunn, Dennis J. *The Catholic Church and Russia: Popes, Patriarchs, Tsars, and Commissars*. Aldershot: Ashgate, 2004.

Dwyer, John. *The Agrarian Dispute: The Expropriation of American-Owned Rural Land in Postrevolutionary Mexico*. Durham, NC: Duke University Press, 2008.

Eckstein, Shlomo. *El ejido colectivo en México*. Mexico City: Fondo de Cultura Económica, 1966.

"Entrevista con Salvador Abascal." In *Hacia una reinterpretación del Sinarquismo actual*, edited by Guillermo Zermeño and Rubén Aguilar, 80–109. Mexico City: Universidad Iberoamericana, 1988.

Escalona Victoria, José Luis. *Etúcuaro, la reconstrucción de la comunidad: Campo social, producción cultural y estado*. Zamora: Colegio de Michoacán, 1998.

Escobar Ohmstede, Antonio. *De la costa a la sierra: Las Huastecas, 1750–1900*. Mexico City: CIESAS, 1998.

———. "Del gobierno indígena al ayuntamiento constitucional en las Huastecas hidalguense y veracruzana, 1780–1853." *Mexican Studies/Estudios Mexicanos* 12, no. 1 (1996): 1–26.

———. *Desastres agrícolas en México. Catálogo histórico II. Siglo XIX (1822–1900)*. Mexico City: Fondo de Cultura Ecónomica, 1994.

———. "El movimiento olartista, origen y desarrollo, 1836–1838: Una revisión histórica." In *Procesos rurales e historia regional (sierra y costa totonacas de Veracruz)*, edited by Victoria Chenaut, 51–74. Mexico City: CIESAS, 1996.

———, ed. *Indio, nación, y comunidad en el México del siglo XIX*. Mexico City: CIESAS, 1993.

———. "La estructura agraria en las Huastecas, 1880–1915." In *Estructuras y formas agrarias en México del pasado y del presente*, edited by Antonio Escobar Ohmstede and Teresa Rojas Rabiela, 177–96. Mexico City: CIESAS, 2001.

———, et al., eds. *Las sociedades frente a las tendencias modernizadoras de los estados nacionales del siglo XIX latinoamericano.* Amsterdam: CEDLA, 2002.

———. "Los condueñazgos indígenas en las Huastecas hidalguense y veracruzana: Defensa del espacio comunal?" In *Indio, nación y comunidad en el México del siglo XIX,* edited by Antonio Escobar Ohmstede, 171–88. Mexico City: Centro de Estudios Mexicanos y Centroamericanos, 1993.

———, ed. *Los pueblos indios en los tiempos de Benito Juárez (1847–1872).* Mexico City: UAM, 2007.

———. "Review of 'Los bienes de comunidad y la defensa de las tierras en a Mixteca Oaxaqueña.'" *Historia Mexicana* 56, no. 1 (2006): 303–20.

———, and Frans J. Schryer. "Las sociedades agrarias en el norte de Hidalgo, 1856–1900." *Mexican Studies/Estudios Mexicanos* 8, no. 1 (1992): 1–21.

Esparza, Manuel. "El difícil camino de sentirse nación: Oaxaca y la guerra contra los Estados Unidos." In *México en guerra, 1846–1848: Perspectivas regionales,* edited by Laura Herrera Serna, 495–522. Mexico City: Consejo Nacional para la Cultura y las Artes, 1997.

———. *Gillow durante el Porfiriato y la revolución en Oaxaca (1887–1922).* Oaxaca: UABJO, 1985.

———. "Los proyectos de los liberales en Oaxaca (1856–1910)." In *Historia de la cuestión agraria mexicana, estado de Oaxaca,* vol. 1, edited by Leticia Reina, 271–329. 2 vols. Mexico City: UABJO, 1988.

Esteva, Cayetano. *Nociones elementales de geografía histórica del estado de Oaxaca.* Oaxaca: Tip. San German Hnos, 1913.

Ewald, Ursula. *Estudios sobre la hacienda colonial en México. Las propiedades rurales del Colegio Espíritu Santo en Puebla.* Wiesbaden: Franz Steiner Verlag, 1976.

Falcón, Romana. "Force and the Search for Consent: The Role of the Jefaturas Políticas of Coahuila in National State Formation." In *Everyday Forms of State Formation: Revolution and the Negotiation of Rule,* edited by Gilbert M. Joseph and Daniel Nugent, 107–34. Durham, NC: Duke University Press, 1994.

———. "Indígenas y justicia durante la era juarista. El costo social de la 'contribución de sangre' en el estado de México." In *Los pueblos indios en los tiempos de Benito Juárez (1847–1872),* edited by Antonio Escobar Ohmstede, 123–50. Mexico City: UAM, 2007.

———. "Poderes y razones de las jefaturas políticas, Coahuila en el primer siglo de vida independiente." In *Cincuenta años de historia en México,* edited by Alicia Hernández Chávez, 341–70. Mexico City: Colegio de México, 1991.

———. "Subterfugios, armas y deferencias. Indígenas, pueblos y campesinos ante el segundo imperio." In *Las sociedades frente a las tendencias modernizadoras de los estados nacionales del siglo XIX latinoamericano,* edited by Antonio Escobar Ohmstede et al., 125–44. Amsterdam: CEDLA, 2002.

Falcone, Frank Samuel. "Federal-State Relations in Mexico's Restored Republic, Oaxaca: A Case Study, 1867–1872." PhD diss., University of Massachusetts, 1974.

Fallaw, Ben. *Cárdenas Compromised: The Failure of Revolutionary Reform in Postrevolutionary Yucatán*. Durham, NC: Duke University Press, 2001.

———. "An Uncivil Society: Mexican Catholics and the Religious Question in Postrevolutionary State Formation." Unpublished manuscript, on file with author, Michigan State University.

———. "Varieties of Mexican Revolutionary Anticlericalism: Radicalism, Iconoclasm, and Otherwise, 1914–1935." *Americas* 65, no. 4 (2009): 481–509.

Farriss, Nancy. *Maya Society under Colonial Rule*. Princeton, NJ: Princeton University Press, 1984.

———. "Nucleation versus Dispersal: The Dynamics of Population Movement in Colonial Yucatán." *Hispanic American Historical Review* 58, no. 2 (1978): 187–216.

Ferrer Muñoz, Manuel. *Los pueblos indios y el parteaguas de la Independencia de México*. Mexico City: UNAM, 1999.

Figes, Orlando. "Stalin's Oblomov." *Times Literary Supplement*, January 13, 1995, 26.

Fisher, Andrew B. "Relaciones entre fieles y párrocos en la tierra caliente de Guerrero durante la época de a insurgencia, 1775–1826." In *Religión, política e identidad en la Independencia de México*, edited by Brian F. Connaughton, 306–46. Mexico City: UAM, 2010.

Flores, Jorge D. *La revolución de Olarte en Papantla 1836–1838*. Mexico City: Imprenta Mundial, 1938.

Ford, Caroline. *Creating the Nation in Provincial France: Religion and Political Identity in Britanny*. Princeton, NJ: Princeton University Press, 1993.

———. *Divided Houses: Religion and Gender in Modern France*. Cornell, NY: Cornell University Press, 2005.

Fowler, Will. "Carlos María de Bustamante: Un tradicionalista liberal." In *El conservadurismo mexicano en el siglo XIX*, edited by Will Fowler and Humberto Morales Moreno, 59–85. Puebla: Benemerita Universidad Autónoma de Puebla, 1998.

———. "The Compañia Lancastriana and the Elite in Independent Mexico, 1822–1845." *Journal of Iberian and Latin-American Studies* 2, no. 1 (Summer 1996): 81–110.

———. "El pronunciamiento mexicano del siglo XIX. Hacía una nueva tipología." *Estudios de Historia Moderna y Contemporanea de Mexico* 38 (2009): 5–34.

———. "Mexican Political Thought during the 'Forgotten Years.' An Analysis of the Beliefs of the Creole Intelligentsia (1821–1853)." *Bulletin of Latin American Research* 14, no. 3 (1995): 287–312.

———. *Mexico in the Age of Proposals, 1821–1853*. Westport, CT: Greenwood Press, 1998.

———. *Santa Anna of Mexico*. Lincoln: University of Nebraska Press, 2007.

———. "Valentín Gómez Farias: Perceptions of Radicalism in Independent Mexico, 1821–1847." *Bulletin of Latin Amercian Research* 15, no. 1 (1996): 39–62.

———, and Humberto Morales Moreno, eds. *El conservadurismo mexicano en el siglo XIX*. Puebla: Benemerita Universidad Autónoma de Puebla, 1998.

———. "Introducción: Una (re)definición del conservadurismo mexicano del siglo diecinueve." In *El conservadurismo mexicano en el siglo XIX*, edited by

Will Fowler and Humberto Morales Moreno, 11–36. Puebla: Benemerita Universidad Autónoma de Puebla, 1998.

Fowler-Salamini, Heather. *Agrarian Radicalism in Veracruz, 1920–1938*. Lincoln: University of Nebraska, 1978.

———. "The Boom in Regional Studies of the Mexican Revolution: Where Is It Leading?" *Latin American Research Review* 28, no. 2 (1993): 175–90.

Fraile, Francisco. *Cristo. El Señor de los Corazónes*. Huajuapan de León: Diócesis de Huajuapan de León, 1997.

Frazier, Donald S., ed. *The United States and Mexico at War: Nineteenth-Century Expansionism and Conflict*. London: Macmillan, 1998.

Freeze, Gregory. *The Parish Clergy in Nineteenth-Century Russia*. Princeton, NJ: Princeton University Press, 1983.

Friedrich, Paul. *The Princes of Naranja: An Essay in Anthrohistorical Method*. Austin: University of Texas Press, 1986.

Galindo y Galindo, Miguel. *La gran década nacional: La intervención extranjera, 1861–1864*. Mexico City: Imprenta y Fototipia de la Secretaría de Fomento, 1905.

García Alcaraz, Agustín. *Tinujei: Los Triquis de Copala*. Mexico City: Comisión de Río Balsas, 1973.

García-Gutierrez, Blanca. "La experiencia cultural de los conservadores durante el México independiente: Un ensayo interpretivo." *Signos Históricos* 1, no. 1 (1999): 128–48.

García Martínez, Bernardo. *Los pueblos de la sierra: El poder y el espacio entre los indios de norte de Puebla hasta 1700*. Mexico City: Colegio de Michoacán, 1987.

García Ugarte, Marta Eugenia. "Church and State Conflict: Bishop Labastida in Puebla, 1855–1856." In *Mexican Soundings: Essays in Honour of David A. Brading*, edited by Susan Deans-Smith and Eric Van Young, 140–68. London: Institute for the Study of the Americas, 2007.

———. "Estabilidad de Querétaro durante la revolución." In *Memoria del Congreso Internacional sobre la Revolución Mexicana*, edited by Gobierno del Estado de San Luis Potosí, 310–22. Mexico City: Gobierno del Estado de San Luis Potosí, 1991.

———. *Hacendados y rancheros querétanos, 1780–1920*. Mexico City: Consejo Nacional para la Cultura y las Artes, 1992.

———. "La jerarquia católica y los gobiernos mexicanos." In *Clérigos, políticios y política: Las relaciones iglesia y estado en Puebla, siglos XIX y XX*, edited by Alicia Tecuanhuey Sandoval, 69–83. Puebla: Instituto de Ciencias Sociales y Humanidades, BUAP, 2002.

———. *Liberalismo e Iglesia Católica en México: 1824–1855*. Mexico City: Instituto Mexicano de Doctrina Social Cristiana, 1999.

———. "Proyecto pastoral de la Diócesis de Querétaro: De su fundación al Porfiriato." In *Memoria de la I Coloquio Historia de la Iglesia en el Siglo XIX*, edited by Manuel Ramos Medina, 241–60. Mexico City: Colegio de México, 1998.

Garner, Paul. *La revolución en la provincia: Soberania estata y caudillismo serrano en Oaxaca (1910–20)*. Mexico City: Fondo de Cultura Económica, 2004.

Garza Quiros, Fernando. *El Niño Fidencio y el fidencismo*. Monterrey: Editorial Font, 1991.

Gauss, Susan M. *Made in Mexico: Regions, Nation, and the State in the Rise of Mexican Industry*. University Park: Pennsylvania State University Press, 2010.

Gay, José Antonio. *Historia de Oaxaca*. 2 vols. Mexico City: Imprenta de Dublan, 1881.

Gerhard, Peter. *A Guide to the Historical Geography of New Spain*. Cambridge: Cambridge University Press, 1972.

Gibson, Charles. *The Aztecs under Spanish Rule: A History of the Indians of the Valley of Mexico*. Stanford, CA: Stanford University Press, 1964.

Gibson, Ralph. *A Social History of French Catholicism, 1789–1914*. London: Routledge, 1989.

Gil, Mario. *Los ferrocarrileros*. Mexico City: Editorial Extemporaneos, 1971.

Gillingham, Paul. "Force and Consent in Mexican Provincial Politics: Guerrero and Veracruz, 1945–1953." PhD diss., University of Oxford, 2006.

———. "Maximino's Bulls: Popular Protest after the Mexican Revolution, 1940–1952." *Past and Present* 206, no. 1 (2010): 175–211.

———. "Mexican Elections, 1910–1994: Voters, Violence and Veto Power." In *The Oxford Handbook of Mexican Politics*, edited by Roderic Ai Camp, 53–76. Oxford: Oxford University Press, 2012.

Goddard, Jorge Adame. *El pensamiento político y social de los Católicos mexicanos, 1867–1914*. Mexico City: UNAM, 1981.

Goldblatt, David. *The Ball Is Round: A Global History of Soccer*. New York: Riverhead Books, 2006.

Gómez Carpinteiro, Francisco Javier. *Gente de azúcar y agua: Modernidad y posrevolución en el suroeste de Puebla*. Zamora: Colegio de Michoacán, 2003.

González, Orea Luis. *El Huajuapan de ayer*. Mexico City: 2007.

González Escamilla, José Pascual. *Memoria de Acatlán: Revolución de 1910, agrarismo y empresa educativa*. Puebla: Gobierno del Estado de Puebla, 2003.

González Huerta, Neftalí. *El tupa: El mito de un ser fantástico en una comunidad mixteca*. Mexico City: CONACULTA, 2003.

González Navarro, Moisés. *Cristeros y agraristas en Jalisco*. 5 vols. Mexico City: Colegio de México, 2000.

———. "The Hours of Leisure." In *In the Age of Porfirio Díaz*, edited by Carlos B. Gil, 123–28. Albuquerque: University of New Mexico Press, 1977.

———. "Instituciones indígenas en México independiente." In *La política indigenista en México*, edited by Alfonso Caso et al., 113–69. Mexico City: INI, 1973.

González Ramírez, Manuel R. *La iglesia mexicana en cifras*. Mexico City: CIAS, 1969.

González y González, Luis. "El indigenismo de Maximiliano." In *La Intervención Francesa y el imperio de Maximiliano. Cien años después, 1862–1962*, edited by Arturo Arnaiz and Claude Bataillon, 103–10. Mexico City: Asociación Mexicana de Historiadores, 1965.

———. *Historia moderna de México. La república resturada. La vida social*. Mexico City: Hermes, 1974.

———. "La Revolución Mexicana desde el punto de vista de los revolucionados." *Historias* 8–9 (1985): 5–13.

———. *Pueblo en vilo: Microhistoria de San José de Gracia*. Mexico City: Editorial Clio, 1999.

——. "Un cura de pueblo." In *A Dios lo que es de Dios*, edited by Carlos Martínez Assad, 165–82. Mexico City: Aguilar, 1994.

Gosner, Kevin. *Soldiers of the Virgin: The Moral Economy of a Colonial Maya Rebellion.* Tucson: University of Arizona Press, 1992.

Grandin, Greg. *The Last Colonial Massacre: Latin America in the Cold War.* Chicago: University of Chicago Press, 2004.

Greenberg, James B. *Santiago's Sword: Chatino Peasant Religion and Economics.* Berkeley: University of California Press, 1981.

Gruzinski, Serge. "Indian Confraternities, Brotherhoods and Mayordomias in Central New Spain." In *The Indian Community of Colonial Mexico: Fifteen Essays on Land Tenure, Corporate Organizations, Ideology and Village Politics*, edited by Simon Miller and Arij Ouwenweel, 205–23. Amsterdam: CEDLA, 1990.

——. *Man-Gods in the Mexican Highlands: Indian Power and Colonial Society, 1520–1800.* Translated by Eileen Corrigan. Stanford, CA: Stanford University Press, 1989.

Guardino, Peter. *Peasants, Politics, and the Formation of Mexico's National State: Guerrero, 1800–1857.* Stanford, CA: Stanford University Press, 1996.

——. *The Time of Liberty: Popular Political Culture in Oaxaca, 1750–1850.* Durham, NC: Duke University Press, 2005.

Guarisco, Claudia. "Indios, cultura y representación política durante el primer federalismo. El caso del Valle de México." In *Prácticas populares, cultura política y poder en México, siglo XIX*, edited by Brian Connaughton, 167–220. Mexico City: Casa Juan Pablos, 2008.

Guedea, Virginia. *La insurgencia en el departamento del norte: Los llanos de Apan y la sierra de Puebla, 1810–1816.* Mexico City: UNAM, Instituto Dr. José María Luis Mora, 1996.

Guerra, François Xavier. *Las revoluciones hispánicas: Independencias americanas y liberalismo español.* Madrid: Editorial Complutense, 1995.

——. *Le Mexique de l'ancien régime à la révolution.* 2 vols. Paris: Harmattan, 1985.

——. *Modernidad y independencia: Ensayos sobre las revoluciones hispanas.* Madrid: Editorial Encuentro, 2009.

Guerra Manzo, Enrique. "El fuego sagrado. La segunda Cristiada y el caso de Michoacán (1931–1938)." *Historia Mexicana* 218, no. 55 (2005): 513–75.

——. "Entre el modus vivendi y el modus muriendi: El Catolicismo radical en Michoacán, 1926–1938." In *Integrados y marginados en el México posrevoluciónario. Los juegos de poder local y sus nexos con la política nacional*, edited by Nicolás Cárdenas García and Enrique Guerra Manzo, 33–81. Mexico City: Universidad Autónoma Metropolitana, 2009.

——. "The Resistance of the Marginalised: Catholics in Eastern Michoacán and the Mexican State, 1920–1940." *Journal of Latin American Studies* 40 (2008): 109–33.

Gutierrez Alvarez, Juan José. "Sinarquismo y reforma agraria: El contexto de una crisis apuntes y testimonios del movimiento en Querétaro (1931–1944)." In *Religión, política y sociedad: El Sinarquismo y la iglesia en México (nueve ensayos)*, edited by Ruben Aguilar V. and Guillermo Zermeño P., 55–92. Mexico City: Universidad Iberoamericana, 1992.

Gutiérrez Casillas, José. *Historia de la iglesia en México*. Mexico City: Editorial Porrua, 1974.

Guzmán Navarro, Carlos. "Perspectivas en la investigación de la religión." *Revista Nueva Antropología* 51 (1997): 105–17.

Hale, Charles A. *Mexican Liberalism in the Age of Mora, 1821–1853*. New Haven, CT: Yale University Press, 1968.

———. *The Transformation of Liberalism in the Late Nineteenth Century*. Princeton, NJ: Princeton University Press, 1989.

Hamnett, Brian. "Benito Juárez, Early Liberalism, and the Regional Politics of Oaxaca, 1828–1853." *Bulletin of Latin American Research* 10, no. 1 (1991): 3–21.

———. "The Comonfort Presidency, 1855–1857." *Bulletin of Latin American Research* 15, no. 1 (1996): 81–100.

———. "El partido conservador en México, 1858–1867: La lucha por el poder." In *El conservadurismo mexicano en el siglo XIX*, edited by Will Fowler and Humberto Morales Moreno, 213–38. Puebla: Benemerita Universidad Autónoma de Puebla, 1998.

———. "The Formation of a Mexican Conservative Leader: Tomás Mejía, 1840–1856." In *Mexican Soundings: Essays in Honour of David A. Brading*, edited by Susan Deans-Smith and Eric Van Young, 122–39. London: ILAS, 2007.

———. *Juárez*. London: Longman, 1994.

———. "Liberales y conservadores ante el mundo de los pueblos, 1840–1870." In *Los pueblos indios y el parteaguas de la Independencia de México*, edited by Manuel Ferrer Munoz, 167–207. Mexico City: UNAM, 1999.

———. "Liberalism Divided: Regional Politics and the National Project during the Mexican Restored Republic, 1867–1876." *Hispanic American Historical Review* 76, no. 4 (1996): 659–89.

———. "Los pueblos indios y la defensa de la comunidad en el México independiente, 1824–1884: El caso de Oaxaca." In *Los pueblos indios en los tiempos de Benito Juárez (1847–1872)*, edited by Antonio Escobar Ohmstede, 189–205. Mexico City: UAM, 2007.

———. "Mexican Conservatives, Clericals, and Soldiers: The 'Traitor' Tomás Mejía through Reform and Empire, 1855–1867." *Bulletin of Latin American Research* 20, no. 2 (2001): 187–209.

———. "Oaxaca: Las primeras familias y el federalismo de 1823." In *Lecturas históricas del estado de Oaxaca*. Vol. 3, *Siglo XIX*, edited by Ma. de los Angeles Romero Frizzi, 51–69. Mexico City: INAH, 1990.

———. *Roots of Insurgency: Mexican Regions, 1750–1824*. Cambridge: Cambridge University Press, 1986.

———. "Royalist Counterinsurgency and the Continuity of Rebellion: Guanajuato and Michoacán, 1813–20." *Hispanic American Historical Review* 62, no. 1 (1982): 19–48.

Hansen, Peter. "Bac Di Cu: Catholic Refugees from the North of Vietnam, and Their Role in the Southern Republic, 1954–1959." *Journal of Vietnamese Studies* 4, no. 3 (2009): 173–211.

Hardiman, David. "The Bhils and Shahukars of Eastern Gujarat." In *Subaltern Studies V*, edited by Ranajit Guha, 1–54. New Delhi: Oxford University Press, 1987.

Hart, John M. *Empire and Revolution: The Americans in Mexico since the Civil War.* Berkeley: University of California Press, 2002.

———. "Mexico Peasants' War: Conflict in a Transitional Society." In *Riot, Rebellion, and Revolution: Rural Social Conflict in Mexico*, edited by Friedrich Katz, 521–60. Princeton, NJ: Princeton University Press, 1988.

Hart, Paul. *Bitter Harvest: The Social Transformation of Morelos, Mexico and the Origins of the Zapatista Revolution, 1840–1910.* Albuquerque: University of New Mexico Press, 2005.

Harvey, Neil. *The Chiapas Rebellion: The Struggle for Land and Democracy.* Durham, NC: Duke University Press, 1998.

Haskett, Robert. *Indigenous Rulers: An Ethnohistory of Town Government in Colonial Cuernavaca.* Albuquerque: University of New Mexico Press, 1991.

Henderson, Peter V. N. *Gabriel García Moreno and Conservative State Formation in the Andes.* Austin: University of Texas Press, 2008.

Hernández, Conrado. "El efecto de la guerra en el conservadurismo mexicano (1856–1867)." In *Los rostros del conservadurismo mexicano*, edited by Renée de la Torre, Marta Eugenia García Ugarte, and Juan Manuel Ramírez Sáiz, 71–98. Mexico City: CIESAS, 2005.

Hernández Chávez, Alicia. *La tradición republicana del buen gobierno.* Mexico City: El Colegio de México, 1993.

Hernández Jaimes, Jesús. "Actores indios y estado nacional: Las rebeliones indígenas en el sur de México, 1842–1846." *Estudios de Historia Moderna y Contemporanea de México* 26 (2003): 5–44.

Hernández López, Conrado. "La 'reacción a sangre y fuego': Los conservadores en 1855–1867." In *Conservadurismo y derechas en la historia de México*, vol. 1, edited by Erika Pani, 267–99. 2 vols. Mexico City: Fondo de Cultura Económica, 2009.

Hernández Rodríguez, Rosaura. "Las campañas de Porfirio Díaz en el estado de Guerrero." *Estudios de Historia Moderna y Contemporanea de México* 2, no. 12 (1967): 147–56.

———. "Los indios durante la Intervención Francesa." *Estudios de Historia Moderna y Contemporanea de México* 6, no. 63 (1977): 43–49.

Herrera Sánchez, Josefat. "Bodas de oro de la Parroquia de la Virgen de Guadalupe de Huajuapan." *Noticias*, June 23, 2005.

Hewitt de Alcantara, Cynthia. *La modernización de la agricultura Mexicana: 1940–1970.* Madrid: Siglo XIX, 1978.

Hobsbawm, Eric. "The Machine Breakers." *Past and Present* 1, no. 1 (1952): 57–70.

———. *Primitive Rebels: Studies in Archaic Forms of Social Movement in the Nineteenth Century.* Manchester: Manchester University Press, 1959.

Hoffman, Odile. *Tierras y territorio en Xico, Veracruz.* Veracruz: Colección Centenario, Gobierno de Veracruz, 1992.

Hu-Dehart, Evelyn. *Yaqui Resistance and Survival: The Struggle for Land and Autonomy, 1821–1910.* Madison: University of Wisconsin Press, 1984.

Huerta Rios, Cesar. *Organización socio-política de una minoria naciónal, los Triquis de Oaxaca*. Mexico City: INI, 1981.

Hvilshøj, Ulrik. "El dialecto pastor. Las afiliaciones dialectológicas del Nahuatl de los pastores." In *La vida volante: Pastoreo trashumante en la Sierra Madre del Sur, ayer y hoy*, edited by Danièle Dehouve, Roberto Cervantes Delgado, and Ulrik Hvilshøj, 103–29. Mexico City: Joral, 2004.

Iturribarria, Jorge F. *Historia de Oaxaca, 1821–1854*. Oaxaca: Ramírez Belmar, 1935.

———. *Historia de Oaxaca, 1861–1867: La intervención, el imperio y la restauración de la república*. Oaxaca: Imprenta del Gobierno del Estado, 1939.

———. *Historia de Oaxaca: La Guerra de Reforma, 1854–1861*. Oaxaca: Talleres Gráficos del Gobierno del Estado, 1939.

Ivereigh, Austen. *The Politics of Religion in an Age of Revival: Studies in Nineteenth-Century Europe and Latin America*. London: ILAS, 2000.

Jacklein, Klaus. *Un pueblo popoluca*. Translated by María Martínez Penalosa. Mexico City: SEP, 1974.

Jackson, Robert H., ed. *Liberals, the Church, and Indian Peasants: Corporate Lands and the Challenge of Reform in Nineteenth-Century Spanish America*. Albuquerque: University of New Mexico Press, 1997.

Jacobs, Ian. *Ranchero Revolt: The Mexican Revolution in Guerrero*. Austin: University of Texas Press, 1982.

Jacobsen, Nils. *Mirages of Transition: The Peruvian Altiplano, 1780–1930*. Berkeley: University of California Press, 1993.

Jansen, Maarten. *Huisi Tacu: Estudio interpretativo de un libro mixteco antiguo: Codex Vindebonensis Mexicanus*. Amsterdam: Centrum voor Studie can LatijnAmerika, 1982.

———. *Tnuhu niquidza iya: Temas principales de la historiografía mixteca*. Oaxaca: Ediciones del Gobierno Constitucional del Estado de Oaxaca, 1980.

———, and Gabina Aurora Perez Jiménez. *Encounter with the Plumed Serpent: Drama and Power in the Heart of Mesoamerica*. Boulder: University Press of Colorado, 2007.

———. *La lengua señorial de Ñuu Dzaui. Cultura literaria de los antiguos reinos y transformación colonial*. Mexico City: CSEIIO, 2009.

———. *Voces del Dzaha Dzavui (Mixteco Clásico)*. Oaxaca: Colegio Superior para la Educación Integral Intercultural de Oaxaca, 2009.

Guadalupe Jiménez Codinach, Estela, et al., eds. *Planes en la nación mexicana*. 4 vols. Mexico City: Senado de la República, 1987.

Jiménez Moreno, Wigberto, and Salvador Mateos Higuera, eds. *Codice de Yanhuitlán*. Mexico City: INAH, 1940.

Johnson, Richard A. *The Mexican Revolution of Ayutla, 1854–1855: An Analysis of the Evolution and Destruction of Santa Anna's Last Dictatorship*. Westport, CT: Greenwood Press, 1974.

Jonas, Raymond. *France and the Cult of the Sacred Heart: An Epic Tale for Modern Times*. Berkeley: University of California Press, 2000.

Joseph, Gilbert. "The Challenge of Writing Narrative Cultural History." *Mexican Studies/Estudios Mexicanos* 15, no. 2 (1999): 359–71.

Juárez, José Roberto. *Reclaiming Church Wealth: The Recovery of Church Property after Expropriation in the Diocese of Guadalajara, 1860–1911*. Albuquerque: University of New Mexico Press, 2004.

Katz, Friedrich. "Introduction: Rural Revolts in Mexico." In *Riot, Rebellion, and Revolution: Rural Social Conflict in Mexico*, edited by Friedrich Katz, 3–20. Princeton, NJ: Princeton University Press, 1988.

———. *The Life and Times of Pancho Villa*. Stanford, CA: University of Stanford Press, 1998.

———, ed. *Riot, Rebellion, and Revolution: Rural Social Conflict in Mexico*. Princeton, NJ: Princeton University Press, 1988.

Kellogg, Susanne. *Weaving the Past: A History of Latin America's Indigenous Women from the Prehispanic Period to the Present*. Oxford: Oxford University Press, 2005.

Kelly, Michael. "Catholicism and the Left in Twentieth-Century France." In *Catholicism, Politics and Society in Twentieth-Century France*, edited by Kay Chadwick, 142–74. Liverpool: Liverpool University Press, 2000.

Kimball Romney, A., and Robert Ravicz. "The Mixtec." In *Handbook of Middle American Indians*, vol. 7, edited by Evon Z. Vogt, 367–400. Austin: University of Texas Press, 1969.

Kirshner, Alan M. "Tomás Garrido Canabal and the Repression of Religion in Tabasco." In *Religion in Latin American Life and Literature*, edited by Lyle C. Brown and William F. Cooper, 106–18. Waco, TX: Markham Press Fund, 1980.

Knight, Alan. "Cardenismo: Juggernaut or Jalopy?" *Journal of Latin American Studies* 26, no. 1 (1994): 73–107.

———. "El liberalismo mexicano desde la reforma hasta la revolución (una interpretación)." *Historia Mexicana* 35, no. 1 (1985): 59–91.

———. "The Mentality and Modus Operandi of Revolutionary Anticlericalism." In *Faith and Impiety in Revolutionary Mexico*, edited by Matthew Butler, 21–56. London: Palgrave, 2007.

———. *The Mexican Revolution*. 2 vols. Lincoln: University of Nebraska Press, 1990.

———. "Mexico, c. 1930–1946." In *The Cambridge History of Latin America*, vol. 7, edited by Leslie Bethell, 3–82. Cambridge: Cambridge University Press, 1985.

———. *Mexico: The Colonial Era*. Cambridge: Cambridge University Press, 2002.

———. "Popular Culture and the Revolutionary State in Mexico, 1910–1940." *Hispanic American Historical Review* 74, no. 3 (1994): 393–444.

———. "Review of *The Power of God against the Guns of Government: Religious Upheaval in Mexico at the Turn of the Nineteenth Century*." *Hispanic American Historical Review* 79, no. 3 (1999): 557–59.

Knowlton, Robert J. "La iglesia mexicana y la reforma: Respuesta y resultados." *Historia Mexicana* 18, no. 4 (1969): 516–34.

———. "La individualización de la propiedad corporativa civil en el siglo XIX, notas sobre Jalisco." *Historia Mexicana* 28, no. 1 (1978): 24–61.

Kouri, Emilio. "Interpreting the Expropriation of Indian Pueblo Lands in Porfirian Mexico: The Unexamined Legacies of Andrés Molina Enríquez." *Hispanic American Historical Review* 82, no. 1 (2002): 69–117.

———. "Los pueblos y sus tierra antes de 1910." Paper presented at CIESAS conference "Repensar la revolución: Tierra, sociedad y agrarismo antes y después de 1910," Guadalajara, May 12–13, 2011.

———. *A Pueblo Divided: Business, Property, and Community in Papantla, Mexico.* Stanford, CA: Stanford University Press, 2004.

Kselman, Thomas A. "Ambivalence and Assumption in the Concept of Popular Religion." In *Religion and Political Conflict in Latin America*, edited by Daniel H. Levine, 24–41. Chapel Hill: University of North Carolina Press, 1986.

Kyle, Chris. "Land, Labor and the Chilapa Market: A New Look at the 1840s' Peasant Wars in Central Guerrero." *Ethnohistory* 50, no. 1 (2003): 89–130.

Ladd, Doris M. *The Mexican Nobility at Independence, 1780–1826.* Austin: University of Texas Press, 1976.

Lafaye, Jacques. *Quetzalcóatl and Guadalupe: The Formation of Mexican National Consciousness.* Chicago: University of Chicago Press, 1976.

LaFrance, David G. *Revolution in Mexico's Heartland: Politics, War, and State Building in Puebla, 1913–1920.* Wilmington, DE: Scholarly Resources, 2003.

Landavazo, Marco Antonio. "El asesinato de gachupines en la Guerra de Independencia Mexicana." *Mexican Studies/Estudios Mexicanos* 23, no. 2 (2007): 253–82.

Lannon, Frances. "1898 and the Politics of Catholic Identity in Spain." In *The Politics of Religion in an Age of Revival: Studies in Nineteenth-Century Europe and Latin America*, edited by Austen Ivereigh, 56–73. London: ILAS, 2000.

———. *Privilege, Persecution, and Prophecy: The Catholic Church in Spain, 1875–1975.* Oxford: Clarendon Press, 1987.

Lara Cisneros, Gerardo. "Aculturación religiosa en Sierra Gorda: El Cristo Viejo de Xichú." *Estudios de Historia Novohispana* 27 (2002): 59–89.

Larin, Nicolas. *La rebelión de los Cristeros, 1926–1929.* Mexico City: Ediciones Era, 1968.

Larson, Brooke. *Cochabamba, 1550–1900: Colonialism and Agrarian Transformation in Bolivia.* Durham, NC: Duke University Press, 1998.

Lauria-Santiago, Aldo. *An Agrarian Republic: Commercial Agriculture and the Politics of Peasant Communities in El Savador, 1824–1914.* Pittsburg, PA: University of Pittsburg Press, 1999.

Legaria Corro, Gregorio Genaro, and Concepción Legaria Guzmán. *Vida, pasión y obra de Antonio de León (1794–1847): Crónica narrativa del ilustre benemérito de la patria, General Don Antonio de León y Loyola.* León: Legaria Ediciones 2002.

Legrand, Catherine C. "Living in Macondo: Economy and Culture in a United Fruit Company Banana Enclave in Colombia." In *Close Encounters of Empire: Writing the Cultural History of US–Latin American Relations*, edited by Gilbert Michael Joseph, Catherine LeGrand, and Ricardo Donato Salvatore, 333–68. Durham, NC: Duke University Press, 1998.

Lempérière, Annick. *Los espacios públicos en Iberoamérica: Ambigüedades y problemas. Siglos XVIII–XIX.* Mexico City: Centro Francés de Estudios Mexicanos, 1988.

Levy, Daniel C., and Kathleen Bruhn. *Mexico: The Struggle for Democratic Development.* Berkeley: University of California Press, 2006.

Lewis, Gwyn. *The Second Vendée: The Continuity of Counter-revolution in the Department of Gard, 1789–1815*. Oxford: Oxford University Press, 1978.

Lewis, Laura A. *Hall of Mirrors: Power, Witchcraft and Caste in Colonial Mexico*. Durham, NC: Duke University Press, 2003.

Lewis, Stephen. *The Ambivalent Revolution: Forging State and Nation in Chiapas, 1910–1945*. Albuquerque: University of New Mexico Press, 2005.

Lira, Andrés. *Comunidades indígenas frente a la Ciudad de México, Tenochtitlan y Tlatelolco, sus pueblos y barrios, 1812–1919*. Mexico City: Colegio de México, 1983.

Loaeza, Soledad. *Clases medias y política en México, la querella escolar, 1959–1963*. Mexico City: Colegio de México, 1985.

———. "El Partido Acción Nacional: La oposición leal en México." *Foro Internacional* 14, no. 3 (1974): 103–25.

———. "La Iglesia Católica mexicana y el reformismo autoritario." *Foro Internacional* 25 (1984): 138–65.

———. "Notas para el estudio de la iglesia en el México contemporáneo." In *Religión y política en México*, edited by Martin de la Rosa and Charles A. Reilly, 42–58. Mexico City: Siglo XXI, 1985.

Lockhart, James. "Introduction." In *Provinces of Early Mexico: Variants of Spanish American Regional Evolution*, edited by Ida Altman and James Lockhart, 3–31. Los Angeles: UCLA Latin American Center Publications, 1976.

Lomnitz-Adler, Claudio. *Exits from the Labyrinth: Culture and Ideology in the Mexican National Space*. Los Angeles: University of California Press, 1992.

Londoño-Vega, Patricia. *Religion, Culture, and Society in Colombia: Medellin and Antioquia, 1850–1930*. Oxford: Clarendon Press, 2002.

López Villaverde, Angel Luis, and Julio de la Cueva Merino. "A modo de introducción: Reflexiones en torno al clericalismo y al asociacionismo católico." In *Clericalismo y asociacionismo católico en España: De la restauración a la transición*, edited by Angel Luis López Villaverde and Julio de la Cueva Merino, 17–25. Cuenca: Centro de Estudios de Castilla–La Mancha, 2005.

———, eds. *Clericalismo y asociacionismo católico en España: De la restauración a la transición*. Cuenca: Centro de Estudios de Castilla–La Mancha, 2005.

Loyola Jiménez, Adolfo. "El problema agrario en la Mixteca." BA thesis, UNAM, 1961.

Lujambio, Alonso. *Democratización via federalismo? El Partido Acción Nacional: La historia de una estrategia difícil*. Mexico City: Fundación Rafael Preciado Hernández, 2006.

———. "Democratization through Federalism? The National Action Party Strategy, 1939–2000." In *Party Politics and the Struggle for Democracy in Mexico: National and State-Level Analyses of the Partido Acción Nacional*, edited by Kevin J. Middlebrook, 95–128. San Diego, CA: Center for US-Mexican Studies, 2001.

Luque Alcaide, Elisa. "Catecismos mexicanos de las primeras décadas de Independencia (1810–1849)." *Anuario de Historia de la Iglesia* 17 (2008): 43–61.

Lynch, John. *Argentine Caudillo, Juan Manuel de Rosas*. Wilmington, DE: Scholarly Resources, 2001.

Mabry, Donald J. *Mexico's Acción Nacional: A Catholic Alternative to Revolution*. New York: Syracuse University Press, 1973.

Magaloni, Beatriz. *Voting for Autocracy: Hegemonic Party Survival and Its Demise in Mexico*. Cambridge: Cambridge University Press, 2006.

Magaña, Gildardo. *Emiliano Zapata y el agrarismo en México*. 4 vols. Mexico City: Editorial Route, 1951–1952.

Mallon, Florencia E. "Entre utopia y la marginalidad: Comunidades indígenas y culturas políticas en México y Los Andes, 1780–1990." *Historia Mexicana* 42 (1992): 473–504.

———. *Peasant and Nation: The Making of Postcolonial Mexico and Peru*. Chapel Hill: University of North Carolina Press, 1995.

Margolies, Barbara Luise. *Princes of the Earth: Subcultural Diversity in a Mexican Municipality*. Washington, D.C.: American Anthropological Association, 1975.

Martínez, Luis de Guadalupe. *La lucha electoral del PAN en Oaxaca, tomo I (1939–1971)*. Mexico City: 2002.

———. *Los primeros ayuntamientos de Huajuapan, 1820–1823: De la época colonial a la instauración de la república*. Mexico City: 1999.

Martínez Assad, Carlos. "Dos versiones de la Revolución Mexicana." *Nexos* 167 (1991): 78–80.

———. *El laboratorio de la revolución: El Tabasco garridista*. Mexico City: Siglo XXI, 1979.

———. *Los sentimientos de la región: Del viejo centralismo a a nueva pluralidad*. Mexico City: INEHRM, 2001.

Martínez Saldaña, Tomás, and Leticia Gándara Mendoza. *Política y sociedad en México: El caso de Los Altos de Jalisco*. Mexico City: Centro de Investigaciones Superiores, INAH, 1976.

Martínez Soriano, Martin. *Monografía de Cosolotepec, Oax*. Oaxaca de Juárez: Colección Glifo, 1994.

Martínez Vásquez, Procopio. *Relatos y vivencias de Huajuapan: Acatlima, el barrio de Guadalupe y la región triqui*. Mexico City: CONACULTA, 2000.

Martínez Vásquez, Victor Raul. *Historia de la educación en Oaxaca (1825–1940)*. Oaxaca: UABJO, 1994.

———, ed. *La revolución en Oaxaca, 1900–1930*. Oaxaca de Juárez: UABJO, 1985.

Masferrer Kan, Elio. "Los factores étnicos en la rebelión Totonaca de Olarte en Papantla (1836–1838)." *Cuicuilco* 14–15 (1984): 24–32.

———. "Los Totonacos y sus relaciones con el clero católico." In *El anticlericalismo en México*, edited by Franco Savarino and Andrea Mutolo, 399–415. Monterrey: Tecnológico de Monterrey, 2008.

Matute, Alvaro, Evelia Trejo, and Brian Connaughton, eds. *Estado, iglesia y sociedad en México, siglo XIX*. Mexico City: UNAM, 1995.

Mcmillan, James. "'Priest hits girl': On the Front Line in the 'War of Two Frances.'" In *Culture Wars: Secular Catholic Conflict in Nineteenth-Century Europe*, edited by Christopher Clark and Wolfram Kaiser, 77–101. Cambridge: Cambridge University Press, 2001.

Mcnamara, Patrick J. *Sons of the Sierra: Juárez, Díaz, and the People of Ixtlán, Oaxaca, 1855–1920*. Chapel Hill: University of North Carolina Press, 2007.

Medin, Tvzi. *El sexenio alemanista*. Mexico City: Ediciónes Era, 1990.

Medina, Luis. *Historia de la Revolución Mexicana, periodo 1940–1952: Del cardenismo al avilacamachismo*. Mexico City: Colegio de México, 1978.

———. *Historia de la Revolución Mexicana, periodo 1940–1952*. Vol. 20, *Civilismo y modernización del autoritarismo*. Mexico City: Colegio de México, 1979.

Medina, Miguel Angel. *Los Dominicos en América: Presencia y actuación de los Dominicos en la América colonial española de los siglos XVI–XIX*. Madrid: Mapfre, 1992.

Melvin, Karen. "Urban Religions: Mendicant Orders in New Spain's Cities, 1570–1800." PhD diss., University of California, Berkeley, 2005.

Méndez Aquino, Alejandro. *Historia de Tlaxiaco (Mixteca)*. Oaxaca: Compañía Editorial Impresora y Distribuidora, 1985.

———. "La Batalla del Cerro Encantado." In *Oaxaca, textos de su historia*, edited by Margaret Dalton, 363–66. Oaxaca: UABJO, 1990.

Mendez G., Cecilia. *The Plebian Republic: The Huanta Rebellion and the Making of the Peruvian State, 1820–1850*. Durham, NC: Duke University Press, 2005.

Mendoza García, Edgar. "El ganado comunal en la Mixteca Alta: Del la época colonial al siglo XX: El caso de Tepelmeme." *Historia Mexicana* 51, no. 4 (2002): 749–86.

———. "La matanza de animales cabrios." *México Desconocido* 225 (1995).

———. "Las cofradías del curato de Coixtlahuaca durante el siglo XIX. Independencia económica de los pueblos." In *Personajes e instituciones del pueblo mixteco*, edited by Angel Ivan Rivera Guzmán et al., 31–55. Huajuapan: UTM, 2004.

———. *Los bienes de comunidad y la defensa de las tierras en la Mixteca oaxaqueña: Cohesión y autonomía del municipio de Santo Domingo Tepenene 1856–1912*. Mexico City: Senado de la República, 2004.

———. "Poder político y económico de los pueblos chocholtecos de Oaxaca: Municipios, cofradías y tierras comunales, 1825–1889." PhD diss., Colegio de México, 2005.

Mendoza Guerrero, Telesforo. *Ciudad de Huajuapan de León, Oax*. Huajuapan: 1984.

Menegus, Margarita. "La territorialidad de los cacicazgos y los conflictos con terrazgueros y los pueblos vecinos en el siglo XVIII." In *Practicas populares, cultura política y poder en México, siglo XIX*, edited by Brian Connaughton, 97–139. Mexico City: Casa Juan Pablos, 2008.

———. "La venta de parcelas de común repartimiento: Toluca 1872–1900." In *La desamortización civil en México y España, 1750–1920*, edited by Margarita Menegus Bornemann and Mario Cerruti, 71–89. Monterrey: Universidad Autónoma de Nuevo León, 2001.

Menegus Bornemann, Margarita. "La desvinculación y desamortización de la propiedad en Huajuapan, siglo XIX." In *La desamortización civil en Oaxaca*, edited by Carlos Sánchez Silva, 31–64. Oaxaca de Juárez: UABJO, 2006.

———. *La Mixteca Baja entre la revolución y la reforma: Cacicazgo, territorialidad y gobierno, siglos XVIII–XIX*. Mexico City: UAM, 2009.

Menéndez Rodríguez, Hernán. *Iglesia y poder: Proyectos sociales, alianzas políticas y económicas en Yucatán (1857–1917)*. Mexico City: Consejo Nacional para la Cultura y las Artes, 1995.

———. "The Resurgence of the Church in Yucatán: The Olegario Lolina–Cresencio Carillo Alliance, 1867–1901." In *Peripheral Visions: Politics, Society, and the Challenges of Modernity in Yucatán*, edited by Edward D. Terry et al., 213–26. Tuscaloosa: University of Alabama Press, 2010.

Meyer, Jean. *El Catolicismo Social en México hasta 1913*. Mexico City: Instituto Mexicano de Doctrina Social Cristiana, 1992.

———. *El conflito religioso en Oaxaca (1926–1938)*. Oaxaca: UABJO, 2006.

———. *El Sinarquismo, el Cardenismo y la iglesia: 1937–1947*. Mexico City: Tusquets, 2003.

———. *Esperando a Lozada*. Guadalajara: Hexagono, 1989.

———. *La Cristiada*. 3 vols. Mexico City: Siglo XIX, 1973–1974.

———. "La Iglesia Católica en México." In *Conservadurismo y derechas en la historia de México*, edited by Erika Pani, 599–647. 2 vols. Mexico City: Fondo de Cultura Económica, 2009.

———. "La junta protectora de las clases menesterosas. Indigenismo y agrarismo en el segundo imperio." In *Indio, nación, y comunidad en el México del siglo XIX*, edited by Antonio Escobar Ohmstede, 329–64. Mexico City: Centro de Estudios Mexicanos y Centroamericanos, 1993.

———. "La Segunda Cristiada en Michoacán." In *La cultura purhe: II Coloquio de Antropologia e Historia Regionales*, edited by Francisco Miranda, 245–76. Zamora: Colegio de Michoacán, 1981.

———. *La tierra de Manuel Lozada*. Guadalajara: Universidad de Guadalajara, 1989.

———. *Problemas campesinos y revueltas agrarias (1821–1910)*. Mexico City: SEP, 1973.

———. *Sinarquismo: Un fascismo mexicano? 1937–1947*. Mexico City: Joaquín Mortiz, 1979.

Middlebrook, Kevin J. "Party Politics and Democratization in Mexico: The Partido Acción Nacional in Comparative Perspective." In *Party Politics and the Struggle for Democracy in Mexico: National and State-Level Analyses of the Partido Acción Nacional*, edited by Kevin J. Middlebrook, 3–47. San Diego, CA: Center for US-Mexican Studies, 2001.

———, ed. *Party Politics and the Struggle for Democracy in Mexico: National and State-Level Analyses of the Partido Acción Nacional*. San Diego, CA: Center for US-Mexican Studies, 2001.

Miller, John D. *Beads and Prayers: The Rosary in History and Devotion*. London: Burns and Oates, 2002.

Miller, Simon. *Landlords and Haciendas in Modernizing Mexico: Essays in Radical Reappraisal*. Amsterdam: CEDLA, 1995.

———, and Arij Ouwenweel, eds. *The Indian Community of Colonial Mexico: Fifteen Essays on Land Tenure, Corporate Organizations, Ideology, and Village Politics*. Amsterdam: CEDLA, 1990.

Mintz, Sidney Wilfred, and Eric Wolf. "Analysis of Ritual Co-parenthood (Compadrazgo)." *Southwestern Journal of Anthropology* 6, no. 4 (1950): 341–64.

Miranda, Jose. "La población indígena de México en el siglo XVII." *Historia Mexicana* 12, no. 2 (1962): 182–89.

Moguel, Julio. "La cuestión agraria en el periodo 1950–1970." In *Historia de la cuestión agraria mexicana: Política estatal y conflitos agrarios 1950–1970*, edited by Julio Moguel, 103–221. Mexico City: Siglo XIX, 1989.

Molino, Arcadio G. *Historia de Tehuantepec, San Blas, Shihui y Juchitán en la Intervención Francesa en 1864*. Oaxaca: Tipografía de San German, 1911.

Monaghan, John. *The Covenants with Earth and Rain: Exchange, Sacrifice, and Revelation in Mixtec Sociality*. Norman: University of Oklahoma Press, 1995.

———, Arthur Joyce, and Ronald Spores. "Transformations of the Indigenous Cacicazgo in the Nineteenth Century." *Ethnohistory* 50, no. 1 (2003): 131–50.

Montalvo, Enrique, ed. *Historia de la cuestión agraria mexicana: Modernización, lucha agraria y poder político 1920–1934*. Mexico City: Siglo XXI, 1988.

Montesinos Cruz, Victor. *Monografía de Juquila de León, Tezoatlán, Oaxaca: Historia de un pueblo en la Mixteca oaxaqueña*. Mexico City, n.d.

Moore, Barrington, Jr. *Injustice: The Social Bases of Obedience and Revolt*. New York: M. E. Sharp, 1978.

Mora Paz, Luis. *Luis Guevara Camacho*. Mexico City: Comision Editorial del PAN, 1992.

Morgan, Tony. "Proletarians, Políticos, and Patriarchs: The Use and Abuse of Cultural Customs in the Early Industrialization of Mexico City, 1880–1910." In *Rituals of Rule, Rituals of Resistance: Public Celebrations and Popular Culture in Mexico*, edited by William Beezley, Cheryl English Martin, and William E. French, 151–72. Wilmington, DE: Scholarly Resources, 1994.

Morin, C. *Santa Inés Zacatelco (1646–1812): Contribución a la demografía histórica del México colonial*. Mexico City: INAH, 1973.

Morrison, Lynda S. "José Canuto Vela and Yucatán's 'Benign' Clergy from Independence to the Reform, 1821–1861." In *Peripheral Visions, Politics, Society, and the Challenges of Modernity in Yucatán*, edited by Edward D. Terry et al., 173–86. Tuscaloosa: University of Alabama Press, 2010.

Mouat, Andrew C. "Los chiveros de la Mixteca Baja." MA thesis, UNAM, 1980.

Mullen, Robert James. *Dominican Architecture in Sixteenth-Century Oaxaca*. Tempe: Arizona State University, 1975.

Murillo, Luis Enrique. "The Politics of the Miraculous: Popular Religious Practice in Porfirian Michoacán, 1876–1910." PhD diss., University of California, San Diego, 2002.

Nájera Espinoza, Mario Alberto. *La Virgen de Talpa: Religiosidad local, identidad y símbolo*. Zamora: Colegio de Michoacán, 2003.

Nandy, Ashis. *The Intimate Enemy: Loss and Recovery of Self under Colonialism*. New Delhi and New York: Oxford University Press, 1988.

Needell, Jeffrey D. *The Party of Order: The Conservatives, the State, and Slavery in the Brazilian Monarchy, 1831–1871*. Stanford, CA: Stanford University Press, 2006.

Nesvig, Martin Austin, ed. *Religious Culture in Modern Mexico*. Albuquerque: University of New Mexico Press, 2007.

Newcomer, Daniel. *Reconciling Modernity: Urban State Formation in 1940s León, Mexico*. Lincoln: University of Nebraska Press, 2004.

Niblo, Stephen R. *Mexico in the 1940s: Modernity, Politics, and Corruption.* Wilmington, DE: Scholarly Resources, 1999.

Noriega, Alfonso. *El pensamiento conservador y el conservadurismo mexicano.* 2 vols. Mexico City: UNAM, 1972.

"Nuestra Señora del Rosario." *Acontecer Católico* 7, no. 69 (March 2009): 12–13.

Nutini, Hugo G. *Todos Santos: A Syncretic, Expressive and Symbolic Analysis of the Cult of the Dead.* Princeton, NJ: Princeton University Press, 1988.

———, and Betty Bell. *Ritual Kinship: Ideological and Structural Integration of the Compadrazgo System in Rural Tlaxcala.* Princeton, NJ: Princeton University Press, 1984.

Ochoa Serrano, Ivaro. "Religioneros en Michoacán: Eulogio Cárdenas y otras." In *La responsibilidad del historiador: Homenaje a Moises González Navarro*, edited by Shulamit Goldsmit and Guillermo Zermeño, 173–84. Mexico City: Universidad Iberamericana, 1992.

O'Doherty, Laura. "El ascenso de una jerarquia eclesial intransigente, 1890–1914." In *Memoria de la I Coloquio Historia de la Iglesia en el Siglo XIX*, edited by Manuel Ramos Medina, 179–94. Mexico City: Colegio de México, 1998.

O'Hara, Matthew. *A Flock Divided: Race, Religion and Politics in Mexico, 1749–1857.* Durham, NC: Duke University Press, 2010.

Olavarria y Ferrari, Enrique. *México: A través de los siglos.* Vol. 4, *México independiente.* Mexico City: Editorial Cumbre, 1962.

O'Malley, Ilene V. *The Myth of the Revolution: Hero Cults and the Institutionalization of the Mexican State, 1920–1940.* New York: Greenwood Press, 1986.

Ortiz Castro, Ignacio. *Apuntes históricos: Personajes y reflexiones sobre Villa de Chilapa de Díaz. Mixteca Alta.* Mexico City, 2009.

Ortiz Escamilla, Juan. *Guerra y gobierno: Los pueblos y la Independencia de México.* Seville: Editorial Grafites, 1997.

———, and José Antonio Serrano Ortega, eds. *Ayuntamientos y liberalismo gaditano en México.* Zamora: Colegio de Michoacán, 2007.

Otero, Mariano. *Consideraciones sobre la situación política y social de la Republica Mexicana en el año 1847.* Mexico City: Valdes y Redondas, 1848.

Ouwenweel, Arij. "Altepeme and Pueblos de Indios: Some Comparative Theoretical Perspectives on the Analysis of the Colonial Indian Communities." In *The Indian Community of Colonial Mexico: Fifteen Essays on Land Tenure, Corporate Organizations, Ideology, and Village Politics*, edited by Simon Miller and Arij Ouwenweel, 1–37. Amsterdam: CEDLA, 1990.

———. "From 'Tlahtocayotl' to 'Gobernadoryotl': A Critical Examination of Indigenous Rule in 18th Century Central Mexico." *American Ethnologist* 22, no. 4 (1995): 756–85.

———, and Cristina Torales Pacheco. *Expresarios, indios y estado: Perfil de la economía mexicana (siglo XVIII).* Amsterdam: Centro de Estudios y Documentación Latinoamericanos, 1988.

Overmyer-Velazquez, Mark. *Visions of the Emerald City: Modernity, Tradition, and the Formation of Porfirian Oaxaca, Mexico.* Durham, NC: Duke University Press, 2006.

Pacheco, Maria Martha. "Cristianismo sí! Comunismo no! Anticomunismo eclesiástico en México." *Estudios de Historia Moderna y Contemporanea de Mexico* 24 (2002): 143–70.

Padilla, Tanalis. *Rural Resistance in the Land of Zapata: The Jaramillista Movement and the Myth of the Pax-Priísta*. Durham, NC: Duke University Press, 2008.

Padilla Rangel, Yolanda. *Después de la tempestad: La reoganización católica en Aguascalientes, 1929–1950*. Zamora: Colegio de Michoacán, 2001.

Palacios, Guillermo, ed. *Ensayos sobre la nueva historia política de América Latina, siglo XIX*. Mexico City: Colegio de México, 2007.

———. "Postrevolutionary Intellectuals, Rural Readings and the Shaping of the 'Peasant Problem' in Mexico: El Maestro Rural, 1932–34." *Journal of Latin American Studies* 30, no. 2 (1998): 309–39.

Pandey, Gyanendra. "'Encounters and Calamities': The History of a North Indian Qasba in the Nineteenth Century." In *Subaltern Studies: Writings on South Asian History and Society III*, edited by Ranajit Guha, 231–70. New Delhi: Oxford University Press, 1984.

Pani, Erika, ed. *Conservadurismo y derechas en la historia de México*. 2 vols. Mexico City: Fondo de Cultura Económica, 2009.

———. *El segundo imperio: Pasados de usos multiples*. Mexico City: CIDE, 2004.

———. "La nueva historia política mexicanista: No tan nueva, menos política. Mejor historia?" In *Ensayos sobre la nueva historia política de América Latina, siglo XIX*, edited by Guillermo Palacios, 63–82. Mexico City: Colegio de México, México, 2007.

———. *Para mexicanizar el segundo imperio: El imaginario político de los imperialistas*. Mexico City: Colegio de México, 2001.

———. "'Verdaderas figuras de Cooper' o 'Pobres inditos infelices'? La política indigenista de Maxmiliano." *Historia Mexicana* 47, no. 3 (1998): 571–604.

Pansters, Wil G. *Politics and Power in Puebla: The Political History of a Mexican State, 1937–1987*. Amsterdam: CEDLA, 1990.

———. "Tropical Passion in the Desert." In "La Dictablanda: Soft Authoritarianism in Mexico, 1938–1968," edited by Paul Gillingham and Benjamin Smith. Unpublished manuscript, on file with author, Michigan State University.

Paredes Colín, Joaquín. *El distrito de Tehuacán: Breve relación de su historia, censo, monumentos arqueológicos, datos estadísticos, geológicos, etnográficos y otros*. Tehuacán: Tipográfica "El Refugio," 1921.

Parson, Wilfred. *Mexican Martyrdom*. New York: Macmillan, 2006.

Pastor, Rodolfo. *Campesinos y reformas: La Mixteca, 1700–1856*. Mexico City: Colegio de México, 1987.

Paula de Arrangoiz, Francisco de. *Apuntes para la historia del segundo imperio mejicano*. Madrid: Imprenta de M. Rivadeneyra, 1869.

———. *México desde 1808 hasta 1867: Relación de los principales acontecimientos políticos, que han tenido lugar, desde la prison del virey Iturrigay hasta la caida del segundo imperio*. 4 vols. Madrid: A Pérez Dubrull, 1871–1872.

Pellicer de Brody, Olga. *México y la Revolución Cubana*. Mexico City: Colegio de México, 1972.

———, and José Luis Reyna. *Historia de la Revolución Mexicana, 1952–1960: El afianzamineto de la estabilidad política*. Mexico City: Colegio de México, 1978.

Peña, Guillermo de la. "Poder local, poder regional: Perspectivas socio-antropológicas." In *Poder local, poder regional*, edited by Jorge Padua and Alain Vanneph, 27–45. Mexico City: Colegio de México, 1986.

———, and Renée de la Torre. "Microhistoria de un barrio tapatio: Santa Teresita (1930–1980)." In *Vivir en Guadalajara: La ciudad y sus funciónes*, edited by Carmen Castaneda, 119–38. Guadalajara: Ayuntamiento de Guadalajara, 1992.

Peña, Moises de la. *El pueblo, su tierra: Mito y realidad de la reforma agraria en México*. Mexico City: Revista de Economía, 1964.

———. *Problemas sociales y económicos de las mixtecas*. Mexico City: INI, 1950.

Peña Espinosa, Jesús Joel. "Desacrilización de espacios y construcción del discurso anticlerical en Puebla, 1856–1934." In *El anticlericalismo en México*, edited by Franco Savarino and Andrea Mutolo, 165–88. Mexico City: Porrua, 2008.

Peralta Hernández, Juan Carlos. *Cuyotepeji: Desde la época de las aldeas*. Oaxaca: Consejo Nacional para Cultura y las Artes, 2006.

Pérez Escutia, Ramon Alonso. *Taximaroa: Hisoria de un pueblo michoacano*. Morelia: Instituto Michoacano de Cultura, 1986.

Pérez-Rayon, Nora. "The Capital Commemorates Independence at the Turn of the Century." In *Viva Mexico! Viva la Independencia! Celebrations of September 16*, edited by William Beezley and David E. Lorey, 141–66. Wilmington, DE: Scholarly Resources, 2001.

Pérez Toledo, Sonia. "Movilización social y poder político en la Ciudad de México en la decada de 1830." In *Practicas populares, cultura política y poder en México, siglo XIX*, edited by Brian Connaughton, 335–67. Mexico City: Casa Juan Pablos, 2008.

Perkins, Stephen. "Corporate Community or Corporate Houses? Land and Society." *Culture and Agriculture* 27, no. 1 (2005): 16–34.

Perry, Laurens B. *Juárez y Díaz: Machine Politics in Mexico*. Dekalb: University of Northern Illinois, 1978.

Pescador, Juan Javier. *De bautizados a fieles difuntos: Familia y mentalidades en una parroquia urbana: Santa Caterina de México, 1568–1820*. Mexico City: Colegio de México, 1992.

Pita Moreda, María Teresa. "El nacimiento de la provincial de San Hipolito de Oaxaca." In *Actas del II Congreso Internacional sobre Los Dominicos y el Nuevo Mundo*, edited by José Barrado, 433–52. Salamanca: Editorial San Esteban, 1990.

Portes Gil, Emilio. *La lucha entre el poder civil y clero: Estudio histórico y jurídico del Señor Lic. Don Emilio Portes Gil, procurador general de la república*. El Paso: Revista Press, 1935.

Portilla, Anselmo de la. *México en 1856 y 1857: Gobierno del General Comonfort*. Mexico City: INEHRM, 1987.

Pottash-Jutkeit, Barbara. "La moral pública en el Paraguay: Iglesia, estado y relaciones ilícitas en el siglo XIX." In *Familia y vida privada en la historia de Iberoamerica*, edited by Pilar Gonzalbo, 133–59. Mexico City: Colegio de México 1996.

Powell, T. G. "Priests and Peasants in Central Mexico: Social Conflict during 'la Reforma.'" *Hispanic American Historical Review* 57, no. 2 (1977): 296–313.

Priestland, David. *The Red Flag: A History of Communism*. New York: Grove Press, 2009.

Purnell, Jennie. *Popular Movements and State Formation in Revolutionary Mexico: The Agraristas and Cristeros of Michoacán*. Durham, NC: Duke University Press, 1999.

Quintanilla, Susana, and Mary K. Vaughan. *Escuela y sociedad en el periodo cardenista*. Mexico City: Fondo de Cultura Económica, 1997.

Quirk, Robert E. *The Mexican Revolution and the Catholic Church, 1910–1929*. Bloomington: Indiana University Press, 1973.

Raby, David. "Teacher Unionization and the Corporate State in Mexico, 1931–1945." *Hispanic American Historical Review* 59, no. 4 (1979): 674–90.

Radding, Cynthia. "Etnia, tierra y estado: La nación opata de la sierra sonorense en la transición de colonia a república (1790–1840)." In *Indio, nación y comunidad en el México del siglo XIX*, edited by Antonio Escobar Ohmstede, 267–89. Mexico City: Centro de Estudios Mexicanos y Centroamericanos, 1993.

———. *Landscapes of Power and Identity: Comparative Histories in the Sonoran Desert and the Forests of Amazonia from Colony to Republic*. Durham, NC: Duke University Press, 2006.

Ram Garmabella, José. *El criminólogo: Los casos más impactantes del Dr. Quiroz Cuarón*. Mexico City: Debolsillo, 2007.

Ramírez Rancano, Mario. *El patriarca Pérez: La Iglesia Católica apostólica mexicana*. Mexico City: UNAM, 2006.

Rangel Rojas, Guillermo. *General Antonio de León: Consumador de la independencia de Oaxaca y benemérito del estado de Oaxaca*. Oaxaca City: Gobierno del Estado de Oaxaca, 1997.

Reed, Nelson A. *The Caste War of Yucatán*. Stanford, CA: Stanford University Press, 1964.

Reed Torres, Luis. *El General Tomás Mejía frente a la Doctrina Monroe, La Guerra de Reforma, La intervención y el imperio a través del archivo inédito del caudillo conservador Querétano*. Mexico City: Editorial Porrua, 1989.

Reich, Peter L. *Mexico's Hidden Revolution: The Catholic Church in Law and Politics since 1929*. South Bend, IN: University of Notre Dame Press, 1996.

Reina, Leticia. "De las Reformas Borbónicas a las leyes de reforma." In *Historia de la cuestión agraria mexicana, estado de Oaxaca, prehispánico–1924*, vol. 1, edited by Leticia Reina, 183–267. 2 vols. Mexico City: Juan Pablo, 1988.

———. *Las rebeliónes campesinas en México, 1819–1906*. Mexico City: Siglo XXI, 1980.

———. "The Sierra Gorda Peasant Rebellion, 1847–50." In *Riot, Rebellion, and Revolution: Rural and Social Conflict in Mexico*, edited by Friedrich Katz, 269–94. Princeton, NJ: Princeton University Press, 1988.

Reveles Vázquez, Francisco. *Partido Acción Nacional: Los signos de la institucionalización*. Mexico City: UNAM, 2002.

Reyes Heroles, Jesús. *El liberalismo mexicano*. Mexico City: UNAM, 1957–1961.

Rivera, Agustín. *Anales mexicanos: La reforma y el segundo imperio*. Guadalajara: Escuela de Artes y Oficios, 1897.

Rivera, Gregorio Eduardo. "Resistance among Mixtecan Indians of Oaxaca to the Official School, 1920–1952." PhD diss., University of Illinois, 2005.

Rivera Farfán, Carolina. *Vida nueva para Tarecuato: Cabildo y parroquia ante la nueva evangelización*. Zamora: Colegio de Michoacán, 1998.

Rock, David, ed. *Latin America in the 1940s: War and Postwar Transitions*. Berkeley: University of California Press, 1994.

Rodríguez, Artemio, ed. *José Guadalupe Posada, 150 años*. Hong Kong: La Mano, 2003.

Rojas, Basilio. *Efemerides oaxaqueñas 1912*. Mexico City, 1960.

Romero, Laura Patricia. "De la religión jacobina al socialismo. Jalisco, todo un caso." In *Religiosidad y poder en México*, edited by Carlos R. Martínez Assad, 243–78. Mexico City: Programa Institucional de Investigación en Cultura y Religión, 1992.

Romero de Solís, José Miguel. *El aguijón del espíritu: Historia contemporánea de la iglesia en México (1892–1992)*. Mexico City: Colegio de Michoacán, 2006.

Romero Frizzi, María de los Angeles. *Economia y vida de los españoles en la Mixteca Alta, 1519–1720*. Mexico City: INAH, 1990.

———. *El sol y la cruz: Los pueblos indios de Oaxaca colonial*. Mexico City: SEP, 1996.

Roseberry, William. "Peasants, Proletarians, and Politics in Venezuela, 1875–1975." In *Power and Protests in the Countryside: Studies of Rural Unrest in Asia, Europe and Latin America*, edited by Robert P. Weller and Scott E. Guggenheim, 106–31. Durham, NC: Duke University Press, 1989.

Rubin, Jeffrey W. *Decentering the Regime: Ethnicity, Radicalism, and Democracy in Juchitán, Mexico*. Durham, NC: Duke University Press, 1997.

Rugeley, Terry. "From Santa Iglesia to Santa Cruz: Yucatecan Popular Religion in Peace and War, 1800–1876." In *Peripheral Visions, Politics, Society, and the Challenges of Modernity in Yucatán*, edited by Edward D. Terry et al., 187–212. Tuscaloosa: University of Alabama Press, 2010.

———. *Of Wonders and Wise Men: Religion and Popular Culture in Southeast Mexico, 1800–1876*. Austin: University of Texas Press, 2001.

———. *Rebellion Now and Forever: Mayas, Hispanics, and Caste War in Yucatán, 1800–1880*. Stanford, CA: Stanford University Press, 2009.

———. *Yucatán's Maya Peasantry and the Origins of the Caste War*. Austin: University of Texas Press, 1996.

Ruiz, Eduardo. *Historia de la guerra de intervención en Michoacán*. Morelia: Balsa Editores, 1975.

Ruiz Cervantes, Francisco José. "Movimientos zapatistas en Oaxaca. Una primera mirada: 1911–1916." In *Lecturas históricas del estado de Oaxaca*. Vol. 4, *Siglo XX*, edited by Ma. de los Angeles Romero Frizzi, 273–88. Mexico City: Instituto Nacional de Antropología e Historia, 1986–1990.

Salazar Paz, Tomás. "Problemas sociales y jurídicas de las poblaciones indígenas de la Mixteca." BA thesis, UNAM, 1963.

Salmeron Sangines, Pedro. "Catolicismo Social, mutualismo y revolución en Chihuahua." *Estudios de Historia Moderna y Contemporanea de México* 35 (2008): 75–107.

Sánchez Silva, Carlos. "El establecimiento del federalismo en Oaxaca, 1823–1825." In *El establecimiento del federalismo en México (1821–1827),* edited by Josefina Zoraida Vázquez, 237–62. Mexico City: Colegio de México, 2003.

———. *Indios, comerciantes, y burocracia en la Oaxaca poscolonial, 1786–1860.* Oaxaca: UABJO, 1998.

———. "La consumación de la Independencia en Oaxaca." In *La consumación de la Independencia,* edited by José Manuel Alcocer Bernes, 43–62. Mexico City: AGN, 1999.

Sanders, James E. *Contentious Republicans: Popular Politics, Race, and Class in Nineteenth-Century Colombia.* Durham, NC: Duke University Press, 2004.

Sandstrom, Steven E. *Agrarian Populism and the Mexican State: The Struggle for Land in Sonora.* Berkeley: University of California Press, 1981.

Sante Croix, Lambert de. *Onze mois au Mexique.* Paris: Plon, 1897.

Santibáñez, Manuel. *Reseña histórica del cuerpo de ejército de Oriente.* Mexico City: Tipografía de la Oficina Impresora de Estampillas, 1893.

Santoni, Pedro. "A Fear of the People: The Civic Militia of Mexico in 1845." *Hispanic American Historical Review* 68, no. 2 (1988): 269–88.

Santos Soriano, Daniel. *Santos Reyes Tepejillo, reseña histórica.* Oaxaca de Juárez: CONACULTA, 2007.

Sau Witte, Hans, and Koo Sau. "Quetzalcóatl: Mixtec Religious Symbolism in Past and Present." In *Mixtec Writing and Society,* edited by Maarten E. R. G. N. Jansen and Laura N. K. van Broekhoven, 423–35. Amsterdam: KNAW Press, 2008.

Savarino, Franco, and Andrea Mutolo, eds. *El anticlericalismo en México.* Mexico City: Porrua, 2008.

Scheper Hughes, Jennifer. *Biography of a Mexican Crucifix: Lived Religion and Local Faith from the Conquest to the Present.* Oxford: Oxford University Press, 2009.

Schmitt, Karl M. "Catholic Adjustment to the Secular State: The Case of Mexico, 1867–1991." *Catholic Historical Review* 48, no. 2 (July 1962): 182–204.

———. "The Evolution of Mexican Thought on Church-State Relations, 1876–1911." PhD diss., University of Pennsylvania, 1954.

Schneider, Luis Mario. *Cristos, santos y virgenes: Santuarios y devociones de México.* Mexico City: Editorial Plantea, 1995.

Schryer, Frans J. *Ethnicity and Class Conflict in Rural Mexico.* Princeton, NJ: Princeton University Press, 1990.

———. *The Rancheros of Pisaflores: The History of a Peasant Bourgeoisie in Twentieth-Century Mexico.* Toronto: University of Toronto Press, 1980.

Scott, James. *Domination and the Arts of Resistance.* New Haven, CT: Yale University Press, 1992.

———. *The Moral Economy of the Peasant: Rebellion and Subsistence in Southeast Asia.* New Haven, CT: Yale University Press, 1976.

———. *Weapons of the Weak: Everyday Forms of Peasant Resistance*. New Haven, CT: Yale University Press, 1985.

Segovia, Rafael. *La politización del niño mexicano*. Mexico City: Colegio de México, 1975.

Segura, Jaime. "Los indígenas y los programas de desarrollo agrario (1940–1964)." In *Historia de la cuestión agraria mexicana, estado de Oaxaca, 1925–1986*, vol. 2, edited by Leticia Reina, 189–290. 2 vols. Oaxaca de Juárez: Juan Pablos, 1988.

Septién Torres, Valentina. "Guanajuato y la resistencia católica en el siglo XX." In *Integrados y marginados en el México posrevoluciónario Los juegos de poder local y sus nexos con la política nacional*, edited by Nicolás Cárdenas García and Enrique Guerra Manzo, 83–119. Mexico City: Universidad Autónoma Metropolitana, 2009.

———. *La educación privada en México (1903–1976)*. Mexico City: Universidad Iberoamericana, 1997.

———. "La Unión Nacional de Padres de Familia: La lucha por la enseñanza de la religión en las escuelas particulares." In *La ciudad y el campo en la historia de México: Memoria de la VII Reunión de Historiadores Mexicanos y Norteamericanos*, vol. 2, edited by Ricardo Sánchez, Eric Van Young, and Gisela Von Wobeser, 927–35. 2 vols. Mexico City: UNAM, 1992.

Serrano Alvarez, Pablo. "Historiografía regional mexicana: Tendencias y enfoques metodológicos 1968–1990." *Relaciones* 72 (1997): 47–57.

———. *La batalla del espíritu: El movimiento sinarquista en el Bajío mexicano (1932–1951)*. 2 vols. Mexico City: CONACULTA, 1992.

Servin, Elisia. "Hacia el levantamiento armado. Del henriquismo a los federaciónistas leales en los años cincuenta." In *Movimientos armados en México, siglo XX*, vol. 1, edited by Veronica Oikon Solano and Marta Eugenia García Ugarte, 307–32. 3 vols. Zamora: Colegio de Michoacán, 2008.

Shadow, Robert D., and María J. Rodríguez-Shadow. "Religión, economía y política en la rebelión cristera: El caso de los gobiernistas de Villa Guerrero, Jalisco." *Historia Mexicana* 43, no. 4 (1994): 657–99.

Sherman, John W. *The Mexican Right: The End of Revolutionary Reform, 1929–1940*. Westport, CT: Praeger, 1997.

———. "Reassessing Cardenismo: The Mexican Right and the Failure of a Revolutionary Regime, 1934–1940." *Americas* 54, no. 3 (1998): 357–78.

Sierra, Justo. *Juárez su obra y su tiempo*. Mexico City: UNAM, 2006.

Silva Prada, Natalia. "Las manifestaciónes políticas indígenas ante el proceso de control y privatización de tierras: México, 1786–1856." In *Poder y legitimidad en México en el siglo XIX: Instituciones y cultura política*, edited by Brian Connaughton, 75–135. Mexico City: UAM, 2003.

Silverblatt, I. M. *Moon, Sun and Witches: Gender Ideologies and Class in Inca and Colonial Peru*. Princeton, NJ: Princeton University Press, 1987.

Simon, Collier. *Chile: The Making of a Modern Republic, 1830–1865: Politics and Ideas*. Cambridge: Cambridge University Press, 2003.

Sinkin, Richard. *The Mexican Reform, 1855–1876: A Study in Liberal Nation Building*. Austin: University of Texas Press, 1979.

Smith, Benjamin. "El Señor del Perdon y los matacristos de Oaxaca: La Revolución Mexicana desde el punto de vista de los Católicos." *Desacatos* 38 (2010): 61–76.

———. *Pistoleros and Popular Movements: The Politics of State Formations in Postrevolutionary Oaxaca.* Lincoln: University of Nebraska Press, 2009.

———, and Aaron Van Oosterhout. "The Limits of Catholic Science and the Mexican Revolution." *Endeavour* 34, no. 2 (2010): 55–60.

Smith, Brian H. *The Church and Politics in Chile: Challenges to Modern Catholicism.* Princeton, NJ: Princeton University Press, 1982.

Sosa Elízaga, Raquel. *Los códigos ocultos del Cardenismo: Un estudio de la violencia política, el cambio social y la continuidad institucional.* Mexico City: UNAM, 1996.

Soto Correa, José Carmen. *Movimientos campesinos de derecha en el Oriente Michoacano, 1867–1914.* Mexico City: Hoja Casa Editorial, 1996.

Spores, Ronald. "Differential Response to Colonial Control among the Mixtecs and Zapotecs of Oaxaca." In *Native Resistance and the Pax Colonial in New Spain,* edited by Susan Schroeder, 30–46. Lincoln: University of Nebraska Press, 1998.

———. "Marital Alliance in the Political Integration of Mixtec Kingdoms." *American Anthropologist* 76, no. 2 (1974): 297–311.

———. "Mixteca Cacicas: Status, Wealth, and the Political Accommodation of Native Elite Women in Early Colonial Oaxaca." In *Indian Women of Early Mexico,* edited by Stephanie Wood, Susan Schroeder, and Robert Haskett, 185–98. Norman: University of Oklahoma Press, 1997.

———. *The Mixtec Kings and Their People.* Norman: University of Oklahoma Press, 1967.

———. *The Mixtecs in Ancient and Colonial Times.* Norman: University of Oklahoma Press, 1984.

———. "Postclassic Mixtec Kingdoms: Ethnohistoric and Archaeological Evidence." In *The Cloud People: Divergent Evolution of the Zapotec and Mixtec Civilizations,* edited by Kent V. Flannery and Joyce Marcus, 255–60. New York: Academic Press, 1983.

———, and Miguel Saldaña. *Documentos para la etnohistoria del estado de Oaxaca: Indice del ramo de mercedes del Archivo General de la Nación, México.* Nashville, TN: Vanderbilt University, 1973.

Staples, Anne. "Clerics as Politicians: Church, State and Political Power in Independent Mexico." In *Mexico in the Age of Democratic Revolutions, 1750–1850,* edited by Jaime E. Rodríguez, 223–41. Boulder and London: Lynne Rienner, 1994.

———. *El estado y la iglesia en la república restaurada, in el dominio de las minorías: República restaurada y porfiriato.* Mexico City: Colegio de México, 1989.

———. "La educación como instrumento ideológico del estado: El conservadurismo educativo en el México decimonónico." In *El conservadurismo mexicano en el siglo XIX,* edited by Will Fowler and Humberto Morales Moreno, 103–14. Puebla: Benemérita Universidad Autónoma de Puebla, 1998.

———. *La iglesia en la primera república federal mexicana (1824–1835).* Mexico City: SEP, 1976.

———. *Recuento de una batalla inconclusa, la educación mexicana de Iturbide a Juárez.* Mexico City: Colegio de México, 2005.

Steffen Riedemann, Cristina. *Los comerciantes de Huajuapan de León, Oaxaca, 1920–1980.* Mexico City: UAM, 2001.

Stern, Steve. *The Secret History of Gender: Women, Men and Power in Late Colonial Mexico.* Chapel Hill: University of North Carolina Press, 1999.

———. "The Struggle for Solidarity: Class, Culture, and Community in Highland Indian America." *Radical History Review* 27 (1983): 21–45.

Stevens, Donald F. "Lo revelado y lo oscurecido: La política popular desde los archivos parroquiales." In *Construcción de la legitimidad política en México*, edited by Brian F. Connaughton, Carlos Illades, and Sonia Perez Toledo, 207–26. Zamora: Colegio de Michoacán, 1999.

———. *Origins of Instability in Early Republican Mexico.* Durham, NC: Duke University Press, 1991.

———. "Temerse la ira del cielo: Los conservadores y la religiosidad popular en los tiempos de colera." In *El conservadurismo mexicano en el siglo XIX*, edited by Will Fowler and Humberto Morales Moreno, 87–101. Puebla: Benemérita Universidad Autónoma de Puebla, 1998.

Sullivan-González, Douglass. *Piety, Power, and Politics: Religion and Nation Formation in Guatemala, 1821–1871.* Pittsburgh, PA: University of Pittsburgh Press, 1998.

Tackett, Timothy. *Priest and Parish in Eighteenth-Century France: A Social and Political Study of the Cures in a Diocese of Dauphine, 1750–1791.* Princeton, NJ: Princeton University Press, 1977.

———. *Religion, Revolution, and Regional Culture in Eighteenth-Century France: The Ecclesiastical Oath of 1791.* Princeton, NJ: Princeton University Press, 1986.

Tamayo, Jorge L. *El General Antonio de León, defensor del Molino del Rey.* Mexico City, 1947.

Tanck de Estrada, Dorothy. "La alfabetización: Medio para forma los ciudadanos." In *Historia de la alfabetización y de la educación de adultos en México*, vol. 1, 111–32. 3 vols. Mexico City: Colegio de México, 1993.

Tarvaez, David. *The Invisible War: Indigenous Devotions, Discipline, and Dissent in Colonial Mexico.* Stanford, CA: Stanford University Press, 2010.

Taylor, William B. *Drinking, Homicide, and Rebellion in Colonial Mexican Villages.* Stanford, CA: Stanford University Press, 1979.

———. *Magistrates of the Sacred: Priests, and Parishioners in Eighteenth-Century Mexico.* Stanford, CA: Stanford University Press, 1996.

———. "Two Shrines of the Cristo Renovado: Religion and Peasant Politics in Late Colonial Mexico." *American Historical Review* 110, no. 4 (2005): 945–74.

Terraciano, Kevin. *The Mixtecs of Colonial Oaxaca: Ñudzahui History, Sixteenth through Eighteenth Centuries.* Stanford, CA: Stanford University Press, 2001.

———. "The People of Two Hearts and the One God from Castile: Ambivalent Responses to Christianity in Early Colonial Oaxaca." In *Religion in New Spain*, edited by Stafford Poole and Susan Schroeder, 16–32. Albuquerque: University of New Mexico Press, 2007.

Terry, Edward D., Ben W. Fallaw, Gilbert M. Joseph, and Edward H. Moseley, eds. *Peripheral Visions: Politics, Society, and the Challenges of Modernity in Yucatán.*

Tuscaloosa: University of Alabama Press, 2010.

Thompson, E. P. "The Moral Economy of the English Crowd in the Eighteenth Century." *Past and Present* 50 (1971): 76–136.

———. "Patrician Society, Plebian Culture." *Journal of Social History* 7, no. 4 (1974): 382–405.

Thomson, Guy P. C. "Bulwarks of Patriotic Liberalism: The National Guard, Philharmonic Corps and Patriotic Juntas in Mexico, 1847–1888." *Journal of Latin American Studies* 22 (1990): 31–68.

———. "Cabecillas indígenas de la guardia nacional en la sierra de Puebla, 1854–1889." In *La reindianización de America, siglo XIX*, edited by Leticia Reina, 121–36. Mexico City: Siglo XIX, 1997.

———. "The Ceremonial and Political Roles of Villages Bands, 1846–1974." In *Rituals of Rule, Rituals of Resistance: Public Celebrations and Popular Culture in Mexico*, edited by William Beezley, Cheryl English Martin, and William E. French, 307–42. Wilmington, DE: Scholarly Resources, 1994.

———. "La contrarreforma en Puebla, 1854–1886." In *El conservadurismo mexicano en el siglo XIX (1810–1910)*, edited by William Fowler and Humberto Morales Moreno, 239–64. Puebla: Universidad Autónoma de Puebla, 1999.

———. "Los indios y el servicio militiar en el México decimonónico. Leva o ciudania?" In *Indio, nación, y comunidad en el México del siglo XIX*, edited by Antonio Escobar Ohmstede, 207–51. Mexico City: CIESAS, 1993.

———. "Popular Aspects of Liberalism in Mexico, 1848–1888." *Bulletin of Latin American Research* 10 (1991): 121–52.

———. *Puebla de los Angeles: Industry and Society in a Mexican City, 1750–1850*. Boulder, CO: Westview Press, 1989.

———, and David G. LaFrance. *Patriotism, Politics, and Popular Liberalism in Nineteenth-Century Mexico: Juan Francisco Lucas and the Puebla Sierra*. Wilmington, DE: Scholarly Resources, 1999.

Tilly, Charles. *The Vendée*. Cambridge, MA: Harvard University Press, 1976.

Toren, Christina. "The Effectiveness of Ritual." In *The Anthropology of Christianity*, edited by Fenella Cannell, 185–210. Durham, NC: Duke University Press, 2006.

Toro, Alfonso. *La iglesia y el estado en México*. Mexico City: Talleres Gráficas de la Nación, 1927.

Torre, Renée de la, and Marta Eugenia García Ugarte. "Introducción." In *Los rostros del conservadurismo mexicano*, edited by Renée de la Torre, Marta Eugenia García Ugarte, and Juan Manuel Ramírez Saíz, 11–34. Mexico City: CIESAS, 2005.

———, and Juan Manuel Ramírez Saíz, eds. *Los rostros del conservadurismo mexicano*. Mexico City: CIESAS, 2005.

Torre Villar, Ernesto de la. *Diario de un cura de pueblos y relación de los señores curas que han servido la Parroquia de Nuestra Señora de la Asunción de Tlatlaqui, escrita por el señor cura don Ramón Vargas López*. Mexico City: UNAM, 2005.

———. "Seminario Palafoxiana de Puebla: Nóminas de maestros y alumnos (1651 y 1770)." *Annuario de Historia de la Iglesia* 15 (2006): 237–58.

Torres Ramírez, Blanca. *Historia de la Revolución Mexicana, 1940–1952: Hacia la utopia industrial*. Mexico City: Colegio de México, 1984.

Traffano, Daniela. "Educación, civismo, y catecismos políticos. Oaxaca, segunda mitad del siglo XIX." *Revista Mexicana de Investigación Educativa* 12, no. 34 (2007): 1043–63.

Trexler, Richard C. *Reliving Golgotha: The Passion Play of Iztapalapa*. Cambridge, MA: Harvard University Press, 2003.

Turner, John K. *Barbarous Mexico*. Austin: University of Texas, 1984.

Tutino, John. *From Insurrection to Revolution in Mexico: Social Bases of Agrarian Violence, 1750–1940*. Princeton, NJ: Princeton University Press, 1986.

———. "Rebelión indígena en Tehuantepec." *Cuadernos Políticos* 24 (1980): 89–101.

———. "The Revolution in Mexican Independence: Insurgency and the Renegotiation of Property, Production, and Patriarchy in the Bajío, 1800–1855." *Hispanic American Historical Review* 78, no. 3 (1998): 367–418.

Underdown, David. *Revel, Riot, and Rebellion: Popular Politics and Culture in England, 1603–1660*. Oxford: Oxford University Press, 1987.

Valdés, D. N. "The Decline of the Sociedad de Castas in Mexico City." PhD diss., University of Michigan, 1978.

Valdes, Norberto. *Ethnicity, Class, and the Indigenous Struggle for Land in Guerrero, Mexico*. Lincoln: University of Nebraska, 1998.

Valenzuela, J. Samuel, and Erika Maza Valenzuela. "The Politics of Religion in Catholic Country: Republican Democracy, Cristianismo Social and the Conservative Party in Chile, 1850–1925." In *The Politics of Religion in an Age of Revival: Studies in Nineteenth-Century Europe and Latin America*, edited by Austen Ivereigh, 188–223. London: ILAS, 2000.

Valles, Patricia. "José Garibi Rivera: Primer cardenal mexicano." In *A Dios lo que es de Dios*, edited by Carlos Martínez Assad, 267–86. Mexico City: Aguilar, 1995.

Vanderwood, Paul. "The Millennium and Mexican Independence." In *The Birth of Modern Mexico, 1780–1824*, edited by Christon I. Archer, 165–87. Lanham, MD: Rowman & Littlefield, 2003.

———. *The Power of God against the Guns of Government: Religious Upheaval in Mexico at the Turn of the Nineteenth Century*. Stanford, CA: Stanford University Press, 1998.

———. "Religion: Official, Popular, and Otherwise." *Mexican Studies/Estudios Mexicanos* 16, no. 2 (2000): 411–41.

Van Oss, Adriaan C. *Catholic Colonialism: A Parish History of Guatemala, 1524–1821*. Cambridge: Cambridge University Press, 1986.

Van Young, Eric. *Hacienda and Market in Eighteenth-Century Mexico: The Rural Economy of the Guadalajara Region, 1675–1820*. Berkeley: University of California Press, 1981.

———. "In the Gloomy Caverns of Paganism: Popular Culture, Insurgency and Nation-Building in Mexico, 1800–1821." In *The Birth of Modern Mexico, 1780–1824*, edited by Christon I. Archer, 41–65. Lanham, MD: Rowman & Littlefield, 2003.

———, ed. *Mexico's Regions: Comparative History and Development*. San Diego, CA: Center for US-Mexican Studies, 1992.

———. *The Other Rebellion: Popular Violence, Ideology, and the Mexican Struggle for Independence, 1810–1821*. Stanford, CA: Stanford University Press, 2001.

Varley, Ann. "Women and the Home in Mexican Family Law." In *Hidden Histories of Gender and the State in Latin America*, edited by Elizabeth Dore and Maxine Molyneux, 238–61. Durham, NC: Duke University Press, 2000.

Vaughan, Mary K. "The Construction of the Patriotic Festival in Tecamachalco, Puebla, 1900–1946." In *Rituals of Rule, Rituals of Resistance: Public Celebrations and Popular Culture in Mexico*, edited by William Beezley, Cheryl English Martin, and William E. French, 213–46. Wilmington, DE: Scholarly Resources, 1994.

———. *Cultural Politics in Revolution: Teachers, Peasants, and Schools in Mexico, 1930–1940*. Tucson: University of Arizona Press, 1997.

———. "The Educational Project of the Mexican Revolution: The Response of Local Societies (1934–1940)." In *Molding the Hearts and Minds: Education, Communications, and Social Change in Latin America*, edited by John A. Britton, 105–26. Wilmington, DE: Scholarly Resources, 1994.

———. "El papel político de los maestros federales durante la época de Cárdenas: Sonora y Puebla." In *Escuela y sociedad en el periodo cardenista*, edited by Susana Quintanilla and Mary K. Vaughan, 166–95. Mexico City: Fondo de Cultura Económica, 1997.

Velasco, Alfonso Luis. *Geografía y estadística de la República Mexicana: Oaxaca*. 20 vols. Mexico City: Ministerio de Fomento, Colonización e Industria, 1891.

Ventura Patiño, María del Carmen. *Disputas por el gobierno local en Tarecuato, Michoacán, 1942–1999*. Zamora: Colegio de Michoacán, 2003.

Vera Soto, Carlos Francisco. *La formación del clero diocesano durante la persecución religiosa en México, 1910–1940*. Mexico City: Universidad Pontificia de México, 2005.

Vigil, José M. *México: A través de los siglos*. Vol. 5, *La reforma*. Mexico City: Editorial Cumbre, 1962.

Villagómez, Castulo. *Memorias de un valiente Zapatista*. Huajuapan: CONACULTA, 1991.

Villa Lever, Lorenza. *Los libros de texto gratuitos: La disputa por la educación en México*. Guadalajara: Universidad de Guadalajara, 1988.

Villaseñor, Guillermo. *Estado e iglesia: El caso de la educación*. Mexico City: Editorial Edicol, 1978.

Villavicencio Rojas, José Mario. *Donde se canta y se baila: Evocaciones de Leonor Rodríguez sobre Coicoyán de las Flores, Oaxaca*. Puebla: Benemérito Universidad Autónoma de Puebla, 2004.

Viotta Da Costa, Emilia. "New Publics, New Politics, New Histories: From Economic Reductionism to Cultural Reductionism: In Search of Dialectics." In *Reclaiming the Political in Latin American History: Essays from the North*, edited by Gilbert Joseph, 17–31. Durham, NC: Duke University Press.

Voekel, Pamela. "Liberal Religion: The Schism of 1861." In *Religious Culture in Modern Mexico*, edited by Martín Austin Nesvig, 78–105. Albuquerque: University of New Mexico Press, 2007.

Wallace, Peter George. *The Long European Reformation*. London: Palgrave, 2004.

Warren, Richard. "Elections and Popular Political Participation in Mexico, 1808–1836." In *Liberals, Politics, and Power: State Formation in Nineteenth-Century Latin America*, edited by Vincent C. Peloso and Barbara Tannenbaum, 31–40. Athens: University of Georgia Press, 1996.

———. *Vagrants and Citizens: Politics and Masses in Mexico City from Colony to Republic.* Lanham, MD: Rowman & Littlefield, 2001.

Weber, Eugene. *Peasants into Frenchmen: The Modernization of Rural France, 1870–1914.* Stanford, CA: Stanford University Press, 1976.

Weckmann, Luis. *The Medieval Heritage of Mexico.* Translated by Frances M. López-Morillas. New York: Fordham University Press, 1992.

Weiner, Richard. "Trinidad Sánchez Santos: Voice of the Catholic Opposition in Porfirian Mexico." *Mexican Studies/Estudios Mexicanos* 17, no. 2 (2001): 321–49.

Weitlaner, Roberto. "Chilacapa y Tetecingo." *El Mexico Antiguo* 4, no. 2 (1943): 1–45.

Welter, Barbara. "The Feminization of American Religion, 1800–1860." In *Clio's Consciousness Raized: New Perspectives in the History of Women*, edited by Mary Hartman and Lois Banner, 137–57. New York: Octagon Books, 1976.

Whetton, N. L. *Rural Mexico.* Chicago: University of Chicago Press, 1948.

White, Christopher M. *Creating a Third World: Mexico, Cuba, and the United States during the Castro Era.* Albuquerque: University of New Mexico Press, 2007.

Wickam-Crowley, Timothy P. *Guerillas and Revolution in Latin American: A Comparative Study of Insurgents and Regimes since 1956.* Princeton, NJ: Princeton University Press, 1992.

Wilkie, James W. "The Meaning of the Cristero Religious War against the Mexican Revolution." *Journal of Church and State* 8 (1966): 214–33.

Wilkie, Raymond. *San Miguel: A Mexican Collective Ejido.* Stanford, CA: Stanford University Press, 1971.

Winter, Marcus. *Cerro de las Minas: Arqueología de la Mixteca Baja.* Oaxaca de Juárez: Casa de la Cultura de Huajuapan de León, 1996.

Wolf, Eric. "Aspects of Group Relations in a Complex Society: Mexico." *American Anthropologist* 58, no. 5 (October 1956): 1065–78.

———. "Closed Corporate Peasant Communities in Mesoamerica and Central Java." *Southwestern Journal of Anthropology* 13 (1957): 1–18.

———. *Sons of the Shaking Earth.* Chicago: University of Chicago Press, 1959.

———. "The Vicissitudes of the Closed Corporate Peasant Community." *American Ethnologist* 13 (1986): 325–29.

Womack, John. *Zapata and the Mexican Revolution.* New York: Knopf, 1969.

Woodward, Ralph Lee. *Rafael Carrera and the Emergence of the Republic of Guatemala, 1821–1871.* Athens: University of Georgia Press, 1993.

Wright-Rios, Edward. *Revolutions in Mexican Catholicism: Reform and Revelation in Oaxaca, 1887–1934.* Durham, NC: Duke University Press, 2009.

———. "Visions of Women: Revelation, Gender and Catholic Resurgence." In *Religious Culture in Modern Mexico*, edited by Martin Austin Nesvig, 178–202. Albuquerque:

University of New Mexico Press, 2007.

Young, Glennys. *Power and the Sacred in Revolutionary Russia: Religious Activists in the Village.* University Park: Pennsylvania State University Press, 1997.

Zamacois, Niceto de. *Historia de Méjico desde sus tiempos más remotos hasta nuestros días.* 19 vols. Barcelona: J. F. Parres, 1877–1882.

Zárate Hernández, José Eduardo. *Los señores de utopía. Etnicidad política en una comunidad P'urhépecha: Santa Fe de la Laguna–UEAMO.* Zamora: Colegio de Michoacán, 2001.

Zavala, Silvio. "Victor Considerant ante el problema social de México." *Historia Mexicana* 7, no. 3 (1958): 309–28.

Zeldin, Theodore. *France, 1848–1945.* Vol. 2, *Intellect, Taste, and Anxiety.* Oxford: Oxford University Press, 1977.

Zermeño, Guillermo, and Rubén Aguilar. "Ensayo introductorio: Iglesia y Sinarquismo en México." In *Religión, política y sociedad: El Sinarquismo y la iglesia en México (nueve ensayos),* edited by Guillermo Zermeño and Rubén Aguilar, 17–30. Mexico City: Universidad Iberoamericana, 1992.

———, eds. *Hacia una reinterpretación del Sinarquismo actual.* Mexico City: Universidad Iberoamericana, 1988.

Zolov, Eric. "Cuba sí, Yanquis no: The Sacking of the Instituto Cultural Mexico-Norteamericano in Morelia, Michoacan, 1961." In *In from the Cold: Latin America's New Encounter with the Cold War,* edited by Gilbert M. Joseph and Daniella Spenser, 214–52. Durham, NC: Duke University Press, 2007.

———. *Refried Elvis: The Rise of the Mexican Counterculture.* Berkeley: University of California Press, 1999.

Zoraida Vázquez, Josefina. "Iglesia, ejercito, y centralismo." *Historia Mexicana* 39, no. 1 (1989): 205–34.

———. "La educación socialista de los años treinta." *Historia Mexicana* 28, no. 3 (1969): 408–23.

———. "Los primeros tropiezos." In *Historia general de México,* edited by El Colegio de México, 525–82. Mexico City: Colegio de México, 2000.

———. "Political Plans and Collaboration between Civilians and the Military, 1821–1846." *Bulletin of Latin American Research* 15, no. 1 (1996): 19–38.

Index

Abelino, Andres, 133
Acapulco, 56, 111
Acaquizapan, 29, 62, 83, 87, 90, 130, 150, 211, 212, 307
Acatlán, 22–24, 28, 30, 47, 48, 50, 53, 58, 68, 97, 136, 146, 147, 185, 186, 190, 194, 195, 198, 208, 209, 212, 264
Acción Católica Mexicana (ACM), 248, 249, 259–62, 267–71, 276–79, 289
Aceite party, 132
Acevedo, Juan (eighteenth-century merchant), 48–49
Acevedo, Juan (nineteenth-century politician), 82, 90, 100, 104, 106, 124, 126, 135
Acevedo, Zenón, 165
Achiutla, 33
Acho, Guillermo, 176, 177
Agrarian Code, 223
agrarismo, 14, 206, 223, 229, 234, 235, 244. *See also* land reform
Aguascalientes, 192, 200, 243, 248, 249, 260
Aguilar, Higinio, 209, 211
Aguilar y Cedeno, Librado, 100
Aguilar y Salazar, Manuel, 275
Ahuehuetitlan, 66, 91, 92, 130, 146, 269, 303
Aja, Petra, 86, 102, 302–3
Ajofrín, Francisco, 46
Alamán, Lucas, 118, 141, 197
Alcaldía, 24, 50
Aldana Rendón, Mario, 4
Alemán, Miguel, 247, 251, 268, 285

Alencaster, Manuel, 104, 126, 142
Alencaster, Vicente, 66
Allende, Salvador, 293
Almazán, Juan Andreu, 208, 211
Alonso, Hilario "Hilarion," 110, 114, 133, 136, 137, 139
Altamirano y Bulnes, Luis María, 235
Alvarado, Lorenzo, 86, 88
Alvarado, María Micaela, 87
Alvarado, Pedro de, 27
Alvarez, Juan, 111, 139
Amador, Ignacio, 66
Amador, José, 90
Amador y Hernández, Rafael, 18, 163, 182, 186, 191–99, 206, 212–22, 234, 235, 242, 264
Antequera, 48. *See also* Oaxaca City
Apostolado de la Oración, 215, 237
Apoyo al Desarrollo de Archivos y Bibliotecas de México (ADABI), 17, 18
Aranguti Aguayo, Antonia, 59
Arenas, Felipe, 174
Argentina, 157, 245
Argumedo, Benjamín, 209
Arias Fuentes, María, 253
Arrangoiz, Francisco de Paula, 118
Arriaga, Dionisio, 137
Arroyo, Vicente, 237
Article 3, 230, 232, 240, 247, 271
Article 27, 204, 223, 251
Asad, Talal, 10
Atenango, 102, 273, 303, 307
Atoyac, 22, 25, 28, 45, 50, 59, 70, 88, 133, 144, 170, 176, 177, 178, 210, 211, 225, 307

Avelino, Andres, 146
Avila Camacho, Manuel, 247, 249, 257
Ayú, 102, 103, 195, 279, 282, 303
Ayuquila, 28, 59, 68, 115, 135, 140, 171, 172, 199, 200, 211, 214, 215, 216, 221, 234, 243, 252, 253, 260, 273, 274, 280, 282, 307
Ayuquililla, 114, 140, 185, 194, 198, 225, 239, 242, 267, 269, 270, 276, 280, 282
Azuela, Mariano, 4

Bajío, 17, 47, 56, 57, 157, 212, 224, 229, 249, 256, 292
Balandier, Georges, 15
Barragán, Arnulfo de Jesús, 260
Barragán, Concepción, 183
Barragán González, Juan, 260
Barragán Leñero, Jesús, 289, 290
Bases Orgánicas, 83, 137
Baskes, Jeremy, 49
Bassols, Narciso, 230
Bautista Cortés y Velasco, Juan, 35
Bautista y Guzmán, Joaquín, 90, 91, 102, 105
Bautista y Guzmán, José Ramón, 62
Becerra y Jiménez, José María Luciano, 95
Bello, Bibiano, 253
Beltran, José E., 274, 282
Blancarte, Roberto, 249
Blessed Souls of Purgatory, 36
Blok, Anton, 113, 211
Borah, Woodrow, 24, 25
Bossuet, Jacques-Bénigne, 213
Boturini Bernaducci, Lorenzo, 42
Bourbon Reforms, 21, 57, 69, 94, 97
Brading, David, 66, 157
Bravo, Nicolas, 70, 127
Brazil, 7, 41, 157
Bruno, Juan, 133
Burgoa, Francisco de, 22, 24, 32, 33, 40, 48
Burke, Edmund, 15
Bustamante, Antonio, 132

Bustamante, Carlos María de, 71, 75, 76, 79, 100, 118, 128
Butler, Matthew, 10, 17, 206, 221, 242

cabecera, 24, 25, 61, 62, 83
Cacaloxtepec, 178, 228–29, 287, 307
cacicas, 29, 30, 35, 45, 73, 85, 86, 89, 91, 92, 102, 182, 187, 228, 302, 303
cacicazgos, 26, 30, 61, 77, 86, 90, 130
caciques, 5, 21, 26–42, 46, 47, 50, 51, 54–71, 74, 79, 81, 82, 85–95, 99, 102–9, 114, 116, 117, 118, 122, 124, 130, 133, 139, 142, 149, 150–53, 164–69, 172–79, 181, 195, 209, 224, 225, 228, 235, 236, 248, 249, 254, 256, 271, 274, 278, 283, 288, 294, 295, 302, 307, 308. See also cacicas; cacicazgos; nobles
Calihuala, 23, 45, 86, 307
Calixto de la Palma, Eduardo, 95, 97, 102
Calles, Plutarco Elías, 16, 227, 230–32
Camacho Pichardo, Gloria, 179
Camacho y García, Ramón, 201
Camotlán, 52, 55, 89, 170, 173, 188, 256, 273, 279, 281, 282, 303
Campeche, 168, 243, 248
Cantu, Miguel, 178
Cantu Corro, José, 194–200, 220–21, 262
capitación, 111, 137–39. See also tax
Caplan, Karen, 129, 142
Cárdenas, Lázaro, 14, 227, 243, 247–52, 283–285, 286, 288, 291, 292
Cardenismo, 14, 257, 271, 275, 285, 288, 292
Carmagnani, Marcello, 68, 131
Carrancista, 209, 211, 212
Carranza, Venustiano, 204, 205, 212, 213, 223
Carrera, Rafael, 157
Carriedo, Juan Bautista, 86, 88
Carrión, Miguel, 116, 135, 138
Castillejos, Vicente, 127
Castillo, Agustín, 90
Castillo, Eduardo, 226

Castillo, Felipe, 175

Castillo y García, José Rafael, 66

Castro, Fidel, 284, 285

Castro, José María de, 86

Catholic Church, 2–20, 26, 30–46, 55–61, 66, 72–81, 87, 92–107, 111, 117–26, 129, 131–42, 145–51, 154–68, 173–75, 180–207, 210, 214–19, 222, 226, 227, 230–38, 241, 243, 244, 247–87, 291, 292–96

Ceballos, Ciro B., 3

Ceballos, Juana, 281

Cedillo, Saturnino, 231

centralism, 2–4, 16, 20, 63, 73–85, 92–95, 108, 109, 110–13, 122, 123, 129–42, 154–55

Cervantes Delgado, Roberto, 51

Chalcatongo, 72

Chalchicomula, 70, 151

Chance, John, 25, 58, 62, 64, 173

Chapultepec, 216

Chassen-López, Francie, 168

Chávez, Gabino, 196

Chazumba, 29, 48, 62, 65, 67, 68, 83, 86, 88, 90, 91, 95, 96, 99, 101, 104, 105, 114, 130, 152, 153, 168, 174, 211, 212, 215, 228, 238, 267, 268, 303, 307

Chiapas, 46, 65, 254, 256

Chiautla, 156

Chichihualtepec, 66, 80, 90, 164

Chignahuapan, 156

Chila, 23, 28, 31, 33–37, 43, 46–49, 54, 58, 66–68, 84, 89, 90, 111, 135, 137, 138, 142, 143, 146–49, 152, 153, 163, 182, 195, 198, 199, 212, 215, 235, 236, 253, 264

Chilac, 68

Chilapa, 111, 137, 138

Chilapa de Díaz, 84, 143, 146, 148, 152, 153, 163

Chilapilla, 55

Chile, 202, 292, 293

Chilpancingo, 94, 155

Chinango, 67, 86, 103, 178, 196, 219, 307

Cholula, 65, 155

Christ cults, 1, 20, 21, 38, 40, 41, 45, 67, 68, 74–76, 99–104, 112, 153, 159, 166, 187, 188, 201, 214–18, 222, 277

Christian, William, Jr., 40

Christlieb Ibarrola, Adolfo, 291, 292

Cisneros, Miguel, 134

Ciudad Hidalgo, 247, 271, 290

Coahuila, 204, 243

Coalcomán, 249

Coatlán, 32

Cobos, José María, 120, 123, 147, 148

cofradías, 2, 10, 12, 13, 18–20, 31, 32, 34–42, 44, 45, 46, 49, 50, 55, 61, 64, 67–69, 71, 72, 81, 83, 84, 86, 93, 99–104, 118, 120, 129, 142, 143, 145–56, 160, 163, 165, 173–76, 179, 181–88, 195, 199, 200, 203, 215, 216, 218, 222, 228, 234, 235, 243, 255, 277, 296, 297, 302–6

Coicoyán, 65, 66, 68, 112, 267, 268

Coixtlahuaca, 31, 59, 179, 190, 194, 251

Cold War, 17, 283–93, 299

Colegio Pío Latino Americano, 162, 182, 192, 193

Colima, 168, 230, 256, 260

Colombia, 17, 157, 202

Comisariado de Bienes Comunales, 250, 254–56

commerce, 21, 27, 46–50, 85, 89, 176, 179

communism, 2, 202, 230, 246, 249, 259–62, 284–93

Concepción Porfirio Díaz, 241

Confederación de Trabajadores de México (CTM), 273

Confederación Nacional Campesina (CNC), 252, 253, 273, 274, 275

Confederación Nacional de Organizaciones Populares (CNOP), 273, 276

Connaughton, Brian, 92, 106, 134

conquest, 1, 20–25

constitutionalists, 204

Cooke Sherbourne, 24

Copala, 91, 93, 108–15, 122, 126, 135–39, 142, 143, 154, 242

Córdoba, 178

Corpus Christi, 35, 37, 40, 42, 245

Corral de Piedra, 228

Correa Zapata, Dolores, 196

corregimiento, 24

Corro, Juana, 281

Cortés, Diego, 27

cosolotepec, 212

Costa Chica, 48, 50, 51, 52, 68, 88, 109

Costeloe, Michael, 112

Coxcatlán, 68, 217

Cristeros, 4–6, 249, 270. *See also* Cristiada

Cristiada, 2, 3, 5, 201, 223, 224, 244, 247, 248, 290

Cristo Rey, 2, 188, 189, 264

Cristo Viejo, 155

Cruz, Cipriano, 236

Cuautepec, 72, 304

Cuba, 284–87, 290

Cubas Solano, José, 236

Cubas Solano, Manuel, 194, 235, 237, 238, 239, 259, 261

Cuernavaca, 69, 190, 191, 192

Cuicatlán, 176

Cuitito, 188, 303, 307

Cuyotepeji, 23, 28, 55, 58, 71, 87, 170, 172, 175, 177, 178, 238, 255, 256, 261, 267, 269, 274, 279, 282, 291

de-Christianization, 13, 14, 93, 108, 111, 154, 155, 158, 213

defensas sociales, 207, 211–13, 222, 226

Dehouve, Danièle, 36, 51

De la Cruz, Jeronimo, 27

De la Cruz, Juan Bautista, 83

De la Cruz, Mendoza, Juan, 87, 303

De la Cruz Villagómez Pimentel y Guzmán, Teresa, 30

De la Cruz y Guzmán, Domingo, 27

De la Peña, Moises T., 268

De la Portilla, Anselmo, 145

De los Angeles, Rafael Francisco, 61

De los Angeles Guzmán, Sebastian Mariano, 62

De los Reyes, Francisca Xavier, 87

Diacon, Todd, 7

Díaz, Felix, 163

Díaz, Porfirio, 16, 78, 80, 121, 141, 150, 153, 154, 160–68, 197, 204, 207, 209

Díaz Chavez, Manuel, 239

Dinicuiti, 240, 281, 282, 303

Diquiyú, 23, 55, 60, 64, 84, 88, 89, 130

Dominicans, 19–22, 24, 31–34, 40–42, 45, 46, 56, 59, 60, 63, 74, 214, 215, 262–65, 295

Ducey, Michael, 169

Duran, José María, 226

Durango, 212

Dzahui, 40, 45

Ecuador, 157

ejidatarios, 206, 227–30, 233, 248–57, 274

ejidos, 204, 224, 225, 228, 229, 230, 239, 248, 250–54. *See also* land reform

Ejutla, 105

El Espinal, 238

El Hule, 179

El Salvador, 171

Escobar Ohmstede, Antonio, 173

Esparza, Manuel, 168

Esperón, Gabriel, 109

Esperón, Tomás, 110

Esteva, Cayetano, 187

Etla, 135, 257, 273

Fabián y Fuero, Francisco, 59

Fagoaga, Manuel María, 88, 302

Fallaw, Ben, 182, 243

federalism, 4, 73, 74, 78–82, 91, 93, 94, 108, 110–43

Fernández y Fernández, Celestino, 258, 259

Figes, Orlando, 244

fincas, 168, 176, 178, 223. *See also* haciendas

Finistère, 202

Flores Ayala, Rufilio, 236, 242

Flores y León, Juan de Dios, 192

France, 12, 96, 107, 108, 190, 202, 214, 292

French Intervention, 2, 76, 80, 142, 150–53, 163

Frente Zapatista, 278, 282

Galicia Chimalpopoca, Faustino, 118

Galva, Matias, 89

Galvez, Mariano, 138

Gamio, Manuel, 220

Gandara, Manuel, 155

García, Antonio, 99

García, Aurelio, 165

García, Santiago, 132

García Correa, Bartlolomé, 231

Garcia Moreno, Gabriel, 157

García Niño, Aurelio, 192

García Peral, Antonio, 223

García Toledo, Anastasio, 232

Garibi Rivera, José, 248, 286

Garrido Canabal, Tomás, 231

Gasca, Celestino, 285

Gay, José Antonio, 109, 188, 264

Gerhard, Peter, 61

Germany, 158, 292, 293

Gillingham, Paul, 272, 274

Gillow, Eulogio, 191, 192, 200

godparentage, 7, 34, 37, 38, 42, 46, 49, 107, 178, 198, 219

Gómez, José, 167, 176, 177, 178, 307

Gómez Ayala, Pedro, 260

Gómez Farias, Valentín, 93, 134

Gómez Morin, Manuel, 276

González, Athenogenes, 172

González, Paulino, 89

González, Rafael, 151

González Torres, José, 286

González y González, Luis, 2, 173, 207, 227, 299

Gosner, Kevin, 7

Greenberg, James, 173

Gruzinski, Serge, 40, 45

Guadalajara, 106, 182, 217, 248, 249, 260, 285

Guadalupe la Huertilla, 225

Guadalupe Morelos, 252, 253

Guadalupe Olleras, 168

Guanajuato, 127, 180, 197, 200, 205, 230, 273

Guardino, Peter, 4, 69, 78, 79, 110, 111, 128, 141

Guatemala, 17, 46, 48, 157, 293

Guerrero, 21, 50, 51, 53, 70, 77, 78, 82, 88, 89, 91, 93, 109, 110, 111, 121, 130, 131, 137, 138, 143, 153, 154, 156, 157, 177, 208, 209, 210, 243, 283, 286, 296, 297

Guerrero, Antonio, 19

Guerrero, José Joaquín, 67

Guerrero, Vicente, 70, 111, 132, 133

Guillén, Gregorio, 249

Gutiérrez Maza, Rafael, 235

Guzmán, Felipe, 62, 63, 64, 135

Guzmán, Gabriel, 33

Guzmán, Jacinto, 67

Guzmán, Joseph de, 51

Guzmán, Mariano, 136, 137

Hacienda La Concepción, 109, 110

haciendas, 21, 25, 27, 109, 122, 160, 161, 168, 169, 206, 223, 224. *See also* fincas; haciendas volantes; plantations, sugar

haciendas volantes, 25, 46, 47, 50–55, 63, 65, 68, 72, 88, 89, 91, 96, 109, 125, 126, 176, 228, 295, 296, 302

Hale, Charles, 160

Hamnett, Brian, 79, 116, 142

Haskett, Robert, 69

hermandades, 44, 68. *See also* cofradías
Hernández, Benito, 32, 41
Hernández Chávez, Alicia, 78
Hernández Cirigo, José María, 183
Herrera, Francisco, 135, 143–45
Herrera, Manuel, 70–71
Herrera Ponce, Manuel del Refugio, 246, 261, 289, 290, 291, 292
Hidalgo, 155, 179, 197, 209, 224, 225, 246, 270, 271, 289
Hobsbawm, Eric, 113
Holy Cross, 19, 20, 31, 34, 37–42, 45, 56, 67, 68, 72, 74, 100, 102, 103, 187, 189, 199, 201, 203, 214, 217, 218, 222, 262, 263
Holy Sacrament, 34, 35, 37, 72, 174, 175, 190
Huajolotitlán, 28, 67, 94, 106, 125, 152, 225, 227, 273, 288
Huajuapam de León (bishopric), 190–200, 232, 236, 257, 259
Huajuapan (town and district), 22–28, 31, 33, 34, 43–75, 82–107, 111–52, 163–69, 176, 177, 183–211, 214–20, 224–26, 230, 232–46, 251–53, 256, 260–91, 301, 302; siege of, 70, 73, 76, 100, 148, 166, 269
Huapanapan, 23, 83, 94
Huasteca, 57, 77, 78, 85, 121, 131, 143, 154, 179
Huastepec, 86, 94, 102, 307
Huatulco, 41
Huazolotitlan, 72
Huerta, Felix, 194
Huerta, Victoriano, 204, 212, 230
Huichol, 84, 156

Ibáñez Soriano, Daniel, 216
Ibarra, Daniel, 194
Ihualtepec, 21, 22–25, 27, 28, 33, 45, 59, 61, 65, 66, 67, 71, 82, 86, 90–92, 115, 135, 164, 276, 282, 302, 307
Irigoyen, Francisco, 94, 100
Italy, 292, 293

Iturbide, Agustín de, 76
Ixtlán, 68, 95, 130, 149, 195, 302
Ixpantepec, 55, 65, 100, 103, 106, 153, 188, 199, 216, 262
Izúcar de Matamoros, 146

Jacobs, Ian, 173
Jalisco, 15, 84, 157, 184, 200, 205, 224, 230, 247, 271, 289
Jamiltepec, 52, 56, 72, 177
Jansen, Maarten, 21, 32, 39, 41, 145
Jaramillo, Rubén, 14, 285, 292
Jesuits, 42, 51, 52, 198, 270
Jiménez, José Aurelio, 270
Jiménez de Esquivel, Jacinto, 29
Jiquilpan, 258
Joluxtla, 83
José, Bernadino, 137, 138
Juárez, Benito, 101, 115, 121, 124, 137, 141, 142, 160, 163, 270
Juquila, 72
Juxtlahuaca, 22, 31, 47, 48, 72, 108, 111–15, 126, 133, 136, 137, 138, 143, 174, 218, 259

Knight, Alan, 12, 160, 212
Kouri, Emilio, 171, 178, 298

La Carbonera, 153
La Laguna, 203, 223, 248
land reform, 2, 79, 80, 81, 85, 122, 124, 162, 171, 173, 176, 180, 205, 206, 209, 223–29, 233, 234, 250, 251, 271
land tenure, 27, 28, 47, 49, 50–54, 58, 59, 84–92, 168–80, 209, 223–29, 250–56. *See also* ejidos; sociedades agrícolas
La Noria, 78, 164
La Pradera hacienda, 169, 176, 178, 208, 209, 211, 224, 225
Larios, José, 208
Las Piñas, 239
León, Antonio de, 2, 85, 88–91, 95, 96, 100, 104, 105, 108–11, 115, 116, 118,

122–26, 128, 131–42, 157, 166, 167, 177,
190, 252, 278
León, Felipe, 104
León, Manuel de (brother of Antonio de
León), 89, 100, 104, 116, 125, 128, 133
León, Manuel de (father of Antonio de
León), 51–54, 63, 70, 72
León, Manuel de (nephew of Antonio de
León), 151
León, Mariana de, 261
Leo XIII, 192, 194, 215
Lerdo de Tejeda, Sebastián, 160, 164, 165
Lewis, Laura, 9
Leyton, Manuel María, 127
liberalism, 2–5, 8, 14–18, 73–85, 92–94,
103, 113–79, 196, 199–204, 245, 252,
267, 270, 271, 297, 299, 307
Llano Grande, 238
López, Juan Guerrero, 66
López Cortes, Francisco, 231, 232, 235
López de Santa Anna, Antonio, 84, 93,
95, 111, 121–27, 132–37, 142, 143, 157
López García, Guillermo, 193–94
López Mateos, Adolfo, 285–86
Loyola, María de la Luz, 125
Lozada, Manuel, 4, 5, 17, 84, 156
Lozeza, Soledad, 286
Luna, Miguel, 143, 144, 148

Machado, Cayetano, 127, 128
Macuiltianguis, 153
Madero, Francisco, 204–8, 222
Magdalena, 130, 195
Maldonaldo, José de Jesús, 112, 116, 138
Mallon, Florencia, 4
Manzano, Gerardo, 140
Mariano Maldonaldo, José, 51
Mariscala, 146, 170, 171, 195, 209, 225, 227,
233, 278, 279, 288, 303
Martín, Feliciano, 110
Martín, Pablo, 116
Martínez, Felipe, 95, 102, 144, 146, 148

Martínez, Luciano, 142, 144, 146–48
Martínez, Luis María, 248
Martínez, Ricarda, 170
Martínez Gracida, Manuel, 187
Martínez Rodríguez, Senén, 278
Martínez Vásquez, Procopio, 276, 277, 290
Masferrer, Kan Elio, 154
Masonic lodges, 124, 132, 198, 202, 232,
239, 289
Maximilian, 81, 117, 121, 123, 124, 151–53
Maya, 7
Mayagoita, David, 284, 286
McCarthy, Joseph R., 293
Medellín, 202
Medina, Manuel, 110
Mejía, Tomas, 17, 121, 156
Melendez, José Gregorio, 84
Méndez del Río, Jenaro, 234–41, 258, 259
Mendoza, Ezequiel, 249
Mendoza, Francisco de, 61
Mendoza, Isabel de, 86, 91, 302–3
Mendoza, Isidora, 55
Mendoza, Josefa Patricia, 66
Mendoza García, Edgar, 179
Menegus Bornemann, Margarita, 28,
60, 61
Mexicali, 205, 223
Mexico City, 31, 46, 49, 50, 53, 56, 76,
78, 79, 88, 106, 113, 117, 123, 126, 128,
132–34, 137, 140, 148, 153, 155, 157, 165,
225, 237, 249, 255, 258–60, 262, 270,
289, 292
Meyer, Jean, 5, 6
Mezquital Valley, 93
Michetti, Emigdio, 192
Michoacán, 10, 30, 143, 154, 155, 157, 165,
180, 184, 200, 205, 224, 228, 230, 242,
246, 249, 258, 271, 284, 286, 289
Middlebrook, Kevin, 272
military, 2, 76, 85, 115, 116, 123–28, 133,
135, 138–40, 153, 156, 162, 163, 166, 208,
211, 212, 246, 253, 280, 287, 290, 291

Miltepec, 28, 50, 51, 55, 57, 58, 68, 71, 72, 94, 103–6, 140, 149, 171, 173–77, 182, 188, 199, 214–17, 235, 238, 253, 260, 267, 307

miracle, 10, 40, 68, 158, 159, 160, 187, 213

Miramón, Miguel, 195

Mixquixtlahuaca, 83, 87, 150, 172, 237, 238, 303, 307

Mixteca Alta, 21–24, 27, 31, 45, 47, 48, 51, 53, 57, 62, 63, 72, 109, 142, 153, 154

Mixteca de la Costa, 21, 53

Mixtecs: and the church, 30–46, 65–68, 72, 73, 75, 76, 92–107, 134, 135, 145, 146, 152, 153, 159, 160, 173–75, 181–200, 212–22, 230–43, 256–71; and education, 12, 16, 33, 59, 60, 93, 95–99, 111, 117, 122, 131, 133, 134, 136, 142, 145, 152, 153, 156, 162, 164, 165, 182–85, 195–97, 200, 202, 205, 207, 217, 225, 230–43, 256–71; and land tenure, 27, 28, 47, 49, 50–54, 58, 59, 84–92, 168–80, 209, 223–29, 250–56; nobles, 5, 21, 26–42, 46, 47, 49, 50, 54–73, 74, 79, 81, 82, 85–95, 99, 102–9, 114, 116, 117, 118, 122, 124, 130, 133, 139, 142, 149, 150, 169, 172, 174, 179, 181, 224, 283, 288, 294, 295, 302, 302, 307, 308; pre-Hispanic history, 22, 23

Molina, Olegario, 168

Molino del Rey, 116, 124, 140, 142, 166

Monaghan, John, 26, 61

Monterrey, 287

Moore, Barrington, 8

Mora, Angel, 262, 276–81

Mora, Avelino, 237, 262

moral economy, 6–10, 16, 18, 20, 25, 26, 36, 45, 56, 60, 69, 73, 81, 92, 117, 179, 207, 229, 295–97

Morales, Domingo, 60

Morales, Francisco Antonio, 66

Morales, Jesús "El Tuerto," 208

Morales, Pedro, 233

Morales de Moran, Angela, 268

Morales Jiménez, Eloy David, 257

morality, 13, 16, 80, 93, 95, 97, 98, 105–7, 121, 122, 131, 135, 149, 150, 155, 156, 185, 196, 220, 243, 261

Moran Rios, Felix, 261

Mora y del Río, José, 183

Morelos, 8, 78, 100, 110, 118, 154, 161, 205, 208, 209, 241, 252, 253, 270, 292, 297

Morelos, José María, 70, 71, 76, 100, 110, 118

Moreno, Miguel, 150

Mouat, Andrew C., 50

museum, 1

Narváez, José Mariano, 133

Navarrete, Miguel, 95, 152

Navarrete y Méndez, Raymunda María, 71

Navarro, Ignacio, 71

Nayarit, 17, 155, 201, 254

Nepomuceno Almonte, Juan, 118

Niño, Geronimo Gaspar, 233

Niño de Rivera, Luis, 165

Niño de Rivera, María Ignacia, 126

Niño de Rivera, Miguel, 261, 275, 276

Niño Pacheco, Luis, 203, 214, 233

nobles, 8, 16, 20, 23, 27–37, 45, 57, 61, 64, 73, 74, 149, 296

Nuchita, 62, 64, 88, 114, 147, 163, 303, 307

Nuevo León, 284

Nuiñe, 22

Oaxaca, 10, 18, 21, 22, 31, 36, 41–43, 46, 50, 51, 53, 63–65, 68, 72, 79, 81–84, 89, 92, 95, 96, 108, 115, 121–54, 157, 163, 164, 167–69, 173, 182, 184, 189–92, 207, 208, 217, 221, 223, 232, 233, 235, 236, 239, 240, 242, 244, 249, 251, 260, 263, 270, 275, 281, 283, 287, 294, 296, 297

Oaxaca City, 31, 53, 63, 65, 72, 125, 126, 127, 128, 130–32, 135, 136, 137, 143, 145,

147, 148, 150, 167, 232, 243, 249, 270, 275, 294

Obando, Agustín, 51

Obregón, Alvaro, 225, 250

Olavarria y Ferrari, Enrique, 3

Olivera, Emigdio, 143, 148

Orizaba, 104

Orosia Torres, Manuela Trinidad, 126

Ortiz Escamilla, Juan, 73

Osio, Juan de, 88

Osio, Tomás, 171

Osorio, Diego, 33

Our Crucified Lord, 45, 100, 103

Our Lady of Lourdes, 176

Our Lady of Ocotlán, 42

Our Lady of Perpetual Succor, 213, 214, 218, 219, 233

Our Lady of Solitude, 101, 112

Our Lady of Sorrows, 34

Our Lady of Talpa, 201

Our Lady of the Rosary, 34, 35, 36, 37, 61, 67, 88, 101, 103, 174, 218

Our Lady of the Snows, 55, 56, 101, 103, 188, 199, 216, 262

Our Lady of Tlacuilac, 201

Our Lord of Clemency, 217

Our Lord of Fainting, 99

Our Lord of Forgiveness, 1, 219

Our Lord of Hearts, 45, 76, 100, 101, 103, 153, 166, 188, 199, 215

Our Lord of Holy Burial, 67, 68, 219

Our Lord of Hope, 99

Our Lord of the Calvary, 101, 222

Our Lord of the Sanctuary, 217

Our Lord of Wounds, 68, 103, 104, 188, 216, 217

Ouwenweel, Arij, 28, 29, 61

Oveda y Berdejo, Joseph Rafael, 66

Pacheco, Tranquilino, 203, 213, 304

Pajacuarán, 258

Palafox seminary, 66, 182, 183

Palafox y Mendoza, Juan de, 42

palm products, 29, 36, 49, 74, 86–89, 95, 97, 102, 129, 177–80, 224, 229, 260, 291, 307

Pani, Erika, 79

Papantla, 82, 93, 154, 171, 179, 200

Paredes, Mariano, 139

Parsons, Wilfred, 231

Partido Acción Nacional (PAN), 2, 15, 16, 230, 243, 244, 249, 257, 262, 271–84, 286–89, 291–93

Partido Revolucionario Institucional (PRI), 4, 247, 266, 271–75, 278–83, 285–88, 290–92

Pasqual, Joseph, 60

Pastor, Rodolfo, 37, 51, 86

Pat, Jacinto, 3

Patlanalá, 23, 27

Paxtlahuaca, 218

Payno, Manuel, 80

Peón, Carlos, 168

Peral Martínez, José, 233, 239

Pérez de Vivas, José, 58

Pérez Jiménez, Gabina, 40, 41

Pérez Toledo, Sonia, 134

Perkins, Stephen, 56

Perón, Juan, 245

Perpetua, Virginia, 219

Petlalcingo, 24, 28, 44, 53, 68, 88, 146, 147, 186, 188, 198, 208, 222, 260, 264, 265, 266

Piaxtla, 47

Pimentel, Bonifacio, 55, 86, 87, 302–3

Pinotepa, 72

Pinotepa de Don Luis, 52

Pius IX, 162

Pius X, 196

Plancarte y Navarrete, Francisco, 190, 191

Plan of Ayala, 161

Plan of Ayutla, 121, 124, 144, 146, 163, 164, 166

Plan of Cuernavaca, 104, 134, 135, 137

Plan of Iguala, 127, 197

plantations, sugar, 25, 88, 108, 144, 178, 224, 251, 273

priests, 1–5, 9–19, 23, 28, 31, 32, 34, 39, 46, 49–60, 54–68, 70–75, 92–107, 111–13, 125, 126, 134, 137–40, 144–48, 151–56, 158, 159, 163, 164, 166, 174, 175, 181–90, 193–208, 211–22, 225, 228, 230–48, 250, 253, 256–71, 274, 276, 277, 282, 286, 288, 290–96

pronunciamiento, 120, 121, 131, 133, 135–40

Protestantism, 108, 123, 140, 185, 203, 206, 213

Providence, 76, 140, 150, 166, 187, 192, 206, 207, 212–14, 219, 220, 233

Puebla (diocese), 31, 67, 94, 134, 145, 201

Puebla (state), 6, 18, 19–22, 26, 30–35, 42, 49, 50–56, 59, 65–72, 78, 85, 88, 89, 93, 95, 97, 98, 104, 106, 107, 125, 127, 134, 144–47, 151–57, 161, 162, 166, 176, 179, 182, 183, 188, 190, 198, 208, 209, 233, 235, 260, 262, 275, 285, 286, 297, 298

Purnell, Jennie, 173, 228

Putla, 21, 48, 70, 72, 91, 93, 108–15, 122, 126, 132, 133, 137–39, 142, 143, 154, 177

Querétaro, 6, 155, 161, 166, 180, 196, 200, 201, 260

Quintero, Calixto, 209

Ramírez, Casimiro, 143, 167

Ramírez, Feliciano, 159

Ramírez, Gerónimo, 51

Ramírez Acevedo, José, 144

Ramírez Arellano, Manuel, 59

Ramírez Pacheco, Vicente, 226, 227, 233, 253

re-Christianization, 13, 14, 80, 92, 93, 99, 108, 146, 155, 158, 181, 190, 201, 206, 207, 212, 213, 222, 234

Régules, General, 75

Reich, Peter L., 257

repartimiento, 49, 69

república, 8, 21, 28, 39, 56–62, 67–69, 73, 74, 80, 82, 83, 99, 112, 118, 119, 123, 129, 130, 155, 245

Revolution, Mexican, 1, 2, 203–22

Reyes, José A., 195, 220, 241

Reyes Aguilar, Saul, 100, 104, 207–9, 211

Reyes Márquez, Ricardo, 208, 209, 212

Reyes Ramírez, Timoteo, 127

Río Balsas, 286, 288

Rios, Fidencio, 194

Rios, Mariano, 143

Riva Palacio, Carlos, 231

Rivera, Cipriano, 233

Robles, Manuel, 72, 73

Rodríguez, Santiago, 92

Rojas, Dionisio, 116, 140

Roldan, Alejandro, 142, 307

Romero, Matias, 121

Romero, Zeferino, 176

Romero Frizzi, María de los Angeles, 48, 51

Rosas, Juan Manuel de, 157

Rosas, Manuel Lazaro de, 67

Rueda de León, Carlos, 95

Rugeley, Terry, 14

Ruiz, Agustín, 134

Ruíz, Ulises, 294

Ruíz y Flores, Leopoldo, 183, 192

sacraments, 12, 97, 190, 197, 198, 204, 212, 220–21

Sacred Heart of Jesus, 208, 212, 214, 215

Sada, Enrique, 278

Sáenz, Moisés, 220

saints, 1, 19, 20, 38–45, 55, 56, 68, 72, 73, 75, 76, 99–101, 103, 153, 187, 188, 215–19, 262–63

Saint Thomas, 40

Salas, Miguel, 208–10

Saltillo, 192

Sánchez Camacho, José Antonio, 95
Sánchez Cano, Edmundo, 271
Sánchez Toscano, Pablo, 67
Sandoval, Rosario, 241
San Francisco del Progreso, 225
San Francisco El Chico, 225, 227–29
San Ildefonso Salinas, 28, 86, 277
San José de Gracia, 249
San José la Pradera, 225
San Juan de las Cañas, 87, 176
San Juan Trujano (village), 276
San Luis Morelia, 277
San Luis Potosí, 106, 139, 157, 179, 224,
   231, 283
San Nicolas Hidalgo, 225
San Pablo Anciano, 233
San Sebastián del Monte, 22, 28, 86, 102,
   145, 149
Santa Catarina Estancia, 105, 140, 225,
   307
Santa Cruz Tlacotepec, 52
Santa Gertrudis, 196, 213
Santander, 202
Santiago, 202
Santiago de Río, 114, 209, 303
Santo Domingo, 34, 37, 218
Santos, Gonzalo, 282
San Vicente del Palmar, 86
San Vicente de Paul, 186, 198, 240, 277
Schryer, Frans, 173
Scott, James, 6–8, 18, 26
Secretaría de Educación Pública (SEP),
   237, 238, 239, 247, 267, 268
Segura, Hilario, 139
Segura y Guzmán, José, 142, 144, 147, 151,
   153, 163, 164, 166, 167
Sesma, Ramón, 70
shrine, 12, 16, 38, 55, 56, 104, 188, 214
Sierra, Justo, 3
Sierra Gorda, 17, 77, 121, 154, 155, 156
Sierra Juárez, 78, 142, 150, 153, 154, 161,
   162, 234, 254

Sierra Norte de Puebla, 30, 78, 85, 145,
   154, 161, 166
Sierra P'urhépecha, 254, 271, 283
Sigüenza y Góngora, Carlos de, 41
Silacayoapan, 22–24, 27, 29, 31, 48, 58, 65,
   66, 72, 90, 95, 97, 98, 115, 137, 146, 152,
   163, 164, 190, 208, 251, 269, 271, 274,
   275, 276, 280, 287, 288
Silacayoapilla, 87, 172, 256
Simarrones, 71, 105, 196
Sinarquistas, 17, 248, 249, 271, 283, 292
Sinkin, Richard, 157
sociedades agrícolas (agricultural
   societies), 151, 163, 179, 205–9, 218,
   224–29, 234, 250–56, 274
Solano, Juan José, 116
Solano, Lauro, 255, 274, 291
Sonora, 155, 230, 285
Spain, 12, 20, 26, 29, 30, 31, 34, 35, 38, 40,
   42, 46, 48, 55, 61, 64, 68, 69, 71, 125,
   126, 127, 129, 158, 202, 225, 244, 245
Spores, Ronald, 23, 32, 61
Staples, Anne, 95
Suárez, Felipe, 236
subject town, 24, 25, 61, 74
Suchitepec, 23, 28, 58, 72, 102, 106, 149,
   175, 177, 208, 225, 228, 229, 237, 238,
   253, 281, 282, 303, 307
sugar production, 25, 48, 50, 58, 70–73,
   88, 108–10, 133, 144, 163, 167, 169, 170,
   176, 178, 179, 205–9, 224–26, 244, 251,
   273, 295

Tabasco, 231, 248
Tacache de Mina, 209, 224, 225, 228, 239
Tacambaro, 260
Tackett, Timothy, 11, 66, 108, 190
Tamaulipas, 246, 289
Tamazola, 31, 33, 65, 66–68, 95, 100, 115,
   116, 138, 148, 183, 216, 303
Tamazulapan, 23, 31, 33, 34, 99, 139, 192,
   261

Tapachula, 249

Tarecuato, 271

Tata Chu, 112, 241

tax, 27, 34, 76, 82, 91, 96, 101, 104, 105, 111, 114, 117, 121, 127–29, 137, 141, 147, 168, 172, 226, 233, 239, 246, 252, 256, 267, 281

Taylor, William B., 9, 11, 34, 37, 38, 173

Tecomaxtlahuaca, 31, 33, 114, 115, 303

Tehuacán, 21, 23, 46, 48, 53, 88, 148, 177, 212, 216, 217, 219, 264

Tejupan, 29, 31, 33, 59, 102, 180, 190

Teopan, 52, 55, 177

Teotihuacán, 23

Teotitlán, 176

Teotongo, 144

Tepeaca, 125

Tepeji, 24, 149

Tepejillo, 67, 302

Tepic, 84, 155, 156, 168, 192, 201

Teposcolula, 22, 27, 28, 31, 48, 53, 58, 59, 65, 95, 136, 274

Tequisistlan, 217

Tequixtepec, 1, 23, 25, 28, 29, 31, 35, 37, 48, 57, 58, 62, 65, 66, 68, 72, 87, 90, 91, 105, 114, 120, 130, 136, 146, 147, 152, 175, 182, 185, 188, 189, 190, 194, 195, 196, 198, 200, 203, 210–15, 218–21, 233, 236, 243, 256, 257, 259, 260, 264–69, 273, 279, 281, 282, 306, 307

Terraciano, Kevin, 23, 27, 45

Terrazas Moctezuma, Lucia de, 29, 30

Tezoatlán, 23, 31, 33, 48, 50, 52, 53, 60, 64, 65, 88, 95, 105, 115, 127, 138, 140–48, 152, 170, 171, 173, 183, 188, 220, 225, 226, 237, 261, 267, 278, 288

Theatro americano, 46, 57

Thompson, E. P., 6–8, 26

Thomson, Guy, 155, 166

Tianguistengo, 87, 112, 114, 302, 307

Tindú, 19, 28, 40, 41, 72, 187, 188, 189, 191, 221, 236, 263

Tiuxi, 146

Tlacamama, 52

Tlachichilco, 86, 94, 95, 100, 115, 138, 152

Tlacotepec, 48, 53, 56, 65, 104, 140, 146, 153, 188, 195, 215–17, 222, 262

Tlacoxcolco, 217, 219

Tlapa, 44, 46, 48, 56, 70, 98, 104, 108, 111, 112, 116, 138, 139, 154

Tlapancingo, 31, 65

Tlatlauqui, 156

Tlaxcala, 155, 205

Tlaxiaco, 46, 48, 70, 72, 136

Toluca, 26, 161, 179

Tomochic, 9, 200

Tonalá, 19–22, 24, 28, 31, 33, 34–42, 45, 47, 48, 55, 63–65, 72–74, 84, 88, 95, 97, 100–103, 115, 116, 127, 129, 138, 139, 140, 143–48, 167, 173–76, 182–89, 191, 194, 208, 215, 217, 221, 225–29, 235, 236, 252, 253, 259–64, 273, 288, 292, 302, 303

Toro, Alfonso, 3

Torreblanca, Fiacro, 192

Torres Bodent, Jaime, 247

Totoya, 146

Traffano, Daniela, 173–74

Triquis, 108–15, 136–39, 241

Tritschler y Córdova, Martín, 183, 192

Trujano, Valerio, 70, 71, 75, 76

Trujapan, 101, 211

Tulancingo, 94, 155, 168, 191, 192, 235, 259

Tutino, John, 56, 85

Tutitlán, 256

Tutla, 23

Tututepec, 23

Tuxtepec, 164, 165, 176, 178, 179, 223

U.S.-Mexican War, 2, 139–41

Valdiviesio, Gabriel, 33

Vanderwood, Paul, 9

Van Young, Eric, 9
Varela, Manuel, 174
Vargas, Isidro, 208
Vasconcelos, José, 220
Vásquez, Marcelo Antonio, 59
Vaughan, Mary K., 5
Vázquez, Bishop Francisco Pablo, 95,
    104, 106, 107, 133, 134
Vázquez, Genaro V., 231
Vázquez, Ignacio, 147, 148, 152, 153,
    162–68, 193, 194
Vázquez, José O., 194
Vega, Gabriel, 233
Vejar Vázquez, Oscar, 247
Velasco, Andrés de, 67
Velasco, Feliciano de, 59
Velasco, Juan de, 27
Velasco, Narciso Jesús, 67
Velasco, Teresa, 86
Velasco y Mendoza, Ignacio, 130
Velasco y Villagómez, Pedro, 95, 101
Vendée, 17, 158
Veracruz, 48, 56, 65, 70, 104, 148, 157, 176,
    178–80, 198, 205, 212, 262, 283
Vietnam, 7, 8, 245
Vigil, José M., 3
Villa, Pancho, 204, 213
Villa Alta, 57, 65, 69, 131, 141
Villagómez, Bernardo, 58
Villagómez, Diego, 50
Villagómez, Gregorio, 29
Villagómez, Iñes, 208, 209, 211
Villagómez, María Josefa, 66
Villagómez, Mariano, 50, 71, 86, 87, 90,
    116, 303
Villagómez, Martín Carlos de, 58
Villagómez Cortés de Velasco, Narciso,
    28, 58
Villagómez Guzmán y Mendoza, Martín
    Joseph de, 28–29
Villagómez y Guzmán, Lorenzo de, 50
Villa Hernández, Narciso, 260, 267

Villaseñor y Sánchez, Joseph Antonio
    de, 46
Villavicencio, Miguel de, 66
Vinagre Party, 128, 132
Virgin of Guadalupe, 68, 181, 206, 214,
    218, 219, 220, 266, 269
Vives y Tuto, José de Calasanz Félix
    Santiago, 192
Voto Libre Huajuapeño, 278, 280–82

War of Reform, 2, 76, 106, 145–50, 299
Weitlaner, Roberto, 51
Wolf, Eric, 25
Wright-Rios, Edward, 10, 99, 186, 217,
    219, 221

Xicayan, 56
Ximénez, José, 62
Ximénez y Enriquez de Alvarado,
    Ramon Antonio, 105, 130
Xochixtlapilco, 23

Yanhuitlán, 27, 28, 30, 21, 32, 33, 48, 50,
    70, 144, 164
Yetla, 36, 102, 174, 175, 228
Yolotepec, 88, 171, 173, 196, 198
Yosocuta, 186
Yosondua, 72
Yucatán, 8, 30, 46, 65, 77, 78, 131, 155, 168,
    183, 231, 299
Yucuná, 87, 307
Yucuquimi, 60, 86, 217, 225
Yucuyachi, 61, 62, 144
Yutandú, 105, 307
Yutatio, 114, 303
yya, 23, 24, 27, 32. *See also* cacicas;
    cacicazgos; caciques; nobles

Zacapoaxtla, 5, 94, 145, 156
Zacatecas, 157, 230, 271, 289, 298
Zacatepec, 25, 65, 66, 71, 114, 115, 135, 173
Zahuatlán, 159, 282

Zamora, 155, 260

Zamora, Vicente, 192

Zamora y Santiago, Ignacia Antonia, 86, 88, 307

Zapata, Emiliano, 3, 14, 161, 204, 205, 208, 209, 285

Zapatistas, 1, 2, 203, 206–15, 217, 218, 222–25

Zapoquila, 150, 254, 303

Zapotecs, 84, 142, 150

Zapotitlán Lagunas, 86, 92, 114, 209–11, 257, 273, 276, 280, 303

Zaragoza Acevedo, Manuel, 291

Zarate López, Ernesto, 232

Zertuche, Albino, 167

Zinapecuaro, 155, 156

Zitacuaro, 93

Zoquiapan, 61

Zuniga y Velasco, María de la Concepción, 87